Inside My Skin

by

Susan Lucas

www.insidemyskin.com

The page most people just skip over ☺....

Copyright © Susan Lucas 2011
　　　　This book is copyright. Apart from any fair dealing for the purpose of private study, research, critique or review permitted under the Copyright Act 1968, no part may be stored or reproduced by any information storage and retrieval system without prior permission in writing from the author. All rights reserved....

Original edition self published in Australia by me: Susan Lucas
Absolutely every bloody step taken was done by me with the help of giving friends....

Mothers Day, May, 2004, I first had the idea my religiously kept journal would make a good read. Fathers Day, September, 2011, a completed 'Inside my Skin' was installed onto www.Lulu.com and the very first copy purchased for printing. Two ends neatly tied ☺....

National Library of Australia
Cataloguing-in-Publication entry:
Author:　　　Lucas, Susan
Title:　　　　Inside my Skin
Edition:　　　1st edition
ISBN:　　　　978-0-646-55438-9
Dewey No:　　920.720994

ABN: 62 026 458 148

Available for purchase through: **www.insidemyskin.com**

Disclaimer
'Inside my Skin' has been written accurately and in fair knowledge. I take no responsibility for bruised egos. What I have written may offend few but to be purely honest that's unavoidable, however, it will be a sad day if honesty becomes illegal....

Dedication

I dedicate this recorded chunk of living to the importance for inner well-being found within the strength of a loving family….

~

Footnote

The purpose for initially starting a journal was to capture precious memories that were turning over so quickly, writing relieved my brain to ensure they weren't forgotten. All the little things, that now would have faded or possibly been lost forever, matter a lot. In the course of a regular evening handwrite I've never run so many pens dry or had a collection of backing cardboard from spent writing pads. Obliviously documenting experiences was pleasantly oblivious as to where it would lead ☺ ….

Rating Special Mention

Without these generous beings big pieces of my life would be missing….

I would personally like to acknowledge and thank every person who crossed my path to find their name written within the pages of 'Inside my Skin'. Every one of you gave, and some continue to give, pieces of knowledge to further enhance and carry forward on lifes little journey….

Deserving of individual recognition for outstanding selfless acts of giving when I had little to offer:
- A loving and caring Mum and Dad (Margaret and Barry), they supported and listened to me waffle week after long week about editing and never once told me to go out and find a real job ☺ ….
- My best mate and furry friend, Tia, for always being there keeping life real and filling any potential dull moment ☺ ….
- Sheila Perry-Vance and Peter Vance deserve mention for the most outstanding surprise event. Doing a fleeting trip across Bass Strait they stepped from their car with candles ablaze to sing 'happy birthday' to me in person. Adding to their repertoire of outstanding they accepted my ask to do a proof-read, even after being warned the pay is lousy but the credits are good ☺ ….
- Mary-Anne Wadsworth and Rita Summers honourably stood out on a limb to outstretch the hand of friendship when I sure could have used it most ☺ ….
- And every book has a hero at the end. On cue and in perfect timing, 'Inside my Skin' found closure when after several thousand kilometres AEnone McRae-Clift drove through the front gate of Rainbow Falls ☺ ….
- Thanks go out to the generous, giving heart of Lesley Nic (Nicklason) for sharing with me her last two spare hours for 2007. After coming off nightshift at St Mary's hospital, through tired eyes, Lesley climbed the ladder in the horizon paddock to shoot the outstanding image decorating the cover ☺ ….
- In keeping with a family of giving, her mother as the hero, Loui Dude (Louise Quinlan) stamped her mark, not only as a friend, but as the person who made sense of all my thoughts transferring them onto paper to design the cover to its perfected completion ☺ ….
- Kindly going over the many thousands of words spilled onto paper for a proof-read, grateful thanks go out to a long-time friendly neighbour, Audrey Bell, who made growing up in Jenkins Place a pleasant experience. Also accepting the proofing challenge of placing etchings on paper is long-time friend and former work mate Splasho (Lyndall Ash). It was for the purpose of Splasho and Geoff's wedding I inherited the pair of tight-arsed gumboots that still torment me to this day, but that's Lyndall's story to tell ☺ ….
- Many thanks go to my grammar 'secret weapon', Ian Summers, for polishing 'Inside my Skin' to a smooth finish ☺ ….
- Rounding off a distinguished list of generosity. Gratitude goes to Joe Brock for sharing his computer knowledge and classy design of www.insidemyskin.com ☺ ….

Most outstanding of all is that every person mentioned above asked for nothing in return, all acts were done from generous kind hearts full of honest giving, that's the mark of solid friendship. It definitely doesn't get any better than that ☺ !!!!

Preface

When I came bouncing into the world, met by one marginally older sister, we grew up in the framework of a loving well-adjusted family. Dad had a love for the bush, Mum had a love for shopping, sometimes their passions overlapped. Surviving the whole experience well-balanced and unscathed, I took on board enough life survival skills to ease my way into adulthood....
Blowing the money saved from many hours spent enclosed in a supermarket working after school, I purchased and threw my leg over a motorbike just as soon as I could. Chaffing at the bit to reach the legal age for my learners permit and the prospect of not having to walk anywhere, the first 100-kilometres were done literally circling the backyard of the family home. Stemming from humble beginnings I saw out five motorbikes over two decades. Not scared to have a go at anything taking a fancy, when my body refused to sprint around a softball diamond, stretch for a volleyball and lost interest in 8-ball, a little spice was added. Stepping outside my comfort zone of heights I sampled abseiling. Heading in the other direction, and holding my interest longer, several trips were taken with the Mildura Desert Divers Club to participate in the underwater adventures of SCUBA diving....
In the tenderness of my early 20's a stable job was secured with the Department of Agriculture. The job financially supported my desires for sampling life on the endless hunt, looking for that something more, to lastingly fill that little piece missing inside to feel complete and content. Starting as an Apprentice Fruit Grower I finished my stint as a 'shiny bum' Project Officer. After 14 years devotion I left with enough experience to be dangerous in a lot of areas....
Cringing at the thought of growing old and dying behind that desk, with the knowing there's got to be more to life, I threw caution to the wind. In an endless search for that something more trying to fill that insatiable void, distracted by sex, I gave up my job and followed a high libido to Kiama....
Time made it quite clear that looking outside myself to fill that void only managed to create a bigger emptier one, but on the flip side I couldn't have remained doing what I was doing either. The only direction was forward????
By the time dust settled on two years of life experiences slowly chiselling pieces away my weight plummeted to a meagre 38 kilos. A visit by the angel of death reversed my thinking and priorities, and my four legged best friend, Tia, give me the elixir of life, simple honest love. It's by my side, with unconditional love, Tia chose to remain returning back to health and quality of life finding a few kilos to wrap around my bones and fill my skin. Unsure of what direction to take next, I bought a car affectionately pet named 'Destiny', and garage sale'd life's possessions down to manageable. The bits that wouldn't fit in Destiny were stored with a friend and we drove out of the Illawarra....
Lacking anything resembling long-term thoughts on life, in a round about trip making friend and family stops along the way, I headed to Tassie to clean-up Rainbow Falls. A property listed for sale I'd bought a couple of years earlier....
A secure offer of sale was faxed through to the real estate agent September 10, 2001, for another changeover of ownership. The following day a terrorist attack on the Twin Towers in America destabilised the financial market, the offer of sale was immediately withdrawn.

Unbeknown at the time what an impact the fall-out of an event worlds away would have on my future????

If anything, Tasmania would give me the opportunity for a direction rethink while simultaneously making Rainbow Falls more marketable. However, the longer I stayed the more that void, that search for something more was being filled, finding it in inner peace and contentment. A course I refuse to deviate from....

Long before the arrival of the Tassie Trio me, Tia and Destiny, on that life changing day of May 21, 2002, ploughing Destiny through scotch thistles from the front gate to reach housing, Rainbow Falls already boasted a long decorated and dignified past. Documented settlement history begun well over one hundred years earlier by an Irishman by the name of Edward Young. Edward poked his flag in a patch of ground in wild mountainous country 1889, built a hut Tia and I adopted as our bedroom, calling his found hamlet 'Dublin Town'....

Seeing four owners over a 117-year period, like myself, Rainbow Falls had very little left to offer. Together we started the healing process, one foot in front of the other....

This is where the wandering Tassie Trio stumbled into an incredible journey and fit into an equally incredible piece of history....

Inside my Skin, let the journey begin....

Tuesday 21, Wednesday 22 & Thursday 23 May 2002
First stepping foot on the soil we now call home, Tuesday the 21st seemed an appropriate number for my final coming of age....

Driving off the 'Spirit of Tasmania I' Tuesday morning I was able to collect Tia from the kennel around 10:30a.m. After a long night confined, I led my best friend walking for a spot of relief but there was no grass so she didn't pee. Free to roam our newly adopted home I fuelled up not far from the ferry and focussed on 'destination St. Marys'. Some time down the track stopping on a quiet road in Conara to give my little mate a stretch of the paws, opening the car door Tia bolted to the first patch of green in sight. The length of time Tia squatted her bladder was stretched beyond capacity!!!!

The whole day felt perfect and just kept getting better. I steered a course directly to the property to get settled while Mother Nature provided free lighting. Arriving at the front gate of Rainbow Falls Tia & I got out of Destiny, opened the gate, and I knelt and kissed the soil that absorbed us so comfortably within, feeling an instant lasting peace. Tia too is beaming, so much to see and do, she'll probably be putting in for overtime ☺....

Getting as settled as we were going to, we wandered back down the hill for food and to sort out a Post Office box. The Post Office was a most pleasant encounter nothing was too much trouble, a refreshing experience....

Aside from a trip to the Post Office, supermarket, and taking the 100 kilometre round trip to St. Helens to purchase a phone, much of Wednesday was spent on the shovel finding buildings behind weeds....

Thursday was lost pulling scotch thistles out in Dublin Town, I've got a job ahead with thistles some are taller than me. At least now the shed can be seen from the bungalow where Tia & I have made our home until the cottage is renovated....

Thistled out, I quit to satisfy my craving for a burger with the lot. The dirt road linking home to town saw the blade of a grader the past two days surfacing sections of small rocks. I think I prefer corrugations? The drive back from town in darkness was interesting with the local wildlife active, counting twelve wallabies, one live roo, one dead roo, one rabbit and one devil....

Sealing us in after bush wee's on the thistle free patch before bed the security system offered a laugh. The padbolt inside the door doesn't quite align due to a lot of reasons and seasons, so I give it a bit of encouragement with the back of a tyre lever. The stud clamp, the bit that covers the wheel nut, acts as a great padbolt opener. The security system is running smoothly ☺....

Friday 24 & Saturday 25 May 2002
Writing until late Thursday I freely slept in Friday. Popping my head out of the bungalow I frightened the shit out of Jeff from Telstra. While making a cuppa for Jeff and myself, Andrew the electrician arrived to join us in a brew. Everyone I've met since arriving has bent over backwards to help in whatever way they can. Jeff left metres of cabling and a junction box advising me to get Andrew to do the work for economics....

Friday expired tinkering with the many half-started jobs I happened to walk near....

Bath preparations were well underway, the first pot of boiling water emptied and another set to boil, going to the dam for more water I returned to find the tub empty! Let down by the new plug, no longer does it take pride and place anywhere near the bath ☺!!!!

Saturday morning was easily absorbed walking to the dam for bath water on a mission for a shopping trip....
Groceries packed in Destiny, it was straight into the hardware store for 80 metres of poly pipe for the purpose of running a direct line from the dam to the cottage. No more walking for water. I feel like a kid in a lollie shop inside a hardware store, extending the excitement to buying a saw and nails also.... Who's a lucky girl ☺ !!!!
Dark by 5:30p.m. sharp, about 6p.m.-ish I walked up the hill to the outside loo and the torch picked up a possum on the roof. For comfort sake the possum was asked to please leave. Thinking I had the loo to myself I went in to sit down, glancing back up at the roof the possum was watching from directly above my head. My personal space in need of expanding, again I requested of the possum to leave. Gone, I sat only to have Tia frighten the poor little thing back into the loo for refuge, this time at my feet. Looking into one anothers eyes, the noises I was making the possum again tried its luck with Tia. There's never a dull moment, living in 'Eden' life can only be good ☺....
Ripping rotten carpet out of the cottage for its next faze as compost, out fell a packet of roll-your-own tobacco, lo and behold there was a stash of hooch inside. Highly likely left behind by one of the squatting ferals that had moved in while Rainbow Falls was vacant prior to our arrival....

Sunday 26 May 2002
Yahoo, shortly after 1p.m. the newly installed poly pipe waterline from the dam to the cottage was successfully flowing, no more carrying water! I can appreciate how the Chaffey Brothers must have felt when they managed to get water flowing for the first time for irrigation, however, I had gravity on side. Reward for effort, a deep soaking bath was prepared with a non-leak plug ☺ !!!! Ahhhh....
It's the first day Tia & I have had to ourselves it was an illusion to think life would be so social nestled in the mountain semi-isolated? What has been obvious, besides a cold southerly, is the clarity of the night sky, star constellations are dense and sharp....
Finally emptying the last possessions from Destiny, the bungalow is being constantly modified to make room. Ms Tia decided on a few bungalow renovations of her own, biting down on and dragging, Tia pulled her bed to the foot of mine, which incidentally sits directly in front of the heater. As I write, Tia's as snug as a bug in her newly positioned bedroom in front of the heater.... Who's the smart one????

Monday 27 May 2002
As saying has it, a beautiful sunny day follows frost. Saying was correct, but the new beaut pride and joy waterline fell victim to an extremely heavy frost taking until 11a.m. to thaw and flow. I was a bit lazy yesterday to dig a 40 metre trench to insulate the pipe ☺....
Filling idle moments, the cottage and bungalow are being found buried behind a healthy collection of overgrowth. Clumps of combined dirt and grass dug out in the process of finding buildings is being recycled as insulation to assist with the water line freezing problem....
Making a quick trip into town, I stepped into the Post Office where I struck up an over the counter conversation with Ruth. Sidetracked chatting, I walked out without paying for a

photocopy, when the penny dropped I about turned straight away and generously Ruth told me not to worry about it. Another nice experience at the local St. Marys Post Office ☺ ....

Tuesday 28 May 2002
Tia and I had a pretty quiet one, aside from boiling water, most of it was spent hanging onto a wooden shovel handle unearthing the path between the cottage and burnt out house. Hidden amongst overgrowth, the shovel's blade found a small bike and a path continuation, a wide concrete strip bordering the rear of the burnt out house. The area has a nice feel, in time I'll endeavour to clean it up. Home is like having a blank canvas to work with I just have to find the canvas ☺ !!!!
Without looking back, from the time of first entering the front gate my energy and eating habits have risen incredibly along with my libido, I had better keep a lid on that I've got enough work to do as it is ☺ ....
Out for last wee's before calling it a night, in her city living unfit slow pace, Tia took off two steps behind chasing anything out of her yard. She must have been only one step behind tonight something cleared the dam fence making a huge splash. If bath water is cloudier than usual it's self-explanatory....

Wednesday 29 May 2002
Keeping its handle polished, the shovel got another run extending freshly revealed paths. For a dash of variety, and secured by a thick concrete retaining wall, I had another go at the elevated garden at the rear of the burnt out house. Sizing up the burnt remains, I reckon slowly but surely using it for a wood supply the burnt house can gradually be demolished going up the heaters flue????
Resting spent muscles to cool with a trip to the laundromat, incorporating a spot of food shopping and dropping film in for processing was enough to fill my plate....
The night sky never ceases to amaze. Without street lighting to detract it's unbelievable the density and clarity of stars and constellations available to the naked eye, tonight is exceptional....
Cold evenings have transformed Tia into a heater hog she sits that close I turn one bar off so she only gets half-baked! It'll probably be her nickname by the end of winter ☺ ....

Thursday 30 May 2002
Lost in the elevated garden with my helping hand, Tia I did some serious pruning, sights are set on clearing a section free of rubbishy shrubs. Just stepping onto the wave of a steep learning curve, the more of this slice of 'Eden' revealed it draws me deeper within a strong sense of home, a feeling only ever experienced within the security of family....
Close behind a heavy frost, like a typical Mildura winters day, calm conditions and a warming sun follow, dressing me down to a t-shirt basking....
Paving covers far beyond the area initially thought, the more I look the more there is to find. Every day opens a new adventure for discovering extending an inner sensation of feeling so alive....

Some useful bits 'n' pieces as well as some not so useful have come to the surface, the treasure booty consists of a one metre long jemmy bar, a clapped out carby, pieces of steel and fencing wire, all stuff to hoard in the shed ☺….

It's probably lucky I'm keeping a journal, without television the daily entry is my only connection to what the actual day is, however, there's no real need to know, everyday no matter what I'm doing feels great….

Friday 31 May 2002
Up 7a.m.-ish, and after doing our morning ritual of milo and shared toast, water flowing meant bathing and getting to the shops at a reasonable time….
I got the 'couldn't be bothered's' with anything to do with gardening. Endurance for physical labour still has a way to go. Sizing up what's left to be done, maybe the army could do a backyard blitz ☺ ????
Venturing further afield I found more pathways, its like I'm in some sort of fantasy adventure everyday something new, exciting, and constantly thought provoking to discover….
The cliché 'make hay while the sun shines' now makes a lot more sense. Dark 5:30p.m. sharp, anything that can be done outside is done during daylight hours everything else waits until after dark ☺ ….
Needing something stronger to write by an electric lamp has made the wish list. The oil lamp creates a beautiful homely feel but doesn't quite cut the required candle power….

Saturday 1 June 2002
Known for spoiling me rotten on occasion, the first thing Tia did when let out was to track down and roll in fresh poo, the white markings on her neck had lost their shine. Needless to say inside was taboo until her scent returned to lavender ☺ !!!!
Raising the celsius working in the elevated garden, a bone warmer in paradise encouraged me to strip down to give bare skin an airing. A liberating freedom and privilege I have wherever I am it just feels more comfortable here….
Well here I am, 3:30p.m. in Tassie sitting on an oversized wooden box fixed under the bungalow window basking behind glass with sun on my back. Warm enough for a lazy old blowie to hang around took my thoughts to Mum's Sunday roast cooking ☺ ….
Feeding Tia from the bargain bought at the butchers, I asked for a couple of bones and some off-cuts and was given the 'Flintstones' pack. Four ribs still attached to the breastbone and enough fresh off-cuts to feed her for a week for only two dollars…. What a bargain ☺ !!!! The 'side of ribs' will make a good all-day-sucker to keep her amused on a rainy day down the shed, however, the meat will go off first if this weather keeps up????
Keeping warm behind glass on the bungalow window ledge to its fading end, on cue at 4:45p.m., the sun starts to set behind the mountain range. Once light has faded there's no wandering without the beanie….

Sunday 2 June 2002
A lazy old Sunday consisting simply of writing, following the sun and boiling bath water, hmm, I can cope with that…. Now I might put that boiled bath water to use ☺ ….

Distracted by the pen I boiled an extra pot, setting the stage for the deepest bath, totally immersed in water except my head and poor little boobies, I was one content woman☺!!!! Winding a lazy day down that failed to wind up I kicked the tennis ball around for Tia. Tia's learnt her new environment quickly, the ball landed smack bang in the middle of a scotch thistle and she definitely wasn't going to get it…. Smart girl….

Monday 3 June 2002
Offering more room to let dear Destiny in and out, attracting attention was the need for the shed gates to swing freely. Shovelling grass clumps, leaving Tia to her brontosaurus burger, I put the radio on in Destiny to catch up with the outside world. The weather forecast predicts 18° all week with a possible shower Thursday…. hmmmm, did I shift to Tasmania????
Thinking, while getting the shed gates free swinging and another patch of thistles cleared, I made my mind up to buy a lawnmower. The yard is starting to take some shape and feel good. It's time to complement clearing☺….
With something bothering her foot, Tia had a rather ordinary experience. Familiar with pulling prickles out, this time a fat slimy leech had nestled in. On the fourth attempt I squashed the rubbery bugger leaving my entire heel imprint in blood!!!!

Tuesday 4 June 2002
As soon as we were up and door open, Tia was out to see what was left of her 'brontosaurus burger', not even the lure of a milo could drag her away from it….
Completing the bits that keep life ticking over, and sharing myself around, I went back to scotch thistle removal. By knocking out taller weeds the yard is being brought down to size and seemingly enlarging. A slow process, but I'm looking forward to the building area looking tidy and homely. When our immediate surrounds feel comfortable then I'll wander further afield. I suppose you have to see where you are going to get there????

Wednesday 5 June 2002
The deepest ever, tonight's bath will become the benchmark until the hot water service is operational….
Taking a peek at just another glorious day in paradise we greeted it shortly after 7a.m. Without distraction I spent it entirely clearing around the huge pile of rocks dumped near the bungalow door. Raising the stack tidying the base perimeter eased the task of eliminating entwined threaded weeds....
Doing her bit in the yard Tia copped a bee sting in the roof of her mouth; it had her pulling a few faces the poor little bugger. However, the sting didn't lessen her appetite a feed always makes things better☺….

Thursday 6 June 2002
Leaving my runners in the cottage overnight, because the bungalow is too small for their odour, before sunrise a mouse had chewed the toe out of one. Guess mice don't have a sense of smell☺????
Slowing the pace a little, a bit of washing was done and a drive was taken to replenish our waning supply of food. Without the confirmation from bathroom scales, I feel like I've gained

more weight in the last two weeks than the past nine. I'm in the right place for trying bloody hard to regain the last ten kilograms to reach body weight, Rainbow Falls offers a sensation of relaxation and healing, I can't help but feel good when everything is a pleasure not a chore....
Waiting on hot water I tinkered the time usefully making more of a dent in pulling out scotch thistles. I don't want Rainbow Falls known as a prickle farm, one foot in front of the other she'll be brought back to a former elegance....
Trampling taller grass tufts unthinkingly barging at the base of thistles to rip out, Tia and I are having an easier time of playing ball. The rough turf is still providing a degree of difficulty with an element of skill involved, but Tia loves using her mind and is certainly blossoming since arriving here....

Friday 7 June 2002
Bugger, the sweet sound of rain offering a sample late last evening didn't linger, I was hoping to wake to it still pattering on the roof to justify burning prickles down the shed. Sun once again shining, deluding bias thoughts on Tasmania's weather, the few showers through the night just wet the ground surface....
Lacking motivation, with shovel in hand I simply took it at my own pace clearing a section of fenceline leading from the bungalow. The crude selection of tools that followed me here aren't designed for fast progress, however, treasures lurking buried at the ground surface are better found with a shovel than machine. The yard is starting to shape up, with the ability to now see from the bungalow directly across to the shed without obstructions....
The make-do emergency repair job on the broken bungalow window also received an upgrade. Taping down the edges and applying pressure on the yellow plastic window pane made a remarkable temperature difference inside....

Saturday 8 June 2002
The long awaited change finally arrived with a few showers finding ground overnight, the sun may have made an appearance but nature's elements threatening from south determined 'prickle burning day' yahoo!!!!
Taking the short walk up the hill to the long drop throne exposed the need for running repairs to the roof, the missing centre piece of tin does nothing to keep the toilet roll or seat dry after rain☺!!!!
Determining their final fate in the face of the heater, some of the prickles had one last go at me by piercing soft skin with thorns. Warm in the shed was the place to be, rain may have been elusive but the southerly was bloody lazy....
Passing the bungalow on a bath water mission I caught a phone call from Kylie, a friend from my Wollongong life. Mentioning she's into her tenth day of quitting ciggies with patches, Kylie might be just the inspiration I'm looking for. I had better go cold turkey the patches may be stronger than what I'm smoking now....

Sunday 9 June 2002
Literally shitting in its own nest, war has been declared on residing in the same space as rodent's pooing on my doona pushed the limits of decency. Mice can join the rest of the fauna outside or face a determined woman ready to kill!!!!

Knowledge that's come with experience is my bladder must be empty before tipping a boiler load into the bath otherwise there's a merry jig. Another observation is food takes longer to spoil, a loaf of bread lasts two weeks without moulding and the fridge quietly ticks over rarely cycling on its lowest setting, less energy and noise can only be good ☺ ….

Conserving a little of that precious energy myself I indulged away the better part of the day finalising a book. A recommended read from Anna's collection, 'The Alchemist' by Paulo Coelho is a simple read with a captivating story line, a book I could probably read again in time. Anna being a kind friend, and host at our final stopover in Melbourne before daring to venture across Bass Strait into Tasmania. ….

Monday 10 June 2002
Wild gusts striking through the night tested temporary repairs almost dismantling the bungalow window 'plastic gap filler'. Straight into maintenance, it was out with hammer and nails first thing. While inspiration lasted I tackled broken windows in the cottage also to take the wind chill factor off bath time ☺ ….

Perched on the bungalow window box behind glass, separating the strong cold southerly element from robbing the sun of its warmth, I'm not moving! Indulging in plunger coffee and coffee scrolls catching the last fading daylight, the setting sun lit the distant mountain ranges to life in a fiery red adding atmosphere to the moment ☺ ….

Without having passed through Rainbow Falls front gate since Thursday one day soon I'd better go and check there is another world out there, gather more rations and return to hibernate in paradise….

Tuesday 11 June 2002
Driven by the need for food Destiny was taken out to stretch her rubber. Utilising the trip to organise a radiator hose, I experienced another great moment of trust and simplicity that can exist living in a small country town. Grant looked at the radiator hose and simply said "no worries, I'll get one by tomorrow", I only introduced myself as he was walking off, how good is that ☺ !!!!

Getting outgoing and adventurous, I remembered to drive past the front gate to the end of the road to check on the state of the bottom paddock gate. Like everything else it needs to be cleared to swing freely, it's only a matter of time before the shovel finds its way there….

Returning a little quality with the recipe of plenty of sleep, food, fresh air and exercise, my health is rising to inspirational levels of wanting to participate in life. Taking a walk to the streams, Tia led me along wallaby tracks bringing us out at the top of the waterfall, exploring with my little mate is not a bad way to spend an afternoon at home ☺ ….

Wednesday 12 June 2002
Pounding at regular intervals for several days, wind finally abated taking a few casualties with it. Out of desperation and improvisation I did a balancing act on a half pallet, the closest thing resembling a ladder, banging a few nails in the roof to hold things together….

Low cloud draped itself over South Sister Range giving it a soft fluffy hug, filling the space wind so freely flowed only hours earlier. The dam got a bit of a stir up, bits 'n' pieces coming through in bath water are bringing me closer to my earthy environment ☺ ….

Entering the other world for things I can't get locally a drive was taken to St. Helens, sticking only to business before pointing Destiny's nose homeward. Pulling in on the way back to pick up the radiator hose, Grant offered to fit it but would be about an hour, not blessed with tools I thought that great. One hour to kill is bloody slow with nothing to occupy myself with so I asked Grant if I could borrow tools and do the job myself. Obliging my request, I was on my way home within a half-hour one happy camper ☺....

Thursday 13 June 2002
All are good, some exceptional, today was bloody beautiful, calm as, with a dash of cloud. Great to be out on the shovel clearing scotch thistles and weeds surrounding the carport, then going on to follow along the shed wall, a visually pleasing advance in the yard....
Heavily shaded in long shadows and still harbouring enough warmth outside, I watched a beautiful sunset to fading while Tia had her dinner. Transforming to darkness the atmosphere was motionless, time stood still and sound seemed three-dimensional travelling lightly to great distances, a pin could be heard dropping....
The organised chaos created first putting what Destiny could hold of our lives where it fitted in the bungalow, as time has passed is slowly being sorted. A rainy day spent inside coupled with a dose of inspiration should finish it off....

Friday 14 June 2002
Up early in the company of energy and my little mate, I put in a big one walkabout with the shovel venturing into the emerging yard. Finally conquering this season's crop of scotch thistles between the bungalow and shed, where larger weeds have been removed and grasses trampled have rewardingly greened up. It's good energy to watch progress slowly unveiling and physically evolving ☺....
Protesting muscles made the decision to put the toys away and soak in a relaxing, hot, deep bath....
It's funny when your home environment changes so too do priorities. In a former life hot water flowed from a tap and bathing didn't have much thought put into it, now my everyday evolves around it. No matter what's going on, I'm aware that every three-quarters of an hour the 10 litre boiler will be ready and blowing off steam....

Saturday 15 June 2002
Anna brought their tour to my attention. An outstanding favourite band 'Concrete Blonde' played in Melbourne the past two nights, oh to have been part of the audience. All that could be done was to glance back over my shoulder because life's journey was leading me in the exact opposite direction????
At 7:45am sitting at my seat to the world milo'd up, gazed out the bungalow window at rain, just perfect, my body was grateful for a rest from the shovel. Isn't it funny, when it rains the little things that need fixing when the sun shines, like the toilet roof, come to mind....
Keeping an idle brain occupied, I focussed on bungalow maintenance modifying the temporary window repair with a more secure windproof, cardboard temporary window replacement ☺....
My window box perch was cleaned inside and out and refurbished with a hall runner across the top, simply encouraging me to spread further ☺....

Independently thinking more for herself Tia comes and goes from the bungalow at will, stemming from that a doorbell system developed, when enough fresh air has been had she rings the doorbell by releasing a low bark at the door. Adopting a several hectare area surrounding housing as claimed territory, Tia proudly stands on the rock pile looking over her kingdom.... She's glowing with health and happiness ☺....

Sunday 16 June 2002
Charging like a bull at a gate, up at seven by nine was out in the thick of it. A cool start but it didn't take long to warm a body swinging on the end of a shovel ☺....
Finding the fence belonging to the cottage side yard attracted shovel blade attention. Already green, once mowed the side yard will look great. Cloud progressed with the morning, coming good with its promise of moisture permitted the shovel to be put down with a clear conscience ☺....
Sick of soggy socks, the old boots are only good for dry days new boots have made priority one on the wish list. Bearing a split across the right sole, like the loo roof, is only noticed when it's raining....
A sudden change in climate has spurred on a thickening growth in Tia's fur the new outfit is a deep chocolate colour supporting a noticeable shine....

Monday 17 June 2002
The baking tray under the flue, where the heater once upon a time sat in the cottage, was three-quarters full. A measurable sign the heavens opened overnight....
A burst blister caused from soggy socks rubbing yesterday secured light duties today and another good reason for new shoes....
The day started easily down the shed eyebrow plucking at the only available mirror, Destiny's rear-view. Taking in my view from the driver's seat, coupled with inclement weather, the thought of burning prickles became appealing. And so it was to be, from under the five metre high by five metre wide by ten metre long pile of thistles the shed emerged ☺....
Feeding the heaters appetite a boxthorn thorn wedged itself deep into the flesh of my arm making eyes widen pulling it out, unfriendly bugger. I, however, had the last word!!!!

Tuesday 18 June 2002
Not one of the hottest, snowing to 800 metres and nursing a sore arm, light duties were declared and more sense was made inside. The bungalow just happened with possessions placed on shelving on arrival and has been evolving to need since. Positive steps today helped evolution along in the direction of comfort and homeliness....
Going for a walk with my best friend to break the monotony of cleaning, disappearing amongst trees behind the shed uncharted waters opened a voyage for discovery. Finding the used machinery dumping ground, the recognisable bits are of an old hay bailer and quite a car collection. Taking on earthy tones, a rusted shell of a XP Falcon rests wedged between trees in the company of a Dodge truck cabin, amongst the collection is a Landrover 4WD station wagon, the oldest and most interesting one of the lot is an old Humber....

A quiet stillness hung on the evening, a mouse chewing on draught proofing attempting to come in could be clearly heard and location pin-point identified. Tapping quite sharply on the wall I put an end to the destruction, if the poor bugger ever dares come back it'll be deaf☺!!!!

Wednesday 19 June 2002
A postcard perfect white frost established itself overnight putting the waterline insulation to the test, water and icicles flowed at 9:30am, ice added time for water to reach boiling point ☺....
Reversing the use of foil for gap filling insulation, time has taught me it's a great conductor of cold and is noisy when mice chew it!!!!
Woken by a bloody mouse six times last night trying to chew its way in near the head of my bed, when cussing settled I promised myself there wouldn't be a repeat. Being proactive 'Plan B' was instigated, step aside noisy cold foil for tried and proven, and quieter when chewed, cardboard strips. Cutting to size and wedging strips into gaps, cardboard strips sit firmly psychologically feel warmer, and amber side up, even blend with the timber décor....

Thursday 20 June 2002
Bloody cold and not daring to wander too far from a heat source, warming Destiny's motor a flow of hot water was pumped through her heater going to the outside world. Taking a remote snatch at an easy way out, I put the winning lotto numbers on for Saturday. With clean clothes and food to decorate shelves again what more does a girl need, maybe just to get home and enjoy it☺....
Whenever cardboard becomes available it's cut to replace foil, thoughts have sprung to mind of giving the bungalow the pet name 'Cardboard Cubby'. I'm beginning to lose count of the number of boxes carved up and poured into timber gaps ☺....
Amongst opened mail was an envelope from APRA, Australian Prudential Regulatory Authority, I then wasted what remained of daylight chasing up yet another of their bloody errors. In the process of accessing Superannuation Scheme funds they first sent documentation to the wrong address, an error I was left to deal with, this time it's the wrong scheme name. Bloody bumbling fools!!!!

Friday 21 June 2002
Aimless, not really knowing what to get my teeth into, was probably caused by what awaited, taking steps to rectify the wrong Super Scheme name!!!!
Occupying an idle mind one-month to the day of our arrival, I touched the surface at applying a loved look to the cottage. Used as a shed in a former life, a few metres of chicken wire walked out the door and anything else that had 'didn't belong' written over it followed me down to the shed....
Running shy on energy for anything manual decided cutting cardboard and filling gaps fitted the mood, sticking with it while the light was good....
Daydreaming out the bungalow window sipping brewed coffee as the curtain opened onto night, at that precise moment I didn't want to be anywhere else ☺....

Saturday 22 June 2002
I offered the world very little in the way of groundbreaking. Destiny's request for attention was answered by having a tinker with her carby attempting to loosen a sticking choke cable. She'll soon enough let me know how well I fared ☺ ….
Losing what remained of the day spreading myself between the cottage and cardboard cubby I dabbled at a bit of everything. Complementing nature's nice warm offering I was able to open housing for a good airing, fresh air adds lightness to a room.…

Sunday 23 June 2002
A fair bit of activity was going on in the garbage bag hanging from the wall, waking a sleeping household 4:30am wasn't greeted with approval. A mouse happily fossicking in the bag heard the effects of the tyre lever when I gave the bag a few swipes. Like a scene from a cartoon, the mouse sprang half a metre into the air while simultaneously projecting itself forward with such speed even I was impressed. Vermin activity has slowed since the 'cardboard cubby' commenced creation, although a couple of mousetraps should help slow activity even further.…
Filling in a lazy old Sunday on personal maintenance, the neighbours, Troy and Paul drove over and introduced themselves. Troy and his young family lease the house and Paul leases the 500 acres attached farming beef cows. Conversation with them showed interest in grazing cattle on home soil in return they'll slash and keep the paddocks tidy…. Sounds reasonable????
Running out of ciggys instigated a wander down the hill, making the drive worthwhile Destiny was filled with the aroma of a burger with the lot for the trip back. Sharing the experience, Tia got what I couldn't eat, lettuce, beetroot and alfalfa were left to last but didn't remain.…
Capping the whole experience with coffee and Tim Tam slams, yeah.…

Monday 24 June 2002
On the drive home from a Post Office and groceries trip a wave of risqué came over, being a bit rash a step was taken on the wild side detouring to South Sister lookout. Challenging my fitness level she was a hard walk to the top but well worth it the 360° view was spectacular, offering an illusion of seeing forever. Spread through the vast expanse, St. Marys and surrounds fit into the picture along with never ending mountains, ranges and ocean, an ideal spot for a picnic.…
Complementing all the bloody gaps I've filled with cardboard four mousetraps slipped in with today's shopping. All traps set and strategically placed throughout the bungalow tonight I feel pretty vermin proof. Those couple of persistent, pesky little mice will have to be very, very careful ☺ !!!!

Tuesday 25 June 2002
Curiosity killed the mouse one pesky little varmint went to heaven in a snap and already the great indoors feel cleaner.…
In a desperate attempt to add life to my near on white boots I gave them a lick of nugget to look as reasonable as they could for a town visit, their days are numbered.…

Ground softening welcome rain also gave Destiny a rinse doing a mountain dash to St. Marys Medical Centre. Still needing to put more meat on my bones left with a medical certificate buying two more months to do just that, a drive to St. Helens finalised the required paperwork to go home and heal. Driving away from the coast back into hilly country yet another rainbow presented itself. The frequency of rainbows is regular at home South Sister Range is a magnet for the colourful arches....

Wednesday 26 June 2002
Walking between the cottage and bungalow last night, stopping me in my tracks, one couldn't help but notice a powerful spotlight through trees by the top boundary. The angle of the bright beam was so low, large and split by trees initially I didn't recognise it as the moon, an exceptional planetary performance of light mingling through nature....
Filling out documentation for the overdue release of superannuation funds and a dash of financial freedom stole away the morning. Loading the family in the car the mountain was tackled to post the paper bundle, we then headed to St. Helens where I treated myself with shopping, laundry, and no trip feels complete without going to the hardware store, which is expanding, yahoo!!!! Without walking out empty handed, technology at Rainbow Falls was extended, a measuring tape and pliers was added to the tool collection my fingers say hallelujah....
Doing the usual pull up and shut the front gate routine getting home, the neighbours dog offered a moment of cuteness, he had been over to check out the new girl that has moved in across the road. Unsure and lacking in confidence he meekly exited as we entered. A beautiful looking dog, predominantly white with a couple of black patches, cute and shy, he is similar in size to Tia....

Thursday 27 June 2002
Totally unmotivated, I made myself get up at 9a.m., by placing one foot in front of the other we were fed and watered. Sitting quietly in the bungalow eating and browsing yesterday's paper a trap springing broke the silence, mouse number two has now gone to heaven....
Looking for direction I wandered into the cottage armed and dangerous with the new measuring tape. Sorting through a stack of cut timber for the purpose of cottage renovations, an area of wall was wiped over preparing it for banging a few planks onto....
Working in the cottage certainly added some needed spring into my step. Getting serious and inspired I made the measuring tape earn its keep, finalising the last five metres of skirting board I also measured, cut and nailed the first wall finishing board on, leaving me feeling pumped....

Friday 28 June 2002
With the selection of crude tools consisting of handsaw, measuring tape, hammer and nails, nineteen boards were measured, cut and found a spot on the cottage wall....
Other than having an idea of what bits should go where carpentry has never been a feather in my cap. Achieving in unfamiliar territory has given confidence a huge boost, leaving me feel I could tackle almost any job ☺ !!!!

Ducking down to the Post Office, rain on and off the past couple of days has wet up the dirt track making the trip a lot slower. Well compacted, the road surface can vary from firm to slippery and exposed rock in short stretches. One thing is for certain, owning another road bike while living up here is out of the question....

Saturday 29 June 2002
There is never a dull moment living in a semi-isolated environment. Dabbling around in the cottage I heard the sound of voices, four in fact. Introductions established my visitors to be brothers John and Roger Lohrey, both raised at Rainbow Falls, in the company of Rogers' daughter and her boyfriend....
Soaking in a little history on offer, the first registered settler of Irish descent, Edward Young, having no siblings, left Rainbow Falls to the Lohrey family of German heritage. It was some time after Edward settled that the Lohreys too established home in Dublin Town. John and Rogers' father, Norman Lohrey, was given Rainbow Falls for his 21st birthday. When Norman married Doris they had built the house that has since been burnt....
Before leaving John and Roger gave me their mother, Doris' contact details, 88 and living in Launceston, mentioned she would love to tell me the history of Rainbow Falls over a cup of tea or two... Lucky I like tea and history ☺....

Sunday 30 June 2002
A third mouse fell victim through the night. With no fresh poo evident in the bungalow the vermin population is feeling under control....
Pleasant enough to leave the door open for an airing, I warmed my bones cutting another empty water box contributing to draught proofing the bungalow. Incorporating a bit of variety around boiling bath water, my eyebrows were plucked, a couple of boards were measured and cut in the cottage and weeds were chipped. Chipping weeds is where I crossed paths with a cute little frog....
Fresh from the bath, hair washed beanie free and free flowing, I perched on the window box sipping at coffee and eating chocolate royals, hmm, don't call me I'll call you ☺....

Monday 1 July 2002
Superb to be outside, I didn't hesitate to get out amongst it. With the help of my little mate we found the base of some fenceline, but for the most, we focussed on polishing the impressive view from the bungalow window box perch by sharpening the border of the rock pile ☺....
Sticking with the low-key quiet mood I slipped between North and South Sister's Mountains doing a Post Office and supermarket run, those little white plastic bags were filled with enough to keep us up the hill until Thursday at minimum. Pointing Destiny's nose homeward we re-immersed back into the sanctuary of not having to be anywhere at any specific time, working within a sense of freedom is good for the soul ☺....
A few celcius added to the air has encouraged a second consecutive beanie free day. Without having had a haircut since departing my Wollongong life, the faithful old beanie has been the only thing keeping hair out of my eyes!!!!
In the psychological lead up to quitting smoking, Sunday I took a step forward by reducing to 1mg menthol, puffing my way through twelve yesterday and the same number today. I'm

calling the 1mg's my patches, I think they release less of a hit into my system than real patches do, they're a lot of work for not much. Reeling in the habit by not smoking after 5:30pm, I'm slowly working the little buggers down....

Tuesday 2 July 2002
Procrastinating my way around, I settled into building a 'Sue nest' in the cottage, measuring, cutting and hammering until the nails ran out. The section under construction that wall finishing boards are being added to is now about two-thirds complete. Working towards habitable, the cottage will be comfortable enough for guests once the heating problem is resolved ☺....
Lucky my little mate is young and blessed with a good bladder. Giving myself permission to roll with listening to a lean body's healing requirements, I have hibernation sleep averaging ten hours, lots of catch up to do.... zzzzz....

Wednesday 3 July 2002
In bed at 9p.m. and up at 9a.m. is a loud scream out to slow down and put the rest and recuperate wheels in motion. By simply doing what energy allows you wouldn't want to be paying me wages, sometimes doing a lot sometimes just a little, but always moving in the right direction ☺....
Underweight, a period has the capacity to wipe me out, knocking the wind out of my sails for a week this time. Ongoing physical work does me no favours, but full of excitement for discovery it's hard to hold back....
Near on out of patches to satisfy cravings I ducked down the hill for ciggys and a check of the mail. A stock-take count of unburned butts revealed only seven passed my lips for an impressive, most refrained, will-power tester.... Another psychological step toward quitting ☺....
Forms and fees lingering amongst mail, harbouring penalties if neglected, make it bloody difficult to step back from an economic world that is so easy to get into. Companies are empowered with the ability to force a direction that not necessarily suits needs, lifestyle or health, and for the most, rigid, cold and unbending, lack humanity, compassion and understanding. Piece by small piece I've been shedding the gadgetry and wallet full of plastic, the 'must haves' that once fulfilled my complete life. Getting some of the monkeys off my back I live for the day obligations are reduced to the bare bones of living expenses!!!!

Thursday 4 July 2002
Rising from a hibernating coma, my little mate and I were set-up with breakfast, luckily, it supplied enough sustenance to chat with my sister Kerry for the following two hours ☺.... yarp, yarp, yarp, yarp....
Observing the world from the loo I was impressed by an eye-catching clump of various sized juvenile trees having a healthy go at life. Extending a helping hand, I got off the throne, got the long handle secateurs and got into eliminating non-native competition. Working near the waterfalls is a nice part of the world to get lost in ☺....

Friday 5 July 2002
A full day outside the front gate, once bathed, fed and watered we went to town. The laundromat is a great place to have a chat, I struck up a conversation with Craig, "but everyone calls me Alf", so it was Alf. Masses of hair tucked under and out of his beanie for insulation against cold, Alf's speciality is crayfishing. Staying out on the boat working pots for up to seventeen days at a time, he only recently took a television for company after eight years of listening to sounds the sea offers…. Another who likes the peace found in absolute silence…. Tumble drying done the supermarket came into sights to keep our bellies full a bit longer. Adding a twist from the norm on our big outing I pulled into the curb out front of the recently established local radio station 'Break O'Day FM'. The radio station is constantly advertising for volunteer announcers, reckoning I'd enjoy giving it a go walked to a closed door. The buggers closed at 12 noon and I was standing there at 2p.m., not good, on the positive I at least now know where to find them next trip to St. Helens☺….

Saturday July 6 2002
Chance opened a voyage for discovery. So nice outside, I just wanted to be out there. Wandering outdoors with the intent of tidying about the entrance gate to have Rainbow Falls take on an occupied look, I only made it a few steps beyond the bungalow. Warming up the shovel bringing to light a large rock free of shadowing tall growth I didn't get any further, there was another rock and another, and another, but wait there's more. Absorbed in the excitement I started an excavation site, exposing several large slabs evenly laid like paving???? An amazing amount of metal bits 'n' pieces also surfaced with each load of dirt removed, from a horseshoe, old rusty gate hinges and metal pins, all signs that an old gate once existed. Feeling like a kid on a treasure hunt every shovel full unearthed something new and exciting, detracting from rusty metal, the largest worm I've seen was brought to the top, extending from the tip of my middle finger to my wrist, it was bloody huge☺!!!!
Breaking the large green expanse, the freshly revealed slabs of rock once buried under centimetres of soil add earthy colour to the yard. All good intentions for the entrance gate will have to wait for another time☺….

Sunday 7 July 2002
A pretty sure sign its nice out is when the little weather forecaster is keen to get out of bed, if Tia's content to snooze, its beanie temperature☺….
Motivation still fresh and hungry the excavation site was a magnet, the more soil turned the more treasure found, curiosity has now extended the diggings over a seven metre by five metre area. The dig site is really evolving into something quite big and exciting, what's left to be discovered remains a mystery but there's a hint of a buried past from Edward Young's Irish era☺????
Sitting in soft lighting from a single candle burning I noticed something odd on the carpet, putting the candle closer for identification illuminated a blood bloated leech content with life's offerings, but not for long!!!!

Monday July 8 2002
Out the gate early in anticipation of a healthy super cheque arriving, it had, ya-fucking-hoo, returning choice, we're as free as life permits....
Waiting friendly mail was aplenty, a welcome letter sent from Mary, Joan and Judy filled my hand reaching into the Post Office box. I prefer to hold and read a hand written letter there's something very individual and personal about it. Mum and Dad also forwarded on local Mildura newspapers containing Uncle Terry's tributes, not letter writers, they did however attach a hand written note. Dad writes only when he has to so I handed him a challenge to write one word in a letter for every journal page I write, fill that fountain pen with ink Lukey ☺ ....
Collecting mail is a big thing, the 16 kilometre return trip to the little black box is not taken thoughtlessly, and made all the more exciting when there's something friendly to collect, quality thoughtful friends make sure of that ☺ ....

Tuesday 9 July 2002
Softening the ground nicely, rain from 5a.m. through to 8a.m. set the stage for ideal shovel conditions. Starting by the west side of the cottage facing the driveway, the site there's supposed to be a septic tank, offering hope of a flushing toilet I've just got to find the septic ☺ ????
My interest led a curious mind astray, after some rough treatment a dose of tenderness was applied to the burnt out house front veranda, offering a cared for look....
Delivering a bit more of the same, moisture falling from the sky nearing 3p.m. cleared the playing field driving those without webbed feet inside for a half-hour. Still keen for the outdoors, returned to the car garage next to the burnt out house having a go along the side of the concrete retaining wall leading up to the entrance. Standing on top of the wall slamming the shovel down levering out clumps, and job just about complete, the shovel found a tough spot. Slamming the shovel in a few extra times, levering the clump forward I saw colour and muscle movement that didn't belong to grasses. Unaware if I killed or injured my first snake but I wasn't hanging around to find out, calling Tia away without fuss it was time to call it a day....

Wednesday 10 July 2002
Waking, Tia wanted out straight away, the barometer indicated nice weather waiting the other side of the door and the forecaster was true to character. Having heard its lure the past couple of trips up the hill to the loo, obeyed the instincts of nature taking the remainder of the trip strolling to the waterfalls with my little mate. A magic performance turned on by the elements made the experience all the more pleasurable ☺ ....
Reptiles not being one of my strongest traits, following yesterday's accidental encounter with the snake thought I might wait to purchase a brushcutter to finish the job off by the car garage. The excavation site was a safer bet for those who don't need too much excitement, when leeches, worms and frogs are enough ☺ ....
Vermin activity finding its way inside the bungalow has gone quiet since the third mouse went to heaven. I hope it stays that way ☺ !!!!

Thursday 11 July 2002
Tidying a few loose ends in the outside world I pointed Destiny's nose at the front gate and she led the way. The big excursion couldn't have started more perfect, going to pay bills the Post Office stop was made all the more pleasant with friendly mail waiting. A beautiful letter from Kristy-Lee and girls gave me the warm and fuzzies the entire envelope contained nothing but love ☺ ....

Ducking over next to St. Marys friendly mechanic Grant, made a booking for next week to have Destiny's carby receive more attention than I can give her, then it was express all the way on the final leg to St. Helens....

Taking it in stride waiting for washing to do its thing I went to Centrelink, newsagent, supermarket and the hardware store. Putting in a big committing finish gluing stray threads together to join the 'Natural State', and St. Helens having the closest Service Tasmania for anything to do with car registrations, I pledged allegiance to our new home State. My license changeover breezed through the system to spit out the vital piece of plastic confirming my Taswegian status, failing with Destiny's new identity, absent one vital piece of paper she gets a roadworthy 10a.m. tomorrow....

Friday 12 July 2002
Tidying the remaining loose identity thread returned to St. Helens for Destiny's scheduled 10a.m. appointment. Preferring to be punctual usually find myself early, so I filled the gap beforehand in search of a haircut, threatening to go home and shave it off if I couldn't get one, it was my lucky day ☺ ....

Destiny in having her gadgets pushed, twisted and pumped for that all-important roadworthy piece of paper, idle waiting time was invested wisely at the mower business buying a brushcutter and accessories, look-out weeds and grasses. The guy at the mower business said to bring the brushcutter in for a free service after five hours of use, my reply was, "I'll see you Monday" ☺ ....

Still filling wait time, while I was roaming through a shop Tia was tied and waited patiently at a shop door, a passing Jack Russell terrier decided it owned the street and was promptly told to share. Those little dogs are full of spunk and no fear they're to be admired for courage. During my wander tried the radio station again but Friday isn't good either, office hours are Monday to Thursday, I guess it will happen when the time is right ☺ ....

With my fist loaded with the entire collection of paper Destiny completed her transition to a fully-fledged Taswegian, proudly displaying new number-plates. They are the cleanest part of her ☺ ....

Nothing left to hold us in town and the draw to play with the new toy strong I didn't look back. One and a half hours tackling fenceline along the driveway made a fast impact on applying a loved look, a week's work with the shovel!!!!

A great day was topped with the most perfect phone conversation with my mate Mary from Mildura. Oddly, Mary rang to advise me on the best brand of brushcutter to buy, as fate happens it was the one brought home and exactly the same as hers. Our conversation turned into a brushcutter bonding session, entering into accessories boasting Mary won she has a stihl stubby holder ☺ ....

I can't wait for the sun to come up tomorrow to get back out there....

Saturday 13 July 2002
One wouldn't have needed a crystal ball to predict my movements. Productively revealing, I was straight into brushcutting tidying fenceline following the driveway from the cottage to, and including, the driveway entrance. Slowly exposing Rainbow Falls' hidden beauty ☺ ….
Working the machine a great little system fell into motion, the brushcutter tank took a half-hour to empty and pot for bath water three-quarters of an hour to boil. When the brushcutter stalled empty and was prepared for another round, it was spot-on time to empty the boiler. Then I'd do it all over again ☺ ….
Consecutive days of sunshine have cast a little warmth over the cottage adding lingering pleasure to bath time. Fitting in with obsessive amounts of brushcutting an extra pot was boiled, spoiling myself with a 'nipples under' bath. Five boilers they're out, six they're under ☺ ….

Sunday July 14 2002
Leaving my mind to wander, I filled the morning with personal grooming while Tia went about protecting her yard making sure everything was where she left it ☺ ….
Supporting a squeaky clean body we loaded into Destiny doing the mountain dash to satisfy my need for a couple of things in town. Acting on impulse, while still on bitumen I made a rash decision to travel on fresh ground and wander somewhere we haven't been. Taking in a good mix of windy mountain forest to coastal views, Destiny took us around the triangle. Winding through Elephant Pass to the Coast we followed the Coast up returning back via St. Marys Pass. Elephant Pass has some outstanding scenery winding through roads carved into mountain, from beautiful trees, an assortment of ferns, bloody long roadside drops, road kill, an array of plant varieties, oh, and other traffic to keep your eyes busy….
Enough of the life as a tourist it was back to Rainbow Falls for more land reclamation….
The side yard to the cottage was today's beneficiary to feel the effects of the brushcutter upon it. Knocking the life out of grass clumps makes ground outstandingly easier to walk on, however the tidiness has openly exposed the waterline to frost ☺ ….
In the past I've never been much of a stargazer, but far removed from city or street lighting the depth of clarity of space and density of constellations stops me in my tracks and beckons gazing time….

Monday July 15 2002
Before diving in with a spinning blade, while etching a brushcutter safe distance around a couple of obvious large rocks with the shovel I stumbled upon a familiar story, there were more rocks, and lo and behold the cottage side yard now has a fire pit ☺ ….
As predicted the first five hours of operation took no time to clock-up. Bathed and on the go early, the brushcutter was taken in for its first service….
In my latest phase of getting to know the extended backyard and alternate routes, returning from St. Helens I left bitumen taking the Upper Scamander Road toward home…. It's certainly not designed for comfort….

Tuesday 16 July 2002
Tia gave me a worrying start to the morning. Responding to her request for outside at 7a.m. I dived back into bed, after a reasonable toilet break time I went to let her in, having other ideas she was nowhere to be found. Searching obvious places and still no Tia, jumping in Destiny to broaden the search drove to where the road ends at our bottom paddock gate, there be one white and one brown dog. Tia and the neighbour's dog have developed a beautiful friendship, worry settled and thinking shifted, the dogs can exercise one another and have a little fun ☺.... Interestingly watching Tia's intent concentration sitting outside under the bungalow window, looking towards her playmates house white dog was trotting down the road. Watching them through binoculars, white dogs' tail began wagging and was as eagerly met by a brown wagging tail, after initial hellos it was off to play at white dogs' house.... Happy days ☺....

Wednesday 17 July 2002
At the front gate yesterday I told cows in the adjacent paddock to escape and of their pending fate, taking me literally, I was amused to see four cows on the road this morning. I guess I didn't tell them where to go ☺....
Taking a courtesy drive over to the neighbours to tell them about straying cows, I also established there were no problems with the dogs socialising, leaving more informed I was told white dogs name is Snowy. Parting the inseparable pair I took Tia for a drive to St. Helens to bring the serviced brushcutter home....
Doubling the trip with a dash of forward planning I walked through the door of the travel agent booking me, my car and me dog onto the Spirit of Tassie. Setting a Bass Strait crossing for 4th September leaves plenty of time to make Mildura for the up and coming big event of Kristy-Lee's 21st ☺....
Met by open doors everywhere, I went and found another open at the radio station to offer my services as a volunteer.... Let's see what happens ☺????
Without fear of cobwebs settling I began working on hour number six, but brushcutting was brought to an abrupt halt the instant the blade hit the 2-inch irrigation pipe fed from the dam. My thinking immediately went to finding the nearest in-line main to stop the gushing flow, bleed the line, cut and repair. Ha bloody ha, there was no in-line main between the cut and the dam, adding to the challenge the exact location the pipe was sunk in the dam was also a shortcoming. Sorting out the irrigation system hasn't been a priority, guess it just shifted it up the list fuck it!!!!

Thursday 18 July 2002
Starting on the obvious, there was no idle bum scratch and look around my brain was active with thoughts of gushing water the moment my eyes opened. Trying to locate the irrigation pipe in the dam gave me no luck, beaten by the moment decided to just let the bastard empty. One paddock should green up nicely, a couple of thousand litres of water helps ☺????
Appearing like Tia had injured her side I took her inside to clean blood away for a better look. Finding nothing major, rolling Tia over merely revealed she was well and truly in season, if Snowy's not desexed the puppies should be cute ☺....
Warming Destiny's oil doing the mountain dash a wonderful box of goodies waited at the Post Office. Stacey and Kerry had pieced together a survival kit. Opening it was better than

Christmas, it contained a big chew bone for Tia, a packet of flower seeds, gardening gloves, novelty band-aid's, two girly calendars, secateurs, photos of Stacey's unit and more, the box gave a lingering feel good effect ☺ ....

Toiling the afternoon away in the cottage I cut finishing boards for the wall, leaving them lean against their designated spot they looked pretty good just sitting in place....

Sealing into the bungalow for the night young Tia settled straight into bed with her present from the survival kit, having a passionate gnash at the bone in doggy utopia....

Friday 19 July 2002
Seriously not having a good time of it, I well and truly should have stayed in bed, no matter what I had a go at I fucked up! With dust settling on the near on 100 kilometre round trip to pay land rates, beginning my bad run I pulled up out front of the bank in St. Helens to find I'd forgotten my wallet, great start! Minor dilemma sorted, I got myself comfortably home and in the safe hands of the shovel but didn't have the energy for its weight. Feeling a bit testy, I pitted myself against a few nails and ended up throwing the hammer to the shit house, so I gave that away quickly. Feeling left-wing cranky is a bit like having a headache, going when it's ready!!!!

Making less noise when thrown, I sidetracked a restless mind paper shuffling. Preparing the annual tax return was enough to sober my shitty mood.... Thank Christ....

Tia took an evening stroll over visiting Snowy, checking her whereabouts later found the two of them snuggled together by the bungalow door. Dear Snowy is a little flighty, unsure of me, interrupting his cuddle he took off home. It'll only be a matter of time before I win his confidence and he'll feel comfortable to freely visit and stay a while....

Saturday 20 July 2002
Of recent, opening the bungalow door holds no surprises, freed to the day Tia and Snowy seek one another out. Separating best friends for a short time a drive was taken to fulfil my duty of compulsory voting. A thought regularly rising to the surface looking for a solution, while in town I stopped into Grant's to buy hose clamps for the purpose of slowing the dam emptying process....

Squinting with water giving me a dousing, there was no easy way, working with gushing water under pressure I persistently kept turning the nut on the hose clamp turn by slow turn pulling the horizontal irrigation line split ends together. Only a band-aid fix, the pipe split still leaks but a few hose clamps have greatly reduced the flow rate....

Returned to positive, my attitude is far easier to be around. Regaining enough confidence to pick up the brushcutter, other than a little shovel work, the cottage side yard is complete. Surfacing from underneath the removed outer coating are clumps of flowering bulbs. A delicate, small, down turned bell shape white flower known commonly as snow drop is a visually refreshing change to weeds and grass clumps ☺ ....

Sunday 21 July 2002
It's hard for my brain to harbour the concept we've been living at Rainbow Falls now for two months. Time hasn't stood still????

Wandering a little further afield the brushcutter was taken for a drive to the end of the road freeing up bottom paddock gates. Leaving gates to swing freely I drained what remained in the tank at the front entrance. Returning the troupe inside home gates then further polished the shovel handle in the cottage yard....

Kerry and Stacey wouldn't recognise the gloves sent in the survival kit, the colour has changed somewhat through serious work usage....

Lounging around outside on grass enjoying the warmth of late afternoon sun, reaching to pat Tia my hand found a small stick clinging to her fur, nothing unusual, but what held it in place was the thorn it was attached to. Wedged firmly into her side she let me pull it out without a whimper, I haven't known a time Tia's encountered so many injuries, the little bugger has no fear and is in the thick of everything. On the flip side it's the healthiest and happiest she's ever been, one by one the problems causing injuries are slowly being tidied...

Monday 22 July 2002

Returning from a quick trip down the mountain I destroyed more fossil fuel making in-roads in the front yard of the cottage. Another small step taken onboard in the learning curve of outdoor life is the importance of the correct choice in shoes. Non-selectively a deep grooved tread collects a massive amount of poo, whether it's wallaby, possum or dog, the grooves pack it in....

Coming in overcast and cool we retreated for a more sedate pastime of prickle burning down the shed, there I had a major breakthrough with Snowy. Leaving him to build confidence at a safe distance, hanging around while I was brushcutting, burning prickles Snowy came into the shed hopping under Destiny initially for safety. Slowly at his own pace Snowy came over and let me touch feeling an act of kindness from a human hand ☺....

Letting the fire die down to finalise prickle burning I sparked up a ciggy and was going to gaze out the shed gates lazily, but smoke billowing from the cottage roof changed that mood, not something that was supposed to be happening?!?!

My feet didn't touch the ground racing over to find an area of wall alight, without a second thought I worked on turning the situation around. Having me moving it didn't take long to douse naked flame, however, the timber being so dry I kept pouring water on anything smouldering. All over in a half-hour, it was excitement I could well do without!!!!

Unbeknown how a burning candle placed in a kitty litter tray of sand fell smouldering the edge of the tray into flame it progressed onto the wall. Sustaining a couple of burns to finger tips and a little smoke inhalation but nothing serious, it certainly put me on edge. I reckon I've nearly had enough of life's tests a run of luck that is not 'bad' would be pleasant. If this is a test of my strength of character then I'm feeling strong enough!?!?

Other than the obvious scorched wall the only other known damage is to phone line cables, attempting to phone out nothing positive happened stopping all communication to the outside world until it's fixed.... What a day, leaving me in disbelief because I'm so careful????

Tuesday 23 July 2002

My jitters made it through the night, good thing because by the time my boots were pulled off I was exhausted and slept solidly. Looking back with the luxury of hindsight not much was in favour, gravity fed, the waterline to the cottage was empty due to splitting the irrigation pipe and lowering the dam water level. Without power the landline doesn't work, my mobile had no credit and the neighbours weren't home. Hmm, the potential, only a lesson to learn and grow from....

Today is a new day, yesterday is behind, time to just get on with it and getting on with it meant cleaning up after the action. Poking my head through the access hole into the roof inspecting wiring, the only damage being to telephone cabling gave me confidence to return power....

Seeing how fire seems to be the theme, showing no fear resumed prickle burning down the shed. Keeping me alert, a shift in breeze directed the heater's smoke over the cottage causing a second take ☺.... Phew!!!!

Wednesday 24 July 2002

Snowy woke the bungalow occupants four times through the night scratching and whining at the door to come in. It just about tore my heart out to leave him outside knowing how cosy we were on a cold night just the other side of the door. He sure could use a bit of love. I'm certainly no tough farmer there's no way I could run animals for slaughter, I'd go broke, they'd get pet names and die of natural causes ☺....

When we did greet a delighted Snowy and the new day, a most beautiful rainbow stretching from the falls arching perfectly to the bottom of the property was on display ☺....

Putting wiring repair into action, I'd just finished bathing when Roy turned up to re-connect us to the outside world. Having travelled to Mildura with the Ulysses Motorbike Club and familiar with the Nangiloc, Colignan areas, gave us plenty in common to talk about. Playing around with wires Roy extended technology setting up a phone socket in the bungalow....

Feeling my way around the municipality I deviated from the norm sampling grocery shopping at Bicheno, it's about the same distance but in the opposite direction to St. Helens. Uninspired for anything physical a drive suited me perfectly....

Thursday 25 July 2002

Unwilling to take the final step letting dear old Snowy inside, he copped some harsh words through the night with continual whining at the door. My words made such an impact Tia didn't move from bed, not game to wake the grump!!!!

Taking the trek into St. Helens to the closest laundromat the trip was utilised to incorporate something more pleasant, responding to a telephone message I called into the radio station. Greeted warmly, I was shown through the building and introduced along the way to those working. Completing the volunteer application form an interview was set for Monday at 11a.m. with Rita, Station Manager, and a personality behind the microphone at Break O'Day FM. Well, I guess the ball's rolling now ☺....

A few more boards felt the effects of nails and found a position on the cottage wall but the lure of reading by the heater to escape cold won over....

Friday 26 July 2002

On a mission to do a food stock-up for the weekend first poked the key into the Post Office box retrieving out an official invitation to spunky bum, Kristy-Lee's twenty-first. A pretty invitation with an envelope full of bloody glittery sprinkles, I'm definitely going the ferry is already booked ☺....

Fiddling around with the shovel in front of the cottage rain drew outdoor activity to a halt stopping play shortly after 2p.m., grateful, by then I'd had enough. A treasure long grown over, an old rusted rabbit trap was today separated from its overgrown captor finding a spot amongst the rusty pieces of treasure stored in the shed. Weather elements taken into consideration, like a smart farmer, adjourned to the shed ☺….

Our regular visitor Snowy must have been tied up, he hasn't been sighted since yesterday. It's been nice to have a break, whining at the door through the night is a bit much. I do feel sorry for the poor bugger, not too pampered, he's a very nervous flighty dog….

Saturday 27 July 2002
With more than my fair share of jobs to choose from it's just a matter of picking a spot that takes a fancy and starting. Being the focus of today's attention I edged along the front of the cottage. A stash of surfacing treasure amused a mind not overly taxed by shovel work. Seeing first daylight in a while was an old saucer, a ten cent coin, a gnome, plastic lizard, plastic horse and two metres of picket fence lying idle on the ground….

My everything hurt after a big day working the shovel even a long soak in the hot water of a bath didn't cure aching muscles….

While doing a bit in the yard a couple of blokes turned up after following posted 'For Sale' signs looking for a hobby farm to run a few cattle. At this stage I'm not keen on selling and the longer we remain it will become less likely, I feel in my heart me, Tia and Destiny will be here for quite some time. It's a peaceful haven escape from the rest of the world offering personal decision making freedoms and forcing me to think, a struggle to find bombarded in advertising, systems and the lots of advice associated with living amongst the masses….

Sunday 28 July 2002
A fiery red sunrise welcomed in the fresh day. If the old cliché, 'red sky at night shepherds delight, red sky in the morning shepherds warning', is correct, then moisture should be lurking about, and it was, 3:30p.m.-ish gentle, steady rain hovered above….

It feels like forever ago we were last there, so the cycle of half jobs on the go must have done a complete circle, delving back into the elevated garden armed for some serious pruning made a good impact. Observing human behaviour in a simplistic manner we spend our lives moving things, every task undertaken involves moving something in one form or another. It brings a smile to my face observing daily tasks a bit like worker ants we spend our lives shifting things. If I had to collectively describe the human race in one word it would be 'movers' ☺….

No job being complete until it's cleaned up after. Me and my little mate took a few trips to the shed carting today's load of cut prunings, filling up the floor space just found and giving me fuel for the next rainy day. I reckon if the heavens seriously opened, and long after Noah considers building another Ark and starts loading them in two by two, I could still be down the shed burning prunings and prickles ☺ !!!!

Monday 29 July 2002
A follow up courtesy call determined my interview with Rita was postponed until 10a.m. this coming Wednesday due to a forgotten board meeting. Instead, dear Destiny was the lucky recipient receiving a long overdue wash to expose her hidden colour and windows ☺ ….

Displaying a clean car made the trip to the tax agent all the more enjoyable. Shy of a group certificate the annual drudgery is all but finalised....
Filling the remaining daylight hours was done at the elevated garden, the worthless sample of non-native plants and shrubs only have value for shoving in the face of the heater, they're a pretty trashy selection. A pruning saw would be useful, the long handled secateurs and me don't have the strength required to tackle some of the thicker branched buggers....
And so winds down another glorious day in paradise ☺ ....

Tuesday 30 July 2002
Preparing my psychology, I basked in sunshine on the window box doing Tim Tam slams with a coffee. Smiling contentedly with an indulgent sugar and caffeine load took my passive mood into town. A wonderful present waited from Kylie, a friend from my Wollongong life, sending much needed film for the camera ☺ ....
Feet planted back on the ground and sharing my muscle groups around I played on the shovel unveiling more concrete pathway. With a pathway separating them, the clearing journey is progressing down the side of Doris and Norman's now burnt out house, with sights set for the perimeter of the fenced 'potential' vegie patch on the other side of the path....
I love a long leisurely bath on a warm day, its there I think I've discovered how to slow the ageing process without expensive lotions and potions. There's nothing like a thorough skin exfoliation with a face washer after skin has softened soaking in hot water, ahhhh ☺ ....

Wednesday 31 July 2002
Rattling my dags to get ready I drove the 100 kilometre round trip to St. Helens for the 10a.m. interview with Rita. Creating a comfortable environment, the interview was more of a relaxed chat. Leaving so soon for Kristy-Lee's 21st in Mildura training as an announcer is going to be left until after I return. Being multi-skilled I extended my volunteer generosity to reception, offering to work Fridays to extend office hours to five days a week commencing Friday week. Not walking out empty handed, I left with an invitation to pizza pow-wow for Tuesday 27 August 6:30pm, nearly my bedtime. A great concept, pizza pow-wow is an opportunity for staff and volunteers to congregate in the one place talk out any ideas or suggestions and meet and greet new faces over food ☺ ....
Prior to leaving St. Helens, and looking for assistance with the issue of running for a ringing phone and missing calls, reached for the solution in more white goods putting an answering machine on order. Delivering the outstanding group certificate my tax return will more than cover the white goods extravagance, a two and a half thousand return printed from the computer guaranteeing keeping a roof over our head a bit longer....
Finalising the day and my energy, played around extending concrete paths with the aim of making Rainbow Falls look lived in before leaving for Mildura....
Looking to settle in and relax young Tia changed that course, she received a sponge bath because there was no way we were sharing the same space with the aroma she was wearing around her neck!!!! Phew....
Not something to be done indoors, partaking in my smelly unhealthy smoking habit outside wasn't judged by nature for pollution, instead I was treated to a motionless calm, so still the

sound from a single owl calling echoed through the gorge travelling great distance....
Ahhhh....

Thursday 1 August 2002
Planting our feet and spending a day home, lost the morning pruning anything that got in the way inside the fenced 'potential' vegie garden. Keeping us company working outdoors was quite a large population of kookaburras, along with brilliant coloured wrens and robins they're gorgeous little birds. A lazy cold wind nudging me one too many times helped with the decision that there's something better I could be doing, making an executive decision to give it away....
Cleaning up after inroads made by the secateurs I boiled an extra pot of water for a 'nipples under', 'don't call me I'll call you', bath ☺ ....

Friday 2 August 2002
Visually, Rainbow Falls is taking on some shape complementing time invested, working like a termite, I simply make a hole and just keep working at it. Returning to an established termite hole armed with long handled secateurs penetrated into the dense wall of a shrub with small, densely entwined, leaf decorated limbs in the elevated garden.... Still got a long way to go with that termite hole ☺ ....
Having a change of scenery with established termite holes, I emptied a couple of tanks of juice in the brushcutter between the bungalow and dam. Every patch of ground touched by the brushcutter blade is transforming, greening up, and further inspiring me on. The housing area is beginning to breathe and feel good on the soul, watching positive change is uplifting, a different story now to when we first arrived not knowing where to start, a start has been made ☺ ....
Snowy still hasn't been sighted its been over a week even Tia's lost interest in visiting, a link in the chain somewhere is preventing the regular appearance of his face. Dogs don't have to talk observing actions speak volumes....

Saturday 3 August 2002
Breaking the tranquillity of last evenings peace, a car taking off from across the road flogging the cars engine left at a crazy pace, my request a couple of weeks back to slow down apparently fell on deaf ears. Car maintenance is their own issue, affecting us is their attitude putting Tia and me at risk, sharing and wrecking our only access road. A few days after first stepping foot on the soil of Rainbow Falls, early evening, a pair of old Holdens doing alley rings in front of the house and leaving from across the road, raced over and back through the mountain. My initial thoughts were the kids were mucking up while their parents were out, finding out they are the adults they have good skills to hand on to their kids. There is no such thing as 'boys will be boys', there are only responsible and irresponsible people, I'm glad I'm getting to know them from a distance because our common threads are few....
Putting my feet on the floor tackling the new one ahead I was inspired and full of energy for more brushcutter activity, however, Mother Nature had other ideas. The heavens spilled some much welcome moisture causing a shift in thinking but only for a short while. Utilising softened ground a pathway linking the burnt out house to the nearby car garage was exposed.

From observation there only seems to be one pathway at the burnt out house left to clear but like everything else time will reveal ☺....

Also putting her heart and soul into the transformation of Rainbow Falls, and always in the thick of it when there's work to be done, Tia showed obvious signs of discomfort finding the culprit to be a leech. Attached to her front leg the buggers certainly lodge themselves firmly into skin, this one won't be doing it again!!!!

Sunday 4 August 2002
Wandering aimlessly procrastinating my way around having a go at whatever tickled my fancy started by lowering the population of mosquito larva in the cattle trough. The elevated garden received a dose of my limited concentration span, and a few more progress photos made it into the camera adding just a little extra life to the words regularly written and stored in the journal....

My 'nipples out' bath water received a second use, much to Tia's disdain her scent was altered to lavender. Taking a lot of work to smell as beautiful as she did I turn around and ruin it within five minutes ☺!!!!

With the passing of each sunrise giving life only what's spare I'm growing back into my skin, the old healthy me is returning. My lungs almost function solo weight too must be finding bones because I now have tits. I'm eating enough for two people and sleeping pretty solidly, not to mention plenty of exercise and as much fresh air as desired, I'm starting to feel dangerous again ☺....

Monday 5 August 2002
Nothing is more pleasing than reaching my hand into the little black box to retrieve friendly mail. Taking a brief drive over the hill to keep home life ticking over, a very thoughtful niece Kristy-Lee and girls had taken the time to write. I love each niece dearly each reminding me a little of myself. Kristy-Lee is the quiet achiever and very creative, while Stacey knows what she wants and grabs onto life with both hands, young Tegan has a good heart with a bit of a rebel inside. I remember sitting down the 'rowers' in Mildura smoking rum tipped cigars when Kristy-Lee was born, it doesn't seem that long ago, and now the young woman is turning twenty-one ☺!!!!

Needing a job to warm-up with I mixed up the freshly purchased fuel for the two-stroke and only pulled up after emptying the fourth tank load in the brushcutter, the right job for the appropriate temperature ☺....

Most spurs and flowering bulbs are now exposed and easy to work around with the brushcutter. It's a slow moving job taking the time to grub back to ground level, thinking for the future, a lawnmower should then go over it with little effort. Eliminating lumps and bumps back to hugging the ground contour makes it far easier to walk on and play ball. Inspiring progress inspires progress it's a passion to bring Rainbow Falls back to her former glory ☺....

Tuesday 6 August 2002
Without getting out of bed the day was planned, ears tuned into inclement conditions determined the shed was the place to be....

It's a pure pleasure opening the bungalow door looking out over the ever-expanding tidied area with flowering bulbs dancing in the wind and rain. Overdue for a good soaking, pipping two months there's been nothing substantial.....
The sun popped out but didn't make much of an impact so Destiny supplied music to keep 'prickle burning' company. Keeping warm on weeds, chipped away shoving around ninety percent of them up the flue exposing a good deal of floor space only to make room for more ☺ ....

Wednesday 7 August 2002
So close to finishing, and as a bonus the heater drum still offered coals, so I let the whim take me back to the shed and prickle burning....
Slipping out of the haven on a brief mission for food I was meant to catch a phone call from my mate Bernie Bear, who by chance will be in Tassie tomorrow on a 'boat buying' trip. Wishing to cross paths, I couldn't think of anything better, bursting to show someone around I can only hope he's got enough energy to keep up ☺ ....
After washing prickle burning smoke from my body Tia and I ducked down the hill to stock the shelves and again friendly mail waited, this time from dear friends Sheila and Peter. I aspire to have a relationship like theirs, after seven years together, they don't always agree, but haven't exchanged a cross word. Not too many relationships could boast that level of caring consideration ☺ ....

Thursday 8 August 2002
The brushcutter lured me back under its spell to expose even more flowering bulbs. Another outing pushing the blade above the ground surface should complete the area between the shed and bungalow. Its amazing what weeds survive hidden within tufts of grass, eliminating a bloody lot knocking grass down low should save a lot of future work ☺ ????
It was a pure pleasure being outside with absolutely no wind and a warming sun, the mood of changing seasons is beginning to make an impression, even the days are longer maintaining daylight until a more respectable hour of 6p.m.-ish.... Not that I get anymore done ☺ !!!!
Wow, tomorrow my association with Break O'Day FM radio station commences, I'm looking forward to 'nine to two' in the office and the opportunity to expand my social life....

Friday 9 August 2002
Up by 6:30am to make the radio station by 9a.m., and loved it, sharing an amazing few hours with exceptionally nice people. Reception wasn't too taxing, what I enjoyed most is the friendliness in a relaxed atmosphere and the encouragement and enthusiasm towards creativity, it felt comfortable there....
Destiny's nose pointed toward home and tuned to the radio, on-air Rita dedicated a song to Bret and me for giving voluntary time at the station. I was deeply moved by the compliment of recognition ☺ ....
Bypassing the turn off to home, Rita's consideration sent me off to Launceston uplifted to pick Bernie Bear up....
Energy still flowing high managed a park out front of the bus depot a half-hour ahead of Bernie Bear. Arriving, we didn't take a breath constantly talking and hugging for ten minutes

before considering driving anywhere. For a dash of local culture, on the return trip home we stopped at a small town pub to wash the dust off a few kilometres over a beer, some local lads decorated the bar sleeveless flannel shirts offered a very country feel. Onward to our destination, St. Marys and the 'Ranch Diner' for dinner where Pamela has never failed to please a healthy appetite ☺ ....

Grabbing a nightcap bottle of port we headed up the hill to Rainbow Falls and the shed heater where we sparked a few candles into life, stoking the heater and chewing one another's ears off sipping port polished a bloody magic day ☺ .... Ahhhh....

Saturday 10 August 2002
Working with limited time, we got straight up and into a day of discovery for both Bernie Bear and me. Touring of the living area and waterfalls complete, Bernie, Tia and I headed down into the valley paddock at the bottom of the property to investigate the lot. Meandering up the rocky stream leading toward the base of the falls Bernie clearly demonstrated his passion for rocks and nature in general, his enthusiasm was infectious....

Using the principle of 'no point covering the same travelled ground', returned Bernie to Devonport via a scenic route through St. Helens to Scottsdale. Making fast grabs at worth seeing attractions along the way, while light lasted made St Columba waterfall a priority simply by being the largest and longest drop waterfall in Tasmania. The 'pub in the paddock' was next with the local icon 'slops' the beer drinking pig. After stopping in Scottsdale for a counter meal then followed the wiggly road kilometre after fucking kilometre until finally getting onto freeway after Launceston....

The guy Bernie is buying the boat from owns a motel in Devonport and extended the offer to put us both up with compliments, I'm going to run the hot water service dry ☺ ....

Sunday 11 August 2002
Settled into the motel for the evening, I was on my way out to take care of Tia's comforts, in passing was stopped by Frank at reception inquiring very diplomatically whether our accommodation was fine. In a round about way he was asking if we required a double bed, very tactful, I politely replied our accommodation was fine the hardest decision is what single bed to sleep in. Frank must have met some unfaithful people in his time????

Bernie left at an ugly hour for an early flight, he was on his own, I slept on until ready to leisurely turn those taps for a bottomless pit of regulated water ☺ ....

I really enjoyed the energy and enthusiasm of Bernie Bear's company he's a thoughtful sweetie.

Cleaning Destiny out at home the promotional Mars Bar wrapper found on the floor was a winner offering a free bar, although, I reckon I've been a winner all weekend ☺ ....

Lacking enthusiasm, with a fist full of newspapers escaped the elements and built a Sue nest reading and having a token go at the crosswords. Improvisation is at times amusing, without a dictionary and spelling skills that could use sharpening, which makes doing crosswords at times a little difficult, I've resorted to the index of the phone book.... '101 uses of a phone book' ☺ ....

Monday 12 August 2002
Following a pumping high-energy weekend with Bernie Bear, Tia and I slept like babies. Surfacing and poking my head out the bungalow door to face what the elements presented it was decided there and then, prickle burning ☺ ....
Setting daily life up to claim what time remained to adjourn to the shed for as long as desired first ducked down the hill to top up on tucker....
Music for company, through favourite songs my vocal chords got a stretch in between feeding the fire and kicking the tennis ball for Tia ☺ ....

Tuesday 13 August 2002
The shed was the place to be, if it wasn't icy wind and sunshine it was icy wind and rain for a bit of variety. Weather reports confirmed snow down to 700 metres, situated at about 300 metres wind comes with its own built-in chill factor ☺ ....
Anything could have been happening outside, playing with the heater, doing so well at keeping warm, found the floor and run the shed dry of trashy shit to burn until we make some more and drag it in ☺ !!!!
During Bernie's visit he discovered the guitar that's followed me through life the past twenty years that I still don't know how to play a chord on. Helping my cause, Bernie Bear wrote down three chords with finger placement and numbering to practice with. Unsure if by chance or a subliminal planted message, but the chords in sequence are D, A and G, was he trying to tell me something ☺ ????

Wednesday 14 August 2002
A little body maintenance, another battle with the crossword, eating and making a bath was all it took to keep me amused....
In quiet moments young Tia still wanders over to check for Snowy, going for a roam this morning a car pulled in and she came straight back....
Filling waiting time for a pastie to heat I practised the DAG chords on the guitar, Tia's reaction said it all she headed for the door. Food being Tia's priority, the aroma outmatched her need for retreat. I'm not going to have much company learning the guitar ☺ ....
When procrastination subsided two tanks of the brushcutter vaporised outside the bungalow, progressively opening progress gives a pleasing feeling of inner well-being ☺ ....
Striking at random, projectiles are propelled directly from the brushcutter blade into some unprepared part of my body, bath time reveals each new injury my shins lead with the greatest number of bruises....
No cloud to obscure the changing over of the guard into sunset, for a transient moment the entire length of the gorge was ablaze with the red of fiery setting colours. Trees lining the top of the gorge held the glow within while simultaneously casting shadow over paddocks and housing.... A magic moment in time ☺ ....

Thursday 15 August 2002
Rewarded with a 'bone warming' beaut after enduring a few coolies it made it easier being outside. I didn't feel much like changing the world even my hard working offsider preferred a lazy one basking in sunshine....

Diverting from the original idea of unearthing more concrete path, in hindsight, wish I had stuck with the idea. While collecting water at the cattle trough I did the regular 'mosquito larva population decrease' scooping them out with the bucket and tossing the load onto the lawn much to Tia's delight. Motivated by moving water I progressed to shifting the poly line for the cottage further out and deeper into the dam. Playing around inside the dam fence also moved the line to the cattle trough filling it with air. My initial thoughts went to it being only a matter of siphoning air out of both lines and all systems go, think again!!!! I sucked until my lips and tongue could take no more. The accidental half-metre drop in the dam water level is making it tough for surface floating pipes in a gravity system….

Friday 16 August 2002
With a cup full of enthusiasm, I had Tia and Destiny comfortably taking care of one another and myself punctually ready and available at the radio station by 9a.m.….
Doing the morning shift Rita asked if I would take and hold a call from Dr Harry, the TV personality Vet, until she was ready to take the interview live-to-air. I felt like a kid having the opportunity to chat with Dr Harry, but he was busily ordering food with someone in his immediate company, not real interested in my dog conversation….
Delivering brochures to local sponsors of the station, working at the CD Centre, Therese asked if I would consider joining the 'Grassy Bottom Regional Arts Group', promoting music and arts to the local area, it sounds like something I could enjoy….
Out roaming shops I purchased two folders for storing the neat stack of hand written pieces of paper keeping a record of life at Rainbow Falls, each folder is capable of holding about one and a half months of living on average. It will be amazing after filling a dozen folders to have a record of comparison to progress and change, so much to look forward to and so much to look back on ☺….

Saturday 17 August 2002
An absolutely pristine winter's day in paradise, Tia kept busy basking behind glass in Destiny sleeping leaving me to sweep the shed. Pushing the broom around a floor space twice that of the cottage, I'm now confident enough to walk in there without shoes….
My get up and go got up and went, not inspired by anything strenuous, roamed doing light duties only. After pruning a hydrangea in the front yard of the burnt out house, I moved onto a lavender, there scratching around I noticed, so far, about one metre of concrete path. I don't know exactly where it leads to or how long it is, but one thing is for sure that's a discovery to be made another time ☺….
Troy and Kristy, the neighbours leasing the house across the road, with kids loaded into the Ute paid a visit. It was a courtesy visit to let me know they'll be laying 1080 poison soon for the purpose of killing the native and non-native competition that's eating grass meant as cattle feed. I hope it coincides with us being in Mildura, I don't condone or like the idea of using poisons to kill native animals….
In keeping with a low impact mood I practised the three guitar notes. My chord change is improving however the 'D.A.G.' song still needs sharpening ☺…. Tia wishes I knew more chords ☺!!!!

Sunday 18 August 2002
Waking without relief from a night of healing sleep, still a little congested with persisting chest pain assumed to be the start to bronchitis, predetermined whatever happened was to be gentle and restful. Unable to lift the pace beyond lazy I only managed a bath and drive for a paper....
Parked in full sun near the shed I lifted Destiny's tailgate and built a nest spreading myself over the back of the station wagon, Tia didn't budge an inch from her Destiny sunroom basking either. Reading until the sun disappeared under cloud, then adjourned to the bungalow continuing with the theme of read, eat and crossword, that suits me but young Tia had some pent up energy simmering just below the surface ☺....
A regular at practising the DAG chords on the guitar, however, the stage has arisen I'm hungry for more knowledge for fear of boredom and loss of interest taking over, I'm floundering with a head full of questions and nowhere to source answers????

Monday 19 August 2002
Stripped down to a t-shirt unveiling the most recent concrete find in the front yard of the burnt out house, revealed it to be garden edging running parallel with the path leading to the front gate....
Sharpening her skills as a field mouse catcher, on a trip to the loo Tia was nose down bum up on a mission busily digging. Checking on her walking back, one mouse took off seeking refuge in a nearby clump of grass while she was being kept busy with a second. Tia's success rate isn't that high but she's certainly stirring them up ☺....

Tuesday 20 August 2002
Finally greeting a day with energy, the past few I've been feeling as strong as a half-sucked peppermint!!!!
Getting current with life on the outside world took the drive between the Sister's Mountains. Mail sorted and groceries stowed appropriately I put my new-found energy to use with the brushcutter, and use it I did, bringing an area in front of the cattle loading ramp down to size....
One thing is for sure there's going to be a few hundred less scotch thistles this season, between the brushcutter and my boot a potential good crop has been harnessed ☺....

Wednesday 21 August 2002
Shit, with one foot standing on a banana skin three months of living at Rainbow Falls has dissolved, passing so quickly, I guess we'll just have to keep living it to the fullest ☺!!!!
After a pretty casual start I eased into a drive to St. Helens specifically to pick up the answering machine, no more missed or chased calls. On a fact finding mission for answers to first aid for all the bitey things most likely to affect Tia I called into the Vet clinic, also getting my head full of knowledge on 1080 poison. That conversation led to the short drive to the Department of Primary Industry, the blokes there were again extremely helpful, addressing my concerns over the use of poison and the horrible death it causes....
The final stop was for a haircut, with my hair shorter and head full of knowledge it was back home to Rainbow Falls....

Setting up the answering machine took priority getting home. With only a double power point in the bungalow and one outlet catering for the fridge and clock, to expand choice the other has a four-plug power-board plugged in. The phone and answering machine take up two spaces on the power-board, so cooking, heating, and other needs are a juggling act ☺.... Lucky lighting is by candles....

Saturday coming young Tia turns four, it dawned on me she had her first birthday in Mildura, her second in Kiama, third in Wollongong and now her fourth in Tasmania, she has travelled and experienced more of life than some humans may ever dream to....

Thursday 22 August 2002
Factoring in the usual level of procrastination led to a wander into the front yard of the burnt out house where the decision was made to tidy up the last of the concrete chase. Its hard to catch a moving target, lo and behold I finish edging one strip of concrete and find another, again a job for some other time, tools were downed for a 1:30pm appointment with a doctor.... Granted another three month medical certificate lets my body stay at a pace it feels up to at any given moment and take a balanced path forward of both participation and healing. Moving in a positive direction another couple of kilos have found my lean bones ☺....

Back within the comfortable arms of paradise I reluctantly began taking prunings from the burnt out house to the clean shed. In the midst of carting a load of prunings, Russell the building inspector decided to pay us a visit. During the course of conversation Russell mentioned he'd let himself in and gone through housing on occasion when I was an absentee owner, saying the heater, kitchen sink and bench, along with the copper header tank were all in place when he last let himself in for a look around. Pondering my conversation with Russell prompted me to phone the Council asking why I never received a courtesy call, and if Russell wants to come up here again to first make an appointment!!!!

Reducing the smelly ciggy habit to one milligram, cutting back the amount I damage my lungs with daily, I'm having trouble taking the final step. Reaching for more experience I took positive action by phoning the 'Quit Line' and speaking to a counsellor and reformed smoker Eve. Every time thoughts and excuses ran to the safety of my habit, Eve would switch the light of logic on, our conversation left me empowered with strength sealing the decision to be free of the burdening smelly habit. Helping my cause a 'quit pack' should arrive with Monday's mail....

Friday 23 August 2002
Hitting the ground running for a dose of social interaction at the radio station, the latest progress photos were collected on the way. Taking a nice shot from the front yard of the burnt out house captured the window view to the ocean and the two little off-shore islands....

Being the face for Friday reception proved to be another enjoyable experience. The work isn't difficult what I enjoy most is the interaction with creative, giving people and the prospect of always meeting new personalities ☺....

Home not long after the stroke of three I got stuck into revealing yet more garden edging, carving a neat rectangle strip following the path to the burnt out house front entry gate, getting about halfway through it before running out of puff and calling it a day....

Another small step in the journey of life was reached with a second journal folder jam packed with our life's adventures now complete. Reading back over it, appropriately placing photos with the relevant occasion and date, early accomplishments feel like a lifetime ago. There's a long way to go and we've already achieved so much ☺ ....

Saturday 24 August 2002
Going through our usual morning cuddles, loves and scruff up routine, I went that bit further and sang 'happy birthday' to the big four-year-old then included a treat of schmackos with her special birthday milo ☺ .... Life's pretty good!!!!
A dangerous time for weight loss, a period determined nothing too strenuous, even if the body is willing the brain has to override without being tempted to join in. Phone calls, eating and practising the three notes on the guitar occupied idle hours along with plenty of love and attention for the birthday girl ☺ ....
Spreading solar panels for a re-charge we laid around outside on the grass taking in some sun. I attempted to write, but sleeping with one eye open, Tia lured me into a game of 'get the sheepie', a game that instantly activates her natural round-up instincts. A tennis ball being the prized 'sheepie' is placed between us, standing a few feet back and without forming patterns, I walk clockwise and anti-clockwise around the ball verbally and visually instructing Tia to either go round or back. Standing the same distance from the ball, Tia keenly and eagerly remains directly opposite the ball and me. A game only draws to a close when the final step is taken, stopping motionless in my tracks causes a flow-on effect with Tia, holding her concentration with my hand pointing directly at the ball repeat the words of "focus", at that point nothing else in the world exists. Holding motionless for varying lengths of time, Tia's taut muscles hold her in a 'ready to spring at any second' pose, waiting in full concentrating anticipation for me to slowly step up to the ball and kick it. Aerating the lawn, Tia hunts the escaping beast down bringing the ball back we do it all over again ☺ ....
Lacking substantial rain for quite some time the bulbs are looking a bit stressed, offering a token drink I've been recycling bath water to quench the thirst of a few. The value of water becomes blatantly eye-opening obvious when it isn't delivered by an external service, but the only thinking it eliminates is paying a bill. Scarce and precious, the resource has to be used to its fullest potential. Receiving a haircut with Kellie she asked "how's the water supply at your place", in the next breath asked if it was still flowing, dry conditions are capturing the topic of many a conversation....
Seeing out her birth date day one happy woman, for a special 'fourth birthday' celebration dinner Tia had beef and vegetable stew with pieces of fresh lamb throughout slightly warmed. Doing the dishes beautifully, when Tia finished her bowl couldn't have been cleaner ☺ ....

Sunday 25 August 2002
A precious occasion surplus energy filled my body. Breaking out of the termite hole maintenance cycle, used the freed up ability to scale the spectacular country immersed within South Sister Range on the hunt for the spring fed poly line feeding home's 7000 litre water tank. Only carrying scratchy knowledge of a conversation had sometime back with the previous owner, it wasn't a shock to have no luck finding the poly line. The entire outing

ending up being a lung pumping, spectacular, up hill walk learning the importance of following well worn wallaby tracks in thick mountainous scrub ☺....

Before driving back inside home gates a trip was done down the hill for ciggy's and paper, then it was time to lose a bit of that energy load on real work. Putting myself into action with the high revving whirly machine I grubbed around the carport in the driveway, even going as far as to finalise the side of the carport where the snake was encountered, an area I've been avoiding ☺ !!!!

With outcomes to measure, I could sit down with a clear conscience read the paper and relax....

Reading through earliest journal entries last night offered a laugh at the difficulty Tia and I first had playing ball, now I can't kick it far enough, my how times have changed ☺ ....

Monday 26 August 2002
The massive dose of energy that found my body lingered on. Dipping my oar in many waters started in the front yard of the burnt out house finding the last of the hidden concrete and severely pruning a dead hydrangea....

A quick trip down the hill, a feed and a read of the newspaper, I went to work with the brushcutter complementing the edging revealing paths. The plan of making Rainbow Falls look lived in and loved before we go to Mildura is coming together she's evolving beautifully ☺ ....

In town, sealing and joining tape made the grocery order, adding it to the split irrigation pipe pulled the slow leak up even slower, robbing Tia of one less spot to grab a quick drink from ☺ ....

Enhancing an already outstanding view from my window box perch in the bungalow, directly in front a beautiful display of flowering daffodils are adding a splash of lively colour. Popping spurs through the ground everywhere, the housing area resembles more of a market garden. Quite a variety of flowers and an assortment of colours are having their seasonal burst ☺ ....

Tuesday 27 August 2002
Such a mild start I didn't even bother turning the heater on, the seasons they are a changing ☺ ....

Because I can only concentrate on one thing at a time, Destiny is never far away taking good care of Ms Tia, permitting me put full focus into the spinning blade knocking down tall stuff....

Working around the burnt out house hasn't been without its surfacing treasure, a useful one-foot jemmy bar about the length of a hammer exposed itself, its half the size of the one found a while back. Other finds have been three shovel heads of varying shapes, seems to me that tools resembling hard work were buried throughout the yard ☺ !!!!

Tools away and squeaky clean, written onto the calendar so it was definitely happening tonight was the night to dust off social skills over pizza at the radio station. Always utilising a trip to St. Helens I spoilt myself doing laundry first....

Only ever meeting a small sample of the total staff and volunteers that make the entire station tick, pizza pow-wow brought a great number of them together. Rita's management sets the stage for a relaxed comfortable environment in which to get to know the faces behind the names, and to also offer ideas and suggestions value adding to the Station's operation....

Wednesday 28 August 2002
Pulling up at the front gate last night the sight of a powerful light in the distance, and what I thought to be gunshots, attracted attention, listening in it dawned the loud cracking noises were falling trees, turning out to be a logging coupe operating. I read with amusement in the last Council newsletter an article about issuing fines for excessive smoke omitted from the family home chimney, yet endorse a municipality forestry logging operations coupe burn???? Playing a double hand????
Starting slow I eased into the day, quietly waiting for a burst of inspiration to find me I took the team for a drive over the mountain to make a booking with Grant to give Destiny a check over before we head off....
Sitting content with bellies full, my mind wandered to finalise grubbing between the bungalow and shed, doing just that pulled the starter cord and filled the airwaves with the noise of the brushcutter. I'm happy with progress the evolution of Rainbow Falls is pleasing ☺....

Thursday 29 August 2002
Stirring briefly at 5:30am heard the start to good solid rain, the welcome sound on a tin roof without insulation put a smile on my face and sent me straight back to sleep....
Fed and watered, we roamed around checking benefits from the welcome moisture. The market garden of bulbs is now standing tall and proud with buds bursting to open. Even the less than happy violets are now standing to attention. Wet, everything looks sharp, healthy, clean and full of natural energy, in the short time as a resident it's the best rain I've known us to receive....
Doing a dash into town for the special purpose of posting Dad's Fathers Day card, straight away Destiny returned Tia and me to further evolve Rainbow Falls....
Working with the elements, picked up the shovel because it's a lot easier to break the ground of moist, soft soil. Rising to a return of confidence, cleared a brushcutter blade safe distance either side of the 2 inch irrigation pipe, no more gushing surprises! Following the irrigation line digging, opened to sunshine from its sheltered position an outlet with about ten metres of one inch hose connected, woohoo, potential ☺ !!!!
It was a great night to get a wet arse with the Grassy Bottom's, the sky closed in with the inclusion of thunder. Making town for the 4:15pm 'Grassy Bottoms Regional Arts Group' meeting helped me decide to stick to radio only I'm more mainstream arts than alternative, one less voluntary thing to commit myself to....

Friday 30 August 2002
A sound offering inner peace, tranquillity, relaxation and brilliant to get a day started, water flowing over the falls could be heard from the loo ☺....
Slipping into a Friday routine of up and at'em and into the radio station, I was having a chat to the breakfast announcer Adam at the 9a.m. shift-changeover and we quickly established common threads. We both arrived in Tassie from the Illawarra this year and his grandmother lives in Mildura. I'm going to make an effort to pop in on his grandmother visiting Mildura for Kristy-Lee's 21st. It would be nice to give Adam and his grandmother news of one another ☺....

Destiny booked in for a health check before she's due to face the many, many kilometres ahead, we ventured into St. Marys. Grant waved a sample of his collection of tools over her, pressure tested the radiator, tightened a couple of screws, heart rate fine, she's now as ready as she'll ever be for the trek to Mildura ☺ ....

It's time to do it. A slap in the face reminder filled the space of the Post Office box the 'quit pack' had arrived. Browsing contents, the words it contained however useful it was the colour pictures that offered the greatest impact. Chiselling away at wearing down and kicking the filthy, unhealthy habit of smoking I've become a clock watcher, not allowing myself to have a ciggy within one hour of the last, eliminating the thoughtlessly grabbing without thinking habit. Leaving the colour picture of the cancerous, tar stained lung by my cigarettes should help inspire the quitting attempt ☺ ....

Saturday 31 August 2002
Snapping thoughts away from 'have to's', reached for a shot of brain therapy with an optional, getting the blood and appetite pumping went scaling mountainous country exploring with my little mate, initially lured by the sound of the flowing falls ☺ ....

Given a cup full of energy from the environment I had a go at emptying it by the base of the dam trimming the boxthorn. New growth scotch thistles also felt the effects of my boot....

Rainbow Falls is benefiting from the campaign to quit smoking, without allowing myself to have a smoke within an hour of the last I've been keeping a mind and body preoccupied and busy. Taking the shovel to tidy around a fencepost I ended up edging right along one side of the shed. I'll sleep well tonight I feel buggered my little mate is already asleep by my side....zzzz....

Sunday 1 September 2002
The first Sunday in September, a date tattooed in a loving child's mind, made my first move to ring Dad for Fathers Day. Had it fallen next Sunday I would have been in Mildura, saving my hug and kiss for Thursday's arrival ☺ ....xxxx....

Owning few possessions, and noted for its absence, the razor had disappeared from the ledge of the bath a couple of day's back, I assumed it had just been knocked onto the floor and obscured by the bath. Ready to rectify the situation was surprised to find both razors gone, neither one was to be found under or around the bath? Concluding a bower-bird is present in the cottage collecting shiny objects, their disappearance remains a mystery????

Staying firmly on the rails the psychological lead into quitting smoking hasn't wobbled at all, not that I didn't think about just one extra won't hurt, every bloody one does, but I refuse to weaken. Pushing it further each morning before sparking up the first and sticking like glue to never having another within an hour of having the last, I'm starting to get a head rush from 2mg menthol winding my body down from the addiction. Heading in the right direction.... Yahoo!!!!

Keeping idle thoughts occupied during a craving I took the shovel into the front yard of the burnt out house playing around edging fencing....

A pleasant gain in weight is measurable by what was once a 'nipples under' bath is now a nipples exposed ☺ ????

Monday 2 September 2002
Walking out of the shed with the brushcutter harness slung over my shoulders and the aim of grubbing the remainder of the burnt out house front yard, achieved beyond expectations. With plenty of petrol left in my motor I also cleared a strip outside the entire length of the front yard fence. Absolutely stoked, Rainbow Falls looks beyond the 'loved look' I hoped to achieve before going to Mildura ☺ ….
Clumps of bulbs still popping up en masse all over the place has left me in disbelief, four different varieties have emerged so far. The paint brush swipes of colour decorating cleared ground is reward for the many laborious shovel and brushcutter hours that's gone on ☺ ….
Recently gazing out the bungalow window over coffee saw a black figure spring at a distance in the paddock directly ahead, unable to identify the black figure, thought it odd for native animals to be active at that time. Returning from a trip over the mountain a large jet-black cat cut across the driveway into that same paddock, confirming what I saw. It was mentioned to me to get a cat and you won't be troubled by snakes, that no maintenance critter may be doing us a favour as well as keeping the mouse population down ☺ ???? Sadly its destruction isn't isolated!!!!

Tuesday 3 September 2002
In contrast to yesterdays major manual effort outside today my wheels fell off. Changing down a gear with energy exertion and having a shift in thought patterns, I began focussing on the fast approaching trip. Keen this Mildura visit to really enjoy quality time with family, a gain in weight with an equivalent rise in energy is dealing a kind card permitting me keep up….
A few light showers found ground through the night hours encouraging the dam to slowly rise, hopefully in our absence Mother Nature will supply a few more litres, enough to get the line to the cottage flowing again. Taking water from the cattle trough is keeping the mosquito population down and a healthy population of frogs is looking after the dam. On a still night frogs supply a constant chorus line and backing vocals to all other nocturnal sounds, tuning themselves into an available airwave frequency, compete to deliver messages ☺ ….
Polishing off the working day Destiny was parked in the shed packed with everything possible for taking off in the morning…. Let the journey begin ☺ ….

Wednesday 4 September 2002
Pure wind force shoving in the occasional shower woke me around 5:30am, sure the roof was still on went back to sleep conserving precious 'get up and go' for the big days ahead….
Leaving no stone unturned, down to flicking the main power switch off, packed in Destiny shut the front gate behind for the adventure in the big beyond. The drive to Devonport is the easiest leg of the journey to board the good ship 'Spirit of Tasmania II', where my little mate and I endure our dose of separation anxiety….
On board one of the new twin ferries, now running a daily service, I had to be assisted in the end to find my cabin, its a bloody maze, and lacking in an outstanding sense of orientation for me to find cabin 8202 was a pain in the arse. Settled inside the reassurance of the cabin hunger caused me to get brave enough to venture out and I made it back unassisted! The shower set-up is better designed in the new ferries than the recently retired 'Spirit', the entertainment is more compact or maybe I should have walked slower ☺ ….

Thursday 5 September 2002

Off the boat by 7:30am, and with minimum difficulty made it out of the City of Melbourne and onto the Tullumarine Freeway where the brain's known road maps kicked in and it was all systems go to Mildura....

Getting clear of the big smoke and hungry I pulled into a roadhouse. Putting the snack of four dim sims in Destiny while having a ciggy and Tia toilet break, a brief sniff around and wee Tia wanted back in Destiny, unthinkingly I let her in. Staying out to finish my ciggy only to watch Tia nose down bum up eating a dim sim ☺.... Little shit....

Destiny's tyres didn't get a chance to cool making our destination. Briefly disturbing work environments began the social circuit with nieces, starting with the birthday girl Kristy-Lee for a warm greeting hug. Stacey's desk chair was empty the poor bugger was off sick, and Tegan, well she could be anywhere she chooses at any given moment ☺....

Sights then fixed firmly onto Mum and Dad's, it felt wonderful seeing, hugging and chatting with missed loved ones. Betty and Aunty Claire called in while I was there it was almost like a 'Ford' family reunion ☺....

Crossing town for my one and only sister, met another warm greeting with Kerry, Kristy-Lee was also there busying the kitchen with party catering preparations. Visiting the sick patient Stacey at home was brief, she looked as flat as a tack and I didn't want what she had. Ready to set-up my swag for the evening headed to Mirro's where a home-made pizza and bottle of red waited ☺.... And so the curtain is lowered on another day....

Friday 6 September 2002

A few domestic duties and the privilege of hot and cold running water I did what would have taken the complete day to do at home in a couple of hours ☺....

Taking a familiarising stroll through town, being born and raised in Mildura, pleasantly it didn't take long to meet familiar faces and stop for a chat ☺....

Being her exact birth date, the travelling Tassie Trio packed into Destiny and took the short drive for a brief work disturbance to wish the birthday girl Kristy-Lee many happy returns, personally delivered with a hug and kiss....xxxx

Without letting the social dust settle and still out disturbing businesses called in on Peter at Sunraysia Steering Service, the span of our friendship keeps bridging the years. With minimum fuss I made contact with Adam's grandmother 'Nana Edith', she invited me to her home for a cuppa and chat in the morning, rapt I'll be able to take news back to Tassie. Another long-time friend and former work mate, Fred phoned and we're going to cross paths Sunday, Monday plans have been made with the lovely Mary, Joan and Judy, for an update on their new house and shifting plans. But tonight I'm looking forward to a family dinner at the 'Regal Chinese Restaurant', having the entire immediate family together in the one place is an event that's getting harder to achieve ☺....

Saturday 7 September 2002

Kristy-Lee's actual birthday dinner with family at the 'Regal' was an exceptional evening incorporating plenty of friendly banter. Rounding off a huge night for Kristy-Lee, following a birthday speech and still holding everyone's attention, her boyfriend Brenton knelt on one knee and proposed marriage. There wasn't a dry eye, a very romantic birthday dinner for Kristy-Lee a memory of lasting quality....♥....

Carrying a little jet lag from party celebrations, I was slow but punctual for the arranged morning tea with Adam's grandmother 'Nana Edith', and what a sprightly lady, she turned on a lovely cuppa and array of snacks. Taking more than a photo back for Adam, Edith also gave me his birthday and Christmas present....

It was my intention to busy the afternoon away at Kerry's chipping in helping with party preparations instead I ended up in her bed. Waking this morning with a sore throat, as time progressed I began aching all over, sleeping the afternoon away dosed myself up to enjoy Kristy-Lee's party....

Sunday 8 & Monday 9 September 2002

Sunday's journal entry never made paper through total lack of energy and interest, unable to think of anything other than bed hit the wall 4p.m.. Supposed to go to Fred's for dinner I struggled getting myself out of a horizontal position, reluctantly phoned and cancelled then collapsed my bones back into a heap in bed....

Feeling reasonable Sunday morning, Mirro, Andrew and myself went out to the car boot sale cum auction at Lindemans winery. Swallowing cake and a cuppa at Mirro's parents afterward, Jilly phoned asking if we wanted to join them on the recently purchased Tasmanian houseboat for a cruise upstream and a barbecue. Boat loaded for a scenic arvo on the Murray, as Bernie Bear proudly untied ropes current moved the boat breaking a propeller blade on rocks. Ropes again securing the boat, we had a barbecue on the bank from there we looked at the proud new Tasmanian purchase☺....

Monday was a pretty quiet state of affairs dividing my energy evenly amongst family, visiting Stacey and Kristy-Lee on the job, had a cuppa and yarn with Mum and Dad then picked Tegan up from school for lunch together. Out in the Irymple area returning Tegan to her institute for learning called in on friends formed from a Fergie Tractor Rally, Mary, Joan and Judy. Over a cool beer I was given a progress tour, they've certainly sunk many hours work into the house and yard since my last visit May....

Tuesday 10 September 2002

Slowing the pace to suit the mood I occupied myself absolutely relaxed over socialising. Like a homing pigeon started at my favourite place spending precious quality time with Mum and Dad, leaving only to collect Tegan from the bus stop at 4p.m.....

Bridging absent time, together Tegan and I visited Kerry, met with open arms and a friendly smile comfortable conversation settled in no time. A 7p.m. arrangement at the cinema had us rattling our dags, fish 'n' chips in a hurry, Fred, Stacey, Tegan and myself met in the foyer deciding on 'Orange County', a light-hearted comedy. Prior to calling it a night coffee at the Grand Hotel was a popular choice....

Cruising streets in their car, a signatory pastime set aside for the just licensed generation, Kristy-Lee and Brenton were doing laps. Seeing them as we left the Grand, and excited to share more news they pulled in for a chat. They had just left the 'Setts' following a wedding exhibition, the legendary Kristy-Lee won the raffle taking home a beautiful orchid bouquet☺....

From the moment of arriving in Mildura I got a good dose of the flu, Stacey was just getting over it, now Mum and Dad have come down with it, it's been spreading like wild fire. Flu aside, it's been very friendly, social and overall enjoyable visit ☺....

Wednesday 11, Thursday 12 & Friday 13 September 2002
Wow, the last few days have merged....
Saying farewells broke the back of Wednesday. Wishing we had the convenience of living closer I miss family dearly but my heart and life journey keep us apart. Destiny packed and all travellers on board Mirro and I said our farewells, saving the hardest one for last waving Mum and Dad out of the distance, that moment cuts deep in my heart but we must keep moving forward....
Taking a small step in the trip toward home went only far as Colignan where I was greeted warmly by Bernie and Jill offering a sincere depth of friendship. Over food and wine there was never a lull in conversation ☺....
Roaming around the beautiful grounds in an idyllic location set on the banks of the Murray and bordering the Hattah Kulkine National Park, took my sweet leisurely time leaving Thursday for the next leg where us Tassie travellers terrorise the streets of Melbourne ☺!!!!
Taking the friends tour home weaved my way through City traffic to Newport, returning to an old stomping ground of many years earlier, there Trudy waited offering the next warm greeting. Time and life had kept us apart for a while and again another evening vanished in conversation. Trailing a huge night I collapsed into bed and didn't resurface until 1p.m. Friday, by then Trudy had already been busy filling our social calendar ☺....

Saturday 14 September 2002
Being my desire to be submerged in sisterhood culture, Trudy granted the wish immersing me into every night-club open on a Friday. Packing the social hours in together, and unable to keep up, I fell into a few hours sleep before Saturdays social agenda item waited for attention. Trudy had arranged for us to reunite with a long absent friend Jodie. Settled into a beer garden the afternoon blended into evening and into more night-clubs. By stumps at 'My Sisters Lounge', I was beaten so me and Tia left a pumping Trudestar to it ☺....

Sunday 15 & Monday 16 September 2002
Sunday consisted of anything that didn't require thought, fitting the need began with a fast food drive-through, with a belly full of greasies we then collapsed in the lounge room in recovery watching DVD's.... perfect....
If my eyes were open we were on the go doing something, Trudy only has two speeds, go and stop. I wasn't shocked waking to find Monday had arrived ☺....
Without the soles of my shoes getting time to cool, Destiny was once again packed and nose pointed toward the Port of Melbourne to endure a night on the 'Spirit' ferrying us back to paradise....
Making bobbing about in the ocean more pleasant I shared a cabin with a woman by the name of Aliki, she was also starting a new life in Tassie. We had plenty of newcomer experiences to exchange and parted company planning to catch up sometime in the future....

Tuesday 17 September 2002
Off the boat reaching home soil Tia's comfort was catered for, then, as if drawn by some powerful magnet, thought concentrated on returning to our peaceful nest in the mountain. Pulling into the curb of St. Marys township I checked the post, grabbed some groceries, then it was straight up the hill to get reunited with our beloved Rainbow Falls..♥.. Home sweet home....♥....
Unpacking Destiny simulated a prosperous Christmas everyone we visited had a little something that might be useful on the farm. Mary and Joan offered an orphaned kitchen sink to replace the one stolen from the cottage, and I accepted a pick from the array of garden tools Bernie had on offer. Mum and Dad added to the booty two much needed canvas fold up chairs along with a gift wrapped birthday present that came with instructions 'not to be opened till the actual date' ☺ .... Still to be revealed????
Offering surplus goods Kerry contributed to our loot a CD player, yahoo, an iron, hmm, and a bundle of shade cloth.... Destiny was full of treasure ☺ ....
It was a pretty nice feeling sitting in a beloved new canvas chair listening to a CD and reflecting on the love and generosity shown to me on the trip. It fills my heart knowing the love and depth of friendship I'm lucky enough to be surrounded in, family and friends make life whole and complete....

Wednesday 18 September 2002
Coming down from trekking and socialising around the mainland my wheels fell off, tucking myself in by 8p.m. last night didn't see daylight again until 9a.m. this morning....
Windy, cold with an occasional shower, Mother Nature encouraged a lazy day conscience free to stop and play with new toys....
New chairs and a CD player have added another dimension of luxury to Rainbow Falls, it's wonderful to have a seat with back support and the privilege of selecting music for the mood, woohoo, life only keeps getting better ☺ ....
Physically the brakes have been put on I pretty much spent the day reading and eating. On a shopping expedition in Mildura I bought a self teach guitar book, reading over the first twenty-seven pages it made sense, I reckon the timing must be right for me to learn????

Thursday 19 September 2002
The elements turned on a repeat performance of yesterday promoting another idle one to scratch my bum and catch my breath....
Once again, far removed from the press button tap turning conveniences found in the average home, it was back to making the most from what we have. Tools of any fitting description would be of useful assistance setting up the sink and taps, and heaven forbid, have water constantly flowing to the cottage. No more walking for water or boiling the large pot, a day I look forward to ☺ ....
Hospitalised with asthma shortly after we left Mildura, I phoned my little mate Tegan out of caring to check progress. Tegan's lungs are back to a healthy solo function enabling a green light for release to go home....

Friday 20 September 2002
Any wonder getting out of bed was a struggle. The topic of the moment at the radio station was we had just experienced our coldest night leaving winter, dropping to a chilly -7°. It was great to be back amid a wonderful group of people at the station, giving Adam his present, told him of my visit with his grandmother he was rapt. A personalised BOD FM nametag waited for my return, and the news that when I cross paths with Mel and make a time she'll commence training me for the announcer's seat ☺.... Bring it on!!!!
Leaving a tidy desk I followed on by doing the washing, a grocery shop, checked the post box and fuelled Destiny. Life's needs catered for we headed up the mountain for the weekend without any need to move until Monday at minimum.... Yahoo....
Sitting writing, distracting movement outside the window was the black cat crossing the driveway back into the same paddock. It too seems to have set-up home at Rainbow Falls....

Saturday 21 September 2002
Our reception home has been rather chilly to date, very little to warrant running for sunscreen. Dampening the ground, the sound of a few brief showers filled my senses waking to face a fresh one, pulling to a stop just as soon as the bungalow door was opened. Its only a southerly nip carried with wind holding back the prospects of a bit of warmth on offer, it certainly robs the 'linger' out of bath time ☺....
A document that had been wedged in the cottage door in our absence stated 1080 poison had been laid across the road while we were away. I've been noticing quite a lot of black tar spots on the ground, a sure sign of unhealthy poo from a poisoned animal enduring a slow painful death. I hope it was worth something????
The twenty-first, a brain tattooed calendar number, represents living at Rainbow Falls now four months, time has vaporised. We hit the ground running in the achievement stakes both on the domestic front and socially, there's a long way to go but the journeys a positive one ☺....
Like sliding your hand inside that perfectly fitting soft wool lined glove, we slipped into a lifestyle easy on the soul I can't imagine living anywhere else. Me and Tia have feathered long-stay nests ☺....

Sunday 22 September 2002
A splash of warmth on a perfect day inspired outdoor activity. A play in the elevated garden and nearby fenceline was the focus of attention and enough to keep me busy....
Family might not be here but everyday their love surrounds, the simple pleasure of a CD player is a constant reminder of Kerry's generosity, another gift making an obvious change for the better are the chairs from Mum and Dad that followed us home. I'm lucky to live in paradise and to also be immersed in so much love and thoughtfulness, being very content with the direction life is heading in now ☺....

Monday 23 September 2002
Paradise turned on a beaut, soaking in the elements took the picturesque mountain drive into town posting Tegan Termite's birthday card and, hopefully, purchasing my last packet of ciggy's????

Putting a concentrated effort into quitting I've been leaving it later before letting the first pass by my lips, and pushing my comfort boundaries, have extended the time before having another to one hour and fifteen minutes. Yesterday nine ciggy's found my lungs, the day before ten, each day tightening the reins just that little bit more without falling off the rails. Preparing the brain for the separation and feeling strong going cold turkey isn't far away, I so want to be a non-smoker!!!!

Tuesday 24 September 2002
Working with the shovel had become difficult with the ground as dry as a chip, so when the dull moisture laden sky began gently releasing its booty 9a.m.-ish it was most welcome to soften things up. Inclement weather is a genuine clue from nature to participate in a conscience free lazy day eating and energy building…. Suits me ☺….
Falling as slow soaking heavy droplets from thick fog cloud, immersed in its weight, visibility dropped to enchanting blocking the existence of another human from view ☺….
The umbrella found practical use taking the short uphill walk to the toilet and collecting bath water. Applying a bit of warming assistance to bath time the electric heater found its way into the cottage, and that's where we settled. The bungalow feels too confined on a rainy day for Tia and me, so with chair, heater and journal we set-up camp next door, a much larger dry area….
Bowing their heads carrying a heavy water load, daffodils are a tough bulb, they've been flowering for a month enduring some of natures most trying elements in that time and surprisingly still look fresh….

Wednesday 25 September 2002
Yahoo, exceeding my expectations with ciggy's yesterday I only had seven with a set target of eight ☺!!!!
Down the shed filling my lungs with the first ciggy poked my head out the back door sizing up the work involved in clearing the cattle holding yards and sighted my first male wren. A beautiful little bird displaying an outstanding vivid blue cap and tail-feather, spectacular….
Rain pulled up but it was still a bit of a lottery anything could have happened, making use of soft soil did a bit of shovel work while energy held out. Sights set on clearing the base of fenceline surrounding the dam got a quarter of the way around before running out of puff….
Packing idle time I pulled the guitar out of its box and got comfortably to lesson three in the 'teach myself how to play' book. A quick look forward to advancing lessons advertises a steep learning curve it's like getting your brain around learning a new language♫…. Reckon I'll repeat today's lesson a few more times before moving on ☺….

Thursday 26 September 2002
My mind was fixed, when the remaining few ciggy's went up in smoke it was cold turkey. Unbending in psychological preparation I put in a huge brain effort last night convincing it to set today as quit day. Having the last cigarette in the pack I officially went cold turkey 12:20pm, may I remain a non-smoker ☺!!!!

Just letting my brain get used to the idea of doing one less thing, Wendy, an out of view neighbour from the property bordering our bottom boundary, came over to introduce herself staying long enough for a chat over coffee....

My big test came with a trip to town a few hours into cold turkey, so ready to quit made it back empty handed, I'm even calling myself a 'non-smoker' ☺!!!!

Friday 27 September 2002

Proving a point you don't die from not smoking, I made it through the night unscathed to be driven from bed by the alarm to honour my voluntary role doing a community service at the radio station....

Without having many other thoughts for conversation, at my time on reception bragged about being a quitter and going cold turkey, there was nothing but positive responses. So far cravings have been minor, I get rid of them simply by thinking of all the reasons why I quit ☺!!!!

Saturday 28 September 2002

A body having gone into shock and a brain focussed on quitting gave me writers block yesterday thoughts weren't too free flowing ☺....

Hearing the magical sound of rain steadily falling stirring sometime from sleep, it continued solidly until 8a.m. then broke up into passing showers, every drop is welcome....

Within ear shot of the phone made the designated rings to catch a call from Aliki, better known as Al, the woman I shared the cabin with on the ferry returning from Kristy-Lee's twenty-first. Al has a relaxed personality and is very easy to talk to we left our conversation planning to cross paths sometime at the halfway mark in Launceston....

Since the brushcutter has found the ground surface I've developed a habit of kicking out new growth scotch thistles with my boot, I can't walk past them. It always takes twice as long to get to wherever I'm going ☺....

The afternoon plan of tuning into a radio station broadcasting the Collingwood and West Coast Eagles football grand final didn't falter, listening to the only game for the season I'm semi-interested in....

A Saturday afternoon tuned to the radio listening to football rekindled fond childhood memories.

Both my grandfather, Pop Luke, and my Father were like two peas in a pod, trying to gain either of their attention during a radio broadcast game both would look at you and say, 'aayyee', remained leaning on their elbows tuned to the game ☺....

The afternoon plan didn't remain on track I was left shattered Collingwood lost another grand final. Delivering a crowd pleasing close game it kept little old cynic me engrossed, entertaining, neither side would give in....

Sunday 29 September 2002

Eating my way through cold turkey, I ducked down the hill to grab a paper to keep my idle mind occupied....

Mum phoned to pass on the news Uncle George had died. Within the space of a few months Uncle Terry, a long-time Jenkins Place resident Betty, and Uncle George have passed on, if I live to their accumulated average age then I'm over halfway through the journey. The sobering

realisation life isn't forever and possibly half it has already passed and how quickly it went, leaves what's remaining thought about with consideration and respect....
The cottage and bungalow withstood the buffeting of strong wind gusts offered over the past few days but a piece of iron from the carport attached to the shed threatened to escape, under pressure, it lifted a wide gap from the roof. Fixed in one point, from below I twisted the sheet of tin jamming it underneath shed roof overhang, holding it firm buying time to purchase a ladder with the money saved on ciggy's ☺.... Oh, to be able to reach the repair jobs....

Monday 30 September 2002
I must have left my 'get up and go' back in Mildura because I haven't really fired up since coming home at all, today being no exception. Doing very little beside follow the mood, ate, carted water, ate, went for a wander, ate, emptied water into the bath and ate ☺....
So nice outside I parked myself in a chair and soaked it up struggling with yesterday's crossword, ahhhh, the start of another working week ☺....
Day four of cold turkey arrived in a blink, it still feels weird, a sensation of being able to smoke just as easily as not, I'm at a delicate stage but refuse to regress!!!!

Tuesday 1 October 2002
First move on this important occasion was to call Tegan Termite celebrating her 15th birthday, phoning just prior to 10a.m. got a yawning Termite out of bed.... ☺....
Reciprocating a visit, I phoned Wendy planning to drop in on the way home from town. Making a strong statement, my directions were to look for the gate with the sign 'Off World' posted, short for 'fuck off world'. The big social outing managed to tire Ms Tia out....
A phone call to the radio station took life on another exciting turn, confirming a start to being trained as an announcer this Thursday 6:30pm with Mel, yahoo....

Wednesday 2 October 2002
A pleasure to be alive and participating, I stripped down to a t-shirt and with the help of my little mate collected off-cut timber boards left strewn, now overgrown, from a portable milling site just inside the paddock by the shed. Only good for poking in the face of the heater, they're now drying in wait. Once freed of timber the area surrounding the shed can then be tackled with the brushcutter to find ground before reptiles get active....
Cold turkey six days now, being a second time quitter, from memory this time I'm finding it more difficult. If a ciggy found me in a weak moment I'd sniff it in passively, bottom line is I purely and simply just don't want to smoke so I'll just keep riding that wave....
My little mate's big outing socialising yesterday must have worn her out because she disappeared for a snooze in Destiny, not interested in anything but rest and recreation. It's a difficult life when the most pressing decision to make is which spot to sleep ☺....
Sitting an idle evening away in the bungalow with the door open watching the world go by, was content watching a raven turning over clumps of dried grass on the hunt for a snack. That was until it was noticed by Ms Tia and cleared from her personal space ☺....

Thursday 3 October 2002
The first peek outside revealed mystical dense fog cloud had blanketed down isolating us from the world, rain pulled up 8a.m., but always lurking was a chance for more....
Stepping outside the bungalow door, time and wear had exposed the edge of an oven rack now poking out of the ground. Getting onto it with the shovel levered it out, laying flat underneath the rack was a composting phone book, but wait there's more, also striking some rocks seemingly laid as a path???? Another day's adventure today had other priorities....
Putting a trip to St. Helens off, to coincide with taking a fresh step outside my comfort zone starting training as an announcer at 6:30pm with Mel, created a list to fill beforehand maximising the 100 kilometre trip. Reliably early, stepped inside the radio station to hear the words 'the studio was double booked and Mel was supposed to phone to reschedule'.... hmmmm....
Certainly an evening better spent off the road. Coming home, mountain fog reduced Destiny to a very slow second gear, the most testing driving conditions encountered that without local knowledge I would have turned back....
One week since putting that last ciggy out, it's been a long one convincing my brain it doesn't need a smoke. Without saturating thoughts as it initially did, each day the hazy cloud is lifting and I'm gaining strength in one of the few areas I'm proud to be a quitter☺....

Friday 4 October 2002
The horrible buzz of the alarm made sure I wasn't late for reception at the radio station. Wishing to avoid a repeat of studio double booking caught up with Mel to seal training dates in concrete. Set in stone are both Monday and Friday evenings 6:30pm, training can only be at that time because then the live broadcast ceases and crosses to the National Community Radio Network, freeing the studio to imitate the real thing....
Concerned about either doing two trips to St. Helens on a Friday or trying to fill the time gap between reception and training, I spoke to Rita, applying a dose of logic it was decided I give up reception while in training....
Clean, dry laundry neatly folded in Destiny we headed home to paradise, ahhhh, no place like home....

Saturday 5 October 2002
With all good intentions of making an honest woman of myself earning a keep physically I toddled to the dam shovel in hand, only managing a half-hour before the heavens gently released a sample. Lingering in the area a few days, gathering cloud banked saturating itself over South Sister Range, building until the weighty load tumbled its way down engulfing us in heavy mist....
Settling in, mist forced a direction reassessment placing indoor activities definitely on the agenda. Seeing brief glimpses of sun, the only variation in weather came with visibility dropping between twenty and one hundred metres.... Feels magical☺....
Stretched out in bed obliviously content chewing a bone, Tia left me to concentrate between journal writing and gazing out the window appreciating our submerged atmosphere of mystery....

Sunday 6 October 2002
Yesterdays mist opened into some really heavy showers throughout the night, easing off by sunrise to a soupy fog. Wandering through the dense hovering moisture greeting the morning, with my little mate, walked through this soft wall simply to enjoy the sights and sounds of flowing water at the falls ☺ …. ahhhh….
Late morning cloud lifted permitting the occasional attempt by the sun to cast shadows. Taking in the entertainment provided by the elements, and excited by soft ground me, Tia and the shovel headed for the potential vegie patch. Completing a lap around the boundary clearing all bordering obstacles, worked on getting the gate free swinging, cleared around a preparation bench then around hydrangeas, then the boarders increased in depth, then time slipped away, then I got hungry and stopped ☺ ….
Beyond the obvious change in season symbol of being annoyed by a few blowies, now extending daylight and a warming earth enables the bungalow door to stay open longer leading into evening.
Watching the variety of busy birds, listening to the dam alive with frogs, the dense rising vegetative covering of South Sister Range surrounded the entire event like a natural amphitheatre, the smells, sights and sounds satisfying all senses. Remaining with the performance until after sunset faded, night noises then come alive, nature's version of the changing of the guard…. I don't need television the environment is my screen ☺ ….
Having a snack gazing out the bungalow window; two native hens went scampering past racing up toward the toilet. Bursting into laughter watching the hens busy stick legs disappear from view through the open door, there's no other place I've lived where this would have happened, it's a different side to life at Rainbow Falls ☺ ….

Monday 7 October 2002
Thinking 9a.m. a reasonable time to pick up the phone, celebrating their wedding anniversary I dialled the numbers for Mum and Dad. There was one small hitch in my good intentions I overlooked the fact Victoria doesn't start daylight savings until the end of the month, catching sleepy heads not long out of bed ☺ ….
Doing fluff around jobs from collecting water to cleaning mosquito larvae from the cattle trough, all the little life maintenance bits stopped a mind from becoming idle. Starting off fine and warm the elements shifted course to direct south, by 11a.m. no shadows were cast….
A very thoughtful Rita delivered a courtesy call to let me know studio one was being used from 6:30pm for a 'Country and Western' special, cancelling training eliminated the need to leave home….
Turning on an absolutely beautiful bone-warming afternoon, for a change of scenery catching the sun on offer, I sat on the front steps of the burnt out house taking in the window view to the ocean….

Tuesday 8 October 2002
Raising the curtain on a night of entertainment, Mother Nature slipped into the evening a thunderstorm with lasting power rattling Tia's cage for what seemed forever. Adding to the excitement, following some pretty weighty showers, taking the next step a deafening dump of intense hailstones hammered the roof, powerful stuff ☺ !!!!

Easing to a more regulated pace showers remained. Refusing to budge from under the doona tuned to the sweet sound of rain I stayed snuggy having a chat with Kerry. Contact with family is a pleasant way to ease into any day ☺....

In town for a Post Office, supermarket trip, hailstone conversations were abuzz, measuring somewhere between the size of ten-cent coins and golf balls, word had it they were the biggest hailstones seen in this area....

Fun mail had been tucked into my post box containing birthday wishes from the perfect couple Sheila and Peter the card also included a scratchy and lotto ticket. The ticket can only bring better luck than the scratchy. The mail cache also included an invitation to attend the official launch and opening of 'Break O'Day FM', the first, and only, local station has simply been operating a few months longer than we've lived here in Tassie ☺....

Sun broke through in the latter part of the afternoon, escaping outside Tia and I returned to the soft soil of the potential vegie patch. Carving the large area up into sections, breaking the entire job into smaller patches is helping the brain see it as a manageable size.... Anything that pleases the mind ☺ ????

Wednesday 9 October 2002
Awake but still lounging, the first thoughtful birthday wishes arrived via the phone from Kerry. The day arrived I was finally able to open the much travelled present brought back from Mildura that has sat on a shelf looking at me for the past three weeks ☺....

Besides the much needed and loved chairs given to me by Mum and Dad, the decoratively wrapped little box contained the gift of cash and a tongue in cheek birthday card titled, 'from the dog', adding a feel good injection of humour. No more than five minutes after opening the present Mum and Dad phoned to wish me the best. Today had a magical feel, my energy and health feel like they are aligning and life really is beginning, I couldn't have hand selected a more exotic location to have my 40th ☺....

From my Wollongong life, Ms Kylie rang, her first words were, "where the fuck have you been" and "happy birthday", hmm, or was it the other way around ☺ ????

A little more polite were Sheila and Peter, young Stacey, Kristy-Lee and Tegan Termite also made contact to wish me many happy returns, perfect. Only emphasising how important families and quality friends are for maintaining inner health and well-being, we derive energy from the mental support ☺....

Thursday 10 October 2002
Another day older and feet firmly planted on the ground, Tia and I worked like we owned the place. The brushcutter was kept busy carving a path up hill to the water tank, clearing an access track in anticipation for future walks in the process to get running water back on tap in the cottage....

Fresh from the bath, and in the company of my little mate, went for a walk enjoying the outcome from a day's toil, discovering the area least frequented by the water tank has the best view. Time meant nothing standing at the top boundary taking in the 360° view from the ocean to mountains and neatly contoured ranges diving to the valleys below, purely magnificent ☺....

Naturally extending daylight hours and the illusion of more time daylight savings offers, it now doesn't get dark until 8p.m., first arriving it was 5:30pm sharp! The days and evenings are developing an air of warming, an overall feeling of winter exercising a departure ☺....

Friday 11 October 2002
Voluntary reception duties relinquished the alarm stayed silent, more pleasant on the brain first thing ☺....
Never a job to rush I took it pretty gentle feathering the nest doing domestic duties, the sink now shines and my bed and surrounds are aired and cleaned. Easily distracted by idle grey matter, thoughts flashing to the available view by taking that short walk up the freshly cut access track to the top boundary by the water tank, I didn't resist the notion. It absolutely takes it all in up there. Checking out hoses entering and exiting the water tank the reticulation system is piecing together in my head, knowing what bit does what and runs to where ☺....
Putting myself through a bit of pre-excitement, excitement, before training I proudly entered the hardware store purchasing a new wheelbarrow spending my birthday present from Kerry, another step towards simplifying life at Rainbow Falls ☺....
And what a prelude to taking a step into the unknown, wheelbarrow and groceries loaded neatly into Destiny, I delved into an exciting alien world having the first hands-on training with Mel. Learning what gadget does what in studio one I settled in comfortably, leaving me with more questions than answers and a head bursting to learn ☺....
By training's end I was comfortable with how three CD players fitted with the mixing board and series of volume switches. Confidently pushing buttons and making music before having to walk out the door.... Yahoo ☺....

Saturday 12 October 2002
An outstanding event I didn't see coming from extreme left field changed any plans I may have had. Beginning no differently to any other, filling a bucket at the cattle trough a car drove around the back, which in itself isn't an uncommon event it was the occupants that generated the big hurrah!!!!
At first I thought the car to be a service vehicle, when it got closer and the number plate entered my focus reading [Sheila], Sheila and Peter had ducked over from Melbourne for the weekend simply to wish me happy birthday. Candles ablaze they stepped from the car singing. What's an appropriate word for that moment? I was left gob smacked speechless, disbelief took some shaking they're exceptional human beings ☺!!!!
What's one to do but blow out the candles put the kettle on and try to absorb the moment ☺....
Taking in a long leisurely look around Rainbow Falls we kept the sight-seeing wheels in motion taking in some local attractions. Starting at The Shop in the Bush went on to St Columba Falls and back to the Pub in the Paddock, finishing at the Ranch Diner for dinner....
Phew ☺....
If Sheila and Peter are after a reaction they certainly know how to go about it ☺!!!!

Sunday 13 October 2002
The birthday surprise still hadn't sunk in when the tricky travellers had to make their way back to the ferry. I was remained struggling for adequate words to express the appreciation for the

love, caring and generosity freely offered as we bid farewell. Sheila and Peter left me with a generous cup full of love and memories that will last a lifetime ☺ ....

Pleasantly considerate to wait until after our sight-seeing outing, sometime late evening it started raining and only got heavier. The baking tray catching water under the dangling piece of flue where a heater once sat in the cottage began bearing quite a load. At a rough 'baking tray' guess I reckon we had around two inches before bed, without an end in sight, the baking tray was full to overflowing by morning and just keeps filling up....

Watching from a more comfortable position behind glass, low cloud moved past so quickly it almost resembled smoke, one minute the bottom of the property was in view, the next visibility was down to twenty metres. A good one spent indoors looking out. The ground is struggling to slurp up the deluge, puddles formed into small streams and for my limited experience this rain will be a benchmark, a measuring stick for the future....

Constructively using a brief intermission in the rain show, Tia and I took off in the direction of the incredibly spectacular, heavy flowing falls. It was easy to stand motionless and get lost in the awesome act of nature pumping out strong energy ☺ !!!!

For a time leading into evening the rain stopped, wind dropped, sunshine broke through and a heavy silence fell over Rainbow Falls, however, the sheer force of water rushing over the rock face of the falls extended through the silence to reach the bungalow ☺ ....

Monday 14 October 2002
Still walking tall with a light heart, a lingering carryover from Sheila and Peter's surprise visit, I used the given energy wisely investing it with my best mate and the shovel tidying more fenceline around the dam. Stepping down a couple of metres for a change of muscle groups, collected water to pump up the supply in the cottage, topping up my full cup incorporated the occasional stroll to the falls. A roaring strong flow is forcing its way over the top splashing down to the base of the gorge and forming a stream to destination unknown.... Magnificent, a pure pleasure to be near....

Accepting a 'get to know bordering neighbours' invitation for coffee, took a slow trip on wet ground to Wendy's doing as planned chatting over cuppa's. Settling in yet again, rain made the decision to leave while Destiny could still make the top of Wendy's steep dirt driveway. Following the road carvings in mountain contours back home the trip was slow, having trouble shifting the deluge, water was on the move along and across the road....

During the course of conversation with Wendy I happened to mention the black cat that's been seen on occasion, I now know its origin: it's her son's cat. He moved the cat to Wendy's, day four it disappeared and that was around two months ago....

Tuesday 15 October 2002
Quite a few conversations with Wendy yesterday slipped into the topic of snakes and fire, it helped inspire the emptying of three tank loads in the brushcutter. One tank found dam fenceline the other two were exhausted along the driveway....

After washing the physical labour from my body I then eagerly did the dash to St. Helens for another training session. Revisiting last weeks knowledge learning by pure repetition, again went through the procedure of setting and selecting tracks on the CD players, fading songs in and out, and going over what switch does what. Everything is repeated over and over until it becomes second nature. Mel added a new dimension to keep me thinking introducing the simplicity of selecting tracks from the computer. The increasingly late hour brought to my attention, next thing I knew it was time to pack up and go home???? I must be enjoying it ☺ ….

Wednesday 16 October 2002
Without a second thought we were up and into the potential vegie patch with the shovel turning in clods and grass. Turning one third of the total area it's starting to take shape, breaking the job up into sections has certainly given me a psychological advantage. Taking the shovel for a walk led us to the front gate, until now it never made the priority list because it worked, but it could have worked better. Refusing to swing freely, to close the front gate the last metre offered resistance, relocating rocks and soil it's now a pleasure ☺ ….
Listening to Mels radio program toiling away outside, stepping out on a limb we talked about it and she went through with it, playing a song containing the word arse many times Mel made it the last one of her shift so she could do a quick runner. Mel said over air, 'Groove Amarda – I see you baby' is for Tassie Sue who had better be listening, and I was ☺ !!!! Tassie Sue is the on-air name I've settled on ☺ ….
Early evening a light mist pushed in, pleasantly the air temperature was mild enough to sit with the bungalow door open simply to appreciate a tender moment from nature. Coated in gentle spring rain everything looks fresh and clean, enhancing the back-drop a short distance away, South Sister Range was dimmed buried in entwining low cloud…. A relaxing environment….

Thursday 17 October 2002
Slowly gaining on the body mass filling my skin, 13 kilograms is not quickly found in a delicate balance with keeping active, but forward is the only direction. Every little bit more I grow into my skin energy equally rises, moving to levels I haven't experienced in quite some time there's less procrastination and more getting on with it, good health is important to life enjoyment….
The potential vegie patch again received the day's energy ration turning grass face down to expose soil. The seasons' soft warming sun made shovel work more pleasurable, stripping the t-shirt from my body I fully absorbed the moment….
Specifically chasing a new black pen caused a late afternoon trip down the hill. I've never run so many pens empty: they're usually lost or borrowed before ever running dry ☺ ….
Stepping up introducing himself in town I was invited by Rodney, another resident living a little further down the mountain, for a cuppa. Taking up his offer after securing a black pen, I enjoyed listening to his philosophies on life, it's always nice to keep an open mind and accept new knowledge….
Week three off ciggy's, time has evaporated, far more comfortable than the first two I ate my way through them but that can only useful. There are bloody difficult moments to keep my mind convinced it is a non-smoker, it still needs reminding occasionally, however, I'm feeling much healthier for the perseverance….

Friday 18 October 2002
Catching a glimpse of rushing water over a waterfall from the toilet almost lets me forget what I'm there for ☺ ….

A warmer airflow is starting to lift the soil temperature, and luckily for Tia, it makes drying after a bath more pleasant. My plan for a relaxing afternoon took a slight deviation. Out on a stroll little Ms Tia found fresh poo to smear over her neck, rather unpleasant to view, touching the pasted odour with bare skin was out of the question, warm water and gloved-up, to Tia's displeasure fur again shone ☺ !!!!

With both of us smelling beautiful, foregoing training instead had a big night out in St. Helens attending the official opening of Break O'Day FM....

Saturday 19 October 2002
Starting cool and wet the elements added brief glimpses of sun and wind as time progressed, between showers me and my best mate did a tad more in the potential vegie patch. Returning after dodging a shower, was stopped in my tracks and reduced to laughter watching an event that wouldn't have occurred for some years, wind freely played with the vegie garden gate pushing it open and closed ☺ ....

Looking for a change of scenery with the shovel took in the view from dam fenceline, a high point that dries fast....

The air temperature gained a few celcius and rain left, but wind only lifted in performance, near on blowing my beanie off on a couple of occasions ☺ ....

Sunday 20 October 2002
Enduring a bloody wild night, Mother Nature rushed in a few gusts that did their best to blow us away, hearing tin slide up nails did nothing to add to comfort!!!!

The rough elements showed no signs of relenting. Frustrated by having no ladder to help myself I phoned Wendy who willingly loaned me hers to relieve my anxiety of the roof blowing off. Gaining access to the cottage roof justified my anxiety, climbing up revealed a section of roofing iron that wouldn't have endured another repeat pounding like the last, a number of nails had loosened and the right gust would have sent iron sailing....

Turned loose on the roof hammering in nails I also put re-calibrating the rain gauge on the cards, in passing pushed the hood over the flue more securely now less rain should find its way into the baking tray....

Lighter than the previous night, wind picked up with the setting sun, not a murmur was heard from the roof until 11p.m. when tin again slid on nails!!!!

Monday 21 October 2002
Stepping inside home gates I put one foot on a banana skin, five months is now water under the bridge as residents of Rainbow Falls. Time passing fast is a sure sign of enjoyment ☺ ....

Firmly impressed in waking thoughts is the fast approaching fire and reptile higher probability season. Focussed on clearing a halo around housing will offer the best opportunity my energy can muster....

An allocation of time was absorbed with the shovel finding hidden obstacles, or as many as possible, before taking in obstacle flinging spinning machinery. Happy the ground surface was pretty tidy I emptied one tank from the brushcutter below and around the immediate bungalow window view. Working along the western side of housing, I smiled unravelling the mystery of a razor that disappeared off the bath. Finding the razor on the ground outside, and directly

below, the site blackbirds are nesting in the cottage roof.... The little buggers are getting inside☺!!!!
Content winding down another evening peacefully gazing through the open bungalow door, I tuned into the varied activity making its presence known both visually and on the airwaves. Through observation it's amazing what difference climatic conditions make as to what wildlife is active, frogs however are pretty good on any night.... Television couldn't fill my every sense with the sights and sounds provided freely by just looking out the door☺....

Tuesday 22 October 2002
As part of a balanced day sampling a bit of everything I ducked down the hill to restock empty shelves. I'm starting to feel more localised bumping into known faces in town for a chat☺.... I love our new home ♥....
Returning the borrowed ladder on the return trip from town, I left Wendy's with an electric kettle until we get one of our own, that'll save many trips into the cottage to boil water on the stove top....
Socialising over it was back to unearthing a hidden property with the assistance of a brushcutter. Having another go at sharpening the scenery in and around the bungalow, edging towards the front of the cottage, I'm making sense of exactly what lurks under that long grass bit by bit☺....
Feeling a bit woolly tickling my ears, eyes and generally giving me the shits, a haircut was put on the agenda gaining an appointment with Kellie for tomorrow. This time, along with finding my face, I'm going to have tips to blend the dusting of grey creeping in☺....
A courtesy call from the radio station confirmed there'll be no training for at least two weeks, dreams of becoming an announcer have been postponed☺....

Wednesday 23 October 2002
Unwilling to falter from leisure my body dictated the pace I virtually got up, got ready and got my bum perched on a seat at the hairdressers. For near on two hours Kellie spoilt me rotten, from foils, washing and trimming, my hair not only looks good it feels great also☺....
Coming down to earth from a pampering the laundrette was targeted to put choice back into the wardrobe. Comparable to watching grass grow is waiting on the spin cycle, adding life to a dull moment the elements delivered a dash of thunder with the added impact of a hail shower. Ms Tia was not impressed at all!!!!
Before taking off for St. Helens Ms Tia had picked up the scent of a possum trying to snooze daylight hours away on top of a shed wall beam. Returning from our outing the ball of fluff was still on top of the beam☺....
Able to measure life its rapid passing becomes evident, three journal folders packed with Rainbow Falls' history have now been completely filled. The regular entry is an important record of our progressive journey discovering life's little wonders, unaware what its future holds or when I will ever stop contributing its like existence itself, evolving????
During Sheila and Peters' visit we discussed the prospect of running a few head of cattle. Pondering the idea thoughtfully and thoroughly, my brain was tortured by the thought of sending them off to the slaughter yards. I can't do it, my conscience won't let me fatten

animals to have them killed. It was giving me nightmares I need sleep and positive thoughts ☺ !!!!

Thursday 24 October 2002
Tia's need for the great outdoors and a patch of ground got the day underway. With the start up routine over, we took off to the viewing area from the loo severely pruning unwanted shrubbery….
In need of a change of muscle groups long handled secateurs were traded for shovel. Going ahead of the brushcutter removing the many and varied obstacles hidden in grass makes for slow forward movement, but movement however is in the right direction….
Mum called with the sobering news that she'll be having day surgery next Thursday to remove a polyp from her bowel, all going well that should be the end of it. Worst case scenario involves a ten-day hospital stay to recover from a partial bowel removal, only the desired outcome is preferred. These are the times I wish we lived closer to be present and available for family at the drop of a hat!!!!

Friday 25 October 2002
Yesterday's phone conversation with Mum left me with plenty to think about????
Struggling with finances to travel to family on desire, and tired of living in poverty using everything just to exist without anything spare, I thought out a solution. Phoning the friendly tax agent for advice on how to calculate capital gains for taxation assessment purposes, left me feeling inclined to sell the Mildura house…. Freeing up some choices now rather than later….
Hearing a chainsaws high revving motor on Lohreys Road working on a tree that had given in to the elements, a new concept to me is fallen trees blocking the road. A regular occurrence here, a fallen tree covering the road would have made front page news anywhere else I've lived????.
Handed a perfect moment in time, laying back in my nipples out bath enjoying the initial penetrating heat deep into every muscle, sun obscured by cloud dimly lit the room and perfectly on cue a gentle shower did a tap dance on the tin roof….hmmmm…. Don't call me I'll call you ☺ ….

Saturday 26 October 2002
Rising out of bed I was met with a 'can't be bothered attitude', so I only left my cosy cocoon long enough to open the door for Tia….
On the phone yacking to Ms 'sick with a bad hangover' Kylie, exchanging latest news I happened to look outside the bungalow door and over the hill from the direction of the waterfall Wendy rode up on her horse 'Daphne' with two dogs in tow. Taken by surprise with something so big coming into her yard Tia let Daphne know it's a one-dog yard ☺ !!!!
Wendy and I had spoken earlier about agistment for Daphne today confirming the decision Daphne can help keep the grass down….
A small step in a marathon has been reached, one month of abstaining from ciggy's is leaving me feel more energetic and a bit heavier, assisting weight gain is non-stop eating….

Sunday 27 October 2002
Exposing myself to new experiences I took Wendy and an open mind to St. Helens for the 'blessing of the fleet'. The blessing of the fleet is, for the most, an out of doors church service, not holding my attention like the donuts at the foreshore takeaway van. Browsing the moored boats there was an extreme mix, from five star luxury models to those that left me in wonder how they still floated ☺ ????
Adding choice, a wind free evening offered ideal conditions to sit with the bungalow door open watching the changing of the guard until night fell. Young Tia breezed in and out keeping her world in order, I'd love to attach an odometer to clock the number of kilometres she now covers since landing in doggy utopia ☺ ....

Monday 28 October 2002
Planning ahead for Daphne's arrival we loaded in the car and trotted down the hill for brushcutter fuel with the intention of freeing up a couple of paddock gates to easy opening stage....
Turning brushcutting into a career I went crazy emptying a tank at each required gate then set sights onto the driveway entrance, packing up tools having had enough by 4p.m.....
A sense of taste, enhancing flavour, is returning since the big quit, I'm particularly enjoying the taste of tea, quitting has opened an entire new world to flavour ☺ ....

Tuesday 29 October 2002
Finalising property preparations for the arrival of a horse, tidying up where I left off yesterday, with minutes to spare Daphne was here for a stay. Daphne's presence is adding a visual dimension to gazing out the bungalow window to see movement in the bottom paddock....
For varying reasons, including not wanting to get it dirty, the wheelbarrow hasn't been used, being christened today its maiden voyage was clearing timber off-cuts from along the front of the cottage ☺ ....
Ms Tia trialled her latest scent by pasting her neck in horse poo, it's like any other poo it bloody well smells. Reverting Tia's pasted state it was then a good time for a cleansing myself. At 22° a nipples out bath enables a soak until toe and finger tips wrinkle, ahhhh a taste of what's to come ☺ ....
Wandering on a mild, still evening, taking in all the sounds filling senses the reliable chorus of frogs had the company of an amazing amount of varying birdcalls. So calm, sound had a three-dimensional sharp clarity arriving clearly audible from all directions....

Wednesday 30 October 2002
Motivated, and with Tia and Destiny parked comfortably nearby, I continued adding a lived in and loved look to the front entrance gate finding contours with the brushcutter. Exceeding expectations, however, it was me who ran out of puff to finish the job ☺ ....
Tia is turning 'Daphne watching' into a sport, very aware of her presence, in idle Tia moments she sits below the bungalow window keeping a keen eye on Daphne's movements. The best insurance Daphne has, if anything odd occurs in her paddock, young Tia will sound the alarm.... bark, bark, bark, bark ☺ !!!!

Thursday 31 October 2002
Strongly influencing every waking thought I got on the phone to extend my love and to wish Mum well for today's trip into theatre. Letting my fingers keep dialling, Kerry had told me Kristy-Lee had been passing out, concerned, she was my next call. Dosed up with the flu and having the remainder of the week off work, rest can only help....
Having been a happy recluse hunger drove me from the mountain. Loaded with groceries I next pulled into Grant's booking Destiny in for a service and a full check over. I feel pretty confident we'll take off to Mildura next Thursday that way catching both Stacey and Mum's birthdays, double bonus ☺....
An incoming call from the radio station requested my availability to train next Tuesday between 10a.m.-1p.m. with David, an experienced announcer from Hobart. Glad to be back training I've missed it the past two weeks....
Harbouring an unsettled brain I phoned on and off throughout the afternoon for any word on Mum. Around 6p.m. Mum surprisingly answered the phone theatre news wasn't good cancer was found. To what extent is not yet known, what is known is that Mum will be readmitted to hospital Monday for whatever treatment is needed. The news pushed my desire to be in Mildura forward to Sunday to stay for as long as needed. In shock, my body saturated in stunned numbness, the news has knocked the wind out of my sails.... I want to be woken from this bad dream....

Friday 1 November 2002
Feeling helplessly useless pacing like a caged bird, I channelled thoughts and actions positively into bring forward travel plans, and pulled it together. Seemingly in a blink with no time to wallow we were on board the Spirit of Tasmania preparing to disembark....
A need to be with family is far stronger than my patience, and too much idle time lets my eyes betray me. Home life put on hold the plan is to stay with Mum and Dad for as long as needed....
Raising a restless head 7:30am I didn't muck around, arrived near opening to see if Grant could squeeze Destiny in for a quick health check, he kindly did so without problem. Step two in my plan, booking the ferry meant a drive to St. Helens travel agent where we got the thumbs up for the evening ahead. With doors opening in every direction, before stepping into them, I did a courtesy stop at the radio station relinquishing voluntary commitments for a period unknown. Holding my composure, Margaret's act of compassion reaching out with a hug to take with me got tears flowing. Assured that whenever I return I'll be welcome to resume training....
All obligations taken care of, main power switch flicked off, packed and unable to sit still me and my little mate pointed Destiny's nose in the direction of Port Sorell. Fifteen minutes from the ferry, Aliki offered her uplifting personality a beautiful meal and a nice drop of red ☺....

Saturday 2 & Sunday 3 November 2002
Off the boat and bladders comfortable for a few kilometres, most of Saturday dissolved watching white line after white line pass. Fortunately saved by a layer of high cloud taking the harsh edge off, it was supposed to be 35° the drive was warm enough overcast....

Turning into Mum and Dad's driveway 1p.m.-ish, following a warm greeting, we shared an hour together before being joined by Kerry and Kristy-Lee. The format changing very little, it felt reassuringly nice immersed in the strength of a family united ☺....

Mother Nature had a different welcome of her own in mind she put together the messy combination of a dense low visibility duststorm in the company of a thunderstorm. Comforting Tia in Destiny it began raining mud. A kind act, I appreciated Dad's voluntary car wash he re-found windows and body paint below the mud ☺....

Coming to grips with the unwelcome new-found knowledge, it was no surprise no one slept well Friday. United, come Saturday evening the energy wheels fell off and we all had heads on pillows by 8:30pm and slept like babies....

Unable to go inside, Tia was released Sunday morning from her best friend and makeshift holiday bedroom Destiny, she then busily went about claiming real estate in the yard. Content, I jumped back into bed contemplating the world in comfort waiting until Mum and Dad's shower routine was over and the bathroom was free....

Getting on with a fresh day Tia helped Lukey in the garden, I vacuumed Destiny and Mum cooked a delicious roast lunch before handing the kitchen over to Dad and me. Limited to a liquid diet in the lead up for tomorrow's hospital visit, I let Mum know how much I appreciated her cooking when she was unable to join us in the eating ☺....

A welcome stream of well-wishers continued with visits from Yvonne, Stacey and Kristy-Lee. Healing strength is found in simple acts of caring and love....

Monday 4 November 2002

Filling the slow minutes found in waiting, with words of strength and encouragement riding the emotional rollercoaster, it's probably the longest day of Mum's life....

Enduring a liquid diet since Saturday lunchtime, slowly losing weight, today being Mum's most trying with nothing to eat or drink from 7a.m.. Due for admission 1p.m. the surgeon was running behind and Mum never made theatre until 4p.m. by that time extreme hunger, dehydration and nausea had taken a hold. Three hours to complete the procedure, Mum was then admitted to the Intensive Care Unit, not because of a life threatening condition it's the best ward for high quality attention and a quiet recovery....

A few phone calls and a lot of nervous waiting, 8:30pm family were finally allowed to visit, what we learnt was a section of bowel and lymph nodes had been removed. With a rather large incision taking in the lower half of Mum's stomach, she's being administered with morphine to numb shock and curb pain....

The biggest hurdle behind only speed humps to go. An important big part of my life, Mum is irreplaceable!!!!

Tuesday 5 November 2002

Up and mobile, I took a few incoming calls from concerned friends and family. One caller being my little mate Tegan Termite, making arrangements to pick her up later for a hospital visit, and a dear friend Miriam also dropped in to offer supporting friendship ☺....

Picking Tegan up in perfect timing for Intensive Care visiting hours, I was pleasantly impressed at how well Mum looked day one following surgery. However, coming as no surprise, Mum's energy is all over the place tiring very quickly....

Revisiting again in the evening I was able to stay around a half-hour before Mum tired, her courage and strength is exceptional its to be admired. Ending up half the person Mum is I'll be an asset to this world....

Wednesday 6 November 2002
Folding neatly into one another, keeping the journal is helping me keep track of what day it is????
In general conversation Mum mentioned she must wash the kitchen curtains, making a point of doing just that for a nice feel good homecoming. Another piece of conversation taken onboard was to encourage Dad out golfing. All wishes thus far have been fulfilled ☺....
Reliably there at the opening of visiting hours, daily I'm impressed by Mum's rapid recovery. Today the catheter was removed, being mobile enough to take the toilet walk unassisted, Mum only needs help to unplug the gadgets to wheel the entourage of technology attached to her body behind....
Shifted to an end room with ensuite and view to the carpark, the evening visit turned on an antidote of innocent laughter at the expense of a curious young girl. One way glass screens Mum's room from the carpark, a young girl pressed her face flush against the window in an attempt at discovering what mystery lay beyond. Without luck, the young girls many facial expressions fell to expressionless, amusing the audience hidden behind the reflection ☺....
Making a point of going to the hospital a little earlier Dad and I looked in on Mrs Millward, another long-term resident of Jenkins Place, not so fortunate, Mrs Millward's cancer is at an advanced stage. Sharing memories she was happy to hear word on Mum. A very giving natured lady, my outstanding memory of Mrs Millward growing up in Jenkins Place, kids included, she knew everyone's birthday and never failed to stop to wish many happy returns ☺....

Thursday 7 & Friday 8 November 2002
First priority Thursday was to pop into Stacey's work and sing that timeless tune 'happy birthday' delivered with a gift. It's always a pleasure to have your Aunty do that to you at work ☺!!!!
Still lurking about in town put my Chrismas present plan into action, rattling my brain under pressure placed an order for personalised stamps using existing photos.... That should be a family pleaser ☺....
Each afternoon hospital visit Dad and I are making a point of also calling in on Mrs Millward, sitting up looking bright and cheerful her company is always easy to be in....
Better by the day, Mum had her first oral intake, a step in the right direction for going home. So Mum could share in Stacey's birthday available family met at the hospital 6p.m. until we wore the patient down. Thursday finished with a barbecue dinner and more birthday celebrations at Kerry's ☺....
Announced at Stacey's barbecue dinner, Kristy-Lee and Brenton have set a wedding date, planning the big event for February 9, 2004, February 9 being the date Kristy-Lee met the groom to be ☺....
With nothing coming from left field Friday ticked over without surprise, a few odds 'n' ends around the house, a grocery grab in town then onto the hospital....

Returning from an afternoon visit of patients I took the malting Ms Tia for a cool swim in the mighty Murray at Apex Park on yet another bloody hot day, 30° by lunch and 37° is forecast for Monday, yuck! Turning the thermostat up, Ms Tia's fur has been jumping out of her skin, in one go I brushed ten brush loads of hair out, her body has gone into shock with the sudden rise in temperature ☺ !!!!
Settled in for the evening Dad and I took refuge by feeling the full effects of the air-conditioner with a cold beer ☺ ....

Saturday 9 November 2002
Domestics complete and Lukey golfing, Tia and I squeezed in a dash of socialising reacquainting where life left off since last visit with Fred. Leaving Fred's for visiting hours the popular lady already had a room full, Kristy-Lee, Kerry, Aunty Claire and Betty filled the room. Mum is looking terrific, yesterday the morphine drip was removed today the saline drip and the bowel drain plug was taken out. The bandage covering the surgical cut and staples was also removed extending more freedoms to move around. Mum's diet of solids is also increasing, I don't think we'll be visiting the hospital much longer ☺ ????

Sunday 10 November 2002
In conversation with Mrs Millward we established we both have a passion for writing and photography, mentioning in idle chat she'd like something to write with, having a few spares at home Mum told me to take a pad and pen from there....
Visiting Mum first, she wrote a short note to Mrs Millward in the writing pad before I took it across. Constantly asking after one another but unable to visit it was one way they could communicate. Mrs Millward greeted the gift and note warmly, now she can release every emotional thought she's inspired to write.... The simple things in life can make a big difference ☺ ....
Hospital staff waited on my predictable evening visit to alleviate any surprises associated with walking into an empty room, Mum had been shifted from Intensive Care to ward 2, room 5. At this stage Mum still has an ensuite room to herself keeping recovery restful and as comfortable as possible. Hospital staff have been brilliant making life extremely pleasant....

Monday 11 November 2002
Coming back from doing a few chores in town, harbouring a little emotional overload Dad and I locked horns having a couple of quiet words. For a change of scenery I escaped to Kerry's for some time out. Ready to leave Kerry for hospital visiting hours Tia was nowhere to be found, it's out of character for her to jump a fence and the gates were still shut? Sure she wasn't inside the yard I jumped in Destiny and began searching nearby streets, extending the search further afield rang veterinary clinics, radio stations and the pound. Feeling helpless, unsure of another avenue, some three hours later crying into a beer Kerry rang to say Tia had turned up in her backyard, I was there in a flash ☺ !!!! Following a loving reception Tia jumped into Destiny reunited with safe familiar friends and refused to budge....
Back to walking on air a better frame of mind to take with me to the hospital, is where I found a very tired but welcoming beautiful mother. Looking like she could sleep for 24 hours without any effort I didn't overstay my welcome. The good news shared in our short time together was

a release home is likely within the next couple of days, hopefully tomorrow for an ideal birthday present ☺ ????
Emotionally and physically drained, I'm glad this day is in the closing stages....

Tuesday 12, Wednesday 13 & Thursday 14 November 2002
Well, life threw a curve ball while my guard was down....
Celebrating Mum's birthday and homecoming Tuesday, the news that followed her home was cancer had made its way outside the bowel and was found in every thigh lymph node removed. The surgeon told Mum she has a 'C' class cancer, placing her in a 50% category for beating the disease. Without a course of action to take, cancer is a very humbling experience....
Playing her trump card of attitude, determination and strength, a winning combination, Mum is not going to lay down and take it rising up to look it in the eye to again live a full and active life ☺ ....
Thirteen of the twenty-six staples from the surgical cut were removed before Mum was released home, what remained was becoming increasingly uncomfortable. By Wednesday the lower area of the cut in particular was reddened and sore with a burning discomfort, causing concern enough for me to phone and bring a doctors appointment forward. Without Mum even making it out the back door a volcanic eruption of fluid wept from the infected area releasing internal pressure. Mum not only brought antibiotics home from the doctors but favourable test results also, no abnormalities showed in any blood tests her liver also screened cancer free ☺ ....
With the luxury of freedom to be anywhere at anytime at the drop of a hat, staying until Christmas was on the cards, now Tia and I will remain until we reach our expiry date. Holding strong family values everything else is secondary, there's only one chance to do it right!!!!
Willingly slipping into a carer's role, Thursday evaporated dutifully honouring my matronly bedside manner. With limited flexibility while the surgical cut heals I've become Mum's lifter, bender. Two weeks of basically a liquid diet has been pretty harsh on Mum's slight body, losing a considerable amount of weight she dropped to a mere 40 kilograms, a quick drop of about ten kilograms, try as she might it's not surprising Mum runs out of puff quickly....
Also released home to Jenkins Place, I took the short walk continuing regular visits with Mrs Millward, she told me her cancer has now reached her spine making its way into her bones and each day she's feeling more tired than the last. Another person who spent her life only giving to others, so undeserving and cruel, a bloody indiscriminate uncaring disease.... Fuck cancer to hell!!!! Why my Mum, why anyone's Mum????
Even in the face of extreme hardship Mum is still giving and unselfish wishing she knew what caused her cancer so she could warn others not to do the same thing.... An idol and mentor!!!!

Friday 15, Saturday 16 & Sunday 17 November 2002
Anything outside of family I'm struggling to keep up with, time is just flying by and days are blending. Visitor after visitor and regular phone calls maintains a healthy social scene....
An excited young bride to be has a date set in concrete, the closest Saturday to February 9, 2004, happened to be Saturday the 14th, Valentines Day, a doubly romantic day. Without fear of the grass growing under her feet already Kristy-Lee has her wedding dress on lay-by and bridesmaids have selected their dresses, wedding plans seem to be unfolding smoothly....

Finally the infection around Mum's staples is beginning to subside, dressing the area each morning before showering I'm seeing positive change, the operation alone was enough to endure without the added stress of an infection! I wish I could carry the load for a while to give Mum a rest from the constant discomfort she so bravely endures....
On a personal level Tia joined me on a night out sampling food dripping from human hands while I had a few ales with Chris and Ann, it was nice to relax in the company of friends. I reckon it was the delicious spread of antipasto that soaked up a hangover saving my grace for Saturday's 10a.m. appointment at Roccisano's Real Estate. Francis and I discussed the sale of the Mildura house and got the ball rolling....

Monday 18 November 2002
An end to an era in Jenkins Place arrived with the news of Mrs Millward's passing, another victim of damned awful cancer. A beautiful, giving soul now at rest and out of pain.... Mildura has a very high incidence of cancer????
Another stinking hot unproductive afternoon spent in self-preservation, what doesn't get accomplished beyond the air-conditioner in the morning just doesn't get done, skin burns rapidly at 38°!!!!
Monitoring it daily, the reddened area surrounding Mum's infection is constantly reducing and looking more comfortable. However, the gaping hole the escaping pus blew open isn't reducing in size or showing signs of closing over, opening a real window view to internal workings....

Tuesday 19, Wednesday 20 & Thursday 21 November 2002
By days end my brain struggles for words, three days passing without ink finding paper is slipping into routine, well here we are Thursday already????
Quite a few big steps have been taken toward selling the Mildura house. Moving paperwork along I saw Francis and Tony at the real estate agents Tuesday, Roccisano's have been brilliant rental managers, their professionalism being no different now its time to sell....
Following up on all the other little bits and pieces associated with selling, like sorting the mortgage, meant a visit to the friendliest bank manager, Helen, at the Bendigo to advise of the sale. The final missing thread in the selling link, I arranged with Allstate Conveyencing to deal with the legalities....
A phone call from a pretty excited Kerry shared welcome good news, Tegan decided to move back home with her ☺....
This time last week I was visiting Mrs Millward in her home this Thursday I attended her funeral, I'm pleased to have had the privilege of sharing time with her ☺....

Friday 22 & Saturday 23 November 2002
Mildura is turning on stifling unseasonable heat, knocking the wind out of my cooler climate sails!!!!
Using an energy spurt wisely, Friday Mum took a roam through Jenkins Place to hand out a string of thank you's beginning with Lorry and Vicki diagonally across the road. Wandering further afield Mum ventured to Don and Norma's to show appreciation for their kind thoughts, then onto Jimmy's to offer condolences for his loss of Mrs Millward....

With rising energy permitting extended freedoms, doing that bit more has increased the length of the stomach hole at the infection site to around four centimetres in length. It's a whole new world viewing internal workings, the gaping hole is a concern, it's a mystery to me how it is ever going to close over and heal????

In Miriam's company, just as we did years earlier, Friday night we revisited bars and pubs once patronised. I must be earning that 'old' status because going out without direction doesn't interest me anymore. My preference for socialising is with friends over a meal and a good red, something with purpose. Home by 11:30pm satisfied we had been, seen and conquered....

On just another bloody hot day in Mildy, after Lukey left for golf Saturday, Mum and I had a restful one home together....

Sunday 24 & Monday 25 November 2002

Finally Sunday brought with it a cool change, a day under 30°, heat takes its toll on how active one feels like being. Cooler conditions returned the spring to my step, participating in the great outdoors away from the sane security of the air-conditioner I paid a couple of bills and hit the laundromat sprucing up Tia's bedding. The laundromat was a pleasant experience, on duty within Karen was extremely helpful assisting me with forgotten soap powder and invited Tia inside in air-conditioned comfort. Winning me over is as simple as offering a sincere act of kindness☺....

Mobility and independence rising, I just do the things Mum can't and have no problem going out and leaving her to her own devices, if I'm not mistaken I think she's happy to have some quality time alone. Since hospital there's been a welcome flow of well-wishing visitors, important in the healing process, or there's been Dad or me underfoot☺....

Complementing the cool change Mum cooked Monday's entire evening meal, and a perfect night for spaghetti in the company of Stacey, rain dropped the temperature making a hearty meal more enjoyable....

Tuesday 26 November 2002

It weights my body with lead helplessly watching Mum pour her heart into returning to known capabilities and at how quickly her body betrays and tires. The unrelenting, out of season soaring temperatures are of no bloody help for stimulating a desire to get motivated either. Staying up beyond 7p.m. is big, but not tonight, without quibbling over leaving me to prepare dinner is a give-away Mum's tank is empty....

While it cares to remain, the cool change inspired my legs into action taking my little mate for a walk blowing a few patiently stored cobwebs off pent up energy. In a more relaxed state, Tia stayed with Mum and Dad and plenty of shade while I took Destiny to Dazzlers and an industrial vacuum cleaner to remove Tia fur without help☺....

Wednesday 27, Thursday 28, Friday 29, Saturday 30 November & Sunday 1 December 2002

Gone before I realised it had, the past week didn't stand still. Breaking into December, we've been here a month with Chrismas fast approaching????

As punctual as ever, Wednesday at 2:30pm I went to sign my will, apparently the appointment was for Tuesday, right time wrong day, oops. Rescheduling for Thursday, I later received a call

from the office asking if I could reschedule because the solicitor wouldn't be in on Friday, my reply was simple, "my appointment is for Thursday".... Hmmmm, who is confused ☺ ????
Thursday saw me at the conveyancer finalising paperwork for a 'section 32' in preparation for the sale, nothing more can be done now until the house is sold....
Contributing a huge appreciated effort, Kerry offered to made dinner Friday evening, cooking everything at her home, she walked through the door with an instant feast at Mum and Dad's. I sampled a bit of everything from chicken and corn pie, beef and mushroom pie, along with an array of vegetables in a creamy white sauce. Following a sample of butterscotch pudding food was the last thing on my mind, when I stood to leave the table unfortunately dishes were the next thing to enter ☺ ....
Unearthing an inkling and desire, Mum requested we do a spot of shopping while Lukey golfed, a request readily fulfilled. It's pleasing and fills my heart seeing Mum comfortable and active regaining independence and quality of life....
During our stay Tia has managed to turn on the charm and win hearts, she's like a pet lamb following Lukey around the yard and on warmer days Dad gives Tia a cool hosing off catering for her obsession with water. Dad was quietly out the front gardening with Tia shadowing, I watched from the kitchen window, a car slow at the driveway near Tia and a Sunday paper was tossed out. Watching the whole event without too much expression, Tia as casual as you like picked up the paper and took it to Lukey, not for him to read but to throw it again, and again ☺ .... Life is just one big game....

Monday 2, Tuesday 3 & Wednesday 4 December 2002
With energy to burn following a visit to the doctor we hit the mall, only having ever lived in Mildura Mum has established long-standing friendships. There was a series of conversations to catch up on in the social circuit through town following a few weeks of noted absence. Finalising a successful outing at Grannies Antiques, satisfying Mum's passion for antique lamps, she didn't leave empty handed ☺ ....
With a power of leftovers, Stacey chipped in to help joining us for dinner Monday. Adding a freshly cooked quiche to the heap of vegetables, the four of us put an end to the foil covered bowls decorating the fridge. Letting dinner settle pleasantly, we adjourned outside giving Tia victims to throw the ball ☺ ....
A firm offer not far off the asking price was phoned through from Roccisano's, what I'm asking is fair so I'll just wait a bit longer....
Tuesday I treated myself to the luxury of a haircut from my favourite and long-standing Mildura hairdresser Steve located at the Centre Plaza, and as usual a pleasant experience. Without wandering too far in the shopping complex I bumped into a couple of old friends Mandy from softball days and Jan from secondary school years, rekindling fond memories ☺ ....
A phone call came through Wednesday from an unrelated friend Margaret Lucas, with the news a dear friend Juney Mallum had died. Juney was a drinking buddy of my deceased Grandparents Nan and Pop Lucas, an end to an era of an ageing group that once met regularly at the Workers Club. A one-eyed blues supporter, Juney and I had a standing bet of a bottle of beer each time Collingwood and Carlton met in football, I proved to be a regular milking cow Juney benefited many bottles from our bet ☺ ....

In Mildura just over a month and this will be my second funeral, I'd better not stay here too long!!!!

Doing a processed photos pick up, pill gathering and pie craving for lunch dash into town, was met appreciatively at home by hungry bellies. Then, offering Mum some of that precious little time alone, while Lukey golfed, Tia and I disappeared for a cool down splash in the mighty murky Murray....

Topping a nice day Tony called to say the asking price had been reached but he would like to do a little more bartering, leaving me feel pretty confident the Eighth Street house will be sold by the end of the week ☺....

Thursday 5 December 2002

After breezing through keeping the home nest feathered Mum and Dad then treated me to lunch at O'Malleys tavern, the lunch and company couldn't have been better ☺....

Losing the afternoon in idle chatter that relaxed into beer o'clock, guessing our way through 'Wheel of Fortune' Tony phoned through a freshly offered price for the sale of the Eighth Street house, confirming there and then I was prepared to settle, time to begin finalisations....

Friday 6, Saturday 7 & Sunday 8 December 2002

Taking healing to the next level, Friday Mum completed a circuit around the block and her stomach hole is also healing over at a remarkable rate. Unable to imagine how it ever would, what was a gaping hole of about 6cm x 3cm has reduced to a pinhole with flesh covering the entire wound. Mum's mobility and independence is rapidly returning I feel confident me, Tia and Destiny will be returning to our Tassie home not long after Christmas????

Beyond being a homebody, Saturday I ventured visiting dear friends Mary and Joan, over a couple of beers we kicked back into some nice relaxing chat ☺....

Following Mum's traditional roast, Sunday was a pretty quiet affair tinkering with Christmas cards preparing them for posting....

Monday 9 & Tuesday 10 December 2002

Monday evaporated doing bits 'n' pieces around the house until the time for June's funeral came around. Turning out to be the best funeral service I've attended, with no pretence, it was as down to earth as Juney herself. Proceedings began with the Carlton Football Club song, then prompted by the person leading proceedings, mourners got involved sharing their personal June stories. What struck me when the service was over was the amount of loud conversation and laughter that lingered outside the chapel ☺.... June would have been pleased....

Leaving the chapel Destiny took me no further than Roccisano's Real Estate to activate the paper shuffle. Signing contracts for the sale of the Eighth Street house, now confirmed in ink, the cooling off period finishes 5p.m. Wednesday, December 11, and settlement January 15, all systems are in motion without any consideration of turning back....

A high priority, and the last stop before daring to enter home gates, was to replenish the supply of tennis balls for my little mate, trashing six since arrival there's now another four to do with as she wishes ☺....

Tuesday didn't gear into hyperactive. After doing my bit helping the household tick over, staying with a casual theme took my best friend to Apex Park for a run and play in the murky

River Murray. Tia's concentration was busy chasing water ripples along the shore left from the wake of a passing boat, entertaining me a cute moment arrived with a curious pelican. Tia was obliviously happy running back and forth chasing moving water until the curious pelican paddled in too close and gained her full attention. Raising her curiosity in return, Tia started to swim out to the pelican, when she got too close it paddled out of reach and Tia would return to the bank with the pelican again paddling not far behind. The repetitive pattern of behaviour kept me happily amused for a half-hour ☺ ....
Making it back inside home gates returned to where a quiet beer and glass of wine was being enjoyed ☺ ....

Wednesday 11 & Thursday 12 December 2002
As Lukey took off for his regular Wednesday golf, I took Destiny to the industrial vacuum cleaner eliminating river sand and fur before considering the idea of taking Mum shopping....
Sand free and furless, we loaded into Destiny then Mum proceeded to wear me out with her favourite pastime, shopping, I wasn't sorry when she was Christmas shopped out....
Home long enough to slightly rest worn feet, I then walked Tia the short distance to the dog groomers for a puppy pampering. Murky Murray shampooed from her body, blow waved, fluffy soft with nails clipped, she looked beautiful ☺ ....
Thursday didn't have me on the edge of my seat or change the course of the world, a visit to Medicare, optometrist then Centrelink, before spoiling myself going home to vacuum. That was enough to keep me honest and out of trouble ☺ ....

Friday 13 & Saturday 14 December 2002
It may have been Friday the 13th but it certainly wasn't a black Friday. Leaving a 2:15pm appointment, answers following Mum out the door of the surgeons practice put a spring in her step. Confident there's years of life ahead, Mum's now determined to resume walking with her sister Claire and die from old age in her sleep ☺ .... Attitude is nine-tenths of the healing process....
Putting words into action, and very ready to participate in life, leaving the surgeons Mum lured me into town for a spot of shopping. I have trouble keeping up with Mum's refined shopping and socialising skills, she's definitely coming good ☺ ....
The gaping hole I never could fathom how it would ever heal over has now closed completely, steadily gaining weight and rapidly gaining the desire to participate, Mum's also doing most of her own lifting and bending. I reckon planning the journey home to our beloved Rainbow Falls can be pencilled in....
Scanning the bombardment of Christmas catalogues squeezed into the letter box Saturday morning, I spied a good priced chrome kettle and was immediately instructed by Mum to race in and grab one as a Christmas present for me.... And they were popular....
Ticking over an aimless day I dragged a garden hose around the corner to the Eighth Street house splashing water around, it's my responsibility to keep the garden happy in the lead up to settlement....
Sparking my social life into gear, my mate Mirro phoned to say she'd be at the 'Retro Bar' all afternoon helping potential new local music talent gain a public performance and confidence.

An afternoon out with a few beers, a good mate, and random samples of music was greeted with 'I'll see you there'♫♪♫♪....

Sunday 15 & Monday 16 December 2002
Not a common occurrence because of a couple of nomadic members, the entire immediate family met at the Gol Gol pub Sunday for a meal to celebrate Mum's belated 60th birthday. Fitting for the mood the meals were superb, not even the harshest of critics could raise an eyebrow. The restaurant has the perfect ambience for a nice occasion, full length tinted windows overlook a large maintained lawned expanse meandering a short distance to the river. An easy place to settle into and we did, forgetting about the 38° temperature lurking outside and the inability to find a park in shade until it was time to leave, walking out into a wall of stifling heat was a blunt reminder. Increasing the thermostat a few degrees was to travel home in a car without air-conditioning that had been sitting in the sun☺!!!!
Escaping the harsh elements and self-preservation was the only option, succeeding in that plan ripped the lid off a few cool ales with air-conditioner pumping down and watched the Aussies beat England in a one day cricket match....
She who prefers shopping and heat least, being a good Aunt offered to pick Tegan up Monday for a spot of Christmas shopping. Tackling extreme heat, dense traffic and mobs of last minute Christmas shoppers, I know how to spoil myself. A cooler airflow was supposed to find us predicting only 37° as the day's top, reaching that by 10a.m. it nicely heated the pavements for us shoppers. Going on to excel expectations, peaking at 42°, try and find a park in the shade on a day like that is near on impossible ☺!!!!

Tuesday 17 & Wednesday 18 December 2002
It seems unseasonable high temperatures are at the forefront of everyone's mind. Waiting for the moment the suns magnification had the edge taken off by a small band of high level cloud, I did a dash to the conveyancer's to sign finalised paperwork for the house sale. Catching a weather report on the radio driving in, with cloud cover, it was 41.2° with a predicted overnight low lurking ahead of 28°, something to look forward to. Doing nothing to raise spirits, there was nothing forecast below 40° until the end of the week, bloody beaut!!!!
Waiting to sign the paperwork I was chatting to the woman at reception discussing the obvious heat, she said during her lunch break the thermometer shaded underneath her carport read 51°!!!! How comfortable....
Resembling a wilted flower, helping keep Tia's thermostat stable by a favourite method she's being given a regular hosing down, on average eight times a day, she then buries herself under the pergola amongst the shade of shrubbery waiting for that cool change also!!!!
Amusing herself giving Tia a regular morning biscuit smeared in vegemite, Mum then indulges in watching her style of eating. The biscuit travels quite a few metres pushed by her tongue before the vegemite is cleaned, only then is the remaining soggy biscuit thrown down the hatch ☺....
A long-standing part of Lukey's morning routine is to duck around the corner store and grab the local paper. Having a glance through in an idle moment, I read in disbelief the death notice of a known friend Max at the tender age of forty-seven. Looking for confirmation phoned Fan to affirm what I read to be true, Max had a massive heart attack and was unable to be revived. I

was only chatting to Max and kids in the mall a few weeks earlier???? Far too bloody young!!!!

Thursday 19, Friday 20 & Saturday 21 December 2002
Outside of self-preservation bugger all has been happening the past few days, merely trying to survive the continuous onslaught of fucking heat is enough. Only leaving the house and air-conditioner when absolutely necessary, I'm beginning to feel stir crazy with the stifling limitations!!!!
Disappearing outside of the front gate merely once in three days was to book Destiny in for a service and look over with a long-time friend, front-end specialist and mechanic, Peter, at Sunraysia Steering Service.... Step one in the return home process....
Enforced limitations is taking a toll on everyone we're all wilting, there hasn't been a break for the past two weeks, the range has hovered between 39°– 42°.... Insane!!!!
Roccisano's asked me to maintain the garden at the Eighth Street house until settlement. During days of total fire ban there are no fixed sprinklers between 10a.m. and 10p.m., I'm forced to wait until near on sunset for a cool enough temperature to stand outside with a hand held hose. Dad's chipped in helping splash water around on his morning walk to get the paper, for that I'm grateful.... A change has been forecast and it won't come too soon, I've had enough of the ridiculous oppressive heat!!!!

Sunday 22, Monday 23 & Tuesday 24 December 2002
Sunday too, was spent eating and avoiding the bloody magnifying UV rays, although plummeting down to mid thirties it was still an unpleasant mongrel heat. The eternally teasing forecast change finally arrived Monday, offering a release for pent up energy to participate in this world and what a full day of participation....
Activity began outside the house meeting a 10a.m. scheduled arrangement with Pete at his workshop to give Destiny the once over. Young Tia looked cute with a bemused expression peering out Destiny's window riding the motion of the rising hoist☺....
With a spring back in Destiny's step she was put to work scooping up Mum and battling town traffic so we could finalise those last minute Christmas needs from bonbons to brown sugar. Continuing with her good deeds, when night finally fell Destiny took me, Mum and Tia traipsing all over town looking at the festive Christmas light displays fulfilling our viewing need☺....
Within a blink here we are the day before Christmas, the eve of a day traditionally known for over indulging. In training, I spent Tuesday home resting and eating, a prelude to the main event....

Wednesday 25, Thursday 26, Friday 27, Saturday 28, Sunday 29 & Monday 30 December 2002
I now have the privilege of writing with a beautifully engraved gold pen, a Christmas gift from dear Stacey. And with the obvious six-day neglect from journal writing some of that ink was spilled onto paper☺....
A gathering of the clan at Kerry's to celebrate Chrismas left me showered in practical presents. Tegan Termite bought me a great reference book on Australian natives, the beautiful Kristy-

Lee had gift-wrapped a sandwich toaster, a useful gift when food is a priority. Generously, pillows and power tools were given from Kerry, and from Mum and Dad the chrome kettle, now I'll be able to give back the borrowed kettle returning home ☺....

Without getting overwhelmed by the spirit of Christmas, we festive travellers wandered back to our side of the city late afternoon to finalise a quiet one at home. If that was Christmas its now over....

The days following Christmas have been pretty low-key, just getting on with life healing the sick, watering the Eighth Street house garden, exercising and hosing down Ms Tia, contributing inside the house and going shopping ☺....

The humming busy atmosphere of town eased with the passing of Christmas, it was a pleasure pacing the pavement in a more relaxed atmosphere with Mum Saturday morning. Idly taking our time browsing in and out of any desired shop, stopping to chat on occasion and sitting for coffee, it was nice quality time together ☺....

Making plans and following through with an idea rolling around in my head, decided to take the long way home via the New South Wales Coast visiting friends and collecting another car full of stored possessions from Kiama. Leaving early in the New Year will hopefully coincide with a cool change....

Tuesday 31 December 2002, Wednesday 1, Thursday 2, Friday 3 & Saturday 4 January 2003
I have to get the hang of writing 2003, and a better year it's going to be, with more meat on bones I'm ready to face it head on ☺!!!!

Turning on some bells and whistles of her own leading into New Year's Eve, Mother Nature mustered up a thunderstorm, getting active in the wee baby hours I spent considerable time in Destiny calming a very stressed, barking Ms Tia. There wasn't much sleep going on in my bed, fireworks equally activate the Tia stress meter, they arrived with the welcoming in of the New Year. Fortunately fireworks had a known time limit....

New Years Eve was a quiet affair Mum and Dad were in bed early and I sat out the back quietly over a couple of beers with Tia. Still a bit tired from sleep deprivation caused by the previous night's storm, I retreated to bed until my fragile furry friend was disturbed by the start of midnight fireworks....

Light celebrations and a pleasant change in direction New Years Day, by Mum and Dad's invitation, we went to the Gateway Tavern for lunch redeeming a voucher the champion won playing golf. Lunch turned into quite a social event, meeting up with family members on the Lucas side along with friends. A flutter on the pokies filled the afternoon of our social outing, managing to walk away with a ten-dollar profit is rare for them thieves ☺....

Pushing the boundaries of exercise, Thursday Mum, Ms Tia and I took a stroll to the Chaffey graves along the riverfront walkway. Taking almost an hour to return, it's the longest walk Mum has comfortably done since the operation ☺....

Lunch at Colignan with dear friends Jill and Bernie Bear took care of Friday, plenty of good food and healthy conversation is always on their menu and they turned on a lovely time. Indulging in a farewell haircut with Steve Friday evening kissed the day away....

Following a milo and almost a packet of biscuits between us, Stacey took me shopping Saturday morning specifically to help me select sunglasses. Stacey mentioned that while swimming at Apex Park Friday they became involved in helping with the recovery of a victim of drowning. A body was recovered with the help of a fish finder but was unable to be revived, his young family watched on hopelessly from the riverbank, not a pleasant experience....

Sunday 5, Monday 6, Tuesday 7 & Wednesday 8 January 2003
Consuming days saying farewells preparing to leave Mildura has been an emotional rollercoaster, after sharing home and having family at hand for two months we've settled into a comfortable routine. Tia's available presence in the yard will also be missed. Mum slips Tia regular treats and she follows Dad around outside like a pet lamb, mostly throwing a tennis ball under his feet, Tia is the best help pleasantly doubling the time it takes to get anything done ☺ ....

Tuesday was set as the date for leaving. A predicted 41° for Mildura prompted the decision to drive off into the sunrise at the tender hour of 6a.m. to escape the scorpion's tail. Climbing toward the Coast of New South Wales still didn't offer any relief the overall day for travelling was bloody hot. Making regular stops so Destiny included could cool down, radiating heat, bitumen itself was close to a sticky melt down. Ms Tia travelled wonderfully under trying conditions, both back windows were down to create a bit of breeze and she was smart enough to keep herself out of direct sun....

Adjusting the speed to suit her temperature gauge, Destiny took us to Kiama without missing a beat putting in a long hot day. It was worth every kilometre to be greeted at Denise's warmly with welcoming smiles and hugs. My wheels didn't take long to fall off Tuesday night, exhausted with eyes hanging out of my head following a thousand kilometres in searing heat I searched for bed ☺ ....

With a head for conversation after sleeping away the white line etched into my vision, Wednesday morning vanished chatting idly with Denise as a cool ocean breeze drifted through a full-length open window.... ahhhh....

Overlooking the ocean, it's an ideal location for whale spotting. Staying only a stones throw from where I once lived those fading memories now seem like a lifetime ago....

Thursday 9, Friday 10, Saturday 11 & Sunday 12 January 2003
Days melted catching our breath in Kiama putting in energy conserving relaxed time. Simply doing a social circuit I visited those who left a positive impression carried through from our former life before leaving NSW for Tassie....

Without doubt a trip to Unanderra was inked in, Carola and her Mother Lisalotta put a roof over mine and Tia's heads when we needed it most, and Carola's brother, Torsten, is how Destiny entered our lives.... Lasting fond memories ☺ ....

A bit of a scallywag, I drove those few kilometres further to Wollongong popping in on little Ms Kylie, taking in a tour of her new unit ☺ ....

Eating and staying cool was where priorities started and stopped in Mildura, not too much physical activity happened, exercising Tia walking hilly coastline near the little blow hole in Kiama highlighted a drop in my fitness....

My brain distracted by thoughts of home is a sign its time, we've been a long time absent. Settlement from the house sale this Wednesday permits concrete plans to be made and financed....

One element I've been extremely enjoying is cooler climatic conditions, averaging in the low twenties and backed by a sea breeze its adding life to a wilted body…. Ahhhh, revitalising….

Monday 13, Tuesday 14, Wednesday 15 & Thursday 16 January 2003
Time in Kiama literally breezed by finalising travel plans and farewelling friends. A return trip to Unanderra was a certainty, sitting for cake and coffee with Lisalotta, found Carola and Torsten at his mechanics workshop in their element up to their elbows in grease ☺ ….
Settlement found the bank Thursday, doing a quick redistribution of funds got my credit card under control, paid a chunk off Rainbow Falls mortgage and offered each niece $500 to go toward a trip to visit. Still with the luxury of a few spare bucks in my back pocket, set travel plans in concrete booking the ferry to cross Bass Strait….
The steps involved in casting off from the Port of Melbourne Saturday evening, after showing Denise appreciation for opening her home, is to stay with Kylie in Wollongong Thursday evening getting me a close distance to entering onto the Hume Highway. Come Friday, we'll take the drive full steam ahead along the Hume Highway to Melbourne, stay with the beautiful Sheila and Peter, then sail out of Melbourne Saturday evening…. Just a few more kilometres to cover to fulfil plans ☺ ….

Friday 17, Saturday 18, Sunday 19, Monday 20 & Tuesday 21 January 2003
Mother Nature sure knows how to treat a girl by turning on yet another bloody hot day to travel in, needless to say there were plenty of stops, Destiny included we were feeling the heat. The roadside was beginning to resemble a car gravesite we must have passed at least ten cars broken down running out of puff in extremes, our beloved Destiny just kept soldiering on ☺ ….
I can't say I was sorry to have finally arrived in Melbourne to be greeted by the beautiful Sheila and Peter, softening an end to many hot kilometres. Twenty-four hours in Melton disappeared in a conversation, hardly having time to catch a breath and Melbourne City was in sights en route to the 'Spirit of Tasmania' for the next leg of the journey home….
The trip over Bass Strait on the 'Spirit' was endured in a cruise seat purely for sheer economics due to inflated prices coinciding with school holidays. Quite a number of people filled the cruise seat room and not one of them snored, was it a miracle????
Disembarked, and after an easy drive across State Sunday, a quick supermarket stop, it was full steam ahead to Rainbow Falls. On our precise arrival at the front gate met Wendy leaving for the last time with Daphne, she warned me of a tiger snake by the bungalow door that made its way into the rock pile…. Happy homecoming ☺ ….
Long grass had re-established and the yard gave me a sensation of the day we arrived. Collecting water from the dam a copperhead snake lay quietly at the edge where I stood, nervously raising the shovel, it swam deeper into the dam…. Snake two spotted for the day!!!!! No more doing it the hard way, first thing Monday we were straight into St. Helens and didn't come home without a lawnmower and new blade for the brushcutter. While in the neighbourhood I made a courtesy trip into the radio station and was greeted by a lot of change in a relatively short absence in the big scheme of things. Introduced to Rose, the new receptionist, another nice personality, the former receptionist Maria had stepped into Rita's shoes managing the station. Without letting the dust settle, Thursday coming from 9a.m. to

12p.m. I'm pencilled in to recommence training with Mel live to-air, it hardly feels like I've been away simply just stepping back in where I left off....

Re-entering home gates 4p.m.-ish offered enough time to empty two tanks of fuel christening the lawnmower. Carving through the growth spurt hiding the state it was left I began finding the ground contour again with relative ease and speed ☺....

Tuesday was more of the same, cutting loose with the new toy emptied two tanks before heat got too much. Finishing the day officially being Taswegians eight months, we have achieved a lot in that short space of time....

Wednesday 22 & Thursday 23 January 2003
There's been no time for contemplative thought I've hit the ground running coming home....
Excited by the fast moving progress made by the convenience of a lawnmower again went for it Wednesday until heat stopped play. Migrating under cool cover of the shed roof I gave the mower a spruce up to deliver it clean for its five hours of operation service....

The horrible sound of the bloody alarm broke blissful silence Thursday morning. Without thought was up and into it having the mower dropped off and walking inside the door of the radio station all before 9a.m.....

Sitting one-on-one through Mel's entire morning program, watching the real thing happen, asking questions and incorporating some hands on with equipment live helped instil confidence. Edging me further out of my comfort zone and into hands on, next training I'm going to introduce myself live and play a couple of favourites to start finding my feet....
Loving the 'outside of my comfort zone' challenge, its exciting ☺!!!!

Washing over, mower picked up, Destiny's nose was pointed homeward to hang washing on the line, there was no need to tumble dry it's that bloody hot ☺....

An ambulance screaming out of St. Helens ahead of us didn't take long to meet up with, just a few kilometres out and emergency vehicles had both lanes blocked. Being second vehicle in the traffic line-up to arrive at the scene, from our parked position I saw a motorbike lying at the side of the road with paramedics working on the rider behind the bike's rear wheel. Around ten minutes of being parked at the scene paramedics stood placing a yellow tarp over the rider; that wasn't a good sign. A family will be getting news they don't want to hear....

Police arrived clearing the accident scene of the traffic build-up, listening to the radio winding through St. Marys Pass a warning was issued 'that due to a serious accident the road will be closed for some time'....

With more events than is needed in a single day, home in a tad more sedate environment, heat slowed activity making it more pleasant to be under cover. Before retreating out of the elements I found the occasion fitting to spruce up around the clothesline, treating the mower to a quick few laps....

Mountain ranges and valleys filling the expansive north-westerly view have harboured a smoke haze the past few days fouling the gorge to the falls dulling natural beauty. Without the experience of a summer at Rainbow Falls an environmental learning curve is on its way. My limited knowledge is aware of the delicate balance of a precious water supply, of high snake activity, drought, fire risk, and am already familiar with the bloody healthy population of flies they are plentiful....

Friday 24 January 2003
This patch of paradise we call home offered a memorable moment last night. About 5a.m. a possum trying to scratch its way through the bungalow window woke the household forcing me from bed. Tapping on the window politely asked it to move on and my wishes were granted, then it was back to where we left off, sleep zzzz....
A bit daring, for comfort sake I broke out the shorts it's the first time here to be driven to such rash extremes, I'm proud to say my habits are so much like my fathers ☺ ....
The day ahead contemplated over a milo, Tia was left resting in Destiny in the cool of the shed while I gave the mower another serious workout. The housing area is almost back to where it was before grass again took over, this time only taking a week to find its surface with the mower on clean ground ☺ ....
Pulled to a stop by stinging UV rays I retreated inside to wash the sweat and dust from my skin. Slowing down on the indulgent use of water, warm conditions have taken the edge off the need to be totally submerged, reducing the amount of work to make a bath also. Feeling clean and fresh participating in anything physical was out of the question, parking my bum in a Mum and Dad canvas chair indulged the day away with my nose buried in a book....

Saturday 25 January 2003
Up and into it without hesitation, after breakfast the brushcutter was pulled out giving the lawnmower a rest. It's that bloody hot that when I stop that's it physically for the day if it doesn't happen in the morning then it just doesn't happen ☺ !!!!
Starting adjacent to the cottage following fenceline with the brushcutter, space was cleared around where I'm now collecting water from the irrigation pipe outlet I then worked back towards the shed. Emptying four tanks in total, the new blade is taking the hard work out of clearing doing more with less effort....
Smoke that has been hanging around is at its thickest today. The series of mountain ranges in the distant west are totally obscured, the gorge to the falls and surrounding mountains and valleys, silhouetted, are also full with smoke. Acting like a dense cloud, suns rays were blocked from reaching the ground giving natural light an amber tinge, re-igniting memories of Christmas 2001 in Wollongong and the long month of bushfires with smoke constantly permeating the air....
Giving up on the brushcutter around 1:30p.m.-ish the boiler was put on for hot water, with heat and dirt combined I was searching for a wash....
Clean and bellies full we settled into the cottage for a relaxing afternoon of conserving energy. Initially writing and listening to the radio, body conservation was topped by burying my nose into my current book....

Sunday 26 January 2003
Carrying a dose of the 'couldn't be bothered's', bed held me like a magnet, offering inspiration required to get up, young Stacey phoned pleasantly for a simple natter ☺ ....
Dull, overcast, with smoke filled air blending with cloud, I joined the elements on offer and again got in rhythm with the swinging motion of the brushcutter. Having a shift in behaviour giving air quality a bit of a lift it was rain that stopped play not the intense rays of sun.

Embracing the direction chosen by Mother Nature with both hands got comfortable in the cottage with a book....

Losing focus on the pages with fading light, Tia and I adjourned to the bungalow to start on dinner. Like I do, gazing out the bungalow window I stopped motionless watching a wallaby casually inspecting the freshly cut grass then just as casually make its way around toward the dam and out of sight, only in paradise ☺ ????

A benchmark date, the 26th signifies I've now been a non-smoker for four months. I rarely get cravings but they pop up occasionally, it's still just as easy to smoke as it is not to but I choose the latter, everything smells and tastes better ☺ ....

Monday 27 January 2003
The horrible droning sound of the alarm annoyed life into the bungalow. My nervous brain couldn't be distracted from the thought of the first live moment on-air, facing it head-on when the time arrived....

What I'd rehearsed in my head isn't exactly what came out of my mouth. I don't know where the breakdown occurred but began my live moment by saying good afternoon when it was morning, not earth shattering stuff but I'm hoping that is the end to nervous bugs. Adrenalin pumping, it was an awesome experience going live to-air and I can look forward to doing it all again same time same place tomorrow ☺ ....

Once again, taking laundry home to dry got us there sooner. Leaving clothes to dangle from the line, and as predictable as the sun rising, I gave the brushcutter a workout tidying ahead for the lawnmower to give it the final close shave....

Tuesday 28, Wednesday 29 & Thursday 30 January 2003
Eager, and nervously excited, I was back at the radio station Tuesday. Gaining enough confidence to hijack the microphone for a half-hour, I enjoy the character strengthening challenge of stepping outside my comfort zone experiencing life without fear ☺ !!!!

Time at home is seemingly becoming carbon copy. Planting my feet firmly back on the ground Wednesday, surprise of all surprises, grubbed back more contours for the mower to trim up taking the shine well and truly off the brushcutters new blade....

After washing raised dirt and grass from skin and polishing bruises, packed the team together in Destiny and took off to St. Helens for a 6:30pm announcers meeting. Leaving with Rita as Manager also went the tasteful décor, timber has been replaced by laminex and plastic.

Treating myself to an easy dinner of pizza stopped at the St. Marys Coach House Restaurant on the way through to home, perfect for the moment....

Rain welcomed in Thursday, a sound that will green up the areas grubbed down. Mother Nature on the other hand was giving me the hint to do something else other than yard clearing. Cloud continued to fill the sky and misty rain persistently fell along with the temperature to cool and comfy ☺ ....

A very healthy population of skink lizards has made a home amongst the rock pile outside the bungalow door the little buggers are everywhere, including inside. Investigating the sound of a blowfly stuck tracked it lifting the mat on the window box, a skink had a blowfly abdomen in its mouth, wing flapping, the fly was still trying to take-off.... Not likely!!!!

Claiming territorial rights inside, lizards occupying westerly facing windows definitely aren't going to feel the effects of hunger ☺ ....
A bit of excitement finished Thursday. In the cottage brushing my teeth daydreaming out the window feeling the warm and fuzzies watching wrens with young dancing over the red hot fire poker shrub, looking for a feed, from the drain a snake joined in. The little birds scattered and the snake meandered its way along the driveway. With my 'never lived in the country' city mentality, as a figure of speech 'I pissed my pants', jumping into Destiny I tried to run the snake over merely to watch it disappear in the paddock out front. Managing only to achieve an adrenalin rush for myself and a rough car ride for Tia ☺ !!!!

Friday 31 January 2003
Packing in another satisfying day in the life and times of the Tassie Trio....
Out the gate, I hit the road fuelling up in St. Marys then was on the way to St. Helens to mix it with quite a few members of the police force. Representing the radio station in a combined 'Road Safety Task Force', accident prevention promotion, assisted Mary-Anne handing out soft drink and sausages to the masses. At 11:30am we adjourned to the front of the Post Office where the promotion took place. Visually in your face, a large billboard with the catch phrase 'Just like that' was propped on a trailer and a tow truck carted around a pretty nasty car wreck. A sausage sizzle, plenty of give-aways, along with a bit of humour and good organisation, and of course no party is complete without speeches, made certain the promotion was positively met by the public....
The euphoria wound down, cleaned and packed up after, I continued on with a spoiling treating myself to laundry and groceries. By the time the front gate was sighted again the day was a bit long in the tooth. Destiny unloaded, groceries put away, clothes hung out and water collected that was enough to finish up with ☺ ....

Saturday 1 & Sunday 2 February 2003
A simple trip to the loo dished out a healthy dose of adrenalin, on the short walk up the hill Tia and me in the company of the shovel met up with a copperhead snake. Facing a fear I took a wobbly swing with the shovel missing my target, making a quick exit, I threw the shovel like a spear after the retreating snake, but it was safe ☺ ....
I don't like surprises like that, offering a fair chance walking to the loo I sparked the mower into life and carved a ten metre wide strip to the throne ☺ !!!!
Remaining with carving strips Sunday, this time with Destiny in mind and the potential unleaded cars have for starting grass fires, gave the brushcutter a turn trimming within and beside the driveway.... That's enough to keep a girl honest and out of trouble....

Monday 3 February 2003
Shit I hate that bloody alarm, but it's worth the torment to be seated in the studio at the radio station. Taking over the headphones and microphone following the 10a.m. news, I hijacked the studio for an hour. Picking the eyes out of a few personal favourite songs they were played between sponsorship live-reads and setting sponsors messages on the mini disk, I also included a few errors to learn by ☺ ....

Taking the slow trip home incorporated the supermarket, Post Office, and more pleasantly Rod's offer of a cuppa in passing, by then we're at least nine-tenths of the way home. Rod offered useful tips on how to better deal with snakes, I can't always be running for Destiny ☺!!!!

Finishing the trip up the hill to home I didn't muck about, firing the lawnmower into action I had another go tidying up where the snake was met yesterday. Unable to keep up the pace the poor mower is falling apart already, replacing a screw that vibrated loose on the plastic engine cover was a wasted exercise because it too had the same fate. Both screws have come adrift from the exhaust cover also they just don't make things like they used to ☺!!!! It's probably worked harder the past two weeks than it should in a lifetime....

Tuesday 4 & Wednesday 5 February 2003

Like two peas in a pod, both Tuesday and today were pretty much carbon copies....

Both mornings Destiny and Tia were made comfortable together while I psyched Tassie Sue's confidence to take-over the microphone following the 10a.m. news. Less reliant on my trainer wheels, confidence is growing, comfortably settling in for longer stints now extending to ninety minutes. Human error is becoming less of a distraction, I'm loving it, the radio challenge is giving me heaps of energy!!!!

Tuned in while I was cutting my teeth on-air, phoning through a request for 'Cat Stevens and Peace Train', Rod also extended the offer of a cuppa and platypus viewing in passing heading home. Accepting the invitation, pulled up at Rods to him happily singing 'Peace Train', a better, appreciated welcome I could not have received ☺....

The cuppa and chat were reliable but the platypus didn't show, saying farewells I made the last leg of the mountain climb to home for a little physical labour....

Tuesday the brushcutter got a run outside the cattle yards, alternating muscle groups, today gave the mower a workout having a re-run over a woolly cottage side yard....

Watching a large fly buzz back and forth along the bungalow window ledge couldn't understand why a skink wasn't attracted by the wing flapping buzz for a juicy feed. Lifting the mat laid neatly across the box below the window revealed a skink with a wing hanging out either side of its mouth, an answer soon became evident ☺....

Thursday 6 February 2003

Ahhhh, thank the lord, finally a sleep in, no bloody alarm clock!!!!

Without rushing the day, over a cuppa and procrastination I contemplated the world, easing into the decision for an update on family events over a yarn with Mum and Dad ☺....

Finding a little 'get up and go', further advanced the unveiling of Rainbow Falls having my hips rhythmically swivelling in motion with the brushcutter. Timely, a tank had just run dry when a car pulled up at the front gate, encountering the first person lost. Armed with a fist full of maps he was steered back on the right dirt track....

Keeping an eye on slow banking cloud gently draping and thickening over South Sister Range, beginning to feel its effects, was pulled up in my brushcutting tracks to shelter in the great indoors....

First to accept the offer of $500 towards visiting Tasmania, a phone call from Kristy-Lee confirmed early March to be a sure thing. I can't wait to see family here to share the backyard of my newly adopted home. Visiting Port Arthur is high in Kristy-Lee's agenda, along with waterfalls and the ocean. A trip to the seaside is a must when you live 400 kilometres from the nearest beach ☺....

Friday 7 February 2003
The sound of brief showers stirred sleep patterns to conscious brain awareness on a few instances through the night, but only waking long enough to comfortably register the sound then eyelids slid snugly back to shut tight....
Barely enough to wet ground, low cloud lingered until early afternoon drifting the occasional misting shower through and offering a legitimate reason to leave tools packed away, instead I eased up for a spot of socialising ☺....
Enduring car problems, leaving Rods Wednesday I made arrangements to pick him up on the way through today so he too can keep a bit of variety on the menu. Supermarket, Post Office, newsagent, petrol for the toys and a stop for a brew, Rainbow Falls was then set in sights. Dense mountain cloud hung heavily on the high point of the pass between North and South Sisters, both driving over and back we were immersed in soupy poor visibility, offering a pocket of mystical enchantment crossing the mountain ☺....
Like a magician raising the cloth from a hat, within ten minutes of being home cloud lifted and sun broke through convincingly enough to bring out the brushcutter.... It's a pleasure to watch stroke after stroke of the overgrown mass recede to tidy....

Saturday 8 & Sunday 9 February 2003
Saturday, like a woman possessed, didn't stop the mission in the yard, gnawing away like a termite kept my hips in swing with the brushcutter. Concentration was robbed briefly by a rock leaving the blade at a pace and finding my left knee, unable to take a breath until endorphins kicked in, the impact drew blood, not much, but blood was drawn ☺!!!!
Plans of overdoing it outside were placed in the sane basket, cranking up the dial Mother Nature turned on a stinker. Changing locations, and with the thought of visitors in mind, made a start on the cottage. Carcasses removed from ledges, windows received attention inside and out, they're an absolute pleasure to daydream through now ☺....
Infected with a massive dose of the 'couldn't be bothered's', it was only the need for food that finally drove me from bed Sunday....
Take it easy, short-term concentration stuff was all my head would take onboard, simply tidying up small jobs. Ash went up to the toilet for use as deodoriser, water was collected and I did whatever else got in the way and pleased....
Young Tia showed no respect for the glistening clean windows, successfully catching a fly, she left behind a nose and tongue smear ☺....
Relaxing over a cuppa and snack, patiently waiting for an offering Ms Tia had built-up a healthy amount of drool, leaning forward accepting a sample of food she emptied her load of drool into my sockless slippers, what can you say???? Another treasured moment ☺....
A late call Sunday from the radio station, short of an announcer, questioned whether I felt confident enough to do the entire morning program tomorrow. Without hesitation confirmed a 'yes' to unleashing 'Tassie Sue' for her first maiden voyage, it will do my confidence the world of good to jump in the deep end.... Yahoo!!!!

Monday 10 February 2003
What a fulfilling, exciting day!!!!
Following the phone call my brain did the program over and over all night, not even the alarm going off gave me the shits. Tassie Sue was focussed for the first solo, voluntary community radio broadcast ☺ ....
My stomach may have been in a knot but I was ready to tackle the challenge head-on, concentrating hard on concentrating nothing else entered my body. Freshly baked, Mary-Anne brought in a scone laced with jam and cream but my stomach wasn't at all ready to receive it. Bugger scones are a personal favourite ☺ !!!!
Settling into the headphones and microphone quite comfortably, following the format for sponsors live-reads and news relays the entire morning flowed smoothly. Placing a feather in my cap was very happy at how the morning unfolded, feedback was also encouraging. I didn't walk away empty handed, before leaving I was set-up with 'drive show' shifts for tomorrow and Wednesday from 3 to 6p.m.. Taking it as a compliment being considered ready to do follow up programs, I'm enjoying every moment it feels good ☺ ....
Riding on a wave of high pumping energy burnt some of it moving or removing bits 'n' pieces from the cottage floor expanding the transformation. Used at one time as a shed, for many years the cottage hasn't received too much pampering, being long overdue for a dose of tender loving care....
Russell the plumber and I finally got co-ordinated over the phone, suggesting he'd be here sometime over the weekend to size up the cottages needs....

Tuesday 11, Wednesday 12 & Thursday 13 February 2003
Preoccupied with too much free time to think, leading up to the afternoon 'drive' program, procrastinated Tuesday away until it was time to leave for radio. A concentrating mind is hard to distract to do anything else constructive ☺ ....
The initial ten minutes of entering the studio are those most intensely concentrated on, the studio take-over happens in a rush within the few minutes of a news break. One bum slides out, and another slides in the chair, at that point a slight sense of urgency takes over. Satisfying that sensation only when a CD is set-up, the weather report is rehearsed in hand, the news wind up line etched in as a 'must say', volume switches checked and headphones on. When the dust settles from a rushed beginning so do I. A confident beaming beginner, I felt pretty comfortable the entire program, mistakes made were mainly tongue tangle mispronunciations nothing to drive me from continuing ☺ ....
Fun over and homeward bound 6:30p.m.-ish, driving with an empty belly in a hurry for dinner I pulled up out front of the Ranch Diner, biding the wait time washing a dry mouth with a beer ☺ ....
With one drive program under my belt it didn't help much with Wednesdays, same as yesterday, thinking too much to be of any use at home my brain only had thoughts for the shift ahead....
Once the initial urgency of needing to get organised passed and my heart rate was again reasonable I settled in to making minor mistakes. Again, happy with the overall program the feedback is an incentive to continue ☺ ....

Sharing the wealth around in the economy of St. Marys I patronised the Coach House Restaurant for pizza travelling home Wednesday evening. Making a slight deviation, dropping a newspaper off to Rod we shared the pizza, conversation and a brew….

Taking it quietly into Thursday, unable to maintain the high paced energy levels of the past couple, and perfectly suiting the mood, Rod phoned to let me know the platypus was active in the dam, who could say no to an offer like that. Loaded in Destiny, we rounded South Sister to Rods for a cuppa, chat and a gentle performance by the platypus ☺….

Following a few days of abstinence, after lunch the brushcutter got a run continuing on from where the last outing left off extending impressions on land reclamation….

Friday 14 February 2003

A rare occasion, but my feet hit the ground with a spring in their step and a body as readily obliging to tackle anything presented. Harnessing the energy into constructive use I slid the shoulder strap over and swivelled my hips in tune with the spinning blade. Making a lasting impression from today's outing a small stone tried wedging into my shin after leaving the blade. Taking a moment to catch my breath, my skin was left intact but slightly misshapen forming a nice egg…. Ooooh….

Dashing over the mountain to the supermarket and Post Office, on the return trip I dropped a paper off to Rod and stayed long enough for a cuppa then it was home to paradise to prop for the weekend ☺….

Blissfully oblivious of a fire that had flared up a few kilometres down the road from home yesterday, two CFA Ute's are still there today keeping an eye on the area incase of flare-ups. Apparently there was a fair bit of action with fire trucks and personnel yesterday, missing the lot, it was a good day to have stayed home….

Saturday 15 & Sunday 16 February 2003

Betrayed by my bladder was driven from bed early Saturday and stayed up. Pleasantly walking out onto cloud completely engulfing South Sister Range, creeping towards us effortlessly in the stillness, fine mist followed me back from the loo. Continuing to roll forward like a tumbling duststorm, totally immersed in the heavy damp air, satisfying senses, it dropped visibility opening the curtain on a favourite climatic condition. A frosted dusting of fluffy grey, as painted within the pages of a fairytale book, fog offered the sensation of stepping out into unknown magic and mystery….

As with all good fairytale books they have an end, and like a woman possessed with petrol to burn I forged forward finding ground surface with a spinning blade emptying four tanks. While giving both the brushcutter and my motor a rest, I caught a call from Russell the plumber, arranging 4p.m. to size up the cottage. After a look and a chat said he was unable to make a start at Rainbow Falls for around three weeks, there's at least light at the end of the tunnel, hot and cold water on tap will eventuate!!!!

Sunday morning was so motionless calm and quiet just drawing breath was clearly audible. The occasional birdcall, ever reliable frogs and sprinkling of lazy old blowflies broke the rigid silence with sound travelling with precise clarity….

Shattering the silence on and off for a couple of hours I threw the strap over my shoulder and had another full body workout emptying four tanks along the driveway. Clearing a strip of

around fifty metres of fenceline, another good day should see grubbing back reach the front gate however, hidden rocks slow things down a bit☺!!!!
Come knock off and waiting on bath water to boil, I stood by the shed beer in hand looking down the driveway simply enjoying the expanding cleared view.... I was feeling pretty bloody good☺....

Monday 17 & Tuesday 18 February 2003
Slipping into routine and becoming set in concrete, Mondays are up and onward to St. Helens for radio....
Its rare to leave home without a list to fill, starting with putting household rubbish in the bin, checked the post, fuelled up, did banking, put film in for processing and lotto on, then into the radio station for a regular Monday program leaving no time for an idle mind☺.... Happy at how quickly I'm settling behind the microphone....
The 3p.m. news broadcast and shift changeover signified another three hours experience as an announcer had been chalked up. Running a fine line to meet business closing times made a bee-line to the laundromat, closely followed by supermarket, petrol for the brushcutter, and topped it with a quiet night in☺....
A cooler start Tuesday made lazing in bed easy. Idling through the morning bits, incorporating a dose of procrastination, wiping yesterdays grass from the brushcutter only made room for today's load. Grubbing back the last furry section linked a clear strip the entire 100 metre length of the driveway to the front gate.... One proud moment☺!!!!
Sounding a little off-colour toward the tail end of action the brushcutter is seemingly screaming out for a rest????
Sunset fading and bellies full, the end to another perfect day.... hmmmm....

Wednesday 19 February 2003
There are times in life when enough is enough and self has to come first. Whinging from the brushcutter instigated the decision to have one off too. The world won't stop turning if we do to smell the roses....
A day off is merely a state of mind because I only get on with the usual things that keep home life ticking over. Placing the old pot on the boil I tubbed up for a dash to the supermarket because there was only enough milk for a milo and no bread for toast....
Staying in town only for as long as necessary then turned back up the hill to home. Tia resumed where she left off, on the scent of a possum safely snoozing on top of a shed wall beam, aroma alone kept her entertained for hours☺....

Thursday 20 & Friday 21 February 2003
An end to a trial era at getting flowing water to the cottage, Thursday, the poly line I so proudly took water from those months back was rolled up and put into storage. Taken from the same water source, I've got used to collecting it at the tap above the cattle trough by the dam....
Still showing interest in the untouchable scent of the shed possum, Tia was more loyal to her stomach today. Enjoying afternoon sun, biscuits and a hot cuppa, with a very attentive Ms Tia sitting ready for anything that might go her way, a lazy blowie flew in to join the party. Tia had

different ideas for the intruder swinging her head quickly to have a snap at the blowie the quick action released built-up drool over my legs.... Priceless ☺ ....

Also out basking, five swallows, at intervals, did their high wire performance around the power cable strung across the view outside the bungalow door....

Pushing the lawnmower out early when it looked hopeful I might use it, but after cracking a stubby declaring beer o'clock, just as easily, it was pushed back into the shed and left as a thought for some other time ☺ ....

Endeared friends, Peter phoned out of courtesy to inform me of Sheila's colonoscopy result. A simple day surgery for a polyp removal turned into a return trip to theatre for major surgery to remove a cancer growth from her bowel. Peter feels confident that the entire cancer has been removed, with no recommended follow up treatment beside regular check-ups. Supporting the same surgical cut as Mum, with the road to recovery being plenty of loving support and rest Sheila should heal quickly ☺ ....

Not once did the sun consider poking its head through Friday, the only delivery from above was misty rain that developed into some heavy showers. Weighty dense cloud sunk to immerse us in its magical, enchanting appeal, blocking the rest of the world out dropped visibility to less than 100 metres ☺ ....

Before misty rain drifted down I was occupied pushing the mower around, happily retreating under cover, it was a pleasure to watch a measurable drop fall giving the parched ground a much welcome drink. Might I say, resting my elbows viewing life through clean cottage windows gave great clarity to a good shower of rain ☺ ....

The twenty-first of May 2002 we arrived on the shores of our newly adopted island home, now nine months later to the day, hearts are contentedly being consumed by our adopted home....

Saturday 22 & Sunday 23 February 2003

Reluctantly budging from bed after buying every possible extra minute pressing the snooze button, Saturday morning it was a bare bones basic breakfast a bath, then Destiny's nose was pointed in the direction of St. Helens to unleash Tassie Sue to the airwaves. Picking processed photos up on the way, got a dose of the warm and fuzzies viewing heart warming photos of Mum and Dad taken on the recent Mildura trip, setting the mood for a feel good afternoon of radio ☺ ....

Confidence is quietly growing in the announcers' seat I'm coping thinking on my feet to recover quickly from those left field moments that aren't seen coming. With a strong station support base live transmissions began for the first time this weekend, I put my hand up for Saturday afternoon. Unbeknown to me news isn't transmitted after 12p.m. on weekends, trying to cross was just another on the job learning curve ☺ ....

Burning up energy behind the microphone, the express went straight home to feed a hungry belly and let young Ms Tia stretch her little legs, to again contentedly settle to a quiet night in....

Ya-bloody-hoooo, Sunday spelt relief from the droning alarm. Easing into the day with breakfast, a bum scratch and look around, made a couple of calls, carted water to the cottage then gave the mower an outing....

Paying excessive interest to her girly bits, a close inspection confirmed Ms Tia was well and truly in season.... hmmmm, another level of alertness required....

Unthinkingly gazing out the window towelling off after a bath, large reptile movement outside gained my full attention, adrenalin quickly came down with the realisation it was a shingle back lizard…. No cause for alarm ☺ !!!!

Monday 24 February 2003
Taking all the time in the world getting ready, Destiny thoughtfully loaded with required bits I took off early for radio cramming in a few odd jobs en route. Post Office, bank, a get well card for Sheila, and hardware store for citronella oil to keep the writing lamp burning and two-inch self tapping screws with washers to hold the roof on this winter, I then did a bit for community radio….
Expanding the number of known people in the area I was extended an introduction to Lou, another female announcer, previously having only heard her program I've enjoyed her choice in music. Happily pushing dials and turning switches a message entered the studio, phoned through from a woman by the name of Donna, expressing how much she enjoys the music I play and hope's I'm with the station on a regular basis. Compliments don't come much better than that ☺ !!!!
The three hours of announcing passed in the press of a few CD players, and before I knew it a tips cap was firmly planted on my head sitting in front of the hairdresser's mirror ☺ ….
Safely home to Rainbow Falls, Destiny unloaded and everything put away, it was time to kick my feet up enjoying a beer letting the days events unfold in the journal ☺ …. Another fulfilling day in paradise almost behind…. Ahhhh….

Tuesday 25 February 2003
Contemplatively roaming aimlessly eating until a spark went off pointing the radar at the lawnmower as the targeted toy to play with ☺ ….
I was pulled to a halt running out of petrol, but not before making a considerable impression both on me and in the yard. Feeling quietly proud, visually, the entire living area is mowed neatly back to the same evenness all over, it looks fantastic. Mowing under the bungalow window struck another treasure in a splitter head, a tool that has the potential to be very useful, I don't want to spend too much time using it of course ☺ ….
Toys packed away and bath water on to boil, in the company of my best friend walked the yard basking in its appearance over a stubby, I'm proud for visitors to arrive now ☺ ….

Wednesday 26 February 2003
Up and about full of energy I pulled the reins in conserving it, after a contemplative breakfast then took the drive to town. Checking to see if Rod needed anything in passing he jumped in for the ride. Petrol supplies replenished, I stopped at Rods long enough for a cuppa before re-entering the front gates of home….
Finding a good patch of reception driving the mountain the mobile phone woke from sleep to receive text messages. Kylie sent a text apologising for not ringing over the weekend, Stew, her rabbit ate through the phone line….
Broken cloud with concentrated sun drenching every gap, pushed by wind, presented a spectacular light display dancing like an orchestrated performance over South Sister Range,

special effects as never before seen ☺.... Suns rays reaching through to find skin burnt quickly, the thought of any physical task outside was shelved!!!!
Walking into a sun drenched bungalow four skink lizards were sunning themselves on the floor. Ms Tia, who doesn't socialise with most creatures other than human, surprisingly doesn't react to the lizards.... A happy union....
Officially a non-smoker five months, cravings come and go, but most importantly they pass ☺ !!!!

Thursday 27 February 2003
Choosing to do whatever tickled my fancy, left the front gate shut making the decision to bring the lawnmower out for a tad more manicuring....
Stopping yard maintenance over lunch, me and my little mate went for a roam and observation tour, movement in the potential vegie patch attracted attention, I could only but watch a healthy tiger snake slither out to the side yard of the burnt out house!!!!
Mower parked cooling its wheels, waiting on water to boil I commenced a token gesture shed clean up. Spruced and sitting down to beer and bikkies the moment was entertained by nature's elements. The distant view of mountain ranges, extending from west to north, was drenched in sun and blue sky while directly above a token shower of rain, hardly worth mentioning, fell. The dusting was complements of a passing thunderstorm, giving us a wide berth but let its presence be heard!!!!

Friday 28 February, Saturday 1 & Sunday 2 March 2003
Days vanish like the passing of an hour without a word put to paper....
Casting back, Friday began abruptly with Tia's bark breaking the silence along with a thunderstorm at precisely 4:45am. Unsettled conditions, both inside and out, lasted for around one hour before another wink of sleep was permitted....
Having a second go at approaching the new day, filled it tinkering in the yard edging around the bits that are meant to be there polishing the manicure. Extending a leisurely lunch made it all the more pleasant having a yarn with Mum and Dad, keeping myself close to family through conversation ☺....
Putting time aside to load the 'don't forget' things into Destiny, planning ahead for Saturday's trip to St. Helens, took me through to knock off....
Cool to start off with Saturday, I wanted to stay in bed but my little mate had other ideas, she's better than an alarm clock. With one foot in front of the other I got organised for St. Helens, doing what was necessary along the way to get myself into the announcer's seat. I'm getting very comfortable behind the microphone, reeling my brain back from the invisible audience to the little room occupied alone, I've relaxed in my own company. As time does it passes, throwing in a dash of fun at shift changeover I gave Mel a huge build-up before vacating the seat ☺....
Changing hats, displaying other hidden talents like poking coins into washing machines, supermarket shopping and considerate friend, I dropped a newspaper into Rod in passing....
Unrelenting, Ms Tia gave me the paw tap in the wee baby hours of Sunday morning for a toilet break, such a rare event that when she wakes me its genuine. A nippy night made it difficult to enthusiastically stir from a warm bed....

In a failed attempt at sleeping in, following breakfast and water collection Sunday got absorbed expanding on the tidy image outside without the use of machinery….

The last desired job finished, the brushcutter and lawnmower were cleaned and packed into Destiny to deliver for servicing. All jobs complete, it was time to call it a day and settle into the more leisurely side of life ☺….

Returning a missed call from Stacey, and in for a chat, she shared the news she had split with her boyfriend because together they had stopped having fun, good enough reason to move forward. In the next breath Stacey told me details of her big night out single and celebrating. Aware I was talking to a wall of silence, a wave of nausea had Stacey consumed, a lot of salivating could be heard through the receiver. Long quiet minutes passed, Stacey said "I got to go, I'm going to be sick, bye, I love you"….beep….beep….beep….beep…. Thank you for letting me keep that moment forever ☺ ….ha, ha, ha, ha!!!!

Monday 3 & Tuesday 4 March 2003

Fuelling up on the way to St. Helens Monday, Destiny was also booked in to have her water leak tracked down Grant pencilled her in for Thursday afternoon. In keeping with the mechanical theme, parted company with the brushcutter and lawnmower dropping them off for a service before radio….

Monday's stint behind the microphone wasn't such a picnic in the park I was taken sailing into uncharted waters being extended new challenges. With no prior warning two live interviews were placed in my lap, adrenalin assisted I took them in stride. The seat wasn't even warm before doing the first interview from a job network was advertising vacancies live via the phone. The next and most challenging, a one-on-one live in the studio with a woman by the name of Jo, working in the field of sexual assault. In the area once a month, Jo and I are scheduled for a regular segment the first Monday of each month. Happy with both interviews again I had a great time in the studio ☺ ….

Borrowing a double bed mattress for Kristy-Lee and Brenton's pending visit picked it up on the way home from radio. After chasing groceries for Rod, he came for the run up home to help unload. Mattress set-up, cuppa's complete, 400 metres up the road taking Rod home Destiny decided 'that's enough' she refused to continue. Her engine would turn over but she wouldn't run, a rolling start too failed, conceding I'd exhausted my minimal knowledge declared it was out of my hands. Throwing Destiny into angel gear steered her in silence rolling down the hill attempting to get as close as possible to home. Down hill all the way Destiny was picking up pace, however, the tight bend leading into the flat home straight slowed things down a bit. I think I can, I think I can, Destiny had just enough puff to make it over a slight rise about 40 metres from home giving her the oomph required to roll the distance into the driveway entrance area….

Rod's legs and lungs got a good workout walking between the mountains I waved him off smiling at least. A follow up call assured he got home safely ☺….

In impeccable timing Kristy-Lee and Brenton arrive tomorrow, they might take me to see Grant to turn Destiny's life around????

Knowing we were going nowhere, being was pretty much our plan for Tuesday anyway, in the good company of my little mate spent much of it preparing for the expectant arrival of our dear visitors, making the cottage as comfortable as possible ☺ ….

Wednesday 5 & Thursday 6 March 2003
Waiting unsettled, continued to feather the nest filling the gap before Kristy-Lee and Brenton arrived. A couple of phone calls talking them through the right turns to make, weary travellers arrived at the front gate after a long night enduring cruise seats on the good ol' Spirit of Tassie....

Taking their physical condition into account, catered for it Wednesday by taking a leisurely look around Rainbow Falls and following it with a home cooked meal, a gentle paced card game playing poker for matches filled the evening ☺....

Catching their breath and in holiday mode they greeted Thursday in no rush. Fulfilling Kristy-Lee's wish we headed in the direction of St Columba waterfall, Tasmania's longest drop waterfall, and took in every tourist stop between here and there....

Taking a guided tour of the radio station I introduced Kristy-Lee and Brenton as we walked through, while there I also shared the news of my inability to make shifts until Destiny is repaired. I was astounded to leave with the offer of a car on loan. Accepting the generous offer picked the car up on the return trip from the falls, unbelievable ☺!!!!

In full tourist mode, it was worth the drive to see the pure appreciation St Columba Falls presented in their eyes, and in passing, Kristy-Lee bought a couple of take home samples from the Pyengana Cheese Factory. Returning to St. Helens I picked up the limo and headed back to Rainbow Falls....

Following a big day takeaway got the thumbs up, then onward to home to resume cards. Getting serious there's no matches with tonight's game we're in it for the big bucks playing for lollies ☺!!!!

Friday 7 & Saturday 8 March 2003
Doing my bit for community radio I left visitors with a lust for adventure to their own devices, driving a car with Victorian number-plates had Tassie tourist written all over it. Taking in the coastal strip of Bicheno and idling up, they explored Coles Bay, Sleepy Bay and Wineglass Bay areas. Arriving back 7:30p.m.-ish armed with a feed of hamburgers and stories of impressive venturing through some beautiful scenery, as an added bonus Kristy-Lee and Brenton made two friends on their big day out ☺....

Trying to redeem a few lollies in another game of poker snuggled under sleeping bags, Kristy-Lee and I had a successful evening making a dent in Brentons pile of lollies and boasting. Donating winnings to a happy travelling box, it's a sugar hit that will drive out the gate with visitors ☺....

Time only stands still for those who stand still. Saturday was upon us and the happy travellers were making plans of meandering to Devonport to take the sting out of an early rise Sunday boarding for a day trip on the good ol' Spirit. Bathed and packed ready to go by 10a.m. it only feels as though they just arrived. I do miss and love family dearly ☺....

Waving visitors out of the gate I wasn't far behind, heading to St. Helens to animate and share Tassie Sue over the airwaves. Slipping into a groove, Saturday has become a regular shift. Rose initially joined me in the booth expanding her need for knowledge training as an announcer, reluctantly leaving for her paid job. Seemingly in the spin of a CD, I slid out of the seat and out the door pointed toward home....

Nearing St. Marys Pass the borrowed car began chugging running out of fuel. With a limited service history the car isn't real economical on fuel and of no assistance the fuel gauge doesn't work, adding a little guess to the equation. With that knowledge and being a smart cookie I put a 5 litre container of fuel in the boot, I must have known!!!!

Feeling the effects of welcome rain it wasn't a good day to be walking, it was enough just to stand in the elements delivered from above to empty the can of fuel into the car. Moisture falling from the sky gave Tia some sport pitting her skill at catching water dripping off the front of the shed roof. Food and a comfy warm bed put a stop to that game for the evening ☺....

Sunday 9 March 2003
The new day burst into life with a powerful energy explosion from above, the tin roof copped a pounding, staking a claim rain settled in. Sound alone gave all the reason needed to remain in bed Ms Tia offered no objection whatsoever she too was content to cuddle in ☺....

Rain pulled up long enough to do a dash carting water to the cottage for bathing staying out of the elements we settled into the bungalow. First a healthy yarn to Mum and Dad passed my lips, then parking on the window box I went over a hardcopy of all music available on computer at the station. Browsing the wad of paper highlighting songs I knew I liked simply to add more variety to programs....

Initially Ms Tia was reluctant company in the bungalow preferring to be outside in the rain catching water falling off the end of the shed roof, although she warmed to the idea of a dry, cosy afternoon ☺....

Monday 10 March 2003
Driving out of the mountain heading for radio passed a grader working on the road, my only hope was it would find its way further up and drop its blade on the road closer home. After an afternoon away, to my surprise the only road to have altered was the dirt road to home.... A driving pleasure....

Highlighting songs on the hardcopy play-list expanded music variety, also sped up selection, easing pressure it's an uncomfortable sensation running short on music. The shift passed quickly and quietly, quietly because it's a public holiday and for most of the program I was the only person in the building ☺....

A quick load of washing, and due to most shops being shut for the public holiday, I found a break in traffic and drove home without the brushcutter and lawnmower. I won't know what to do with myself ☺ ????

The presence of rain is transforming the yard it can almost be seen with the naked eye greening up. Although petering out, small pockets of moisture are still hanging about. Over the duration of the front, catching water from under the flue in the cottage, the baking tray was emptied two-and-a-half times. If I source the actual number of millimetres that fell I'll be able to do a rough calibration with the baking tray doubling it as a rain gauge ☺.... From memory it's been the best soaking rain since October....

Tuesday 11 March 2003
Able to penetrate easily below the surface, I was game enough to bring the shovel out after breakfast and water carting. My little mate always on the ready with our tried and proven system, I dig and toss Tia sorts and composts, together, weeded the perimeter of the rock pile outside the bungalow door ☺....
Taking a quick trip into St. Marys, aside regular things, I dropped a key into Grant for when it becomes convenient to make a start on Destiny....
A favourite composure, roaming with hands buried in pockets, the greater part of our afternoon melted following the trail of countless young scotch thistles leaving them with a lasting impression of the heel of my boot....
Happily amused after a hard day's work, Tia rested her paws winding down over a meaty beef bone ☺....

Wednesday 12, Thursday 13 & Friday 14 March 2003
There hasn't been a pass made through the front gates of Rainbow Falls since parking the car in the shed Tuesday, near on the same time I stopped applying ink to paper....
What also followed us through the gate Tuesday was the answer to how much rain we received, having somewhere between two and a half to three inches, that sum fits tidy with two and a half baking trays. As a rough rule of thumb, I'll run with the theory that one inch in the baking tray equals one inch of rain....
Wednesday was put to good use taking advantage of soft soil, warming the shovel clearing around the cattle trough by the base of the dam. That action in turn led to emptying the trough of composting leaf litter and the cloud of mosquito wrigglers with a very short life expectancy, leaving it refreshed to start all over again....
Getting out of hand in the potential vegie patch comfrey drew attention to itself, making the next priority. Although it has worthwhile uses comfrey is a feral weed if planted in the ground, a sliver of root left behind will re-shoot. Painstakingly slow moving, I'm sorting through every shovel load to slow comfrey down a bit. Before walking out the gate in long shadows and with the sun on my back, one-third of the potential vegie patch had been turned....
A soak in a warm bath was muchly appreciated on muscles after a long one spent shovelling ☺....
Inspired by Wednesday's visually progressive labour, we were drawn like a magnet back to the potential vegie patch Thursday to continue the mission....
The grapevine had been working well. Living on a neighbouring property, Charles pulled up offering to take a look at Destiny putting a halt on shovel work. Playing apprentice, and up to our elbows in grease eliminating theories, a clean break in the crankshaft was tracked down, thanks to Charles' help there's a starting point for fixing.... Turning on toasted sandwiches and a cuppa to show a little appreciation....
Drawn like bees to the honey pot, returned to further expose fresh soil in the potential vegie patch Friday. I'd hardly warmed to the idea of the shovel and Charles returned offering a freshly home baked loaf of bread still oven warm. Only after my belly was full and unable to swallow another bite of warm bread laced in melting butter, did my brain even consider the idea of returning to the shovel ☺....

Entertaining an afternoon in the garden, the amazingly fluorescent male flame robins were dancing around being very showy impressing a harem of nearby females....
With every shovel load turned finalising the job became achievable, toiling until the last clod was turned could we then walk away without looking back, well at least for a while ☺....

Saturday 15 March 2003
What can I do to slow time down, another day is so quickly drawing to a close????
Up before the alarm, ready early I pulled in for a chat with Grant on the way to radio, Destiny's immediate fate is to remain where she is at the front gate until a replacement part is sourced. Following a long separation and serviced and waiting to go home the brushcutter and mower were picked up ready to take the trip....
I did myself a huge service writing all known and liked available music in a personal scrapbook, giving me a beaut quick reference sheet. I'm also playing more music from the computer simultaneously creating greater choice for myself and listeners.... That can only be good ☺....
Winding down the working part of the day and starting on the eating wind up part, Tia was noticed by her absence. Calling, she let out a bark from the front of the burnt out house, initial thoughts raced to snake, promptly investigating found an echidna with its spiky defence up. Giving the echidna plenty of time to make a slow getaway distracted Tia inside cooking dinner ☺....

Sunday 16 & Monday 17 March 2003
Rapidly gaining momentum, another two days in life have almost passed since the last journal entry ☺????
Walking around bum scratching I put in a pretty lazy old Sunday, the most strenuous task accomplished was to bath the beautiful Ms Tia. I chatted with Ms Stacey for a while, kicked out a shit load of bubby scotch thistles and got Destiny packed organised for the trip to St. Helens, that's about all I remember doing besides eating ☺....
Back to reality Monday, after fuelling up it was onward to the radio station for another few hours of play. Leaving me with a pretty good feeling, three unprompted requests were phoned in, each arrived with a compliment voicing enjoyment of music selection. All feedback exchanged has been positive which is very encouraging, good for my confidence and on-air energy ☺....
Headphones handed over and a load of washing later we were on the way home to hang it out. A very mild evening offered the items dangling from the line time to dry before the curtain fell on light....

Tuesday 18 & Wednesday 19 March 2003
What can be done to slow fast disappearing days down????
Back in St. Helens Tuesday for an 11:30am appointment with some contracted sub-branch of Centrelink, I took a smart direction trading off voluntary work at the radio station incorporating the hours as a 'Work for the Dole' project....

While still in the neighbourhood I took up Rose's offer to tune my guitar. About to do a shift change, Loui was waiting in reception and tuned it before Rosy switched over to the news. A better sound may help my waning interest ☺ ????

Nothing measurable happened at Rainbow Falls Tuesday afternoon, rising mercury robbed the desire for anything other than knocking the lid off a couple of coolies ☺ ....

Some serious family catch up filled a good chunk of Wednesday morning. Landing in Mildura from Vancouver Monday, I phoned to hear how the Ford family reunion was going with Uncle Len ☺ ....

Bouncing about running to the bungalow door responding to the sound coming from inside, Tia alerted me to the ringing phone. A return call from Mum shared in the rare phenomena of a duststorm, saying its the worst she's ever encountered blanketing everything in its path and dropping visibility to extremely low. Content no stone was left unturned I disappeared into the yard chipping weeds....

Such a big event, the Mildura duststorm made it onto our local news broadcast, reporting visibility down to as low as twenty metres and winds of up to 100 kilometres per hour. Raised dust originating from the Mallee blanketed Victoria rolling on to Melbourne. That's a lot of topsoil the wheat paddocks now don't have....

Pleasant outdoors, a couple of little polishing jobs were done with the shovel before bringing the mower into play knocking the fluff off new growth following rain. Threatening on and off, however nature's elements let me put in an honest day's work, opening the floodgates only after toys were put away.... Timing is everything ☺ ....

Thursday 20 March 2003

Making itself at home rain persisted throughout Wednesday evening and into Thursday. Adding an interesting twist, about 3a.m. a thunderstorm settled in, according to the Tia stress meter it lasted around two hours. A burst of hail and extremely heavy rain muffled the sound of thunder rumbles offering a distraction to bring Tia's heart rate down a bit....

Following the endured level of broken sleep, and with showers still persisting, I took no encouragement to stay in bed, grinning, counting my blessings for mowing the lawn yesterday ☺ ....

As expected judging by the deluge the baking tray rain gauge had overflowed, receiving beyond an inch....

Dodging showers with shovel in hand, I made a solid start clearing the external base of fenceline surrounding to the cottage side yard. Beaten by the elements as the afternoon wore down, rain intensity just increased, chalking up somewhere close to three inches. Overnight, freshly mowed ground has taken on a lush green appearance....

Friday 21 March 2003

A bit nippy to point bare toes out from a snuggy warm nest I was reluctant to budge from bed....

When time came around for my walk up the hill, nearing the loo, not only could the sound of running water be heard from the falls it could also be seen from my perch on the throne, leaving me happy to remain seated ☺ ....

Looking for something to warm up with I got blood pumping revealing more overgrown fenceline hemming the cottage side yard. The yard itself is a nice shade of green neatly mowed with sharp edges it looks the best ever ☺ ....

Dropping a paper into Rod returning from town he had measured four inches the past forty-eight hours, not a bad drop. Rather than exchanging coin for the paper Rods offer of organic vegies from his garden is a much healthier idea....

Tia's taken an interest in eating walnuts fallen from the tree, cracking into a few she's developed a taste for the flesh.... You have to be quick around here....

Stepping inside the front gates and onto the soil of Rainbow Falls for the first time I pushed the time machine lever onto fast forward on the way through, with another passing month tallies number ten as Taswegians ☺ ????

Saturday 22 March 2003

Coming from left field, the day that panned out before me was nowhere near the plan!!!! Breakfast had, bathed and organised for radio we drove out the gate. Only 100 metres shy of where Destiny broke down the Falcon followed suit. The battery died within a couple of turns of the key so I reverted to the practised roll down the hill trick, adding an element of skill this time by doing it in reverse. The obvious front gate being the target, the Falcon ran out of steam 20 metres short ☺ ....

There was no way I was going to make St. Helens for a radio shift, so me and my little mate walked back up the driveway and I got onto the blower. First courtesy call went to the station, then wishing to sort out at least one of the broken down cars now sitting out front, phoned Grant to ask him to tow and fix Destiny when it next suits....

Cleaning the badly corroded battery terminals didn't entice much interest from the battery. Resting an exhausted brain from bloody cars and nutting out mechanical solutions, gave up in frustration and disinterest putting pent up crankies to work on the shovel until mustering the spirit for another go!!!!

Seemingly fuel related the car wants to start but just won't complete the task, fitting Destiny's battery in the Falcon it still refused to start. Checking the fuel filter and other basics, it dawned that the fuel injection is electronic and may require a fuse, stumbling onto a blown 20-amp engine fuse. Lo and behold when replaced the engine started, a one-dollar fuse kept us grounded and me frustrated most of the day. By that stage I'd had enough of anything mechanical, parking the Falcon in the shed I simply walked away....

Sunday 23 March 2003

Physically and mentally off the boil, I eased from procrastination into light duties actually daring to put dirt in the new, unmarked, red Kelso wheelbarrow ☺ ....

Between food breaks and dodging the occasional dusting of mist, never shy when there's work to be done, my little mate was by my side the whole way taking clumps, legacy of fenceline clearing, and depositing them into driveway wheel ruts. Transferring quite a number of wheelbarrow loads is a slow way of levelling the driveway with recycled products, but very little gets wasted at Rainbow Falls ☺ ....

Coming to the surface and seeing the light of day due to extensive and intensive clearing, objects exposing themselves to the ground surface are of quite an assortment from rusty pliers to a variety of metal objects, timber, clothing, to rocks, rocks, rocks, and more rocks ☺ ....

Monday 24 March 2003
If I had to pre-empt writing a script for what I thought I'd be doing today it would have been way off course....
Monday began like any other focussed on preparing for a midday radio shift. Without getting much further down the road than Saturday the Falcon blew another fuse, taking a fuse from the indicators put it in the engine slot, ready for a re-start the recharged battery shit itself.
Extremely frustrated at yet another breakdown, in sheer helplessness rolled the Falcon to the side of the road and walked the short distance home, beaten, but only for the moment. True to his word Destiny disappeared from out front, Grant had her towed out of the mountain to make a start on repairs, one down one to go....
All planets aligned to keep us on home soil so I took the hint and just got on with it. Keeping a brain distracted in the garden put the wheelbarrow to use carting tired hydrangea flowers. Ending up in the potential vegie patch I turned the entire space within a few hours, the ground is soft and I'm getting fitter ☺ ....
Slipping him $10 to run me into the supermarket, Charles arrived around 4:30p.m.-ish, smartly grabbing a few spare fuses while in town. Pulling up next to the Falcon blown fuses were replaced but the tired battery even refused a jumpstart. Going nowhere this evening we conceded defeat, Charles offered to charge the battery and we went back to Rainbow Falls for a cuppa????

Tuesday 25 March 2003
What a bloody huge day, only making time to sit and write 10p.m.....
Doing a bit more on the shovel polishing edges in the neatly mowed yard, set sights next to tidy the scruffy temporary patch up on the broken bungalow window. Tired of looking at the clutter of timber planks with large rocks wedged at the base leaning against the temporary window fill to hold it in place, put an end to temporary window Mk II to make way for temporary window Mk III. Lapping around the perimeter of the heavy duty yellow plastic window fill upgrade with sealing tape blocking ventilation gaps, for extra insurance tapped in clouts to hold it all in place ☺ ....
Working nearby, to check messages I put the mobile phone on a fence post outside the bungalow where it got reception, three skink lizards already occupying the space weren't fazed by the intrusion. A skink boldly walked straight over and climbed on top of the moby, seemingly claiming ownership ☺ ....
With the arrival of Charles and a charged battery offered an air of optimism, but still the Falcon just wouldn't start. A dose of fuel directly down the throat of the carby and the bastard burst into life, only taking me 100 metres before shitting itself again, the slightest hint of an incline and working the engine, it pops a fuse????!!!!
Reverting to rolling backwards down the hill, I pulled up on the flat stretch close to home and poured another dose down the throat of the carby then drove the burden into the shed, leaving no broken down cars to litter the road....

Extending one final test before giving in, parked in the shed the ignition wouldn't turn off, resorting to pulling the engine fuse out to stop it only the plastic casing pulled away leaving the car running. Wishing only to shut the car door behind me and walk away, out of frustration managed to pull a remaining metal bit from the fuse box finally severing life from the beast. I didn't look back....

Wednesday 26 March 2003
Today I'm pretty happy to have behind....
I phoned Grant to nut out 'Bluey' the Falcons problem, with cars lined up waiting for fuel said he'd phone back when he could. A try at the radio station and no one was answering the phone there. I took it as a strong message to give up on communicating and retreated outside....
Returning to have a rediscovery play at the long neglected excavation site, and drawing attention to themselves, a few weeds taking off between rocks were responded to accordingly. Shovel work wearing thin, and with little choice left in the wardrobe and water quality high, I got into a spot of hand washing giving my wrists a workout....
Any day numbered 26 means I've reached another milestone with the quit ciggy's campaign, clocking up six months. Blowing about $50 per week up in smoke my habit averaged two hundred dollars a month, equating to a saving so far of twelve hundred dollars.... My health is the biggest winner☺....

Thursday 27 March 2003
Being the norm of late, I rang the station with another courtesy 'unable to make my shift' call, chatting with Mary-Anne an offer came from the background from Rose offering a loan of her car, I asked if she was game enough with my track record the past few weeks. Roses offer also extended to a pick-up service, travelling the 90 kilometre round trip from St. Helens to pick me up so I can have her car, that's pretty outstanding ☺ !!!!
A couple of hours up our sleeve before Rose was due we spent it playing at the excavation site careful not to get hot and dirty....
Rose was offered and accepted a brief tour, keeping to a tight schedule for paid work we were soon bound for St. Helens. Free to roam the streets at will I pulled in to pick Grant's brain to possible cures for the Falcon, without a look it was difficult for him to be sure but he offered good news for Destiny. Managing to locate a second-hand camshaft she's not far away from being a goer.... Yahoo....
Final stop Rainbow Falls for dinner and a quiet night in ☺....

Friday 28 March 2003
Slowing momentum to a pace I can keep up with I got busy doing very little ☺....
The hazy mechanical cloud is lifting, efficiently on the job 8:30a.m.-ish Grant phoned letting me know the camshaft is replaced, it was a perished engine hose spewing oil slowed things down until a replacement hose arrives. A man that doesn't muck around, Grant already placed a hose on order and everything going well, Destiny should be home next week ☺....
Life back into gear with a reliable vehicle, and cutting a fine line to make the actual day, priority one was post Dad's birthday card. Breakfasted and bathed, picked Rod up on the way to hit the shops to again keep our bellies full....

Hoping to pull off a birthday surprise to assist with celebrating Dad's 65th birthday, I tried to second guess he might be agreeable to a meal out, sending Kristy-Lee home with $200 to organise picking Mum and Dad up in a limo and buying their meal. The breaking news that Dad wants an afternoon home with family caused a 'Plan B' rethink????
Doing another of my least favourite chores, let my mind wander preparing dinner, free ranging, a 'Plan B' sprung to mind. Every family gathering deserves good food, doing a family ring around 'Plan B' is off and running with many thanks to Kerry. On a 'gourmet food buying spree' at short notice, Kerry's going to attempt to track down crayfish and prawns so the sausage rolls can stay in the freezer ☺ ….

Saturday 29 & Sunday 30 March 2003 'Happy Birthday Dad'
As with our former Saturday routine prior to mechanical failure, it was up and organised for St. Helens, and yes, we made the entire distance to unleash Tassie Sue ☺ !!!!
First opportunity at the beginning of the program, I personally thanked everyone who helped me with mechanics over the past few weeks their help being invaluable….
The stint behind the microphone over and still lacking in mechanical confidence, stopped at the St. Marys pub bought a box of beer and went straight to the security of home to sample a couple ☺ ….
Slowly easing into Sunday feeling a bit ordinary from that 'one too many', roamed listlessly with hands in pockets kicking out scotch thistles ☺ …. Perfect….
Waiting for an opportune time to catch as many family members as possible at Dad's backyard birthday reception, I called shortly after 2p.m.. Including the birthday boy and Mum, I also struck
Stacey, Aunty Claire, Uncle Len, nice of him to drop in from Vancouver, and Kerry, offering opportunity to thank her very much for arranging the food platters at short notice ☺ …. I wish I could have been there….

Monday 31 March & Tuesday 1 April 2003
With confidence to arrive at our destination, Monday was up and get ready for a dose of community radio. Stopping at the St. Marys Post Office Peter sent me off with a request….
Religiously sharing a pie with my best friend prior to any program I've sampled most of what's on offer between here and there, a chicken-mornay would be amongst the best. With a sample of pie, bowl of water, and Tia and Destiny set-up in shade, I walked into an office abuzz preparing for Wednesdays AGM….
Time ticking away behind the microphone, the newly appointed Manager Maria and brother-in-law Bruce entered the booth, impressing upon me the importance of becoming a financial member to vote. Handing me a 'who to vote for' card supposedly to stop a minority religious group from taking over the radio station, stressing that reading religious announcements would become norm. In trust of management I became a financial member to vote and help carve the future of the station….
Ms Tia put in a day she would rather forget Tuesday, feeling the effects of two baths. Disappearing for ten minutes she returned with her neck smeared in pasty poo that received immediate attention to remove it, however a determined young Tia had other ideas. On the

phone to Mum Tia walked into the bungalow again wearing her more favoured poo scent that too was short-lived ☺ ….
Putting daylight hours in pretty gently I just fluffed around airing bedding, taking clothes off the line and moved a piece of carpet into the driveway wheel ruts. My intention to get busy with the brushcutter never eventuated ☺ ….
An air of excitement loomed at Rainbow Falls Tuesday evening with the lead into a big night out at St. Marys Hall to watch a series of short films, collectively called 'far flung flicks', they're documentaries filmed in Tasmania and New Zealand….

Wednesday 2, Thursday 3, Friday 4 & Saturday 5 April 2003
Wednesday through to Friday offered little variation, only small differences ☺ ….
Stirring into consciousness Wednesday morning the sweet sound of rain filled my senses.
Plans for putting machinery to work were shelved for a re-think, and what better place to do it than in bed. Horizontal 'Plan B' sprung to mind, and without hesitation lit up the shed heater tackling the dumping site for prunings and weeds, ideal ☺ ….
Packing up tools to clean up for the 7BODFM Annual General Meeting, was surprised on arrival by the sheer number of people interested, filled to capacity, the room housed about 80 people. Early into the meeting there was an attempt at disruption but it was quickly stifled, something's brewing below the surface????
Thursday was cold windy and mostly overcast, the obvious choice to stay warm was burning prickles down the shed. Quickly settling into the routine of feeding the heaters face with prunings, kicking the ball for Tia, feeding the heater and kicking the ball. Our routine was well polished when Rod pulled up in his repaired car and warmed his hands by the heater for a while ☺ ….
The daylight hours of Friday were extinguished further finding the shed floor and a trip to replenish cupboards and eating sorted that remaining ☺ ….
Saturday was so quickly upon us. Bathed, car packed, a random pie stop along the trek to St. Helens, newsagents, then around to the radio station to settle Tassie Sue in. Having the most fun from memory, a flow of listener interaction over the phone placing unprompted requests lifted an already good mood ☺ ….
Lucky I'm having fun because I now have an extra shift. Helping with a shortfall of announcers to fill shifts due to recent resignations, I can also enjoy Wednesdays ☺ ….

Sunday 6 April 2003
In my haste to get home yesterday I didn't stop at the supermarket, paying the penalty for breakfast there wasn't even a slice of bread for toast ☺ ….
Being one of the few shops to open on a Sunday, the newsagent also gets a bakery delivery, half way home the thought of 'forgetting milk' crossed my mind, letting it pass through to the keeper decided I'll survive until tomorrow ☺ ????
Wendy's sons' black cat has again been making its presence known seeing it cross the driveway last Thursday. Today Tia sniffed the cat out and gave chase. Dumping a wheelbarrow load of carpet into driveway wheel ruts Tia's barking gained attention. From the front yard, Tia chased the cat into the burnt out house, they did a screaming lap amongst the burnt debris and within seconds, the cat, closely followed by Tia, exited the same doorway

entered moments earlier. The cat made it safely up a large pencil pine to reassess how many lives it had left, giving Tia cause to check on the pine at regular intervals throughout the afternoon....

Beside cat chasing, young thistles were cleared from the west facing side of the shed, rotten carpet laying by the cattle loading ramp went into a wheel rut, and anything laying around that could be burnt took over freshly cleared floor space in the shed ☺....

I was surprised to see a bloody mouse in the bungalow, one hasn't been sighted in months, the only way to receive action is to attract attention ☺!!!!

Monday 7 & Tuesday 8 April 2003
The view of a motionless mouse greeted the explosion of light flooding the bungalow with the removal of the cardboard curtain. Hygiene feels lifted without them!!!!

Monday means radio. My confidence behind the microphone has thrown the trainer wheels free and reeled in speech stumbling, although, a few errors keeps me on my toes and makes the whole experience more enjoyable....

Spotting a wombat Easter egg doing the grocery shop bought it for Peter and staff at St. Marys Post Office, alias 'wombat post'; I've never thought to ask why. Sharing a bit of fun with those who enjoy sharing a bit of fun, on occasion I find lollies in my post box, and they're regularly phoning requests or faxing through a shit-stir giving me stick ☺....

Dozing awake to greet a fresh one Tuesday, giving my best mate a pat or two began hearing the occasional tap, tap on the roof, then down it came and developed into a bloody close, loud thunderstorm with a pretty lightning flash display. Personally I love the untamed burst of energy storms muster: Ms Tia on the other hand, and my priority, has stress attacks, so their duration is spent pacifying little one hoping for the storm to pass and as always they eventually do....

With heart rates back to reasonable, a rainy day gave me all the reason needed to spark up the shed heater to have a go at the latest accumulation....

Doing all the hard work in the morning measuring a quick inch in the baking tray gauge there wasn't much to talk about after that. Sun emerged and there was the occasional scattered shower, but it was still good to be warm feeding the heater....

The quick burst of moisture got an equal reaction from the falls. Amid one of the sunny moments I took a peek at water bursting over the top of the rock face with forceful energy, ironically the falls untamed wildness offers internal peace and tranquillity ☺ ????

Wednesday 9 April 2003
Breakfast had, bathed and at the St. Marys Post Office by 11a.m.-ish, was greeted by a small parcel waiting from Mum and Dad. The gratefully accepted bundle contained snippets from a local Mildura newspaper, capturing some pretty impressive photos of the massive block-out duststorm that recently top-dressed a layer of soil over everything in its path. Amongst the bundled goodies was a card containing a voucher for Easter cheer, the unexpected funds can go toward a new pair of elastic sided work boots ☺....

Feeling pretty good with life went in and did the additional twelve to three radio shift, nine-tenths attitude, enjoyed my time having a little fun along the way. A string of announcers

resigning recently has opened a gap in shifts to fill, stemming from the recent AGM there has been quite a turnover on the board and faces now frequenting the station....
A three-hour shift doesn't take long to tick over, washing completed its cycle we were heading home. Fuelling up before tackling the mountain Grant broke the good news Destiny was ready, yahoooo ☺ ....
Home phone still not working since the thunderstorm, Charles noticed Destiny being worked on and dropped in to see if I could use a spare driver, timely. During the course of chat over a brew we got onto rollerdoors, in need of repair, I mentioned the desire to remove the one from the car garage in the driveway, he was happy to take it off my hands, a win, win outcome ☺ ....

Thursday 10 April 2003
Yahoo, I finally tracked refills for the pen received from the beautiful Ms Stacey for Christmas, St. Helens newsagent had three black refills in stock so I bought all three ☺ ....
Driven by my desire to be punctual was ready to pick Charles up by the arranged 10:30a.m.-ish. Given a courtesy clean and packed with everything required, I took off in the Rosy mobile for possibly the last time....
Finer details sorted with Grant, we traded keys, taking Destiny's I handed him in return the Falcons.... One happy ending, one to go!!!!
A nagging thought crossed my mind collecting Charles, remembering one of Destiny's battery terminals had broken through doing a battery changeover, unperturbed Charles drove her to St. Helens anyway. Unwilling to push luck, left Tia in the company of Destiny at a garage for an hour and like magic new battery terminals were fitted, a wise $15 investment ☺ ....
Destiny repaired and ready to go, I rounded the trip to St. Helens at the hardware store before venturing back to St. Marys a happy camper with the Tassie Trio again united and mobile.
Taking refuge in the cottage during an afternoon shower, glancing through a window caught sight of Destiny parked in the shed and the sight gave me the warm fuzzies ☺ ....

Friday 11 April 2003
Still horizontal basking in morning ambience contemplating the day showers narrowed possibilities. From my position formulated a plan to simply duck into town, without lingering, come home and do whatever took my interest working with the elements....
Heading back up the hill, I pulled off the road meeting Grant who had just left Rainbow Falls looking at the Falcon. Grant went on to say he'd rectified the fuse blowing problem and was attempting to drive out when he thinks it ran out of petrol, oddly not far from the other breakdowns. Leaving it to me to test the petrol theory, failing that, Grant said he'd arrange for it to be towed out. I'll be happy to see the back of the Falcon it hasn't been much fun....
When I had myself to the point of pouring petrol and turning the ignition, I called on Rods voluntary assistance as a driver. Not leaving without a final test, the battery faded quickly, throwing jumper leads on Destiny drove life into the lame duck, bursting into action Rod drove the trying pest out of the mountain and didn't look back, spending the night at his place ☺ ....
Turning into the front gate of home two vehicles occupied the driveway for the purpose of repairing the phone line. Apparently lightning did a bit of damage to communication equipment located on top of South Sister Mountain. A power surge had also burnt the brain of the answering machine!!!!

Losing traction in a strip of soft wet ground in the driveway, one of vehicles on-site to repair telephone communications made sure of leaving a bloody mess behind for me, putting the vehicle into 4WD ploughed along the driveway then without a word drove out the gate!!!!

A funny thing happened in town this morning whose origins began Wednesday airing a request for 'wombat post'. On-air I mentioned not to put any bills in my Post Office box, a service account waiting in my Post Office box had written in large font over the front of the envelope 'no bills for Tassie Sue' ☺…. Good sports….

Saturday 12 April 2003

If we were in drought then we're well and truly out of it now, I'm contemplating building an Ark ☺ ????

Several strong showers impacted on the tin roof through the night, stopping for a short while initially getting up, from then on rain only altered in degree of intensity, the likes of nothing I've seen. Before considering a trip into the outside world Destiny first had to make the length of the driveway without getting bogged. Avoiding wheel ruts she slipped and slid but made it to the compacted dirt road surface to take a quiet drive out of the mountain….

Concerned by the deluge, before leaving I phoned Rod offering him choice to deliver the Falcon in more favourable conditions. Rod was just happy to escape four walls to meet at shifts end helping me part company with the last surplus car come rain, hail or shine ☺….

I put in another fun program in the invisible world of a booth talking into a piece of foam and moving volume switches. A sprinkling of requests joined in on the action helping the hours zip by and in no time the smiling faces of Rod and daughter Hannah were standing in the doorway having arrived safely with the Falcon ☺…. Grateful to drive home with the saga of the Falcon now only left to memory!!!!

The deluge had shifted the moorings of three large boulders. Rolling onto the convict carved mountain road of St. Marys Pass the boulders blocked an entire lane on a blind bend. The deluge had me driving slow enough to miss the large obstacles, being community minded we reported the rock fall to police reaching St. Marys….

Meandering back up the hill bloody slowly, veins of washaways forming in the road rushed excess water out of the mountain. Water rushing from above, below and along the sides, and at times the dimension of poor visibility was added, the trip was done quietly. Rounding the final bend toward home I stopped to size up the 20 metres of road under water between Destiny and the front gate. Decision being, I could either drive it or walk it, an overwhelming sight, it was a slow first gear without stalling. Taking my first breath reaching the shores of the other side, I simply pulled up and parked in the driveway entrance because taking Destiny any further was sheer ridiculous, the driveway was almost under. Traipsing across the soggy ground, I walked on highest points because wheel ruts were just channels of water, easing for our walk to the bungalow the heavens let us arrive high and dry…. Unbelievable amount of water ☺ !!!!

Out of need, I gave up on the baking tray rain gauge and put a bucket in its place, I've never witnessed rain like this in my life, ten inches plus the past four weeks. The water flow rushing from the falls can be seen going off from the toilet. This deluge will be a benchmark to compare all future downpours….

Sunday 13 April 2003
Tia and I shared our breakfast ritual, then camera in hand, headed to the falls where we met Charles and children who had just passed Ashley leaving on their way in.... Popular spot after rain for neighbourhood trespass ☺....
While the camera was still slung over my shoulder we walked to the opposite boundary with the thought of grabbing a happy snap of the lake Destiny so bravely negotiated. I was stunned to find the only water left on the road was captured in pot-holes????
From a slow draining, flat ground, deluge flood prone, semi arid background, the sheer volumes of water that are so quickly slurped up or moved along in this chalk and cheese terrain keeps my learning curve steep. Channels in wheel ruts, flowing so full yesterday, were reduced to etchings trailed in soil and sand within hours. Keeping to high ground I had confidence enough to return Destiny to the shed....
The past 48-hours has delivered around three plus inches of rain, in that entire time sun didn't break through until 3p.m.-ish this afternoon, when a sneak preview of fifteen minutes of sunlight was felt. A major bonus to this impressive quantity of moisture is the strong water force at the falls can be heard from the bungalow, natural energy delivered to the door. How good is that ☺!!!!

Monday 14 & Tuesday 15 April 2003
Before going on-air Monday I patronised the electronics shop for a replacement answering machine, apparently Tuesdays thunderstorm generated quite a bit of business ☺....
Big John was playing around with sound effects in studio two, separated by a pane of glass and linked to studio one via intercom, my stomach was tested by Big John sharing the sound of someone spewing. Taking the only course available, put the headphones on and turned the music up ☺!!!!
Going directly home after radio I wasn't long inside the door and Mum rang with results from a specialist visit. The specialist is happy with progressive healing, but to further cover bases of the cancer possibly spreading Mum's booked in for a kidney x-ray tomorrow. Experiencing some discomfort in her kidneys the waiting game is back on. Mum deserves good news after what I recently watched her live through....
Waking Tuesday the sound of rain again filled my senses, easing with the morning, left no reason to stay inside. Drawn by the sheer might filling airwaves we made the pilgrimage for the third consecutive morning to the falls ☺....
Idling back from the falls I stood tall on the dam wall to check the water level, there and then made the decision to remain tidying fenceline while ground is soft. The Rainbow Falls gardening team co-ordinated, I shovel and toss Ms Tia sorts and composts, we are a balanced combination ☺....
Taking an extended lunch from shovel work I got comfortable over a birthday chat with the beautiful Sheila. Keeping my fingers busy over the keypad phoned Mum also for x-ray results. A very elated Mother told me her kidneys were clear of cancer, although the x-ray did reveal one of her kidneys to be misshapen, something that has existed since birth and nothing of concern.... A happy way to end the day....

Wednesday 16 April 2003
Out for last wee's before bed, the moon almost full, coupled with a clear sky, visibility was very good enabling Ms Tia to quickly catch sight of movement and clear her claimed real estate. Tia's strength and fitness have increased out of sight her restricted residential life and limp muscles are stepping aside for high performance ☺....
Loaded in Destiny we made bitumen headed for St. Helens for the, now regular, Wednesday radio program. Collecting mail en route there were two little Easter eggs sitting in my post box, poking my head inside the Post Office front door said thanks ☺....
Dropping the bloody mower in for more repairs mentioned I would verbally be good advertising to sell a lot of brushcutters but not one lawnmower, pleasantly of course. Not a tough build they rattle apart with a work-load....
A final stop at the hardware store before radio, I walked out the proud owner of a shiny new ladder. I told the bloke at the hardware store 'if it fits in Destiny you've made a sale'. He made a sale and everybody's happy ☺....
I look forward to going to radio for the interaction. It's nice to have a job (if I could call it a job) I'm passionate about and get pleasure from. As usual the shift zipped by quickly and I was soon at the laundromat waiting for the washing cycle to finish....

Thursday 17 April 2003
Since the wind up of daylight saving I've been waking like clockwork around 7a.m., without responding to my conscious state I stay in bed contemplating the world until either Tia or myself decide its time. Psychologically daylight saving is missed, losing the sun 5:30p.m.-ish, shortening days already offer less daylight hours....
Out and about Ms Tia checked out all the fresh overnight scents, reclaimed real estate then settled in for breakfast. Listening to the 'laid back Loui' doing her morning radio program, enjoying her music selection inspired me to phone in a request, setting the mood before a stint with the brushcutter....

Friday 18 & Saturday 19 April 2003
Determined to turn loose with the brushcutter again Friday, as the day progressed, pleasurably, so did the temperature, following a designated dose of procrastination only then did I make a start emptying another three tanks, this time around the top and base of the dam. It's a must to stop to bath before sunset because with nightfall comes a temperature fall then it's too nippy to be naked in the fully air-conditioned cottage ☺....
Stripping down to a t-shirt its the first bone warmer we've had in a while even Ms Tia contentedly basked in the rays on offer. With each refuel of the brushcutter I'd open a car door for Ms Muffet to do Tia things, choosing to stay and bask she didn't budge once from behind glass in Destiny ☺....
Saturday provided a sun drenched t-shirt day up the mountain. Taking off for radio I was comfortable leaving in short sleeves, rounding the bend at the base of South Sister for a quick descend on the town side of the mountain I met an ocean of white with a blanket of fog covering St. Marys, unbelievable, worlds apart. Taking a nose-dive down into the dense mass of foggy mystery the air temperature also took a nose-dive and my t-shirt decision was being questioned. Reaching St. Marys Pass we were returned back into sunshine???? Magical....

With my little mates comfort taken care of I went and had a look at 'Shop One' 900 items auction, particularly with a bed in mind, but it wasn't to be. Waiting in reception for shift changeover, Rita and Ian arrived to free their daughter Heather of the seat. In conversation I mentioned having no luck at the auction for a bed, coincidentally from a recent garage sale Rita and Ian said they still have two beds for sale, or should I say had two beds for sale. Both older style with mesh bases, one is a solid timber double the other a three-quarter hardwood slat single, suiting home décor perfectly ☺....

Another pleasant experience was had behind the microphone. With no distractions outside the booth having the station to myself the entire shift, applied the extra dose of energy into the program opening the phone line encouraged requests for company....

Sliding from the seat at shift changeover with my energy quota spent the last thing I felt like doing was cooking, saving me from the chore I called in to see Pam at the Ranch Diner for a burger, beer and chin wag....

Sunday 20 & Monday 21 April 2003

Easing into Sunday I started the boiler for a hair wash and tub as Mum called with thoughts at Easter. Immersed in conversation I remembered the water on the stove, excusing myself, I took a quick intermission doing a runner to the cottage to turn it off. Returned to the bungalow and concentrating, Mum said she and Dad are having a day with family going to Kerry's for lunch ☺....

Not many surprises were in store for me, swivelling my hips moved with the brushcutter working around the dam, mindful of quitting to bath while it was still warm....

Squeaky clean, and working day spent, I kicked the ball for Tia watching a most fiery red spectacular sunset....

Shorter daylight hours are being felt, dark around 6p.m.-ish I'm finding myself looking for bed earlier and get up earlier. Rarely sleeping beyond 7a.m. since daylight saving ended, although getting out of bed is another matter ☺ !!!!

Waddling off for radio Monday, doing a random bakery pie stop en route, had Tia settled in with a sample and I got on with the program ahead. Passing quietly due to a public holiday, the office was empty but the roads were full of traffic leaving the area....

The high number of empty spaces on supermarket shelves displayed telltale signs of a tourist destination Easter impact. There was still a bit of slow moving traffic migrating out of the area as we headed home, a wise time to display patience particularly with people unfamiliar with local roads, it was nice to reach the sanctuary Rainbow Falls front gate offered within ☺....

Tuesday 22 April 2003

Eyes open, but a non-responsive body refused to rush out from under the doona....

Opening up before breakfast I flicked the radio on in the cottage and Loui was on and played 'Kate Bush and Wuthering Heights', one of a few songs that inspire me to sing badly, literally starting the day off on a high note ☺....

Destiny and Tia cosy under the shade of a tree, I'd just made a start with the brushcutter and Charles and his kids arrived to remove the rollerdoor. Tank empty, I offered my services arriving in time to help manoeuvre it into the trailer. Leaving Charles to tie down I organised biscuits and cuppa's to celebrate the tidy state of the doorway ☺ ....

Wednesday 23 & Thursday 24 April 2003
A preferred option for greeting the morning, coinciding with daylight savings end, there's been no need to set the alarm my body clock is ticking perfectly....
A leisurely breakfast, bathed and car packed with camera, laundry, CD's and rubbish, spelt organised for the Wednesday trip to St. Helens. Key slid in the Post Office box, petrol in the tank I then merged to blend into the heavier than usual holiday traffic. There are plenty of campaigns encouraging drivers to slow down however other drivers are hazardous by their slow pace, some needing a rocket placed up their arse to get moving ☺ !!!!
Quickly and quietly an afternoon of radio passed without fuss, remaining in town I hung around filling time to attend the 6:30pm announcers meeting....
Parked outside the station I let Tia out for wee's and to share a bite of food prior to the meeting, all was going well until she spied Rosy's cat and not a word passing my lips would stop her. Trinny luckily made it across the road and over a fence, lucky for me too. The burst of action in a quiet court drew attention from Melanie at the real estate agents next door, introducing ourselves, she praised Tia, Trinny hasn't been making a good impression in the neighbourhood catching birds....
The new format announcers meetings resemble nothing of the open style pizza pow-wow offered; now it's more of a manager's update only. The meeting outcome for me, without a word of thanks, I was simply told 'you'll no longer be doing Wednesdays'. Back to two shifts per week is a better balance of time at home....
With intentions of going nowhere outside the gate Thursday, and a lot of good intentions inside the gate, I didn't advance the world far at all. Taking long enough to get organised for brushcutting a passing shower let me put it away without getting started. A dash of procrastination standing in the bungalow doorway pondering looking out, decided to tackle cutting a few limbs from a bloody pest sycamore tree by the dam. Dodging the occasional shower I appreciated the convenience of a light ladder ☺ ....

Friday 25 April 2003
Without wandering outside the front gate now for two consecutive days, and in that time having no contact with another human being, my batteries again feel charged....
Not a habit of mine is to rush into any day. Breakfast, a bum scratch and look around, leaving Tia and Destiny to strengthen their bond I tackled more ground surrounding the dam giving it a mechanical shave. More is generating more, every patch of ground tidied makes me feel pretty bloody inspired to do the next, and so the termite hole expands ☺ ....
Running out of fuel was fast closing in so was running out of daylight and warmth, it was down tools for a bath before being naked was out of the question ☺ !!!!
Utilising the last of the fading light outside Tia and I went for a roam about purely following whim....

Saturday 26 & Sunday 27 April 2003
Saturday's routine held no surprises, leaving a little earlier I made time to browse the stall holders market to purchase chemical free potatoes. A ritual sharing of the pie, Tia and Destiny comfortably acquainted, I then feel assured to leave for an afternoon of filling airwaves with music♫♪♫♪....

The afternoon had quietly ticked over and was getting close to a wind up when I dedicated 'Billy Idol – Dancing with myself', to myself. Waiting in reception for shift changeover, Phillip entered the studio and started dancing with me and said "now you can't say you were dancing by yourself", mentioning what occurred over air for a harmless bit of fun ☺ ....
Clocking them up, I've now been off ciggy's for seven months!!!!
Jaw agape yawning getting a gob full of fresh air on a new day Sunday, me and my little mate did the building open up and yard roam about thing. A distinct changing in season has now established a strong presence and is influencing weather. Reptiles have crawled back under their rocks and are no longer active adding confidence to unrestricted wandering shovel free....
Tinkering in the yard I happened to notice the front gate had been closed. Taking precautionary measures, the neighbour leasing the paddocks was about to drive cattle down the road, with home paddocks full of feed an open gate might have been too much temptation. First we 'herd' the protesting 'moos', then about thirty large black frames click clacked their way down the road for a shift in paddocks....
Excited to share the news of a new man in her life, Stacey called and no stone was left unturned ☺ ....

Monday 28 April 2003
Post Office box checked in passing, I indulged in a chicken in white wine sauce pie and stuffed a birthday card full of goodies destined for Kerry. Appropriately accompanying the card I inserted a 7BODFM sticker, scratchies, and twenty dollars for a taste of birthday cheer. Sealed, addressed and posted, I walked into the booth and placed the earphones on for Monday's shift ☺ ....
For the duration of around one-hour, individually, I had company in the booth of two new volunteer announcers, Julie and Roger. Having a natter in reception Mary-Anne mentioned she'd be in St. Marys tomorrow on business, we arranged to mix it with a dash of pleasure....
Fun over and Destiny tucked into her bedroom motor cooling I got on the phone to Mum following up on an appointment with her surgeon today. Mum's back problem is something common with a hard to pronounce name, which boiled down, is nothing to worry about, causing discomfort at times but all the same a good outcome. X-ray images measured Mum's regular shape kidney at twelve centimetres while the odd shaped kidney measured fourteen and a half, without interfering with normal function again it was nothing serious to worry about, all good news. To cover all bases, a favourable outcome with this coming Wednesdays CT scan will give Mum a perfect score of negative for every test administered, she's feeling confident and dangerous again ☺ ....

Tuesday 29 April 2003
Aiming for punctuality mixing business with pleasure, meeting Mary-Anne in town she first took me to the Coach House Restaurant where the face to Tassie Sue wanted to be identified. On to the business side we went to Peter and Ian's, wildlife carers and station sponsors, they had two pademelon bubbies being rehabilitated for release. Driving to the other side of St. Marys Peter introduced us to Pam and Terry, also wildlife carers. Converting their yard into smaller fenced paddocks Pam and Terry simulate comfortable environments for rehabilitating

animals. The rascals that stole the show were two wombats, still pouch snugly they were cute little teddy bears to cuddle ☺….
Invited for Pam's home baked cake and biscuits, along with fresh brewed coffee and great company, sealed a really enjoyable outing. Topping Mary-Anne's experience with a tour of Rainbow Falls ☺….
After waving Mary-Anne off I pulled the lawnmower out until beaten by poor light. On the overall a very rewarding fulfilling day ☺….

Wednesday 30 April 2003
Sights set on returning where I left off mowing yesterday, although nothing came of it, glancing over my shoulder at a few close attempts at moisture shelved those thoughts, instead got my teeth into tinkering with weather suited jobs….
Following 'For Sale' signs the best he could, a chap took a chance and drove in, greeting the car explained that Rainbow Falls is off the market because I plan on sticking around a while. I'd only removed the real estate sign from the front gate an hour earlier ☺!!!!
Looking the best ever, while the bath water pot was heating I grabbed a beer and in the company of my best mate taking in all the new scents, walked around the yard absorbing the evolving fine look from all angles and was left feeling pretty bloody happy ☺….

Thursday 1 May 2003
Putting the body anchors on, I put in a relaxed one….
Jumping straight into important business I phoned the birthday girl Kerry and settled in. Family happenings current, I turned the big pot on for a tub up in excited eagerness for haircut day ☺!!!!
Car packed with essentials, fuelled up, then moved with and weaved through some painfully slow traffic to make a 1p.m. appointment in St. Helens. Young Sara whisked me in and gave me a cut I'm extremely happy with. Recklessly treating myself, continued with the extravagance buying a new pair of Blundstone boots with the Easter money from Mum and Dad….
Finishing off the way it started, on the phone to family, I called Mum and as yet no results are available from the CT scan. After our chat I had a stubby of Guinness and called it a successful day ☺….

Friday 2 May 2003
Abruptly woken by my uterus wall tearing, commonly known as period pain, almost folded in half I walked to the loo retching with nausea and a body burning up. Within five minutes, as quickly as the fuss started it stopped. Not an event one would want to endure for too long. Ready to perform more accordingly I put my body to work carting water. Life waits for no one you just gotta get on with it….
Towards the end of emptying tank two in the lawnmower I was searching for a cuppa and a biscuit and perfectly on cue Charles drove around the back. Offering to help bring the recently purchased beds home, before leaving Charles and I made arrangements for Monday….
Returning to mowing, I caught up with the carved path forged by the brushcutter ☺….

Saturday 3 & Sunday 4 May 2003
Shit, there go another two!?!?
I put in a bloody big one Saturday not something my body is practised at....
A simple trip in for radio armed with warm clothes to attend foreshore entertainment afterwards, we drove out the gate. From mail, pie stop, to chemical free spuds, the usual sequence of events led Tassie Sue to the announcer's chair. Incorporating a bit of contact from outside the booth keeping me company, quite a few unprompted requests came in, along with a live cross to Loui at the somewhat quiet foreshore entertainment reaching the pack up stage....
Migrating to the foreshore after my shift, being able to park close wasn't a good sign, other than live entertainment everything else was being dismantled or towed away. After strumming out a few numbers, Loui asked if I could give her a lift home with the suggestion we make a stop at the Bayside Inn for 'a quiety' in passing. That simple suggestion turned into a 'longy', a few games of pool, more impromptu music from Kim and a couple more songs from Loui, Destiny's headlights sighted the front gate 11p.m.-ish....
Tia insisted bungalow occupants rise from bed Sunday morning, so I did, feeling surprisingly bright I filled the daylight hours ahead doing tinkering bits 'n' pieces around the yard....
With the all-important water bucketed to the cottage, I then cleared one of the many sod and charcoal mix piles from the path out back of the burnt out house. Prunings taken to the shed I topped the outdoor experience by replacing as many nails with 2-inch roofing screws the drill battery would withstand until flattening. More secure, at least some iron will stay on the cottage roof. A few nails replaced didn't involve much effort to remove. The ladder has paid for itself over again, a bloody wise investment ☺ ....

Monday 5 & Tuesday 6 May 2003
Life keeps escaping here I am a day behind in the journal again ☺ ????
Monday takes no guessing, being of course a radio day, means a trip to the big smoke. Leaving early, I met Charles at the Post Office 10a.m. for the Camira fan club to travel in unison to Rita and Ian's. Loaded with the proud purchase of the two beds dismantled and packed into every crevice, I took off for radio and Charles went to the dentist....Lucky bastard ☺ ....
First Monday of the month represented the live studio interview with Jo, a sexual assault social worker employed by Laurel House. In any case I have about 30 minutes to prepare, this time the entire interview was scripted taking the pressure off thinking on my feet....
Loaded to the hilt, squeezed groceries in gaps and excitedly took off home to relieve Destiny of her booty of bed fittings. Enthusiasm kept me going, assembling the base structures in anticipation of their wooden framed wire gauze inserts loaded with Charles to complete the picture ☺ ....
With her persistent manner Tia insisted when it was time to get up Tuesday. Flicking the radio on had a listen walking in and out carting buckets of water. Catching the tail end of Mary-Anne's breakfast show, still traipsing in and out, Loui began her 'morning tea' program making comment of how we should all try living without water on tap for 24-hours, ringing Loui to share the news I've now done it for near on a year ☺ ....
Pruning a way into the dense wall of competing shrubbery in the elevated garden of the burnt out house filled idle hours of daylight. The only deviation came with the arrival of Charles and bed bases. Setting up the double bed in its new home left the three-quarter single dismantled.

Fitting in beautifully suiting the style and décor, it gives me the warm and fuzzies looking at it standing so proudly in the cottage ☺....

Wednesday 7 May 2003
Another day slipped by and almost beaten but contentedly participated in....
The laborious plan to keep an idle mind occupied for a few hours was directed at clearing the driveway side of the cottage, the last scruffy patch remaining in the housing area. Relieving the brushcutter of two tanks of juice to complete the circuit, standing at the shed door I can now see the distance clearly through to the front yard of the burnt out house, a period in time never visualised beyond dreams. My knowledge starting out was simply the job was huge, working persistently like a termite taking small bites, continually gnawing at the hole made it bigger materialising a vision ☺....
Of late, having a regular knock off beer I bloody well enjoyed one tonight wandering the yard appreciating it from all angles, change perpetuates change ☺....

Thursday 8 & Friday 9 May 2003
Blending, playing in the yard another couple have slipped by catching me with my pen down ☺....
Thursday morning evaporated tackling more of the overgrown mess in the elevated garden, a strip that hasn't felt direct sunlight or rain in many moons. A couple of the shrubs now making their way up the shed heater flue were so dense I couldn't see in to begin cutting....
Morning basking gave in to a cooler change, for warm-up exercise I skirted the dam doing swivel hips with the machine. Instead of playing catch up Rainbow Falls now has a forward moving feel.... Beer, bath, beer, food, another day over ☺....
Still motivated, Friday I had another go with the brushcutter grubbing around the dam, only getting as far as emptying the first tank before rain put paid to the idea. Snookering me from getting comfortable by the heater burning prunings the bloody rain stopped, trading machine for manual, picked up the shovel edging cottage surrounds. Pulling up in plenty of time for the beer, bath, beer, food, ritual ☺....

Saturday 10 & Sunday 11 May 2003
An inner feeling of being so in tune with life lately: it feels great ☺!!!!
Making a donated delivery for the animals to Pam and Terry on course for radio Saturday I was invited in to see the latest family member. A baby wombat around four months old supporting only a 5 O'clock shadow of fur pink skin was still exposed, it looked so vulnerable....
Life continued in a nice direction, chicken mornay pies were available ☺....
Comfortable and talking more freely, unprompted requests came in for company, for the rest I was content to yarp a bit of bullshit. A call came through from Loui requesting 'men are not nice guys', coincidentally sitting queued on the computer I followed on with 'baby did a bad bad thing', phoning back, Loui requested we finish the spontaneous set off with 'I will survive'.... Women scorned!!!! Ouch....
Winding the program up on a note of sentiment, I devoted time, thoughts and music to the approaching occasion of Mothers Day. Dedicating a song to my Mum, who I miss and love

very much, 'Bryan Ferry – Let's stick together'. A reminder of a time in our family life when we danced in the lounge room on a Saturday night bumping the needle around on the record player, very fond memories ☺ ….

Arriving home to find a message of thanks on the answering machine, Mum had already received her flowers. Returning the call told Mum what I did for Mothers Day over the radio, she got goose bumps and teary eyed…. I love Mum dearly….

We may have spoken Saturday but Sunday is officially Mothers Day. Taking the time to call again to wish Mum a special one, they were preparing to have lunch at Kerry's ☺ ….

Family sentiment lingering, I had a bit of a fluff around time, collected water, mixed a fresh batch of 2-stroke fuel and pruned back tree overhanging almost blocking the path running between the vegie patch and burnt out house. Polishing off a day containing a bit of everything I emptied two tanks of the brushcutter around the dam….

Monday 12 & Tuesday 13 May 2003
Passing ridiculously fast, limited daylight hours gives an illusion of time accelerating exaggerating the shortness in a day, applying the domino effect offering a much earlier sunset…. Still, that's no excuse for not writing yesterday ☺ ….

Making the Monday microphone pilgrimage, tackling the mountain I pulled off to the side of the road for a yarp with Rod and left with a request….

During the program I had a visit from Phillip inviting me for coffee in a little café after my shift to get to know one another outside the radio environment, I had a lovely time. Following coffee we did not pass go, did not collect $200, I aimed Destiny straight at Rainbow Falls and our cosy nest ☺ ….

Fluffing the morning away Tuesday I put life in order before burning another two tanks of fossil fuel into the atmosphere swivelling my hips finding the face of the dam….

Supplies looking pretty grim I pulled the plug on toys early to make the supermarket. The trip into town has been made more comfortable a grader has been knocking the tops off corrugations and shifting a few rocks shaping a more pleasant drive. It was also novel to stay on the right side of the road rather than ducking and weaving all over the place chasing smooth spots….

Wednesday 14 May 2003
I started the fresh morning a bit grumpy after having contact with Centrelink. Speaking to a female at a call centre in Queensland, she requested I travel a 240 kilometre round trip to Launceston for a fifteen minute interview. Persisting for a dash of logic we rearranged to have the interview done via the phone????

Back to the practical side of life, it was maintenance time….

Threatening rain clouds gathered about, but without hampering the advancement of securing the cottage roof, I emptied the entire packet of 50 screws in short time. No sooner had tools been packed away and moisture fell from the heavens, justifying sparking up the heater and vanishing into the shed ☺ ….

A few hours of poking bits into the heaters face, and body temperature still hot from the fire, I comfortably tubbed up. Over the indulgence of a beer, dried my hair by the warmth of the remaining hot coals….

Thursday 15 May 2003
Without looking back I hit the ground running to make a surprise birthday morning tea in Loui's honour at the station. Making it by the briefest of margins, St. Marys Pass was going to be closed from 9:23am for TARGA Tasmania, a popular car rally....
Armed with Lavazza coffee, plunger, and a chocolate mudcake, Mary-Anne decorated pancakes with jam and cream, together we got busy in the tea room to have the goodies ready for the 10a.m. news cross. Waiting to surprise Loui, we filled the cake with candles and made enough coffee to go round. For maximum effect we waited until Loui crossed live to the weather bureau then walked into the studio with candles ablaze singing happy birthday, leaving her with few legible words. Helping make Loui's birthday a memorable experience ☺ ....
Exhausting time waiting for St. Marys Pass to re-open I did laundry, groceries and browsed the hardware store. Running short on ideas and shops I escaped into the Bayside Inn for a quiet beer watching the last of the cars pass. That tasty exercise took me to road opening perfectly ☺ ....
Staying in tune with perfection had no sooner unloaded Destiny and rain, only varying in intensity, impacted on the ground. Fairly pumping, the falls are loud and clear from the bungalow....

Friday 16 May 2003
The machine in me ran out of petrol managing only to do a lot of nothing ☺ ....
Quite intense through the night, rain pulled up as I munched on my toast, measuring in at a quick three inches. Sun found daylight poking its head out between broken cloud, starting to show promise, a huge blanket had us endlessly immersed again by 1p.m.....
Like a magnet the distant beckoning sound drew us to the falls to catch peak flow, it was hard to identify sounds outside of the intense roar from the heavy rush of water. Two separate watercourses, generated by rain, meander their way from the direction of South Sister Range to the top of the gorge rock face, finding the edge within ten metres of one another....
Loaded with a dose of natural high energy I removed a few more branches from the pest tree by the dam until bath, beer, and browse time came around. Not much action may have happened today but a lot of thought and planning went into the future ☺ ....
Teeth brushed and cottage locked I was walking back to the bungalow to settle in, a message from Ms Tia bluntly reminded me to let her out of the locked cottage.... Oooop's....

Saturday 17 May 2003
On the usual Saturday pilgrimage for community radio, a peek inside my post box found friendly mail from Stacey. A standard pie stop, market for chemical free vegies, film in for processing, I then went to-air....
Tracking down a copy of a song, I followed up on a request for Max from a couple of weeks earlier. Showing appreciation, within twenty minutes of playing the request he arrived at the studio with a card and chocolates, being my first official fan. Turning shift changeover into a big song and dance, Phillip and I have continued having a regular dance, I give the moment a big build-up leading into some 70's disco song and announce it as 'boogie in the booth' ☺ ....

About to settle into the evening journal write, Tia lovingly wandered into the bungalow after having done her bit to clean up the environment covered in her fair share of buzzie burrs, affectionately named pom-pom prickles due to shape and capacity to break into a hundred smaller pieces. Damp from rain and wet ground, the condition of Tia's fur added another degree of difficulty in removing them!!!! It's definitely love....

Sunday 18 May 2003
Rain again made touchdown overnight. Following breakfast, an arse scratch and look around, me and my little mate took the short walk to purely enjoy the natural high energy at the falls.... Leaving the falls with oxygen flowing through my body at rates beyond standard I shared my uplifted mood with Mum and Dad over a yarn. Dad's ability to chat with me for longer periods via the phone is improving out of sight, once a man of very few words we now chat easily for fifteen minutes, that comfort feels nice ☺....
Mild and mostly overcast it was a relief to have a day without some measurable rain. Soil is at saturation point, around fourteen inches has found the ground the past eight weeks, incredible. The dam is to capacity and overflowing, adding to sogginess underfoot....
Frittering away time armed with a pruning saw finished removing limbs from the pest tree by the dam and felled its smaller neighbour of the same pest sycamore species....
Signifying knock off is beer o'clock and walkabout, a point in time I just simply enjoy the fruits of labour with my best friend ☺....

Monday 19, Tuesday 20 & Wednesday 21 May 2003
It feels like another lifetime has passed since the last journal entry, so much and yet so little can evolve in a twenty-four hour period????
Rewinding life back to Monday, it was the regular routine of making the usual stops on the way to radio. Settled in behind the microphone, Loui phoned mid shift inviting me over to have a look at the fruit trees in her orchard I offered to help prune....
Spoiling myself with radio afters' I got the suds agitating at the laundrette and Destiny loaded with more tucker. Utilising the last daylight, I received a tour inside and out having a pleasant social time with Loui and her kids....
For two consecutive evenings, and out of character, Tia has been picky with her food and doing a little whimpering. To satisfy any element of doubt first thing Tuesday I made an appointment at the vet for that afternoon. The latter part of Tuesday decided I was snapped back into the present. Standing in the doorway of the bungalow, and dropping to my knees, I was bitten on the base of the skull by a European wasp. Once endorphins took over pain management I rang St. Marys Medical Centre to enquire if there was anything to be concerned about, advised to come in if I had a reaction. Not sitting around waiting for a reaction, with the help of my little mate went about shifting rocks away from the bungalow door....
With my health showing no adverse effects, it was Tia's turn, her prognosis was a little constipation is causing the discomfort, something easily fixed is what I wanted to hear ☺....
Sticking around for the 'managers' report' announcers meeting, both Loui and I were awarded with certificates of competency as radio announcers.... Woohoo....

Sparking up the lawnmower Wednesday, my little mate has devised a way to keep the job more interesting, she's learnt to drop a ball in its path making me stop to kick it out of the way. Managing to make it through two tanks before rain stopped play ☺ ....
Escaping the elements we migrated under the roof of the shed, too mild to spark up the heater, instead prepared for a cold day breaking and stacking prunings into heater sized bits....
A huge turning point in time, the 21st represents Tia, Destiny and I have officially been Taswegians for one complete year, with many more planned ☺ ....

Thursday 22 May 2003
On one of those rare times Tia wanted out in the wee baby hours, thoughts shot directly to the dose of paraffin oil administered and the request wasn't ignored, hopefully leaving her tummy a bit more comfortable....
A gentle evolving one for us settled Rainbow Falls inhabitants, the morning vaporised turning soil, removing rocks and anything else not belonging in the chook pen structure in the cottage side yard....
Scattered showers developed after lunch, like bees to the honey pot entered the magnetic field strong inside the shed gates and menaced prunings down to heater size. Having ideas of her own, Ms Tia snoozed peacefully in Destiny ☺ ....
Sipping a quiet cuppa with the bungalow door open enjoying fading evening light a native hen darted across the yard, in short time the hyperactive little legs went darting back to the safety the fenced dam offered ☺ .... I can't imagine living anywhere else....

Friday 23 May 2003
Phoning to confirm a wildlife carers' series had been approved for radio, while talking to Pam asked whether a visit by myself, Loui and her clan, was convenient for Sunday. Everything hunky-dory, I text messaged Loui confirming wombat hugging.... A great family pastime....
When finally organised to exit home gates we made a trip down the hill to replenish life's little needs and catch up on the outside world. A bit of an awakening occurred in the supermarket, highlighting my weakening desire for meat, it didn't matter how long the meat section was browsed nothing appealed. I don't call myself vegetarian or plan to be but all those dead animals packaged in front of me I didn't find appealing....
Enjoying the lingering last of the beautiful sunny conditions and daylight, replenished the water supply, and emptied the shed heater taking anti-odour grey ash to the toilet.... A nice recycle system....
Indulging in the pleasantries of beer o'clock, I took a stubby for a walk to the highest point at the top boundary by the water tank to enjoy the magnificent view in pristine elements. The window view to the ocean and off-shore islands, along with rambling mountains and ranges, was sharp, offering a three-dimensional depth of field with articulate clarity, extending a sensation of standing on top of the world. Adding to the visual splendour, cool, clear evenings open the curtain to a night sky dense with stars, a spectacular sight, constellations so crowded they resemble a patch of cloud ☺ ....

Saturday 24 & Sunday 25 May 2003
Pretty much consumed going to and fro, Saturday afternoon radio is starting to evolve into a public interactive good time shift. Around eight requests came in, one from a regular caller I've adopted as Nana Raye, without fail, she requests 'Country and Western' music that doesn't suit the style of the program. Having a dag about, leading into the song I give the duller tones of Country a big build-up and always play her selection. Never one to let a chance go by, following through with an idea asked Nana Raye, and without hesitation, she agreed to do a regular segment featuring 'Nana Raye's pick of the week', turning her Country and Western selection into a bit of fun☺....

Topping an interactive program and pumped up, I gave shift changeover 'boogie in the booth' a huge lead in build-up, breaking into a seventies disco track we danced in reception☺....

I was able to laze Sunday because Loui cancelled the planned wombat cuddling. Remaining horizontal under the doona is where Mum's call found me and we kept our lips busy for over an hour. Visiting a friend, it came as more of a shock than surprise when Mum said Dad had gone to Balranald for an overnight stay. Besides going bush, I've only known Dad to stay away from home once around thirty years ago☺????

Getting an idle body moving, the main focus centred on waterproofing the cottage, leaking around a few windows and still down the flue, I selectively distributed a tube of silicon....

Monday 26 & Tuesday 27 May 2003
Stopping reliably at a bakery on the drive to Mondays' radio shift, settling in for a start is followed never too far behind by a finish....

During the drudgery of laundry a fellow by the name of Allan introduced himself, mentioning he was new to the area buying a former takeaway shop in St. Marys. He's using the shop as a residence and extended an invitation for coffee. A coffee invitation has many hidden agendas, now with the privilege of hindsight he proved himself nothing more than a dirty old man, offering everything from presents to pornography to loosen my loins when I was clear to him of my sexuality from the start?!?!

Life as organised as it was going to be, Tia and I settled in front of the heater for the evening. Remembering Mum's visit to the surgeon I phoned for results, the CT scan showed cysts on both kidneys, without being a bother they're to be left untreated but monitored. The extremely exciting news is no advanced cancer was detected.... Yahoo!!!!

Paraffin oil having gone to work making her existence a little more comfortable, Tia woke playful and full of energy Tuesday morning, the first in a few....

Sick of the visual clutter of cut branches littering the base of the dam from the severely pruned pest tree, further cut them down to down to size for drying and throwing up the flue one cold day, its a dull burning timber but it still burns....

Wednesday 28 & Thursday 29 May 2003
Since driving up the hill Monday I haven't, other than verbally over the phone, crossed paths with another human being, a time of peaceful solitude....

A perceived ideal day, light sun with that perfect tepid temperature, Wednesday was appreciated by the base of the dam cutting down branches for removal. Tia grabbed, tossed, shunted, growled and filed until the next branch arrived☺....

Enjoying the fruits of labour sipping satisfied on a beer, with my little mate, wandered the yard simply enjoying the massive number of bulbs popping up. That alone is a one beer walk☺!!!!
Following close behind a magic taste of autumn Thursday was a different kettle of fish, cool and overcast, without faltering beyond. Taking my time over breakfast I put plenty of thought into gathering tools to make a start on the shed roof….
Stepping off the ladder and out of my comfort zone, stepped sure footedly onto the apex base of the rear, chapel steep, vee section of the roof, replacing nails with two inch roofing screws and filling holes with sealant, wind and waterproofing in passing….
Off the roof and back on terrafirma, tubbed up and enjoying a beer, I made a certain decision there was no need to leave Rainbow Falls with enough of everything to stay up the hill and isolated…. Happy alone with my furry friends ☺….

Friday 30 May 2003
Tia had me up by 8:30am, only fair she had an earlyish night☺….
A gentle beginning eased into clearing the last of the pest tree from the base of the dam, placing them neatly, created a homely looking wood stack under the shed carport☺….
Tia was a great help taking pieces of timber out of the wheelbarrow and putting them back in the yard, credit where credit is due, she did carry one piece from the yard to the carport. Another invaluable helper was the wheelbarrow, proving its useful worth saving my back and legs a few trips….
Rounding off a successful day, I dusted off my social skills to have a few drinks over dinner, with complements, as a thank you to station volunteer staff. I think Destiny is capable of driving herself to St. Helens unassisted☺????

Saturday 31 May & Sunday 1 June 2003
Did I have a night out Friday, I'm glad to say haven't tied one on like that for many moons, capable of carryover next day writers' block…. Lucky I don't go out much☺!!!!
Pizza, pasta and wine was washed down at the Bayside afterward with a few pots over the bar, Loui offered me the couch at her place so there was no counting drinks. Asked politely to leave the Bayside so they could lock-up we were far from ready to call it quits, the manager opened up and we continued on back at the station. Without a yawn in sight, Loui and I had a few more beers back at her place where the rising sun found us. Putting the kettle on, it was a waste of time going to bed with my shift only a few hours away….
For the first half-hour with a head a bit cloudy I had trouble settling behind the microphone, making it over that hurdle got comfy in the seat and time moved on. Quite a few requests came in and Nana Raye joined me for 'boogie in the booth' in Phillip's absence. Still capable of having the usual level of fun, I was, however, happy the shift was over and I was making progress towards bed and sleep zzzz….
Deteriorating the closer I got to home, Destiny parked and all obligations met, my health failed having a spew that came from my boots, it was lights out 6:30pm sharp….
Sitting upright in bed a few hours into recovery, was orientated enough to respond to a ringing phone. A friendship made, and lasting from a former lifetime working together at the Department of Agriculture, David warned me of his pending visit in a couple of weeks. He is a genuine sweetie whose company I look forward to….

Unwilling and unprepared to move from bed Sunday morning, I received the perfect solution to keep me there with a call from Sheila. Entrenched in a healthy natter, it was after midday when the hot receiver was replaced ☺….

Getting out of bed before it was time to go back, toast and a milo went down well and stayed down. Demanding recovery, obeyed my body by tinkering, cleaning and finding homes for accumulated bits 'n' pieces in Destiny, taking it slowwwww…. One thing is for sure, beer o'clock never made the menu ☺ !!!!

Monday 2 & Tuesday 3 June 2003

My body certainly bucked up being pushed beyond its limits by punishing me with 'hangover lag' up to, and including Monday, losing many brain cells for thought through a healthy alcohol poisoning ☺ !!!!

Monday was the usual 'up and at'em' for another afternoon of filling the airwaves. Being the first Monday of the month I packed the time before going to air familiarising myself with the script for the live studio interview with Jo, representing Laurel House, assisting survivors of sexual assault. The program behaved itself accordingly pandering to my flat lining brain by going smoothly and quickly. The Tassie Trio made it back to Rainbow Falls just before seven, unloaded Destiny and settled in to prop!!!!

Tuesday didn't inspire much the big, big night out on the town is taking some recovering from. Tinkering in the cottage gradually finding homes for misplaced stuff kept me off the street and out of trouble….

Before the cool day turned cold I spruced up, feeling squeaky clean and recovery complete I enjoyed a beer preparing dinner ☺ ….

Wednesday 4 June 2003

To this point there's been around seventy nails replaced by roofing screws. Strong wind crept in through the night and not a creak or groan was heard coming from roofing iron sliding on loose nails… A comfort while trying to catch a bit of shut-eye ☺ ….

Until late afternoon, cloud blanketed and showers struck at random. With an abundance of thick cloud loaded with moisture draping South Sister Range catching the odd hit of direct sunlight, I was lucky enough to see five rainbows at different points and times perfectly arched close to the falls ☺ ….

Easily distracted and literally with my head in the clouds, I didn't get teeth into anything in a serious way, finding a last minute spurt of energy put it to work slicing into a few branches of a pest tree by the cattle yards. Ms Tia being her usual helpful hard working self, filed as I cut, we're a well-matched team ☺ …. Day at a time we forge forward….

Thursday 5 June 2003

Abruptly woken by the automatic thunderstorm detector, the bungalow is a small space for a big bark, an ongoing pacifying process, the detector reactivated with every new rumble. Tia and the weather a little more settled, pretty much the same as yesterday, showers came and went only varying in intensity. One moment it appears there is no way it will rain, then rotating a complete 360°, left you think you've seen the last of sunshine????

Aimlessly wandering with a concentration span not extending beyond five minutes I found inspiration in a hot soak. Taking the cool edge from the corner occupied by the bath I had the electric heater going trying to make naked a little more pleasant ☺ ....
With muscles feeling limber I grabbed the shovel and gloves and watched the setting sun poking around in the cattle yards finding the loading ramp....

Friday 6 June 2003
It seems I don't know what to do with myself when it rains, again wandering unfocussed I found direction by bathing in readiness for a quiet moment in the weather to duck down the hill. Fuelled up and food loaded, making it the last stop, replenished long depleted beer supplies where I scored a bonus, with every carton of beer sold a box of chocolates was thrown in. They know how to please a girl ☺ ....
Pulling into the shed the skies opened with a twenty minute burst that was ridiculous to step foot out into, preferring instead to listen to the deluge amplify under the tin roof looking out....
The sudden outpouring from the heavens got the falls cracking, the first sign of rain easing in one of Mother Nature's quieter moments, Ms Tia and I just followed the sound ☺ .... Magic....
Out wandering near the front gate of the burnt out house I approached with caution what I thought to be a snake, a closer look identified there was nothing of concern. It was the site Tia's dose of paraffin oil went to work, no wonder she had a belly-ache and was making so much fuss....
Continuous deluges have put waterproofing efforts to the test, demonstrating some areas could use revisiting, but on the overall gains far outweigh losses.... Not perfect but forging forward....

Saturday 7 & Sunday 8 June 2003
Spontaneity, I love it, I went out yesterday and arrived home today ☺ !!!!
Oblivious to what exactly was ahead left Saturday for an afternoon of radio....
Picking up a steady following with regular listener interaction calling in messages and requests,
'Nana Raye's pick of the week', and 'boogie in the booth', helped pack a fun program. Evolving from humble beginnings, last week Nana Raye danced with me this week both Phillip and Rosy Girl, where will it end ☺ ????
Before leaving the studio I read waiting text messages from Loui, one making funny comment about boogie in the booth the other inviting me over for a beer before leaving town....
One beer led to another, and another, and a sleep over on the couch. The couch may be sighted by the free-standing heater but that's a wolf in sheep's clothing, the area comes with children full of energy at 7a.m. precisely ☺ !!!!
With regulated water at my fingertips I luxuriated in the ease of a shower brightening my body for the drive home....
Returning to the comfort of Rainbow Falls utilised the warming sun turning re-growth in the potential vegie patch before it goes to seed. Working the patch until sunset, a protest was lodged appealing against poor light, there was a stop-work meeting, and all workers walked off the job to cook dinner ☺ ....

Monday 9, Tuesday 10 & Wednesday 11 June 2003
Struth I'm good at getting behind in journal entries????
Monday was the regular trip to St. Helens for radio. A public holiday ensured both the office and town was quiet. The shift went quickly, a couple of requests accompanied my verbal bullshit then it was off to the laundromat wrapping up the outing ☺ ....
Striking cooking from the waiting list I stopped for a Coach House Restaurant pizza, while the pizza cooked Tracey struck up a conversation saying "over the radio today I heard you say"....
It's refreshing to know people are listening and time spent behind the microphone is worthwhile. Sitting alone in the booth talking to an invisible world it's pleasant to be reminded I'm not ☺ ....
A nice greeting waited at home, Snowy, the neighbours' dog, is making his presence felt again, the only known dog Tia enjoys the company of ☺ ....
Monday covered, now onto Tuesday where I was struck by a fit of the lazies. Inactive, I responded to text messages and had a family update with Mum. I just remained fused to the bed because I couldn't be bothered getting up, there does come a time however, something is forced to give to drive me out of my cocoon....
Finally fired into activity more of an impression was made on the cattle loading ramp and holding pens....
I didn't give myself much to write home about Wednesday either, doing much of the same, migrated back into action at the cattle yards. Shooting through to bath before the cool day turned cold, squeaky clean with a couple of daylight hours left, for a change in scenery and big finish the shovel was taken for a short walk winding down with fading light in the evolving vegie patch....

Thursday 12 & Friday 13 June 2003
Greeting it as my first waking encounter Thursday morning, was one neat pile of vomit, Tia just leant over the side of her bed keeping her little nest clean to continue snoozing.... At one time Tia would have at least made an effort to reach the nearest exit ☺ ????
Toiling with my best friend and shovel further evolved the vegie patch until muscles decided it was time to use a different group, I then gave my legs a stretch changing gears doing a town run. Phoning, Rod caught me before leaving, saying he and daughter Hannah were keen on visiting so they followed us for the camels hump trip between the Sisters Mountains home. Sliding into a state of decadence the touring party explored the falls with blood pumping we kept the shell warm adjourning to the shed and stoking the heater. Candles burning and heater glowing, waving visitors off, Tia and I stayed settled. Contented watching a couple of evening showers I was only drawn from the warm spot for food and beer....
Rising Friday to face a cool wet one that didn't allow the mercury to rise much at all, dodging showers, fluffed around doing all the little bits that hold the threads of our existence together....
Tidying up after the night before swept the top section of the shed, not taking long to drag limbs in to begin refilling the cleared, clean floor space ☺ ....
Bathed, beer'd and bikkied up, with my best friend went wandering simply enjoying life at Rainbow Falls....

Saturday 14 & Sunday 15 June 2003
Waking Saturday by feeling the lagging effects of the coldest overnight temperature encountered this winter. Reading the local weather report following the midday news, heard myself make mention of snow down to the 500 metre level, that's bloody close to home ☺ ....
Creating a character, I've been giving 'Nana Raye's pick of the week' a huge lead in build-up having a bit of a dag about, obliging my whims she's a genuine good character to share fun with. A sprinkling of requests kept me searching for music, I then delivered a big build-up finish with 'boogie in the booth'.... That's all folks ☺ ....
This weather is no good for a healthy sex drive, preferring to put more clothes on than take any off. Expecting to wake Sunday to the sight of snow but the only evidence of the extreme cold was a few icicles that flowed out of the tap collecting water....
Snowy has again become a regular visitor, spending time together collecting real estate, both he and Tia busied a couple of hours outdoing one another pissing and pooing everywhere....
A good site to keep warm, and with two dogs with active bodily functions, they happily followed the shovel and me in the direction of the cattle yards to claim real estate there ☺ ....
Bathed, fed, dishes done and words on paper, time now to settle by the heater for the evening ☺ ....

Monday 16 & Tuesday 17 June 2003
Monday passed in a blink. My program whizzed by quickly and quietly. Leaving washing going, I ducked to the hardware store for lamp oil and did groceries before returning to tumble dry. A check of the Post Office box in passing, Destiny took us home without hesitation....
Feeling the effects of another bloody nippy night, Tuesday turned on a perfect defrost solution by stripping me down to a t-shirt, a rare event of late ☺ ....
As soon as we stepped foot outside Snowy was there enthusiastically to join in. Getting the small ongoing jobs done, water carted, heater emptied and grey ash taken to the loo, bedding aired and bungalow cleaned as best possible of Tia fur, Snowy and Tia did their thing leaving me to mine with the shovel. Another session in the cattle holding yards should see it ready for the brushcutter....
Spruced up, roamed the yard beer in hand admiring the present and dreaming of the future. Around 4:30p.m.-ish heavy fog started rolling in completely obscuring the sun before setting, dimming visibility to 100 metres offered Rainbow Falls the 'only place on earth' magical feel ☺ ....

Wednesday 18 June 2003
Whimpering at the door 7a.m. Snowy was promptly told to demonstrate patience until we were ready to get up. Waiting in a manner more socially acceptable, Snowy stayed with us all morning and drifted in and out during the afternoon. It beats me how they manage to muster such a 'flow on demand' amount of wee following one another around pissing and shitting. Snowy received a verbal addressing from me for peeing just ahead of the shovel where I was about to dig!!!! One couldn't afford to stand still with those two in action for fear of being pee'd on, they certainly kept me on the move in the cattle yards ☺ ....

Enjoying a beer taking in the day and planning the future, still with a bit of daylight in credit, used it manually getting in and giving the potential vegie patch a tickle up before calling it quits….

Thursday 19 June 2003
Contemplating the world from bed got it fixed in my head to finish turning the area beginning to resemble more of a vegie patch. Start up routine complete, radio blaring, I did just that….
Trying to make a phone call out before a supermarket dash got no response from the piece of technology, currently it's just there for looks? Determined to finish turning the vegie patch did a quick supplies run and resumed where I left off….
Turning sods, Snowy rolled up with a blood covered face, beside myself at first glance, however he was contentedly happy. Tia proudly led me to a road kill wallaby just outside the front gate Snowy had literally been feeding his face with. Creating a blood mask with circles of natural white colouring rimming his eyes, Snowy looked like he was going to a masquerade party ☺….
The last sod of soil was turned on the setting of the sun in ideal timing for beer o'clock. Retreating to the bungalow to write, Tia munched on a bone outside while Snowy intently watched native hens from behind the security of the fence surrounding the dam…. Life's perfect….

Friday 20 June 2003
Paradise complete, outside waiting was a bloody white frost and Snowy, confidence building he's staying for longer duration's….
Firing into action, I had a go at cutting to size a spike covered prickly tree in the cottage side yard and packed its dismembered bits in a clean shed. Working with radio for company, unsure if it was due to our recent text message, but Loui signed her program off as 'Tassie Lou', oops, handing out a good belly laugh ☺….
The spice to life is variety. After lunch the shed was targeted for cutting branches to heater sized pieces. Yard clearing is now feeling beyond catch up. Aiming to tidy entirely around housing is in sight and feeling achievable….

Saturday 21 & Sunday 22 June 2003
More of our precious existence has zipped by with minimal time to absorb it and here we are Sunday????
Sampling every desired pie, leaving the valley travelling the coast to St. Helens, didn't break with tradition heading for Saturday's stint behind the microphone….
Left to concentrate on a program announcing is something I enjoy, needling at me slowly, the new direction administration took doesn't always sit well with my sense of morals….
Loui came in to use a computer during my program and she also extended an invitation for a roady afterwards. A forming habit, we settled into conversation and one roady leads to two and this occasion included a bonus dinner ☺….
The spell of bone warming days came to an end Sunday with cold wind pushing a little rain our way. Initially ignoring Tia and Snowy's early pleas to run amok, I had to move sooner or

later, and after completing daily start up bits 'n' pieces me and the team again adjourned to the cattle yards digging out pest sycamore seedlings....

Rain stopped digging 1p.m.-ish and settled in so me and the team migrated for the cover of the shed roof. Trimming down to size the last branches neatly finding a bit of floor space, I almost get the shed tidy before routinely filling it up again. I'm not going anywhere fast with the shed but the yard is looking great ☺ ....

Cosily nestled into the bungalow by the electric heater for the evening playing happy families, David gave a courtesy call confirming his holiday details he'll be arriving at Rainbow Falls Tuesday week for a short stay. Former work colleagues at the Department of Agriculture, we left within months of one another, me to Wollongong and Dave to Melbourne to start a cadetship with the Salvation Army.... I'm looking forward to his light company ☺ ....

Monday 23 June 2003

Going early doing the coast run, I hit the laundromat being washed and dried before releasing Tassie Sue to the airwaves, eliminating the chore afterwards. I find waiting for a washing machine to finish a tad unstimulating....

Heading out of the booth to quench a thirst generated from hot electrical equipment, I happened to walk through the office at same time Max arrived offering a cherry ripe and drink. Max loaned me a CD with the song he requested Saturday that was unavailable in the station library, I gave him a brief tour of where the noise is transmitted, happy, he left and seemingly not too much longer so did I.... Ahh, to be home cosy in the Rainbow Falls nest....

Tuesday 24 June 2003

Tia and Snowy are never far away or apart. It fills my heart to see Tia socially interact with another dog. The helping paws kept a close eye on me clearing the last cut limbs from the yard. Is the shed ever going to be free of prunings and remain clean????

Returning to eliminate more sycamore seedlings, the three of us have found a niche, I dig, Tia files and Snowy cruises, an effective system, above all it works ☺ ....

Wednesday 25, Thursday 26 & Friday 27 June 2003

Its been my intent to update the journal before this but Wednesday struck me with a dose of 'couldn't be bothered', last night I enjoyed a few extra beers and couldn't in the end ☺ !!!!

Back to the 'couldn't be bothereds'. Wednesday was quietly spent home in the company of Tia and Snowy. Disappearing into the black hole of the shed I cut every last branch down to fit the heater. Becoming aware my company had disappeared tracked down their destination in a neighbouring paddock. Snowy was teaching, a fast learning, Tia the value of fresh cow afterbirth, that's worth ignoring me over. I don't want Tia to get comfortable roaming after food. The further away she is from home soil the more unmanageable variables are probable....

All tubbed up, put an end to Wednesday taking off for a 6p.m. announcers meeting picking Heather up on the way....

Snowy patiently waited for us to get up Thursday. Considering mowing, I got the lawnmower out only to put it away again without using it. Procrastinating long enough a shower came in saving me from the decision of starting it. More suited to the mood a cracking heater held greater appeal, once again putting an end to unwanted prunings laying around….

It was a long hot job finding the shed floor, taking us late into the evening it required many extra beers. It was somewhere in that 'working hard down the shed stage' I lost interest in writing…. hic☺….

Wallowing in the big effort put in the night before, sipped a milo in bed listening to Loui's morning tea program, spontaneously she dedicated a song to me inspiring a feel good return call of thanks. Loui's kindness offered the energy needed to inspire me from bed, but that's about it, the morning disappeared without much to show for it☺….

Nursing a bit of a hangover I took a gentle drive into St. Marys. Stopping at Rods on the return trip he offered the cure with a cuppa and cake, settling the ill feeling to 'almost forgotten about', where I prefer them☺!!!!

Better part of the day over, I roamed to the shed with the intent of emptying ash from the heater, finding red-hot coals, it was stoked up instead☺…. hmmmm….

Saturday 28, Sunday 29 & Monday 30 June 2003

I've certainly had myself sidetracked, no journal entry since Friday, it's time for catch up….

The radio station was a hive of activity on Saturday upgrading and networking the computers. Ready for the big shift changeover, Phillip arrived supporting a migraine unable to do 'boogie in the booth'. Dancing was out of the question so we faked it, a bit like sex without an orgasm☺????

Accepting an invitation for a 'head home roady', I stayed at Loui's long enough to also get a dinner invitation. Later, making our way through light patchy fog to find Rainbow Falls….

Sunday was slow out of the blocks, with one foot in front of the other carting water returned from a trip to the cattle trough to find a message on the answering machine from Loui, calling back we settled in for a yarn….

Rain set in early afternoon so I poked a stick in stirring coals and got the heater cracking, only moving for food or beer☺….

An eager white wagging tail, like so many other mornings, was there to greet us Monday. Tia and Snowy played until it was time to leave for St. Helens for the regular dose of radio, spoiling myself after with my least favourite pastime, the dreaded laundry. Washing everything a bloody mouse crapped on created an extra load, and the bugger won't be caught!!!!

Tuesday 1 July 2003

Waking happily with the thought of Dave's anticipated arrival, I feathered the nest not wandering far from the phone waiting on his call to let me know when he'd arrived. We planned on meeting in town so he could follow me up home eliminating the need for directions. Finding a message on the answering machine I downed tools and we were off. Meeting Dave was like we've never been apart he's so comfortable, we just picked up where life last left us☺….

After extending a tour of Rainbow Falls to a weary traveller, we set-up camp by the shed heater for a quiet night in, suiting Dave, he was ready early to climb under the stack of blankets he brought with him☺….

Not ready for bed myself, I poked a bit more wood into the heater and Tia and I remained toasty together. Surprisingly, Snowy left early not staying until stumps, it was either the new company or he had something worthwhile leaving for ☺ ????

Wednesday 2, Thursday 3 & Friday 4 July 2003
Opting to just simply enjoy Dave's company I gave myself a couple of nights writing free ☺ ....
A homely personality, wishing only for time away from a busy world, Wednesday Dave was happy to gently drift around Rainbow Falls. Asking for something to do to contribute, I suggested Dave collect firewood for the shed heater from behind the cattle yards, with purpose, I left Dave to his own and carted water. Taking beyond the time required and ready to put the kettle on, checking on Dave's whereabouts, I pulled him up with a cuppa and reminded him about this holiday thing he was on. Not only was there ample firewood, but Dave started making sense of the strewn and tangled timber dumping ground directly behind the cattle yards, stacking several pallet sized piles, he made a tidy impression on the scattered mess....
Carrying out Dave's suggestion of cooking dinner on top of the shed heater we had soup heating one end, party pies the other, and Dave toasted bread by the open front.... We got through ☺ ....
Stepping outside of the quiet life, if only for a short while, Thursday David's backyard tour was expanded outside home gates doing a little exploring and socialising. Emptying my head of local knowledge playing tour guide en route to a favourite tourist destination St Columba waterfall, I called into Break O'Day FM introducing Dave. Pulling up at 'The Shop in the Bush' in passing I unearthed a take home treasure buying a beautiful round bevelled edged mirror, adding choice beyond Destiny's rear-view mirror....
Taking a slow trip home we had coffee with Phillip, visited Loui for introductions, and last stop St. Marys Coach House Restaurant for takeaway before the express returned us home to the heater, Dave's favourite holiday destination ☺ ....
Getting his lungs working first thing Friday, Dave took a walk exploring the obscured valley end of Rainbow Falls, returning invigorated, Dave resumed brain therapy timber stacking he says he enjoys it ☺ ???? But not as much as me, tidier, the area looks terrific....
A mountain dash for a pizza dinner, then at Dave's request and a forming pattern, you guessed it, we spent the evening at his favourite holiday destination by the shed heater, and what a nice place. It was Dave's aim to retreat from the hustle and bustle of the city for a rest in the country: he did pretty well in that area....

Saturday 5 & Sunday 6 July 2003
Ending in a blink, leaving for radio Saturday morning I bid the gentle giant Dave farewell, treading lightly on the world his company is comfortable to have around....
The office was a hive of activity working on the computer system upgrade, one major bonus of extra bodies in the building someone took all incoming calls and simply delivered messages into the booth....
An arcade style walkway separates full glass fronted units from the station, from the safety of their doorway John and Leanne amused themselves watching 'boogie in the booth' in full

swing. Beckoning them to join only caused a panic run to the safety found behind a closed door ☺ ....
Catching a glimpse of South Sister from Scamander on the drive home she was draped in cloud; a sure indication there was mountain fog to travel through, happy to be tackling it through daylight....
Competing with a draught problem, a Saturday night in highlighted the poor old electric heater in the bungalow is overworked and could be more effective. Going to sleep with that thought in mind put rectifying the issue into action Sunday. The external edge of the door frame is a piece of angle iron that is filled with overlaid timber boards, looking for a quick fix to block airflow, filled the gap between angle iron and timber with the proven reliably of effective draught proofing cardboard ☺ ....
Without wandering far from the bungalow, cleaned up mouse poo tidying up loose ends, so to speak, and declared war on pesky mice!!!!

Monday 7 & Tuesday 8 July 2003
What a whirlwind 48 hours now put behind....
A busy program Monday, incorporating the live interview with Jo, a tough topic helped along by a well-written script, Loui popped in also extending a traveller invitation....
Washing done and a few groceries onboard, I did the couple of kilometres to Loui's. With a child home sick and without an end in sight, Loui asked if I would fill her 'morning tea with Lou' Tuesday radio program. Unable to say no without a reason, and I didn't have a reason to say no, again braved the couch lured by a home cooked meal and hot shower....
The last words heard leaving Loui's Tuesday morning, "I'll be listening", lingered ☺ ....
A brain geared to afternoon shifts only, I managed to confuse everyone including myself reading from the afternoon program format, having a go at creating chaos until put on the right track.... Oops....
Surviving the experience, afterwards grabbed a couple of pies, dropping Loui's CD's off I stayed long enough to eat then run....
Feeling good driving home, a great day got better, not far from home saw a pair of eagles feeding on road kill. Already disturbed from feeding, I appreciated the brief eagle encounter then passed through quickly and quietly so they could get back to tearing strips off the carcass....
Raising visibility in the cottage for meal preparation, I replaced one missing globe, one blown globe, refreshingly one actually worked, generating a beacon in the night with three working electric lights ☺ ....

Wednesday 9 July 2003
After having the best solid sleep in a while is a good way to enter a beautiful winters' day. Morning stuff done, shovel in hand and two dogs in tow, worked on exposing the large slabs of rock positioned for steps elevating to the cottage front door. Staying with the dogs and shovel theme, doing more of the same, shifted position to the cattle yards clearing fenceline until dusk, using the fading moments to appreciate achievements over a beer ☺ ....

Removing a rotting wardrobe, weathered and collapsed and destined to go up the flue to finalise life as grey ash for the toilet, coupled with a neatly trim fenceline, the cattle yards are losing the closed in drab look....

Hazing the clarity of being outside, a nearby burn off of unwanted bits, being a standard procedure following a forestry logging operation, smoke filled the expansive view from the gorge right around to the ocean....

Exercising her favourite pastime next to eating Tia does nothing but run, her fitness level is at an all time high, she's one sharp ball of proud muscle living in doggy utopia ☺ ....

Thursday 10 July 2003
Repeating a tried and proven performance, Tia, Snowy and I adjourned back within the cattle yards, more real estate was claimed and reclaimed, and the distance of tidy fenceline was lengthened. Treasure surfaced from under a tall grass camouflage, tidying across the front of the little shed in the corner two glass cream bottles came to light, and not much further on the shovel found poly pipe. Without doing any damage with the shovel blade, I forged through the clutter finding a working tap fed direct from the dam....

The wind direction wasn't blowing in favour bringing full throttle our direction smoke from a logging coupe burn off. The thick intensity of the smoke took me to the last Christmas spent in Wollongong, during the month long bushfire devastation....

Friday 11, Saturday 12 & Sunday 13 July 2003
Looking at the wrong 'J' month on the calendar thought I had until Monday up my sleeve to pay Destiny's registration, it was with a rude awakening of realisation when it dawned she was going to run out of rego Saturday. Getting my arse into gear Friday to meet the deadline, and the nearest point for payment being St. Helens, always looking to maximise a trip gave Loui a ring running past my idea. Suggesting I do what has to be done in town then make a start pruning her orchard, stay overnight, and forge on with pruning Saturday morning until I'm due at the station. Everything went to plan except the excessive amount I had to drink....

Pruning gear quietly packed away said my farewells to Loui and headed for the station where on and off waves of nausea found me, budging mid afternoon, nausea stepped aside for the tiredies. Without letting what was happening internally affect external events, managed to sink every last drop of energy into having a fun afternoon of radio while simultaneously supporting a good poisoning ☺ ....

Stopping only for milk and chippies in St. Marys, struggling with heavy eyelids, I gave in without resistance 7:30p.m.-ish....

Lying in bed pondering Sundays' adventure in paradise, a gut full of fresh air fitting the need, made the decision to scale South Sister Range to locate the spring and water supply pipe connection to home. A wild walk through some thick scrub located the water source, I initially walked past the rusted out tank hoping it wasn't the one, ours being further ahead. Resigned to the fact it was our rusted out leaking water settling tank, decided to make sense of it. Devising a solution to direct connect the rusty tank inlet and outlet hoses using the overflow hose to link the two pipes, bypassing the settling tank altogether. Without tools and in need of a couple of poly joiners the job will be done some other time my blood could use another good pumping ☺ ....

Monday 14 & Tuesday 15 July 2003
Monday didn't pass quick enough, wow, I woke in a cranky mood that wouldn't be shaken and it was enhanced by a call to Centrelink, an experience rarely found pleasant....
Taking the drive for radio, I was distracted from personal crankiness with the realisation there hadn't been a car in front of me the entire trip, encountering the first on the bridge entering St. Helens. It was as if someone had been ahead warning of a pre-menstrual woman approaching ☺....
A new trainee announcer, Sue, joined me in the booth the entire shift, taking over the reins between 1 & 2p.m. she did an impressive job. Tassie Sue finished for another shift I did only what couldn't be avoided then retreated to the sanctuary of our little feathered nest....
Long tucked in with a few zeds under my belt, strong wind gusts stirred me to eyes open, listening and hoping. Wind force pushed in one of the remaining pieces of glass from the broken bungalow window and it landed neatly on the box below, the gusting intensity eased for a splash of rain 8a.m.-ish....
Roaming leisurely shovel in hand Tuesday morning saw me wander into the cattle yards, and in a short time added pruning saw to the repertoire of tools. Hours evaporated concentrating on removing free standing and entwined dolly bush from fence wire....
Attention grabbing, the sheer number of bulb spur clumps breaking ground at differing stages of development throughout housing exceeds the display of last season. The front yard of the burnt out house looks like a market garden.... A nice distraction of alive colour....

Wednesday 16 & Thursday 17 July 2003
Possessed by progress, the magnetic force drew Tia, Snowy and me back to the cattle yards Wednesday. Just getting on with it, a car came up the driveway and the dogs formed a welcoming committee for Charles. Settling in for plunger coffee, bikkies and chat, was followed closely by a bulb and progress tour during which we picked a nice take home bunch of flowers ☺....
Soaking in a mid afternoon bath on a heater free warm one, from my comfortable position noticed a mouse had committed suicide in a bait free trap, one less to cause grief....
Missing them and needing to hear their voices, I spoke with Mum and Dad before me and my four legged friends returned to clearing until poor light stopped play ☺....
Following a scratch and a look around, added to the shine on the face of the shovel lining it up for another workout Thursday. Meandering to the cattle yards stopped on the way to eliminate the woolly base from an old wooden paddock gate by the shed to raise its profile to a feature....
A water leak under Destiny couldn't be ignored, having a rest from the shovel ducked into town booking her in with Grant for tomorrow. A spot of socialising, a Post Office and supermarket stop, it was back up the hill armed with friendly mail from Kristy-Lee, only to pass myself going back down for a big night out at St. Marys Pub to be part of Loui's audience....

Friday 18 July 2003
Nothing brings Loui to life more than being behind a microphone singing, a crowd pleaser she brought the pub to life last night. A huge social event for my sheltered life, Roz, Roger and me

were later joined at the pub by Allan, the bloke I met at the laundromat who proved himself just a dirty old man. Allan liked nothing more than to talk about himself and a has-been music past, doing his best to establish how wonderful he is then humbly left. Seeing opportunity, a guy called Ross then came and introduced himself. A little more practical thinking my conversation with Ross led to horse agistment, leaving the pub with loose arrangements of trading agistment for paddock slashing.... Sounds good to me ☺....

Filling idle hours leading up to tracking Destiny's water system leak with a pressure test, in the company of my furry friends Tia and Snowy, worked on getting water flowing to the cattle trough. Just a breeding ground for mozzies when water is left sit idle, first emptied and cleaned the trough. Sinking the inlet deeper into the dam, dashed around to the tap turned it on and relieved the line of air then wrapped my lips over the end of the tap for a siphon start. A beaming smile was produced to see water flow and not look back....

Saving me hours of frustration, in short time Grant set-up the pressure tester gave it a couple of pumps and seeping coolant gave the leaks location away. Pleasantly a simple fix, needing only to tighten a couple of screws and Destiny was on her way home under pressure for a cosy night in ☺....

Saturday 19 & Sunday 20 July 2003
Winding down on a weekend full of positive caring experiences....
Saturday unfolded as any other for an afternoon of filling airwaves with Tassie Sue and music. Nana Raye popped in briefly to proudly deliver a hand knitted Collingwood beanie, knitted straight from the heart by her own hands, her clacking needle action was prompted by a little football banter over the airwaves. Stoked, I pulled the beanie over my head straight away and it fit like a glove. While I had Nana Raye's attention asked if she'd consider recording some promos to use live to air, adding a fresh dimension of fun to 'Nana Raye's pick of the week', she isn't one to balk on a challenge ☺....

Painting their unit across the arcade walkway from the office, John and Leanne stayed a comfortable watching distance from 'boogie in the booth'. Easy targets, we danced our way to them getting the desired panic reaction. At a safe distance John made the gesture of a dance move, I know he's itching to break out ☺....

By invitation I stopped into Loui's for a roady before heading home on the no stops express run....

Ross phoned Sunday morning with plans of bringing his tractor around if it will start.... Was this really going to happen????

Me and the dogs vanished into the yard, raising its head, a useful piece of treasure was unearthed finding metres of heavy-duty tow chain supporting metal hooks at either end. Relocating the chain to the shed in impeccable timing to see Ross coming up the driveway on the little grey Fergie tractor followed closely behind by his daughters loaded in the Ute. While I made cuppa's Ross did a few laps with the slasher in a paddock. The scene unfolding left me emotional, with each slashed strip laying flat the tall grass revealed an image I've never experienced. Life got even better I was left with a dinner invitation ☺....

Standing on top of the dam wall getting a good overall view of the cattle yards and slashed runs, beer in one hand twisties in the other, life gets better but not today. My eyes kept

wandering to the shed in reassurance the little grey Fergie and slasher are real, I'm not dreaming ☺ ????
Slipping the other side of North Sister Mountain to take up the dinner invitation so did Snowy, tracking our scent he joined in on a night out. Quick on his feet, a four paw all terrain sort of chap, he was only a couple of minutes behind going home also ☺....
What an amazing weekend of friendship and change....

Monday 21 & Tuesday 22 July 2003
Good intentions of writing in the journal daily are genuine but life keeps escaping, demonstrating the need to enjoy it because it disappears when you're not watching....
Taking off earlier to do washing before radio Monday is a mistake I won't repeat. The laundromat was extremely busy, and machine problems are dealt with by the grumbling Mr Misery from the business next door, adding to an already unpleasant experience. Mr Misery's unfriendliness helped with the decision to commence hand washing at home!!!!
Entering inside the studio my escapism began and any baggage was left outside the door. Having light-hearted fun along the way, Roger joined me in the studio the entire program and took over the microphone for an hour feeling the water before hosting his own program....
With a few groceries loaded, I then chatted over a cuppa with Loui before heading home to paradise....
Synchronised, Sunday morning neither me nor Tia was in any rush to rise up from horizontal to exit the bungalow door to face whatever presented itself....
Unthinkingly idling through the daily routine bits that keep our existence ticking over allowed myself to be sidetracked being lured by pure sight alone to walk the slashed strips. Reaching the dividing boundary fence gate noticed the irrigation pipe took a wide berth turning into the horizon paddock to again pull back flush against fenceline. Placing the job as priority on the agenda, the pipe was exposed to view with the shovel rather than have it found with the slasher....
Squeaky clean come beer o'clock, armed with stubby, twisties, and dogs in tow, went for a walk starting in the slashed strip returning via the boundary tracing the edge of the gorge. Observing progress and smelling the roses ended the day the way it began, gently ☺....

Wednesday 23 July 2003
Persistently sure she wanted out, Tia had me mobile 8:30a.m.-ish, after an extremely long night of loud and ongoing flatulence I wasn't game to ignore her desire for outside ☺....
Ready to face the world, Tia, Snowy and I steered a course down the slashed strip, entering the horizon paddock exposed more of the irrigation line from being accidentally found. Opening a voyage for discovery gaining access to areas previously too overgrown to consider entering, the only way is up for my learning curve. Tinkering with the shovel along the irrigation line tracked a working tap adding to the repertoire of home knowledge....
Retreating from the physical, rain put an end to outdoor activity, sent under a roof washed the day's workload from my body. Staying with indoor activities dialled the numbers and Mum and I got our money's worth over the phone. Receiver still running hot Lukey arrived home from golf, raining in Mildura also, he'd been out playing in it. An honest golfer, I've not

known any climatic condition stop him, rain, hail, duststorm, thunderstorm and extreme heat, he's played in it all ☺ ????

Thursday 24 & Friday 25 July 2003
Betrayed by the speed days, and in turn, life passes by my time will be up before anything is seriously accomplished ☺ ????
Cruising softly into Thursday I avoided anything resembling work instead quietly massaged the direction toward a pampering at the hairdressers....
A good hour of tips, washing, trimming and a blow wave, I was reduced to putty, probably the right mood to face the supermarket where I met up with Loui and was invited back for a brew. Cuppa tea'd out I took the drive to settle for an evening home ☺ ....
I've got the leisurely start down pat, freedom to choose the direction and speed the day takes is purely done by listening to my body's energy. Well that's how Friday began....
Leaving the pot to boil, and in the company of Tia and Snowy, did a spot more clearing.
Tubbed up for a mountain dash, particularly for fuel, going to town has become a social event, waving to Roz on the way to the service station, chatted to Pam in the supermarket and Allan found me outside the Post Office reading mail....
The afternoon was getting a bit long in the tooth to start anything new, instead filled my fist with a stubby and went walkabout. Escaping a lazy breeze, shielding from the elements, stood in the rollerdoor free car garage in the driveway gazing out towards rolling hills and the ocean and time passed unnoticed....

Saturday 26, Sunday 27 & Monday 28 July 2003
I wasn't sorry Saturday passed, I had a fit of the crankies wouldn't be shaken. As flat as a shit carter's hat I sustained enough energy to fulfil my community radio obligation and get us safely home again....
Rather a quiet drive, the 100.3 signal sited on South Sister Mountain was down, only being able to pick up the 93.7 signal from Scamander to St. Helens. Regularly dedicating a song to me after shift changeover, Phillip's timing was spot-on, the song finished with two minutes to spare before driving through Scamander and losing signal ☺ ....
Crankies gone a fit of the lazies moved in Sunday, it was only due to Tia's pestering that drove me out into fresh air and sunshine. Needless to say afternoon came around quickly, merely idling quietly in the yard with my best friends what remained of the day vaporised....
In concentrated beams as the sun was sinking, and bursting through clouds pushed by wind, entertaining beer o'clock I watched an amazing moving light and shadow display decorate South Sister Range....
A little over-sexed of late, young Tia has been offering, an entire Snowy, invitations that rarely come by but he just stands there wagging his tail with no interest in raising a leg. Tia has demonstrated on him the correct position but still Snowy doesn't raise a leg, he is safer than a contraceptive. Rarely leaving Rainbow Falls Snowy protects his girlfriend, marks territory, does everything but the deed, Tia may think contrary, but in my book a puppy safe dog is welcome ☺ ....

Just like clockwork Snowy was there to greet us opening the bungalow door Monday morning, Tia gave him a sex education lesson that fell on deaf ears while I tubbed up for a trip in for radio....

Program passing without event, Loui phoned directly into the studio and on the spur of the moment we went live talking about a two-year-old female border collie/kelpie cross in the pound with a short life expectancy. A woman phoned in with an enthusiastic response but didn't follow through. Later finding out the dog had been put down....

Program finished, Nana Raye joined Big John and me in studio two recording voice-over snippets to incorporate in Saturdays 'Nana Raye's pick of the week'. Transferring five brief messages onto computer, Nana Raye enjoyed the experience that much she asked to keep the recycled paper I quickly wrote the one-liner scripts on as a memento ☺....

Tuesday 29 July 2003

Pleasant to wake knowing there's no obligations to meet I took advantage of the occasion....
Tia and Snowy followed nearby busily watching me drag prunings from the cattle yards to the shed. Completing what I set out to do and taking a quiet minute to ponder the next move spotted an eagle, flying overhead close enough to make eye contact, then with ease it glided to the bottom paddock disappearing down the valley.... A special moment....

Ross mentioned he had garlic that needed planting out, agreeing it could find a home in the vegie patch, with that thought in mind and little helpers on the ready prepared a patch of soil beyond requirements....

Not a hot day by any means, but physical labour warmed the blood enough to cope with nakedness without a heater to shower. Holding onto a thread of mildness, scattered showers followed knock off, but the mention in weather reports of snow down to 500 metres could explain why it's a bit nippy....

Wednesday 30 July 2003

I'd be concerned if the white face and wagging tail wasn't waiting to greet the opening of the bungalow door ☺....

Doing a rehearsal in St. Marys, Loui invited me down from the mountain for a listen in, singing is something she does passionately well and her voice is very easy on the ears....

Making a detour up home to look at the bulbs on display before picking her kids up from school, turning into the driveway to see Ross slashing, keen on gaining Loui's attention the paddocks are a winner ☺....

On cue a shower of rain put a stop to all outside activity, sending us in to socialise I flicked the switch on the kettle....

Excitement over and like peas in a pod, Tia, Snowy and me adjourned to the shed by the heater for a warm one in....

Thursday 31 July 2003

The power of suggestion, well sound for that matter, hearing a cool wind blowing didn't encourage me to race out of bed to get amongst it....

Drawn by the magnetic force of vast amounts of flattened grass the dogs and I went walkabout exploring, roaming the boundary of the half slashed paddock I enjoyed the tidy look and newly accessible areas. Personally, I've never seen the paddocks cleared its overwhelming....

Roaming the boundary with Tia and Snowy I was stopped in my tracks to watch three eagles gliding in thermals above the drop away to the valley at the bottom of the property....

Water being plentiful with good clarity I had a go at a spot of hand washing, its time to do laundry at home and avoid the bloody awful laundrette. I refuse to give that miserable bugger another cent ☺ !!!!

My wrists must be getting stronger, hand washing that usually takes a week to dry in a stiff breeze was on and off in the same day ☺ ....

A pleasant surprise phone call came through from Nana Raye, mentioning she'd be in Hobart Saturday visiting her twin sister Nana Kaye, organised her 'pick of the week' early and in her absence is going to have my program taped ☺ ....

Friday 1 August 2003
Hand washing soaked up every last drop of stored water, passing myself going to and from carting more, left it to settle and had a yarn with Mum and Dad ☺ ....

Putting the boiler on the stove for a tub left 45 minutes wait time for it to reach boiling point for a walk around the slashed boundaries alone. Tia was put in Destiny for going out the front gate, Snowy also got a roasting but the determined bastard won't leave ☺ !!!!

Slashing has opened a whole new world for discovering, the paddocks I'd watched from the outside looking in offer much new knowledge and views being in the thick of it. Cutting short daydreaming being aware of a boiling water time limit....

Keeping fuel up to the tractor I took the jerry can for a drive to the service station and did all the routine things while in town....

Definitely not on the list of high priorities, purely necessity, the iron was brought out for first time ever here, preparing my shirt to keep Ross company at a wedding Sunday, a look at the instructions was required before starting ☺ ....

The wedding had no entertainment so Loui is now onboard, and I can't leave Tia behind, Ross is borrowing a van to cart three adults, one dog, kids and Lou's equipment.... The trip alone should be good ☺ ....

Saturday 2, Sunday 3 & Monday 4 August 2003
Oops, here I go again, intentions of writing daily are good but lack of discipline lets me get led astray. Following Saturdays radio program I've more often than not got nothing spare, walking away drained writing usually comes a poor second. Failing to write Sunday was another matter, it was entirely balked at by the effects of excessive alcohol on brain and hand co-ordination ☺ ....

Back to the start an obvious place to begin. Hanging in the wings Saturday waiting for the moment of rush at shift changeover Big John introduced me as crazy Sue, my return comment going to air was, "you have to be a little crazy to survive in this world". Lining up Nana Raye's voice-overs and pushing buttons on cue added another dimension of daggy fun to her segment. Including requests and 'boogie in the booth' four hours escaped and flowed ten minutes into Phillip's shift before I finally left the studio ☺ ....

What is becoming a ritual, I stopped into Loui's after radio I also met her sister, Serena, visiting from England. When finally making the front gate of home, a patiently waiting Snowy with a strong wagging tail was happy to see us, well, maybe Tia in particular ☺ ....
It was a rude shock to the system Sunday having to get out of bed by 7a.m., something I don't consider. Tia and I were organised and ready to be packed into the van by the designated 8:50am, picking Loui up in St. Marys, drove onward to Evandale for an 11a.m. wedding. Married in their backyard, Ross' friends home borders the airport runway, the lone sheep in the paddock next door grazing didn't mind, it could have been the very location scenes from the film 'The Castle' were shot ☺ ....
A spot of sight seeing before being chauffeured home, new to me, we went into Launceston and City Park to see the monkeys sealed in a huge perspex enclosure. Having had a few beers, I enjoyed relaxing taking in the view being driven home....
Alcoholed out and curled up in bed I hadn't quite warmed the sheets and heard a car come up the driveway, surprised to see my neighbour Troy, Snowy's owner. A formal complaint had been made about Snowy, and being his recently adopted home it was an obvious point to start. I told Troy, Snowy had been giving me the shits lately but the complaint wasn't mine, Rainbow Falls is a safe place for the fella....
My get up and go had got up and went come Monday, staying at the one forward moving pace got myself to St. Helens and completed a radio shift. An air of happiness filled the office, a pleasant distraction away from my stomach ☺ ....
Included in the supermarket grab was the request of a dozen eggs to take to St. Marys for Pam and Terry, they won the eggs on Loui's morning tea program. A planned cuppa with Phillip, then over to Loui's for another, by the time I got to Pam and Terry's I was cuppered out, declining their offer. Inside home gates there was no waiting wagging tail, although nice to have a break, Snowy's absence was noticed????
Out of the goodness of her heart Loui sent me home with a small lamp, its novel to have an electric light to write by, the thought of reading can also be considered in the evenings ☺ ....

Tuesday 5, Wednesday 6 & Thursday 7 August 2003
Here I go again, another three days down the track, where is time and my life going????
Removing the cardboard curtain from the bungalow window Tuesday revealed a splash of yellow from the first opened daffodils, a colourfully pleasant start. On the flip side, Snowy's happy face and wagging tail hasn't been there to greet the opening door, he was last sighted Sunday????
Up and into it, I made a big impact removing timber from the milling site just inside the paddock by the shed. Pulling me up in my tracks, Pam and Terry rolled up to accept the offer of slashed grass for their animals, chipping in, I happily helped rake to fill the trailer. A tour, coffee and plenty of chat made for a very comfortable relaxing time, steady rain arrived as Pam and Terry parted company ☺ ....
Doing only a few small jobs, Wednesday was a pretty gentle one for participation. Getting me started I emptied ash out of the heater and transferred it to the loo, charged the mobile and wrung out a heap of hand washing. Home life sorted, Ross called in for a visit, getting the heater cracking down the shed I kept beer flowing and we sorted out the world....

Loui asked if I wouldn't mind recording her Thursday 'vinyl vortex' program, still content in bed I simply rolled over and pushed the right buttons setting the wheels in motion.
Endeavouring to use studio two to accommodate a record player, the differences between the two studios generated controlled chaos, causing a retreat back to studio one and Loui's known comfort zone. Loui told me to listen in because she was going to do a 'morning tea' tribute to 'boogie in the booth'. The moment arrived and it consisted of much sniffing and snorting, she has too much spare time ☺....
After fulfilling my promise of recording Loui's program the afternoon was lost on a trip between the Sister's Mountains. Stopping at Rods on the way home he put on a brew and I was introduced to a visiting friend, Suzanne....
Using the last hour of daylight I feathered the home nest to settle in for the evening....

Friday 8 August 2003
Active hormones abating, Tia has pleasantly come out of season, enjoying time alone with her is simply relaxing, with Snowy present I was constantly kept alert with the buggers trying to wander out the front gate. Although welcome, Snowy still hasn't been sighted since Sunday....
Walking back and forth collecting water the elevated garden gained my attention, focussing the working day there. Armed with pruning saw and long handed secateurs I did some serious pruning, another half job to return to when the occasion fits....
Ending the same way it began, with a shower of rain, like good girls do when moisture falls, adjourn to the heater with my best friend and a beer ☺....

Saturday 9 & Sunday 10 August 2003
Usually bushwhacked Saturday evenings with zero inspiration for writing after a radio shift, I proved the theory to be correct ☺....
Although ticking over routinely, Saturdays program was that busy both on-air and off, the shift touched down only after walking out the door for home. Winding the program down for changeover I dashed out to the loo, passing through the 'brains room' housing all the computer gadgetry it was hard not to notice water seeping in from under the door slowly engulfing the floor. Tracked to a washing machine overflowing from the adjoining unit laundry, faking 'boogie in the booth', the problem was found, conquered and fixed while maintaining a regular sounding program ☺....
Over dinner and drinks at Loui's, before making tracks for home, plans to revisit wombat cuddling were again ignited, striking while the iron is hot, Sunday was pencilled in for a day of discovery for Loui, Serena and kids....
Following through with plans, Sunday also celebrated Evie's birthday. Banana pancakes made the wish list menu before wombat cuddling. It's hard not to enjoy yourself at Pam and Terry's, a kids and adult paradise with animals to touch and hold, plus a divine afternoon tea....

Monday 11 August 2003
Forced out of bed on one of those rare occasions by the dreaded alarm clock.... arrrr!!!!
The reason behind enduring the awful beep beep sound was a pleasant one Mary-Anne asked if I would assist her in doing a little community education at a primary school for the radio station. Asking the kids a series of questions, Mary-Anne was going to patch together a

segment for air. The kids were easily worked up and eager. Producing quite a load of megabytes for Mary-Anne to extract a cute interview with the kids, the recording also included a promo with the kids in unison saying, 'our favourite station Break O'Day FM'…. A fun time….
Pulling up at Mary-Anne's for a brew afterwards rounded off a pleasant morning ☺….
With minutes to spare got myself into the announcer's seat and never really settled in. Holding the interview back a week, the shift incorporated Jo from Laurel House. Studying the survivors of sexual assault faxed script, familiarised myself with the topic to give it the dignity deserved….
Around the time Jo left the studio the computer decided to muck up, getting through the program doing the best I could with what I had survived to tell the tale….

Tuesday 12 August 2003
In contrast to yesterday's hectic start up pace, no alarm clock just pure self-indulgence met this fresh one ☺….
Sun broke through on a couple of occasions, but for the most, heavy cloud threatened without succeeding….
Striking a blow I had a go at a couple of half jobs on the go. Starting in the elevated garden with secateurs I tackled more of the overgrown jungle. After lunch we migrated to the cattle yards, shovel in my hand, to reveal several more metres of fenceline. Giving in for beer and bath o'clock ☺….

Wednesday 13 August 2003
Paradise turned on storybook want to be out in them elements….
Simply letting it evolve without much thought applied, roaming led me into continuing a couple of half jobs on the go. Rifling through the milling site, I feel close to confident in saying one half job has been completed. Shifting the strewn mess only a few metres, it was stacked more neatly in the shed and under the carport for drying. Moving the timber disrupted an ecosystem in progress, the timber shift exposed a couple of large worms, several skink lizards and a frog, who would have been more content to see the timber remain ☺ !!!!
Satisfied I could see no more timber littering the paddock then disappeared into the vegie patch digging out new comfrey shoots missed on the first round. Digging about, treasure exposed itself to the surface when the shovel turned up a 1927 threepence, another keepsake to put in the trophy room ☺….

Thursday 14 & Friday 15 August 2003
Transience, and the speed it quietly happens, is realised when it can be measured and seen evolving on paper, but not on my paper last night ☺….
Here I am Friday evening, not long put Loui's kids to bed doing the child minding thing, catching my breath seated at the kitchen table, only then could I consider emptying my brain to write….
Ahhhh, returning to Thursday's recollection….
A job that's been plaguing, and now accomplished, was to find homes for a couple of rolls of processed progress photos placing them in appropriate spots through the journal. Still working

with my hands got busy with laundry and the associated ongoing carting of water. Needing to stay on the move to keep warm because wind was coming off snow somewhere close, kept my blood pumping in the vegie patch using the shovel....

When the physical work stopped by the heater was the place to be where the beers slid down easy. Deciding to call it a night and just warming the sheets the phone rang, fumbling a little uncoordinated in the dark knocked the phone and base over reaching toward the sound.

Tracking the phone I had all the trouble in the world trying to hear Loui on the other end, hanging up due to sound quality, it dawned on me later the phone was more than likely upside-down, not something I'm going to brag about.... It was all too hard for me to work out at the time ☺ ????

A very endearing way to begin Friday, Tia wanted out after cuddles, preparing to get up she walked around and did a loving spew by the head of the bed.... How precious, that's love ☺ ....

Lucky there's been gale force winds the past twenty-four hours it got my hand washing dry ☺ .... Clothes put away, the vegie patch got another look in. During a food break I phoned Loui to clarify last nights attempt at conversation. By the end of our call the outcome was, I look after the kids and stay the night, she goes to the Beaumaris pub to set her equipment up for a 'jam' night.... Who got the best deal????

Saturday 16, Sunday 17 & Monday 18 August 2003
Another three on, life is passing at an insane head rush pace!!!!

Late nights are easy but sleeping in is out of the question at Loui's, 7a.m. sharp the lounge and couch are reclaimed for television and cartoons. Waking with no choice but early Saturday, and resigned to the fact sleep was over, took Tia from her Destiny bedroom for a walk stretching our legs. One luxury I enjoy at Loui's is turning a tap for regulated water and letting the hot water beat down on my skin. Showered, and with orchard pruning finished, I took time to prepare for the radio program ahead....

Nana Raye is developing a following, keeping the segment fresh by adding new dimensions is enhancing the fun ☺ ....

By invitation, a change in cuppa stops after radio I pulled into Rods. Still visiting, was greeted by both Rod and Suzanne. Suzanne asked if she could come up for a stay at Rainbow Falls, I explained the lack of amenities but she was still keen....

Head nestled into the pillow dozing, and having the same rating as thunder, hurting her ears, distant gun shots repeatedly disturbed Ms Tia setting off the barking stress meter. Sounding like a cull across the road, lead is faster and preferable to poison, the stress meter was finally let simmer just after midnight!!!!

Without rushing the job, wandered into the vegie patch Sunday morning turning soil in. From my position in the vegie patch the noise heard rattling down the road, and getting closer, was Ross rolling up on the tractor with a couple of extra attachments for the three-point linkage. Settled into a hot brew, Ross had news on the plight of Snowy he'd been sitting in the pound and was due to have a lethal needle. Living next door to the dog-catcher, Ross heard of Snowy's pending fate and took him home....

Throwing a match to the heater I luxuriated in the ambience of the crackling fire and got settled cosy, still a little off-colour, Tia voluntarily put herself to bed in the bungalow. Sitting quietly in my own company noticed movement, a possum was casually strolling up the shed

ramp to the top level oblivious it was walking toward me, parallel, I said "g'day" its feet hardly touched the ground making a quick exit ☺ ....
Any day I crave a lay-in is the one needed getting up for that's how Monday started....
Doing the community radio thing propped behind the microphone, a fax came through from Peter at St. Marys Post Office mentioning I had a big parcel to pick up, he's not shy at joining in on a bit of fun banter....
Wishing to make the Post Office before the five o'clock closing, and to meet and greet Suzanne now moved to Rainbow Falls for a stay, I didn't muck around, there was no cuppa stops Destiny's nose was pointed homeward....
The amazingly large parcel was a surplus vacuum cleaner sent by Peter and Sheila. Not one of my favourite pastimes, their generosity however continues to humble ☺ ....
Socialising the evening away by the heater with Suzanne the possum returned, adding a little life to the party running around on roof beams and teasing Ms Tia to distraction ☺!!!!

Tuesday 19, Wednesday 20 & Thursday 21 August 2003
Day two extended to day three by having that extra beer by the heater ☺ ....
A storybook warm sunny day set the mood Tuesday, along with music for an enjoyable relaxing time shared working in the vegie patch. Suzanne pitched in offering help, no sooner were we up to our elbows in dirt and Ross and Snowy arrived with additional garden tools and garlic to plant.
Incorporating many food stops, I turned soil, Suzanne raked behind, Tia and Snowy got reacquainted and Ross squared up garden beds and popped the cloves in. Not a garden tool remained active when a pair of eagles was sighted in the distance. Sharing plenty of conversation and had a few laughs generated a pleasant time planting ☺ ....
Unprepared to give in socialising, day rolled into evening, and decisions were made to each contribute to create a meal. Ross had a meatloaf prepared, Suzanne cooked vegies and I heated pies for dessert.... Hmmmm, I got the best deal ☺ ....
Our evening of food, drink, conversation and laughs continued down the shed by the heater until one by one we called it a night. Watching Snowy leave with Ross, unbeknown at the time, was to be my last sighting, sadly, under mysterious circumstances the four-paw all terrain lad disappeared....
Picking up rocks found by the brushcutter, and left at the base of fence posts as a collection point, with the company of my best mate idled a bit of time away Wednesday pushing the wheelbarrow back and forth adding to the enormous rock pile outside the bungalow door....
Before settling in next to the heater and keen to hear how Mum's visit to the surgeon went, phoned my Mildura home. Healing and progressing well, the next testing time arrives November, twelve months on exactly Mum's booked in for a colonoscopy. Content everything was as good as it could be with Mum and Dad I grabbed a beer and adjourned to the heater finding the end to Wednesday ☺ ....
Before it got out of hand, ha, ha, Thursdays main focus was pretty casually spent catching up on washing....
Settling to shed culture easily, Suzanne got the heater cracking, now the journal is up to date my conscience will let me relax and join in.... Does it get better hmmmm????

Friday 22 August 2003
Sent off to sleep with showers of rain dancing over the tin roof and woke to the same pleasant rhythm☺....
Perfect justification for self-indulgence, densely weighted cloud blanketed our world down to 50 metres blocking everything except immediate housing from view, a magical feeling of complete isolation and peacefulness.... Ideal conditions lured the faithful to the shed ☺....
Never one to let my brain sit idle for entertainment, at the end of the first music set of a Saturday program I've started a segment 'My week at home in St. Marys', putting a small script together talking about some appropriate thought provoked since the last program. Drawing from plenty of experience, the script for tomorrow touches upon the importance of a bloody good shed, written to produce a smile ☺....
Script ready, journal nearly up to date, the last things left to do are bath and eat, hmmmm reckon I'll cope.... Oh, and put more wood on the fire ☺....

Saturday 23 & Sunday 24 August 2003
Saturday as predicted it was onward to radio....
Allan popped in for a visit 2:30p.m.-ish and stayed the remainder of my shift. Roger and Mary-Anne called in 4p.m.-ish, getting the office jumping, five of us danced to 'boogie in the booth'.... I had a great time ☺....
Holding an invitation to Mel's 21st at the Bayside Inn, I hung out at Loui's after radio until it started. Taking Loui with me, I stayed nice as designated driver. A couple of hours at the Bayside, a brew and snack at Loui's, it was my little mates turn for a little freedom so we headed in the direction of home. The trip was an adventure, leaving Loui's in rain there was a tree down covering my side of the road at Diana's Basin, encountering fog in St. Marys Pass that continued the remainder of the way. Driving the mountain cautiously in the heavy rain and fog combination, the usual twenty metres of road out front was under water, a first gear slow drive got us to the shed high and dry.... Destiny again proved herself capable in all conditions ☺....
Tia was the recipient of many extra scruff ups Sunday by reaching the tender age of five. We must now finally be settled because she's had two consecutive birthdays in the same town ☺....
Rain remained incredibly heavy all night, a quick assessment of the conditions we headed straight for the shed getting a crackling sound from the heater. In a quiet moment in rain transmission we followed the deafening sound of a powerful amount of water thundering over the edge of the falls, breathtaking....

Monday 25 & Tuesday 26 August 2003
Suzanne and I said parting farewells prior to leaving for Tassie Sue to do her bit for community radio Monday....
With a distracting abundance of high energy I did a bit of mucking around over air, listening in, Loui called inviting me back for a traveller afterwards. Dagging about, time flew, so did time in the supermarket and the social visit with Loui, then it was nice returning home to an empty house.... ahhhh....
It was Tia's choice we get out of bed Tuesday, I'm always happy to stay longer ☺!!!!

Procrastination wandering over, focus was then directed at keeping the shovel running hot having a go in the elevated garden of the burnt out house. Still calling a spade a spade, I progressed to a change in location, exposing to the light of day the 2-inch irrigation pipe and following it along the driveway into the paddock. Happy with achievements then enjoyed a beer or two ☺ ….

Wednesday 27 August 2003
Paradise was perfect, simply spent home alone following whims of doing just as we pleased. I love waking up knowing there's nothing obligatory waiting and the entire day ahead is freedom of choice, which doesn't mean any special exemptions its just a pleasant state of mind….
Disguised with a feel good mood, I used my state of mind on updating laundry. Washing, rinsing, carting water and pegging out the hand wrung clothes filled a good chunk of the day, squeezing in a little more fenceline clearing after….
The ground temperature beginning to rise, coupled with longer daylight hours, is taking the edge off winter, spring is feeling close. The buzzing from a couple of lazy old blowflies hanging around the window ledge is a sure sign of warming….

Thursday 28 August 2003
A ringing phone added lively activity to the bungalow. A call from the radio station was a request for a little assistance, apparently music being played from the computer wasn't being transmitted from the 100.3 frequency located on top of South Sister. Playing phone tennis, I reported outcomes of a few live-to-air trials attempting to track the problem. I felt for Loui trying to maintain normality in her program amid chaos, the problem was eventually isolated to the computer in studio one….
Doing a mountain run I crossed paths with Ross in town, he mentioned Snowy had disappeared without a trace now for almost a week, suspecting foul play. Poor Snowy was only ever mistreated or misunderstood by humans….

Friday 29 August 2003
Edging her way closer, Tia has taken small step by small step to find her way under the doona, when under she's not game to move for fear of being asked to hop out. A win:win outcome, I get to lay in bed longer ☺ ….
Fed and watered, again ventured forth shovel in hand to follow the irrigation pipe digging away, at minimum, three years competitive growth. During a daydream moment resting muscles I observed a pair of eagles at a distance, remaining in and out of view for a couple of hours they created a nice distraction from the shovel….
Stopping to watch eagles, stopping to simply enjoy the view and stopping to eat, you wouldn't want to be paying me wages ☺ ….

Saturday 30 & Sunday 31 August 2003
A bloody quick forty-eight hours!!!!
A good day to be behind the microphone rather than the shovel, wind and rain filled the airspace Saturday….

The computer in studio one was still plagued with problems, the network being down minimised the play list to CD's only, robbing the program of Nana Raye's voice-overs. Surviving with the limited music experience caused a bit of creative improvising with 'Nana Raye's pick of the week', but still added that dash of Tassie Sue fun along the way right up to 'boogie in the booth' and dancing my way out the door ☺....

A couple of travellers with Loui, that's exactly what I did, made tracks for Rainbow Falls.... Hearing myself read the words 'snow to 500 metres', air travelling with it came with its own built-in chill factor making for a bloody cool night....

Taking the shovel walkabout chipping away at progressive change was the best way to stay warm Sunday, returning to follow the irrigation pipe along fenceline. A sense of achieving moved in surpassing the halfway mark, the targeted strip of fenceline is closer to the end than the beginning. A shower of rain stopped play just prior to 4p.m. that soon transformed into hail, an even clearer message to call it a day ☺ !!!!

Bath time is still the no bullshit, in and out, too bloody cold to muck around, get straight to the point, wash, wipe, dry and get dressed....

Monday 1 & Tuesday 2 September 2003

There go another two, I can't seem to do enough quick enough, hours, days, months then years slip by, really in the end what does it all mean????

The ritual Monday radio pilgrimage steered a course to the announcer's seat where again time and the program buzzed by. Only a couple of hiccups remain with the computer, not all music is available and the mouse couldn't be used while the volume was up otherwise the clicking sound would go live to air, nothing that couldn't be worked with....

The manager came into the studio during my program pushed a piece of paper under my nose and said here sign this, a form she called an announcers agreement. Reading the A4 sheet with about a dozen dot points, one point being 'I promise to wash my coffee mug after use', I laughed and said "you're kidding, I think that's proved already". Unwilling to leave the booth, and put under pressure trying to run a program, Maria further insisted on a signature, I signed the paper as 'wank', the more she persisted I expanded it to 'wanker'. In the end, we respected one another's point of view and friendship and decided to continue on without unnecessary formalities. Maria agreed it was a load of wank further going on to say, "don't worry about it I'll take care of it"....

Doing a regular stop at Loui's before leaving town, she popped the question of whether I'd consider babysitting for her next Saturday evening. Meaning a sleepover, further meaning a 7a.m. wake up on the couch, I like kids but babysitting as a pastime is up there with laundry and cooking for me..... Hmmmm, not a decision to rush....

On the road travelling around 6p.m. is obviously not a good time, I had a couple of 'just missed' with active feeding furry animals but we all made it home in one piece ☺....

Treating myself to a little indulgence, Tia left me to blissfully lounge in bed Tuesday, and I did.

Cold mornings I've been letting Tia under the doona, more so Tia has trained me to lift the doona to put her cool fur against me to warm-up, oh, and a pat wouldn't go astray while you're at it. When Tia's ready to get out she walks through to the bottom of the bed pulling anything

tucked in apart. Brushing the bed down and a remake has listed itself on the daily 'to-do's' ☺....
First job tackled was to cart cut shrubs from behind the cattle yards into the shed, finding a supply and demand has entered the equation, there's a need for fuel to keep warm on those cool evenings over beer and bullshit....
Doing what I set out to accomplish remained in the great outdoors progressing with fenceline following the irrigation pipe. Beaten by poor light I was forced to retire the shovel for beer and a bath up.... Hmmmm, some things a girls just gotta do ☺....

Wednesday 3 & Thursday 4 September 2003
A jam-packed couple of days....
Wednesday began with a phone call from Phillip, he'd heard on the radio it had been snowing in St. Marys. None of the white stuff only the air temperature reached this side of the mountain....
Driven by the mission of posting Kristy-Lee's birthday card and Dad's Fathers Day card to arrive on time for the respective occasions, a run into town was made. Thoughts to family on their way, Tia and I settled into irrigation pipe and fenceline clearing....
In the neighbourhood, Loui came up home for a traveller before passing through. Wiping the froth from my mouth I returned to the shovel, managing to surpass the halfway mark by clearing around the end post of the short stretch of fenceline to begin the shovel journey back ☺....
Thursday began on the same note, with a ringing phone, this occasion the voice on the other end belonged to Stacey. Doing a spot of forward planning, Stacey called to say she and her new boyfriend Leigh will be accepting the $500 on offer and visiting early November ☺....
The seed planted in my head of family visiting was just the stimulation required to tackle the laundry head-on and on and on. Maybe my wrists are getting stronger or the extremely windy day helped, but washing was taken off dry the same day????

Friday 5 & Saturday 6 September 2003
Maybe I'm only meant to write every second day because there go another two ☺????
Woken 3a.m.-ish Friday morning by some pretty strong gusting wind, staying awake with ears and brain fully alert and tuned, for around one hour hoped the roof was going to stay intact.
Feeding from my emotion, Tia too was a little unsettled, requiring extra cuddles, that's always a pleasure ☺....
Seeing an end in sight continued the fenceline project, what I initially sized up as a couple of days work has stretched to a week!!!!
By invitation, I had a big Friday night out in St. Marys having beer and pizza with Allan spending the evening in front of the television, giving me a TV fix for another twelve months....
With the knowledge of the minimum amount of time required to prepare for and take the short run up the Coast, after soaking in every last available minute, only then forced myself from under the doona....
A moment of excitement raised its head on the drive to St. Helens, overtaking a Ute before entering St. Marys Pass, by his own omission later, he was unhappy at being overtaken and

gave me a close tailgate. With no room for error the Ute driver's attitude found Destiny's arse end giving her a gentle nudge. Pulling over outside the Pass, joined by boy Ute driver with lame arguments about not liking being overtaken, I kept our discussion factual continually reminding him he was simply travelling too close!!!! Young and dumb and now a little better informed, with no sustained damage to Destiny we moved on....

Armed with chemical free vegies I strolled to the radio station to do my bit for community contribution. Stepping into the booth on a fast moving down hill rollercoaster, packing a little fun along the way boogied my way out the door????

Unable to find anyone else willing, I gave in, taking the drive around to Loui's after radio to babysit rather than follow the wriggly road home. Again I get the kids and Loui goes to a footy tipping dinner, I'm not doing something right ☺ !!!!

Sunday 7 September 2003

Gone prepared to stay the night at Loui's, noisy neighbours kept me awake, Loui put in a late one, and with the knowledge of the kids reclaiming the couch early I put in the extra effort to drive home, collapsing into bed for a comatose sleep at 5a.m. sharp!!!!

The sun was well and truly over the yard-arm when I phoned Dad to tell him how great a Father he is on that one day of the year its officially recognised ☺....

The moment the bungalow door was opened Ms Tia was off like a rocket assertively barking. A free ranging neighbours' cow had wandered onto home soil making itself comfortable until the Tia factor stepped in fearlessly rounding it out the front gate. Unfazed, several cows roamed at will grazing along the road. Pretty casual farming practices????

Several rather loose calling cards were left by the visiting cow unfortunately I wasn't the only one to find the poo. Ms Tia pasted her entire back rolling in a large cow pad needless to say what she copped next ☺ !!!!

Without getting my teeth into anything too strenuous, I opted instead to fluff around tidying up and tinkering with some radio programming preparation stuff. Settled into the bungalow after dinner I heard an unfamiliar noise outside, Ms Tia soon tracked a cow drinking from the cattle trough by the dam and got it 'moo'ving along. Roaming cows are a new concept to me and rather a daunting size....

Monday 8 September 2003

Onward to St. Helens for another exciting adventure in the life and times of community radio and Tassie Sue....

A regular segment given the sensitivity of simple explanations separated from in-house jargon, in an attempt to reach listeners who may need a helping hand surviving within sexual assault, had the interview with Jo, tackling the topic of 'how to leave a violent relationship'. The topic of sexual abuse is difficult but I am enjoying the challenge of trying to reach people through radio, offering a possible first step to a solution assisting them out of a bad situation. I was happy with the way the interview presented itself....

Nana Raye was good company joining me in the studio around 2p.m.-ish and sitting in until the end, dagging about we had a bit of jovial fun both on and off air, becoming a local personality she's a good sport ☺ ....

Phillips for coffee, Loui's for a ritual traveller, then Destiny did not pass go or collect $200, taking the express, she was unpacked and put to bed by 6:30pm....

Tuesday 9 September 2003
While doing a shift changeover last Saturday I made arrangements with Scoots to pick her up in St. Marys for a visit while Grant serviced the family car......
Tia knew how to turn on the charm, with no time to spare for a bath before picking Scoots up she rolled in cow poo, enough to give a good odour. Not overly warm, a window had to be down to dilute the precious aroma☺....
Ooing and arring in all the right spots, Scoots was given a personal tour of the grounds. Leaving food to warm we picked a take home bucket of flowers from the amazing amount of bulbs still going crazy. Completing Scoots visit a pair of eagles I've sighted in the area lately showed. Following food and cuppa, Scoots was returned back into town in perfect timing to find her car ready to drive away ☺....
Still early and with energy to spend gave it away to the irrigation pipe fenceline project, making an impression, broke the back of the job. It's nice on the eye to see nothing but bare soil along the stretch of fenceline, soothing on the soul.... The unearthing of Rainbow Falls is forging ahead☺....

Wednesday 10 September 2003
Loui phoned at a respectable hour of the morning to say her and the kids were paying a brief visit. Receiver still warm, the station manager, Maria, called asking for feedback on a potential problem with the 100.3 frequency on South Sister....
Up and at'em harbouring a dose of determination, I completed the fenceline clearing project as Loui and kids turned into the driveway.... Perfect☺....
Lou and I headed for the comfort and warmth offered by the shed heater, with Tia's company, the kids followed their hearts and imaginations in the yard....
Showers followed Loui out the gate robbing heater decadence of justification. Reluctantly leaving the heaters comfort, me and Tia travelled the entire length of the driveway with the wheelbarrow ferrying back every last rock and stray fencepost. Deviating to have a go at bracken fern on the barrow pushing travels, knocking it down left a clean, green strip very easy on the eye....
Driveway stripped of anything unwanted, drizzling rain again found ground, and we once again found the comfort of the heater☺....

Thursday 11 September 2003
The planets aligned to enhance my domestic side. Incorporating all bedding in with the standard laundry pile, I did nothing but cart bloody water☺!!!!
Squeezing it between environmental and human created elements, I washed while the sun shone, yesterday smoke filled the air and more rain is predicted. Most laundry items made it inside folded and returned to appropriate spots, at sundown I dangled what remained off furniture to dry in the bungalow by the heater. Tia now has both doonas clean more pleasantly all bedding is fresh with no remnants of cow poo☺!!!!

Friday 12 September 2003
Contemplating the world and how to participate in it Loui phoned snapping me from daydreaming. Loui mentioned it was totally clouded over and raining in St. Helens, on the contrary, a corridor of blue sky sat above Rainbow Falls leaving us bathed in sunshine, our part of the world only disappeared under cloud for short periods….
Morning in order and water supplies replenished my little mate and I wandered out to the front paddock by the road having a go at cutting dolly bush down to size, cleaning up ahead of the tractor….
With free time to have a go at a bit more slashing, after a cuppa, Ross fired life into the little grey Fergie. Moving into the paddock Tia and I were in, an unknown area for debris, the slasher found a solid rock jolting the PTO shaft to a standstill cleanly snapping the gearbox universal joint. Putting paid to any slashing for a while it was a good time to down tools for a beer, solving the problems of the world over a couple….

Saturday 13 & Sunday 14 September 2003
A courtesy call from the station late Friday was for the purpose of letting me know the computer had again crashed and Saturday would be CD's only. Without the convenience of a computer the program was kept tight, there was no time for setting up sets, working the three players it was go, go, go, one CD in one CD out. It was fortunate Nana Raye paid a personal visit to the studio with her grandson Dylan, browsing the music selection available she took the improvising out of her 'pick of the week'. Getting the bug for going on-air, Nana Raye and I amused ourselves promoting a bingo bus, she needed twenty-two bums on seats to organise a trip to the Launceston Casino to play bingo ☺….
Preparing to leave the station Loui phoned, nearing St. Helens returning from Launceston after picking Dom up from the airport, she had spent my Bunnings birthday voucher courtesy of Sheila and Peter. Suggesting I hang about in St. Helens so I can take possession of the new screwdriver set, drill bits, router bits, and meet Dom…. What girl could say no to that sort of offer ☺….
Home comfy by the heater for the evening one bar of the much-travelled faithful electric heater fused out. The one bar still aglow kept the edge off night air, but for how much longer????
I didn't tackle the world head-on Sunday. Feeling a bit second-hand I put some fuel in my tank and headed out to the front paddock with the intent of focussing on dolly bush, instead, stepped sideways chipping out a large patch of establishing scotch thistles….

Monday 15 & Tuesday 16 September 2003
Feeling a bit clagged after a long day in St. Helens Monday journal writing was out of the question then, but not now….
On a rather nippy night Tia put her cold nose on me around 6a.m. Monday morning looking to get under the doona…. Give them an inch ☺….
In a fresh episode in the life and times of Break O'Day FM Kristi joined me for the entire program as part of her announcer training, taking over the microphone for a half-hour she did a brilliant job. Walking from the booth at shift changeover I was greeted by the smiling face of Nana Raye chasing a phone number to get the bingo bus rolling ☺….

Bringing the Centrelink payslip home in its addressed envelope failing to post it travelling to and from St. Helens instigated a 'must' drive to St. Marys Tuesday…. Bugger!!!!
Getting ready to leave Tuesday, Allan phoned inviting me for a cuppa, suggesting I bring laundry to use a fully automatic machine and rubbish to fill his half-empty wheelie bin…. All offers accepted….
A call from Loui also firmed up plans for Wednesday, I'm to pick Dom and her kids up in St. Marys while she rehearses then she'll meet us up home later…. It's shaping up to be a social week ☺ ….

Wednesday 17 & Thursday 18 September 2003

Wednesday turned out to be quite an adventure….
Loui phoned from Scamander giving me warning to warm Destiny, they were getting close. In chat Loui mentioned St. Marys Pass opened one minute before they arrived, a tree had fallen on a woman's car in the Pass causing the closure, fortunately the woman got out unscathed to tell the story….
With Dom and the kids loaded in Destiny the plan was coming together beautifully. Within the 20 minute duration of me leaving the mountain, a couple of kilometres before home and stopping any possibility of a loaded Destiny making Rainbow Falls, a large tree had fallen blocking the road. There was no other place to go but back down the hill, report it and wait….
Tired of cartoons and being invisible through rehearsals me and my little mate took a walk to the police station to have my ears filled with good news of a re-opened road, I readily escaped the confines for a bit more space up home….
Dom was given a brief tour before the lure of the shed heater had our bums decorated around it. Tia wore the kids out burning off pent up energy, being joined after rehearsals for a roady by Loui….
Remaining propped on my perch surrounding the warm drum after company parted, enjoying the ambience I partook in a couple of extra quiet ales, adjourning to the bungalow then purely for siesta…. zzzz….
Treading lightly on the world Thursday I didn't get overly inspired. Cleaning up after the night before noticed a couple of temporary windows needing more temporary maintenance, responding to bits falling apart, I tinkered on. Gaining attention is the first step in being repaired….

Friday 19 September 2003

Its a cosy sensation being snug and warm in bed listening to rain on a tin roof, that's exactly how the day started….
The phone burst into life 8a.m.-ish, answering it with confidence said, "good morning Phillip", planning to visit rain frightened him away his courtesy call was to cancel….
Making use of the new cushion grip screwdriver set I assembled the coat and hat stand waiting patiently for the very moment to arrive. Unmotivated for very little both inside or out, instead just fluffed around, making use of the mirror purchase did the eyebrow plucking, pimple squeezing, thing….

When sun poked its head out briefly in the afternoon I made use of the warmest moment to strip down for a bath. I'm looking forward to taking my time in future warmer elements, being naked is something I don't want to be for to long ☺!!!!

Saturday 20 & Sunday 21 September 2003
Pretty much a textbook Saturday for us Rainbow Falls' folk doing the usual up and at'em and into St. Helens....
It's been a testing time with failing equipment both in and out of the booth for a few consecutive weeks, this week the computer is working but the 93.7 frequency covering the St. Helens district is down. A new phone system too was being installed blocking anything incoming until 2:30p.m.-ish. Concerned Nana Raye was unable to get through with her 'pick of the week' I phoned her, without radio coverage she had her ear tuned into the footy instead. Early Collingwood, Port Adelaide results were favourable for Collingwood in a preliminary final leading to the grand final. Calling in on airwave action, Janine from St. Marys phoned through to let me know Collingwood were twenty points up, I started getting Collingwood grand final confident live-to-air handing out a bit of banter ☺....
Getting us home early for a Saturday, and missing Mum and Dad, I called for a chat. Striking a premium family moment, Kerry and Kristy-Lee were also visiting. Being a Collingwood supporter Dad proudly confirmed they won convincingly, my on-air confidence paid off, lookout grand final. Speaking with Dad of the desire to publish my journal his sincere reply floored me, mentioning 'if anyone can do it you can, you do anything you put your mind to'. Hanging up I was left feeling quite emotional, just writing the words again made my eyes well up with happy tears ☺....
Tia decided when it was time to rise Sunday. Attempting to rest my weary bones, the longer I tried ignoring Tia the more adamant she became persistently giving my horizontal body the paw tap on the shoulder ☺....
Up and inspired, pitted the dose of inspiration against the shovel making sense of the driveway side of the cottage, unearthing timber and plumbing bits that lay immersed amongst grass and weeds....

Monday 22 September 2003
Recording a single days events to paper in one sitting is more pleasurable, beyond one psychologically requires that much more energy....
Checking Tia's whereabouts before bathing, found her in a paddock feasting on the carcass of a poor possum kindly donated from some animal that wouldn't miss a few bites ☺....
Before settling into the studio Tia was made comfortable in Destiny. Tia didn't sample today's pie offering, full on possum she was unable to fit another morsel in....
Stepping into the booth I entered a trying time. Walking through the door a new mini disk player was being installed. I was instantly handed a lost two hours of sponsor messages to catch up on. Gremlins were still striking at will the newly installed mini disk would only produce volume if the volume switch of the computer was up?!?!
Thinking booth life was sorted the headphones snapped, one challenge would be fixed and the next was lined up waiting, but I still managed to walk away smiling ☺.... Weird stuff????

Hearing myself read the weather report out loud determined we go straight home after my haircut, the words 'westerly change with 120km winds' was enough to push the decision....
Making it home we were initially bathed in calm sunshine that feeling was short-lived watching the change quickly approaching. Taking only a half-hour to move in and wind to pick up, the sun was totally blocked by 5:15p.m.-ish, no pretty sunsets tonight. Not much a girl could do but have a couple of beers by the heater and watch the whole scene evolve with a spot of rain. Not as fierce as predicted, wind wasn't worrying, 8p.m.-ish rain stopped and the evening had a gentle calmness, I hope it's not the calm before the storm☺????

Tuesday 23 September 2003
The front passed with little fuss, as the elements, life and time does, we too just got on with it....
Settled into finding ground and strewn bits at the side of the cottage, I kept warm manoeuvring the shovel. It's my aim to give Rainbow Falls the best chance against fire and snakes as well as look sharp on the eye☺....
Doing a sprint to the bungalow door where she then bounces around is a Tia signal the phone is ringing. The call was from Business and Employment, Launceston, my case managers for 'Work for the Dole'. The purpose of the call was to ask if I'd consider being nominated for some sort of 'Work for the Dole' achievement awards. Good publicity for Break O'Day FM and St. Marys, and with the possibility of securing some funds if the nomination is successful, to put towards a computer to take home and to love and keep for my very own to start a book. I agreed to participate☺....
Excitement behind, I resumed my sedate life with the shovel☺....

Wednesday 24 September 2003
Eased into consciousness to the sound of a pit-a-pat on the roof, I remained content under the doona listening to passing showers....
Having a morning walkabout and bum scratch, checking on the garlic, Mother Nature has certainly been looking after it. Strolling through the turned soil noticed a smooth round shape, rain had washed the dirt from and exposed a 1939 one halfpenny coin, Australia was still reigned over by a king then☺....
Striking a blow, we were sent packing under cover dodging a shower for a half-hour waiting for it to pass. Resuming the tidy up at the side of the cottage until rain seriously set in 5p.m.-ish, driven in, found a message on the answering machine from Ross extending a dinner invitation. I love eating and love it even more when someone else cooks, but Mother Nature turned on some conditions I don't want to be travelling around in at night, keeping me from a somebody else cooked meal....

Thursday 25 September 2003
Struck by a fit of the lazies, that one extra beer last night slowed me down a bit....
Letting Tia out for a wee, I plugged the radio in, we then snuggled back into bed until a message arrived from above, the cardboard curtain fell from the window letting sunlight flood in, I took that as a sign to get up☺....

In my happy 'put another log on the fire' mood last evening, put my finger somewhere I obviously shouldn't have, a 3mm splinter found its way under my fingernail and that's a long way when you're a nail biter…. Ouch….

Passing myself carting water I got into the washing, pegging the last of it on the line just in time for a final rinse or two with passing showers….

Easing into sunset kicking the ball for Ms Tia, in hot pursuit she went charging through a clump of daffodils taking a single stem and flower cleanly out of the ground, I thanked her for picking me a flower and put it in water ☺….

Friday 26 September 2003

What an achievement, one complete year off ciggy's ticked over, my lungs are whistling a happier note and so is my wallet to the tune of $2400 at the quitting rate…. It's all good….

Hyperactivity didn't take-over my body, touching lightly on jobs already on the go also tinkered with the shovel at the side of the cottage. Turning soil and clearing around existing clumps of flowering bulbs, the area is displaying a splash of being loved. Starting to tidy up nicely, little by little the elegance and pride is being returned to Rainbow Falls….

Running out of milk forced a trip into town, and in staying with a minimalist mood took home a St. Marys Coach House Restaurant pizza for dinner…. Yumo….

Saturday 27 & Sunday 28 September 2003

A nice reward and much needed injection into my wardrobe, Tuesday a $100 clothing voucher was offered for doing 'Work for the Dole', the only catch was the offer expired in two days. A good performer under pressure, I phoned 'Suncoast Variety Store', Brenton faxed details to 'Business and Employment', Friday, Brenton made a return call to say the cheque had arrived…. How efficient ☺….

The thought of new clothes had Saturday morning focussed in the direction of the Suncoast Variety Store. Blowing the budget on a pair of beloved Levis and a jacket, stoked with my bag of goodies, grabbed chemical free vegies from the stallholders market and piled the booty in Destiny before radio….

Generating a bit of entertaining fun with the usual segments, in addition I gave Collingwood a one-eyed build-up to the start of the AFL grand final, that's about where my bragging ended. A stop at the Bayside Inn after radio revealed dismal results, Collingwood were lagging badly, swallowing my beer, and the result of the obvious outcome I shot through home in the last of the daylight….

Sealed cosy in the bungalow for the evening comfortably snug by the heater, when at exactly 10:04pm the last remaining bar of the electric heater died, needless to say to stay warm we were snuggled into bed 10:05pm ☺….

Tia let herself out when she was ready Sunday morning because I forgot to snib the door again, oops….

For a change of pace I concentrated on dragging prunings and burnable unwanted's into the shed, reacting to the death of the electric heater I'm anticipating the need for plenty of fuel….

Late cloud cover kept air temperature to a tepid mild, comfortable enough to spend the evening heater free in the bungalow, saving the beautifully stacked fire ready just to light for another social occasion ☺….

Luck with electrical equipment didn't change, last night the heater tonight the globe in the lamp blew, some force is looking after the electricity bill???? Candlelight offers a calming soft atmosphere ☺ ….

Monday 29 & Tuesday 30 September 2003
It's now 8:30pm Tuesday and here I am thinking about Monday….
A bloody cold night with interesting sounding rain, Ross phoned 6:45a.m.-ish Monday morning and said "look outside", dropping the cardboard curtain told him I could see plenty of green grass, astounded, marginally lower down the mountain there was an inch covering of snow. Unable to join in on the excitement I retreated back into the warm nest until it was absolutely necessary to get ready in time for radio….
A thick layer of sludgy ice outside the bungalow door, on the shaded southern side, harboured our entire collection of snow. Driving out of the mountain, and contained to the highest altitude between the Sisters, a beautiful white coating of snow still lined the side of the road 10:30a.m.-ish, any sign had long disappeared before reaching bitumen. Living in a microclimate and in a world of our own ☺ …. Seekers????
Packing the usual level of entertainment and enjoyment into my program it breezed by, supermarket then Loui's, Destiny's headlights next turned into the driveway at home ☺ ….
A bone warmer blossomed in paradise Tuesday, tinkering outside the cattle yards interest in the shovel measured zero, quitting due to lack of concern. Remaining outside I basked following the glorious sunshine and whatever took my interest….
A government agency phoned to arrange a release back to another government agency so I could continue 'Work for the Dole' for another six months. It's a bloody complicated process to keep doing what I'm already doing; the outside world creates unnecessary work, they're admin junkies ☺ …. Give me paper, give me forms, sign here, phone there, post this, blah, blah, blah, blah ☺ ….
Bullshit behind and back on the phone, the next call created a once in a lifetime experience by confirming two tickets to 'Fleetwood Mac'. Promptly contacting Kerry to let her know she can seriously start getting excited the idea has become a reality ☺ ….

Wednesday 1 & Thursday 2 October 2003
October 1 being an important date for family, my first move was to phone Tegan Termite for her birthday. My youngest niece '16', kids are a reminder time doesn't stand still????
Placing myself in ideal circumstances to listen to Loui's additional shift, I indulged in washing and collecting water, passing myself carting more. With the last item hung on the line, the laundry was converted back to a bathroom to tub for a trip down the hill….
Not a day you would break out the sunscreen, the bungalow didn't capture any heat to survive it without heating. Kissing Wednesday goodnight I had a 'quiet ale' in the company of my little mate sitting by the hot drum buried in the shed watching the world go by ☺ ….
Recently gained knowledge filled Thursdays waking thoughts, South Sister Mountain had been given a coupe number and many hectares are scheduled for logging. Left with a head full of 'but's and why's', from nesting eagles to native animals and flora, including St. Marys and surrounding district water supply????

In and out collecting water listening to Loui's program she announced, "for defacing my Tex Perkins picture pasted in the booth this next song is for you Taz, I know you hate it", 'Bill Haley's - Rock around the clock', she was right. A text message in response, my fingers clicked out the words, 'shit hot program Loui, 95% hot, 5% shit' ☺....
Sun broke lingering until mid afternoon, long enough to dry clothes and empty the line but not bone warming by any means. Weighing up options the only plan that sprung to mind was food, beer and shed.... What's a girl to do when she's cool and uninspired ☺????

Friday 3 October 2003
Etching itself in my brain by seeing it out walkabout and thinking about it afterward, my mind was made up before rising from bed to free an overgrown gate to free swinging. An extension and access to the rear of the cattle yards, to make exploring access easier only when the gate shut by gravity alone was the shovel given away....
Concerned about a loose filling in a front tooth, after a succession of eight phone calls from St. Helens to the Launceston dentist clinics, I managed to secure an appointment at the end of October.... Bonus....
With zippy legs too quick for Tia's, chasing a couple of bush chooks around the dam she took a dive in making me feel bloody cold at the sight of her. I was having trouble psyching myself getting naked to face hot water a dunk in a cold dam was totally out of the question ☺!!!!

Saturday 4 & Sunday 5 October 2003
Having trouble keeping up with the pace of life I heard the word Christmas mentioned last week, shit!!!!
Like all Saturdays, Tassie Sue did the usual 'midday to four' radio program and man did it fly by. All requests were coming through on the office phone the only active line into the station, dashing into the office between sets I took what calls possible and it was a big day for listener interaction, catching around ten calls. Then following up on requests, including regular segments, sponsors messages and live reads, four hours disappeared into a piece of history in no time....
Nana Raye also popped in during the shift, she expressed a desire to do a little something more on radio, leaving my mind ticking over for some creative new fun angle. Driving away from the radio station listening to Phillip he mentioned Sunday as being the start to daylight savings, the words took me by surprise I wasn't aware????
A brief stop at Loui's for our ritual catch up, then without looking back, steered a course for Rainbow Falls....
Confused as to which way to alter the clock Sunday, chasing daylight saving answers was about to phone Loui, but the phone burst into life before I could pick up the receiver and it was Loui on the other end???? Who needs a messenger pigeon, spooky....
Going for a walk out front for a 'smell the bulbs' look around I noticed thistles getting ready to flower, there and then it was decided that was the days Rainbow Falls repair job. With the clock confidently turned forward, daylight hours seemed to go on and on....

Monday 6 & Tuesday 7 October 2003
Well here I am, 10:30p.m.-ish Tuesday evening and just sitting down to write daylight saving has been tricking me into staying in the yard longer....
Regularly done on Mondays, that is, migrate to St. Helens for a stint behind the microphone. Step one in the planning stage, before going to air I spoke to the manager about a couple of ideas rattling around in my brain. Incorporating Nana Raye's offering to contribute more I also expressed a personal desire to start a segment to find homes for pound puppies, dogs needing new humans to escape the deathly needle....
The first Monday of the month symbolised the regular live interview with Jo, representing Laurel House. Happy with the direction the interviews are taking, getting more personalised, I want to reach our target audience not just blurt regulation words out about sexual assault....
With a fair bit packed into the program it was needless to say three hours flew. A quick stop at the supermarket, Loui's, and then it was home....
A rare achievement requiring a lot of work for couples to remain united for a lifetime of marriage, Tuesday's first thoughts were sent to Mum and Dad for their wedding anniversary, 43 years together deserves recognition ♥♥♥♥....
Marking a day of special significance by doing something exceptional, me and Tia scaled South Sister Range and by 1p.m. the poly hoses at the spring were joined bypassing the settling out tank, but still no water flowed to the tank at home some several hundred metres away???? Hmmmm, back to the drawing-board....
Done with mountain climbing I made use of dry ground pulling out and firing up the lawnmower. Between eating breaks, four tanks were emptied making a huge impression on the yard, by day's end my arse was dragging on the ground....

Wednesday 8 & Thursday 9 October 2003
I was going to give myself the night off writing, but not quite ready for beer o'clock by the heater, and having already missed Wednesdays entry my conscience acted up ☺!!!!
Wednesday was nice and low-key, in my 'one step at a time I'll be ready when I get there' pace, loaded into Destiny for a drive between the mountains. The Post Office box was brimming with treasure waiting was a birthday card from Mum and Dad, plus two tickets to 'Fleetwood Mac', sharing the excitement of concert tickets with Peter inside the Post Office. Groceries, petrol, a cuppa with Rod and a mid-afternoon visit from Loui and family polished off a 'dust off' of the social cobwebs....
Thursday, my actual birth date, it was heart warming to know so many people had thoughts of me in mind, receiving five phone calls of birthday wishes before getting out of bed, Mum and Dad were first to warm the receiver. My weekly allocation of talking was done in one morning ☺....
Listening to the radio Mary-Anne gave me a lovely birthday announcement on the breakfast show, Loui opened her 'morning tea' program with a 'four play' of songs dedicated to me accompanied by heart warming words. Everyone's thoughtful consideration started a fresh day perfectly, and perfect it stayed ☺....
A day one can afford some indulgence, taking a sedate option me and my little mate went walkabout taking photos of progress adding pictures to the words I so regularly write. Ordering a double set of prints at each processing, one set make the journal the second are posted home

to Mildura with comments written on the back of each print, a nice way of personally staying in touch ☺....

Friday 10 October 2003
Still snoozing when the phone rang quite early, an eager Rod on the other end suggested I look outside at that point a wave of deja vu came over me. This time dropping the cardboard curtain revealed an expanse of white as far as the eye could see.... It was seriously snowing ☺ !!!!
In excited eagerness made a few phone calls of my own then grabbed the camera to record more of Rainbow Falls' exceptional events....
Also being Ms Tia's first exposure to snow, when the bungalow door was opened Tia sniffed the air turned and hopped back into bed, smart girl. When Tia did venture out she showed no signs of bewilderment just got on with it, taking great pleasure in walking back inside covered in snow and shaking, love has no boundaries ☺ ....
Weather wise it was a doozy, feeling the effects of snow, hail, rain, wind, sunshine and calm all by 2p.m., never a dull moment ☺ ....
It was still snowing when I took the regular pilgrimage up the hill to the loo, the missing sheet of iron from the roof allowed two inches of snow to coat the seat. Threading the umbrella through the roof gap to keep snow off, while I got myself comfortably seated it did a Mary Poppins and was whipped up by wind, not to be reclaimed, left me exposed to the elements ☺ ....
A four-inch coating of snow made everything simply look pristinely beautiful. With limited knowledge being a first ever experience of living anywhere it has snowed, appeared it would linger on. A halo of blue sky appeared 11:30a.m.-ish causing a rapid melt down from that moment, transforming pure white to lush green shortly after lunch????
With the variety of elements delivered by Mother Nature there is only one thing a girl could do, besides taking photos, that was to view it all seated by the warmth of the heater barrel ☺ ....

Saturday 11 & Sunday 12 October 2003
The first stop on Saturdays St. Helens trek was to empty the Post Office box. I was stoked to find a letter from my sister, and not so stoked to have to wait until Monday to pick up a parcel waiting inside the locked doors of the Post Office ☺ ....
A new phone system with no extension to the booth, as yet, generated another fast program attempting to catch calls in the office between sets, keeping me on the move ☺ ....
Home and settled in for the evening, Tia was showing signs of discomfort whimpering with the purple ball in her mouth, a soothing tummy rub eased the discomfort. Tia spent the night in my bed to be at hand when the occasional rub was needed. Unless Tia's bellyache gets worse beforehand, she's off to the vet as soon as radio is over Monday for a check from head to tail ☺ ....
Sunday was set aside for laundry. Before striking a blow thought I'd check the water tank on the hill to see if by some divine intervention water started flowing from the spring. Only getting as far as passing the dam and a healthy tiger snake made its presence known, me, Tia and the snake happily went our separate ways, a bloody clear sign to be more aware....

Coming up to plant a few more bits 'n' pieces in the vegie patch, before he got started I asked Ross to help me lift and replace the dam gate, keeping Ms Tia and other passing wildlife out and its own ecosystem in....

Monday 13 & Tuesday 14 October 2003
The time machine still in fast forward, has ticked the meter over on another 48-hours????
Coming around to solve curiosity, Monday led straight to the St. Marys Post Office. Pulled from the box in the wall was a lovely birthday card from Kristy-Lee. Stepping inside, the waiting parcel was sent from Sheila and Peter, packed neatly together was a card and rain gauge, what a practical useful gift☺....
A few birthday 'thank you's' were caught up on in the office before my three-hour shift disappeared into a piece of history and Destiny steered us to the dreaded vet....
There was not a hope in this world Tia was going to sit there smile and take it with a thermometer poking from her bum, sedated, there were no holes barred. Getting a thorough look over Tia was given a clean bill of health, including her bowel and stool. Maybe the 20mls of oil administered the night before got the pain moving, woken at 1am for the toilet is possibly when the problem self repaired.... Opting to let Tia come out of sedation naturally I carried her out to Destiny making her comfortable for the long trip home....
Leaving the sleeping patient snooze in the car I ducked into the hardware store, contributing to a gift voucher I purchased a small electric heater to return choices to home life....
Placing a wobbly Tia comfortably in her bed it tore my heart out to see her so vulnerable and uncoordinated, she was definitely zonked, I ate leftover satay kebab and she didn't move a muscle. The vet said Tia's body would heat and cool easily and shivering is not uncommon also keep her mouth and lips moist to avoid dehydration....
After lights out, heavily sedated and negotiating wobbly legs, Tia made her way around to the head of my bed for the security the doona held underneath, resettled she was asleep again in seconds....
A much brighter energetic Ms Tia greeted Tuesday with an appetite to match☺....
There was no rest for a patient with a big heart: she was straight into a hard, hot, working day assisting with the important job of moving sand from the pile by the shed into wheel ruts near the driveway entrance....
Didn't Mother Nature turn on a warm one, stripping me down to a t-shirt it too has been the most pleasant conditions I've had to bath in for a while.... Just keeps getting better☺....

Wednesday 15 & Thursday 16 October 2003
I've stopped trying to resist the speed life is passing by trying only to enjoy the journey instead☺....
Settled in for the evening Wednesday the only globe blew in the lamp, the oil lamp was near enough to empty, the remaining candle was only a stub not throwing anywhere near enough light to write by, so it was declared relax only.... I never argue with the boss☺....
Wednesday's intentions of going into town got stuck in the yard, finding every reason to postpone the event. Clunking the shovel around rocks having a go at clearing a border around the rock pile ahead of the mower, the whirly machine came into play after lunch. Two tanks covered a lot of area between the bungalow and dam, on certain angles the mower produced a

rattle initial thoughts went to the broken mesh exhaust cover. The true origin of the rattle later revealed itself, a rather large section of the curved undercarriage surrounding the blade literally fell out, I couldn't believe it ☺ !!!!

Coinciding with warmer weather and a trip to the vet, it's been me encouraging Tia out of bed lately, rare. Milder nights, Tia is also less reluctant to bury herself under the doona choosing instead the half in half out option, bum pressed against me somewhere with her head hanging out from under the doona…. Priceless ☺ ….

Finally getting the hibernating bear Tia from bed I followed up on the postponed trip down the hill. Once the lawnmower and the tractor jerry cans were full, with fuel on board its straight home with no stops….

Putting the fuel purchase to use I sparked up the lawnmower finalising between the bungalow and shed, then ambitiously cleared a strip either side and around every fencepost the entire length of the driveway. Ross popped in for a visit right on beer o'clock, indulging with me in a new concept of sitting on the back lawn ☺ ….

Friday 17 October 2003
Tackling the day without hesitation we worked like we owned the place ☺ ….
Pleasant not having to do battle with wind got washing dangling to dry, leaving it alone to do its thing we busied ourselves with the lawnmower again. Tia has become very skilled, sometimes too skilled, at dropping a ball in the mower's path for me to kick out of the way. Putting a quick end to our game, giving the ball a good boot it went under the back of the mower and was spat out the side not as happy as it went in ☺ !!!!

After tidying the side and front yards to the cottage, the last of the fuel was used in front of the car garage in the driveway. I'm absolutely stoked the way the yard is shaping up, hard work and investing plenty of time is paying off….

Saturday 18 & Sunday 19 October 2003
I rose marginally earlier yesterday to achieve a few things before sliding into the announcer's seat. Eager, following a long weeks wait, I collected processed photos, their existence being the only visual remaining memory of snow reaching the ground at home ☺ ….

Following a browse of the market I then satisfied my stomach feeding it the energy required for several hours of running a program providing entertainment for the districts masses….

A regular visitor during a shift, Nana Raye popped into the station to deliver a gift, a lovingly hand crocheted black and white chequered Collingwood lap rug, she's a generous soul. Keen to do more on-air stuff, while we were together chatting I shared a couple of ideas. The main being a 'Nana Raye request fest', she takes requests for a half-hour and one lucky caller goes in the running for a genuine Nana Raye hand knitted beanie, choice of colour…. The idea received the thumbs up ☺ ….

Rod also phoned through during the shift inviting me to call in on the way past, making his place my roady stop. With complements I took home a small bundle of strawberry runners, some made it into the ground before putting my bat and ball away due to poor light ☺ ….

A 'proposed logging of South Sister' information session held at 'Seaview Farm' Sunday roused my attention enough to attend the 11a.m. gathering. With a head full of community emotion and local knowledge I left to ponder what might be….

A minor shower beforehand was a nice way for the remaining strawberry runners to be introduced to soil, adding to the stocked look inside the vegie patch confines....
Helping finalise the clearing of the border of the rock pile, Tia then put in a big finish manoeuvring and juggling four legs over the rock pile as I moved a few kilograms enlarging the walkway between the pile and bungalow.... Another day beaten ☺....

Monday 20 & Tuesday 21 October 2003
Getting my act together fuelled up and took off to Monday's destination radio....
The station displayed posters advertising the 'choirboys' playing on a Saturday at the 'Top Pub', the penny dropped I'd have to sound excited plugging them over air. Chance had me in the audience when the bands lead singer threw a tantrum live on stage doing a gig in Mildura the act of foolishness was unworthy of any respect. Unable to bring myself to promote the fools I offered to forego shifts on days relevant to saturation publicity....
As much as I relish in shifts spent on-air, with an active office time at the station doesn't excite me much, since the current management take-over the office atmosphere is energy robbing. The managers' brother-in-law and station treasurer, Bruce, in my view is an unpleasant sleazy practical joker who keeps pushing the boundaries of decency for reaction....
Not exploding into activity, Tuesday I tuned into Loui's 'morning tea' program and contemplated options....
The words 'capital gains tax' have kept me reluctant to ring the tax agent, biting the bullet I phoned for an appointment committing myself to face the outcome of the past twelve months actions....
Putting myself to work several wheelbarrow loads of sand from the pile by the shed were relocated to fill deep wheel ruts in the driveway. A habit of mine is getting sidetracked, deviating from sand lugging, chipped bracken fern enhancing the visual appearance of the driveway entrance. My protesting body unwilling to go another step further gave work away surrendering to 'beer and bath o'clock' ☺....

Wednesday 22 October 2003
A quiet one spent home together. With my little mate always on the ready we emptied anything that fit into the deepest driveway ruts keeping the wheelbarrow and us on the go. During a break I got the phone running hot, long settled into a marathon conversation with Mum, Aunty Claire's arrival to visit Mum pulled us up to take a breath ☺....
By tidying the pile of sand by the shed, the grass and weed growth that had been slowly engulfing, now relocated to the driveway, it looks as if the sand pile was freshly dumped....
Carting the last barrow load for the working day I decided to wind down chipping away at new growth bracken fern, two hours later it was well and truly beer o'clock. Daylight saving tricked me into staying outside working seemingly longer ☺....

Thursday 23 October 2003
A big effort shovelling yesterday, physically putting muscle groups to work, took the stride out of my step today, by no means was I ready to rush the day waiting....

With one foot in front of the other, like good little squirrels, collected water filtered it and left it to settle. Water clarity is rising putting the gate back on the dam has stopped animal traffic, including Tia's, stirring things up ☺!!!!
The finer points of our existence organised, like writing in the journal, fittingly suiting the mood rain started falling and the lure of the shed beckoned. The heavens offered enough moisture to christen the new rain gauge with a huge 3mm: it's exciting being relatively accurate in small increments ☺….

Friday 24 October 2003
In her quest for ultimate attractiveness late last evening Ms Tia rolled in fresh poo, not a chosen time to deal with such matters, I just plodded forward to reach a solution and my pillow ☺!!!!
Feeling a bit second-hand and out of energy I jumped out of the blocks like a turtle.
Attempting to reschedule the cancelled dentist appointment, following 12 minutes on hold at STD rates, I packed the shits and hung up deciding that would be better pursued at a later date!!!!
Laundry is always a way of distracting my mind back to the basic simplicity that a practical, hard earnt, manual home lifestyle offers. To keep me deeply enthralled, adding to the spoiling, pushed the vacuum cleaner through the bungalow, I know no limits!!!!

Saturday 25 & Sunday 26 October 2003
A change pushed in late Friday, by Saturday morning 4mm had been measured in the new rain gauge….
Preparing for the trek to radio the elements had sunk us in low cloud and limited visibility offering my interpretation of a fairytale book mystical existence….
Sweet talking a girl, a check of the Post Office box passing through I was stoked to find a couple of lollies inside, whatever the occasion it made me feel good. Sharing an acknowledgement to Peter over air in appreciation, a good turn goes a long way. Putting me in the right mood, it was a pretty relaxed program making fun with the regular segments ☺….
Settling in a little at Loui's, I didn't get home to Rainbow Falls until after 9p.m. arriving in misty rain to unload Destiny….
Dropping the compulsion to work Sunday I relaxed the entire day away having invited Max for a visit. Arriving on his 250 Kawasaki dirt bike, I took up Max's offer of a ride having a squirt through paddocks it was a blast, not having ridden since selling my 850 Suzuki in Wollongong ☺…. Following sun, eating, drinking and chatting, it was a nice afternoon….

Monday 27 & Tuesday 28 October 2003
Monday started as a dream come true for Ms Tia, pushing open the bungalow door to greet the morning there lay before her a victim of the previous evening, a dead possum. A treasure to be guarded, Ms Tia soon took control of the situation claiming the newly found wealth and marking boundaries ☺….
Stopping to sample pies at most outlets on the coastal pilgrimage between home and radio I had the best sitting in my own backyard, pleasantly discovering the St. Marys bakery, supplying a few flavours to my liking not available anywhere else….

With an active office available energy input into my radio program was pretty average rising to nothing outstanding then it was over. Stopping at Loui's after my shift I hung around for an announcers meeting, more so a managers report, dropping Loui home afterwards I did the same, went home....
Feeling as strong as a half-sucked peppermint, Tuesday I took my time with light duties. Spending the morning either receiving or making phone calls, I managed to lose the afternoon just making a trip into town???? If I went any slower I'd be going backwards☺!!!!

Wednesday 29 October 2003
Aware of a 1p.m. tax appointment, indulged myself in a leisurely preparation over breakfast and bathing. With hours to go and working well under pressure I lifted the lid off the shoe box sorting receipts into logical piles. A quick phone call to the bank for a taxable interest figure I was shocked to hear $1.32 from a large sum sitting idle, how insulting. I don't even think the tax department would bother with that piss farting amount☺????
A bit apprehensive because the sale of the Mildura house incurred capital gains tax, the final key pressed on the tax computer the total amount payable didn't go beyond my budgeted bank balance, only then was I aware of taking my first breath.... Able to survive another year, phew!!!!
The economy's obligations up to date the next couple of days can be spent at home in contentment, a nice feeling☺....
Slowly sipping a glass of red by the heater sitting snugly on the window box I sat with my back against the fridge watching a beautiful sunset.... What more can I say, hmmmm☺....

Thursday 30 October 2003
Starting like any other, the sun came up. A short time after letting Tia out I took a peek spying her gumming on her treasured possum, eating three day old dead possum wasn't an appealing thought. Leaving Tia to her own devices I too had a, somewhat fresher, leisurely contemplative breakfast....
Collecting enough water to get a load soaking, the following couple of hours were spent carting water, eating and washing. Wandering further afield shovel in hand, Tia and I walked the entire driveway strip chipping any evident baby bracken fern poking their heads through....
Dinner on the cook, content life was under control, it was time to settle into the nest....

Friday 31 October 2003
Shortly after the standard level of procrastination over breakfast, a phone call came through from the dentist rescheduling an appointment for next Thursday. I'm happy to have light at the end of the tunnel????
It was Destiny's turn for a bit of attention being spoilt rotten with a vacuum throughout. Returned to her bedroom a shower of rain stopped outside play. Keeping dry indoors with a roof over our heads enabled me to catch a phone call from Loui for idle chatter sharing our weeks' events. Leaving myself remain idle, I got engrossed preparing for tomorrows radio program writing a 'this week in St. Marys' script and selecting music to start the program. Efficiently organised, also gave myself a sample of overdue attention with a winter hair removal leg shave finding flesh from the hips down; it had been a long cold winter☺....

Comfortably snoozing in the bungalow by the heater, Ms Tia left me in complete still silence to watch the dim light fade and a shower of rain peacefully begin....

Saturday 1 & Sunday 2 November 2003
Taking the Saturday trek, stepped inside the St. Marys bakery for the best pie or pastie tasted on my travels between here and there, a spinach and cheese pastie.... I'm a convert ☺....
Leaving St. Marys it didn't take long to catch up with a couple of trucks tightly weaving their way through the winding Pass, out the other side and overtaken I got cracking. Passing through the town of Scamander I saw a mature aged male fall and roll down a small grassed embankment, not one to be able to drive by stopped to be sure he was fine, he replied "sure, I'm just stoned". Happy he was happy walking back to Destiny watched the trucks again pass by.... Life can be testing at times ☺ ????
Struggling with energy and enjoyment for radio, unsettled in the seat it was an effort to sound enthused and energetic I can't be Mary Poppins each week. Ongoing, persistent calls from the treasurer, Bruce, is taking its toll, robbing radio of enjoyment and the station of atmosphere. I didn't even have the energy to turn Destiny's steering wheel toward Loui's, using the last of my petrol getting home....
In need of time out alone, arriving home I shut the gate behind, a rare occurrence, blocking out anyone who wasn't serious....
Enjoying sunshine patiently waiting for Sunday breakfast, Tia's patience was aptly rewarded....
Setting up a drum over the fire pit in the side yard to the cottage for the purpose of boiling bulk hot water, levelling the drum I pilfered a few bricks from a stack by the cattle yards. Nearby, Tia's manner at sniffing the ground was different, close to Tia's nose, she alerted me to a tiger snake. My verbal firm attitude caused both Tia and the snake to head in opposite directions!!!!

Monday 3 & Tuesday 4 November 2003
A public holiday Monday meant the office was empty, no manager or brother-in-law strong family bonds on staff, my program passed without torment or fuss. Mel phoned asking if I'd stay on an extra hour so she could remain at her paid job. Reading the local weather report following the 4p.m. news a rushed Mel burst through the door, with youthful high energy she was ready to keep going....
A couple of hours evaporated in the company of Loui, then beginning the wind up the mountain to fluff the nest, met up with Ross along the track pulling over for a chat. Stopping in daylight managed the last few kilometres after dark....
Determined, I made an impression on the lawns for the purpose of tidying surrounds so I can relax in the company of Stacey's visit next week. Emptying one tank saw me through what fuel remained, driving my arse briefly between the Sisters and out the other side to town, did the necessary and returned quickly while the momentum remained....
Going hard at it didn't finish until 7p.m.-ish, when the mower ran out of fuel so had I, but not before breaking the back of the total mowing job. Feeling happily content with the outcome settled in for a second bath and beer....

Wednesday 5 November 2003
Observing Tia doing two fresh poo's on an area of lawn destined to be mowed I wondered if that's a dog's idea of a bad joke☺????
Bordering on harassment, the radio stations 'make it up as you go' Miss Manager Maria phoned me yet again at home. Taking no responsibility for her own words of 'don't worry about it I'll take care of it', holding her to uphold her word, she continually pleads 'I'm only the messenger'. Whoever she is the messenger voice piece for is pissing me off I'm nearly over it. Miss Manager was more efficient as receptionist before she decided she wanted to run the show. Backed by her brother-in-law and station treasurer Bruce, and Bruce's drinking buddy and station chairman, Neil, they created a fictitious station restructure that shafted previous management to place Ms Maria's unprofessional inexperience behind the helm. Robbed of fun, I spent idle brain time pushing the mower contemplating my future I don't think radio fits into a positive healthy path....
During the last phone call I was told by Miss Management Maria to just conform, office politics is making announcing hard to enjoy and the ongoing phone calls following me home even less pleasant. I'm not enjoying the attached unprofessional 'CRAP' that goes with radio anymore. Conforming means accepting being the brunt of gay jokes, sexual innuendo, practical jokes and dumb sexist paraphernalia that is draped through the station. Bruce has decorated the station in anything crass from degrading posters to a mirrored mat in the toilet, further pushing the boundaries of unprofessional Bruce's blow-up-doll has become a station mascot. With no limits imposed, and encouraged by the manager, from verbal to visual, the more Bruce is left unaccountable the further he pushes boundaries....

Thursday 6 & Friday 7 November 2003
On a mission to be at the dentist by noon I got up and into it Thursday. Collecting water from the hose connection at the 2-inch irrigation pipe by the driveway Tia gave me 'that look' saved purely for the occasion of a snake. A tiger snake eased passed the tap and continued along the nice strip of cleared fenceline. Shortly after the snake encounter a skink lizard dropped from the bungalow door opening it to walk in, jittery it frightened the shit out of me☺....
Quite warm, it took some searching to find shade for Tia and Destiny while I was being drilled and filled....
Loui was playing at the St. Marys pub from 7p.m.-ish, re-packing the family in Destiny returned back down the hill almost on time. A voice easy on the ear and doing covers I enjoy, Loui always provides an entertaining night....
On the drive home on a very mild evening in paradise there was plenty of native animal action moving under cover of bush and darting across the road at random strikes, staying alert and taking it easy we all reached our destinations unscathed....
The first thing a self-respecting Aunty does on Friday 7th November is to ring through 'many happy returns' to her beautiful niece Stacey. Keeping the phone active I got onto the Launceston dental clinic to get myself back on the waiting list for another recommended filling replacement in St. Helens.... A very roundabout cumbersome system????
I must have carted around 100 litres of water to wet up a fast drying vegie patch, a huge task without a hose on site. Nice out, my little mate and I roamed with the shovel edging anything

that got in the way. Bathed and fed, was then content to relax burning up candle wax and ink ☺ ....

Saturday 8 & Sunday 9 November 2003
The usual Saturday morning disorganised organisation. Fuelled and pastied up in St. Marys, I enjoyed the aromas of my favourite 'cheese and spinach pastie' all the way to St. Helens where Tia helped me share in the greens ☺ ....
Surprising for a weekend Miss Manager Maria was in the office to meet and greet, we had stilted conversation being disillusioned by phone calls received at home from her. Joining me in the booth beginning my shift she wanted to start talking deep, not good timing while I was attempting to deliver an uplifting, entertaining program. I suggested our conversation wait for a more suitable moment, thinking better of it she left the booth and me to it. It came as no surprise that after she left my energy skyrocketed, feeling extremely high for the entire shift enjoyed the program right up to 'boogie in the booth' and leaving the hot seat ☺ ....
A partying group gathered in the cul-de-sac outside the station. With radio blaring and esky stacked they joined in on the Saturday afternoon entertainment celebrating. Tia must have been a bit confused waiting patiently in Destiny hearing my voice over their radio and I was nowhere to be seen ☺ ????
A leisurely Sunday breakfast sustained my energy for collecting water, then even more water for laundry. Down to the last item of clothing, Ross arrived, adjourning to the bungalow for a cuppa and staying comfortable in the afternoon sun, we moved onto a beer before he parted company....

Monday 10 November 2003
A stop at the St. Marys bakery happily found chicken camembert pies on the menu, thank you very much. Nostrils breathing in the aroma gently filling Destiny from the contents of the paper bag sitting beside me, the pie only made it as far as Scamander ☺ ....
Waiting for shift changeover I did a quick cram familiarising myself with the script for the Laurel House interview, since the regular segment has been going Jo has, to this point, had three referrals… Hopefully a positive turning point forward!!!!
Jam-packed, the program buzzed by, afterwards priority one was to get Mum's birthday bits 'n' pieces posted off. Car loaded with groceries on a warm one I only made a brief stop at Loui's....
We made it inside the front gate with enough remaining daylight to replenish cottage water and give the vegie patch a drink. It would be nice to see rain, not only to ease my load by offering a bucket lugging break, but the ground is so dry in places cracks are developing....

Tuesday 11 November 2003
Driven from bed for a pit stop, from the moment my head raised off the pillow I hit the ground running. Stopping in my tracks only briefly watched an echidna cross the yard toward the dam and waddle up the hill and out of sight…. Only at home ☺ ....
With the knowledge the Spirit of Tasmania had docked and a family fix had hit the shores, Stacey and I exchanged progressive text messages clueing me into when they were close. Arranging to meet in St. Marys, and hushing our excited emotions because of the

Remembrance Day Service only 20 metres away, Stacey introduced me to her new boyfriend Leigh then there wasn't a moments silence. Taking the tourists for a drive putting Rainbow Falls' boundaries into perspective, as our journey continued along the bone rattling road Destiny's exhaust noise got louder. Reaching the end of the tour whatever was just holding the exhaust together had separated a job filed in the shed marked for attention tomorrow....
Cramming it in, after a brief look around the grounds of Rainbow Falls the dust didn't settle and Stacey and Leigh tackled the goats track climb to the top of South Sister Mountain for a look at life from on top of the world ☺....
Utilising the time alone, phoned to thank Mum and Dad for the Christmas gifts arriving with Stacey. A fold-up outdoor chair, stainless steel steamer, a set of knives in a wood block, and kitchen utensils were all very useful, practical and most welcome.... A brilliant day, so happy for a family fix ☺....

Wednesday 12 & Thursday 13 November 2003
November 12 is tattooed inside my eyeballs, no other thought besides calling one's Mother for her birthday is considered first thing on that date ☺....
Burnt out from packing it in Tuesday, Wednesday got off the ground quietly roaming. Stacey and I were in the cottage front yard where she pointed out a very healthy snake and I quickly lost my strolling company. Unwelcome around housing, I made a nervous start with the shovel being forced to face a fear.... Not an act I enjoyed carrying out....
Having a peek, Destiny's rear tailpipe had separated from the muffler, sounding bloody loud, there's no sneaking anywhere particularly climbing to cross the mountain delivering her to Grant. Packing into Stacey's car we took off on a favourite tourist route stopping at everything of interest between here and St Colombia Waterfall. Making a song and dance of it, Stacey was crushed Tia deposited fur in her car.... Ooooops....
Having done the walk myself several times, I left Stacey and Leigh to stroll the track into St Columba waterfall, opting instead to stretch Ms Tia's legs amongst the trickle of tourists coming and going. A day for echidnas, exercising Tia I watched another cross the road, amazingly seeing a third reaching bitumen leaving St Columba waterfall ☺....
Stopping at every whim between here and there, we returned buggered, I cooked up a feast of bangers and mash to satisfy an appetite and we finished the evening off by the shed heater....
Being courteous, Thursday morning I vacuumed Tia's fur from Stacey's car while she and Leigh bathed in readiness to leave. Moving on to continue packing in a Tasmanian adventure, they left for Coles Bay to follow the Coast along to gradually make their way to Hobart....
Too bloody insane hot to do anything outside, and left standing with the vacuum in hand, I put the monster to use placing the nozzle on everything from the ceiling to the floor in the bungalow....

Friday 14 November 2003
Getting on with the more important things in life, like laundry, assisting the event was another bloody hot one, wind picking up on occasion made it 'a great drying day', (quote: Margaret Lucas ☺....). My hand washing dried within hours, that alone takes exceptional circumstances ☺....

Fiddling around with my 'this week in St. Marys' radio script Ross pulled up out back to take us to be reunited with a quieter Destiny. As a gesture of thanks I shouted him a drink at the pub....
Watching the action from the bungalow door, to cool down with this sudden blast of heat Ms Tia's been submerging her body in the cattle trough by the dam, a few degrees cooler, she then contentedly rolls on the grass next to it.... Happy days ☺....

Saturday 15 November 2003
Fortunately having sense enough to set the alarm, a big week coupled with a late night and a warm restless sleep didn't culminate for a good start up recipe....
Struggling to find long-term shade close to the radio station for Tia and Destiny, and the studio thermometer reading a temperature of 34° justified bringing Tia into a more pleasant ten degrees cooler booth. Appreciating the conditions she was well behaved ☺....
The phone didn't stop ringing during my shift I managed to take sixteen calls amid all the other bits that had to be dialled, pushed or twisted needless to say time didn't drag....
Making a one-beer stop at Loui's, visiting, I also had a yarn to Gary and the kids before the lure for home got strong....

Sunday 16 November 2003
Out making a mark on the world I walked a path back and forth bucket watering the vegie patch, initially not flowing extremely clear, the vegie patch got a good soaking until quality rose for bathing in....
One thing led to another, and like a black hole, the vegie garden drew us in to toil away many an hour turning in unwanted weeds to compost before setting seed. I find working in the garden very cleansing for the mind, a place for thinking, therapy for the brain....
Reflecting on the day's events I enjoyed a cool beer or two while waiting for bath water to boil. What remained of the evening was soon swallowed finalising the settling in routine of eating, de-furring my bed, and of course a passion, writing in the journal ☺....

Monday 17 November 2003
Struggling to get up without the assistance of the bloody awful sounding alarm, a cool change left me in the mood for snuggling....
The St. Marys bakery is becoming my regular pie stop en route to radio. Sitting in the announcers chair was pretty routine, the only variation I was joined in the booth by a trainee announcer Trish. Another program disappeared quickly, dedicating the final song to Annie, not only was she relieving me of the hot seat but she was also having a birthday, finalising the shift into the news with the 'Beatles and Happy Birthday'....
The in town 'to-do' list incorporated a stop at the vets to replenish worm tablet supplies, the only thing Tia would have been happy about is she didn't have to go inside ☺....
Packed with groceries and forgoing the regular Loui stop, headed full steam ahead to Rainbow Falls....

Tuesday 18 & Wednesday 19 November 2003
Spending the lion's share of daylight transforming the vegie patch by day's end it looked fantastic. Fast drying ground began making soil turning a chore cementing the decision to finish the job after rain. Getting in on the act Tia started some purposeful digging of her own, hot on the trail of something, she sniffed out a long buried tennis ball from a previous occupant ☺....
Cooling muscles leading into laying the shovel to rest I chipped away at some new growth bracken fern in the driveway....
Ongoing excessive phone calls to harassing levels, of up to eight per day, received at home from Miss Managers brother-in-law and station treasurer Bruce, he's insisting I sign the announcers agreement Miss Manager said she would take care of. One call alone would be enough to get the message across. It's disappointing when people don't hold true to their word giving trust I'm being left feel empty by unprofessional management. I like broadcasting and staff associated, but the lack of leadership and 'make it up as you go' management is draining the enjoyment out of community radio.... Disillusioned and let-down, and enduring excessive calls, for peace, Tuesday evening I was forced to pull the phone plug out of the wall to make myself inaccessible!!!!
Wasting a lot of precious energy over the phone, I rested a drained body Wednesday signing up for thoughtless brain therapy recovery doing repetitious activities requiring the least amount of thought. Carting water to the cottage and prunings to the shed fit the bill ideally....
Mustering up the brain power required, I called the secretary in order to clear up the driving force behind excessive harassing calls and tidy up fine detail bullshit, no progress was gained....

Thursday 20 November 2003
Pretty much unfolding of its own accord, I just followed my feet ☺....
In my relaxed bumbly way I got organised, pulling on the last pair of socks predetermined that washing was to be done. The windiest day of the week and surrounded in thunderstorm activity, we may have missed moisture action, instead received a bloody fast drying day ☺....
On two separate occasions out wandering saw an eagle glide over South Sister Range, it saddens my heart their home is earmarked for logging. The economy hard at work????

Friday 21 November 2003
Taking the last cut prunings from the elevated garden to the shed created another job to burn them ☺....
Concentrated efforts were applied at making sense of the rear of the burnt out house, establishing another termite hole. Gloved up and shovel handy, I pulled and chiselled at growth from gaps between concrete paving leading into the rear gate entrance. Tidying a short strip of fenceline surrounding the elevated garden then made a start finding the buried concrete path running parallel to it. A two metre wide strip of paving, now loaded with a thick layer of composting charred remains from the fire, mixed with germinating blown in weed seed and what arrived in the soles of shoes with foot traffic, is a career alone....

Saturday 22 & Sunday 23 November 2003
Easing by without too much fuss, just the way I like them....
Making the Post Office box the first stop, then that all important Saturday special pie stop, leaving St. Marys bakery the Destiny express headed to the radio station....
I'm going to have to consider hired help, managing to answer fourteen calls for requests and incorporating them into the program inevitably it didn't take long and I was walking back out the door I entered. Phoning through her 'pick of the week', Nana Raye and I also made plans to meet for coffee Monday to relax away from a work environment unrushed for a yarn. Doing the regular shift changeover dance, a light-footed way to end a program, boogied out of the booth to the supermarket ☺....
Having a fair sleep in Sunday, and just as leisurely, I got up to face whatever lay ahead. With something in our bellies, de-furring the bungalow is now a usual start up agenda inclusion item, the amount of fur Ms Tia is dropping has fortunately peaked....
Radio in the background, Ms Tia and I took another termite bite out back of the burnt out house, having been consumed by tragedy and neglect, progress is not fast but rewarding. Ms Tia decided to mark territory, a little raw on the nose, she passed a motion only a few paw paces from where we worked the little darling.... Phew!!!! Just a small reminder she loves me ☺....

Monday 24 November 2003
Given the opportunity reckon I would have rolled over and revisited the land of nod, lucky for me the alarm is out of reach ☺!!!!
A pretty predictable sequence of stops en route to the station. Following up on a shift changeover chat last week I took Mel a St. Marys bakery chicken camembert pie as promised, I said if she enjoyed it mention it on-air, going beyond, she said it was the best pie she has ever tasted ☺!!!!
My program passed pretty routine nothing outstanding occurred, and as pre-arranged Nana Raye was there to meet me walking out of the booth. Blocking my path to walk past, was Miss Managers' puppet, Bruce, for a weekly dose of harassment, to freely leave begrudgingly I signed the announcers agreement that Miss Manager Maria was going to take care of????
Surely now there's nothing left to badger me over!!!!
Rising above and wading away from the mess, befriended by Nick, he joined Nana Raye and me for coffee. Expressing my desire to meet Charlie, Nana Raye's other half, it was decided coffee was at her home same time different location next week. I also gave Nana Raye a bundle of wool and knitting needles being a gift from Loui, she was stoked and said she would get into the wool that evening....
Breaking evening peace I stirred Tia up in the bungalow, worked up she took it out on her bed shaking the shit out of it. Her bed ended in a tangle one side of mine, her doona the other side, and conveniently her treasured bone landed smack back right on top of my bed ☺....
Tonight saw an end to yet another writing pad I don't have a memory of honestly completing so many, I'm gaining a collection of cardboard backing from spent pads....

Tuesday 25 November 2003
One of those rare occasions that's never ignored, Tia woke me from deep sleep wanting outside, it took some time to again return to the same level of unconsciousness....
When my reluctant body got moving it wandered only as far as the back of the burnt out house, making inroads at clearing more of whatever built-up or grew over the deep layer of charcoal covering the path. The wheelbarrow got a workout ferrying the cocktail mix to the worst of the wheel ruts....
Stopped with feet up having lunch, watched a swallow through the open bungalow door collect brushed out discarded Tia fur for nesting material. Fur would create a warm palatial suite or make snuggy doonas???? It worked for Tia ☺ ....
Taking a liberating positive step away from material need I phoned cancelling the burden of a money eating credit card, my shoulders lifted just hanging up the receiver ☺ !!!!
Organised surprisingly early, almost including writing by 8p.m., left nothing to do but relax....
Hmmmm, a new concept ☺ ....

Wednesday 26 November 2003
I may have surprised myself last night being organised so early, tonight it's a different kettle of fish, it was 8:50pm before making a start on writing ☺ ....
Falling behind at home through time spent on the 'Save South Sister' from being logged campaign, I offered Rod a day's labour and today was it....
After sharing in a cuppa with Rod and Paul I unloaded the mower from Destiny and got busy bringing the yard down to size. Paula arrived with a freshly baked flour free cake, loaded in fruit it was the nicest cake I've eaten, sustaining our get up and go. Paula helped Rod in the vegie patch while I mowed, a comfortable, friendly time....
Pulling up, I stopped long enough for a cuppa and another piece of that yummy cake before Tia, Destiny and I meandered back the way we came and home to Rainbow Falls....
With thoughts of this time last year still strong, I phoned my Mildura home offering positive thoughts of love for Mum's pending colonoscopy. Feeling confident tomorrow's outcome will be what should have been for Mum's 60th birthday.... A bill of good health ☺ !!!!

Thursday 27 November 2003
Waking thoughts went directly to Mum. I called before the scheduled colonoscopy to tell Mum I loved her and wished only for a good outcome....
Due at the hospital 12:15pm, I kept an unfocussed waiting mind occupied on the mundane activity of washing clothes. Unable to apply my mind to anything requiring concentration, and filling time around laundry, watered the vegie patch, cleaned the vacuum bag and filter, de-furred my bed and other fiddly bits in the wait....
Thoughts constantly wandering to Mum, I was pleasantly surprised to speak to the woman in question first attempt at post theatre contact. Last year bad news was instant, this year Mum was instructed to see her surgeon the 10th December, I'll take it that 'no news is good news'....

Friday 28 November 2003
It was an absolutely amazing day for eagles. In the first instance, becoming aware of one near South Sister Range, it flew in my direction and did a close overhead pass then glided in the

direction of the ocean re-grouping there with another two. Later in the afternoon I heard a sound similar to that of a hot air balloon releasing gas, rousing curiosity I went outside to see what was causing the unfamiliar sound. Attention fixed skyward, plummeting from a height at a rate of knots, wings repelling air and falling feet first, positioned to strike unsuspecting prey, in close range an eagle disappeared out of sight in the gorge directly behind the shed. Awed by what I'd just witnessed, within the space of a few short minutes was treated to a second eagle taking the exact same action…. Breathtaking strength!!!!

A day to be entertained by birds. A pair of swallows collecting discarded Tia fur felt threatened when a kookaburra flew into their personal airspace, with no fear both swallows gave the kookaburra a stern warning to move on with tight circling, invasive passes….

Being entertained indoors as well as out I found the bungalow floor under Tia fur. An incoming call forced a shut down of the vacuum cleaner, promising myself I'd thank the voice on the other end stopping me from self-imposed torture…. Loui's a good friend ☺ ….

Saturday 29 November 2003

Tassie turned on a bloody hot one, the studio thermometer read on average 32° outside the entire afternoon, for respite, once again took Tia into the ten degree cooler studio with me…. Nothing out of the ordinary happened behind the microphone, I was happy to have the window wound down circulating hot air through Destiny driving toward home. Aware of the need for energy conservation during times of heat I stopped into the St. Marys Coach House Restaurant for a pizza ☺ ….

Comfortably home, observed another trait in me inherited from my Father, that is a reluctance to take my shoes off, stinking hot and they're still on. Everyday, habits observed in myself are images of my parents. Inner strength, uncompromising honesty and a feel for the environment, strong traits my parents uphold I'm proud to have adopted ☺ ….

Settled in for the evening a vehicle came up the driveway, being a courtesy visit by Michael, a professional shooter, letting me know he'd be shooting in the neighbours' paddocks. It's a preferable option to 1080 poison….

Sunday 30 November 2003

Turned on in a big way, heat has forced the rash decision to put butter in the fridge ☺ ….

Morning idled away with fiddly bits, pulled up for lunch I was gazing out the bungalow door watching life pass. Seeing what I thought to be leaves spiralling during free fall were actually smaller birds being pushed along by wind that quickly whipped up, catching a few with their tail feathers down ☺ ….

A large log used as a doorstop outside the cottage entrance made the shed to ease into retirement, instating an unearthed gnome as official door opener, a much tidier option….

Mum called giving me stick about a phone message I left two days ago, not real regular at checking their answering service, and with that knowledge I started the recording with "when you receive this message in a couple of days"…. Learning by repetition my intuition was correct ☺ ….

Monday 1 December 2003
After putting petrol in Destiny's tank then put a bit of petrol in my own diagonally across the road at the bakery....
Canvassing ratepayer's signatures beforehand for the 'Save South Sister' petition, stepping into the booth radio then passed pretty routine. Walking from the booth I caught a few minutes with the Station Manager Maria voicing my concern over crass, personally discriminating, harassing, offensive, and downright insulting behaviour that she encourages and her brother-in-law and station treasurer acts out at both the station and social functions. Bluntly honest, told her the office looked like a 15-year-old boys' dormitory, from the mirrored mat on the toilet floor to the tasteless posters decorating the treasurers office space. Maria laughed in reply and said "lucky you didn't go to the staff Christmas party, Bruce took his blow-up-doll there"....
Well lucky me!!!!
Driving away from unpleasantness, it was onward to Nana Raye's to meet her 'other half' Charlie over a brew. Both keen gardeners, I was given a tour of knowledge around their vegetable and flower gardens, a pleasure they put plenty of pride and time into ☺....
Running a delivery dropping a donated heater into Pam and Terry for the animals, responding to my knock, Pam in the company of two young wombats stood in the opened doorway. One of the little rascals being a much chubbier Earl, he was a frail vulnerable looking pink skin when I first saw him, now very active and playful at a healthier 5kg ☺....

Tuesday 2 December 2003
Garden watering revealed the recently planted strawberry plants had been badly mauled by a raiding possum sometime overnight, knocking the plants about, however the runners will come back....
The sun didn't show at all, on the other hand we didn't see any rain either, far from cold it was bloody warm mowing all the same ☺....
Ongoing fiddly bits sorted, the bulk of the working day was spent pushing the mower around opening new ground on top of the dam wall and surrounds, giving the walkway strip, 'the 80-yard dash to the loo', a tickle up also. Working on the dam wall Tia was intense sniffing through the fence, sure enough she was pointing out a snake, all going our separate ways????
Mowing till I could mow no more, it was time for 'beer and bath o'clock'. With dinner ticking away I ducked back to the bungalow briefly, returning to the cottage found Tia enjoying the diced bacon.... Little shit....

Wednesday 3 December 2003
Pleasantly, light drizzle kept me company locking up shop before turning in, stirring briefly through the night was happy to hear it persisting....
Better than an alarm clock thunder activated Tia's stress meter and the bungalow into activity. Up until 9a.m. a welcome 12mm had fallen delivered slow and soaking is beneficial. Received almost two months back, I had more of a concern of the rain gauge perishing from sun than being overworked, up until yesterday it had only measured a meagre 6mm in total....
Fogged in by low cloud with visibility down to 50 metres greeted the opening of the door and the great outdoors. That magic scenario sets a pretty slow appreciative pace, letting the day evolve around a trip to town for groceries, post and more mower fuel ☺....

On a random pat I felt a small lump on Tia's chest, in the dim evening light of the bungalow thought I was dealing with a splinter, pulling it with the tweezers, and offering resistance, the lump proved to be a tick, a first experience for both of us....

Thursday 4 December 2003
Beanie extracted from my head is a certain sign of warmer times ahead, damn I don't enjoy heat!!!!
Offering a fair chance of seeing what's on the ground doing the '80-yard dash', with sights set on exposing the loo I began mowing, mowing, and for something different more mowing ☺ ....
Pushing the overworked, falling apart machine towards two sycamore seedlings on the lawned expanse in front of the loo, saw more weeds in need of mower attention and got totally sidetracked tidying beyond expectations....
The aroma of fresh cut grass stirred the nostrils of cows from across the road, proving too much of a temptation, at any one time there were up to five free ranging in home paddocks. The buggers!!!!

Friday 5 December 2003
Over the top obsessed, endured another bloody big one pushing the lawnmower around....
Last time in town getting mower fuel Grant asked me what I used super petrol for, going on to say he only uses it for washing parts with: he wouldn't use it for anything else. With no shortage of unleaded at home I didn't hesitate to change my way of thinking....
Impressed by the yard transformation, to truly enjoy the experience is to idly walk it sipping quietly on a beer ☺ ....

Saturday 6 & Sunday 7 December 2003
Refining practices to daily journal entries, a party Saturday evening left me with writer's block....
Without checking, I stuffed the uninteresting looking lot of mail into the glove box, called into the St. Marys bakery then drove the winding road leading to the radio station for Saturdays shift....
From answering the phone taking requests to doing all the bits in between the four hour shift disappeared, at one stage I had programmed ten requests in a row ☺ ....
Hanging out at Loui's until the invited time arrived to help Kathie celebrate her 40th, credit for a well catered party. A big afternoon left me yawning before Cinderella was due to leave the ball, while my eyes were prepared to stay open headed home....
Pouring a cup full of energy into a Saturday afternoon program I've perfected the art of being a slow starter the day after. Feeling as strong as a half-sucked peppermint Sunday I made a token effort wandering with the shovel sharpening an already inspiring yard....
Ross and daughters popped in and we sat in shade on freshly mowed grass sharing a chat over a brew. Unable to leave without first patronising me enduring a progress tour, wandering the dam the resident tiger snake was again sighted in the same area as two days back....
Clearing mail from Destiny's glove-box late afternoon, and disguised in a Council letterhead envelope, to my surprise dated two days after expressing my sexual harassment and discrimination concerns to Miss Management, and every other offensive behaviour endured

from her brother-in-law, I received a disciplinary letter from the BODFM Board. The letter outlined possible breaches of announcer's guidelines I may have infringed. Reactive fools. Looks like management supports inflaming problems in a struggle for energy rather than solving them, blood is thicker than water????

Monday 8 December 2003
A crazy one I'm glad to have behind!!!!
The obvious Monday was of course radio day and with my new-found knowledge it was the last place I wanted to go. It didn't come as a shock to see the hunting pack and welcoming committee of intimidators there to meet and greet on arrival. Driving into Pendrigh Place to begin my scheduled program, the Boards chairman and treasurers drinking buddy, was on cue walking into the street towards the station. Pulling up and stopping Neil where he stood, I accepted the offer mentioned in the letter to discuss its contents, arranging to meet following a hair appointment directly after my shift....
Unwilling to accept one moment of intimidation I smiled politely rolling with the 'I know you know and you know I know but no one is saying anything', with a dash of stilted politeness thrown in over three long hours stifled any breathable oxygen in the atmosphere....
A stop at the hairdressers being the only light moment of the St. Helens trip, even there the chairman phoned checking up on progress. Pampering behind I went to decipher the letters contents. The chairman's professional approach was to introduce the treasurer and source of my problem into our meeting, objecting to Bruce's presence Neil insisted he stay as his witness....
The only breach outlined that I had no clue about was the second of the three points so I continued with the hunting pack. Slow progress established the letter wasn't worth the sacrificed piece of paper it was printed on they were simply on a witch-hunt. When the chairman allowed his witness to take the floor, at that point I regained control of the conversation and left, nothing more constructive was going to occur. Odd, I complain about sexual harassment and discrimination and I'm being persecuted????
Constant persecution is taking its toll I've stopped having fun and was bloody happy to arrive home....

Tuesday 9 December 2003
I didn't think ink would make paper following a rollercoaster of emotions; energy and inspiration were resting....
The morning evaporated on the phone. Neil the chairman phoned sparking a succession of calls, with no substance to beat me up with in the initial witch-hunt letter, our phone conversation was brief and concise. Neil said that because of the way I spoke to a board member, namely Bruce, at Monday's meeting until further notice I had been suspended as an announcer, gearing up the energy struggle and still avoiding my initial complaint voiced to Miss Management Maria. Because I wouldn't conform, it was easier to make me go away than deal with sexual harassment and discrimination....
The grapevine regarding my suspension was switched on causing a wave of communication. The saddest call I made was to Nana Raye letting her know our segment was over, her words "they've buggered it up now then, haven't they", stuck in my mind. Pledging her loyalty said

she wouldn't freelance with any other announcer, her words were the only thing to move me throughout this stupid ordeal....

Back to full-time farm body, with the help of my best friend had a go at tidying bits the mower couldn't reach. Feeling as flat as a shit carter's hat, again I didn't get too hyperactive before calling it a night....

Wednesday 10 & Thursday 11 December 2003

I began Wednesday quietly by getting ready for town to restock the cupboards. Stepping into the Post Office to pay an account, and willing to share the news, Peter and Krystal were shocked to hear of my suspension, likewise Rod????

My mind however was preoccupied with more important thoughts, like those relating to Mum's visit to the surgeon and colonoscopy results. Heart beating hard in my chest, Mum answered the phone with the brilliantly fantastic news of 'all clear' ☺ !!!! What a determined strong woman, 'my Mum', a deserving result for a deserving person ☺ ....

To finalise a perfect day, icing on the cake, it tried to rain but only enough to tease not of any great use....

Celebrating Mum's brilliant results, uncontained, I shouted out loud from the bungalow door, 'I love you Mum', with a broad beaming smile. The phone hasn't been a friend for a while, thank Christ the bubble has burst ☺ ....

Following restless sleep, I rolled over Thursday plugged in the CD player and stayed in bed for as long as Tia would let me listening to 'morning tea with Lou'....

Catching me before I left for a doctors appointment, Mum and Dad gave me a courtesy call, after reading tributes in their local paper they informed me Fan's father was now at peace with his battle with cancer, Fan herself phoned later....

Giving the doctor a brief personal history I was prescribed rest, leaving with a medical certificate for three months to go home and do just that.... I'm looking forward to the time out....

Following recent events I might just sample relaxing at home enjoying a humble lifestyle....

Friday 12 December 2003

Usually come Friday my mind is gearing up deciding music to play and what to script for the 'this week in St. Marys' segment. Eliminating preparation to make a program sound presentable opened my eyes to the number of hours slurped up outside of on-air time. It's nice for the time being to not have to think of anything outside our boundary fence....

My get up and go has got up and went, with a body that flatly refuses to endure long stretches of physical activity simply keeping up hygiene takes what's on offer, from carting water to laundry was enough to keep me honest and out of trouble today....

Daring them with laundry dangling from the line, rain cloud built-up on and off, sending me running for the line a light shower stopped almost as soon as I got there....

Saturday 13 December 2003

Bed de-furred, aired, sponged over and re-made ready for me to find my way into this evening, and a cold beer sitting patiently for me to finalise this journal entry, its a well organised combination ☺ ....

I do miss the 'Tassie Sue' high listener interaction and characters a Saturday program offered, but since my suspension it's been a relief to return more personal choices back learning to breathe again....

Without having struck a blow, Rod phoned with a South Sister update, hanging up from solving the problems of the world and keeping the receiver imprinted on my palm, Mary-Anne was close behind extending a dinner invitation for Friday. Settled in for a chat, Mary-Anne mentioned she played a song for me during her Wednesday evening program, 'You'll never walk alone' a heart warming gesture. She also made mention that not all committee members knew of the formulation of the letter I received???? That comes as no surprise....

Quite a number of announcers have thoughtfully taken the time to call, Neville expressed surprise but wasn't shocked by my suspension he said I was the seventh announcer this year to leave due to management???? I've become a bodfm statistic ☺....

My curiosity had me listening to Kristy start the program that I once did, to her credit she did a good job and played good music, I wish her well....

Doing anything that meant being shaded under a roof out of the bloody heat didn't offer too many options, I resorted to tinkering around cleaning. Now it's time to murder a couple of beers ☺ !!!!

Sunday 14 & Monday 15 December 2003
Sunday began rather hard and fast at 6:45am precisely, being sick, Tia vomited three times from my bed to the door....

Treating myself to a little decadence I pulled the reins in escaping the heat with a book doing a re-read of 'The Alchemist', a simple enjoyable story line. My little mate wasn't too active either Tia was happy to keep her thermostat down snoozing by my side....

Bellies full and settled in for the evening, perfectly on cue Sheila phoned and the rest is now history ☺....

Monday started with cuddles rather than vomit, a preferred option ☺....

Needing food to decorate the bare shelves steered a course for the hill. Not mucking about to escape another hot one, unloaded rubbish, went to the Post Office, did a quick shop then went straight home....

Sitting in the bungalow doorway cuppa'd up on the step, watched for some time a pair of eagles gliding in thermals above South Sister Range. Remaining seated and observing from my doorway perch, the colour change in the yard is becoming blatantly obvious, lush green is quickly transforming to fast drying amber. The earth is screaming out for a drink, each day sees less water and quality in the dam. Its sobering at the realisation of how vulnerable we mere mortals are to the elements, nature has the upper hand....

Tuesday 16 December 2003
Making a firm decision, taking the first step outside, that I would only migrate under a roof somewhere.... I'm definitely no reptile....

Quick at wilting in direct stinging rays, I took respite in the cottage scratching the surface altering its function from a makeshift store everything to liveable and homely....

Listening to the radio distracting my brain from cleaning, in an act of spontaneity Mary-Anne dedicated to me a personal favourite, 'Concrete Blonde – Close to home', she's a thoughtful

sweetie. Someone else was tuned into Mary-Anne's program, the following request came from Ross to Taz, 'Cheap Trick – I won't back down'…. What a pick-me-up ☺ !!!!
On a trip into the bungalow I found a message on the answering machine from Nana Raye, she hates answering machines so the effort was huge ☺ !!!! Brief, but straight from the heart, "Hello Tazzy, its Nana Raye here, when you coming back up St. Helens again, catch up later"….
Returning her call, and in town Friday, we made plans to get together before my dinner invitation, she misses her 'Nana Raye's pick of the week' segment….

Wednesday 17 December 2003
Cooking in paradise, nature's thermostat is stuck on furnace, one benefit of the unrelenting oppressive heat is it has stopped lawn growing. Escaping from ridiculous mercury levels the cottage was again the beneficiary further expanding on the interior image change….
A visit from Ross gave me all the reason needed to down tools for a brew. Bringing his gun, following up on the snake sighting at the dam and still in the same area as both previous sightings with one shot it was put to sleep. Killing animals is not a decision made easy or I go out of my way to do, the dam frog population might support the decision however….
It hardly passes unnoticed on a terminating single lane dirt road when in a 48-hour period somewhere between thirty to forty earthmoving trucks towing trailers rattle past out front. Entering fully loaded via a makeshift road running through a paddock at the neighbours, loaded for road construction, sadly at a guess I reckon they're opening a road for log truck access. At this point my concern is the safety aspect, the only access road is a single lane it can be tight to pass another car let alone a 55-tonne fully loaded truck!!!!
The valley and surrounding mountain ranges were silhouetted with a smoke haze. Smoke to the intensity that anywhere else I've lived would raise alarm bells, a sad complacency not to be concerned, highly likely a burn off following forestry operations, a common sight here….

Thursday 18 December 2003
A car coming up the driveway got me out of bed and grabbing for clothes getting the fresh day started. A courtesy visit from a Gunns Timber Company representative was to explain what's going on across the road. John quoted there would be four trucks daily leaving the site, Monday through to Friday until the end of February. With the knowledge of hindsight, John proved to be a smokescreen front delivering a load of bullshit. Gaining access to log state forest through the neighbours' property, state forest is supposed to belong to the people of the state not owned by the elected government????
I prayed for rain to keep truck traffic out and my wish was granted, starting 3p.m.-ish it remained steady. Watching rain cloud move in was enchanting, cloud draped the range and lazily tumbled down tiredly dragging the weighty load through trees, magic…. A welcome drop on a parched earth….
Surveying the cottage to make a start, before striking a blow Charles popped in for a visit giving me good reason to put the kettle on….
The back of the working day broken, I called it a day before firing up. By 8p.m.-ish low cloud dropped visibility obscuring the latest roadwork from view, a mystical feel, with showers resuming more is welcome….

Friday 19 & Saturday 20 December 2003

As planned, Mary-Anne's and a drive to St. Helens were on the menu for dinner Friday. That occasion alone was enough to give myself permission for the night off writing....

Wandering out bucket in hand on a mission for water to spruce up for a big Friday night out I crossed paths with yet another snake, this one on the lawn between the cottage and vegie patch. Territorial, and too close to home, pumped full of adrenalin while simultaneously holding the shovel, I applied Ross' tip to use the back of the shovel head rather than jab at it with the blade. Quickly, shaky hands sent it to snaky heaven....

Making my dinner invitation with Mary-Anne and Theo was achieved in a round about way. Beginning the round about I dropped books back to Ross, slipped the key into the Post Office box, returned a CD to Max, stocked up with non-perishables, then had a yarn over a cuppa with Nana Raye and Charlie finding them both dosed up with the flu....

Reaching the final destination, I walked in totally surprised to see Mary-Anne's niece Rosy girl sitting there large as life, having left the area six months earlier she snuck back for Christmas, there was plenty of warm cuddles exchanged. Keeping me out until midnight, I had a lovely time sharing a very social evening ☺....

Needless to say Saturday was slow out of the blocks. For a change in sounds, instead of being woken by heavy machinery warming up across the road it was the bellowing of three cows happily snacking in the yard. Cows freely wandering in is becoming a regular event????

Tia's natural instincts kicked in and she willingly accepted the challenge without hesitation to 'moove' the old lumps of lard out the gate. Challenged by a reluctant cow, Tia didn't back down, having all three out the gate within seconds like a true champion she was in her element. Full of adrenalin Tia walked tall and proud keeping a watchful eye on the herd grazing in the paddock across the road, daring one to cross the line ☺.... Cows out, the gate was shut and left that way....

Back into transforming the cottage I vacuumed everything in sight from the roof to the walls and floor, no spider web or blade of grass was safe, always advancing forward....

Sunday 21 December 2003

With my little mate content with her tummy full, I contemplated life over a soup bowl of milo watching the world pass from the bungalow door for as long as it took ☺....

Firing into life, it was the bungalows turn to benefit from the vacuum, happy with the outcome I replenished water supplies in the 'clean' cottage before taking one of the seldom walks to the falls. The largest of the two waterfalls fed from South Sister Range has reduced to a dribble, the hillside is going to take some wetting up, however the expansive view at any given time is spectacular....

Strolling back from the falls an object not fitting into the natural colour scheme raised attention enough for a look, identifying the mangled object as the umbrella that escaped from the loo in the snow shower. Breaking into laughter, the umbrella corpse was lodged under the boundary fence where the stream feeding the second waterfall enters Rainbow Falls ☺!!!! No more wondering ☺????

Monday 22 December 2003
Easing my brain into conscious activity, far exceeding the abrupt harshness of heavy machinery, was the soothing rhythm of rain. Overnight 48mm found its way into the gauge, near enough to 2-inches, a good soaking. Even the falls could be heard flowing from the loo, a first for a while.
A few short, sharp showers followed up to supplement last nights soaking, pleasantly slowing heavy activity across the road is nice....
I don't know where my energy's been lately but I'm not inspired to break out and tackle anything requiring it. Making a token effort with long handled secateurs and pruning saw I started breaking pruned branches down to heater size, storing and stacking firewood like a good little squirrel ☺....
This welcome rain has nicely lifted bath water quality, being a bit ordinary of late it made me wonder if I was gaining anything by bathing????
Starting tonight on page 401, the previous page peeled off the writing pad was officially the 400th hand written to finalise journal folder number ten!!!! Who would have thought ☺????
Well, we've eaten, dishes done, journal up to date, 9:34pm now the night is my own....
Ahhhh....

Tuesday 23 December 2003
Again pleasantly waking only to the sounds of nature active. A 'get up' paw tap from Tia much sooner than hoped, I took life in stride at my usual sedate pace. Forward thinking to stock up for the holiday period shut down, prepared the family for a dash over the mountain.... Rubbish finding a bin, Destiny's fuel topped up, a must visit to the bakery, and generously, a Post Office box stop found chocolates rattling around inside. Feeling good I then packed enough groceries over the front passenger seat to survive a few more days....
Happening to be walking by and in for a bit of Christmas cheer, Allan invited me back to his place to share a Christmas beer that was accepted. Leaving Allan's, I met Pam out front and went there next to deliver a bag of donated bits for the animals from Mary-Anne. Staying for a healthy chat, a quiet trip into town turned into quite a social occasion ☺....
Having a beer in town didn't inspire any action at home, so I didn't resist the mood ripping the lid off another beer instead ☺.... The end....

Wednesday 24 & Thursday 25 December 2003
There was no hope of writing last night I lost the evening entirely. Starving by the time dinner was ready I couldn't dish it up quick enough, with a content tummy and empty plate only then did I remember the fried mushrooms and onion left waiting to be dished up.... Oooop's....
After dinner beer assisted tiredness caused a lay down, waking fully dressed on top of the bed with the bungalow door open around 11p.m.-ish ☺....
Wednesday was pretty sedate simply putting bungalow life in order. Waiting patiently for me to finish the mundane task Tia parked her bum in a favourite spot outside under the bungalow window. Letting loose with a warning bark, never before has Tia barked at anyone approaching, with the beauty of hindsight she's a brilliant judge of character....
Walking up the driveway our visitor turned out to be a bloke by the name of Terry, living the other side of North Sister at German Town he walked in the front gate with the agenda of

wanting to manage home paddocks for contract hay. Coming with a reference being a friend of Ross', after negotiation, we decided to have his cattle eat the paddocks out first. Standing in the driveway over a handshake deal, leaving money out of the equation, we traded cattle agistment for plumbing help in the cottage....

Seemingly under control, I left the front gate open Wednesday only to find a cow helping itself to a Christmas feed inside the front gate Thursday. Pleased with a green light, and in her element, Tia short shifted the cow out the gate in quick time ☺....

Extending the spirit of Christmas, I called family then took a couple of wrong turns to find Trout Creek Reserve and Kathie and Roger. Over a couple of light beers, the afternoon was relaxed. Trout Creek Reserve is a pretty spot its surrounds however are scarred by stripped bare logging coupes robbing the beauty from the drive of getting there....

Coming down from the festive excitement life resumed its mellow pace....

Friday 26 December 2003

Just like that, Christmas is gone for another year.... Click....

At a reasonable hour Tia extended the 'paw tap' treatment moving me from horizontal. Winding down an almost spent year doing nothing extraordinary, after a leisurely breakfast enough water was collected to break the back of the washing....

The 48mm moisture drop has encouraged the tap over the cattle trough to flow again, on its own separate line it scoops from near the top of the dam. Water quality from the tap is transparently sparkling. The outcome makes it a pleasure waiting for the bloody slow flow rate to fill a bucket ☺....

Partaking in a 'quiet ale' at day's end my little mate left me with a lasting impression. Dying on home soil for the claiming, Tia took over management of a dead possum. Deciding to sample the wares, I glanced over at the precise moment to witness the intestine being pulled out like a piece of elastic. The mouth full of beer I had just taken took a lot of effort to swallow.... She really does love me ☺....

Saturday 27 December 2003

Well blink, and there goes another snapshot in life ☺....

Spoiling me with her caring, sharing, Tia dragged the rank aroma of the dead possum beside the bungalow, what a treasure....

Without letting the grass grow under his feet, Terry in the company of his son arrived to set-up electric fencing along the driveway to cow proof paddocks. With only the top wire being electrically active it won't affect Tia if she decides to duck under the bottom wire....

Putting my get up and go to work I mowed while Tia constantly dropped a tennis ball in its path ☺!!!!

Adjourned to the shed taking time breaking down small branches for firewood, I first heard the clackety clack of a lot of hooves, then a herd of cattle in view passed the front gate with an entourage of vehicles following up. A 4WD and trailer of calves chased by cattle and followed by three motor bikes got the large bellowing frames settled into their holiday home. Initially taking Tia for a walk on lead to gauge her reaction she didn't seem to care, meeting the entourage at the front gate I invited the crew back for beer o'clock....

Tia seems to be adjusting to all twenty-seven of the new residents without fuss, off lead it was business as usual....

Sunday 28 December 2003
Cow watching has turned into an occupation. Never having ever lived this close to them I'm enjoying observing their habits nearly as much as Tia. Large black bodies sitting in the afternoon shade the blackwood tree provided were seemingly invisible. Tia has accepted the cow's presence quite readily, that makes life easier for the next few months.... Phew....
I didn't get too excited outside, merely exposing a few metres of fenceline by the cottage before taking sun smart advice from cows and heading under cover in the shed. Pruning saw on the ready I cut branches to heater size pieces, only winding down from there ☺....

Monday 29 December 2003
A bloody hot, dry, stinker, one would be excused for thinking they were back in Mildura. Nearing 10p.m. and no sea breeze arrived for relief left me shoeless and in a t-shirt. Motionless calm and deathly quiet outside, individual sounds are heard with exact clarity....
Stripping my feet free of shoes is a rare occasion, I'm soooo much like my Father, breaking new ground I confidently walked from the shed to the bungalow bare feet, very liberating. Recollecting a time in the early stages it was near on impossible to even play ball with Tia in the yard ☺????
Today's movements aren't actually going to create a best seller, I bathed in readiness for town, discarded rubbish, made a bakery, Post Office and supermarket stop, pulled into Rods on the return trip, without finding him home continued onward to Rainbow Falls....
Occupying idle hands with the pruning saw making firewood, stifling heat drove me into energy conservation and I was forced to sit down over a cool beer. With the setting sun we adjourned to the bungalow for a spot of cow watching. Sitting outside below the window, with only two thin strands of wire separating her from grazing cows merely five metres away, her first exposure to cows Tia's just content to watch, making me very proud ☺....

Tuesday 30 December 2003
Another bloody skin scorcher in paradise, 6:30p.m.-ish and its still 35° outside, bloody, bloody hot for us Taswegians, that severe even butter had to be refrigerated. I'm moving closer to the South Pole!!!!
Slipping into self-preservation I wasn't motivated to go hard at all, keeping a slow pace I migrated to the coolest hidey-hole being the shed, once again fiddling around with the pruning saw breaking down branches. Moving from the sanctuary only for the 5p.m. chemist script delivery to St. Marys for asthma puffers, leaving it to the last minute to battle heat made no difference: the sting was still active in the scorpions' tail!!!!
Turning back for home is where our journey took the slow road, overheating and starving for fuel Destiny decided she would stop for a cool down. Requiring just a short wait before getting cracking again Destiny took us only a couple of kilometres further before a repeat performance. A sit in shade for three-quarters of an hour helped her with the remaining distance to reach home soil.... Certainly not a good sign....

Wednesday 31 December 2003 & Thursday 1 January 2004
I've all but stopped in my tracks without relief from punishing heat....
Oblivious to it being the last day of the year, Wednesday at Rainbow Falls proceeded as normal as it ever does. Driven in to escape what was happening out favoured the idea of the large space of the coolest building. Time spent down the shed is showing results, the largest branches are now firewood size, and if only momentarily floor space is reclaimed.... Yahoo....
Getting Mum and Dad's answering service phoning through New Years thoughts they should get the message in a couple of days ☺....
Settled in the coolness the shed offered, feet up with a beer ready to kiss the old year goodbye and welcome in the new one, Ross arrived in perfect timing to join in kicking back over idle chat.... Making the transitional changeover into 2004 quietly....
Harsh intentions of the elements didn't falter from extreme, greeting in the fresh day of a New Year with all furnaces firing!!!!
Brain jet lag from having worked within the framework of the economy, and officially a recognised public holiday, I had it off also. Choosing to fill self imposed decadence I simply elected to take a leisurely bath with music to suit the mood, morning tea moved on to lunch, afternoon tea to beer o'clock and dinner, now here I am and its nearly bed time. If the remainder of this New Year stays as relaxed as the start my wrinkles and grey hair shouldn't increase too much ☺....

Friday 2 January 2004
Well bloody hell here we are full steam ahead into the New Year as if the euphoric fanfare associated with the previous few days never existed????
Just getting on with maintaining the comforts of home I heard a voice in the distance, thinking it was kids across the road paid no attention. The calling out continued and got closer going out I met a wandering soul, Jude, with car problems, actually one big problem. Skidding out of the T-intersection at Lohreys Road and failing to negotiate the turn her car went over the embankment, not a healthy practice in mountainous country, only the boot and rear wheels were visible from the road.... Ooooh.... Needing something heavier than an overheating sick Destiny to tow with, I left after doing what I could at getting car assistance to the next level of recovery....
Warm and still active, kept Destiny's nose pointed in the direction of town, making the highest point passing between the Sister's Mountains she began chugging, reaching the apex it was down hill all the way. Grant's was an obvious stop. An important link in our chain, Destiny was booked in for a health diagnosis. Parking under a large shady tree I left the team as cool as possible resting while I did the supermarket, bakery, pub thing. Loaded, I took the Destiny express as far as she chose to take us, with a few chugging second thoughts she gallantly made the highest point, even rolling in neutral she'd get us home from there....

Saturday 3 January 2004
It wasn't until late afternoon that respite arrived with a change, without producing any rain it did however drop the mercury to a functioning temperature. Constant unforgiving heat is wearing thin, zapping inspiration my get up and go got up and went....

Doing the latest craze of cow watching, their behavioural pattern altered signalling a change in weather by spending no time under the blackwood tree. Since their introduction to home soil, and observing patterns, I could almost set my watch by where cows are positioned in the paddocks at any given time of the day ☺....

Sunday 4 January 2004
Mid morning I heard the click clack of neighbouring cows swinging their lardy hips down the road moaning and groaning. Bemused watching home cows, particularly the bloody huge Murray Grey bull, stand up and take notice of their passing neighbours....
The tap over, and including the cattle trough, responding to a drop in dam level through evaporation have stopped flowing: until rain rectifies that situation I've resorted to commando rolls under the electric fence to get water from the hose outlet at the irrigation line. It's easier to get water in the morning, cows graze by the driveway evenings....
Breaking loose with an energy spurt the bungalow benefited with a vacuum, without going too crazy I escaped the electrical goods allergy darting to the haven. A quick sweep, and everything in neat piles, the shed looks cleaner and spacious, only requiring the combination of rain and a cool night to burn the fiddle fart pruning off-cuts to find the floor once again....
The festive season brought a standstill to logging; the arrival of a couple of trucks with heavy equipment is a reminder it's not over....

Monday 5 & Tuesday 6 January 2004
Not every night words flow out of the pen easily....
Woken 4a.m.-ish Monday by the first of a steady flow of trucks, approximately fifteen in total, carting loads used for road construction. Driving the mountain for town is like playing Russian-Roulette with heavy traffic. A local resident told me a group lobbied to get a school bus operating in Dublin Town but the idea was rejected due to terrain, yet 55-tonne loaded log trucks are acceptable????
The course for the day was set on Destiny, she received a pampering starting with a vacuum by the bungalow before intense stinging UV moved in. We retreated to her bedroom for windows and a sponge bath until the water ration ran out ☺....
Hearing the seemingly slow trip of a truck braking its way down the mountain began 5a.m.-ish Tuesday morning, disruptive, loud and intrusive it's hard to compress feelings of anger.
Rattled apart wondering what the hell to get out of bed for, and emotions in need of stabilising, as if scripted, Rod phoned and a good chat brought my feet back down to the ground. By conversations end I was ready to manage whatever the daylight hours ahead decided I should have a go at. Friends make life worthwhile ☺....
The routine morning job of doing commando rolls under electric fencing to fill a bucket with water was momentarily foiled when no water flowed from the hose. By grazing around it, cows sabotaged their own water supply turning an inline main tap off, a flick of the wrist and water was again rushing....
Affording myself an afternoon of plucking and pampering, topped it with the main event of bathing. A dirty irrigation line is offering ordinary quality water currently it's hard to know whether bathing is making me cleaner????

Wednesday 7 January 2004
Fortunately now an occasion as rare as hen's teeth, and it's a plan to keep it that way, was up with the beeping alarm....
Leaving Destiny in the honest capable hands of Grant, an ever on the ready attentive Allan took us home via St. Helens. It was fantastic to be in the passenger seat, a road travelled literally hundreds of times and so much is missed concentrating from the driver's seat....
Calling in on Mary-Anne, a woman who knows how to set a comfortable socialising environment, she decorated a table in food and cuppa's on the ready, her Mum, Theo and Rosy helped fill the house with homely chatter. In the midst of renovations, I accepted Mary-Anne's offer of taking home a piece of carpet to assist with warming the cottage. Socially primed, we moved to the next social appointment with Phillip doing more of the same ☺....
Returning to a waiting Destiny, Grant feels pretty sure she's got a radiator blockage, again getting warm running the gauntlet home, its time to bite the bullet and book her in for a radiator overhaul....
Cosy and warm behind glass in the bungalow watching a cow grazing, it raised its tail, pee'd, and not once did it stop shovelling the food in????

Thursday 8 January 2004
An important link in home life, without a second thought made the call and Destiny's scheduled radiator overhaul begins Monday, we'll be without her at home for about one week. The radiator has to be sent to Launceston for an intensive clean, by weeks end she'll almost be entirely recycled ☺....
Tearing myself away from the bungalow, Tia and I got into our routine doing the daily water games around carting the stuff for bathing and a drink for the garden.... A splash for Tia, and a dash for the bucket ☺....
A wolf in sheep's clothing, weather wise its hard to select a suitable wardrobe, wind arrived with its own chill factor, in opposing contrast, when wind dropped sun had enough magnifying sting to burn skin quickly. Pleasurably unpredictable, my only philosophy on Tasmania's weather is to go prepared for all occasions????

Friday 9 January 2004
Facing the world with energy to burn I got on with it....
A quick bush mechanic job on the mower to hold the falling apart bits together, I squeezed a couple more tanks out of it. Making a start on the front yard of the burnt out house, for something new to think about and a fresh wound, the mowers front end collapsed.... There and then I packed up my bat and ball and went home!!!!
Putting thoughts into a mountain trip to stock up, being hot and windy didn't want to push my luck with Destiny overheating, I also didn't fancy the idea of getting stuck on the road looking down the barrel of 55-tonnes of log truck bearing down on us. An executive decision was made to stay home????
'Plan B', take a leisurely bath, pamper oneself, write in the journal early (nearly done ☺), indulge in a couple of relaxing beers preparing dinner then have the evening off.... Most of the way there ☺!!!!

Saturday 10 January 2003
What I love about life is everyday it offers something different to experience....
Targeting Rod's for 10a.m., a trait inherited from my parents, I was courteously punctual. Unable to handle the complete distance to St. Marys, I took up Rod's offer suggesting I hop in with him from his place for the drive into town, minimising Destiny's chances of overheating by only doing half the trip and having a rest in between.... The plan worked perfectly....
Jumping in with Rod and Hannah for town, keenly sighted by Rod, we pulled over to watch a pair of eagles until they shifted thermals....
The morning morphed into early afternoon eventuating into a relaxed social occasion of shopping, chatting, cuppa's and more chatting, then home to Rainbow Falls. Destiny treated us to a 'one go' trip to get there ☺.... Phew....
Refining 'cow watching' comforts I put Tia's bed on the window box in the bungalow so she can keep an eye on her world in luxury. A regular family evening entertainment, I feel like a parent that plonks their child in front of a television, Tia however, is watching a real life documentary....
Bum pressed against a 'cow watching' Tia, writing pad on top of the bar fridge, I sat to write....

Sunday 11 January 2004
In keeping with a pattern suiting all players, morning is the time to commando roll under the temporary electric fencing for water....
Checking on his cows, I invited Terry in for a brew, full of good intentions and a fella who says yes a lot, over cuppa's we talked about fulfilling his end of our handshake deal of getting flowing water to the cottage....
Preparing dinner, Robert, an elected board member at the radio station phoned, not happy with management and feeling helplessly outnumbered, he was going to tackle the issues of my suspension at tomorrows scheduled board meeting but it had been postponed for a month. Telling Robert I was going to take the matter further, he supported my decision.... I can only hope sanity prevails ☺ ????

Monday 12 January 2004
The start of another fresh week, it won't be long before we kiss January goodbye....
A bloody big test was placed on the patience of us timid Rainbow Falls folk, being woken by the first truck blurting its engine brakes coming down the mountain 6a.m.-ish. Not a happy camper, I phoned John, the Gunns logging company representative, expressing my dissatisfaction of way beyond the stated four trucks per day striking anytime in a 24-hour period!!!! John said he would see what changes could be made and would get back to me 'this afternoon' or maybe he should have said 'that afternoon', maybe in the morning????
Unloading and getting past dissatisfaction I re-snuggled for a restart at 8a.m., turning attitude around got back to the basics of being thankful of who and where I was....
The day arrived for Destiny's stay with Grant, loaded with enough groceries for a good stint at home, Allan couldn't offer enough help ensuring Tia and I got safely up the hill....

Tuesday 13 January 2004
It was rather a bureaucratic bullshit morning. Woken rudely early by bloody trucks again, I tried phoning John to share my waking thoughts but luckily for us both he wasn't answering. Returning my call 8:15am, John's solution to my problem is to run trucks from midnight through to 6a.m., go figure that logic???? My main issue with sharing our access road was glossed over....
Having endured enough bullshit, Tia and I slipped into water collecting giving the vegie patch a drink while on the trot. Happy to be distracted, so happy with the distraction in fact, remained in the vegie patch weeding leaving my little mate to sort and compost, administering a wonderful therapy session....
Temporarily repaired windows were treated to more temporary repairs, if anything, just to keep bugs out because it certainly doesn't know how to rain....
Contradicting any offered time schedule, a truck entered the site 7:30pm, operating whenever is bloody unfriendly and unfair....

Wednesday 14 January 2004
Wind offered respite carrying the sound of 24-hour operating trucks away in the direction of the ocean and taking the edge off sleep disturbing, full blast, braking sounds!!!!
Staying in sync with cows me and my little mate began the usual morning water carting routine starting with the cottage and winding up in the vegie garden. Without rain to enhance, water quality has risen to very good, it seems cows taking their water 100 metres further down the line has given the pipe a much needed flush ☺....
Wandering doing bits 'n' pieces I began the wander pruning limbs from the pesky sycamore tree in the cottage yard, gaining attention and close by, the flue on the cottage roof was re-covered causing another rain gauge re-calibration. Still with a bit of get up and go, relieved a tube of silicon sealing cottage windows attempting to eradicate water leaks, dare I say 'waterproofed'....
Going in for a big finish I made inroads vacuuming timber shavings, legacy of Mary-Anne and Theo's home renovations, out of the piece of carpet I so kindly accepted. Pulling the plug on the beast is where I gave up for beer o'clock ☺....
All but given up in hopelessness on the issue of 55-tonne trucks towing trailers along our shared single lane dirt access road, kept on the back foot, by the time responsive action can be mustered the job will be over. Searching for a quick shot at public awareness I phoned the Examiner Newspaper. Liz left a return message, stating they wouldn't run the story because there is going to be a meeting early February to discuss log trucks and road usage.... That doesn't bloody well help me now however the issue of shared road suitability for log truck use should be tackled....

Thursday 15 January 2004
Making a conscious decision, for sanity sake, to better manage the random truck noise invasion by remembering to enjoy what I have and knowing limitations, gave myself permission for tranquillity....

Routinely doing the water thing enduring another bloody hot dry stinger, brittle grass crackles underfoot walking over it with little greenery left. The reverse transformation is just as quick from brown to green after rain it just has to happen....

Ready to have another go vacuuming the piece of carpet, I opted to chat with Mum and Dad instead, smart choice. Still waiting for me to return to the deed, I put in a solid effort, timber shavings entwined in the pile are a bastard to budge....

A phone call from Grant brought with it good news, Destiny was ready to come home ☺!!!!

Friday 16 January 2004
The only measurable achievement today was bringing Destiny home regaining our wandering freedom ☺....

Willingly volunteering to pick us up to be reunited with Destiny, Allan walked the last couple of hundred metres to home. Causing Allan to walk, a stretch of fresh spray-on tar was laid on the road out front to help settle the major dust problem stirred, and to slow the rapid erosion the impact from the arrival of every truck makes. On the up side, I've received kilograms of topsoil free....

Grant had Destiny running like a champion, leaving me feel confident to take her anywhere, a refreshing business trait, Grant is a true value for money, bloody honest bloke.... A breath of fresh air....

An internal magnet wouldn't let me pass drawing me into the bakery, supermarket and a beer restock Destiny's nose was pointed at the mountain. In the short absence we were in town a truck had driven smack bang up the centre of the wet tar stripping its wheel marks back to dirt partially destroying the mornings work. The exercise in waste offered Destiny a tar free trip to the front gate....

Saturday 17 January 2004
Contemplating rising out from under the doona Loui gave me all the reason needed to stay put, ready to have a chat, together we broke the back of the morning nattering. Mentioning to Ross I'd pop in for a brew late morning rescheduled for early afternoon ☺....

A long time between drinks, we're at last feeling moisture from rain, beginning early afternoon it steadily eased its way in for a spell.... Yahoo!!!!

Fulfilling a promise I'd planted in my brain, the first cold wet day that presented itself would be spent down the shed cranking the heater converting rubbish to heat. In all reality I'm just simply making way for more. That day arrived so don't call me I'll call you ☺....

Sunday 18 January 2004
What was to be an afternoon of burning prunings down the shed yesterday extended into evening. It was a pure pleasure watching the yard transform to green with a quick inch of rain from my perch inside by the hot drum, in a dry, warm, comfortable position ☺....

A power surge or stoppage through the night sent the clock flashing for a reset, unaware of the exact time I soon jumped to attention with the sound of a vehicle arriving....

Terry was checking on his cows, putting the kettle on we discussed the probability of opening other grassed areas for grazing, he mentioned the extreme dry has dominoed into a shortage of bail feed. My grass covering is someone else's treasure???? We all see value differently....

A total of 43mm fell from the sky a very welcome almost 2-inches, washing raised truck dirt from cows their pelts glistened....
Excited by soft wet earth, I got lost with my little mate having soothing brain therapy in the vegie patch planting out tomato and corn seedlings complements of Rod, certified organic of course. Resembling a garden, now supporting beds of garlic, strawberries, tomatoes, corn, lavender, a climbing rose and rosemary, my how times are changing ☺ ....

Monday 19 January 2004
Watering the garden highlighted another surfacing challenge, having to outsmart the natives to collect the fruits of labour ☺ ....
The threat of the yard getting out of control woolly drove my reluctance for mechanics to do a bush mechanic job with limited resources patching up the mowers front end, soon there will only be wheels and a motor. The mower proved a bit flimsy to handle the pace at Rainbow Falls, after a little imaginative thought it's held together for a bit longer....
Planning a trip to St. Helens to book the ferry to reach the shores of the mainland, and in need of escaping the damaging invasive sounds of log trucks, I turned the occasion into a pleasant social outing. Phoning around made arrangements with those wanting to catch me for a chat over a brew....
As a last resort over my concern of sharing the road with trucks I contacted the police, entering conversation I then exited politely and quietly, with almost the first words exchanged being, "my husband regularly drives a fuel truck up there".... Ok, another avenue closed....
Shot down in flames again by the outside world I headed to a place of comfort, the institution 'the shed' happy with the only sure thing 'me dog' ☺ ....

Tuesday 20 January 2004
Rattled awake absolutely pissed off at 4a.m. by the first five minute blurt of brakes winding the couple of kilometres down from between North and South Sisters' Mountains, with many more trucks following suit in succession.... Thanks a fucking lot!!!!
Struggling to block it out of my mind having my cage rattled and shoved at random strikes, kept my drive alive to rationalise the number of trucks back to the initially told amount daily, and have residents considered in the use of the road.....
The few kilometres of road leading to Rainbow Falls being Council managed, fuming, I made the Council the first stop reaching St. Helens. Looking for a solution with someone who could make decisions to do with road use, had an audience of five staff members and made no ground, walking out as empty as the faces I spoke to....
Leaving politics to rest I met Nana Raye, her identical twin sister Kaye, Scoots and Phillip over lunch at the 'Wok Stop Café'. Nana Raye and Nana Kaye were first to stand to leave, I told them to go insisting I'd cover the cost of their coffee, once they had gone we had a bit of banter with staff telling them the two Nana's had done a runner without paying. Approaching the counter to cover what remained of the account was politely informed Scoots had cleaned up the tab, what a generous soul. Scoots mentioned that the positive effect of my suspension from radio was the office had cleaned its act up removing posters and paraphernalia from the station made it a better place???? Nana Raye told me to drag Miss Manager out into the street and she would run her over, the thought felt nice if only for a moment ☺ ....

Ahh, a nice social distraction that put me in the right mood for the drive home. Calling in at the bakery, Evelyn sent us on our way with little sausage rolls on top of the order just because it's that time of the day. That was nice ☺....

Wednesday 21 January 2004
That one extra beer last night made the desire for kick starting the day a little reluctant ☺....
Earning and finding an appetite for breakfast I got cracking in the mornings cool watering the vegie patch. Before bread made the toaster the phone rang, beginning a stream of calls both in and out....
Starting the flow of calls the first arrived from the Launceston Community Legal Centre. A brief exchange of questions and answers regarding sexual harassment and discrimination concerns, the outcome being, when I'm ready to return to work contact them to start the process. Feeling like I've been yelling into the wind, it's a good sensation to finally open a door addressing positive action ☺ !!!!
Keeping the receiver warm, Loui phoned, and I also spoke to Mum and Sheila respectively, it would seem I was in the mood for a chat. Besides talking, recently cut branches littering the yard made it into the shed for the next stage in the process of the break down....

Thursday 22 & Friday 23 January 2004
Life is passing by at a rapid rate, progress however seems to evolve at a much slower pace????
Thursday passed with no hope of scribing ink on paper, the combination of the late hour and alcohol stopped the inspiration in my brain ☺....
Copping sweet the usual 4a.m. fucking log truck wake up call, consideration of people living anywhere near forestry operations doesn't enter into the equation....
Hot, dry and dusty, I stayed out in it without a roof covering long enough to splash water around the vegie patch. Seeing a truck leave knew traffic flow was in favour, following after it for a brief dash over the mountain. Not taking long to catch up to the truck, and pulling to a stop, the whites of my eyes showed when reverse lights came on and I was at the trucks rear, forcing me to jump on the horn to get noticed. Oddly, it was a visitor for me causing the truck to reverse to make room for passing....
Making it home without a scratch, Ms Tia left herself comfortable in Destiny parked in the shed, I got on with cutting down branches escaping heat and keeping an idle mind occupied....
Generously extending a sleep in the bastards first woke me at 6:20am Friday morning....
Tia and I only endured the water routine before escaping inside protecting skin from a frazzle. Keeping me inside was to the benefit of the cottage, adding to the homely transformation I displayed personal pieces that have followed me through life ☺....

Saturday 24 & Sunday 25 January 2004
Getting into a regular routine of writing daily I've only tripped over on a couple of occasions....
Always suggesting ways we should spend time together, I agreed with Allan to pack in a big one at St. Helens Saturday simply for a day to be entertained away from home. Beginning the big adventure on a happy note we dropped in on Mary-Anne and family. Taking interest next was a flower show exhibit in Portland Hall. With my mind at rest having Destiny and Tia in

survivable conditions of long-term shade, we then immersed into the hive of activity at the festival along the foreshore. Alive with side-shows, plenty of food, a wood chopping competition, water sports, more than enough to keep all senses full even after drinking raspberry cordial. Packing in a years' entertainment in one day, went on to the cinema for a movie, visited Loui, then took the wriggly road back to St. Marys….
Opening more area for cows, I pulled up at the front gate after dark to endure the new internal electrified temporary gate across the driveway for the first time. Squat inside the entrance gate, contentedly resting in the driveway, a cow seemed unfazed driving around her in Destiny…. It was nice to be home, ahhhh….
Late Saturday a change came in offering a meagre token barely measuring in the gauge, hanging around into Sunday, for what it was worth, didn't stop me from working in the yard. Feeling good about life, the phone burst into activity, calling out of the blue for friendship maintenance was a long time friend Laureen, several years of absence to catch up on the call ended when it was ready ☺ ….

Monday 26 January 2004
Making it difficult for cow watching, the only traffic occurs when they cross over from the freshly opened front paddock into our view swaying their lard up to get a drink at the trough….
Saturday evenings 'spits and spats' at moisture did no real favours, wearing my legs out lugging water to the vegie patch remains on the 'to-do' list, only kicking over dry soil…. Bugger☺!!!!
Gearing up on the shovel put it to work removing bracken fern and a healthy crop of thistles from the driveway side of the cottage, pipping them in their prime before flowering to eliminate the next generation….
Leaving that half job swinging, I defected to the milling site by the shed where more scraps of strewn timber keep surfacing. Making sense of the inherited mess, carted salvaged timber bits to dry under the shed roof to indulge a need for warmth sometime in the future over a little beer and bullshit ☺ ….
Concerned enough, Charles phoned airing his concern over shared use of our access road with trucks, gauging interest in taking action as a group to have our views heard if necessary….

Tuesday 27 & Wednesday 28 January 2004
What ended perfect, didn't start out so perfectly Tuesday. Not such a good start, I was rattled into consciousness with the blurting brakes of a 5a.m. log truck wake up call. Wearing thin on my sense of sanity, and in search of a little equality, I tried talking to the timber company representative, John, to rationalise the number and times the trucks run. John merely suggested I phone the police????
Looking for someone to take responsibility for our access road I contacted the palm greased Mayor, his attitude was far from helpful, dismissing me and road use concerns as trivial….
Getting a bit frustrated talking to unwilling ears fate put me in the hands of Sergeant Gregory, the most impartial person I've spoken to. I told him of my plans to barricade the road out of sheer frustration at being treated as invisible, in his wisdom he re-opened negotiations between me, and a more willing, John. Refreshed negotiations opened the door at meeting in a café in

town so all concerned residents have the opportunity for voice also. Finally beginning to be heard, and as a group we are stronger, one small victory....

Resting a brain that hazes over at the mere mention of the word politics, I couldn't have ordered a better remedy rain settling to deluge proportions was a perfect pitch on the shed roof. Heater ablaze, a beer in hand and my little mate snug by my side was a nice end to Tuesday, hmmmm....

Rotating shifts, instead of log trucks, Wednesday burst into action when Tia's stress meter was triggered by a thunderstorm, far preferable and more pleasant sounding....

The two inches finding the gauge overnight had no intentions of stopping there, that intense, by 2p.m. I had to empty the rain gauge it was heading to overflow, resulting from the heavens bursting five fast inches. If the temperature could be regulated I'd only need to step outside with soap to shower any trip amid the intense elements offered a hard fast soaking....

Spoiling me rotten, its Mother Natures way of saying I can have a spell from watering the garden, also demonstrating the necessity that there's not much one can do except try and stay put under a roof....

A couple of passing thunderstorms, coupled with the serious amount of rain turning roads into rivers, caused me, with reluctance for safety, to postpone the meeting with John to reschedule at a smarter time....

Back down to the shed to spark up the heater, don't call me I'll call you ☺....

Thursday 29 & Friday 30 January 2004

What a bloody amazing 48-hours, rain, rain, rain and then it got heavier. I dream of that pressure in the shower ☺ ????

Waking Thursday to the same sound I went to sleep with, it was decided there and then the only thing a girl could sanely do was retreat to her shed reading the rain gauge in passing. Gob smacked, and still persisting, the total had risen to 229mm or nine inches, Mother Natures out to break records ☺....

The benchmark downpour activated water leaks in the wrongest of places in the cottage, for safety reasons I pulled the plug on power. Making a logical choice, to watch the wall of water fall from the sky migrated to the shed to one of the few dry spots, parking next to the dry spot that surrounded the heater....

Hunger drove me from the cave to cook up a feed. Preparing food, a figure came walking up the driveway, knocking on the cottage window I waved Ross in. Amazed to find anybody wandering in these conditions, my first question was, 'what the bloody hell you doing out on a day like this', and secondly, 'would you like to join us in a meal'? Going stir crazy he dared to venture. Without being surprised, Ross mentioned the usual sections of road were under and flash-flooding and road closures further down the mountain were common....

It was nice to share a meal and red wine over conversation, any day at Rainbow Falls is a good day ☺....

A self-imposed power blackout, and with the only remaining candle stub having about five minutes left in it, Thursdays thoughts and ideas were jotted in the last of the fading daylight listening to the twelfth inch drop out of the sky ☺ ????

We were croaked into the land of nod Thursday evening to the sound of a chorus of frogs in plague proportions ☺....

Just one of the many pluses to the unbelievable deluge is no bloody trucks are moving, sleeping patterns as they should be I'm waking with energy and cheerful, as I did Friday. Happy to stay snug with her body buried under the doona, Tia had her head hanging out the foot of the bed resting by a tennis ball.... Ultimate cuteness ☺....
As showers began to ease offering a glimpse of blue sky, a sight not familiar lately, daring to venture out to look around the deluge certainly has the vegie garden standing to attention and lifted the yard to a shimmering green....
With the lulling of one natural element another could be heard from no matter where I stood, lured to the sound of the raging falls, a massive amount of water is thundering over the edge!!!!
A small bonus of the power being turned off is the freezer got defrosted by chance, a job that needed doing. The little bar fridge with no freezer cover takes no time to ice up, I'd carved enough space in the ice for two stubbies to fit perfectly, an ideal cooling set-up that'll be back soon enough. It was however, a lot of loose water to find inside the fridge by chance ☺!!!!
Parking itself above us Tuesday, the amazingly intense front, up until easing Friday morning, measured a total of 357mm pipping fourteen inches ☺!!!! That amount of water certainly highlights all shortfalls in buildings; the cottage displayed many....

Saturday 31 January 2004
Easing to a drizzle a meagre 5mm patiently waited in the gauge this morning, taking the total to a staggering 362mm!!!!
Waiting its turn and bursting out at the first break in cloud, sun beamed down creating humidity levels that sparked thoughts of planting tropical fruits....
A proven reliable spot in any elements, found refuge from the oppressive heat in my favourite location 'the shed' cutting more branches into firewood size pieces, and so the cycle continues ☺....
Rainbow Falls is looking trim, taut and terrific. From the bungalow window view the paddocks look like an extension of the mowed yard, they too have transformed from brittle underfoot to lush green....

Sunday 1 February 2004
Oops, here goes another year with one foot on a banana skin, had better make it count!!!!
Striking garden watering off the daily 'to-do's' has been a special treat the greatest reward of all is the growth spurt in plants. Collecting bath water has also been as simple as leaving buckets out in the rain, no pressure at all ☺....
Terry offered to chainsaw a sycamore tree I'd been chiselling away at with the handsaw down to ground level, an offer kindly taken up, a weeks work for me done in ten minutes. I then spent the lions' share of the working day carting chainsaw'd bits from the cottage side yard to their final destination ☺....
An afternoon thunderstorm made its presence known from a distance, slowly rumbling toward and around us for four consecutive hours stirred Tia to very excitable. A light dusting of misty rain dropped the temperature enough to put an end to the marathon of rumbles!!!!
The art of cow watching offered an unfamiliar behavioural pattern, every calf had followed the bull into the small triangle paddock near housing: he grazed keeping an eye on them without

an adult female in sight as if babysitting. Any cow considered to be of womanhood had congregated in the newly opened paddock out front, seemingly having time out from mothering duties. A nice thought, but more honestly the bull separated the calves encouraging mothers to prepare for the next generation....

Attempting to make an outside call the phone wouldn't play ball, not a priority or a state of emergency to be disconnected from the outside world, so I just got on with the day. Checking individual components later in the evening found that by disconnecting the answering machine caused the phone to work, walaa, back in touch with the outside world ☺....

Monday 2 February 2004
Another 4mm found ground overnight; legacy of the deluge the tap over the cattle trough is again flowing and commando rolls under electric fencing have been put on hold. Time spent waiting for a bucket to fill is put to good use removing scotch thistles from the face of the dam wall....

Staying inside doing a little business I phoned the friendliest bank manager, Helen, looking to refinance Rainbow Falls, step one in bringing repayments back to survivable!!!!

Keeping an eye on a change pushing in it carved a definite line of thick draped cloud through South Sister Range, one of the many brilliant and varied moods offered by Mother Nature. The mere sight of the dense cloud I turned the power off and adjourned down to the shed. In fading daylight I emptied 24mm from the gauge, an inch dropped between 4p.m. and 9p.m., good inspiration to stay seated in the haven ☺....

Tuesday 3 February 2004
To satisfy my mind for sleep, for safety reasons power was again left off last night. Well practised at resetting the minimal 'electricity reliant' gadgets, I've stopped reaching for the answering machines instructions ☺....

The benchmarking deluge easing gradually to a stop deposited another 2mm overnight, following up behind sopping up the major spill the sun did its best all day....

Maximising time, I had a catch up yarp with Loui while bath water boiled, then onward to town.

A priority stop being the St. Marys bakery for a chat with the lovely Evelyn, and never leaving empty handed, doing the rounds left the pub for last. Beginning the mountain climb I pulled into Rod's for some more social interaction over a hot brew before home....

Wednesday 4 February 2004
I'm sick of waking up shitty, if it's not from the random burst of noise from log trucks, creating work, it's the neighbours' cows free ranging, counting eight having a sit-in at the front gate. Herding them to a home paddock gate in Destiny, preferring to stay put one old girl rebelled, doing an about turn she left an impression of her arse imprint firmly imbedded in Destiny's passenger side front panel!!!!

Needing to be somewhere not requiring too much thought that also makes me feel good, administered a dose of therapy immersed in the haven sweeping. I spend more time cleaning the shed than living quarters, merely metres apart I only find one a pleasure ☺ ????

Taking the direct route to the loo for the ash drum I dived under the bottom wire of temporary cow fencing, a clicking sound generously gave me the answer to voltage flowing through electric fencing. Curiosity solved ☺ zz..zz..

Changing venues with the shovel a snake crossed our path. My passion for life and all its little critters hasn't softened to living with snakes yet....

Actively riding the wave of the extended wet I endured my second leech, the first finding the calf of my right leg, the second just got comfortable in my left sock before solving its salt deficiency.....

Thursday 5 February 2004

There is no way in the world did I wake prepared for what I was about to encounter, actions I never imagined myself capable of, surfaced. With my back to the wall I drew a line in the sand taking a huge step into the great unknown for equality and consideration!!!! A minority challenging a monopoly is certainly a big ask....

Turned 5:30am, the first truck braking its way down the mountain drowned many frequencies with noise. Pissed off by inconsiderate actions, put my woken energy into the phone starting with the Mayor, who had previously said to me, 'isn't everyone up at 6a.m.'. Today's Mayoral sympathetic response was almost word for word, "nothing I can do I suggest you phone the police, and there will be no rebate on your rates for the inconvenience"....

Snoozing between arriving trucks isn't ideal quality. Redirecting thoughts into a more positive direction, perfectly on cue, Stacey called with excited eagerness to share the news of a new job and life in Melbourne....

Working at keeping a lid on emotions triggered by the seemingly endless blurt of engine brakes, feeding off my high emotion, Allan willingly joined in barricading the road to find an ear that wasn't deaf and a door that would open. Using Allan's vehicle to block the road, causing two fully loaded log trucks to sit idle on the narrow mountainous track, soon drew plenty of attention. Receiving poor reception on my mobile phone, I called the police informing them of the action and need for a clear thinking mediator. A nice local Constable by the name of Triffid softened my emotion simply by listening and opening a communication link for negotiating action, he had the stand off diffused within an hour.... I don't generate millions per year but I count!!!!

Making it the short distance back inside home gates a message waited on the answering machine from the logging companies representative, John, apologising for running trucks out of designated hours?!?!

My daily dose of energy spent out the gate nothing groundbreaking happened within....

Friday 6 & Saturday 7 February 2004

Oooop's, a relaxing evening by the heater enjoying a couple of beers, light mist keeping the ambience alive, the journal came a poor second Friday night ☺.... Thank you Mother Nature!!!!

Staying in sequence, back to yesterday I procrastinated the morning away collecting water, bathing and preparing for a town trip....

In our absence a light mist began finding the ground, fed, watered and life in order the haven drew like a magnet. As I set the fire, Ms Tia let out a yelp; like myself, had her first feel of an electric fence ducking under....

Without going beyond, a mist dusting that fell during the evening and through into Saturday morning didn't make a measurable impression at all in the rain gauge....

After a leisurely breakfast consisting of crumpets and a soup bowl of milo, eased myself into Saturday with a spot of relaxing jaw exercise on current family events with Mum and Dad....

Raising the pace of the day to physical, measured the fall until liquid was located down the bore, being a reasonable 3.8 metres before crystal clear water is reached is a confident reason to shop around for a pump....

Kneepads I once slid around a polished wooden floor playing volleyball with these days protect my shins from flying missiles mowing. An enduring test was laid on my patience that set trial after bloody trial. Making a good start mowing raised dirt clued me to the left rear wheel area having collapsed, with that repaired a front wheel did the same, I patiently repaired that, when a cutting blade broke I gave up!!!!

Sunday 8 February 2004

Horizontal, listening to a gentle pitter patter on the roof daydreaming, pondering thoughts of vacuuming the bungalow forced its way to the front of my brain???? How little did I know the plan was about to be foiled....

Negotiating a deal back to the original forestry plan of four trucks per day on weekdays only, meeting on middle ground, an empty log truck entered the site gates. The deal is weekends are log truck free, hmmmm, I was surprised by the stupidity....

Phone calls made and questions asked, again the road was blockaded to bring answers to the surface. Around an hour of sitting below North Sister answers soon arrived after the neighbour's wife Kristy passed us on the road. Reporting back, the cavalry came out of the woodwork. A carload of fellas pulled up, beginning some lengthy discussions between us, and the neighbour Troy and site workers. Threatening to move us dole bludgers with their equipment wasn't a good start to negotiations. Moving past their name calling we established our reason for being on the road, wanting to rationalise the use of it and forcing drivers to stick to designated heavy traffic times, residents need to be assured of truck free travel times....

Everyone having their point heard a truce was called, all leaving a lot wiser....

After more conversation than I would have in a week within a couple of hours it was time for a beer or two.... And so the page closes on another thrilling chapter in our lives ☺ ....

Monday 9 February 2004

Politics hopefully put to bed for a while. Needing to relax and clear my head, for grounding the shovel got a workout, a tool that's able to keep up at any pace. I settled into clearing on the driveway side of the cottage. Pleased with the clearing outcome it was time to head inside and begin preparing the cottage for Mum's impending visit, she's returning back to Tassie with the travelling Trio after Kristy-Lee's fast approaching wedding.... Will I have enough time ☺ ????

Thoroughly enjoying a quiet day home brought my energy back up and turned my attention to the Mildura trip almost on top of us ☺ ....

Tuesday 10 February 2004

Shit, closing in, I haven't had any time to put thought into it and now it's happening tomorrow????

I'm as prepared as I'm going to be....

Formulating a plan of attack, I walked the vacuum cleaner in the cottage for a bit of exercise preparing for Royalty visiting. I hadn't turned the vaccy's wheels more than a few metres when the phone saved me from the noisy beast. Ross was a bit stressed, his dog was spooked and ran off when he cracked a darky throwing a temper tantrum at his horses, I offered to help search for Trogg.... Fortunately it didn't take long for a happy outcome ☺ ....

Replacing the handle of the vacuum cleaner in my anticipating palms I returned to finish the job ☺ ....

Calling in later to dig up garlic, Ross and I first stopped for a glass of red, then I leaned on the fence watching and talking while he dug, the shovel also turned up some small potatoes. Loaded with comfrey, potatoes and the entire crop of garlic, Ross headed home. A sample of the garden fresh potatoes in hand I headed for the kitchen to satisfy a hunger ☺.... yumo....

Wednesday 11 February 2004

Travel day....

Feeling relaxed, my little mate and I let the day naturally unfold the only plan was to leave for Devonport 2p.m.-ish....

Squeaky clean, and all loose ends tidied, once the main power switch was flicked to off it was time to make some miles. The road into St. Marys is the worst I've known it making the bone-rattling trip bloody slow, surviving the experience I fuelled up and made stops at the bakery and Post Office. Peter happily agreed to store my collection of journals in the Post Office fireproof safe to give me piece of mind while I'm away.... Bloody nice bloke....

A quiet run to Devonport, stopping only once for conveniences, arrived with plenty of time up my sleeve. Parking close by at a grassed area near the ferries mooring, we snacked, exercised and relaxed for a while before boarding....

The boarding set-up in Devonport has changed. All traffic is diverted away from the ferry terminal to an adjourning car park reducing the former congestion and bank-up of traffic out on the road. A better system, the kennels are now on board for loading, waiting with Tia a staff member asked if I'd prefer to leave Tia in the car, without hesitation said yes, thanking him for being flexible and compassionate. I'm certainly able to settle easier myself knowing Tia is far more comfortable in Destiny rather than in the cold steel of the kennels....

Looking for a comfortable spot to sit and update my journal in rather a packed house I asked two women if I could join their table. Introducing ourselves, Bernie and Gabby, with a spirit for adventure, had just completed a trip around Tassie on postie bikes, their only travel plan was just to keep turning left and turn right when they had seen everything left. Both very interesting women, Bernie a Ph.D. in linguistics, and Gabby being Gabby Kennard the woman who followed Amelia Earhart's footsteps in aviation history....

Thursday 12, Friday 13, Saturday 14 & Sunday 15 February 2004

Another bloody warm, wilting, Mildura greeting. Not a day yet under 40° has proved very limiting, leaving the cool sanctuary the family home provided has been only to attend Kristy-Lee and Brenton's wedding....

Third last driving off the boat Thursday morning, priority one was a Tia comfort stop then we got cracking to make a few kilometres....

The further inland our journey took us in the direction of Mildura the sharper the mercury climbed. Stopping at Ouyen for a cool down, me, Tia and Destiny caught our breath under the shade of a large peppercorn tree before completing the final leg. Driving into Mildura City a digital display board showing time and temperature boldly illuminated a welcoming 40° at 2p.m.....

Turning into Jenkins Place I started tooting the horn and didn't stop until we were up the driveway. Phone calls are good but it was brilliant to actually hug and hold Mum and Dad in the flesh. Over a couple of drinks conversation didn't sit idle ☺....

Destiny went exceptionally well both performance and fuel wise, leaving home with a tank full I squeezed $14 in at Devonport. The $20 put in at Wycheproof got us to Mildura, using around $60 in total for 700 kilometres.... I'm happy....

Friday continued with limiting, bloody stinking hot unforgiving conditions. The furthest I wandered from the air-conditioner was to move Destiny freeing Dad and car for grocery shopping. Self-preservation is all the searing temperature permits the sudden extreme heat is a shock to the system. Ms Tia is receiving plenty of hose downs to combat overheating in the insane furnace. Leaving the air-conditioner is a matter of have to, not choice!!!! The local paper forecast a wedding day temperature of a record breaking 45°????

Forecast close to the mark, the air-conditioner has rarely been switched off since I arrived....

In an optimistic attempt at beating the heat Lukey went golfing early Saturday, he returned back through the gates shortly after midday soaked through with perspiration. A 3p.m. wedding taking place in peaking heat on a very difficult day to venture outdoors, even shade offered no comfort....

Aunty Claire, in the company of Betty, picked us up in an air-conditioned car that struggled to cool making the dozen kilometres to Cardross for the wedding. Smart thinking hosts ensured there was plenty of ice water on hand, that and umbrella's were very popular. A thermometer read 47° or 112 farenheight in the shade.... Cruel heat!!!!

Kristy-Lee and Brenton's marriage was celebrated at a beautifully manicured private rose garden. With perspiration dripping, to their credit, all members of the bridal party endured the elements through the ceremony with dignity. Lingering for idle chatter afterwards was left for the reception at Coomealla Club. The reception hall was tastefully decorated and the meal equally as nice, heat aside we had a terrific night of dancing, eating and drinking with plenty of laughs. A little wine, food and song, and a lot of familiar and not so familiar faces to chat with ☺....

Leaving the club around midnight we walked out the doors into a wall of heat, the outside temperature hadn't altered from unpleasantly hot!!!!

After a long hot social day exposed to the elements bed wasn't an option until a shower replaced a nice feel to skin. By official records Saturday reached 46°!!!!

Sunday wasn't much cooler, limiting weather conditions don't inspire anything but the need to stay close to an air-conditioner. The rate I'm going I'll leave without crossing paths with any friends, I just can't deal with the extreme conditions....

Monday 16, Tuesday 17, Wednesday 18 & Thursday 19 February 2004
I haven't made time for writing I've simply been jotting daily thoughts in the quiet of evening as memory recall prompts for when the occasion struck and ink found paper. Every waking minute in Mum and Dad's company is precious ☺....
Winding back the hands of time to Monday, waking, I become conscious the air-conditioner had been turned off, only offering a few hours reprieve before the motor, barely cooled, got fired back into action....
Up and cracking at only the speed a fully equipped modern home can produce, Dad took me shopping looking at pumps getting prices on one for home. Dad and I complement one another shopping we stick to business then return to the nest like homing pigeons....
Back in the nest I fluffed around never far from a cool airflow. After pressing buttons on the washing machine, I cooked a quiche, and on occasion hosed Tia down to again re-bury herself under the pergola amongst shrubbery....
Staying sane-ish until early afternoon, Tuesday delivered the coolest day encountered only reaching 36°, ten degrees cooler than experienced over the weekend.... Fucking insane heat!!!!
Tia being the only known living being that can keep up with Mum beating the pavement, together they did Mum's regular 12 kilometre power walk slug following the walking track along the river to Apex Park. Taking a softer option, Dad suggested we zap up and purchase the pump we looked at yesterday, being a gift from them both.... Outstandingly generous ☺!!!!
Tuesday's heat being a little kinder, I was game enough to tear myself from the life sustaining air-conditioner and venture out alone to call in on a long time friend, Fan, over a couple of quiet ales ☺....
Feeding Tia in my absence, Mum and Dad obviously gave her a healthy meal, struggling to lift her she feels ten kilograms heavier since arriving in food heaven ☺.... Holidays are for being spoilt....
Wednesday exploded into a hive of activity with social plans of helping celebrate Aunty Claire's birthday at O'Malleys Tavern. All punctual, within one minute of one another, Aunty Claire, Mum, Betty, Tegan and I met on the front step. Leaving a lovely chatty lunch to relax full tummies we walked across the road to the refrigerator cold cinema taking in a movie ☺....
The evening was quietly spent in the company of Mum and Dad until one by one they left me for bed....
Sharing quality time together, after lunch Thursday Mum, Dad and myself visited both cemeteries tidying graves and paying respect to loved ones. Staying with a sedate pace, we continued our bonding session together back home under the air-conditioner over a coolly or two ☺....

Friday 20 February 2004
It just won't let up, another fucking, fucking hot day in a fucking furnace, arrrr, unrelenting it's an endurance test!!!!

Ridiculously limiting, keeping me sane is being in the company of Mum and Dad, oh, and the air-conditioner helps, I'm having trouble functioning, 42° is intolerable!!!!

Planning our trip to Tassie together, Mum and I shared a shopping expedition doing everything from buying ferry tickets to cross Bass Strait to supermarket supplies. We survived the outing by ducking from shop to shop following shade and air-conditioners…. Pulling into the driveway arriving home to a familiar sight, Dad was busy hosing Tia off to keep her cool…. Unable to postpone it any longer the laundromat had to be faced, in the heat of the day Tia's bedding and my doona saw a few cycles. Waiting for a cool day to do anything I'd be left hanging. Within a half-hour of putting the doona on the line it was dry, drying clothes isn't an issue fading colours is the problem!!!!

A forecast change is due, around 8p.m. a breeze lifted offering a sign of relief I hope it extends beyond being more than just a hot northerly, I can't take much more!!!!

Saturday 21 & Sunday 22 February 2004

Finally my pleas for mercy were heard a cool change arrived holding my thin threads of sanity together☺!!!!

Saturday turned on a more sensible temperature. Lukey drove out the gate before lunch to hit that little white ball around golfing, not long after Aunty Claire arrived for a regular visit. I sat and socialised for a while, then took off to demolish a couple of beers doing last minute drop in visits on friends….

Reluctantly leaving Fred, because we still had plenty of conversation left, endeavouring to be home at 5p.m. to catch a planned phone call from Sheila and Peter, then headed to Mary and Joan's to demolish beer number two. With difficulty in tearing myself away I didn't do so well with punctuality. Missing Sheila and Peter's call, when I returned it, they're kindly making Mum and I welcome for a stay in Melbourne, two very beautiful people….

To Tia's delight we ventured outside on a pleasant evening enjoying the cool change and one another☺….

Picking Tegan up to join us for one of Mum's traditional Sunday roast lunches, during table talk Tegan mentioned she wasn't doing it easy. Slipping me money so she could sleep well at night, Mum asked me to take Tegan grocery shopping before delivering her and food home…. Both Mum and Tegan can now have a good night's sleep☺….

The afternoon passed packing Destiny in preparation for tomorrow's trip to Melbourne. Time in Mildura passed in a sweltering blink, happy Mum's coming with me, the only wish is Dad had Mum's travelling spirit….

Monday 23, Tuesday 24, Wednesday 25, Thursday 26, Friday 27 & Saturday 28 February 2004

Well, bloody hell, nearly a week down the track and not one word on paper. Casting my remembery back to where I left off, Monday 23rd February….

Turning on a sensible temperature, and able to leave at our leisure, 11:30a.m.-ish Mum, Tia and I squeezed ourselves into the last remaining free spots in Destiny and waved Lukey off driving out the street. Changing through the gears and a few sets of traffic lights put Mildura in the rear-view mirror and we looked down the barrel of the Calder Highway. Passing through the sprinkling of towns until the kilometres of Melbourne closed in….

The long drive passed effortlessly having company that could use the English language that would talk back, just plodding along made Melton and Sheila and Pete's at our expected 6p.m.-ish. Arriving, we hugged and chatted our way through preparations for a dining out experience. Taking the last kilometre home following dinner, Monday and me were pretty much kissed goodbye ☺....

With plenty left unsaid, Tuesday morning was talked into readiness until it was time to tackle the public transport system into the City for a night of nights at the Fleetwood Mac concert. Kerry simply said "sorry I can't go" so Mum got to share in the experience. Taking no wrong turns we had enough time to relax in the 'Young and Jackson' pub for a drink and nibbles before the main event. Four songs into the concert justified buying the $150 tickets, playing for over two hours covering songs from their Rumours album, Tusk, and most recently released album, I was a content woman. My senses were kept busy trying to absorb the overload. The high energy packed house was treated to a sound expected from Fleetwood Mac, the big screen display, lighting, and onstage performance that included two drummers supporting Mick Fleetwood, it was awesome to watch three drummers complementing each other. A once in a lifetime opportunity Mum and I got to share together, the concert left me on a natural high ☺....

The final train to Melton left 9:30pm and the concert finished 11p.m.-ish, Mum and I caught the last train going as far as Sunshine by minutes, where the outstanding generous giving souls Pete and Sheila were there to pick us up ☺....

A restful start to Wednesday was where the rest bit ended. Going to the concert Mum was dazzled by all those lights and hypnotised by the endless streets lined with shops, so we trained our way into the City to satisfy Mum's shopping fetish. My feet beat the pavement covering most of Bourke, Elizabeth and Swanston Street's before they could again rest on the train back to Melton for a quiet night in with Sheila and Peter.... Ahhhh....

Thursday caught up with us all too quickly. Sheila and Peter are quality people who are easy to be around, both Mum and I enjoyed our brief stay. But Thursday meant making our way across the City to the Port of Melbourne for the Bass Strait crossing taking us to the shores of Tasmania....

Roaming public areas checking onboard entertainment, Mum and I had a couple of drinks and a brief play on the 'pokies' before attempting sleep. Avoiding our booked cruise seats Mum and I got as comfortable as one can on a lounge, horizontal, we managed around five hours sleep....

Come morning, propped up in Destiny watching the hive of activity going on, Tia was happy to see our familiar faces approach. As always, as soon as we reach the shores of the other side Tia gets priority one by having a well-deserved comfort stop....

In no rush, leaving the ferry and Devonport we spent a leisurely day slowly making our way to Rainbow Falls stopping en route at any shop displaying an antique sign or looked like it should. Destiny unpacked and bellies full we put our much travelled, shopped out, tired bodies to bed.... zzzz....

Falling into a coma sleep I didn't move a muscle until the sun again shone. Agreeable for a bit of time out so I could catch my breath we put in a tinkering day feathering the nest. The biggest outpouring of energy went into a town trip, bringing home enough food to carry us through the weekend....

Filling our lungs with fresh air, Mum helped gather a bit of limb wood, just light stuff to get the fire cracking. Not prepared to overdo hard work we called it a day relaxing in the shed over a quiet ale or two. Loving the quality time I've been privileged to share with Mum for me that's inner contentment ☺ ….

Sunday 29 February & Monday 1 March 2004
Well bloody hell there go another two of the precious things…. Zoooom….
Two of the treasured best days because they were spent with Mum, a million phone calls cannot replace one moment of her physical presence ♥♥♥♥…. It could be doubly nice if Dad was here also ☺ ….
Casting my mind back to Sunday, Mum was convinced into another relaxer at home because my get up and go got up and went, I needed to fully recharge my driving legs before hitting the shops again. Instead, I whet Mum's appetite patching together a much-travelled map of Tassie and loosely planned the week ahead on its surface. Port Arthur, markets and antique shops seemed to be a winning combination of words ☺ ….
With many things to look towards, and many kilometres to travel, Mum and I prepared Destiny for comfort with a quick tidy up. Top dressing the yard sweeping the bulldust off from one trip up the hill, I drew the short straw doing the vacuuming and Mum got into the windows….
As if watching our working movements, finishing up Ross and girls arrived with a home baked cake. Definitely time for introductions and a cuppa….
Value adding to Mother daughter bonding, Mum has taken to shed culture, the heater helps. Stoking its embers, we perched around the heat on offer for a nightcap and a dash of bullshit ☺ ….
A repetitive, rhythmic tearing sound roused me from sleep 7a.m.-ish Monday, a quick peek behind the cardboard curtain confirmed my thoughts a cow and calf were in the housing area again. The calf quickly ducked under the fence, the cow, reluctant to leave such lush green feed offered more resistance. Finally encouraging the cow back in the paddock, I turned to see Mum at the cottage window amused watching her pet named 'Farmer Sue' trying to be a farmer ☺ ….
In holiday mode, with money burning a hole in her pocket, sitting home another day wasn't on the cards. A day away from home was planned in St. Helens, up with munching cows I then stayed up. Breakfast and bathed, we took the rough as guts mongrel road over the mountain in search of bitumen….
Beginning the big adventure I treated Mum to introductions and my favourite pastie at St. Marys bakery, Evelyn's famous 'cheese and spinach pastie'….
Dropping the mower off for a patch up job in passing, ventured on to the 'Shop in the Bush', not only could Mum shop she also got to meet two more friends, Margaret and the gorgeous Mary-Anne. Tia and Destiny always comfy and catered for, we did over every shop that represented second-hand, old or antique, plus a few more heading north along the coast for 60 kilometres. Final stop was Scamander for 'fish n chips' before catching the express to Rainbow Falls ☺ ….
Content with full tummies and a successful day shopping, we settled in for shed culture and bonding by the heater over a couple of quieties ☺ ….

Tuesday 2, Wednesday 3 & Thursday 4 March 2004
Packing in full days and preferring to spend maximum time with Mum, for the brief privilege just the two of us have to share, the journal waits for idle spare moments....
Turning the cogs in my brain back to Tuesday, it was consumed inside home gates. In need of fuel to keep shed culture alight we salvaged what dry timber remained at the milling site. Two people working together make short work of any job....
A cow and her calf have persistently been jumping the fence to graze around housing, pissed off constantly herding them out I rounded them into the horizon paddock and out of mischief, sealed in solitary confinement!!!!
Enough sitting around it was time to rub shoulders with the movers and shakers. Spoiling Mum rotten putting faces to the names I've mentioned so frequently over the phone, we had a big Tuesday night out in St. Helens playing bingo, specifically to meet Nana Raye and Janine. With no need for a security escort, Mum and I had a fun night both calling a bingo winning four dollars each ☺....
Brought into consciousness Wednesday morning by Mum's voice at the bungalow door releasing those words, "are you awake" ☺....
A planned big day out began by grabbing a bite to eat with Evelyn at the bakery, sustaining me for the trip to Campbell Town antique shopping, remaining with the same theme we shifted camp to Ross then Launceston....
My feet were relieved when the point arrived we were tucked into the bungalow over drinks and snacks finalising a full day, a well travelled and shopped 300 kilometres....
Unable to keep up with Mum I placed a bid for a rest day being granted Thursday. Doing little other than shift location yacking we didn't do it too hard, mustering the energy required for a couple of big ones ahead, starting with Port Arthur tomorrow....

Friday 5 & Saturday 6 March 2004
Fridays loose plan, raising dust leaving the front gate, was to head to the coast follow it along to Port Arthur, stop overnight somewhere, and make our way back up the centre Saturday just going with the flow....
Settling hunger pangs at Bicheno was the first of many stops incorporating food, toilet, or any shop displaying the word 'ANTIQUE' ☺....
Making our destination, the Port Arthur convict settlement, we joined a 3:30pm half-hour guided tour, spending a further two hours going back over areas of interest amongst the ruins. A huge afternoon of walking and exploring stirred a hearty appetite, deciding on a counter meal at the first sighted pub venturing our way to Hobart....
Bellies full, the final step in the days plan was find accommodation in Hobart and make ourselves comfortable, that was easier said than done! Inquiring at a couple of motels incurred the same response "sorry we're full". The words at the last inquiry, "you'll be lucky to get accommodation anywhere tonight", helped make the decision to point Destiny's nose homeward....
Leaving Hobart City, and the entire trip for that matter, I didn't strike one service station open, hoping what petrol we had would stretch to home. Holding my breath to reach St. Marys, running on empty, I didn't dare breathe tackling the mountain, sighing with relief I began exercising bursting lungs with the driveway in sight 1a.m.-ish....

Destiny performed at her best, not only gallantly getting us home, but me back down the hill Saturday morning making it to a petrol bowser, I'm sure on fumes only. Life in the outside world current, a day of rest was declared, cooling Destiny's rubber for Sunday's trip to Evandale market….

Low cloud and misty rain hung about, the 4mm offered was enough to just settle the thick bulldust the road has been pulverised to by heavily loaded trucks. Without argument, rain also justified beer 'n' bullshit down the shed by the heater ☺ ….

Sunday 7 & Monday 8 March 2004
I'm not documenting the events daily with Mum but loving the daily events with Mum ☺ …. Sunday went as planned, starting with delivering Mum breakfast in bed, sharing toast and a cuppa over a chat, we progressed to loading in Destiny headed for a 9a.m. start at the Evandale market as arranged by the heater in the shed the night previous ☺ ….

Doing over the market in quick time buying not much more than food and a bag of tomatoes the path ahead led to antique shops. Expectantly waiting outside for the antique shopper to emerge to tell of her latest experience, Tia turned on her appeal introducing me to a few passing humans. Leaving no stone unturned, there aren't too many antique shops left unexplored ☺ ….

Prizing my foot from the accelerator pedal I had Destiny parked and fire set ready for the transition adjourning for beer 'n' bullshit….

Released from solitary confinement, teamed up every hour on the hour Tia and I are removing a particular mother and calf from the housing area, they've been bloody insistent visitors since driveway temporary fencing was reduced to a single wire!!!!

Mother Nature dropped 4mm overnight, drizzle persisting on and off rendered Monday good for one thing, disappearing into the haven stoking embers. Hanging low, cloud left us fogged in for the most, sun momentarily emerged just in time to set closing the curtain we were again submerged in cloud….

Making room for more, I emptied heater ashes into the tin and took it up to the loo for deoderiser before setting up a fresh fire. Taking the pilgrimage, Mum scooped a couple of live coals from the ash drum and before her eyes the plastic scoop started a melt down, which was promptly dropped into the drop pit toilet. Smouldering paper and plastic caused smoke to billow from the loo, not sure what to do next Mum went looking for my attention and help, finding me in fits of laughter watching the event unfold, I couldn't stop laughing. Unharmed, and a bucket of water later, the subject was raised on several occasions in jest ☺ ….

Getting hooked on 'shed culture', Mum and I shared morning tea, lunch and pre dinner drinks by the heater, adjourning back after dinner…. A bloody great institution ☺ !!!!

Tuesday 9 & Wednesday 10 March 2004
Driving off the ferry initially stepping foot in Tassie time together felt endless and now we're beginning to think about the airport????

This visit is etched deeply into my heart and feet, in the future I will always talk of the time we had together particularly Mum's arson attempt on the loo, and the 3000 km's travelled to make the entire event happen…. Every precious moment cherished forever ♥♥♥♥….

Another 6mm fell overnight to Tuesday without making an ounce of difference to our only plan of dinner at the St. Marys pub there the weather doesn't matter....
Playing home catch up I fluffed around not getting too serious doing a spot of washing, Mum kept water up and did a little reading, taking regular food breaks together, it was simply a brilliant wind down....
Looking for a release site for rehabilitated possums Pam and Terry tackled the mountain for a visit. Following plenty of natter over a brew, for a pleasant distraction all of us joined in on a walk following the top of the tree lined gorge in search of a suitable release site. Reciprocating a visit, I took Mum to see the menagerie of animals they surround themselves in before dinner....
Never having eaten a meal at the pub I was left happy to return for another. Walking out the pub door we stepped straight into a cold blast, wind and rain had locked together, their delivery synchronised, it was in extreme contrast to when we first walked in. A rare occasion we haven't wanted the 'bone rattling' trip up the hill to end, Destiny's heater was very effective ☺ ....
Woken firstly by some heavy engine starting up, later by cows munching very near, giving up on sleep I opened the bungalow door being met by the usual few cows grazing around housing. And so began Wednesday....
Too quick for me, I failed again attempting to give Mum breakfast in bed, having it vertical instead. Feeding another of Mum's insatiable hungers we packed more antique shopping in, satisfying holiday wishes tackling the 60 kilometre stretch of coast between home and Pyengana....
Culinary needs taken care of, and without the need to encourage, Mum and I settled into shed culture enjoying a couple of nightcaps, the heater, and one another's company.... For quality, it doesn't get any better than that ☺ ....

Thursday 11 & Friday 12 March 2004
If only I could freeze time, Mum's visit is over far too soon ☺ ????
Without a rush, taking our time getting ready for Launceston Thursday, simply let life evolve....
For a last minute take home memory, I gave Loui a brief call through her shift requesting 'Bryan Ferry – Let's stick together' be dedicated to Mum, taking it one step further Loui devoted a complete set that received the desired response all round ☺ ....
Making some easy kilometres we cruised to Kings Meadows booking into our motel, I then drove to the airport to get my bearings for Friday morning and answers to Mum's luggage questions. Life's psychology in place and packing it in all the way we headed to Launceston filling the afternoon, shock of all shocks, beating the pavement doing more shopping....
Shopped out and loaded with food I willingly returned us to the motel, equivalently as clean as, and more outstanding than some humans, Tia found a place inside with us. For the short-term I enjoyed the luxury of hot and cold running water along with a flushing toilet close by....
Returning to Mildura on the ugly hour flight, Mum's in-built alarm fortunately went off 5:15am because the alarm in the motel room didn't. Hitting the ground running Friday, incorporating a Tia comfort stop, we made the airport with minutes to spare....

Luggage booked through for a connecting flight, boarding passes secure, in a quick wave of activity Mum was on the plane and disappearing from view, tears flowed watching the plane leave returning Mum to an eagerly awaiting husband ♥♥♥♥….

A much travelled Tia, Destiny and I made our way back to Rainbow Falls, fog, quite thick in places, distracted my reflective thoughts. Stocking up in St. Marys I headed up the hill to hibernate cooling my shopped out feet ☺….

Stabilising emotions I gave myself a true grounding wielding the vacuum cleaner through the bungalow, satisfying the moment with a mindless job when the brain wants to be alone. A combination of tears, tiredness, and a small dose of hayfever left me a tad unclear….

In search of a solution, a bail of hay was delivered for the cows to stop them wandering into housing, but that idea lasted as long as the hay…. About two hours….

Saturday 13 March 2004

It's hard to believe Mum has been home in Mildura in excess of 24-hours, time shared together in Tassie morphed into precious memories in a flash. Mum affectionately named me 'Farmer Sue' during her stay, back to being a farmer the holiday is officially over ☺….

Getting the gear together to strike a blow with the mower I was pulled up idle by the approaching sound of a cavalry of vehicles. With a small crew of helpers, Terry herded the cows from Rainbow Falls ending their ten-week holiday. Without the courtesy of exchanging a single word the cavalry and the cows travelled out of sight. Getting on with 'Plan A' I cranked up the lawnmower….

Perched on the bungalow step with a glass of port listening to the evening sounds watching daylight fade, an amazing stillness filled the air. The paddocks and housing were ghostly quiet not a twang could be heard from cows ducking under or over strained wire….

Sunday 14 March 2004

Meant to do something else, a token 4mm overnight put a stop to plans of mowing….

Not taking much to keep me busy I got on with a bit of life maintenance, emptying grey ash from the heater into the tin destined for the loo a broad smile broke out memories came flooding back at Mum's efforts at burning it down ☺….

Terry stopped for a cuppa before removing some of the temporary fencing, leaving him to his own devices I adjourned back to the shed setting the heater in readiness for the next 'beer 'n' bullshit' session ☺….

Since the ol' moo cows left Tia is expanding her personal space she's confidently sprinting out into the paddocks barking reclaiming territory….

A damp start did a turn about to be quite warm drying the ground to mowable, but by then I was uninspired…. We didn't get co-ordinated ☺….

Monday 15 March 2004

Taking off on me like a greyhound after a rabbit, my feet didn't touch the ground until 'beer and bath o'clock'….

Water collected, and midway through a hair wash, Pam and Terry called in to accept my offer of cow poo and the chook pen steel frame in the cottage yard. Briefly leaving them to it I made a dash into town, offering cake and coffee on return….

Forging a late start with the lawnmower I broke the back of the housing area before giving in to the inside evening bits....

Tuesday 16 March 2004
Gearing the morning towards a haircut in St. Helens, I filled a little idle time drafting a letter to the Board of BODFM. Close to final draft, it can be finalised when a much-needed writing pad is purchased....
I called in on Loui with time enough for a brew before receiving a favourite hypnotic sensation of going to the hairdressers. Having a haircut is like receiving a scalp massage Kellie left me feeling totally relaxed....
Checking whether the ordered 2-inch poly pipe had arrived was assured it would be there Friday. The pipe offers choice to play with the new pump....
Stopping in on Bruce at the pub I got a box of my usual then took the bumpy road back to Rainbow Falls. With very little daylight left, Tia and I were fed, watered then settled in for the evening.... Happily ever after ☺....

Wednesday 17 March 2004
After breakfast and a little procrastination, I laid out the new writing pad and prepared a final draft letter to the Board of BODFM, included was a covering sheet for faxing a copy to the Launceston Legal Centre. Unexpected, but welcoming and pleasant, Loui arrived and hot on her trail Ross joined us not long after. Fittingly, Loui treated us to a Guinness for St Patrick's day ☺....
Guinness gathering disbanded, Destiny's everything was tested driving the trashed mountain road for a spot of faxing and posting....
Completing what I set out to do I made it back up the bone rattling hill to home, a slow second gear for quite long stretches is robbing any enjoyment and making it a bloody annoying painful trip!!!!
Here I am almost 9p.m., ready to call it a day and wind down in readiness to face another....
What is our purpose????

Thursday 18 March 2004
Another one put behind and I don't have a great deal to say about it. Outside of daily ongoing stuff the main achievement was getting the washing done, not something stored to tell the grandkids about ☺....
Attempting to phone out, the latest fandangled new hi-tech gizmo, was feeling a little temperamental only letting me make out calls whenever it felt like. Striking on a good phone moment I introduced myself to 'Bpay' paying the tax bill deducting funds direct from my savings account via the phone. I'd much rather walk into a shop and hand someone cash, more personalised, Bpay proved itself a cumbersome button pressing process....
The washing had progressed beyond my weak wristed drip-dry stage and a few spots of rain had both the bungalow and cottage transformed into drying rooms....

Friday 19 & Saturday 20 March 2004
It would be nice to have someone document my life so I can have some documented time off☺….
Friday centred on being in St. Helens for the dentist at midday. Slipping in a little earlier I got a few bits 'n' pieces done before climbing into the dreaded chair. Walking in bravely ready to face the known procedure awaiting was greeted on arrival with the words "are you Susan Lucas", with the obvious reply was told my appointment had been cancelled due to a couple of emergencies, just like that. Mentioning I had driven from St. Marys was met with a simple, "sorry"….
Beaten by the moment, went to pick up the poly pipe and there is no way 150 metres of 2-inch pipe was going to fit in the back of Destiny, strike two….
Pulling into Scamander Panels making my way back to St. Marys I got a quote on Destiny's cow bum imprint, grabbed a few items from the supermarket, slid the key into the Post Office box and it was back up the hill to hermit up for the weekend. Destiny's shoes hadn't had time to cool when Megan called to say she was ready to take up my offer of accommodation and was in St. Marys from Mildura that current moment. Making Rainbow Falls' front gate via phone directions we settled into a yarn over a couple of beers. Joining in on introductions and a drink, Loui dropped in before her night out at the St. Marys pub to see Mossy. Friday was quite social from start to finish….
Leaving Megan to busy herself with a fist full of maps planning ahead her next few days in Tasmania I did a couple of small jobs in the yard. The most energy exerted Saturday was going for a walk showing Megan around the grounds, other than that eating, beer, bath and bullshit polished the day off☺….

Sunday 21 March 2004
Having the kettle and toaster tucked away in the bungalow, and up and about long before Tia and me, Megan was searching for a cuppa. Over breakfast she shared her travel plan, heading in the direction of the coast she was moving on to Bicheno and the beach, around 400 kilometres from the nearest, the beach isn't a common sight in Mildura. Getting on with wandering around the State Megan left us to clock up a few kilometres….
The good fairies hadn't visited while I was socialising and not looking, the laundry still awaited wrist action. During a food break the landline gave me no joy attempting an external call, however, it's receiving incoming calls without a hitch???? Go figure….
In a token effort at contacting Sheila and Peter, who arrived yesterday in Tassie, I sent them a text message and they phoned arranging a visit to Rainbow Falls Wednesday☺….

Monday 22 March 2004
Preparing for the big moment, and arriving to release three of their possums now mature enough to go it alone, Pam and Terry saved me briefly from the vacuum. I had almost finished the chore when they returned from their release hike, pulling up then for a cuppa, biscuits and a chat….
A 2:45pm doctors' appointment steered us away from home, making the trip worthwhile I stopped into my favourite bakery. Evelyn recommended a vegie sausage roll, and what a recommendation, I wasn't happy until I'd eaten both they were bloody yumo☺….

Bedding off the line and bed made up, dinner cooked and a bit of fluffing around, another day is almost behind....

Tuesday 23 March 2004
Leaving the harshness of summer the changing of the season sun rays feel kinder on skin, a pleasure being in the great outdoors we spent the morning there, losing a mild overcast afternoon doing more of the same.... Feeling pretty relaxed....
Collecting water for ongoing needs, in passing, the hydrangeas outside the cottage door got noticed looking a little worse for wear. Cows had made a start and I finished with dead heading and a little reshaping....
An ulterior motive had me seated early to write in the journal, enabling a clear conscience, it's a plan to sit down the shed with my little mate by the heater to take the edge off the drop in temperature....

Wednesday 24 March 2004
Watching daylight fade from my perch in the shed idly sipping a port Tuesday evening, mild enough, I left matches in the box and the heater set for another session....
Beginning overcast and making attempts at rain the shed is a magnet in those perfect conditions. Bugger it, not supporting the cause the weather fined up driving me outside to get busy on the shovel. Rising up from the dead leaving its gravesite overnight, still lifeless, a parrot was again interred first shovel job was to re-bury it just a little deeper, sadly breaking its neck on a cottage window....
Patting the soil on the parrot the next shovel job to display itself was a healthy crop of weeds in the elevated garden, turning them in to display the rich chocolate soil underneath. On a bit of a wander, I pulled a damp and willing clump of grass out from under the side of the cottage where an open gap allows access underneath, and that's where I remained. Exposing bare ground to dry out where bath water flows, in clearing, found the plumbing buried amongst the grass and reconnected the pipe to the bath redirecting water away from under the cottage ☺....
Reward for effort????
An even greater reward, Sheila and Peter arrived not long after with the added bonus of lunch, their company is always a pleasure. Our limited but precious few hours exhausted itself touring Rainbow Falls, chatting, eating and chatting. Leaving me with a token gift pack from their trip to the Cadbury Chocolate Factory, there's enough chocolate to see me through a few period cravings ☺....
Following through with Tuesday night's plan by the heater, I simply indulged charging a body full of natural energy watching the view fade to silhouettes in tranquil silence.... Pure peace ☺....

Thursday 25 March 2004
A bit like jogging on the spot, some days a lot happens but I get nowhere fast ☺ ????
In the starter's hands for the second time, I got ready for a midday dentist appointment, this occasion successfully having a filling replaced. In the dentist waiting room is where I met up with Loui, through idle chat we made time for a hot brew afterward....

Photocopying relevant pages of Mum's visit from my journal I added them to a birthday card along with a set of holiday action photos and packed an envelope destined for Dad's birthday…. He can be part of the holiday action ☺….

Back in familiar territory I stepped foot into St. Marys' pub and Bruce walked out with a carton before I got the chance to place an order, how good is that service. The service being just as good as the St. Marys bakery, another must stop incorporated into the slow trip home ☺….

Out of daylight Tia and I settled for a relaxing night in….

Friday 26 March 2004

Wild gusty wind blew up late yesterday without calming until late this evening, in that short space of time it stirred up whatever tortures my sinus buggering a potential good nights sleep….

In conversation with Loui yesterday I spoke of my ongoing problem with the home phone, for a short-term band-aid fix she suggested I put the battery in the freezer overnight. I did, it worked and I've been able to make a few out calls….

A mild but cool start, grass was dry enabling me to get the mower out and have a go. Opening new areas never before mowed, constantly expanding the termite hole, assisted in filling a few idle hours and realising a dream. Having spent many occasions gazing from a north facing cottage window I looked forward to the day when I saw nothing but short, green grass all the way across to the road. The combination of cows, slasher and lawnmower, that long awaited moment arrived and a vision unfolded. It's an amazing sensation to fulfil what merely began as a thought amid a daydream out a window ☺….

Saturday 27 March 2004

Paradise turned on a 'beaut' one would perceive as perfect weather wise, a pure pleasure to be alive….

Happening to be in St. Helens and towing a trailer, thankfully Ross is going to put an end to the issue of getting the 2-inch poly pipe from there to here….

Reaching out to get dressed my hand returned with the tracky daks with the hole in the arse, that single action determined it time to do washing. Organising myself for the laundry task the bath plug was nowhere to be found, a rodent had swiped it overnight!!!! Does everything have to be bolted down ☺????

One of us was having a relaxing time, Tia moved herself following sun snoozing keeping one eye on me progressively loading the clothesline ☺….

Maximising a magic time of it outdoors, my little mate, wheelbarrow and me did the rounds picking up strategically placed rock piles either found with or avoided by a blade of some sort….

Doing all the washing and rock moving I was going to for one day, I'd just knocked the top off my first beer when Ross arrived with the poly pipe, perfectly in time to share in one as a gesture of gratitude….

Sunday 28 March 2004
Taking a sample from the Sheila and Peter Cadbury's Chocolate Factory tour sample pack I fumbled opening a 'freddo frog', the chocky frog sprung from the wrapper conveniently landing near Ms Tia.... Oh, and she said thank you very much ☺ ....
Concerned by the overfull look of the dam answers were quickly found, in their pursuit of water, trampling ground, cows had dammed up the overflow raising pool level. Shovelling mud I reshaped and scaled down the excess water run-off channel, getting a little stream flowing gave a strip of the yard a drink as it meandered to, and along the driveway. Dropping the dam level several centimetres releasing a couple of hundred litres it took a load of pressure off the dam wall....

Monday 29 & Tuesday 30 March 2004
So entrenched by the heater, I gave myself the night off everything Monday. The day however got cracking under cover of low cloud, refusing to leave its fixture draped over South Sister Range it delivered gentle soothing rain. Dropping visibility to as low as 20 metres at times, a favourite mystical element of nature, applying the domino effect generated another favourite justifying a shed day ☺ ....
Mainly for the purpose of posting letters, also stocking up on enough food to see us through a few, I took a drive in rain to St. Marys. Exempt from any obligation we disappeared from the outside world to be temporarily freed for a few days. Minimum requirements met justified sparking up the heater. Five millimetres having already fallen I enjoyed watching the next 5mm in warm comfort ☺ ....
For a slight deviation in momentum sun poked its head out long enough to activate a thunderstorm, it toyed around with the Tia stress meter for a half-hour!!!!
Indulging in an extra sip of port and already consumed in shed culture, the writing was on the wall for an evening off ☺ .... Hic....
Another 10mm found ground overnight into Tuesday, an ideal time to bring the shovel out and that I did after phoning Dad. There is no other way I would think of starting this particular day of the year other than phoning Dad for his birthday. Where have the years gone Lukey, 66???? The beginning of an admirable feat, congratulations ☺ !!!!
Wandering the yard shovel in hand I got busy on the driveway side of the cottage, driven away by heat and following a spot of shade, adjourned to the vegie patch where a few spuds were turned up and quickly put on the menu for dinner ☺ ....

Wednesday 31 March 2004
Setting the heater ready just to put a match to, I returned with my little mate to the gold mine digging up enough potatoes to last a few meals, yumo, lovely white fleshed crunchy spuds full of flavour ☺ ....
As pre-arranged, Ross called in with his crew of visitors arriving early afternoon, downing the shovel we went exploring the falls, further extending home hospitality back at the bungalow over a cuppa, bikkies and plenty more chat ☺ ....
Returning to a waiting shovel after waving visitors off the following three hours got consumed slowly and thoroughly digging out comfrey shoots. I placed the comfrey shoots on the concrete

path outside the vegie patch gate because comfrey only has to look at soil and begins propagating....

Thursday 1 April 2004
Time to re-adjust my thoughts, the penny dropped: daylight saving finished last Sunday, a few things haven't added up lately, I've been out of sync with the outside world and blissfully oblivious ☺ ....
Wind, only changing in intensity, remained put. Sun bursting through the intense fast moving cloud masses illuminated a shadow display decorating South Sister Range in a spectacular light show ☺ !!!!
Again the shovel consumed another day in the vegie patch now all comfrey is stacked in a heap on the concrete path. A useful plant containerised....
For some odd reason I felt tired early readjusting my brain clock to end daylight saving....

Friday 2 & Saturday 3 April 2004
In contrast to Thursday's wild winds Friday did a 180° turn about to pristinely calm....
Regularly travelling through some pretty thick patches of bulldust Destiny's air cleaner element received a check before tackling it again doing a mountain run. Reaching town hungry is a dangerous time to enter the supermarket so I took care of that beforehand with Evelyn at the best bakery....
Loaded with all the required bits braved going back up the rough bumpy road, breaking the drive midway I called in on Rod for a brew....
A message waiting at home on the answering machine from Ross extended an invitation for a barbecue dinner, someone else cooking. How could I say no ☺ !!!!
Putting in a really pleasant night, joined also by Loui and kids, once our bellies were content there was beer and bullshit around the fire getting doused in drifting smoke....
I've been feeling confident about using the road in the evening now trucks have virtually stopped, that was a false sense of security, within ten minutes of arriving home last night a truck left the site and another five followed within the hour.... Can never be too sure with promises made by forestry, and a job that was supposed to end February????
Saturday evolved around the removal of a rickety header-tank stand shadowing the cottage front door. Taking that extra step after proudly achieving the goal, enhanced the area pruning a ratty looking hydrangea which in turn led to polishing the proud look by neatly clearing a border along the entire front of the cottage....
Tidied up, there wasn't much else to do other than enjoy a beer and feel pleased with another job well done ☺ ....

Sunday 4 April 2004
A section of the window box, just because of convenient location, became the 'in-tray' of things awaiting attention, determined to make sense of the eyesore, did. Proving most time consuming was finding relevant homes in the journal for three packets of progress photos taken over several months. Making the job as pleasant as possible, knowing it was going to take a while made myself comfy down the shed, spreading the photos out on a log I read over the small space in time of life at Rainbow Falls to find appropriate locations. Reading over the

past few months feels like a lifetime ago, all the small bits along life's journey can fade to invisible in a very short time span ☺ ????
By days end the 'in-tray' consisted of a couple of bills and a reminder to ring Helen, the friendliest bank manager.... Life under control briefly ☺ ....

Monday 5 April 2004
Assisting a hibernator into action, it must be the sudden end to daylight saving that shocked my system into getting out of bed voluntarily 8a.m.-ish????
Encompassing a bit of everything I just wandered doing whatever tickled the fancy, beginning the wander at the cattle yards relocating timber and rocks....
Testing out the new Stanley knife I squared off the edges of the piece of carpet given by Mary-Anne and Theo, it cut like a hot knife through butter. While the Stanley knife was still out and active, an empty beer box was carved up for further draught proofing the bungalow, trying for a little less winter inside the cardboard cubby ☺ ....
Venturing lastly to the vegie patch on the hunt for spuds is where my fancy was tickled out....
Chipping in on visual distractions having an outside wander, with two separate sightings, I saw a total of three eagles. Giving its wings a rest one of the eagles landed in a tree next to the water tank on the hill. I watched through binoculars until it effortlessly glided off toward the ocean out of sight.... Magic ☺ ....

Tuesday 6 April 2004
Avoiding Tia's vomit was a great start, she deposited two little piles she no longer needed by the door. Throwing the door open the outside view made everything a joy, the makings of my favourite climatic conditions, firstly 4mm waited in the gauge and low drifting cloud tampered with visibility. Unable to see the front gate offered an illusion of total isolation and inner tranquillity ☺ ....
The need for food instigated a trip, taking the rough-as-guts bastard drive into town. Buggering up a good excuse for vanishing into the shed sun began to poke its head out through breaking cloud before leaving. Driving up between the Sisters Mountains our heads were immersed back into thick cloud, exiting the town side sun again shone????
Sliding the key into the Post Office box Easter eggs from postmaster Peter rattled around inside, he's a real sweetie, I'll miss him when the business sells....
Easing the let-down of being deprived out of a day in the shed, instead, rationalised rubbish stored within before wandering out from under a roof to the vegie patch....
Putting the shovel into action unearthing more of the vegie patch, I'd been watching bees drifting in and out of the long stemmed flowers of the naked ladies bulbs. One bee in particular made me take notice, never before exposed to a bumble bee, I couldn't believe its large flat dumpy size its abdomen was at least four times that of the standard ol' honey bee.... Bloody amazing ☺ ....

Wednesday 7 April 2004
Shock, I'm struggling to stay in bed. Waking 7a.m.-ish I lazed until 8a.m.-ish, then was carving square shapes and straight lines into the yard with the lawnmower just after 10a.m.????

Offering a close cut trim from inside the cattle yards across to the toilet and surrounds, then out of control like a woman possessed, opened fresh areas mowing a boundary on two sides of the dam. Creating a large rod for my back to maintain but it looks great. Designer elements to be exposed in, warming just enough to drive the shirt from my back to mow topless for a short while, letting the solar panels absorb a good coverage of vitamin D....

Leaving my body to perform ongoing repetition my brain free ranged, dawning that this fast approaching weekend represents Easter and just a couple of the sprinkling of shops in town will be open. A trip to St. Marys tomorrow is inevitable to survive the duration of the shut down....

Having a beer to settle the dust in my throat was rewarded with a beautiful sunset, slivers of cloud stretching across the horizon and mountain ranges were bathed in rich scarlet, a perfect curtain closing ☺....

Thursday 8 April 2004

Yesterdays' limitless body power wound the amps down a few scales overnight slowing the pace quite a bit ☺....

Lying in bed giving Tia a regular morning pat my finger tips found a small lump on her neck, my suspicion was correct it was a bloody tick, lasting only minutes beyond finding it!!!!

Tuned in to Loui's morning program, I played around in the elevated garden of the burnt out house, with long handle secateurs dared to find the centre and branches of a dense out of control shrub....

Both me and natures elements warming up enough to be comfortably naked, I got the boiler cracking for a bath beginning preparations for a mountain dash to cater for the Easter weekend holiday shut down....

Friday 9 & Saturday 10 April 2004

Propped up in my chair next to my little mate's bed teetering with the idea of having the night off writing, today that decision is an obvious piece of history....

Yesterday literally was a 'Good Friday' here at Rainbow Falls, finding and removing the tick from Ms Tia her spark and energy returned to its usual vibrant heights. The good in my Friday consisted of carting water, washing clothes, bringing the bucket back full again to wash even more clothes then taking the bucket for a walk collecting even more water ☺....

Coming down from the euphoria of laundry turned to the vegie patch for an antidote, finding it a complete body relaxing place to be, the view from any angle isn't bad either.... Life's pretty good ☺....

Obviously much darker with the parting of the full moon, on brief trips venturing out the density of stars visible to the naked eye is purely breathtaking....

Taking the dangling colourful display from the clothesline on a mild sunny start to Saturday then catered for short-term concentration doing an array of fluff around stuff, from watering the vegie patch to scooping mosquito larva out of the cattle trough. Much to Tia's delight anything to do with moving water is a game, I scoop and toss from the trough she does her best at catching every scooped toss. Adopting it as a pool, I've watched Ms Tia on occasion use the cattle trough to cool off in, having a quick squat down Tia dunks her body to the neck cooling

her undercarriage then is on her way again. Over and above mosquito wrigglers, Tia's pool sees quite a bit of passing action ☺ ....
Altering the thermostat, Mother Nature dropped it to cool and overcast in the closing stages, declaring beer o'clock from behind glass. Leaning on the perfect height of the westerly window ledge in the cottage simply gazing out, I settled to a quiet night in listening to the sounds of nature.... Perfect....

Sunday 11 & Monday 12 April 2004
Stirred to life Sunday to the sound of a healthy drop of rain, 30mm by 10a.m.-ish delivered perfect conditions to qualify for one lost in the shed following whim ☺ ....
After breakfast a bum scratch and look around I phoned Mum and Dad having a 'what's Easter all about' yarn. Dad is nowhere near as shy on the phone as he once was pleasingly we settle into some quite lengthy conversations these days ☺ ....
Doing the bare minimum to get organised, then like a moth to a flame, was lured to the haven to watch more rain fall out of the sky by the dry warm spot surrounding the heater....
Heading into the second inch, the only person I know to venture out in weather extremes is Ross, and true to form up the driveway he came. Heavy deluges send him stir-crazy, I'm glad they do because it was sure nice to have company. Needless to say, sitting by the heater is where the inability to write found me and the journal come a poor second ☺ ....
The downpour let a dash of the liquid inside the cottage wetting timber surrounding the main power board encouraging a voluntary power black-out. Flicking the main power switch to off severed all communication with the outside world except via limited reception of the mobile phone. Turning the power off I remembered to take the battery out of the answering machine because that runs down quickly, but the thought of the freezer defrosting didn't enter my mind until this morning ☺ !!!!
I don't think this memory will ever fade. Shovelling ash from the heater destined for the loo a beaming smile raised itself watching a few hot coals make it into the tin, the perfect set-up to burn a loo down ☺ ....
Pulling up at 48mm everything was left feeling fresh and replenished, in quieter moments the falls could be heard flowing from the bungalow....
An eagle stopped me in my tracks to watch it circle overhead gliding that large frame with grace and ease....
With cooler weather moving in draught proofing the bungalow made it onto the priority list. Head down bum up, Monday I plugged neatly cut pieces of cardboard into timber gaps in the window box. It's a fantasy of mine to turn the electric heater on and warm the whole room not just a small spot ☺ ....
Elegantly positioned like an ostrich plugging timber with cardboard, a voice calling drew me out. With introductions our visitors turned out to be John Lohrey bringing his Mother Doris Lohrey, now 89, for a look at their former family home. Sighting the house burnt for the first time didn't inspire them to remain long. Exchanging contact details, at a time in the future I would love to hear the many stories of decades of living at Dublin Town Doris has to share....
For a brief taste of the history on offer, was told Doris' late husband Norman was given Rainbow Falls for his 21st birthday. Following their marriage, together in 1942 Doris and Norman had built the now burnt down house. Later settlers to Dublin Town, and of German

heritage, the Lohrey family was bequeath Rainbow Falls by the original registered settler, an Irishman by the name of Edward Young, having no immediate family of his own to pass property onto....

Tuesday 13 April 2004
A blessing to be alive starting a day in this piece of paradise, gentle steady rain greeted the opening of the bungalow door, visually a pretty sight, low cloud hugged South Sister Range obscuring the top....
Ms Tia's energy returned with amazing abundance since the tick was removed, a preferred option, she's back to all day long, anywhere, anytime, nagging me to kick the tennis ball or to play with something ☺ .... I'm happy if she's happy....
Slipping into town to pay an account, waiting for me at the Post Office was registered mail it was a letter of reply from the Board of Break O'Day FM to my sexual harassment and discrimination issues. It seems our thoughts on the matter are on differing wavelengths, I felt the deepest disappointment reading the letter, my issues so easily erased by the Board with a bit of toner on an A4 sheet of paper, too simple....
I'll never falter from equality. A true unbending honest course can be a lonely path to take but never compromised!!!!

Wednesday 14 April 2004
Intending to dig a trench across the driveway to run poly pipe through I laid the shovel on the ground and left it there, easy in soft wet soil I pulled small shoots of bracken fern out by hand instead. The shovel felt heavy to carry, the thought of using it was too much to consider!!!!
Feeling as strong as a half-sucked peppermint determined light duties, and it doesn't come much lighter than the manual that accompanied the pump, browsing the pages to ensure nothing is overlooked....
Going the extra yard I treated myself to a personal pampering from a pluck to a leg shave. The sight of Ross' car pulling up around back put an abrupt end to leg shaving, bearing the gift of organic potatoes I reciprocated with a beer and snacks taken in the yard in mild afternoon air, chasing it down with a cuppa and biscuits....

Thursday 15 April 2004
The 15th of April doesn't pass without acknowledging Sheila's birthday; the thoughtful caring considerate friend I am I phoned first thing but had no luck. Tried phoning the solicitor again with no luck, so I gave up on the phone and went for a sure thing, bucket in hand, carted water ☺ ....
Listening to Loui's morning radio program the forecast she read offered the words of rain predicted, prompting thoughts into action of weather proofing the cottage. Having a go at solving the cause of the power board timber surrounds wetting up during heavy downpours, attached a small blue tarp directly under the eaves with clouts and tacked it onto the outside wall adjacent to the power board....
Continuing with the waterproofing theme, with assistance from the ladder climbed onto the roof in wind that was beginning to picking up. Sealing around the flue with the available tools

on offer, consisting of a plastic Myer bag and duct tape, a tad more advanced, also plugged holes with silicon....

Chuffed with achievements, I relented to the beckoning call of the haven, starting with a warm-up with the pruning saw trimming branches to fire size pieces. Then like good squirrels, collected dried timber from storage under the carport taking it into the shed for future beer and bullshit ☺....

Settled in the shed with a beer and salada I got a front row seat to the floorshow, witnessing a couple of the seasons before I could empty a stubby. Robbing warmth, wind did a quick swing west, spitting out a couple of extremely light and brief showers and leaving as quickly as it came, it was just a moment in time????

Friday 16 April 2004
Bloody amazing, feeling hyperactive I sprang from bed full of life 7:30a.m.-ish and wheeled the mower from the shed for another punishing by 9a.m.-ish ☺....
Continually pushing the boundaries of the termite hole, opening new ground, feeling quite overwhelmed, beside the visual appeal it's an effective way to stay on top of weeds....
With no clear pattern of attack first starting the mower, by days end, incorporating many food breaks, I'd pushed the high revving beast through most of the cattle yards extending a sharp edged view from the bungalow door. I also made an impact on the face of the dam, achieving far beyond expectations....
Over a 'quiet ale' waiting on bath water to boil, I walked with my little mate soaking up the ambience of the amazing transformation ☺....

Saturday 17 April 2004
Pumped and ready to get back outside transforming our world, in my haste getting out of bed put my jumper on back to front, most noticeable because it's a v-neck. Mother Nature had other ideas about me mowing, wetting the ground enough to stop the four-wheeled hard revving beast in its tracks....
Light mist, not much heavier than fog wasn't enough to send me scampering under a roof, undeterred, I got on with the carting water routine. With hopeful anticipation I started taking timber into the shed from the attached carport, rain stopped, looking threatening at times, however the sky produced nothing, buggering up a good shed day by the heater too ☺!!!!
The absence of falling moisture left no choice but to achieve something in the yard. Making it to the edge of the termite hole, and getting noticed, a badly weathered old wardrobe frame struggling to stay upright against the cattle yards fence is now dismantled and waiting its turn to go up the flue. Just cleaning up the yard is keeping fuel supplies stocked enough to keep the heater running in times of need....

Sunday 18 April 2004
Not much of a tale to tell from a termite obsessed, it was pretty much eat, mow, eat, mow, eat, mow, beer, eat, bath, beer, eat.... No more simple than that ☺....
Stepping foot outside we met a cool, yet mild morning, sun shining and itching to get back amongst it, conditions were ideal to get the mower cracking to make more of an impression unfolding a past long buried ☺....

I'm glad it wasn't warm enough to take my top off mowing because Paul, the bloke who leases the paddocks across the road and owner of the cattle, popped in, giving the green light to get Destiny's cow bum imprint repaired. Mowing until I could mow no more, out of energy and feeling grotty, it was time to give it away....
Planning to incorporate coconut milk into dinner the directions on the can said shake well, nothing moved when I shook the can, not a high turnover item it had sat on the supermarket shelf a tad too long???? With that reply it was better left out!!!!

Monday 19 & Tuesday 20 April 2004
Well, after looking at the last journal entry date it's obvious I had a rest, unable to separate myself from the warm drum to reach a light and ink, the night air produced a real keen edge....
No exciting new developments occurred. Monday was a very low-key affair consisting of water collecting, washing, water collecting, and bathing. Topping the beautiful sunny day off with a drive through the picturesque tree and ferny undergrowth lined, truck trashed, rough mountain road into St. Marys....
There's nothing like a good towel dry to locate any new bruise, mowing into new areas has left my legs a storybook of bruises. Hidden obstacles, usually just twigs or small rocks, really pack a punch directly projected from the blade....
Discarding household waste, topped up on mower fuel, did the 'must' bakery stop, closely followed by pub, Post Office and supermarket. Topping up on drinking water, offered from an outside tap at Ross', caught him in scoring a bonus cuppa....
The logging company miss-representative, John, called wishing to arrange another snatch and grab of logs, extending the entire operation two months beyond the initially quoted life expectancy???? When it comes to forestry operations halve your need and double their take....
Ready to adjourn to the heat source, the only bank manager I've seen show an ounce of compassion, giving blood to the system, Helen phoned 6p.m.-ish ready to start organising refinance for Rainbow Falls. I told Helen to go home and put her feet up, accepting my offer, we rescheduled for morning....
Sitting tight to the drum soaking up heat I made a resolution, on days of rain I'll work the heater burning small weeds and prunings, evenings I'll take the face feeding pace off indulging in larger pieces of timber and simply enjoy ☺....
At some unfashionably unkind hour through the night the phone chucked a whammy continually beeping like an alarm clock. Relieving the unpleasantness I pulled the battery out and slipped it into the freezer to be dealt with later....
Battery defrosted and offering just enough of just enough, Helen said refinancing Rainbow Falls through the Bendigo looks like a sure thing. Yahoo, not only can I tell Westpac goodbye and rinse the bad taste from my mouth, life can also be put back on survive.... Phew....
Closing the conversation with Helen left me feeling pretty good. Taking the good mood outside on such a nice day I took clothes off the line then Destiny's bedroom got broom attention. Playing in haven world I got my hands dirty servicing the mower's air-cleaner and relieved the engine of lodged grass from where it shouldn't ought to be....

Wednesday 21 April 2004

The decision was made from the comfort of bed to continue my obsession enlarging the termite hole. Having sustained enough bruises forced a search for the much-travelled kneepads, sliding them on protecting the shin 'high impact' zone....

A bit sluggish to fire on all four paws, Ms Tia moved from my bed to her own and didn't even budge when breakfast was dished up, at that point alarm bells went off. Giving me clues, Tia had been scratching at her right ear quite a bit with her direction and a good place to start I found and removed a tick from her ear. From the moment of the tick's removal Tia tucked into her breakfast then spent the day actively dropping the tennis ball in the path of the lawnmower☺!!!! Happy days ☺....

A big day of visual change puts a clean sweet taste into beer o'clock and a walkabout of appreciation. Everything that could be mowed was in the cattle yards, plus the sharp look was extended outside the back fence.... It looks bloody amazing. Rainbow Falls is moving ahead ☺....

Thursday 22 April 2004

Paradise turned on quite a warm one, with my best mate never too far off we migrated into the cattle yards to make a start finding homes for timber and rocks unearthed by mowing....

Catching a long-term forecast on the radio it seems the more timber finding the shed the better, a southerly change was mentioned....

Making a cuppa Ms Tia wasn't her usual visual self where the potential for food is concerned, whistling walking to the front gate she released a couple of barks from the housing area, a brief search found I had locked her in the cottage.... Oops ☺....

In the company of someone willing to share in a sample of food, Ms Tia and I sat for smoko. Snapping thoughts back from a daydream a sharp crack, crack, followed by a dull thud signified a tree limb had fallen. Tracking the very useful three-metre limb donation by the water tank on the hill, light enough to carry, it went into the timber black hole, the shed ☺....

Friday 23 & Saturday 24 April 2004

A toy that only comes to the surface when she's feeling off-colour, Tia brought her purple ball inside Thursday night. Unfortunately for Tia straight away she was given a dose of paraffin oil, a good sign of a pain in the belly. The purple ball was previously sighted during her last bout of constipation, when she came good the ball was buried again. Still showing signs of discomfort, Friday Tia copped another dose of paraffin for good measure....

Waking Friday to the sweet sound of sprinkling moisture got me excited by justifying unlimited haven time. Fixing a plan in my head there and then to fulfil a 1:45pm doctors' appointment, do a few bits in town then head directly home to the shed and heater. The plan was unfolding perfectly almost with home gates in view a bloody big bugger of a tree had fallen across the road.... Destiny made it onto home soil in time to call it a day....

With the purple ball in her mouth whimpering, my little mate crawled into bed with me some wee early hour of Saturday morning, still not feeling good, begrudgingly Tia took another dose of paraffin and willingly accepted tummy rubs. Pains come and go, one moment she's up firing on all cylinders the next she's giving me her 'rub my tummy and make it go away' sad eyes....

Bloody strong wind gusts blew in waves of rain overnight and continued into Saturday, orchestrating a designer 'get lost inside' day of compensation. With my little mate comfortable, and as organised as I was going to be, made a bee-line vanishing into the haven only to re-emerge for food. Kicking the experience off perfectly, opening the shed gate an owl landed on an internal roof beam, after making eye contact it flew calmly out the open gate.... A nice moment ☺ ....

Sunday 25 April 2004
All up, 16mm spread over the past two days tested the latest token effort weather proofing highlighting only that the water leaking problem was improved not solved ☺ ????
It must have helped marginally with her pain in the belly, taking a step back from a vet trip Tia had a poo, still not perfect but she's moving in a more positive direction....
Fluffing around doing odds and ends I put oil in the mower and removed lodged grass getting it ready for the next round of punishment. Already immersed in my home away from home I set the heater in readiness for more beer and bullshit ☺ ....
Still tinkering with small jobs, I took the measuring tape for a walk taking a bore depth reading collecting details for my brain to establish a total picture for setting up the pump. Offering water at a respectable depth of five metres, a moving target determined by rainfall, the level doesn't remain constant. Regular measuring will give me an understanding of how the bore thinks, or more so how I think it thinks ☺ ....
Rounding off on a bit of everything day, I scribed ink over the bank paperwork for the refinancing of Rainbow Falls through the Bendigo to move life survival from the red to the black. Relieving my shoulders of a load, refinancing left a lingering mood of reassuring comfort offering a secure future ☺ ....

Monday 26 April 2004
Far from out of the woods, some unfortunate chaos raised its head 4a.m.-ish, with a serious pain in the belly Tia pressed herself against the wall pulling clothes off coat hangers en route to curl up on my head. Taking a moment to co-ordinate thoughts from deep sleep, I took the patient for a walk outside, administering more paraffin oil topped with a tummy rub got my little mate resettled....
The cause of Tia's constipation surfaced in the light of day in the front yard of the burnt out house, a partially consumed possum had her full attention. Fur travelling slower through the digestive system coupled with gorging, are causing all her woes....
Daily necessities in order, I got busy on the border of the termite hole by the cattle yards tidying yet another dump site, this time pieces of flue of varying widths and lengths, now clear of obstacles the long grass can be knocked down to size....
Out roaming I took a peek at the dam, still not nsatisfied it's low enough for pool I had a scratch around at the overflow with the shovel, stood back and watched many litres of water meander across the yard and into the driveway....
Having a not so serious one handed tinker in the vegie patch holding a beer in the other, Pam and Terry pulled in on sunset to release a couple of possums, being turned loose in paradise isn't a bad way to start a new life ☺ ....

Tuesday 27 April 2004
Staying in her own bed for most of the night Tia's not out of the woods with constipation but life is becoming a little more comfortable....
The battery problem in the flash walkabout talkabout landline caused it to go off like an alarm clock again, not a sound one can get used to, so I transferred our telephone life over to a electricity free fixed handset....
Waiting until sun hit and warmed air inside the cottage before I could deal with being naked, spruced myself up for a trip into the big smoke of St. Marys. The purpose and priority behind the drive was to ensure my sister's birthday card made her letterbox for the appropriate day. Keeping the ball moving towards living in the black also poked the bank loan refinancing paperwork into the black dark hole of the posting box ☺....
Closing the curtain on another, I stoked up the heater, and with beer in hand firmly wedged into my favourite spot by the barrel appreciated the beautiful colours of evening fade. Tia's behaviour drew me outside obscured from my perch I walked out to witness a mushroom cloud of smoke rising looking like a nuclear bomb had gone off, that sight I've quickly learnt signifies the end to a logged coupe and the beginning of the clean up. I can't understand why locals can't salvage firewood before the burn, it's a crazy waste????

Wednesday 28 April 2004
Being chest x-ray and a CT scan day for Mum, just as soon as I could was on the phone after results. Making us hang, there was no news on offer so current events got a workout ☺....
Planning on using the car garage in the driveway as a work site to assemble poly pipe and fittings for the pump, first gave it a rake out then the area was swept. Establishing a work site in the clean garage, I got oxygen flowing to every point in my body rolling the 150-metre roll of 2-inch poly pipe from the shed to the garage. The garage is a logical site out of the weather and only metres from the bore, I'd rather cut the straps holding the poly pipe in a roll closer to the bore than further away ☺....
Tia's constipation indicator, the purple ball, didn't come inside Tuesday night a sign of either Tia has had a gut full of paraffin or the worst has passed. Still all over the place with energy, unfortunately the purple ball was retrieved and came back in this evening.... Paraffin on stand-by....

Thursday 29 April 2004
Starting on the phone, Helen got the ball rolling letting me know a bloke by the name of Andrew will make a time to visit tomorrow to do a property valuation for the purpose of the loan. Andrew later phoned confirming an 8a.m. start. I'll have to rattle my dags to be ready for the early rise but at least it takes us another step closer to being refinanced ☺.... yahoo....
A light misting rain kept the morning company long enough to drop 2mm, by 11:30am sun broke through forcing a trade off, beanie for sun hat....
Leaving myself to get absorbed in setting up the pump, from engine oil to attachments its now ready to add petrol, attach pipes, include water and go, 95% of the way there ☺....

Friday 30 April 2004
Waking to the alarm.... Hmmmm.... Not something I want to get used to....
Watching a car drive along the road looking unsure, guessed right, it was Andrew. Given a brief tour Andrew took a few measurements and notes and was gone within the hour. Helen told me in a later conversation he gave me a damning report, the bastard recommended not to finance!!!!
Shutting the front gate after the shallow bastard Andrew, Tia let out a warning bark at a roll of thunder it amused me to watch cows in the adjacent neighbouring paddock start to gather towards Tia's bark. Before walking away from the front gate twenty cows had assembled with more curious 'moo cows' slowly waddling their lardy heavy loads heading over.... Neat to watch....
Low cloud accumulated until the bungalow could barely be seen from the shed luckily I was conveniently onsite setting up the heater when the rain began. Producing a short sharp burst of 2mm, by 11a.m. it was all over and didn't return again until 6:30pm....
Forced back outdoors for a directional rethink, I transferred hot coals to the fire pit in the side yard of the cottage, tossed a drum on top and boiled up bulk water for a soaking bath. Learning the limitations of the drums capacity I had a nipples out bath, with some refining that should change ☺ !!!!

Saturday 1 May 2004
A rough plan of attack for the day formulated in my head was, straight away implement my family first policy with a phone call to Kerry full of birthday wishes, vote, and return home to attach the pipe accessories so attentively mantled together to the pump and pull the rip cord. It will be a hoot to have a major achievement, such as setting up the pump and attaching the pipe, fall on such a special occasion as Kerry's 43rd birthday.... Enhancing an already nice day ☺ ....
Family first, Kerry and I got comfortable slipping into a lengthy chat only pulling the plug so she could get ready for work....
Wishing to catch the supermarket before lunchtime closing I pulled my finger out arriving with fifteen minutes up my sleeve.... Phew.... Buying the first newspaper for a spell, I voted, walked inside the pub, did a quick Post Office check then went directly home....
Handing out another 4mm overnight, the threat of rain remained all day and on occasion was more than a treat. All the bits congregated in the car garage out of the weather on the ready, first move was to cut the binding straps from the cumbersome 150-metre roll of 2-inch pipe. Rolling the pipe like a wheel, unravelled it from the bore up the incline to the water tank, one thing in favour was the closer to the tank the lighter the roll became. Taking a few stops to reach the tank, and reading the pipe label after the event, printed boldly was the words 'forklift assist over 30 kg'. I must remind myself I'm not a forklift ☺ ....
Infrastructure in place it was time to place the pride and joy over the bore. A promising beginning, pulling the ripcord the pump fired into life first go, but priming it was another matter.
Through a process of elimination it came to light the pump was sucking more water than the bore could recharge, only getting a few metres of water into the line before the bore failed to provide. Daylight closing in I quickly disconnected the pump packed up toys and put them away ☺ ....

Sunday 2 & Monday 3 May 2004
Any intellectual pursuits were cancelled Sunday due to an indulgence in beer and bullshit ☺ ....
Hic....
Up early Sunday getting ready for a planned mountain walk from the top of South Sister across to The Huntsman's Cap, windy and overcast, a current weather forecast sealed a cancellation for me. With the new-found climatic knowledge I headed for my rainy day hideaway and with good reason, it began 10:45am. Arrangements made with Allan for an afternoon of eating, beer and listening to his sexual innuendoes, with his ability to lick until I come without putting his dick in, and the 'hypothetically, if we were together I would'.... scenarios, afternoon turned into evening.... Ho hum....
A cold snap hanging about deposited snow on Mt Ben Lomond, only a couple of ranges away accounted for the bloody cold wind. Cooking dinner in the heaterless cottage I didn't muck around to retreat back to the hot drum....
Remaining in step with the elements, Monday was without the luxury of rain to justify indulgence so it was back into it, starting with the routine of collecting water, dishes n' stuff. I wasn't enticed to spend too much time outside wind was still arriving directly off snow, a more pleasantly productive time spent in the great indoors ☺ ....
Reactive to natures elements, got my arse into gear getting halfway through putting underlay between the carpet and floor boards in the bungalow, the warmer the better. If the past couple of days are any indication of the winter ahead then it's going to be brrrr....
Suitably impressed, the entire rear of the bungalow now has extra padding. I look forward to feeling the benefit the underlay makes sleeping in my bed roll on the floor tonight. A slight rise in floor level and the toaster that once fit snugly between the fridge top and shelf above no longer does.... Always adapting to change....

Tuesday 4 May 2004
The extra thickness underlay added made an obvious difference, extra padding was a little softer on a body sleeping on the floor. Another major plus is the fridge has become invisible, it runs quiet and smooth with insular cushioning underfoot ☺ .... It's all good....
The morning soup bowl of milo was thoughtfully and slowly sipped basking in full sun tucked inside shed gates, an easy spot to get the bum stuck ☺ ....
Wind had a fair go at dismantling temporary repairs, creating a couple of air leaks in the bungalow temporary window mark II stepped aside for mark III. Motivated, I cut loose with a roll of tape again sealing the void made from the broken window pane the bungalow should be warmer.... Always value adding....
Destiny's oil got a stir up doing my best to get a Mothers Day card posted to arrive on time ☺ ....
While in town I bought small poly pipe joiners required to link-up cottage pipes. With the sink and taps connected the infrastructure is in place for the time water flows.... I'll feel a great sense of achievement that day!!!!
Avoiding the nippy air temperature, I did it a bit more comfortable catching sun from behind glass giving Ms Tia's beautiful outfit some attention. Stroking out three brush loads of loose fur made space for the latest in winter fashions ☺ ....

Wednesday 5 & Thursday 6 May 2004
By the time Wednesday ended the thought of writing became all too hard, and that's where it remained, a thought ☺ ....
Greeting the remnants of a frost pushing open the bungalow door Wednesday morning, with the general rule of thumb of a nice day to follow, we weren't let down....
Pushing the wheelbarrow up hill by the water tank, my little mate helped collect two loads of small limb wood from under the large gums for the fire pit planning on boiling up the drum for a deep bath....
I must have collected about 100 litres of water for the pleasure of a deep bath, but every bucket load carted to the drum was worth the effort. The plan came together 5p.m.-ish, getting to track 13 with 'Enya' before I surfaced from the marginal nipples out bath with a heat penetrated massaged body.... Ahhhh....
My tolerance to forestry's tardy business practices is wearing thin the arranged 6a.m. start for trucks began 4a.m. Tuesday and ran all day. Wednesday too was a 4a.m. start. John told me there would be four trucks a day until the end of February and they're still operating. Their presence is difficult to block out when the constant buzz from a chainsaw can be heard from 7a.m. for hours on end. My first wake up call from a bastard truck today was at 2:20am exactly, then about 4a.m. and on it goes. Nothing pisses me off more than continually broken sleep, dishonour and lies!!!!
Up and at'em, after several truck wake up calls, for a big outing planned in St. Helens beginning with the dentist at 11:30am. In the chair two minutes and the sliver of filling I'd been nurturing was removed, making very little difference it was decided to just let it be. With extra time on my hands before meeting up with Nana Raye, Loui, Phillip and Roger for coffee, the hardware store was a good place to lose it. I was like a kid in a lolly shop getting more bits to patch the cottage plumbing together. Another handy purchase made from the electronics shop was a battery for the phone....
Meeting and greeting the coffee crew we put in a lovely good-humoured hour together topping a most enjoyable day out ☺ ....
Offering an evening smile, gathering her treasure Tia decorated her claimed shrine, my bed, placing a ball on top, a ball in, and one beside ☺ ....

Friday 7 May 2004
Having a waking cuddle with my little mate thoughts wandered to the bag of goodies purchased at the hardware store, but a test on my personal character had different ideas in store taking a course I didn't plan on....
My understanding of the agreement is log trucks are supposed to have stopped running by 8a.m., annoyed another two came in after 9a.m. I tried phoning John only getting voice mail he didn't respond to, one door shut. In search of an ear to negotiate some sort of agreement phoned the contracted trucking company requesting to talk to a manager, reception told me all managers were in a meeting, door two shut!!!!
With doors continually shutting communication frustration got the better of me, parking Destiny out front on the road blocked truck access to the site. Once again, phoning the contracted trucking company told reception what I had just done and got a manager

immediately seems their meeting had finished. My only question being why are the trucks running out of hours, the 2a.m. and 4a.m. ones were wearing me down....

Wishing only to open negotiations with someone prepared and able to make decisions I was chopped down in my prime, without eye contact or a spoken word police and a tow truck arrived with lights flashing. Simultaneously while being charged, I watched Destiny being winched onto the back of the tow truck. Offering to move Destiny, the female charging officer would only talk about her impounding???? Beaten mentally and physically by unfair work practices, and punished for highlighting them for daring to consider myself equal, it seems stopping greed, corruption and injustice is too legally punishable????

Offering his support as an outstanding actor, Allan used his stern male voice to orchestrate a fine victim performance with a succession of phone calls to the timber and trucking company management. Being left to hang for the weekend, the final word was there's to be a meeting Monday between timber company management and the charging officer with the view to dropping the charge against me.... In Allan's words, "that's got to be worth a lap dance?"....

Roaming outdoors in the cool evening chanced a shooting star sighting, leaving an amazing light streak ablaze across the night sky freezing time momentarily, a peaceful end to one of turbulence☺....

Saturday 8 May 2004

Unable to ignore the chore couldn't put washing off any longer, donning gloves while up to my elbows in suds was to prevent more skin splitting around my thumbnail through staying wet. Needless to say a big event like laundry requires carting copious amounts of water, almost wearing a track to the tap....

Collecting water well may soon be a memory. Finally getting around to fossicking through the bag of goodies purchased from the hardware store I installed the 'S' bend under the kitchen sink and only one join leaked, not bad for putting it together by hand.... Raises the issue of seriously needing tools ☺!!!!

Pouring water down the sink for the first time I raced outside to watch the proud moment of remnants drip from the end of the drainpipe.... For a brief space of time life left me speechless.... Girl can do it ☺ !!!!

Sunday 9 May 2004

Taken seriously, my waking endeavour on Mothers Day is to make contact with my Mildura home. Mum said she received a lovely bunch of flowers from Kerry and the card I sent, in no rush, we settled into a good chat catching up on family life....

Motivated and personally pumped, piecing together plumbing, I put energy into joining the poly pipes that feed water to the taps in the cottage that were once connected to a header tank stolen from outside the front door.... Soooo close....

By chance, I come into ownership of a long outdated computer from a sale at the hospital with brains enough to cater for word processing its ideal for digitising the journals written word. Beginning tonight with data entry, Mothers Day is a fine auspicious occasion to start ☺....

Monday 10 May 2004
Three hand written journal pages made it into the computers hard drive last night. Mothers Day commemorated two significant turning points the cottage is ready to accept flowing water and the commencement of converting the journal to digital form.... The beginning of my book and a dream, I'll be happy to be entering these words into the computer ☺ ....

- I'm actually bloody elated entering the words 2004 ☺ !!!!
- Even more elated reading the words again doing a hardcopy edit 21/4/07 ☺ ....
- Passing by again digitising hardcopy edits into a working document 26/8/07. Amused by the past comments ☺ ....
- Massaging my way through the grammatical second edit is a euphoric state to be revisiting the past series of comments 17/12/07 ☺ ....
- What can I say, its 28/3/08 and a long dedicated time coming, its astounding to be close to fulfilment of a dream I loyally dared to follow through with ☺ ....
- 8/11/09 Doing a hardcopy final edit, if I'd have known writing a book was so time consuming requiring much dedication I probably wouldn't have done it, but glad now I persisted ☺ ....
- 15/4/10 Reading over past progress comments makes me very glad I'm at the stage of final edit almost six years on. Nearly time to get my life back ☺ ....
- 30/7/10 Years of dedication have found an end I'm leaving a trail of finalisations ☺ !!!!

The inclusion of a bloody cold wind generated chill factor gave me all the reason needed to stay inside doing data entry. So enthused, I'm finding it difficult to tear myself away, one more page, one more paragraph, just one more line, the computer is like a magnet to be near. Joining me without complaint Ms Tia didn't mind a cold one spent inside by the heater ☺ ....
The outcome from the meeting between forestry management and the charging officer saw a favourable and sensible outcome, charges were dropped, without being too generous I still had to pay Destiny's towing fee!!!!
Tummies full and today accounted for in freshly written words only leaves one thing for me to do, turn the computer back on and get more words digitised ☺ ....

Tuesday 11 May 2004
Pretty much bungalow bound and limited to a small area, the day went from great to bloody fantastic ☺ ....
Rattling the computer keys until midnight last evening, Ms Tia and I got co-ordinated for a nice lay in. Cold, overcast and windy outside, created justification to a focussed brain giving the green light to stay indoors clunking keys again....
Looking for papers requested for refinancing I turned up a piece of paper with Anna's contact details, yesterday her name came up doing data entry, reading that as a sign it must be time to give her a call and was pleased I did ☺ ....
Keeping the computer running hot, stopping only to eat and pee, the contents of one complete journal folder are now sitting on the hard drive, only twelve to go, that's a lot of hours typing?!?!

The results of Mum's CT scan and chest x-ray were made available with a brilliant outcome, no further cancer was found.... Yahoooo.... Life went from great to bloody fantastic ☺!!!!

Wednesday 12 May 2004
There's no need for a crystal ball to work out what consumed waking hours. A mind so focussed, I get up do what has to be done, add power to the white goods and only stop when necessary....
It's an amazing emotional journey revisiting our humble beginnings at Rainbow Falls almost two years ago to the day. Early journal entries feel like a lifetime ago, such distant memories that would have been long lost....
Fingers dancing over the keyboard at a reasonable touch-typing speed, I'm entering page after page seemingly doing a lot and getting nowhere fast. Passing midway through folder two, word processing has amounted to twenty-seven solid pages of text, at 11pt font, for psychological strength I keep reminding myself that everyday I'm a little further advanced.... My cup is half full ☺!!!!
Shedding her summer coat fur is dripping out, de-furring the bungalow and brushing Ms Tia are a daily must. Emptying fur from the brush I walked out the door to greet a rainbow draped over South Sister Range.... Magical ☺....

Thursday 13 May 2004
Thankfully one of those rare times of waking to the horrible sound of the alarm, and I want to keep it rare ☺!!!!
A deposited 2mm added damp to a cool start, the occasional sprinkle keeping the ground moist coupled with the recent cold snap has encouraged bulbs to start shooting all over the place. Beginning in the front yard of the burnt out house two weeks ago, this morning I noticed a spur clump of snowdrops had produced a sprinkling of dainty white flowers. Winter months are a colourful time at Rainbow Falls....
Before being allowed access to Destiny I must first be the holder of a receipt from the towing company. Accepting a lift from the ever obliging Allan to St. Helens, blissfully ignorant, I went to the address on the account where I was shocked by the request for $155, $55 beyond the quoted $100. Expressing my objection at paying beyond the quoted $100, with the swipe of a pen the account was adjusted to the agreed amount. Counting at least twenty gold rings sprinkled over this woman's fingers, she must have taken her jewellery tax from my account.... Bloody thieves....
Onward to the police station receipt in hand to free Destiny and regain independence, the St. Helens police didn't give me the response I was after, hearing the words, "the car compound is in St. Marys, your car is there", in helplessness I could only laugh....
With a phone call to the St. Marys police station I was informed I could have paid the towing fee there, and in the next breath was told they were locking up shop 3:30pm sharp, no more business entered into.... Destiny's freedom will have to go begging one more night ☺????

Friday 14 May 2004
Focussed solely on bringing Destiny home, Tia and I were at the St. Marys police station with hours to spare. Mentioning the tow truck driver was a thief, the police amended their $155

account to my renegotiated $100. Happy to have been blissfully ignorant, taking the charging officers inaccurate advice made it worth the trip to St. Helens to have those chubby gold ringed fingers so easily swipe that bit of ink across the account!!!!
A pleasure to be sitting proudly behind Destiny's steering wheel, independence back, I pulled her up diagonally across the road for a slab of Bruce's best, that box should last because the cooling elements are slowing my appetite for beer. However, any temperature is a good time for my appetite at the bakery, calling in on Evelyn, moved on to slide the key in the Post Office box then groceries. Life once again sustained, we took the freedom run back up the hill ☺....
Unable to bring myself to turn the computer on with such pristine elements outside instead had a play with the pump over the bore trying theories rattling around in my head. Too big a draw on water, I couldn't pump slow enough for the bore to recharge to even fill the line to the tank, sucked dry on ideas give it away for some more thought ☺????
Satisfied I'd absorbed the best that the elements had on offer, with our existence as under control as it was going to be, I felt justified in gliding fingers over the keyboard moving forward dreams....

Saturday 15 May 2004
With both Loui and Nana Raye celebrating their birthdays I joined in on some of the partying action. Breakfast, bath and on our way....
Loui was playing at a charity fundraiser between noon and 2p.m. I went along to be there for the kids while she was preoccupied playing. The kids looked after themselves, filling senses with all the sights and sounds on offer. Cooling off hot vocal chords, I joined Loui for a birthday drink before fluffing up my party frock and moving camp to Nana Raye's for the next round of celebrations. Busy knitting scarves, she'd completed one in St Kilda AFL colours and reminded me that her beloved St Kilda and Collingwood meet tonight.... One way or another she'll let me know about it ☺!!!!
It was a breath of fresh air sharing a nice distraction away from home catching up with the birthday girls. Making it inside the front gate at a reasonable hour, fed and watered, the journal is a few words from being up to date, it's just gone 8p.m. and I can feel the lure of the computer ☺....

Sunday 16 May 2004
Unsettled come bedtime, Tia demonstrated her discontent to distant thunder rumbling, plenty of love and reassurance helped. Stirring through the night I heard steady rain each time, a fleeting thought before rolling over falling back into sleep was 'it will be a great day to spend on the computer' ☺....
Not rushing out of bed set the pace for a placid Sunday. Doing its best work overnight rain had pulled up by morning, the token 4mm was enough to give the plants a drink....
Entering the cyber world after lunch computer bytes are ticking away, opening the pages to the third journal folder, again stopping only for food and comfort stops. I look forward to the day the entire journal is on CD waiting for the first of many edits ☺....
Quality sleep has returned since log trucks have stopped, they know how to rob energy in all areas. Its reassuring to know the pulverised rough road is pretty much back to local traffic only, sanity is returning.... Especially mine ☺!!!!

Monday 17 May 2004
Tia pushed the issue of getting up, a request ignored for as long as possible....
Copping a bone rattle returning up the hill to home Saturday, a fuse blew, taking with it the indicators. Rarely things ignored go away, useful to have, put my brain into 'find and fix' getting Destiny's indicators active again....
A silver falcon sedan driving around the back took me from a phone call. The two women introduced themselves reckoning they have just the god for me, in polite conversation told them that everything I needed was inside of me.... Not a good day for a conversion....
After smoko Tia got to clean the remaining offerings from what I call an empty peanut butter jar, it kept her full concentration extracting the last of the flavour from every surface her tongue would reach. Entrée and mains complete, with the added bonus of a pampering brush, Ms Tia was content to bask in sunshine snoozing ☺ ....
Repetition has entered home life, doing only what screams out for attention then fire up the computer. Typing my way through a milestone, the 50th computer page was generated into the digital world, just over two hand-written journal pages equate to one computer page. From my seat in the bungalow I observed a beautiful day through the window and open door....

Tuesday 18 May 2004
Brilliant for indoors, drizzle and low cloud were the norm and sun didn't poke its head out once.
Turning the computer off to cook dinner I had just made a start on journal folder four, having now entered 120 hand written pages, at 11pt font at single spacing, equates to 58 typed pages on the computer.... A bloody lot of words ☺ !!!!
Everyone's culinary desires catered for and tummies content, journal up to date and only 8p.m., what's a girl to do but let her fingers again dance over a hot keyboard ☺ ....

Wednesday 19 & Thursday 20 May 2004
In the company of a couple of Guinness' I got comfy behind the keyboard, from there making an executive decision to have the night off writing ☺ .... Lucky I'm the boss of me!!!!
Unable to postpone it any longer the need for food cornered me into a town trip Wednesday, driving to and fro without delay, like a woman possessed to get home and fire up the computer....
Destiny's causing me a brain teaser by blowing fuses just as soon as they are replaced a strong clue there's another solution to track down????
Packed with groceries and friendly mail from Peter and Sheila containing pictures of their new home and contact details in Queensland, drawn like a magnet went home to Rainbow Falls to burn up electricity....
Still dripping that change of season fur, Ms Tia decorates the bungalow in random strikes nothing is without a sample....
Wild wind stirred life up Thursday loosening bark from gum trees that could be heard spiralling and flapping. Caught out of the nest a bird did some wild flying struggling in wind, it was covering distances and doing head rush speeds it would never have experienced ☺ ....
Nature's conditions on offer only encouraged my obsession of staring endlessly into the square screen. It's an amazing sensation to step into any given day and have all the memories ignite.

Currently I'm typing in and reliving Mum's cancer operation and recovery re-entering the emotional journey, so many thoughts and memories accounted for that would have long faded.... Priceless ☺....
A huge turning point was reached on the daily hand write side. Commencing journal folder eleven of documenting life at Rainbow Falls, now totalling 520 hand written pages it's near enough to two complete years of our lives.... Bloody amazing, who would have thought I had it in me, not me ☺ ????

Friday 21 May 2004
Like a dog with a bone, yesterday I hung in until 1a.m.-ish with a glint of determination in my square eyes to finalise entering folder four into the computer. I shut the bugger down with one third of the entire hand written hardcopy digitally active, a good feeling ☺ !!!!
From a fairytale book impression of perfect, it was bone warmingly beautiful in paradise to meet our anniversary day. Blissfully ignorant when Tia, me and Destiny pulled up at the front gate of Rainbow Falls two years ago to the day, I don't have words to generalise exactly how that feels two years on. My character has been tested on occasion, overall I feel rich with a sense of achievement and satisfaction with two very rewarding years of self-growth under my belt. Oddly, a couple of days back I unearthed a photo taken when we first arrived, making me reflect upon how far we actually have progressed.... Worth every moment of involvement, it's easy to get consumed within ☺....
I didn't need a fortune-teller to predict the day ahead, after doing the 'have to's' I seated myself back facing the screen. Word, after line, after paragraph, after page, data entry has been slower than I imagined it to be, lucky for me I see the glass as half full, not empty, and any progress is forward movement ☺....

Saturday 22 & Sunday 23 May 2004
So engrossed in digitising the journal Saturday my fingers just kept dancing over a hot keyboard refusing to stop and pick up a pen....
Unable to justify being indoors when such magic elements were being turned on outside, I didn't get typing until mid afternoon then couldn't, or more to the point, wouldn't stop ☺....
A pleasant distraction from my obsession with data entry, Tia and I piled in Destiny to pick Ross up so he could collect his tractor parked in the shed. After downing a cuppa Ross got the little grey Fergie cracking over the mountain....
Finding myself being drawn to the computer 2p.m.-ish, that's pretty much where I remained until bedtime. Once night fell walking outside was done purely by memory, dropping a wall of black and unable to see a hand in front of my face sparked a memory of SCUBA diving in the River Murray on a 'clean up Australia day' ☺....
Lounging in bed Sunday thoughts warmed to the idea of a deep soak in the bath. Taking step one in the bulk hot water process the wheelbarrow was pushed up hill and filled it with small branches from around the water tank. Instead of lighting the fire pit the wheelbarrow full of timber was parked in the shed, quickly caving in, low cloud teased looking like it could drop moisture at anytime, so the idea was put on hold for the time being....

Wheeling the wheelbarrow load into the shed I got sidetracked by the visual openness created by the tractors absence and was driven to expand, moving four 44-gallon drums out by the outside wall opened an area I have threatened to since early times, easing clutter….
Without the need for too much encouragement to glide over the keys, today's unsettled climate helped decision making ☺ ….
We may have graced the doorstep of Rainbow Falls May 21, 2002, but thoughts to start writing a journal didn't eventuate until May 23, today is two years exactly for the journal…. What inspired me to start and where it will end, who knows ☺ ????

Monday 24 May 2004
Following a bloody lot of persistence and a large dose of determination, giving in Sunday night journal five had been digitised. Coinciding, the accumulated folders added up to the words of page number one-hundred being fed down the computers throat ☺ !!!!
Decorating simply everything, Ms Tia has been dropping masses of her beautiful outfit, causing a regular morning bungalow de-fur ☺ ….
Returning to the deep bath idea, there was always a chance of a little drizzle but I just got on with it facing whatever Mother Nature decided to turn on, which amounted to very little. It was pre bath therapy just getting the fire pit cracking and feeding it, then there's that reward at the end. Squeezing every possible drop of water into the boiling drum still only managed a nipples out bath ☺ ????
Feeling pretty relaxed and in need of a fix for my eating habit did only what had to be done in town then headed straight home. It was nice to see a grader doing road maintenance, making the trip in and out a little more pleasant rather than a task….
The day escaped me just getting organised for it….

Tuesday 25 May 2004
Stepping sideways from priority I had a dabble at those 'one day' jobs. Just an eyesore, I severed the connection between the old power supply wires dangling low, draped between the bungalow and an unused power pole, and cut every low branch in between I was tired of bumping my head on ☺ !!!!
Without exchanging a word since Mothers Day, Mum, Dad and me had plenty to jibber about. The older and wiser we're becoming the more we enjoy and respect one another's company and opinion ♥♥♥♥…. I prefer the wisdom of my years than the naivety of my youth life isn't expendable….
With the nest feathered several more pages and a lot of words in 'the life and times of Rainbow Falls' made their way onto the hard drive. A few hours of clunking keys my brain got distracted by thoughts of dinner, no match, beaten by my stomach disconnected power!!!!
Satisfied in the culinary world I returned to the literary world, reaching for the pen, firstly the latest hand written word was made current closely followed by data entry of words now history ☺ ….

Wednesday 26 & Thursday 27 May 2004
Focussed on finalising journal folder six Wednesday achieved the desired outcome, finger dancing my way into obsession and folder seven before closing down everything for the evening, no more literature entered into ☺ ....

The 'Inside my Skin' file had to be split because the floppy disk, and the only way of extracting data from the computer, gave me a full message, it made no sense making the file any larger. Beginning a new file 'Inside my skin part II', with thoughts of later patching the entire book together on a computer with a CD burner that has the capacity to handle the entire document ☺ .... Woohoo, uncharted territory....

Outside on a break from the screen, timing was impeccable to witness a blast of strong illuminated colour from a rainbow formed at the base of South Sister, arching just beyond the waterfall.... Magic ☺ ....

Direct sun stepped aside Wednesday morning to accommodate drizzle, going that one step further icing off for a bloody cold night, brrrr. Being in no hurry to get out of bed Thursday was for good reason, we copped a heavy frost that still lingered at 9a.m.....

Treading lightly on the fresh day I basked in direct sun cradling a brew before considering returning to the inevitable, doing a serious de-furring of the bungalow. A common habit of natures is warm and sunny elements follow the melting frost, so bedding went on the line to be aired and de-furred. Tia only has to be in the general vicinity or walk past something to cover it in fur ☺ ....

Making the mistake of picking up her constipation indicator, the purple ball, and lying with it a while, to Tia's displeasure she was given a dose of paraffin just to be sure ☺ ....

Driven by some unknown force, found myself again seated in front of the computer continuing the challenge of digitising our past life ☺ ....

Friday 28 May 2004
Sizing up the food supply, an executive decision was made to avoid town and stay home....
Sun may have been shining but wind wasn't doing us any favours, coming straight off snow it arrived with its own built-in chill factor justifying another day on the computer. I really need no reason but one helps ☺ ....

Once my fingers warmed to the keyboard hours and the day evaporated....

Putting the cardboard curtain up on the setting sun in the bungalow was timely to see a pair of eagles gliding above the horizon paddock, close to a nesting site: they were being harassed by a couple of ravens....

Saturday 29 May 2004
Air driven directly off snow set the stage for a bloody freezing night, so cold in fact, Tia brought a bone inside because she couldn't stand to be out in it, brrrr.... It was merely a wind gust away from snow reaching home soil....

Basking in direct sun out of the chilly breeze getting my body freed up and willing to move, Tia had other ideas for me to warm-up with, starting with my legs kicking the ball again and again and again and again ☺ !!!!

My fingers impacting regularly on the keyboard is making headway, delving into the past life, it's digitised up to folder eight. Now surpassing the halfway point, thanks to the company of a very supportive co-author and best mate ☺ ….

Sunday 30 May 2004
Nearing 5a.m., wind gusts trying to take the roof off jolted any thoughts of sleep from my head, delivering a battering for around a half-hour. When she finally eased up it was business as usual….
Going one better, advancing water collecting, connected a hose purchased in Mildura to the cottage side yard tap to deliver water close to the cottage door. Pressure isn't going to blow a hole in the bucket but there's less effort involved in getting it. Pressure doesn't matter a zip to Tia as long as its flowing it's a game, flick a bit of water her way on occasion and she's happy ☺ ….
A cup constantly filling, shortly after lunch my fingers were back hard at it digitising a few more pages of 'Inside my Skin', a title set in concrete for the developing book ☺ ….

Monday 31 May 2004
Just reaching into the wee baby hours of Monday morning a mongrel destructive wind tried ripping the roof off from 1:30a.m.-ish onwards. Disturbing any chance of quality sleep, and in no hurry to move on, it wouldn't let up. The only active birds able to pit their strength against the wild conditions a pair of eagles flexed their might….
Doing a little business I dialled the number to book Destiny in to have her cow bum imprint removed, having a date with the panel beater Monday 14th at 9a.m. ☺ ….
Around general living a few more pages of 'Inside my Skin' were digitised for immortality. Little by little dreams evolve ☺ ….

Tuesday 1 June 2004
Kissing the morning goodbye getting ready for a trip down the hill, and getting bloody hungry, I attempted to make St. Marys' bakery the first stop. Parked across the road and reaching for my wallet I got that empty feeling in the pit of my stomach, a couple of 'arr shit's', I returned to Rainbow Falls for a take two. Wallet joining us for the second drive, it was off to Evelyn's to cure hunger….
Planted amongst dreary mail was a cute card with a brief cheery note sent from Mum and Dad, uplifted, and loaded with groceries, returned to resume the self-imposed hermit's life. Having a day off the computer to return choice back into the wardrobe did laundry instead ☺ ….

Wednesday 2 June 2004
Inspired to try and replicate a photo I think is the cottage, printed in the Western Courier Newspaper, 30 July, 1908, back when our little hamlet was a bustling small community, I took Tia and camera for a walk along the road out front fruitlessly looking for the angle. Sadly a century of weathering, and so-called modernisation, has been unkind on the sprinkling of housing history from early settlement that represent the Speers and Britton's homes dotting neighbouring paddocks…. Already quite a bit of Dublin Town history has, or is in the process of disappearing….

Temporary window 'Mk II' in the bungalow hasn't taken the recent wind battering too kindly, beginning to weaken it screamed out for running repairs, that's the only way to get noticed☺!!!!

Escaping the reactivated bloody icy driving wind it had us securely tucked into the bungalow by 5p.m., happy to be inside by the heater hoping the roof stays on????

Keeping my brain distracted from an unrelenting lashing by the elements, I didn't go at it too hard, but still managed to reach a milestone, as large as life, the 150th page was typed into the computer now digitised for the modern world☺….

Thursday 3 June 2004

Serious about putting in a respectable keyboard effort, up and looking life in the eye 8a.m.-ish, strove and organised the day to the point the only thing left to do was eat☺….

Sparking up the computer I didn't look back until closing the pages on journal eight….

Keeping idle keyboard finger dance moments entertained, through my bungalow window view to the world Mother Nature turned on an interesting assortment, offering a splash of rain, some sun and a bloody lot of wind, setting the thermostat to freeze with the sinking of the sun….

Great to watch from behind glass☺….

Friday 4 June 2004

My uterus wall tearing roused me from sleep, altering my eyes from shut to seeing the whites and sending my body into a cold sweat. Nauseous, once I was sick and came out of shock, everything began easing. The entire cycle lasting 20 minutes left as quickly as it arrived, but robbed every last drop of energy in that short space….

Having trouble picking my arse up from dragging on the ground not much happened fast, it took until 2p.m. just to get organised for a trip into town….

Performing well on premium unleaded with a little additive, giving Destiny another dose I saw Brian and Maggie walking and offered them a lift home. It seems a large rock and the fuel tank of their bus had a disagreement…. Ouch!!!!

With just enough remaining daylight to unpack Destiny and get us settled in for the evening today disappeared just going to town and coming home again☺….

Saturday 5 June 2004

Wonders will never cease to amaze, awake, but encouraged out by my furry friend, from the moment the bungalow door opened at 7a.m. Tia ran. She's one content happy girl living in utopia☺…. My best mate's happiness is infectious on my own….

Beginning with all the makings of gorgeous, fairytale book weather in paradise, Mother Nature delivered the promise. We have well and truly earned one. The gusty conditions have been chiselling away at stripping bark from trees and exposing some rich earthy colours like treasure buried below….

Religiously returning with determination to make an impact on the computer I settled in shortly after 9a.m. delving between the pages of journal nine. Leaving the bungalow door open to bring in as much of the day as possible, quite a variety of bird activity going on outside was great company, real uplifting happy to be alive conditions☺….

Looking through the window on a phone call I sighted movement in a paddock at a distance, afterwards through binoculars made it out to be the feral black cat originating from Wendy's, sadly it's still roaming healthy on a diet of small native birds and animals....

Sunday 6 June 2004
A hangover from yesterday, the elements combined to turn on more beautiful winter conditions. Unable to bring myself to spend it entirely indoors, I put in a bit of time but didn't get real serious with the computer....
Doing any small job that represented being fully immersed in the conditions on offer, pushing the wheelbarrow, Ms Tia and I idled up hill by the water tank filling it with a load of fallen limb wood kindly donated by the trees. About as common as seeing a rainbow, are the number of days the depth of field from our elevated perch is sharp at any focal length, the clarity and detail of the valleys and mountain ranges was breathtaking ☺....

Monday 7 June 2004
A bit of a lazy one on the farm, with her belly full Ms Tia was content to snooze from spot to spot following sunshine.... Not a bad life if you don't weaken ☺!!!!
Life for me at Rainbow Falls was also very low-key, doing the necessary bits then settled into the keyboard finger dance, and that I did....
Lost in a daydream break through the bungalow window, a large frame flying through the patch of space in my view and landing in a tree bordering a home paddock was that of an eagle. A good site to rest its wings, although just on a wish list, it would be a hoot to have an eagle's nest on home soil ☺....

Tuesday 8 June 2004
Basking in direct morning sun, shielded cosy from the elements inside the shed entrance pondering the bit of the world in my view over a cuppa, I did the thirty-metre dash to catch the ringing phone. Looking for something to do during school holidays Loui called to say her and the kids were on their way....
The kids with Tia in tow used up a lot of energy playing on the rock pile moulding nests for themselves within, climbing trees and playing chasey. Tia never failed at being the best at hide and seek ☺....
Loui and I took time to literally smell the flowers, picking a variety of bulb blooms to scent her car driving home with a bunch destined for her Mum AEnone also....
With intentions of incorporating a haircut into dropping Destiny at the panel beaters I phoned through for an appointment. The person answering the phone at the hairdressers simply informed me Monday was a public holiday, obviously a minor detail overlooked by the panel beater also, oops. Rescheduling Destiny, the panel beater said I'd be without her for two and a half days....
The dust on socialising settling I clunked a few more pages into the hard drive, trying always to finish the day exiting more pages than entering ☺.... Chipping away at it, the journals digitisation is getting closer to the end than the start I'm beginning to see the light....

Wednesday 9 June 2004
Exposed to sun for a total of five minutes, the first drop of moisture found ground mid morning, staring at the slow moving screen was the logical place to be keeping progress in a forward motion....
My brain and hands are becoming more co-ordinated producing a greater level of accuracy on the keyboard less time is lost amending errors. Pulling up to cook dinner I was a mere three journal pages shy of digitising our life's experiences to the start of 2004.... Yahoooo, I'm on the data entry home trail ☺ ....
With bellies bulging full of spaghetti, the force of the computer drawing me in was too strong to resist with turning into the year 2004 being so close. One small goal at a time will produce the big outcome, see you there one day ☺ !!!!

Thursday 10 June 2004
Catching my breath I put the obsession anchors on, an uneven balance of late, in favour of relaxation. The only plan left to evolve was to make a 1:45pm doctors' appointment and visit Ross afterwards, not too difficult a task. The plan got even easier I received a call to say the doctor was sick rescheduling the appointment for tomorrow....
A good drop of 16mm found ground overnight rain arrived with wind around 1:30a.m.-ish, stepping aside 7a.m.-ish made way for a delightful sunny day....
Striking all the little necessities from my 'to-do' list headed over to Ross' purely to socialise, taking the remainder of last nights spaghetti and a bottle of red to help sustain our energy for chatting.... Going down well ☺ ....
It was nice to have time out it was a reminder there's a little more to life. The break recharged my batteries ☺ ....

Friday 11 June 2004
Some days disappear without leaving too many footprints in the sand this is one of them....
Doing a take-two for the doctors' appointment I walked in the door to be advised their schedule was quite behind. Filling in time I happily disappeared getting enough food to see us through the long weekend, a slip of the key into the Post Office box, then back to fulfil the appointment....
Medical certificate extended for another month to go home and keep fattening up, en route and grabbing drinking water at Ross', he was in and offered a cuppa....
Destiny unloaded, my next move was to cook dinner, by the time life was semi under control I didn't feel much like doing the keyboard finger dance.... Another night off, I feel like I'm on holidays ☺ ....

Saturday 12 June 2004
It didn't come as a shock with the steep decline in the mercury to greet a white frost pushing open the bungalow door. Picking up a weather report, at 3:30pm yesterday it was 4°, by 7p.m. the mercury was at a chilly zero setting us up for a bloody penetrating cold night.... Brrrr....
Betraying the theory of a sunny day following frost sun was short lasting before cloud and overcast conditions moved in, unpredictable, Mother Nature was going to shoot at random....

Anything could have happened outside my mind was set to return to the computer following a couple of day's absence. Psyched ready to make an impact on folder eleven achieved the target.
Also adding strength to unrelenting determination working towards dreams, my 'half full' cup received another shot of encouragement two hundred hand written pages are now digitised....
A bloody lot of words spat out of my fingertips☺!!!!

Sunday 13 June 2004
Throwing in ten dollars to adequately cover fuel costs Ross agreed to assist in picking Tia and me up from the panel beaters. Planning ahead for Destiny's stay away from home, to look her best, with the help of my little mate and running water she received a spruce up. Connecting a hose to the tap above the cattle trough I began to find Destiny's exterior....
Catching the ringing phone midway through Destiny's bath, pleasantly the caller was a dear Mildura friend Miriam. Without speaking for a while the call wasn't going to be brief and we had solid catch up. Through invitation, Mirro suggested if I could travel a few days beforehand, she would like to share them in the lead up to her wedding day, how special is that, looks like there's a definite trip to Mildura on the cards for September. A double bonus, a mutual friend and former co-worker David, who is now a Salvation Army Captain, is going to marry Mirro and Andrew ☺.... A Department of Agriculture reunion....
Leaving no stone unturned before replacing the receiver, Tia helped me finish washing the last of the dirt road from Destiny. Parking her in the shed for a de-furring and a window clean she's elegantly prepared for time away from home to have her cow bum imprint removed ☺....
Washing Destiny offered all the right moves for a rain dance, paying attention, the elements gathered and moisture settled in blocking sun by 3:30p.m.-ish, that's about when my bum found the chair seated in front of the computer. I'm beginning to feel a major sense of achievement. Appreciating the enormity of the detailed recorded history, the moving target entering the hard drive just keeps growing ☺ ????
Out for last wee's before bed little legs shot off in all directions, a couple of sets of legs flashed passed by me in the dark only guessing one set belonged to Tia ☺ ....

Monday 14 June 2004
Offering 8mm overnight a mixed bag of a day followed, moisture eased up, more so blown away, minus cloud cover the sun shines transparently through wind....
In the transition to clearing, heavy mist cloud woven through trees and clinging to South Sister Range, was hit by the suns rays illuminating rainbows. Arched over the range, one rainbow in particular blasted a strong colour range framed against a black sky ☺....
Ross phoned with his plan of getting firewood in the Scamander area directly after dropping Destiny off at the panel beaters. A cheap date, paying Ross ten dollars and helping load the trailer with wood he's got to be happy with that, probably just as happy as I was to finally be taken home....
Destinyless and unable to wander digitisation should benefit. With the help of my best friend and co-author we're steadying to kick a goal with data entry, already immersed into the pages of folder twelve from a total of fourteen ☺....

Tuesday 15 June 2004
Scattered showers played around in the hours of darkness and disappearing before sunrise left behind 4mm in the gauge as confirmation of its existence….
When sun had made impact enough to dry the cottage roof I climbed on with refreshed enthusiasm to make an impression sealing up the problem area that lets water inside, seriously emptying three tubes of silicon between sheets of iron. Once rain can be kept out then I can make a confident start on the inside of the cottage getting it to a comfortable liveable stage ☺ ….
Seeing light at the end of the journal folder stack, persistence is paying off the moving target end is within reach…. That's a time I'm looking forward to!!!!
Doing the hard yards with me admirably basking patiently behind glass in full sun, testing her co-author perseverance, I made Tia's life even more difficult producing a huge bone that put a sparkle in her eyes ☺ ….

Wednesday 16 June 2004
Dropping out of sight 4:30p.m.-ish, early sunsets and sun rises have altered my internal hibernation clock, not something I'm known for is early mornings, but was motivated 7a.m.-ish ☺ ????
Taking a leap into the past visiting the present, I phoned Doris Lohrey expressing interest in sharing photographs and stories over a cuppa. Commitment free next Tuesday 11a.m.-ish, visiting Doris at home in Launceston was inked in. I can't wait to hear and share experiences of Rainbow Falls' past ☺ ….
Plenty of rain cloud accompanied by occasional mist pretty much summed up the morning, thinning to let sun breakthrough for longer periods in the afternoon made it easier to stay indoors. Folder twelve found completion, making a token start on journal thirteen before blurry eyes and a waning interest stopped the day's play ☺ ….

Thursday 17 June 2004
Remaining in sync with the lunar and solar cycle, my new habit of getting out of bed early didn't falter. Opening the door onto a snow white frost, I could have slept in and experienced this one, it lingered until 10a.m.-ish. The ground temperature was bloody cold throwing off a chill, meeting somewhere in the middle and compensating, sun offered a little warmth being naked for a bath was tolerable and quick!!!!
Nothing groundbreaking occurred, the evolving plan centred on Loui picking us up after her shift to collect Destiny and our independence….
The morning got absorbed with cuppa's inside the shed gates basking in sunshine, bathing, and also hanging a couple framed prints in the cottage further extending a more homely feel ☺ ….
True to her word, Loui scooped me and Ms Tia to be reunited with a 'cow bum imprint free' Destiny. From Scamander we continued on to St. Helens, most importantly paying Destiny's registration. Checking on the verdict of the digital phone at the electronics shop, the base was declared dead, as far as I'm concerned it can stay that way! Requesting to keep the dead unit, I instead chose to take it home staff at the electronics shop then gathered and patched together the already claimed and scattered phone bits????

Retreating back for a hot brew, Loui shared a couple of songs she had written and recorded to mini disk, she writes, sings and plays guitar well, her talent has some purpose. Out of an act of kindness Loui loaned me a mini tape recorder to record Tuesdays visit with Doris Lohrey, I can't leave it to memory it has trouble retrieving stored information at times ☺ !!!!

Friday 18 June 2004
A day off data entry didn't dampen inspiration, on the contrary I'm becoming more inspired as the finish line draws near and I'm beginning to see the end of the tunnel ☺ ....
Out of the blue a call came in from 'Business and Employment', the organisation that arranged my Work for the Dole, requesting details as to why I left Break O'Day FM and my sexual discrimination and harassment issues. Giving me hope someone was interested enough to listen, even for a moment....
Unsure of what drove me to look, fossicking through the bag of phone bits pieced together at the electronics store I took the back off the handset finding it minus the recently purchased $30 battery. Phoning the boys at the store, who were fully aware of the battery purchase, the final word was, if I produce a receipt only then will they reimburse the cost of the battery.
Hmmmm, happy to take my dud phone off my hands for nothing yesterday, the St. Helens boys strike me as nothing but a pair of money hungry thieves!!!!
Adding finishing touches and about to put the cardboard curtain up for the evening, the sight of three eagles gliding effortlessly above the valley at the bottom of Rainbow Falls delayed the process....

Saturday 19 June 2004
Elevated to bolt upright 5a.m.-ish sharp to what I thought to be the sound of corrugated iron being ripped from the cottage roof, dimly lit torch in hand, was dressed and out the door in a flash.
A few strong gusts were about but wind wasn't outstandingly destructive. Following Tia and the dimly lit torch she led me directly to the source of the noise, a piece of iron had dismantled from the chook pen structure in the cottage side yard making a ruckus doing a couple of back flips.... Happy for a simple solution....
Bright eyed from the sudden burst of action I plugged in the lamp and fired up the computer, achieving by morning's end what was hoped for the entire day. Getting pretty pumped with the end so close I can almost touch it, enthusiasm is escalating. Robbing life from the slow moving screen to cook dinner the final journal folder, number fourteen, had commenced its digital existence ☺ !!!!
I've been fortunate that busy computer activity and winter have coincided, growth in the yard has been left only to bulbs grass around housing is being well maintained by native animals.... Bonus ☺ ....

Sunday 20 June 2004
Inspired by yesterdays' gallant effort clunking keys, and an end in sight, I didn't hesitate to get up 7a.m.-ish when Tia gave me a paw tap on the shoulder.... I was a woman on a mission ☺ ....

Rewarded for the early rise by a spectacular crimson sunrise, and with solstice passing tonight from here on in days will only be getting longer. I've just got the hang of getting up early now I'm going to have to revert back to sleeping in???? Demanding world☺….

A pleasant distraction mid morning came with my sister Kerry calling to ask if our cool change brought snow it only felt like it….

Page by page, hour by hour my fingers danced, enthusiasm heightened as the end drew near. Pipping 2p.m. I hit home plate and emerged out the end of the tunnel, shutting down having to hand write more to enter more, a preferred option. Just as soon as the floppy disks finished saving, and bursting to share the moment, was on the phone to the people who listen to my every whim, Mum and Dad☺….

The sensation felt just typing the final date took me emotionally to many places, particularly the many, many, many, many hours of keyboard tango, the journal is now fully digitised, the years of hand writing Rainbow Falls unfolding story for that moment to exist. More words now have to be written to continue creating history, right up to today's entry has now found its way into the hi-tech digital world…. A bloody wonderful feeling☺!!!!

Monday 21 June 2004

Investing all spare time the past six weeks into the computer, I'm lost I don't know what to do with myself now I've typed the journal to current☺????

Filling the void of withdrawal from literary pursuits I busied myself catching up on bits 'n' pieces for posting. Supplementing a letter in pictures, I have an extra set of home progress photos printed, write comments over the back of each print and send them off to Mum and Dad, pleasant to receive☺….

Bathing up for town to post Mum and Dad's picture letter I missed a call from my bank manager and friend Helen, the message left on the answering machine confirmed loan approval, refinancing Rainbow Falls is definite!!!! Yahoo, finally living in the black, I could punch the air☺!!!!

Eventually organised for town I had tummy rumbles that only Evelyn could satisfy, fuelling up at the bakery….

Tuesday 22 June 2004

If the brilliant pastel pinks and blues of sunrise was an indicator of the day ahead then it was accurate. Sitting to write this evening I'm struggling with the pen to formulate words to accurately describe just how inwardly warm and comfortable I felt in Doris' company☺….

My feet don't seem to have touched ground and the planned visit with Doris came around warming Destiny's oil taking a run to Launceston….

Doris greeted me with a welcoming hug and words that etched deeply, "we are soul sisters you and I". Sharing experiences living at Rainbow Falls, and without an inkling of knowledge about me keeping a journal, Doris said, and the words stuck like glue, "it's a great place to write"☺????

Coming from fine country hospitality, Doris put on a beautiful chicken and vegetable soup for lunch and never tired answering every question I relentlessly asked. Approaching 89, and very switched on, Doris' memories, that don't seem that long ago, create the stories now considered pieces of history. I had an incredible time listening and recording….

Toying with the idea, I was honoured to receive a copy of Doris' memoirs the six pages speak volumes of an incredible life, an emotional journey. Placing their stamp on the patch of ground, now affectionately known as Rainbow Falls, Doris and her late husband Norman offered the title as Lustleigh. Time dissolved, leaving the same way as arriving Doris and I embraced in a hug, agreeing to keep sharing our strong bonds in common ☺....
Pulling up to shut the front gate behind, Destiny's headlights exposed an owl settled on the third fencepost in, ahhhh, the giver of wisdom, pretty much sums up my day ☺....

Wednesday 23 June 2004
Choosing to rest my brain doing something requiring minimal thought opted for repetition therapy, just letting thoughts free range with new-found friendship and knowledge, the shed was an ideal location ☺....
Setting the shed heater ready just to throw a match onto then collected enough wood to stay there for a week. Simply planning on a gentle evolving day, let myself be led by the shovel to the dam playing with the shape of the overflow channel, the area is remaining too wet too long for my liking....
Out wandering I put an end to a few young scotch thistles, evolving into spending a couple of hours tidying housing fenceline....
In conversation with Doris yesterday about the original use of the bungalow, she said it was the first registered building in Dublin Town. Dating back to 1889 it was fully built with split timber by Edward Young as his hut prior to the cottage being built, then later served as a kitchen....
Happy putting in a gentle day home, I activated the final plan, striking a match and tossing it onto the heater ☺....

Thursday 24 June 2004
Just getting up and getting on with survival requirements each day blends, they're only given different names so time can be measured ☺ ????
Destiny's tail-gate lock dismantled on the trip to Launceston, possibly rattled apart from using the rough as guts road to home, not quite shutting properly. Before taking on another rattling expedition over the mountain, through the process of elimination I worked out why the lock isn't operating and how to open it manually. Most importantly, shutting the tail-gate securely....
Destiny unpacked from town, I somehow ended up on the window box basking in sunshine behind glass giving the newspaper a serious read over a brewed coffee. Lingering over the crossword I got all but one word out exercising the brain a little.... Rare ☺....
Leaving fading sunlight I drifted in next door to the cottage to cook dinner. Today complemented my energy, simple, sane and sedate, perfect ☺....

Friday 25 June 2004
Sunrise blanketed, the bright lights obscured, I woke instead to the therapeutic sound of a shower of rain on the tin roof.... Ahhhh....
Brain and body aligned ready to tackle physical labour I took on the challenge of wrestling with carpet and underlay in the bungalow, more insulation is always better!!!!

Treated to a personal favourite element with low drifting cloud fading visibility in and out, as an added bonus, for stretches time stood still, accommodating perfect pristine silence from any movement of sound, my own breathing could be heard with detailed clarity.... Pure peace on earth ☺ ....

Responding to the noise of rising iron, between showers I hopped on the carport roof attached to the shed and put a screw in an ominous loose piece of tin. A job being saved for more appropriate conditions but it screamed out loud enough for attention to make high priority, because the squeaky wheel gets the oil around here....

Happier off the roof, and still out of my comfort zone, placed the handle of the vacuum cleaner in my palm sucking up everything before and after underlay installation....

Tidying up a progressive day, followed through with the evening plan of sitting by the electric heater assessing the benefit of extra underlay, and updating the last week of the journal to computer life before it gets out of hand ☺ ....

Saturday 26 June 2004

I love weekends, the business side of the outside world goes to sleep, giving life a deeper sense of freedom from wandering intrusive people giving themselves permission to just enter private land unannounced in the guise of doing their job. On the flip side, those restricted by jobs all week wander weekends????

Having smoko just inside shed gates basking it was hard to drag myself away from that bone warming cosy environment to go inside and do washing, but that's what happened ☺ ????

Tinkering, after wringing my wrists ragged, pruned the scruffy dead heads from hydrangeas in the vegie patch then took a fresh tin of ash up to the loo.... Being a constant reminder of Mum's attempt at burning the loo down ☺ ....

A pocket of clear sky separating the horizon from an extended sliver of cloud hovering above, staged a spectacularly colourful sunset. Perching myself comfortably in a front row seat declared beer o'clock and put my feet up, appreciating the splendour of rich colours peaking to a gradual softening of pastels and fading to darkness.... Exceptional ☺ ....

Sunday 27 June 2004

Underlay now removed from its storage site in the cottage, and motivated by its absence, I swept out the cottage in the ever-evolving process of transforming it from a secure storage area to a homely residence only....

Pushing the wheelbarrow to Rainbow Falls' highest point beside the water tank, me and Ms Muffet went about collecting a load of limb wood from the ground, spotting bonus treasure with a small stack of picket posts. Stacking the lot in the shed to use for a beer 'n' bullshit occasion ☺ ....

Strong contours indented in carpet shadowing warped floorboards have noticeably softened with the installation of underlay. The temperature has also softened every insulation modification is useful, particularly helpful tonight with cool wind trying to blow us away!!!!

Monday 28 June 2004

What an absolute bastard of a night, with the setting of the sun strong wind picked up and gave us a caning. In a futile attempt at sleep I saw every hour on the clock laying in hope the roof would stay intact. Finding wind easier to deal with through daylight hours, I was happy to see it come around. A weather report mentioned wind gusts of up to 120kms per hour we didn't go without, copping a pounding hour after long hour....

Without direction, windy, overcast and at times a little rain was blown in, uninviting to be outside, I wasn't inspired indoors either, finding myself feeling at a bit of a loss. Wandering aimlessly, I unpacked a box of books stored in the cottage and displayed them in the bungalow. A reliable place to occupy a listless brain led me to the shed to reduce prunings small enough to put down the throat of the heater. Tuning my ear into what was making the worst noise during blasts eliminated a few scrapes and creaks that exaggerate wind ferocity.... I have soooo had enough of the rough play!!!!

Tuesday 29 June 2004
Tortured sleep from rattles and clunks accompanying gusts over a couple of nights, I fell in a heap out of sheer exhaustion and the roof was still on waking this morning. Like a bad tenant unwilling to leave, although marginally tamer, wind still persisted!!!!
'Red sky in the morning shepherds warning' there was plenty of cloud and a crimson red sunrise waiting outside. Doing a quick cart of water beating a good shower of rain, at that point felt the lure of the shed kick in ☺....
Before heading down to get absorbed in the haven decided to tidy business first. Attempting to make an appointment with the Launceston Bendigo Bank to organise the signing of refinancing papers no one would answer, the clock displaying 8:36am gave me all the answers ☺....
Oooops....
Pulling the carpet out from under my feet, rain shot through not long after it started, doing a rethink over a cuppa on the window box in the bungalow spied a formed rainbow. Leaning back to take in more of the arch my timing was ideal to see an eagle fly through it, moving to the door for a better view watched the eagle fly out of sight toward South Sister.... Magic ☺....
Being constantly shoved into the forefront of my mind I worked on noises created by things moving and scraping in wind. Picking up again after sunset, wind gusts seemed less vicious on the chorus of protesting scrapes, rattles and squeaks, and psychologically better for me. Gale force wind is taking its toll on energy, I've had enough!!!!

Wednesday 30 June 2004
Awake from 2:30a.m.-ish onwards, the impact of a wild gust almost lifted me bolt upright in bed, the worst encounters left me seriously wonder if the roof was going to stay on. The sound alone of a wind fronts building roar as its driven up the gorge heading our way, and the expectant impact its about to have, plays with the mind, remembering to breathe only after the wave passes without taking the roof. Lashing at us until mid morning wasn't a comfortable experience, so concerned by the pounding I had the SES number handy by the phone and remained fully clothed all night ready for anything....
Dropping the cardboard curtain to get out amongst the blustery elements at sunrise, the vivid colours of part of an illuminated rainbow caught my eye, again with an eagle flying past, I'm surprised how active they've been in such wild conditions. The second sighting of an eagle passing a rainbow, magic stuff ☺....

The removal of the cardboard curtain also revealed cloud with serious looking intentions, battling elements outside I got home bits organised and headed for the sanctuary of the shed. By 8:30a.m.-ish the heater was lit and I was watching horizontal rain, with moving water Tia was happy pitting her skill catching the flow falling off the end of the shed roof....
Feeling as strong as a half-sucked peppermint, I didn't change the world just happy to still have ours intact☺!!!!

Thursday 1 July 2004
Up with the rising sun again, for a change of pace we were greeted by a glorious calm winter morning. A solemn promise made to myself, the next calm break in the weather I was on the shed roof replacing nails with screws....
Forced to give it away early to meet a noon bank appointment in Launceston, by 8:45am seventy nails had been replaced by 2-inch screws on the sheds flat front section alone. A few nails could have been pulled out by hand, pretty worrying, how the shed roof was holding together under the wild torment endured in the hands of the elements recently is beyond me ☺????
It felt somewhat special starting a new financial year driving to Launceston to sign refinancing papers for Rainbow Falls and begin living life in the black.... I hope that's a future omen, surviving is good☺....
Making Launceston, busying my brain to lots of fast moving people going somewhere, found a park, fed the meter, and with minutes to spare punctually walked through the doors of the bank.
Signing in appropriate places, and paper shuffle complete, living in the black was officially confirmed☺!!!!
Leaving the bank I fed the meter and did a few chores then with nothing left to keep me hanging around pointed Destiny's nose homeward. Using the windscreen wipers on the drive home I uselessly watched a piece of paper, tucked under the blade, being smeared across the windscreen then disappear into the big compost heap along the highway roadside. The remaining red sticker instructed me to see the details on the piece of paper for my parking meter expiry fine. Now I have to waste money on wasted money to find out how to pay the fucking thing!?!?
Settling in to write, Kerry gave me a courtesy call letting me know Tegan has been confirmed pregnant. I think she is a careless young shit, but there's no point carrying on or resisting life goes on, I'm about to be a great aunt.... Kerry has to get used to Nana☺....

Friday 2 July 2004
Opening the bungalow door greeted the day with a pair of eagles gliding above Rainbow Falls, not a bad way to be met☺....
Ignorance isn't always bliss, so I phoned the Launceston Council for advice on paying the elusive parking meter fine, my ten dollar fine increases to twenty after twelve days, self regulating thieving bastards!!!!
Letting the bad taste dissipate from my mouth I admitted myself directly into brain therapy basking in sunshine tucked inside the shed entrance. Feeling as strong as a half-sucked peppermint I lazed the morning away over plenty of food, milo and sun.... hmmmm....

Taking some inspiring to prize my arse out of the chair, finally firing up more screws found homes in the cottage roof replacing a few existing and non-existent nails, making our grip on life a little stronger. Eliminating more of those squeaking and scraping sounds created when wind and loosening nails are combined, keeps my mind more peaceful ☺ ….

Staying with the momentum of motivation, basking behind glass in sunshine, Tia snoozed to the whirring sound of the computer, I got fingers active staying current with the hand written journal stopping the snail from escaping the hare. From average beginnings my typing speed and accuracy have improved out of sight making data entry less frustrating and slow ☺ ….

It's a bloody pleasure to be sitting relaxed without any destruction seeking wind, a well earnt calm evening allowing night sounds to penetrate silence to reach the desired audience….
Hallelujah ☺ ….

Saturday 3 July 2004
The atmosphere remaining calm, we slept like babies. Feeling uplifted Mother Nature took me beyond removing the cardboard curtain revealed low cloud and equally as low visibility, a magic day to be swallowed up in the institution. Scattered showers being the norm so with my little mate headed to the shed and stayed put….

Nice to have a rest from the insanity of punishing wind it certainly was a very, very testing week.

I once rode a ZZR 1100 road bike to 200kms per hour solving all curiosity with speed, a sensation of feeling equivalent, Tuesday nights' battering air rushed past my ears at similar speeds….

Pretty much wiped off the map, Tia and I spent the entire day by the heater in the shed or not far from it. Tia was happy catching falling water off the end of the roof leaving me to feed the face of the heater…. Any more relaxed I'd be putty ☺ ….

Sunday 4 July 2004
Exhausted following a long week of broken sleep Ms Tia and I were tucked into beddy byes early last night, waking before 6a.m. to the tune of wind and rain and supporting a cranky mood that took some shaking. The dark mood was triggered by pondering over people I've given a cup full of trust to, particularly the unfulfilled hollow handshake deal with Terry for cattle agistment. Terry couldn't wait to empty the cup quick enough, welshing on his promise of piecing together the cottage-plumbing infrastructure instead of doing a money trade….

Still unsatisfied the dam overflow isn't regulated correctly, took my cranky determined mood and shovel to rectify the soggy wet ground problem once and for all!!!!

Thoughts still straying to pumping up to the water tank I measured the falling bore depth, finding air to almost six metres its going to take serious rain for a retry….

Mother Nature extended a harsh lesson in complacency and brain relaxing, building up momentum she dished out a blunt reminder. Eliminating wind generated building noise is allowing a fine tune of the system. The afternoon's rough treatment exposed a couple more spots requiring attention. Being reactive in quieter gusts, I scaled the ladder drill in hand and replaced a few more nails, constantly getting quieter and stronger in buildings and brain ☺ ….

Monday 5 July 2004
Minimal loose bits responding to demanding wind translates to less night noises permitting a more sound sleep, however, there were constant reminders as to how vulnerable we are to the might of nature....
Living in hope the determined wind will pass I tuned into a weather report, that exercise simply kicked the chair out from under, there's not an end in sight on the radar its here for a bit longer and gale force at times. A southerly change due in tonight sometime should slow speeds down a few knots, certainly having had moooore than enough I'm being rattled apart!!!!
Up with sunrise again, I got ready to tackle the mountain particularly to tidy up paperwork loose ends. Faxing a copy of current insurance details to the bank turned on nothing but refinancing green lights ☺ !!!!
Wandering aimless I went to upright a couple of 44-gallon drums that had blown over at the side of the shed then tinkered not too far off at the cattle yards tidying fenceline....
With daylight beginning to fade I retreated indoors to cook dinner and caught a call from Ross extending a dinner invitation for tomorrow, only a fool would say no to someone else cooking. A definite yes was the reply, a haircut and a cooked dinner lined up for tomorrow it's my lucky day ☺ ....

Tuesday 6 July 2004
Wind eventually shifted, driving in a solid southerly blast for variation. A rush of bloody icy air was intense enough to ice over a puddle formed near the bungalow, breaking the ice crust to pick out Tia's bone left to witness the elements. Awake, I couldn't bring myself to expose pink warm skin to the air waiting outside of the doona until absolutely necessary to make the haircut in time....
A pleasing first stop in St. Helens was to the electronics store flashing my $30 receipt to get a refund on the missing phone battery, a brief, polite and successful experience....
Stepping out of the supermarket is where I crossed paths with Loui's mother AEnone. Into genealogy, I picked AEnone's brains on how to track pieces of the past in relation to Rainbow Falls' former tenant Edward Young....
Investing the electronics store refund on a couple of tubes of silicon and another 100 roofing screws was a far better investment for home. Pampered by the lovely Kellie, my head was found underneath a mop of hair and dusted with a sprinkling of tips to disguise the few greys moving in.... I'm aware of cold ears tonight....
Pulling up home with enough time to take a few slow breaths and for Tia to re-establish some of her favoured real estate before driving back out the gate to Ross' for dinner. Over drinks and food we didn't stop yarping until parting company 11p.m.-ish. Prepared to treat myself to the night off writing my mind was still alert and couldn't leave it alone.... Not so alert at this point ☺ ....

Wednesday 7 July 2004
Good to be inside looking out; the mercury didn't look like making double figures 6° at 10a.m. with snow falling to 600 metres. Jumping up on the cottage roof to empty a tube of silicon my fingers took some warming up afterwards, brrrr. It didn't take Mother Nature long to test

waterproofing the existing leak eased and a new one was generated only really shifting the problem, sadly it was an exercise in achieving nothing....
A good place to keep shielded from the elements was to the benefit of the cottage. Chiselling at the slow moving transformation mirrors and windows now have a better clarity and a few 'Sue nests' were deconstructed ☺....
The sun made cameo appearances between passing showers, although for what it was worth made little impact on the mercury, wind on the other hand is finally settling to sensible speeds. Preferring not to be outdoors longer than necessary, late afternoon we transferred from one set of walls to another, retreating to the bungalow by the heater to watch the sun set hugging a warm milo. Ms Tia has shown very little interest in going outside, if cold air is keeping her in then her word is good enough for me ☺....

Thursday 8 July 2004
More therapeutic on the brain, however, rain was shoved aside by wild gusts taking random swipes.... Another night of broken sleep!!!!
First up the air temperature was bloody freezing, dirty looking cloud I've learned to associate with snow was hanging around and southerly gusts were doing their best to push them overtop. Offering a spell, wind dropped permitting the sun's rays to make an impact generating a dash of warmth....
Running short on days to pay the parking meter fine without incurring a penalty, doubling it as a dash for food, took on the mountain for the shops. From town snow could be seen with the naked eye covering the top of Ben Lomond, sun illuminating the mountain gave the illusion of lifting it three-dimensionally, proudly showing off its pure white decoration and looking purely brilliant ☺....
Making use of the calm, bone defrosting conditions, I scaled the ladder back onto the cottage roof to have another go at waterproofing and replacing more nails....
In contrast to morning, where I couldn't pull the beanie any further down over my ears, I was beanie free all afternoon. Amazing what the elements are capable of in a 24-hour period, it's an eye-opening place to live....

Friday 9 July 2004
After almost two weeks of being pounded by random gusts and somehow surviving, last night was so bloody perfectly calm it was taken full advantage of. Pulling the doona over my ears around 10p.m. I fell in a dark hole of zeds, sliding the bolt on the bungalow door around 9a.m. this morning I'd packed in some much needed quality sleep zzzz....
Greeting a soupy fog, as it began to lift cloud clung to and hung from South Sister Range like custard decorating a Christmas pudding, simply looking spectacular ☺....
If my passion for beer and bullshit was to continue the shed needed restocking with timber, raiding the regular haunts took positive steps to rectify the situation. Light physical labour got an appetite active luring my stomach to the great indoors and that's where I stayed. Leaving the bungalow door open maximising the outdoors coming in, and keeping a finger on the pulse, Ms co-author and myself got journal digitising current....

Saturday 10 July 2004
Rewarded for endurance, following another solid recuperation sleep I stepped out into both a beanie and windproof jacket free temperature, exceptional, one could do little more than go outside immerse in and appreciate the elements on offer ☺....
Determined to beat the persistent water leak entering the cottage ceiling I scaled the ladder carrying out the latest idea fitting into budget. Sealing a proposed watertight lock surrounding the flue and rooftop with a solid plastic bag tightly secured by tape, a cheap way of isolating the supposed problem area....
Following up with a bit of shovel work, by the time it was again parked I was buggered and the alarm had sounded for beer o'clock and to feed the worked up appetite....

Sunday 11 July 2004
Still horizontal under the doona pondering the day ahead I psyched myself into cooking up a deep bath, however, the view waiting behind the cardboard curtain determined a re-psyche. Quietly the latest waterproofing was being tested instigating a rethink over a leisurely breakfast while Tia gnashed at a bone....
Waterproofing the cottage ceiling is a moving target, fix one leak silicon only shifts it to another site, keeping me to a fixed location it's the flue where the problem is isolated to.... I'm in need of another dose of inspiration to continue the waterproofing saga!!!!
Moving at a sedate pace with the clearing of the sky, Tia snoozed from one comfy spot in full sun to another, while I on the other hand got a feel for editing the digitised journal. A totally new experience void of instruction and without any known direction, it took a bit of getting my head around exactly how to tackle and get a feel for it, a slow procrastinating start made way for a solid few hours of pencil practice ☺ ????

Monday 12 July 2004
Back on the cottage roof with a renewed dose of enthusiasm, rounding up equipment I climbed the ladder carting with me sealing tape and plastic sheets determined to isolate and put a halt to leaks.... Preferring to use all spare buckets for water storage rather than taken up catching drips coming inside!!!!
My best friend was only ever a few steps away pushing the wheelbarrow up hill by the water tank collecting fallen limb wood, versatile fire starters for both beer 'n' bullshit and bulk bath water.
Loaded wheelbarrow parked in the shed and traded off for shovel, I lost a couple of hours on cattle yard fenceline....
Turning on a perfect mild evening, with a beer in hand, Tia and I roamed simply enjoying the sunset and our gorgeous surroundings. With fading light we stepped foot in the cottage arranging the collected pieces of carpet and lino until satisfying my imagination that was the best positions that could be achieved....

Tuesday 13 July 2004
Grabbing my cage and giving it a good rattle, raging wind has sensitised my brain, activated by the slightest rattle or scrape sets off the chain reaction of my eyes springing open and ears listening in. A sensitively tuned mind woke 5a.m.-ish to listen to a few stronger gusts gently

pushing us around, nowhere near the extreme potential previously encountered. Reassured everything was holding together returned to blissful sleep....

It's hard to believe, from my desert dwelling origins, the sheer capacity of fast weather changes here. Waking me earlier, wind abated to perfectly calm, ideal for lighting fires outside put in motion the idea of a deep bath. In the short time taken to prepare the fire pit a boating weather forecast described approaching winds of up to 30 knots gale force at times. Finding it hard to believe that such a perfect calmness was going to turn on us, how could such serenity be spoilt????

Before striking a match, a packet of fifty screws was invested into the flat front section of the shed roof, planning on doing it soon, but news of more strong wind put it up the priority list, the squeaky wheel gets the oil. Carefully wandering amongst some slightly raised iron and loosening nails made me wonder how it stayed together; its doing a better job than me????

With the psychological upper hand of another fifty screws holding the lid more securely in place, and not a breath having picked up, 'Plan A' was reactivated putting flame under the drum of water. Limited to take it beyond, no amount of breathing in or rounding of shoulders puts my body totally under I soaked in the standard nipples out bath ☺....

A courtesy call from Forestry Tasmania was to inform me they were about to start a burn-off of unused bits at the coupe accessed through the neighbours', I pretty much told them nothing I say or do will change their course of action....

Wednesday 14 July 2004

A wild mongrel of a night copping another hammering incorporating many hours of broken sleep, my brain let me drift off sometime around 4a.m.-ish.... Pretty bloody ordinary.... I don't have a memory of encountering wind this strong in the previous two years of living here, the constant impacts are taking their toll on me not housing!!!!

Dragging a reluctant tired body from bed I put one foot in front of the other to take a mountain trip for a restock. A wolf in sheep's clothing, as the day progressed elements offered a false sense of security, wind abated delivering warm, calm sunshine????

With my little mate busying herself claiming real estate and anything else tickling her fancy I walked aimlessly through paddocks kicking out scotch thistles. Making for a slow pace, the beneficial therapeutic walk eliminated a couple of hundred young plants....

Broken sleep is really robbing my get up and go, feeling as flat as a shit carter's hat if the elements are kind then I'm in for an early one tonight ☺!!!!

Thursday 15 July 2004

The weather forecast did little to lift spirits wind will be hanging around for the next three days one can only hope it gets amended!!!!

There's certainly no trouble drying the washing its keeping it on the line that's the problem!!!! Struggling with clothes in wind I had a dummy spit, in need of time out after a test of patience, expelled pent energy going walkabout with the shovel.... Tia was happy with that decision ☺....

Downing tools feeling levelled out, I used the last of natural light preparing dinner. Leaving dinner to simmer at leisure we took in a bit of evening viewing on television, watching the setting of the sun morph to fading darkness....

Oddly, finalising today's journal entry, now 9p.m., the evening is calm, to be enjoyed while it lasts because peacefulness changes very quickly, weather is by the hour☺????

Friday 16 July 2004
More tormenting sounds playing with my psychology, and the need to go to the toilet, raised me from a broken sleep to face the day by 6:30am beating sunrise….
Weakening under the pressure of a constant battering, the latest cottage waterproofing effort started to dismantle before being tested. Without the need for rain, a new water leak was found in the cottage, a rodent chewed a hole in the fresh water container and a couple of litres found a new home in the cupboard and over the floor…. Not good practice for a long life expectancy!!!!
Catching an early weather report on the radio predicting showers we spent maximum time outside before forced to retreat in. Bringing to daylight a panel of picket fence invisibly overgrown at the driveway end of the vegie patch, inspiration continued, leading from the vegie patch to the car garage the small stretch of fencing was tidied leaving the area quite pleasing on the eye☺….
Driven inside out of the elements, I sparked up the computer investing time updating the regular evening hand written minutes of the days just been, incorporating a dabble at editing…. The mercury fell away with fading daylight hours and with the change brought calm, presenting a well earnt rest, for however long it lasts, from bloody draining wind!!!!

Saturday 17 July 2004
Driven from bed 6a.m., again due to wind is becoming very tiring. Generated sounds trigger the brain to awaken the body giving it both external and internal torture. I'd rather be up and amongst the sounds than laying in bed listening to their torment, making very little difference other than the ability to watch the sounds in action, oh, and be closer to the toilet☺????
To survive the bloody cold start I slipped on all clothes that would fit to stay warm, supporting a t-shirt, skivvy, windcheater, polar fleece and windproof jacket with accompanying accessories of gloves, scarf and both beanies☺…. More was better!!!!
By candlelight, a match was thrown onto the shed heater to stay warm watching life take a hammering leading into sunrise. As usual the housing stayed together while I stayed awake, comfortable to have seen enough sunrises for a while, as beautiful as they are, I'd be happy for less wind torment and more sleep!!!!
Understandably, my body's desire to participate was minimal, making an executive decision early to indulge in a book as a nice distraction. If wind picks up tonight I think I'll sleep through sheer exhaustion anyway…. Yawn….

Sunday 18 July 2004
Falling into a heap at 8p.m., the occasional gust stirred a sensitised brain but on the overall not a bad night sleep, wind speeds were more sedate than recently endured….
For all the right reasons I really felt the cold last night, wrapped up like a mummy to set foot outside the bungalow, on the water collecting pilgrimage found the cattle trough frozen over. Grass crunched underfoot, without moisture in the soil the ground had frozen without any evidence of frost…. Brrrr….

I may have received some quality sleep, but it's going to take a few more good nights to lift my arse off the ground. Quite a bit of the morning simply vanished enjoying a few hot brews basking in protected direct sun ☺....
In quieter wind moments after sun had defrosted the cottage roof, running repairs were applied to waterproofing. My energy directed the day; nothing groundbreaking occurred but it didn't have to ☺....

Monday 19 July 2004
Encountering a false start, snuggling by my side on another cold night peace was quickly broken clearing Tia of bedding when she began heaving. Feeling somewhat lighter we were able to return and rewarm a clean doona....
Roaming about outside, I missed a courtesy call warning of another burn-off in the nearby coupe. If forestry let locals access what they consider uneconomical timber then the township of St. Marys could have been kept warm the entire winter.... What a terrible waste!?!?
Responding to a letter, and unwilling to oblige me a phone interview, a 240 kilometre round trip to Launceston was forced for an interview to justify unemployment benefits. Cold conditions took a toll on Destiny's tyre pressures, fuelling up and before leaving Grants I spoilt her with even inflation that should also help with economy. Performing like she's loved Destiny scooted down the hill into Launceston with the youth of a pup, parked and parking meter fed I punctually made the 11:45am interview. Because I've produced such a succession of medical certificates in a slow journey back to health regaining weight I was referred to the Centrelink psychologist. Going over my medical history, I was referred to the 'personal support program', offering an avenue away from job search and constant medical certificates....
Making use of being in Launceston I called in on Doris and was also lucky enough to meet a visiting friend Barbara. Barbara and Doris worked together nursing, she's now teaching Doris to play chess, at 89 it goes to show you're never too old to learn. Hijacking their afternoon with cuppas, photos and plenty of chat, I left them to an unstarted game of chess. Inspiring women with honest hearts ☺....
Heading home Rainbow Falls could be pin-pointed 50kms out due to the atrocious amount of smoke billowing from the forestry operations burn-off landmark, if that's managing our environment then I'm confused???? Again, my lungs say 'shove it'!!!!

Tuesday 20 July 2004
Following up close behind the light frost a beautiful warm day emerged in paradise.... Bloody hell, we've earnt a few ☺ !!!!
Still a bit quiet on the energy stakes, I basked time away over a succession of hot brews, only then considering what to do with myself. After a decadent level of procrastination, armed with an assortment of gardening tools, returned to a former haunt at the elevated garden out back of the burnt out house re-finding where the termite hole had last finished off ☺....
Intending only to move a few rocks to get at a sprinkling of weeds, intentions grew beyond expectations. A good hour of reshaping the pile and shifting many kilograms established a reasonable walkway between the bungalow and rock pile, reducing a crowded in doorway entrance ☺....

Wednesday 21 July 2004
Forced out from under the doona for a pit-stop 4:30a.m.-ish, then it was clouded and quite mild, leaving the warm comfort of bedding to get out amongst it after sunrise, wind had picked up arriving with a cool edge. Predicted winds at half the speed of those recently endured, it'll be a good time to catch up on that lost sleep ☺ ....
When Forestry Tasmania gave a courtesy call Monday informing of the burn-off in the coupe across the road what they failed to disclose is how many days each burn lasts. Into day three of the second massive burn, spoilt today, chainsaws were doing what they do and the major burn-off visually blocked a chunk of sky. Submerged in the human intervened conditions on offer, unable to avoid them, I opted to tackle another half job on the go having therapy with the shovel in the vegie patch....
Putting in a big one outdoors, I extended a pruning to shrubs and some unknown fruit tree overcrowded in the elevated garden. Chasing the only light available in its tight home, the fruit tree threw a few scraggly shoots to overhang the concrete path below, reshaped and with headroom created it's now exposed to the elements ☺ ....

Thursday 22 July 2004
From our elevated vantage-point up in the eagles nest, exposed in full sun, the valleys below were an ocean of cloud, a sure indication St. Marys is under a blanket of fog. Literally taking the plunge driving the mountain, rounding South Sister to begin the final descent, leaving sunshine we got buried deeper into dense cloud requiring headlights long before reaching town....
Prior to boosting the economy of St. Marys I called in on Brian and Maggie for a brew, before reaching the bottom of my cup, sun broke through warming me to the idea of hitting the shops ☺ ....
Stocked for another few, the remainder of this beautiful winter's day passed into history in the vegie garden. Downing tools I opened a rare newspaper purchase and got lost in crosswords and the jumble puzzle. It doesn't take much to entertain me ☺ ....

Friday 23 July 2004
Teased by the makings of an ideal shed occasion I had to shelve the thought, continuing to clear, sun broke through robbing justification ☺ !!!!
Adding to the stack in the cottage I spotted holes chewed in waiting laundry; shitting on my white skivvy before leaving a rodent just shit in its own nest; war has been declared!!!!
Fluffing around without clear direction doing bits 'n' pieces, I put the moby on the charge, collected water, took ash to the loo and re-set the heater for the next required fire....
Drawn back to the kitchen I continued with the chicken and vegetable soup. Boiling the chicken yesterday left it to cool overnight to remove most of the fat, slicing, dicing, ripping, shredding, frying, boiling, simmering, simmering, simmering, simmering we were ready to feast ☺ ....

Saturday 24 July 2004
Meeting drizzle greeting the fresh day, at that point all immediate thoughts went directly to the haven structure directly in front, sadly the eager excitement was short lived. Unwilling to budge, all cloud did was turn off the tap and block any chance at seeing sun....
Tired of stepping over the single strand of wire running the full length of the driveway and no plans of ever grazing animals in the future, my little mate gave me a hand to remove the bloody thing. It was visually pleasing to see the wire gone also....
The return of misty rain mid afternoon planted the seed for a Saturday evening enjoying a couple of quiet ales by the heater. Germinating the seed of thought I sat my bum down early to write, a woman on a mission, had life under control early freeing my conscience for a night off. When this pen is replaced the only plan in my head is to grab a beer, head to the shed and strike a match ☺ ....

Sunday 25 July 2004
Plans last evening for a big night immersed in shed culture fell short, mild conditions moved in making it comfortable without the heater. There's no point wasting hard earnt prunings and timber ☺ ....
Dropping the cardboard curtain unmasked a favourite, low cloud had visibility down to around fifty metres offering an inner elevation that included a whistle and a spring in my step. Music to my ears to hear convincing rain 6a.m.-ish, rain audible enough to be heard on the tin roof arrived in waves. Staying in tune with the universe I revisited the fire I didn't follow through with the night before....
Banks of cloud lazily dragged their tired weight through trees on South Sister Range clinging until forced to move on. Between showers, Tia and I ducked behind the cattle yards carting timber in to fuel 'beer 'n' bullshit', there's a career ahead just cleaning up that area alone....
Mid afternoon sun broke through and persisted putting in a warm finish, appealing to my conscience I left the fire for the yard. Pruning the last of the hydrangeas in the side yard to the cottage, then roamed into the cattle yards exposing a concrete drain leading away from the side of the shed, a legacy of its time as a dairy....

Monday 26 July 2004
Disappearing quietly without too much fuss nothing groundbreaking occurred, life and time just ticked over ☺ ....
Eating us out of house and home over the weekend, town beckoned. Fuelling up with Grant he alerted me to Destiny's passenger side rear tyre in need of air, I only checked pressures a week ago so knew there was a problem. By the time I walked across the road to Evelyn and returned feeding my face a horseshoe nail had been removed from the tyre. Patched and ready to go, Grant saved me a lot of inconvenience for a mere $11.... A bloody honest business and service, rare ☺ !!!!
Friendly mail sat tidy in my box from Mum and Dad: they sent a newspaper article of interest covering the recent world hot air balloon championships held in Mildura, balloons are spectacular to watch without animals ☺ ....
Disappearing back to the cattle yards Tia and I utilised the remainder of the afternoon and sunshine. Stopping to look around from time to time, taking a moment to reflect upon just how

far we have come, I'm proud of personal achievements at Rainbow Falls boring away at the termite hole ☺ ....

Tuesday 27 July 2004
Overcast with a nippy wind, wrapped in appropriate clothing I warmed with the shovel and warm-up I did....
Drawn by magnetic forces we ventured to the cattle yards, in clearing exploits treasure in the form of a heavy old pick head stopped the shovel in its tracks, walking away having all clumps of tall, dense grass, knocked down to size.... Now mowable ☺ !!!!
When energy for physical labour waned, my little mate and me downed tools going walkabout shutter bugging taking progress photos....
Heading indoors I had a play around in the cottage. Emptying the wood box of stored boxes of much travelled possessions, ready to empty and utilise the contents, now I'm sure we've settled. Looking to call Rainbow Falls' home for life it has reached in and touched my heart ☺ ....

Wednesday 28 July 2004
Finishing the same way it started, bloody cold, however, the in between bit took the edge off chilled bones. Wrapped up like a mummy I threw the bungalow door open, the only piece of anatomy remaining exposed were my eyes....
Beginning the 'mummy unravel' getting blood flowing, I gave the pruning saw a workout generating future firewood from overhanging limbs from a tree at the corner of the burnt out house. In keeping with the physical theme settled nearby in the vegie patch turning soil....
In an impromptu 'praise and pat' moment my fingers detected and promptly removed a tick from Tia's head. I expect a rise in energy over the next couple of days.... As if she needs more energy ☺ ....

Thursday 29 July 2004
Reluctant to emerge from my doona cocoon, when the door was finally opened a good amount of frost was still lying around, brrrr.... As the morning progressed so did the mercury, warming to beanie free ☺ ....
When I could drag myself away from basking and cuppa's I found direction in the vegie patch putting in a healthy day on the shovel. Paying rewards, persistence finalised one of the many half jobs on the go, it felt good to turn that last sod and close the vegie garden gate behind walking out.... Time for beer o'clock ☺ ....

Friday 30 July 2004
It was a one-dog night, the doona was pulled snugly around my ears and Tia cuddled in closely.
Stepping outside onto a crunchy white frost, the day ahead in the life and times of us Rainbow Falls folk passed without leaving even as much as a fingerprint....
Aiming high, I let life evolve around the preparation of a record breaking 'nipples under' bath. A deep bath takes planning and nice conditions, all ingredients were available so a match was thrown on the fire pit....

A soaking exfoliating bath and eating pretty much summed up achievements. A hard life, but I'm glad it's me that has to do it ☺ ....

Saturday 31 July 2004
With a heavy and moist looking sky, water was collected first up to beat any potential rain, if it doesn't get blown away. Wrapped appropriately against the elements I got straight into outside stuff before breakfast....
Virtually only needing bread and drinking water, the trip into town was quick. A friendly letter waited from Doris and her friend Barbara with some helpful advice for a 'wanna be' published author.... Soul warming, true hearted, energy giving women ☺ ....
Late in the day a cool change, or should I say a bloody freezing change, came in from direct south bringing with it a light moisture offering....
Uninspired to be anywhere outdoors, from available choices, elected to add spark to the computer updating the past couple of weeks of journal entries. We didn't see snow but its nearby presence was felt to the bone....brrrr.... Heading for another one-dog night ☺ ....

Sunday 1 August 2004
Life is full of little tests, demonstrating there is more than one way of doing things, always keeping the mind open and being ready to adapt and improvise is useful. Moments prior to starting the night's journal entry the globe blew in the lamp, with no replacement, candles and the oil lamp combined threw just enough light to see what I was doing ☺ ....
Having an ear fine-tuned to sounds of iron moving on nails and loose things rattling around alone caused broken sleep. A bloody cold blast didn't falter a degree from direct south, losing the worst of its velocity before arriving it was still enough to refrain from fully relaxing....
Raising a restless brain off the pillow I took it outside facing the world covered from head to toe 7a.m.-ish and participated in a bitterly cold morning....
From the meagre selection of tools, I slid fingers into gloves and grabbed the wheelbarrow venturing behind the cattle yards collecting wood from an 'out of sight out of mind' dumping site, and that's where we got swallowed up. Replacing wheelbarrow with shovel, uncovered a good stack of heater sized pieces of wood entwined in long grass, tidied up rubbish, corrugated iron and pieces of steel, complementing work started by David quite sometime ago....
A funny moment in time distracted my attention away from preparing dinner. Settling herself in her bed to begin the patient food wait Tia broke loose with a loud fart, frightening herself, she jumped up looking around for the culprit, escaping sheepishly out the door to the comfort of the great outdoors.... Twasn't me ☺ ....

Monday 2 & Tuesday 3 August 2004
Pen never made it to paper yesterday, it was declared a shed day, that's all that needs to be said ☺ ....
Just as soon as life was as minimally organised as it had to be I looked forward and never looked back, psyched to make an impression on prunings and timber, I spent the day clearing shed floor space to make room for more. Treated to a few hours of low cloud, from my perch behind the heaters barrel I could only see as far as the car garage in the driveway, existence beyond that was invisible, pure perfection ☺ ....

Adjourning to the bungalow for siesta after a long indulgence in the haven, by that stage a few beers had passed my lips, there was only a blown globe in the only electric light source, all clear signs it was knock off ☺ ….

A check of the gauge measured a token 4mm, enough to give the bulbs a drink and indulge me….

In need of food I put one foot in front of the other Tuesday taking the required steps that led us to town. Boosting the economy of St. Marys rain found ground, groceries loaded and windscreen wipers in full swing Destiny's nose was pointed back toward the mountain.

Rounding South Sister and with Rainbow Falls in sight, home was sun drenched, cloud was being held back by the Sisters Mountains. A little altitude and several kilometres separating, at times, our climates are like chalk and cheese????

Escaping the clutches of the vacuum cleaner, I grabbed a beer and ran for the hills with my best mate disappearing into paddocks kicking out scotch thistles wandering. Covering no great distance, and getting nowhere fast, I have trouble walking past emerging scotch thistles….

Wednesday 4 August 2004

The three consecutive weeks of random wind poundings has really rattled my cage, a light breeze only has to pick up and the slightest sound from movement instantly triggers a brain message for my eyes to open. The random battering certainly etched a lasting impression in my mind….

Tia happily lazed following the best of sunny spots because laundry is simply a task she can't raise herself to participate in….

Leaving limp wristed hand washing to drip-dry in the breeze I put in a solid performance with Mum over the phone. Hours from a visit to the surgeon, and because a year has passed, Mum was booked in for a colonoscopy November 11, one day before her birthday. May appropriate birthday results be present for a beautiful soul….

Digging out and manually removing for permanency, shovel activity was focussed on a patch of hemlock, getting rid of the nasties before turning soil in the elevated garden. I had just dug the last of the carrot tops out and a couple of light showers were sent our way, sending me into action retrieving almost dry clothes off the line….

Twisting the lid on another one, beer'd up enjoying a moment before making a start on dinner, nothing left to do but eat, drink and be merry. I can cope ☺…. Ahhhh….

Thursday 5 August 2004

Every little bit done inspires progress on that little bit more. Returning to the elevated garden I slid the shovel into a small termite hole to create a blank canvas and started turning soil. Radio for company, I simply got absorbed in the pleasant conditions on offer while making a positive impression ☺….

Looking for a change of muscle groups and visual surrounds, loaded and pushed half a dozen wheelbarrow loads of timber to the shed catering for many hours of beer 'n' bullshit ☺….

The boating weather forecast and the bureau of meteorology's long-term forecast, the two combined, didn't offer too much promise for outdoor activity, winds up to 30 knots, rain and some possible snow coming our way in the next few days…. I can't wait….

Friday 6 August 2004
Doing a demonstration practice start on the day, my little mate was given a quick shift from the bed as her body began the familiar vomit heave. Bone and grass dispensed with it was back to the business of snoozing....
Making a second and more leisurely start on the day, eased into it basking in direct sun over a brew or two, not rushing the decision making of what to do with the daylight hours ahead....
A bone warming sun hat and skivvy temperature, Tia and I migrated back to the elevated garden to relish in the elements....
A couple of wheelbarrow loads of coal were dumped into wheel ruts in an attempt at making sense of the two metre wide concrete path running parallel to the rear of the house. Over time ivy set-up home in the layer of coal lining the path, with nowhere to travel but across the concrete, ivy established a dense root matting entwined through the coal. The weighty mat could be peeled back like a band-aid from the concrete. Turning the cocktail of ingredients back onto itself, concrete exposed wouldn't have seen the sun in many moons. I was amazed at the sheer size and number of worms active in the coal, dirt, weed mix, obviously a healthy environment. Entering uncharted areas, forward moving progress is always uplifting ☺....
Winding daylight down with a stroll through paddocks, looking back over housing from a distance, an overview brings home just how much has been achieved. The yard is looking very tidy.... I'm proud ☺ !!!!

Saturday 7 August 2004
Driven from under the doona by bladder pressure 4a.m.-ish, Tia joined in on the movement reclaiming real estate and clearing the housing of roaming activity. Fuelling up following a quick sprint around Tia stopped at the leaky pipe struck with the brushcutter for a drink, returning with muddy stockings on she instantly lost her privilege of access to my bed ☺....
Resurfacing several hours later we greeted gorgeous elements in paradise, taking a while to drag myself away from wallowing over sunshine and milo....
When a decision was made and tools gathered me and my little mate walked in the direction of the burnt out house. Radio for company, I gnawed away at the creation of another termite hole making some sense of the tangled mess left behind by the fire. Separating and sorting different building materials from, copper, wire, timber, corrugated iron and steel, to trimming back the overgrown garden, little by little we're forging forward and making sense of our inherited mess ☺ ????

Sunday 8 August 2004
Adding a splash of bright yellow colour to breakfast; gazing out the bungalow window noticed the first daffodils blooming. Housing is alive with shooting bulbs, each year the display is more impressive than the last, a pretty and colourful season ☺....
Walking out onto the remnants of a light dusting of frost, wind picked up adding a chill factor to a potentially warming sun. Demolishing a couple of milo's warming our feet, and still holding interest, headed back to the burnt out house pruning in the elevated garden....
Finding a few blackberry shoots after a few found me first, the garden is starting to open up and breathe....

Working with a reluctant body for physical activity, I was easily persuaded by a cooler weather shift to retreat to a more pleasing climate indoors putting in a gentle afternoon on the computer. From my position behind the screen witnessed shed conditions evolve, by 3:30p.m.-ish the first shower commenced ☺ ….

Monday 9 August 2004
Needing to develop brain survival techniques, saving sanity against the battering courtesy of natures elements, during daylight hours I've been identifying what actually creates the sounds that so easily activate wake up triggers….
With only a dribble of milk remaining, after breakfast a trip between the Sisters was an obvious direction. Blow wave finalised and a body moisturise on the go, from where I stood in the cottage sighted a bus resembling Maggie and Brian's returning from the neighbours. Offering enough of everything plus extra from their well-stocked bus, freed the day enabling us to share it together exploring the treasures of Rainbow Falls…. Maggie and Brian's company exceeded anything I had planned, a refreshing way to replenish energy and recharge the batteries ☺ ….

Tuesday 10 August 2004
I've had a gut full of wind lashing out anytime it fucking well feels rattling my cage, breaking sleep, and threatening destruction!!!! This winter will be a bench-marker for the roughest treatment dished out….
Visiting the waterfall, the trickle flowing was defying gravity getting blown back over the top in spray. The boating weather forecast was of no help either, 30–40 knot winds off-shore gaining momentum racing up hill. Resigning to helplessness for tormenting wind as company, it gave in to my complacency panning out to rather calm????
While preparing to face a mountain run, Maggie phoned with the offer of a 2-inch pipe joiner, stemming from her call, we planned a cuppa visit when the Rainbow Falls crew hit town ☺ ….
Extinguishing hunger pangs at the bakery, from there I found the inspiration to move onto the pub, supermarket and Post Office. Managing to spark up conversations along the way, the social cycle was finalised with Brian and Maggie, where a simple stock up run turned into a three hour round trip. After a week of not budging from the hill it did me the world of good to go out and blow a few cobwebs off the social skills ☺ ….
Destiny unpacked and back in her bedroom, with my best mate not far off I took 'beer o'clock' walkabout through the paddocks…. For every step I take Tia takes one hundred ☺ ….

Wednesday 11 August 2004
The boating weather forecast prediction hit 4:45a.m.-ish. Fruitlessly wishing the howling wind away didn't help, beaten, got up to be part of it instead. Intermittent mind torture is wearing me down and wearing thin!!!!
Donning the majority of my wardrobe, with only eyes exposed, reached for the matchbox sparking the heater into flame. Staying warm I watched the invisible mighty force push our world around leading into sunrise. A 7a.m. weather report confirmed more of the same, with the inclusion of rain. Rain is at least soothing on the brain. I can only hope sleep arrives tonight through sheer exhaustion….

Beside the obvious wind, by 8:30a.m.-ish mild sunny conditions were also developing. Feeling surprisingly energetic, and after burning the blackberry canes to reclaim the wheelbarrow, Tia and I hit the yard. Looking after our own interest carted in a good supply of timber to survive a week of unpredictable anything….

Working consistently until 2p.m.-ish is when my energy took a nosedive and body demanded support from a chair, escaping wind I got the journal up to date early because it's unpredictable when my wheels might fall off ☺ ….

Thursday 12 August 2004

Sitting by the heater last evening contemplating the gusting night ahead, I was sure of one thing, unless I was unconscious not too much sleep was going to happen in the bungalow. Chance sat me in Destiny to use ventolin, that simple act alerted me to her outer shell, and insulation, muffling sound. The seed germinated, if I was going to enjoy any sleep it would be in Destiny. Dropping the rear seat I packed in bedding and can't live without bits. Wind eased, and with the knowledge Destiny would muffle the sounds even lower, didn't give it a second thought and climbed in reducing the volume by a few 'brain saving' decibels ☺ …. Not taking long before being down for the count….

Even from within Destiny's shielded cocoon I was woken abruptly 2a.m.-ish when Mother Nature turned on a real head fucking for a solid couple of hours. It was reassuring to know that if the shed roof blew off we still had Destiny's covering us…. Wind at those speeds is crazy mind altering stuff????

Emerging with everything structural staying together, again it was only me rattled apart. Greeting us and the morning also the air was full of smoke it was either a bushfire or forestry operations????

Menacing destructive gusts made a good start dismantling temporary repairs, cussing and swearing in trying conditions, did a couple of running 'please hold together' repairs. For a greater part of the day we copped a hammering, giving Tia a bone, she stayed outside only long enough to bury it ☺ ….

If we didn't blow away first, a change was arriving, and it did by mid afternoon. Wind dropped like it never existed. Excited by the prospect of rain sounds the bedroom was returned to the bungalow…. Ahhhh, relaxed sleep, my body can't take too much more cage rattling….

Friday 13 August 2004

Offering the occasional reminder, but overall I was permitted a reasonable night's sleep. So sensitised, the slightest upbeat gust and my eyes spring open automatically….

With my batteries feeling a bit flat Tia followed my example of doing very little, ash made it to the loo, another fire was set on the ready, and thistles found my boot strolling with a cuppa. Scoring a good quota of thistles, fine mist kept me walking in the direction of the shed ☺ …. Rain is soooo soothing on the brain….

Without too much petrol in my motor I was happy to share a warm, lazy, contemplative day down the shed with my little mate. Not a breath to be felt listening to rain on a tin roof perched by the heater, it was relaxing for my entire rattled body ☺ …. Badly needed….

Saturday 14 August 2004
Being forced at us with speed, rain stayed all night offering a measurable 24mm to 8:30a.m.-ish.
The air temperature bounced directly off snow and with rain never too far off, definitely not one to linger too long outdoors. Offering a bit of everything besides the obvious cold, wet and windy, there was a brief hail shower, and the sun even poked its head out for a couple of hours????
Attention was immediately drawn to an unfamiliar sound of loose corrugated iron the right gust of wind blew freeing iron to do a high kick on the carport attached to the shed. Not far off going solo it couldn't be ignored, in a quieter moment safer to play with moving iron a few screws silenced the chorus. The work put in replacing roofing nails with screws paid off, I don't think we would have fared so well without the extra support, we've taken a punishing????
In impeccable timing, having a break from the computer Mum phoned, getting our twopence worth we settled into a healthy exchange of words. Mum particularly wanted to know how we were coping with the unrelenting hammering, saying Mildura wasn't missing out either, there's no escaping from it anywhere ☺!!!! Wind won't be missed when it leaves….

Sunday 15 August 2004
Becoming aware, through a patch of calming silence, at hearing the falls flowing clearly from the loo, a sound that encourages an appreciative audience to remain seated longer. Picking up the toilet roll it weighed far too much, a small hole in the protective bag acted as a funnel soaking the roll to the cylinder. Hallelujah for a pocket full of tissues ☺!!!!
Gradually easing to sanely tolerable I was only rattled awake on a few occasions, however it was cold conditions that took centre stage, stepping sideways to extreme, to be as cold as I've ever known it…. A genuine one-dog night ☺….
Tools on the ready to tackle out back of the burnt out house a passing shower of mist sent us for cover, reckoning it was a good time to have smoko. Returning for a second restart invested a serious days' work into the elevated garden. Simply hedging smaller shrubs following the fenceline and eliminating several environmental weeds from wasting soil, it's never looked so good….
With beer o'clock and walkabout declared, me and my little mate disappeared into the paddocks where I kicked out thistles in passing. Stepping in to make a start on dinner, Ross called in and surprisingly brought a six pack, sipping quietly on one, we looked at the top paddock for potentially agisting his two horses, available feed is slowing down….

Monday 16 August 2004
Standing with my tongue pointed in the right direction I've fallen into an outstanding energy flow, everywhere I went and corner turned everything turned to gold, very uplifting and positive….
How quickly wind is forgotten when it's gone, a perfect night for sleeping, and turning up the celsius sun with a bit of oomph stepped in to melt the rather heavy white frost….

Making a start carting water, 9a.m.-ish the cattle trough still had a crust of ice sealing a lid on top. How they survive is beyond me, but mosquito larva were happily wriggling around below the ice crust, emphasising the word 'were' ☺.... Those bastards would survive anywhere....
Requiring a trip into St. Helens to sort out possibly my second last banking transaction ever with that big red W bank, I made a food survival stop with Evelyn en route. Gladly opening mail it was full of nothing but good news, two letters supported the theory refinancing occurred August 10. Living in the black is official ☺ !!!! A sensation not known in a while.... Good news for celebrating, also arriving with mail was the official 'Miriam and Andrew' wedding invitation....
With Destiny boldly parked out front, young Nick tracked me in the supermarket sharing a beautiful warm hug, Nick is a big fan of 'Tassie Sue's', a good hearted little guy and a quality friend, absence doesn't fade feelings ☺....
Stocked with food and positive energy, Tia, Destiny and I headed home to paradise to finish off a perfect day and to settle in for a few more ☺....

Tuesday 17 August 2004
With the privilege of hindsight the world offered me a laugh, dealing a double hand, on one hand while we were being terrorised by wind, there was also something positive working in favour. Now refinancing has occurred our future at Rainbow Falls is as secure as its ever going to be????
Leaving the pot to boil for a shower, my little mate and I shared breakfast then collected enough water for the big laundry event....
Finishing smoko basking in sunshine, the bullying arsehole building inspector Russell, with a reputation to match, walked in again doing another uninvited unannounced visit. I told Russell and his offsider that a courtesy call would have been appropriate and their timing was inconvenient.... Hmmmm, showing them the front gate to exit by....
Enjoying a knock off beer I took in the sunset and fading light from a spectacular viewing spot in the elevated garden where a severely pruned holly shrub once took pride of place. Soft pastel paint strokes decorated the setting eastern skyline, in an expansive view, sharpening and illuminating with a simple swivel of my head to the west, golden colours glowed saying goodbye to last light.... Ahhhh, paradise ☺....

Wednesday 18 August 2004
The only contact with the outside world today was via the phone from Loui. Filling Loui's ear with the building inspectors' unannounced visit, she told me she was first on the scene when his son did major damage to his hand making a pipe bomb.... Why????
Tia and I spent a therapeutic one in the garden again clearing overgrown shrubs and weeds. It's a pleasure participating in the great outdoors deleting the torment of the past months from memory ☺....
Finding the ritual very relaxing, we changed course for beer o'clock walkabout and thistle kicking, heading to the area between the loo and waterfall. Sipping quietly on a beer eliminating thistles my mind free ranges solving the problems of the world ☺....

Thursday 19 August 2004
A period starting delivered a couple of unsettled hours so I didn't hit the ground running this morning, choosing a gentle pace....
Up there with wind for destruction, the big black birds I'm not particularly fond of, namely currawongs, arriving en masse did irreparable damage to a tree in the cottage side yard. Without recovering, I took dead limbs from the tree to the shed to wait in line to go up the flue....
A prediction of rain close to the weekend prompted forward planning, collecting a wheelbarrow load of fire starting small limb wood from behind the cattle yards. Leaving my mind to free range tackling any chosen topic, abstractly separated and happy in my own little relaxed world snapping twigs, then pushed the barrow full of brain therapy to the shed to wait for a rainy day....
Keeping a therapy theme flowing, Ms Tia and I went walkabout heading toward the falls then followed the top boundary fence back to the water tank kicking out scotchies on the way. In our travels pleasingly found few scotch thistles, the ground however is extremely dry it's screaming out for a drink.... By the weekend apparently ☺ ????

Friday 20 August 2004
Enough to keep the bulbs satisfied 3mm sat in the rain gauge this morning, shifting southerly and constantly looking threatening, the 3mm total wasn't added to....
Taking a trip into St. Marys there's never any hurry, familiar faces are always happy to pass the time of day, I love that small town side to life ☺ ....
Soaking up warmth offered behind glass in Destiny only then sorted through mail. Of particular interest, a letter from the big red W bank displaying a total of zero on the final mortgage statement, a solid signal refinancing settlement occurred. Withdrawing cash from the supermarket ATM my savings account had swelled a little, absolutely confirming we're living in the black, I'm convinced enough now to begin believing ☺ ....
Walking through the door in a quiet time at the bakery and having become a familiar face, conversation with Evelyn is increasing. Last stop before tackling the mountain was to restock at the pub with my mate and everyone else's, Bruce, to squat home again for a few more sunsets ☺ ....
Bursting to share absolute complete refinancing news targeted Mum and Dad for an audience. Celebrating the occasion more appropriately in an Irish flavour I splurged cracking open a stubby of stout. Wandering around the top of the gorge by the waterfall an empty stubby and cold air sent us packing indoors, and that's where daylight disappeared into evening ☺ ....

Saturday 21 August 2004
Beginning to yawn at 5p.m., I documented home life while still feeling up to it because it's been a long one ☺ ....
Wind returned aggressive and destructive delivering a lesson in relaxation and complacency, beaten for sleep, I got up for the toilet 5a.m. and stayed up. Doing my best at distracting an idle mind I sparked up the computer and was seated staring at the screen by 5:30a.m.-ish....
An 11a.m. weather report indicated the north-east gale force winds being experienced will shift southerly and ease later.... I look forward to later ☺ !!!!

Filling in time waiting for later, I pulled the beanie down hard over my ears and headed for the great blustery outdoors. Keeping busy with distraction tactics from the hammering a solid chunk of daylight hours was consumed in the elevated garden. A three-quarter inch poly pipe revealed itself under the turn of the shovel offering another clue to the plumbing and irrigation infrastructure....
An eagle gliding low over Rainbow Falls paddocks stole the show for a while battling some pretty fierce gusts....
Hanging around with the wrong crowd Tia was playing host to another tick, this one lodged itself by a nipple and almost went unnoticed, with its removal she's one happy, high energy, nearly six-year-old ☺....
Still in the thought stage for a planned Mildura visit September, Mum quickly put in an order for our favourite premium Tasmanian shortbread biscuits. In need of a family fix and social blow out, the wedding invitation ignited all the reason required to travel ☺....

Sunday 22 August 2004
The past twenty-four hours of pounding wind disappeared like it never existed, there's no build-up or ease off it comes bowling in and leaves in the same manner????
My pace being relatively sedate nothing groundbreaking happened. Tinkering with the shovel in the elevated garden I carved access through the jungle following poly pipes deciphering what leads to where and for what purpose....
Wishing to post a letter I doubled the purpose for leaving the front gate. On return I pulled up on the road below South Sister Range, taking a 4WD walk through some thick scrub scaling the hillside on a mission to join water supply pipes. Working from memory, the largest poly joiner carted up with me was too small, in the end being just an exercise in knowledge and health....
Giving Mum and Dad a quick call to see how Dad fared in inter-club golf championships, they had worrying news to share. Of eight brothers they had some pretty serious news about Dad's only sister Jennifer, complications occurred having a colonoscopy. A gas build-up burst the bowel wall and in a short period of time Aunty Jen was taken on a mercy flight from Mildura to an Adelaide hospital, both kidneys had collapsed and she's in a coma on life support.... Not a healthy prognosis....

Monday 23 August 2004
Giving us a taste of what's around the corner, throwing open the door greeting a fresh one met a warm day associated with spring....
Taking time away from doing routine fluff around bits 'n' pieces, I flicked the kettle on and we basked tucked snugly inside the shed entrance over smoko. Sitting quietly with the moment, both Tia and I became airborne when a petrol tin expanded releasing a sharp crack, receiving a follow up surprise, I splashed a dash of hot tea in my lap ☺ !!!! I must have a good heart....
Like flies to the honey pot, returned to the elevated garden where a secret passage is being created pruning a tunnel attempting to discover and understand the chaos, well, trying to ☺????
Calm clear skies pumped out maximum sunlight and heat, in fact, so perfect in paradise I was enticed to stay out in the elements until 6p.m., notably more daylight hours signifies a changing season is apparent....

Tuesday 24 August 2004
As soon as my eyes and brain co-ordinated to make me conscious of what was happening around I gave the birthday girl a scruff up, a big six-year-old☺!!!! The best way to spoil a girl for her birthday is through her stomach Ms Tia had a culinary good one☺....
Flicking the switch on the kettle a couple of times I put in a long smoko watching drifting wisps of cloud vaporise. About as common as rainbows to witness☺....
Getting amongst the charred remains of Doris and Norman's house, traded beanie for sun hat and made a solid start at compacting a stack of scattered roofing iron, easing the number of rattles and clunks in strong gusts☺!!!!
Its been a wish to uncover Doris and Norm's front veranda from under lodged roofing iron and charcoal, its a great vantage-point to take in the window view to the ocean. Running shy on energy I saved some of the veranda tidying for another dose of inspiration....
Heading into the setting sun the birthday girl and I went walkabout, Guinness in hand, the daily quota of scotch thistles was kicked out. Watching the last light fade from the elevated garden to maximise the amazing expansive view, to the east sun had set over an ocean of greys and to the west the setting sun was still bathed in rich orange.... We live in Eden and lucky enough to know it☺....

Wednesday 25 August 2004
Winding up the morning walk around open up routine, Loui called for a yarn, with plenty to chat about, we did☺....
Inspired by fast moving visual progressive change elected for another go at finding the burnt out house veranda. Several wheelbarrow loads of coal and burnt remains found the deepest of wheel ruts and the veranda and doorway entrance were unveiled. If the front door to Doris and Norm's would swing shut it could now, the seized hinges keep a welcoming open look happening☺....
Ducking over the mountain to keep Ms Tia and myself content for a few more sunsets, made it home in time to unpack Destiny for beer o'clock and thistle kicking, wearing out my boots and a few stubbies has got to make a difference☺....

Thursday 26 August 2004
Disguising beauty and stealing quality from breathable air we were presented, without choice, by smoke from a forestry operations mass burn taking care of the environment???? For as long as these practices continue my memory of the putrid air quality during Wollongong's Christmas bushfires will never fade....
Taking it quietly to avoid saturating my body with foul air I pottered detailing Destiny, she was vacuumed, washed inside and out, and windows left transparent, even going as far as oiling her door hinges. Delivering long overdue tender loving care☺....
In the mood for getting things done I mustered enough heart to have one final try at upgrading waterproofing on the cottage roof before throwing my hands in the air.... Obviously the next rain will either inspire or delude????

Friday 27 August 2004
Fulfilling a 'D' day, that's a Destiny day, today is 'B' day, the bungalows turn for a spoiling. Clearing floor space before vacuuming, I removed four of Tia's stashed balls ☺....
Severing vacuum cleaner noise pollution the still air was full with the sounds of a menagerie of spring activity, a variety of birds and frogs dominated airwaves. Making very little noise skink lizards are also getting on the move, my indicator of reptile activity, particularly snakes waking from the cold, windy winter....
Each trip into the shed immediately brought a smile to my face, seeing Destiny sparkle is a pleasure to the eye ☺....
Out and about on the regular evening walkabout noticed blossom flowering on a couple of trees, a definite sign nature thinks spring is here ☺ ????

Saturday 28 August 2004
Enduring a below average dry winter for the terrain's needs, the parched ground has more of a summer look and feel to it yellowing and drying off in patches. By choice, I'm able to leave the mower parked. The herbivore night traffic is keeping the yard tidy, trimming what little growth is happening. Making use of the lean ground coverage I dropped the mower inside the dam fence to make a little sense of it while grass is sparse, dry and wispy....
Before striking a blow I called home for any new news on Aunty Jenny, her prognosis isn't very encouraging, still in a coma her life support is soon to be turned off, offering a five percent chance at any sort of recovery.... Not very good odds....
Starting first go, and blowing a little smoke on start up, as usual I made the mower work hard. With the tank emptying of fuel and cutting out, smoke started coming from the engine, I quickly killed the motor thinking the mower was in the process of dying. Motor cooled and accessible singed grass around the exhaust had caused the problem ☺....
For periods, having a real sting to it, a very intense concentrated heat as I imagine being under a magnifying glass would be like, direct sun burnt skin quickly and ruthlessly!!!!
From the phone, to mowing, the next focus of attention went to beer o'clock and the removal of the usual quota of scotchies from some randomly selected area while taking in a spectacular sunset....

Sunday 29 August 2004
The suns warm impact was lost to cloud building in the west 4p.m.-ish, prior to its disappearance paradise turned on a sun hat and t-shirt temperature. Getting out amongst it I splashed a bit of water on the surviving strawberry plants and wet the ground around a fruit tree sadly overgrown in the elevated garden in an attempt at reviving it....
Moving from the back to the front of the burnt out house, sheets of tin were taken to cover part of a large patch of dense nut grass stuff, both the lawnmower and brushcutter don't like trying to penetrate it at all. Weighting the tin down with several solid rocks incase Mother Nature decides to turn one on we'll see how the grass survives without sunlight ☺....
Breaking the back of the afternoon updating the journal's computer version, pulled up for beer o'clock and putting the boot into the daily quota of scotch thistles....

Along with the changeover of seasons comes a change in active flora and fauna, sighting a shingle back lizard in the elevated garden and a rabbit at the front gate. It's the first time I've sighted a rabbit this far up the mountain, a first and hopefully the last!!!!
If my little mate's going to catch a rabbit she'll have to pick her energy up: she's been a bit snoozy, strong signs a tick is zapping her energy, if she's hosting one it's eluding me I've searched without luck????

Monday 30 August 2004
Leading us into a false sense of security bathed in sunshine and calm nights, once my head hit the pillow last night she blew in a bastard, unrelenting until 2:30a.m.-ish, getting dressed I went walkabout in it to set the brain straight. Visibility being good on the cusp of a full moon, and shielding from the southerly wrapped like a mummy, I stood sheltering on the front veranda of the burnt out house. Feeling better about life returned to a warm bed to continue a poor night's sleep....
Dragging my sorry arse out of bed got it ready for a trip into town....
A potentially quick run over the mountain took about three and a half hours having an impromptu very social time. Lips being about the only muscle prepared to function, with Dad's Fathers Day and Kristy-Lee's birthday cards in the post, I met Rita in the bakery and accepted her offer of a chat over a cuppa. Calling in for drinking water I also found Ross home in the mood for a chat and brew. Making the front gate with enough daylight left to unpack Destiny and get settled in hopefully settled in for a calm, relaxing night of sleep and sweet dreams ☺....

Tuesday 31 August 2004
The southerly calmed enough for reasonable quality sleep. I didn't imagine working at staying warm in the land of nod, finding the cattle trough had frozen over was convincing evidence of a bloody cold one....
Try as she might Mother Nature did her best at warming things up but wind arriving from deep-south betrayed any attempts. Being the resourceful switched on beings we are, Tia and I expelled our daily dose of energy sheltered in sunshine at the front yard of the burnt out house, getting the maximum from the diverse elements on offer....
Feeling as strong as a half-sucked peppermint and perfect for the moment, I caught a call from Loui about to pass through returning from Launceston, she pulled in for a visit just in time for beer o'clock....
Feeling pretty wound down after Loui's visit there wasn't much else left to do but to eat, drink, write and be merry ☺....

Wednesday 1 September 2004
Dangling the carrot in front of the elements by washing the car, and today tempting Mother Nature by doing the laundry, it still won't rain????
Basking over smoko in our favourite spot to catch morning sun, also considering it a favourite spot swallows have taken up residence in the shed and were being territorial. Doing some beak snapping fly byes past us intruders, taking the hint I returned to the waiting laundry and left them to it ☺....

Donning my glad rags for a night out in St. Marys, picked Ross up 6p.m.-ish for a counter meal at the pub being joined by Jack, then over to e.ScApe Café for a 'Save South Sister' meeting. A positive strong attendance, community support was impressive, the passion coming from a diversity of many and varying opinions, people who have never been politically active were rallying together to save a small piece of ground valued by locals from being logged. My small voluntary contribution was to design a poster for the campaign launch, all the little bits add up....

The sun set on a sad note, Aunty Jenny lost her fight for life, life support was switched off and her own body was unwilling to sustain itself....

Thursday 2 September 2004

With my get up and go up and gone, a gentle morning was had attending to personal grooming and basking....

Looking for thoughts to spark a poster design for the Save South Sister campaign launch I phoned the co-ordinator Melanie, accepting her offer to have an ideas session at her home tomorrow to bounce inspiration off one another....

Slipping by as gentle and unassuming as the morning, the afternoon elapsed cooking a dinner to take over to Ross' to help inspire words for a poster, without much success. Coming down with a cold and spending a great deal of time on the phone to his daughters which is a regular anti-social practice of his, I did a rough poster design and left him to it....

During a routine patting moment my fingers stumbled upon the source of Ms Tia's slightly out of sort's behaviour, another tick, she should rethink her social circle ☺....

Friday 3 September 2004

A polite habit of mine, to be on time, I was being warmly greeted by the bubbly Melanie with minutes to spare on our 1p.m. arrangement....

Over a cuppa and an exchange of thoughts, Melanie, Isabel and I eased into a very slow start getting words on paper. Taking five hours to draft a South Sister press release and launch invitation, at times, trying to get three different ways of thinking going down the same track made for slow progress....

Ready for a spell, I had to tear away to catch shops before closing. With words to play with and working faster alone, I disappeared for a while playing with the layout and wording of the first draft. Happy with the simple design I tore back into town to print a hardcopy, returning to Melanie's the press release was reaching its final stages. Leaving the draft copy to pass onto the editing panel for comment, I was content then to wander back to our side of the mountain....

Settled back into familiar surroundings, Ms Tia fed and happily stretching her patient legs, I relaxed my brain with a crossword.... Ah, bliss ☺....

Saturday 4 September 2004

Tired of waking carrying a load of disappointment, feeling let-down by Terry's lack of action towards his agreed side to the cattle agistment deal done on a trusted handshake!!!! Six months have passed since the cattle returned home and Terry disappeared with them. Recently he asked Ross what the feed was like up at my place ready to take a second bite of the cherry, I thought we had better square off on the original deal first....

Disappointed with Terry's greedy and careless use of trust, I woke for the last time with this thought bothering me. Preferring to avoid confrontation, in automatic pilot I drove to the other side of the mountain, gracing Terry's doorstep for eye contact to share my discontent of his absence and in search of a solution. Declining the coffee on offer from his wife I cut straight to the chase, stating to Terry that the purpose of my visit was to renegotiate our agistment deal. With his usual amount of yes, yes, yes', specified I'd like to renegotiate a new deal in cash only. Twenty-seven cows over ten weeks at $5 per head, I said, "you do your own sums Terry", "but taking into consideration slashing done in paddocks, and being a very fair person, $400 will settle the shortfall". Going on further to add, the labour exchange we had a handshake deal on I'd completed myself waiting for him to act. Being off work due to a skiing accident he asked for one month to pay, having a hunch leaving I'd never see the money, the re-negotiation moment was worth every cent☺!!!! ha, ha, ha, ha....

A spineless coward, Terry was full of 'oh yes, yes' making eye contact until I got home, hiding behind his phone and in a desperate attempt at getting some energy back, it rang hot. Terry was worked up and getting rather aggressive, I took control of the conversation having the last word then hung up, leaving him then to the frustration of an answering machine.... Tia was a brilliant judge of character, the only person she ever greeted with a bark ☺!!!!

Five calls in, I intercepted a friendly courtesy call from Melanie, letting me know the launch invitation had been through phase one of the editing panel and the hardcopy is ready for picking up for amendments. I was extremely happy with the text content and final edit and quietly proud of the final product.... One small step in saving a mountain!!!!

Outside world stuff satisfied, the farming cap was put back on. Observing the damage left behind in a short time by cows, from fencing to their sheer weight impacting ground to threadbare, I made a firm decision today there would be no more on site. Putting a firm stamp on that decision by removing the remaining temporary fencing put in place!!!!

Walkabout murdering a quota of thistles, the neighbours' kids were riding a small quad bike along the road showing disrespect for property and me. In an attempt at speaking with their mother, Kristy hung up on me. I wasn't looking for hostility simply desiring to find some middle ground and respect. Directly following failed negotiations, some fool thrashed a motorbike up and down the road demonstrating loud and aggressive out of control behaviour for a half-hour, high revving and peaking each gear to breaking down, racing everywhere making as much noise as possible to demonstrate some dumb point.... Unwilling to join the fools I'll take the legal avenue, there are far more passive and persuasive ways to defuse foolish behaviour....

A day where my survival skills and strength of character was tested, as a strong woman and individual I think I've earnt the right to stand alone!!!!

Sunday 5 September 2004

Because I care, a thought that must be satisfied, by choice, on this auspicious Sunday in September was to offer the best Dad my love on Fathers Day, and that's just what I did ☺.... Rainbow Falls' morning disappeared in my favourite manner, quietly. Collecting water and playing our usual water collecting games, on an impromptu pat I found yet another tick, this

one behind Tia's left ear. With each tick removed from the beautiful host her energy rises, I might stop looking soon Tia wears me out watching the sheer number of kilometres she runs each day ☺ ....
Taking the shovel for a walk after lunch I dropped a patch of hemlock, then poking around chipped young thistles from the side and front yards of the cottage. Content playing around I started edging the footpath linking the cottage and burnt out house, a sharp path edge is visually pleasing ☺ ....
Ready for beer o'clock by the time the path was finished, chose then to wander kicking scotchies goodbye enjoying accomplishments and sunset. Observing a shift in habits with longer daylight hours, I'm staying up later and working outside longer, my psyche is shifting with the season.... Even happier, to be in the calmer embrace of spring ☺ ....

Monday 6 September 2004
For a practising hermit, life has certainly been social. High priority contact with the outside world first thing was to recognise Kristy-Lee's birthday, only managing to leave thoughts on her answering machine....
Putting work into reviving a sad looking fruit tree in the elevated garden, I got a laugh to see Tia had buried a tennis ball at its base ☺ ....
A call from Melanie mid morning offered a clear direction ahead, arranging to meet at the On-line Centre in St. Marys at 2:30pm to print and copy the launch final draft.... Final draft is always a pleasure to say ☺ ....
In the interim, I sat on my bum in the bungalow sorting through paperwork doing the last minute 'shoebox shuffle' preparing the right bits to have my tax done for another year. Doing my best to scale down and simplify life the paper shuffle doesn't take as long as it used to, that can only be good ☺ !!!!
Driving the mountain a little before the scheduled meeting time, I did personal bits 'n' pieces prior to settling at the On-line Centre focussing on the invitation. Happily clutching a hardcopy of the invitation final draft I left Melanie to copying to meet up with Loui, Loui agreed, by request, to do a set of three songs at the Save South Sister launch. With an S.O.S, 'Save our Sisters' theme, Loui was adapting appropriate lyrics for the occasion from ABBA's - S.O.S, with a couple of other songs in the pipeline, the launch night is coming together ☺ ....
Business finally aside, Loui and I cracked open a coolly settling for a dash of earnt beer 'n' bullshit ☺ !!!!

Tuesday 7 September 2004
The greater part of the day was planned long before my eyes opened to greet it. A bit slow out of the blocks, my sleeping patterns have been a little erratic in the wee baby hours I toss for a couple of hours before resettling into sleep zzzz....
Arriving perfectly on time, I took a simple tax return into the agent that took ten minutes to complete and was shocked to hear a bill of $80. With my apparent shock and 'you're kidding' response the account was generously dropped to $70. One hour of basic tax returns like mine would nett an hourly rate of $480.... Hmmmm, only a breeding ground for greed....
Still in the area, I now have one less reason for going to St. Helens, ending my association with the big red W bank closing a savings account stemming from primary school. Leaving home

$201 was the total in the account, by the time fees were taken $188 was left.... One for me, one for you???? Another breeding ground of greed....
Investing the salvaged crumbs wisely I wandered across the road booking me, Tia and Destiny on the 'good ol' spirit' for a trip overseas, setting Monday 20th in concrete. I can't wait to see Mum and Dad ☺....
With Destiny tidily tucked away in her bedroom it was a relaxed state of affairs at home, breaking out beer o'clock I went walkabout and called it a day ☺....

Wednesday 8 September 2004
Soothed to sleep with, and waking to the same gentle rhythm, it was music to my ears to finally hear measurable rain, the countryside received a much-needed 10mm....
Paradise made special delivery of a personal favourite moment of sheer magical bliss, fogged in and feeling isolated, low cloud blocked the world out just for a while. Offering a mixed bag outside, I opted for the great indoors updating the journal onto computer. That alone kept me out of trouble ☺....
Returning with an empty beer from walkabout and thistle destroying was fortunate to walk in and catch a call from Stacey, with no shortage of conversation it was my bladder that betrayed, dancing out farewells ☺....
Car-pooling out of the mountain, I picked Ross up in passing for the 'Save our Sisters' meeting. The mood was positive, within two weeks there has been a great sense of achievement at how much has been accomplished in such a short time!!!! I'm proud to be part of it....
The meeting was fast moving and constructive, making it back to Rainbow Falls 10:30p.m.-ish, at the rate I'm travelling I may get to bed midnightish ☺????

Thursday 9 September 2004
A casual low energy morning at Rainbow Falls was based around flicking the switch on the kettle. Taking the uphill walk with the ash drum, I don't think I'll ever take ash to the loo again without thinking of Mum's effort at trying to burn it down ☺....
A misty shower early afternoon dangled the shed carrot but what fell out of the sky wasn't enough to warrant the construction of an ark, instead, went walkabout finding a good patch of thistles. Staying entertained longer than planned, and heeding a lesson in life, that it's dangerous to be walkabout with an empty beer because there's no way of measuring time. One beers worth of murdering scotchies is a good quota, taking it beyond empty, Tia and I roamed for over two hours ☺!!!!
The old hiking boots aren't as waterproof as they used to be, walking me out of the paddocks with soggy socks ☺....

Friday 10 September 2004
A mild night left 2mm sitting in the gauge, any moisture Mother Nature offers is welcome. Catching a weather forecast prior to breakfast it predicted an inside day and assisted with the decision to do a town run, and only staying in long enough to do the considered necessary bits....

Without being driven by any particular cause, uninspired, I settled into the newspaper over a slow cuppa☺....
Wind picking up momentum late afternoon brought with it a flow of nippy air, little rain was delivered with the change one thing was for sure the heater was the place to be to keep bones warm ☺ !!!!

Saturday 11 September 2004
Forced out with a full bladder bright eyed just before 7a.m., I remained up and just got on with it.
Unsure of what direction the elements were going to turn, I took the safe dry option imposing self inflicted torture lugging the vacuum cleaner to the bungalow. Adding spark to the drudgery chore and creating noise pollution bringing the carpet back to life, Tia lifted the occasion tossing the occasional tennis ball my way, life is just one big game ☺....
Enjoying the comforts of tidy surrounds, I relaxed indulging in a decadent amount of jaw exercise having a long leisurely call to Mum sharing girl talk while Dad golfed. Mum said Aunty Jenny had a nice send off, her funeral resembled a family reunion; a gathering she would have been happy with....
All news on the family grapevine current, the elements beckoned the great outdoors to immerse in the mild overcast conditions with the company of sun on occasion and the shovel....
Stubby time declared, me and my little mate wandered up the hill by the water tank to simply take it in. Within half a beer a fast moving southerly change hit, always delivered hard and fast, hail started proceedings lightening off to a brief dusting of snow, it came out of nowhere, excitement passing just as fast as it arrived ☺ ???? Leaving behind a convincing southerly and a one-dog night ☺ ....

Sunday 12 September 2004
Leaving the warmth of the cocoon wasn't a decision made rashly, ice still hung about in southerly shaded areas, the cattle trough was again frozen over, and wind cut to the bone....
One of Tia's doonas fell from the line through the icy blast, picking it up it was as stiff as a board, frozen solid it was able to stand alone ☺ !!!!
Wandering the yard following hearts desire, hands buried deep into pockets I reduced the number of scotchies with my boot. Roaming led back to the front yard of the burnt out house clearing overgrown, dense nut grass weed from fenceline. Finalising the working day in the vegie patch I scratched around like an old chook with a hoe stirring a few weeds and soil....

Monday 13 September 2004
Only anything revolving around gentle was considered, a period strips my body void of any inspiration, at these times it's one foot in front of the other....
Showing the makings of a bloody great shed day, to immerse myself at will when the desire struck, like good squirrels collected and did the bits necessary to get to that point. Waiting for the change to arrive, Tia and I went walkabout with the shovel knocking down a couple of small patches of hemlock. Well wait we did, we're still waiting ☺ !!!!

Continuing the gentle pace, pushing the wheelbarrow behind the cattle yards we wandered picking up a load of limb wood with a heart full of optimism for rain. In the end the wheelbarrow was parked in the shed fully loaded for some other time ☺ ????

Lurking about the past few days, strong wind has been easing back into our lives. It amazes me how quickly wind is forgotten about when it's gone, and how fast memories are clearly rekindled bursting its presence back on the scene!!!!

Tuesday 14 September 2004
Dosed up on heavy-duty asthma relief I slept like a baby, stirring only once for a toilet break, my body radiated the quality ☺ ....

Greeting windy overcast conditions with the potential to do anything, observing climatic behaviour to make a decision on direction, we went walkabout and I destroyed scotchies....

Getting shy on a couple of life's creature comforts, made only one deviation in town to satisfy hunger, Tia and I took no time to share a delicious hamburger from the Coach House, perfect for the moment ☺ ....

Driving back through the front gate of Rainbow Falls the first spots of rain fell, I didn't even have time to begin psyching myself for the shed before it stopped, leaving only the bloody nippy wind chill factor behind!!!!

Punishing my feet kicking at the ground a funny thought passed, its a desire to walk around Rainbow Falls without shoes and prickle free, the amount of time spent sending scotch thistles to heaven its probably a good thing, I'll have worn my boots out ☺ ????

Wednesday 15 September 2004
Back to unsettled, wind woke at random, just a reminder about complacency....

Nearing 9a.m., a cloud front thickened mattering itself through trees along South Sister Range, lifting to push a bit our way, wind driven rain began wetting the ground of Rainbow Falls. A clear western sky beamed sunshine through to the already existing mixed bag of elements above, illuminating a brilliant rainbow to complete an impressive picture.... Just a moment in time, who would want to be a weather forecaster here ☺ ????

Just beating the rain, an Aurora employee read the meter, their visit means there's a bill on the way.... Ho, hum....

Nothing groundbreaking happened at home, my head is starting to gear up for the Mildura trip and what I'd like to see done between now and then. One unavoidable job is doing the cattle trough dash collecting water, then with choice, moved inside protected from the nippy elements spoiling myself pushing the vacuum.... What a choice!!!!

With blood pumping and another degree raised in the air temperature, Ms Tia and I roamed making short work of more thistles. I always exit from a stint in the paddocks feeling lighter in body and mind, walking with hands buried deep into pockets acting out thoughtless repetition on prickles letting my mind do its own thing winds me down....

Invited to join in on home made pizza prior to the 'Save South Sister' community meeting, I couldn't say no to Ross. Always taking on more than he can handle and struggling with time, the delicious dinner didn't settle before hitting the road into town. I'm impressed with the intelligent, caring and sensible direction the group is heading it's one I'm proud to contribute to.... Another evening midnight has crept up, time to put it to bed.... zzzz....

Thursday 16 September 2004
One of those rare times the bloody repetitious monotone sound of an alarm clock stirred life into sleeping bodies, the snooze button is a brilliant option, buying precious minutes ☺ !!!!
Both etiquette and early, I met Paul, the Centrelink Psychologist, in town for our 9a.m. scheduled appointment. Opening the chapter on my health and future aspirations over a coffee it seems my head survived the body downsizing unscathed. Suggesting a program most suiting my needs, we worked together for a sensible solution to give my bones time to fit a little more snug inside my skin ☺ ….
Staying out and about I took the wiggly road to St. Helens, stopping there to support and mingle with the 'Friends of the Blue Tier' crowd at the foreshore having a visual celebration waiting on a Court outcome. Ten people charged for objecting to logging operations at the Blue Tier Mountain were having their day in Court, and a supporting crowd eagerly awaited an outcome by the St. Helens foreshore….
Rejoining the anticipating crowd at the foreshore after a haircut, and receiving some serious media coverage, around 1p.m. a roar from the Court drew the lingering crowd over. Four people had charges dropped the other six had their fingers smacked with no criminal recording…. A sensible outcome to an act of passionate conservation….
Planning ahead to Monday, Ross let me use his washing machine for a couple of loads. Leaving laundry to automatically do itself and call when finished, I filled the time constructively over a couple of beers and a dash of bullshit. Making it home with enough remaining daylight to hang the clothes on the line to freeze ☺ ….

Friday 17 & Saturday 18 September 2004
It's been a while since I've missed a journal entry, this occasion I was pleasantly distracted by an exceptional evening ☺ ….
Kicking off with Friday, consecutive nights of restless sleep gave me trouble getting my sorry arse moving, so I drifted around doing whatever took the fancy of my short-term concentration span. It was a treat to take dry clothes off the line without the manual effort involved in getting them there, two loads automatically washed put me a day ahead….
Noticing a small amount of coolant on the ground I went into Destiny damage control, with enough pipe length I clamped another 'o' ring to her bottom radiator hose. A trip over the mountain tested and proved the repairs….
In anticipation of the 'Save South Sister' community launch I gave my 'blundstones' a nugget before the big occasion. A very versatile boot, happy to work in the yard all day then with a lick of nugget they're ready for a night out ☺ ….
Filling all available space inside e.ScApe Café, from guest speakers to visual presentations and live entertainment, the entire launch flowed, entertained and informed smoothly. Loui pulled together an outstanding dash of creative talent re-wording 'ABBA's - S.O.S' to complement the 'Save our Sisters' launch theme. Accompanying Loui, Marita and I had the daggiest fun role playing an adapted version of 'Lou Reeds – Take a walk on the wild side', Marita imitated a chainsaw, I sang a chorus of 'don'ts', while Loui did her best to make us sound good ☺ ….
Generating a positive message it was certainly an uplifting fun night….

An evening at the Café wasn't enough, Loui, Marita and I headed for Rainbow Falls to finish it off with a little 'B & B' by the heater keeping the home candles burning. Sensibly throwing a swag down for the night, Tia deserted me choosing instead to sleep on Loui's bed ☺....
Managing a few hours' kip, the pace started off slow and didn't change Saturday. Having drunk enough the night before and still thirsty, we idly chatted over a couple of hot brews. Waving Loui off with the scent of potpourri filling her car, we had packed it with a beautiful mix of flowers destined for her mother AEnone ☺....
The most strenuous accomplishment achieved was carting water to the cottage incorporating our usual water collecting game, I scoop mozzies out of the cattle trough and Tia amuses herself catching the water tossed from the bucket ☺.... Everyone's happy....

Sunday 19 September 2004
It's not a habit of mine to leap out of bed. Spending waking, dozing time contemplating what's in store, today's thoughts went straight into holiday mode. Tomorrow being travel day the thumbscrews were tightened to prepare for our journey, starting with Destiny....
Pulling her up to the bungalow for her pre trip pampering began with a vacuum. Sensing something was up Tia claimed a position in Destiny one thing is for sure she wasn't going to be left behind ☺....
Windows cleaned inside and out, vitals checked under the bonnet, we were as ready as we'll ever be....

Monday 20 September 2004
Nothing ever does stand still, the day is here and its time to pack for the mainland....
Throwing the bungalow door open to a warm one in paradise, blowflies were lazily hanging around and skink lizards were active on the rock pile. A warming ground temperature is stirring reptiles into activity active skinks are my signal to keep alert for active snakes also. Delivering a blunt reminder to stay alert, movement from a shingle back lizard near the cottage doorway gave me a start. When we return from the mainland the change of season should have finished its transformation????
In an evolving manner time at home disappeared, splashing a bit of water on the fruit tree and strawberries, bathing and packing chewed into it. Main power switch flicked to off, padlocks put on and the gate shut behind, we put a few kilometres on Destiny's clock heading to Devonport....
Exercised for a long night in the car and bellies full, we started the boarding process to lose a long night on board the ferry bobbing around out in Bass Strait. Tia comfortably settled in Destiny avoiding the kennels, I'd be happier to sleep in the car to its far more comfortable than cruise seats!!!!

Tuesday 21 & Wednesday 22 September 2004
Wow, where to begin, the past two disappeared in a blink....
The night on board the ferry didn't disappoint being as uncomfortable as expected, sleep wasn't even considered until after 1am. Cruise seats only being for mind altered people, I set-up camp in the prohibited lounge area just to be horizontal. Managing a snatch at somewhere between three to four hours sleep isn't real fancy leading into a big day of driving. Paying

double to be part of a 4-berth cabin doesn't guarantee any more sleep, a previous trip I was bunked in with a woman freely releasing noise omissions from both ends!!!!

Released onto the streets of Melbourne, Destiny ran beautifully, the roads were relatively quiet and without fuss reached our destination 3p.m.-ish. Turning into Jenkins Place I jumped on the horn signalling a loud happy homecoming, it was brilliant to hug and hold both Mum and Dad, an impossible sensation over the phone ☺.... Seeing Mum and Dad is always a reminder of how much I miss them....

Good ol' Mildura hasn't failed to climatically turn on something exceptional as a warm greeting each time we travel, turning up the thermostat to 31°, surprise, surprise, it was the hottest day recorded since winter.... No complaints, a good ten degrees cooler than the last trip over ☺!!!!

Following a huge day of driving and plenty of exchanged love and conversation I fell into a solid nine hours between the sheets zzzz....

A small sacrifice to pay made up for tenfold by food offerings, Tia's not allowed inside, without doing too badly she's got a comfortable bedroom set-up in Destiny. First move Wednesday was to release her from the confines of her bedroom to claim real estate....

A household up and mobile, leaving me to procrastinate, Mum took off on her 12km walk with Ms Tia and Dad off for a game of golf. A shower and washing would normally take me the good part of a day at home, incorporating water on tap and automation it was all over in a couple of hours.... Bonus ☺....

The afternoon took on a pleasant direction of socialising the presence of Kerry, Tegan and Aunty Claire livened up the house. Conversation was at times in competition with heavy machinery in the process of replacing fifty-year-old water pipes through the street....

Seated outside for pre dinner drinks enjoying the approaching cloud and cool change, without complaint, Mum again insisted on cooking dinner, from there we all wound down.... Happy to be here ☺....

Thursday 23 September 2004
Another great day immersed fully with family ☺!!!!

Listening to heavy engines warming up at 7:30am that weren't log trucks, realised it was machinery in the vacant block next door preparing to commence work on water pipes out front. The wake up call put paid to any thoughts of rolling over snoozing. Welcome to city living ☺....

Planning to meet Mum at midday in town after having her nails done, requiring new camera batteries I did a bit of personal shopping before we crossed paths. Not being a stranger myself, Mum and I met up with people we both knew exchanging introductions and sharing conversations.... A pleasant mother daughter bonding session in town ☺....

Still searching to fully recover from travelling I made no plans, simply relished in a quiet afternoon home with Mum and Dad, the only exception being wandering out the gate taking Ms Tia for a walk to stretch her little legs. Tia has happily settled to the idea of being spoilt by three people, landing in doggy utopia where pats and culinary delights fall out of human hands ☺.... Does it get better????

Friday 24, Saturday 25 & Sunday 26 September 2004
The past few have disappeared in a socialising blink ☺ ....
Showered in parent spoiling, Friday began with a milo in bed, my feet hadn't touched the floor and Miriam phoned holding me to my promise of helping with wedding preparations. The easy attained list started with last minute shopping in town, and Fiona having just flown in from Japan, the list ended with picking her up before heading out to Colignan Hall for reunions and all hands on deck ☺ ....
Fiona and I hadn't sighted one another for a couple of years, a warm welcoming hug and plenty of chatter filled the drive to Colignan where we both saw Mirro for the first time, having another warm reunion of absent friends ☺ ....
There wasn't much to do at the Hall so I took a chance paying a surprise visit on Bernie and Jill, living just 10kms past Colignan Hall. Like I was expected, they were both home and were beside themselves turning on the hospitality, my brief visit turned into a couple of hours over a beer and plenty of conversation. Driving out their gate with a return dinner invitation to further the conversation we didn't cram in today over a few more cold ales ☺ ....
Driving back into Mildura 8:30p.m.-ish, more pleasantly done with eye contact Mum and I talked ourselves out....
Knowing a rough timeline I prepared me, Tia and Destiny for a sleepover at Colignan. Activating arrangements made for Saturday, Miriam rang 11a.m.-ish when she was ready to start wedding preparations and photos. Shooting off many rolls of film at Miriam's request, I followed her to Stewart having her hair done, then to Iraak to get dressed at her parents home, to the final destined ceremony ☺ ....
Out of film, I could happily settle into pure socialising and that I did well, the entire mood of the ceremony and celebrations was relaxed and friendly. A fortunate chat with Iany Weeny and Kirsten left me with another dinner invitation for Thursday. This Mildura trip is panning out to be a pleasurable social time ☺ ....
Festivities fading about midnight, the handful of us left standing didn't take much encouragement to call it a night, Ms Tia was very happy for company in the back of Destiny. Parked amongst tents a warm sun belting through the window drove me out sooner than planned, getting up I made a start cleaning up and dismantling, as bodies surfaced they joined in. The small army of people and entourage of Ute's and trailers had any sign of a wedding gone in a mere few hours....
Ready to wind down festivities and shower, the travelling Tassie Trio made our way back to Mum and Dad's, where lovingly, a dished up plate of Mum's traditional Sunday roast waited ☺ .... Perfect....

Monday 27 September 2004
The dust settling on celebration and festivities it was time to catch my breath and share dedicated quality time with family ☺ ....
Somewhat more sedate, I didn't surface in a hurry to tackle whatever lay before me easing into it I exerted the most effort on a few calls. The first call went to Kerry trying to arrange time to catch up around her work commitments we're still fine tuning that plan. Due to health facilities either unavailable or not so conveniently handy at home, I made appointments for a main-

points check while they're at my fingertips. Putting in a big spurt I took Ms Tia for a wander of the streets on lead to claim real estate and check out 'the hood' ☺....
After returning from one of Yvonne's exercise classes Mum still had energy to burn, after lunch Tia and I joined Mum on her 12km round trip to Apex Park following the river. Not a pace I enjoy walking at but said yes to Mum's invitation. About a kilometre into following the river track, leaning against a tree just off the walkway some jerk was making an effort at masturbation. Verbally humiliating him for his careless actions in public ruined his moment. He's been the brunt of many jokes!!!!

Tuesday 28 September 2004
Another day gone, at this rate we'll be home before we know it????
Feet hitting the ground prompt and early 7a.m.-ish, I was roused into consciousness by unrelenting barking inside the confines of Destiny. Two hot-air balloons drifting overhead releasing gas stirred my girl and every other critter in a kilometre radius!!!!
Fresh from the shower blow waving my hair Dad asked if I could shift Destiny, before moving the phone also rang, in a hurried chat Kerry and I briefly organised lunch arrangements at Aunty Claire's tomorrow....
Finishing the hair dry, I then took off to have my tennis elbow x-rayed followed by a spot of shopping. Going into town was a cultural experience, the local Country and Western Festival was in full swing, a dose of yodelling and ten gallon hats, true checked shirt and tassel country clogged the mall, being a case of do only what's necessary and leave!!!!
Zig zagging my way across town destined for a beer, began in search of the electoral office to cast an absentee vote. On the zag stroke buying vegetable seed from the organic shop met Miriam and Andrew out front, inviting me Friday to help eat wedding leftovers, food I don't have to cook is always a pleasure. Making it to the beer stop I dropped in on a long time friend Fan, condensing the couple of years since our last meeting easily over a couple of cans....
A waiting meal being kept warm in the oven, only from the love of a Mother, so gratefully met me walking through the back door. I haven't cooked a meal since arriving in Mildura, Mum said the complement can be returned when she visits Tassie February, my reply to that comment was, 'you get a break for two weeks, I've had a lifetime of being spoilt' ☺....

Wednesday 29 September 2004
Living in suburbia has some fast track advantages, gaining time to gain time, I showered and had laundry done without having to spend the day to do it. Dad left for golf, Mum and I drove across town to Aunty Claire's, joining up with Kerry and Tegan for lunch and an afternoon of good company ☺....
Complements of Dad, and competing with howdy cowdys, Mum and I braved our way through town to purchase lunch. Arriving within ten minutes of one another, we ate our way through a healthy conversation that didn't sit idle. Patiently waiting outside on the concrete patio, Tia decorated it in polka dots spelling out she was well and truly in season, I was hoping to be home before I had to be concerned.... Such is life....
Dad arrived home not too long behind us having had mixed success with golf, blitzing the back 9 holes first, he stumbled a little on the front 9 to finish in a good position rather than an

outstanding one ☺ .... The evening then evolved gently from pre dinner drinks to dinner and relaxation....

Thursday 30 September & Friday 1 October 2004
The morning routine we so comfortably found a groove in was thrown out of whack Thursday. Kettle filled for breakfast, Dad followed Mum in the bathroom turning around and walking straight back out, water had stopped flowing. Other than the obvious cause, we weren't alerted to the disruption, only guessing it was due to pipe replacement work going on in the street???? Darting off for her walk along the riverfront taking Tia, Mum returned with the knowledge that the water interruption was only supposed to be brief but an unprecedented rusted fire hydrant breaking caused a few headaches ☺ ....
Using energy conservatively I filled in a relaxing afternoon home doing a bit of fluffing around. Destiny attracted attention for a wash with the help of Ms Tia constantly chasing the flowing water the job got done ☺ ....
Following pre dinner drinks, Mum and Dad readily babysat Tia releasing me to take the short walk to Iany Weeny and Kirsten's concern free for dinner. Again, with quality low maintenance friends there was years of absence to fill in and we did pretty well at filling in all the gaps. Ian and Kirsten took me for a computer walk through photo albums from their overseas travels, taking me from Scotland to Cambodia and everything in between. When finally taking a breath noticed the time had pipped 1am, unlike my hosts, was happy I didn't have to work the following morning ☺ ....
A convenient morning shower routine tried and proven, I stay in bed and out of the way until the bathroom is free, before getting vertical Mum has brought me a milo in bed. I'm not accustomed to being spoilt ☺ ....
An October 1 baby, Mum and I planned a surprise visit, stopping to buy a cake on our way, found the birthday girl Tegan home. Happily opening the door to her surprise visitors, lighting candles we sang happy birthday before sampling it over a cuppa ☺ .... Now five months pregnant, Tegan proudly showed ultra sound images of bubbies growth stage....
If left to evening, writing in the journal probably wouldn't happen again because Friday night is wedding leftovers. It would be the last thing I'd feel like doing making it through the back door tonight ☺ .... I'll just have to work writing in around my busy social life????

Saturday 2 October 2004
Consecutive sociable late nights, sampling the variety of food on offer with Miriam and Andrew last night, I didn't surface until 10a.m., by then the household was fully functioning. Mum had returned with Tia from their walk along the riverfront and Dad was preparing to take off for golf ☺ ....
Sitting around the kitchen table chatting about life in general Mum and I set in concrete a plan for attending the Red Cliffs market tomorrow. Working up an appetite with our jaws hunger pangs took over, agreeable to fish 'n' chips for a change Mum said she'd shout if I got them, a saying she picked up from Dad....
Rumbling bellies content, and fitting the mood, we left them to settle over a decadent afternoon with our noses buried in books, it was during reading that afternoon morphed into a quiet night at home simply enjoying family ☺ ....

Sunday 3 October 2004
Leaving Dad to the responsibility of Tia babysitting duties, Mum and I took off to the Red Cliffs market to track down some bargains. Hunting for antiques and collectibles, Mum took a liking to a bargain priced old birko electric kettle along with a couple of other knick-knacks to secure a successful shopping expedition. Seeking items of practical use for home, my booty of bargains started with an A4 timber picture frame, windproof jacket, polar fleece and hooded jumper, all new, at $5 apiece.... Very happy shoppers ☺ !!!!
Chief babysitter and boss of cooking the silverside, Dad had lunch close to ready when we made it back from Red Cliffs. All feeling pretty passive after a solid meal, Dad retreated to his garden, Mum and I disappeared back into our respective books engrossed in the adventures they contained....
Downing tools come beer o'clock, I slipped a couple of coolies into Destiny and me and my little mate took off for some liquid conversation with true hearted friends, Mary and Joan. Picking up where we last left off to again get the latest episodes of our life stories current. Pleasantly this Mildura trip will be memorable as a lovely sociable one ☺ ....

Monday 4 October 2004
Without slipping out of our tried and proven groove, the morning started in the usual fashion, I wait patiently in bed until Mum and Dad finish in the bathroom before taking over. Mum disappeared for her hair appointment in town, I did a little washing and the vacuuming while Dad and Tia busied themselves together outside ☺ ....
As the day panned Mum and Dad went visiting Betty for her birthday, Tia kept me company under the pergola with my nose buried between the pages of a book. The tranquillity of our blissful peace was shattered by the sound of the neighbours' head in the toilet bowl having a beefy spew.... A slight over indulgence....

Tuesday 5 October 2004
A day that took me all over the place. Beginning the social wander at Kerry's over a cuppa and garden walk, incorporating the latest developments inside, Kerry's establishing a nice feel to her home. The best business advertising of all is first hand experience and word of mouth, Kerry gave me the good oil on a reasonable priced muffler shop for Destiny, that being the next stop after bidding our farewells....
I mentioned to the chap at the muffler shop that he was recommended because of honesty and being fairly priced. Taking onboard the compliment, the chap quoted $50 and could fit the job in at 2p.m., my favourite way to conduct business, shook his hand and said I'd be back....
Continuing a social meander, with a couple of decades of friendship under our belt I pulled in for a spontaneous yarn with Peter at Sunraysia Steering Service, warmly welcoming, we picked up where we last left off. Catching up over lunch, I had an update with Mum and Dad before heading back to the muffler shop....
Leaving Destiny for an hour to soften her sound I filled wait time in town. Journal folder sixteen close to finished two more folders made the 'to-do' list, enough to keep me out of trouble a few more months. Weaving back across town I called into an irrigation supply shop in Madden Avenue after a 2-inch poly joiner to repair the irrigation pipe at home. The narrow minded jock serving asked me how long it took me to recite the order, quite sure of making

direct eye contact with the ignorant bastard's eyes, piercing into his empty shell told him squarely I wasn't on a errand for some bloke I run the property.... A humbled small talk silence fell on foolish ignorance....

Contrary to the last ignorant episode, Destiny was ready and waiting on arrival. From go to whoa it was a pleasant experience dealing with the Almond Avenue Muffler Shop ☺....

Wednesday 6 October 2004

With plans for a pizza, pasta lunch out, I got through a brief read absorbed in the current book of a non-fiction series on Helen Forrester's trying and triumphant life, prior to Mum and I venturing off to meet Kerry and Aunty Claire to feed our appetites....

Over lunch Kerry gave me an early birthday present of a lovely black singlet top, clothes are always useful, it will go well with the overalls Dad offered that no longer fit ☺....

Continuing on after lunch, in a once in a not very often occasion, we went to the R.S.L. to blow a couple of bucks on the pokies. Sharing a machine, it kept us amused and as a bonus we broke even at plays end ☺....

Talking through our encounters of a day out in the big wide world, with no obligations for the evening I enjoyed beer o'clock with Mum and Dad. After knocking the lid off a couple, and prior to getting too relaxed, took my little mate for a walk to claim a bit of real estate in the neighbourhood ☺....

Thursday 7 October 2004 'Happy Anniversary Mum and Dad'

Around 6a.m. the combination of Tia's barking and thunder rumbles drew me from bed to pull clothes on and walk out the door in automatic. Making the most of the situation I set-up a bed and went car camping, dropping Destiny's back seat laid it down so we could both be comfortable. When a restful hush fell from the heavens above and jaws from beside, I drifted into sleep, being brought from peaceful slumber by a fresh sound, one of Tia heaving. Trying to bring her paws up in the small space we shared, I achieved an outstanding wake up and response desiring Tia to be outside Destiny for the follow through ☺....

Stirring up all the atmospheric fuss, Mum and Dad mentioned it was 26° at 7:30am, rather tropical....

Chasing specials to load in Destiny for taking home, I browsed the bombardment of catalogues that regularly get stuffed into the letterbox on the hunt. Taking a run out to Target Plaza chasing worthwhile specials, I also dropped in on an off chance my favourite bank manager was in Helen invited me into her office for a client yarn ☺....

Out of Helens office comfort and back out into the hot windy elements, I bought up on a good toilet roll special to take home and also restocked beer supplies they won't make it out of Mildura ☺!!!!

Drawn from the pages of my book I had a yarn with Mum helping with dinner, and that's about as energetic as the afternoon got. Settling the tropics, a cool change moved in without a thunderstorm in sight, it should be a useful night for me and sleep zzzz....

Friday 8 & Saturday 9 October 2004

The only one able to keep pace, Tia went with Mum on her fast paced walk along the riverfront in the cool that Friday morning offered. Water main replacement works scheduled a turn off

between 11a.m. and 1p.m. 'up and at'em' all water needs were met prior to shut down. Last in, I was showered and had washing complete before Tia and Mum returned from pounding the pavement....
With the house clean Mum was content to relax with me in silence reading, Dad toggled between the garden and filling his mind with news and current affairs programs....
Evening plans with long time friend, Fan, at her home over dinner and more drinks than one should drive with in their system, Dad delivered me to her doorstep to cab it home at my own leisure. A recipe for good socialising, sharing heaps of conversation, laughs, and of course beer ☺ ....
Getting myself locked back inside home gates for the evening I shared a bit of quality time with my little mate before tucking myself in. Having a charmed sleep until 6:45a.m.-ish, two hot-air balloons passing overhead stirred up every dog within a kilometre radius!!!! Piss off!!!! Heading back to bed just to rest my bones Mum greeted me at the door to wish me a happy birthday, being the furthest thing from my mind, Mum's wishes took me by surprise I hadn't given my birthday any thought at that stage....
Not treatment accustomed to, I've been spoilt with a breakfast milo personally delivered to me in bed everyday with the exception of the rare times I was still asleep.... Who's a lucky girl ☺ ....
Mum and Dad got me out of bed to join them down the shed where they'd stashed a booty of gifts incorporating both birthday and the fast approaching festive season. It was like Christmas lifting the sheet revealing a set of stainless steel pots, set of three frying pans, a microwave oven and a timber caddy to place across the bath for toiletries, all practical useful presents. Mum and Dad's generosity was overwhelming and appreciated ☺ ....
Lunch out and specials shopping were plans Mum and I made when Dad left us for golf, buying lunch from where Kerry works enabled her to offer birthday wishes. Spending a brief snatch at quality time with Kerry before reluctantly having a hug and kiss goodbye, leaving her to a constant flow of customers and a busy shop. Then from hardware to supermarkets and second-hand stores I lucked shade for Tia and Destiny at each stop ☺ ....
During the course of the day birthday wishes arrived from friends, topping a quality day with a quality evening sharing time and a yarn over a couple of cool ales with Mum and Dad ☺ ....
Moments like those are what make irreplaceable memories, simply the times happily shared....

Sunday 10 October 2004
Letting Tia out of Destiny first thing before being punished pounding the pavement with Mum, she started making a fuss amongst the plants outside my bedroom window. Peeking through curtains I presumed Tia was after a mouse, but doing damage to the plants thought I'd better investigate. Huddled under a plant stand in a corner, just a whisker out of reach, was the neighbours' rabbit and Tia was intent on having it for breakfast. Alive, and safe in my hands rather than Tia's jaws, Mum and I paid next door an early morning visit delivering a badly shaken bunny. The grass is not always greener on the other side....
Regular quality sleep is almost an impossibility lately, today the rabbit, yesterday hot-air balloons, and a thunderstorm the night before, I'm feeling as wrung out as the laundry????

The only killing that did go on was when Mum got her traditional Sunday roast cooking, blowflies arrived en masse, where and how they get in remains a mystery but they weren't welcome to lunch....

Lunch and domestics settling, so did I, with my nose buried into a book. Four books in the Helen Forrester series, the first two moved me, finalising book three I was reduced to tears. An amazing, heartbreaking and inspiring story of survival and personal endurance making the most of very little, from food to compassion, that was on offer, a course very few have inner strength enough to pull through to survive....

Monday 11 October 2004

Measuring 20° by 7a.m., designed the stage for a pretty laid back energy conserving one, nothing too strenuous is the only way to self-preserve in hot Mildura elements....

Reaching a very warm 35°, to get air flowing Mum and I assembled a pedestal fan from its box and the roof mounted evaporative air-conditioner got its first run in the lead up to summer....

A need for tampons was the only thing to drive me from air-conditioned comfort, as if attached by a bungie rope, I was drawn straight back to it ....

Using the assortment of vegetables available I put together a quiche for dinner. When the quiche was cooked ready just to heat and eat, I let the final book in the series and the air-conditioner absorb me until socialising over beer o'clock came around ☺....

Tuesday 12 & Wednesday 13 October 2004

Following dinner at Fred's Tuesday, at 12:30am rattling the side gates to get back in at home pen didn't find its way onto paper.... yawn....

A forecast 37° for Tuesday, Mum took off early with Tia to beat the heat for a mini marathon along the riverfront and returned with a bloody knee. An elderly lady had her dog off lead and it ran straight up to Tia, reaching for Tia's collar, and a little bit of a tug and shove, Mum ended up on her knee on the footpath. Continuing without offering a word the elderly lady just walked on???? Not a very compassionate act!!!!

Patient attended to and prescribed rest and relaxation, heeding advice, an afternoon was spent in the cool cinema taking in a movie. Sitting in refrigerated temperatures that make you wish you'd brought a jumper, it was easy to forget what was going on outside, leaving the cinema 4p.m.-ish we walked out into a wall of heat. In contrast, October last year at home I was experiencing snow this year I'm immersed in a record breaking 40° heat....

Kind to leave Tia buried amongst the cool shrubbery, Mum and Dad babysat while I stepped out into the scorpions' tail driving to Irymple for dinner at Fred's. Taking a pre dinner garden walk Fred toured me through the bits 'n' pieces his friend Westy uncovered at garage sales and markets for garden decoration. I asked Fred if Westy could keep an eye out for an old-fashioned cast-iron tractor seat for Mum, Fred said, "do you mean one of these", leading me to a stack of several Fred generously packed one in the car for an 'about to be' very elated Mother. Following a lovely evening of delicious food and good conversation, Fred sent me home with a beautiful little milk jug hand-made by his recently deceased Mother, a moving gesture I happily accepted to top an already lovely night ☺....

I wanted to burst in the door and wake Mum to show her the tractor seat, thinking better of it put myself to bed instead ☺....

The predicted response to finding the tractor seat Wednesday morning filled my heart and I'm sure would please Fred, what he considered a small gesture is big to someone else. Dad's planning a trip to town tomorrow for paint and if I'm not wrong he'll have it sanded and painted before the sun sets ☺ ....

Taking his ritual walk to the corner store for a newspaper, headlines in the one Dad returned with today read 'Record October temperatures leave Sunraysia sweltering'. Mildura never fails in turning on extremes while we're visiting, yesterday reached 40.2° being the hottest October day ever recorded, great!!!!

Taking his chances with stifling heat Dad shot through for golf, Mum and I readied ourselves for an air-conditioned car dash with Aunty Claire for lunch at the Coomealla Club. Returning to the smoke free environment of the R.S.L. we shared a poker machine together for a flutter, again walking away near enough to breaking even after having a bit of fun ☺ ....

Home sharing our day out stories, Dad also had a top one scoring a nett 65 for his round of golf, a score that should see him take-out his division on the day ☺ ....

Thursday 14 October 2004

Hearing the muffled sounds of a dog barking, unsure if it was Tia, I couldn't lay in ignorance out of hope so I got up and investigated. Barking was coming from a neighbouring house, being good sitting quietly I let Tia out of her Destiny bedroom. Thinking it to be a reasonable hour standing in full sun, I went in to get Tia's food from the fridge and was surprised to see the clock displaying a mere 6:30am. Setting my little mate up with all the creature comforts I went back to bed to warm the sheets a bit longer....

Dad's confidence is growing taking Tia with him for a walk around to the shop, while out of sight out of mind Mum and I shot through for a drive to Red Cliffs for a look around the shopping centre simply to solve my curiosity. As many empty shops as occupied it's beginning to look more like a ghost town. Before leaving Red Cliffs I called into the nursing home to visit a fine gentleman and dear friend affectionately named A.B., otherwise known as Arthur Branson, our friendship stems back to 1984 the very year I began work with the Department of Agriculture ☺ ....

As predictable as the sun rising, Dad is unable to leave anything sit idle, in our absence Lukey occupied his time sanding and painting the tractor seat, the finished result pleased Mum immensely. The seat has taken pride of place on the back porch as a treasured ornament displayed beautifully amongst the healthy collection of plants ☺ ....

Friday 15 & Saturday 16 October 2004

Here I am again up for another two-day journal entry session my social life once again took precedence over writing....

Ready to take off with Tia Friday morning for their walk along the riverfront, coinciding with Dad's trip to collect the daily paper, Mum and Dad walked out of the street together, Mum vowed never to do it again. Parting company, Tia was torn between her loyalties, continually looking back at Dad and stopping in her tracks she broke the flow of Mum's walking stride ☺ !!!!

Beginning to think toward tidying loose ends before leaving for home and the only place with a machine large enough to take a queen sized doona, I treated myself to a stint at the laundromat....

Home in time for beer o'clock, Mum, Dad and myself sat around talking our way through a lovely chicken curry and vegetable dinner ☺ ....

A movie night with a few friends at Miriam's 8p.m.-ish is where writing in the journal went begging Friday night. Getting Tia's travelling 'Destiny' bedroom home 11:30p.m.-ish for my girl to get comfortable....

Its a bit of hit and miss with sleeping in, responding to the sound of a barking dog found Tia comfy, content and still snoozing, waking her to let her out of Destiny I was tricked again by a neighbouring dog....

Saturday morning disappeared on me doing a lot of not much. Dad made tracks for his usual game of golf, having made plans earlier, Mum and I patronised the over priced annual Mildura show. Packing it in amongst the swelling crowd we spent solid hours taking in exhibits, displays, and merely watching spew-inciting rides. Leaving no stone unturned and contentedly socialised my feet were happy to be making their way home ☺ ....

Burning the candle at both ends, late nights, particularly the unpredictable early mornings are wearing me down, searching for an early one knew the only obstacle standing in the way of that was the 9:30pm scheduled show fireworks. When Tia is comfortable and content only then am I able to do the same zzzz....

Sunday 17 October 2004

Beginning to feel a bit flat, lacking quality sleep due to outside influences, when Tia's stress factor abated following fireworks last night I was down for the count sleeping in an unbroken coma until 7:30a.m.-ish....

Preciously guarding the hard earnt new-found energy, I was very conservative with it planning only to stay home. Mum asked me to turn the oven on to start lunch just after 9a.m. so she could beat the pavement earlier for a walk with Tia; too easy. Attracting blowflies en masse, finding their way inside through unknown sources is a frustrating ritual associated with the traditional Sunday roast!!!!

Paws content for a slower pace, Tia followed Dad around the yard like a pet lamb always willing to be of assistance throwing a tennis ball in the way, and keeping an astute mind on the ready, Tia too was happy to file and compost any tossed weed. Dad may take twice as long to achieve anything but his patience with Tia displays his enjoyment of her company ☺ ....

With a belly full of Sunday roast I didn't overdo it, keeping the excitement meter idling on passive I had a tinker with Destiny then basked under the pergola nestled in the outdoor setting. Ms Tia attentively not far off, I slipped between the pages of book four and the final one of the series, a true story receiving my full attention....

Monday 18 October 2004

With travel plans for South Australia, Mum was up and into it preparing for a 10a.m.-ish take-off time. The purpose of the trip was to drop John to work in the Riverland, Betty and Mum then planned to meander home antique shopping as they went.... Not a bad life ☺ ....

Dad willingly babysat Tia and together they kept busy in the garden freeing me for a spot of shopping with Kerry and Tegan. While out and about I booked the 'Woodchipping the Spirit of Tasmania' ferry for home, scheduled to leave Sunday evening....

Having a quiet ale together Dad and I were surprised to see the shopaholics returned by 5:30p.m.-ish, joining in, we sat around sharing our days experiences over a couple of quiet drinks ☺ .... Does life get any better, not tonight????

Tuesday 19 October 2004
Looking like sleeping in, Mum roused me with a reminder of a 9a.m. appointment rounding off my health check with a pap smear. Showered and organised I walked to the Community Health Centre less than one kilometre away being my ever-punctual self....

Like a homing pigeon, as soon as I was done I walked back through home gates, where Dad was already on the job bringing back to life a kerosene iron Mum brought home from her antique shopping expedition. Dad made the old kerosene iron sparkle like a new one a big heart and plenty of patience shows in his work ☺ ....

Staying with the self-preservation theme, tucked under the pergola with my little mate, I was either yarning to Lukey or burying my nose into the final book of the series. Dropping everything come beer o'clock for a family congregation and natter, at that precise point in time I couldn't think of anywhere else I'd rather be ☺ ....

Wednesday 20 October 2004
Inviting Aunty Claire over for lunch, and neither she nor Mum familiar with Turkish food, we made plans for expanding their culinary experiences. Tia and I went for a drive returning with a smorgasbord with complements of Dad. Dad left us to eat for his regular game of golf. Good food and good company, Mum and Aunty Claire enjoyed their Turkish experience and time vanished ☺ ....

Home happy following a walk around the fairways and greens, finishing 18 holes and coming in under par, Dad felt quietly confident he'd get a B Grade placing if he doesn't win his division ☺ ....

Thursday 21 October 2004
Savouring remaining days with family, and enhancing savour Kerry stopped in for a visit between shifts ☺ ....

Happy just to hang around the house and get under everyone's feet, I only wandered to stretch Tia's legs. Out walking with my best mate, glancing over my shoulder and picking up the pace I dared rain clouds hanging around to act out their threat. Arriving inside home gates not long after us, a brief thunderstorm stirred things up a bit. The weathers supposed to remain unsettled, for Tia and my sakes I hope the unsettled bit only means rain without the thunder!!!!

Following another lovely home cooked meal we remained seated around the kitchen table filling one another's ears with idle chatter, until one by one I was out of company, journal updated, Ms Tia put to bed in Destiny, I called it a night myself zzzz....

Friday 22 October 2004
Up early to beat the heat, Mum took Tia along for her mini marathon, a fast pounding punishing Tia wasn't going to get from me. Dad on the other hand got sorted taking off to do groceries and a spot of shopping. I was smart enough to stay in bed out of the way ☺....
The action has been given the pet name of 'Tia's television', in the gap between the bottom board and corrugated iron of the tin fence Tia watches the dogs and any movement next door, if the dogs roam too close a burst of barking breaks out!!!!
Time remaining in Mildura is reeling in fast I've gone into family saturation choosing to stay home. The most strenuous thing I achieved was to clean Destiny's windows preparing to send her out onto the highways in a tidy state. The past month has vanished accustomed to being immersed in family now I have to re-train my brain for the separation....

Saturday 23 October 2004
About 6a.m.-ish the alarm clock of neighbourhood dogs started their barking routine, with my ear tuned for a response to barking sleeping is out of the question, being good, Tia set an example to the neighbourhood....
Taking a drive across town, Kerry offered a television for home, that'll be a novel concept, television at Rainbow Falls. With work commitments, Kerry and I said our farewells, I'm going to have to get used to the idea of not having family so conveniently close????
Like peas in a pod, Dad, Saturday, and golf go hand in hand, when the Kingswood was free of the driveway and rocketing out of Jenkins Place I took off to the hole in the wall bank, supermarket then fuelled up. Striking a reality chord at just how close leaving is, continuing on with preparations, Mum helped me pack the stash of treasure in Destiny. In addition, a pedestal fan and a toaster had found their way amongst the collection of gifts ☺!!!!
Come beer o'clock I took the short walk out of the street for a couple of farewell drinks with Ian and Kirsten, very easy people to be around. Finalising the last evening in Mildura I devoted the precious time remaining with Mum and Dad ☺....

Sunday 24 October 2004
Opening my eyes to the day, the realisation flooded in there was only a few hours remaining with Mum and Dad this visit, and Tia, Destiny and I had a huge day ahead....
Tia proved the only being able to keep pace with Mum's tortuous power trek, beating the pavement between Apex Park and home they returned before I was out of bed. Without letting her paws cool Tia got straight into sorting discarded weeds for Dad and followed him around the yard like a pet lamb, much to Dad's pleasure. Tia creates extra work that's just pleasantly taken in stride ☺....
Packed with sandwiches, Tia and I extended reluctant farewells. If only I could have the best of both worlds. Driving away with eyes welled with tears I don't enjoy the initial separation, my brain used to having Mum and Dad around has to readjust to being apart....
Exactly how I like it, the drive to Melbourne was event free and Destiny didn't miss a beat, I also made the Port of Melbourne without referring to my Melways book of maps and with time to spare. One leg of the journey behind the next trial was just about to begin, enduring a night on the ferry. I've yet to have a trip aboard the Spirit that I have lasting pleasant memories of, I'm always happiest disembarking, but sadly it's unavoidable....

Monday 25 & Tuesday 26 October 2004

Waiting for the docking process and in need of a comfort stop, the only toilet available to me was a disabled cubicle. With no clear way of flushing I pulled a cord dangling from the ceiling, when it didn't respond accordingly only then did I read the sign 'pull if in need of assistance', ah, oh.... An efficient service, pushing the cancel button assistance still arrived it seems I'm not the first to have pulled looking for a flush ☺....

Called to our vehicles, I found young Tia comfortably perched on top of our luggage overseeing proceedings, remaining there until we left quarantine being driven around like royalty ☺....

Waiting to disembark I responded 'yes' to a text message from Ross, extending a welcome home dinner invitation. Stopping at the bakery, Post Office and supermarket, we were home around 11a.m.-ish to call Mum and Dad to let them know we arrived safely it was clear during our call that we miss one another....

Treasure unloaded and Destiny resting hot rubber in the shed, the mower got a run to begin the process of reclaiming the yard, that accomplishment can be achieved in little time these days. With limited time before dinner the mower was put away to resume water collecting. Having my abilities and capabilities confused, drove the mountain for a lovely home cooked meal in Ross' company. Hitting the wall with a serious allergic reaction to something at Ross', likely horse related ventolin was struggling to help, needing to separate myself from the trigger I left for home. Mind and body having had enough after a bloody long one, my brain was a haze and unable to string two words together, so I didn't zzzz....

If any clearing was going to continue Tuesday fuel supplies first had to be replenished, without dilly-dally I drove the mountain and a woman on a mission returned straight home. Going great guns, I emptied two tanks before one brief shower wet the ground stopping play. Filling a couple of hours with food, phone calls and a bit of fluffing around, made an executive decision to return mowing, emptying another couple of tanks....

While I still had energy, veered to the kitchen cooking up a feast of spaghetti, putting some petrol back in Ms Tia's and my tank ☺....

Wednesday 27 October 2004

Nature's elements determined a course the writing was on the shed wall for a heater day. Rolling and stirring from sleep on occasion the same rhythmic sound pattered on the roof, rain had convincingly settled in....

Instigating running repairs, I retrieved the blue tarp from the vegie patch where it had blown in our absence, without stress, it was replaced on the outside wall of the cottage to prevent the main power board area from getting damp....

Doing its best work overnight by 7:30a.m.-ish 24mm had splashed into the gauge, recording only another 4mm to noon. Wind displaced rain and gradually picked up speed forcing in a return rush of winter, the wind chill factor lowered the mercury to bloody freezing brrrr.... Getting the shed heater cracking we didn't move too far from it ☺....

Thursday 28 October 2004
A cage rattling mongrel last night, wind delivered a welcome home hammering, a restless brain forced me out of bed to endure the nippy elements of a bloody cold one, unforgiving for a couple of strong hours the intensity then eased enough to re-warm the sheets....
Planning ahead for Mondays public holiday planted the seed for a town trip, assisting in remaining nestled into the side of the mountain to comfortably make it past the shop shut down stage....
Strong wind chasing yesterday's 35mm total didn't take long to dry the ground surface, home from town I was able to put in another excellent effort with the mower. The poor old mower is struggling to keep up, before starting the oil has to be checked and a nut holding the fuel tank to the side of the motor constantly vibrates loose and needs regular attention????

Friday 29 October 2004
When Mother Nature permits I've been sleeping like a baby, affording me a good run under the doona dominoed into waking with plenty of energy, spending that body rush tacking together and punishing the mower. The poor mower has consumed about seven litres since Monday, transforming rapidly within a week what has taken a couple of years to claim ☺....
Food bought yesterday planning a four-day weekend already looks on the dismal side. I can't satisfy hunger, my insatiable appetite has eaten its way through a good deal of the fridge's contents, town looks like a sure destination before noon shut down tomorrow ☺!!!!

Saturday 30 October 2004
As predicted town was the destination before noon, getting enough to satisfy my appetite this time!!!!
Mother Nature delivered a drift of brief misty showers, indecisive for anything inside or outside I settled on having the day off then it didn't matter....
Spreading the newspaper out I read what caught my attention, in the end only gained paper for starting the heater. Out of reading material to stimulate my brain, and gazing out, decided to improve the view from the bungalow window. A couple of obvious patches of thistles, once growing tall and proud, are now doing their best at transforming into compost....
Between us, Ms Tia and I manage to take our work home, the least of my willing desires I gave the vacuum a run putting the grass back outside. Satisfied then to go walkabout at beer o'clock enjoying the fruits of labour ☺....

Sunday 31 October 2004
Early to bed, early to rise, and ready to face anything daylight hours had to offer....
On the tail end of breakfast dishes, and always looking after me, my best mate returned from some bone burying expedition nose and paws covered in dirt, there was no way she was coming inside it was a good time to collect and play water games ☺....
A succession of small jobs kept me occupied. A job that will forever put a smile upon my face is taking ash to the loo, thanks Mum ☺....
Content outside life was pretty tidy, and my right shoulder causing some discomfort, I changed muscle groups idling the afternoon away staring at the computer screen. Holy mother of pearl, it gave me quite a surprise with the realisation it's been almost two months since I last clunked

away on the keyboard. Following a long absence, it took many typing errors for my brain and hands to again get co-ordinated, taking a slow page to get cracking....

Monday 1 November 2004
The ritual of opening buildings before breakfast was going to schedule, causing a slight deviation by bathing in sun on warm concrete, movement by the cottage doorstep of a tiger snake trying to avoid the oncoming traffic took the entire party by surprise. Quickly making tracks under the cottage, it's not a place I psychologically need to know there's a very healthy reptile residing....
A bloody hot blowing northerly, extremely strong at times and keeping company with a fast burning stinging sun, outside wasn't a place one wanted to linger. Looking for a constructive direction, a sensible choice was unanimously made to once again slave over a hot computer ☺ ....
Hour after hour my fingers danced over the keyboard immortalising more of Rainbow Falls' history....
Not wandering too far for beer o'clock I pulled up at the massive pile of rocks increasing the height of the stack, getting even more generous with cleared space for entering through the bungalow door. Shortening in addition to raising, taking up less surface area the pile of rocks is beginning to resemble more of a wall than a dumped pile ☺ ....

Tuesday 2 November 2004
With no clear direction I strolled around procrastinating for a while before transforming the vegie patch took my fancy, finding the thought of brain therapy turning soil appealing. Real estate already long claimed, and looking after them with pride, Tia nudged at soil with her nose reshaping mounds I disturbed digging past ☺ ....
A body unwilling to turn another sod, I turned the corner from day into evening making a start on dinner. Nursing low energy and a full belly I just kicked back sitting in a fold-up chair outside watching the curtain close on another fine performance ☺ ....

Wednesday 3 & Thursday 4 November 2004
Lost down the shed over beer and bullshit with friends its liberating just to give myself permission to take the night off writing on occasion ☺ ....
Wednesday snapped into activity 2a.m. sharp to the tune of Tia's inbuilt alarm responding to distant thunder rumbles. After rattling Tia's cage thunder drifted off, a few disruptive rumbles in parting, it left in its wake strong wind and driving rain. Appearing like it was in for a long stay a promising 8mm fell by sunrise, only measuring another millimetre before quitting. Wind on the other hand took its time leaving and was pretty wild first up. Making my way to the throne perched on the hill the loo provided a rough ride rattling being pushed around ☺ ....
Doing a honeymoon campervan tour of Tassie, and expected, Mirro and Andrew rolled into St. Marys where I met them. Limited to twenty-four hours to show off the neighbourhood we had a brief look around shops, bought lunch from Evelyn, then onward to the hills....
Following me back over the mountain to home, and slowing the trip a little, a tree had fallen over the road. Without even the need to enter into considerations of what choices we had a front-end loader arrived on the scene and within minutes the road was clear....

Rugged against a penetrating cold wind Tia and I escorted our guests on the obligatory history and falls tour, wearing them out, and a little travel weary, they made up the campervan bed for a afternoon honeymoon siesta....
Keen on attending the 'Save Our Sisters' meeting for a gentle night of politics Miriam and Andrew came along. Sparking up the shed heater afterward, Ross and Lesley joined us back at Rainbow Falls for beer and bullshit where a very sociable evening was had. Winding down festivities writing came a poor second to the sight of my pillow ☺....
Slow to get started, we shared a quiet chat over a breakfast of pancakes. Still honeymooning, Miriam and Andrew packed the campervan for the next leg of their journey. Last treat before leaving, they followed Destiny back over the mountain for a pre-arranged visit to Pam and Terry's to cuddle wombats, topping the experience with cake and coffee leaving them with a nice taste in their mouths....
Before departing town I got enough of enough to hibernate time away up the mountain, returning back through the front gate the working day was spent, pleasantly I didn't wind up before it was time to wind down ☺....

Friday 5 November 2004
A soothing steady moisture drop made its presence known in the wee baby hours, not letting up, the hypnotic sound on the tin roof only encouraged Ms Tia and myself to stay snoozing for a comfortable lay in.... Ahhhh....
Varying only in density, under the sheer weight of the heavy cloud mass everything above ground was swallowed from view, magically fogged in and isolated ☺ !!!!
Ideal for justifying a stint in the shed, flipped a coin and put my hands to work instead dancing over the keyboard. Remaining entombed in the bungalow I wandered outside only for life's little necessities not available within. Smelling an end in sight I didn't let up, extracting power from the computer totally up to date!!!!
A check of the rain gauge at knock off and water had risen to the 55mm mark in the tube before the front ran out of puff....

Saturday 6 November 2004
Breakfast, and a quick clean up of the bungalow, put my workshop cap on and with my little mate close by headed to the shed putting thoughts into action at holding the mower together for a bit longer. The poor old thing has done a lot of work with very little attention, taking the air cleaner off gave it a clean and freed up a jammed throttle cable then removed grass from places there shouldn't have been any. It's again ready for another round or two with me in the yard ☺....
Venturing out turning soil in the vegie patch a follow up shower drove us back to the shed to again fill time constructively, putting the pruning saw to use on larger limbs kept me warm in cool overcast conditions....
The second front strengthened and rain was offering a convincing steady drop, leaving the heater to sit idle, cooled my sawing muscles in the bungalow on those 'one day' jobs....
By knock off 4mm had measured in the gauge and it was far from over. Comfortably cocooned in the bungalow for the evening, Ms Tia snoozed and I watched light fade through misty rain for both of us kissing another one goodbye ☺....

Sunday 7 November 2004
The second front that arrived yesterday lingered the entire night and showed no intention of giving in with sunrise....
Popping into the world twenty-one years ago to the day, a feat to be recognised, I got on the blower giving Stacey a call to wish her all the best. The plan for her twenty-first birthday is to share it with Kerry and Tegan who travelled to Melbourne from Mildura for the occasion. Italian in Lygon Street in the City was on the menu ☺....
Groomed ready to face the hours ahead, then over a couple of hot brews, pondered how to fill them. Getting pretty settled by the second cuppa I decided to spend a lazy one down the shed just to simply enjoying the heaters warmth....
Easing off to a finish 3p.m.-ish, I prised my warm bum from its perch in the haven spilling the collected 19mm from the gauge. Cloud drifted apart letting sun breakthrough to make its first appearance in two days, kissing rain goodbye for now....

Monday 8 November 2004
Ready to escape for some brain therapy, shovel embraced in my palm, went no further than the vegie patch value adding to the transformation. Carefully removing the missed bits of comfrey and clearing around self-sown potato plants, it's a good time to be working the soil, complements of recent rains the shovel slides through soil like a hot knife through butter....
Ideal to be immersed in the elements of the great outdoors a fair drift of cloud kept it cool, adding to the scales of balance, sun made an appearance from time to time maintaining a degree of warmth....
Beer o'clock has been a dry argument the past couple swallowing the last two Friday, I broke the drought tonight with a couple of reds over beef schnitzel and veg taming a roaring shovel appetite ☺....

Tuesday 9 November 2004
A very fine mist started before bed, cloud cover blocked out moonlight and hung around to give sunrise the same treatment, staging the scene for great sleeping conditions and proving that theory to be correct ☺....
The simple chain of events of breakfast, dishes and bath, got me into town to be sure I made the post in time for the fat envelope to arrive for Mum's birthday Friday. Keeping one eye on the weather the entire trip, because I still haven't nutted out how to fix the cigarette lighter, and the rattly road into town makes the loose bits at the back of the dashboard short the fuse to the wipers and indicators....
Amongst incoming mail was a bill from 'State Revenue' for $281, always something that can be done without, I wondered for what purpose their money collecting served. Reading the accompanying brochure the words printed before me, 'you're exempt from this tax if it's your principle place of residence', that piece of knowledge got me straight onto the phone with a contact number also found on that little glossy brochure. An exemption form is now on its way in the post; a possible rare happy ending to a bill ☺ ????
Tidying the remaining couple of daylight hours on offer, the transforming team of me, my best mate and the shovel returned to the vegie patch. Hunger drove me in to complete the next stage before knock off, filling our tummies....

Wednesday 10 November 2004

Hitting the ground running and short on clothes laundry couldn't be put off any longer....
Waiting until a respectable time of the morning to ring I took quality time out to offer Mum thoughts for tomorrows pending colonoscopy, phoning early enough to catch Dad for a yarp before golf also ☺.... I love those people dearly....

There's not too much about laundry Tia gets excited about participating in, instead she amused herself digging up a bone for a chew then guarded it from flies or any other passing traffic ☺....

Dad mentioned during our chat that some good rain is headed our way either late today or tomorrow. With advanced warning I put the knowledge to use securing the blue tarp properly on the cottage wall. Still in modifying mode, green shadecloth was attached under eaves and strung across to protect two leaking cottage southerly windows, being anchored at the base drawing the cloth out from the wall with the theory of diverting water away. A quick fix attempt at stopping water from coming inside????

Shy on light limb wood to get the fire initially cracking, the wheelbarrow was taken for a walk behind the cattle yards and returned full to the shed then the heater was set ready for a match. Like a woman with energy to burn, the bungalow was next in sights for a vacuum to get the house in order....

Dad's forecast change showed its first inkling of arriving 6:30p.m.-ish, South Sister Range fuzzed up with cloud offering a faint mist dusting ☺....

Thursday 11 & Friday 12 November 2004

A lot of water soon flows under the bridge????

Lukey's forecast picked up strength Thursday, stirring into consciousness to the sound of a continuous spill. Rewarded with one of my favourites, being fogged in blanketed in low cloud was treated to stifled visibility toggling between twenty and fifty metres until mid afternoon ☺....

Tia amused herself with water falling from the shed roof leaving me to concentrate on a bush repair with Destiny's fusing problem. Lacking the knowledge to dismantle the lighter and unable to see behind the dash to work it out, went the next step to stop the loose bolt moving by clamping a wooden clothes peg directly behind the mobile bolt causing the fusing. Replacing the existing blown fuse Destiny's indicators and wipers are once again a going concern....

I first tried phoning Mum 4:30p.m.-ish after news of her colonoscopy, only making it through the back door 7p.m.-ish, but most importantly Mum brought home the desired outcome ☺ !!!!
With leftovers and the knowledge that life was all good, I took the liberty of throwing a match to the shed heater just to luxuriate in the warmth and simply enjoy the magical fogged in experience and peaceful serenity that goes with it ☺.... Ahhhh....

Basking with a beaming smile in the knowledge of Mum's colonoscopy results and with a head in the clouds ink wouldn't spill from my pen, the only thing one could do was to have a night off and enjoy the moment ☺....

November 12, the date etched on the calendar needed no prompt, Mum's birthday flows fluently from memory. Friday began with a healthy chat to the healthy birthday girl ☺....

Organised for town, me and my best mate jumped into Destiny to get adequate food to see us through the weekend, then did a stint on the shovel to see time through to beer o'clock putting an end to the drought ☺ ….

Saturday 13 November 2004
A couple of brief showers left a 2mm deposit before sunrise leading me back to toiling with soil while it remained moist. Keeping the thermostat dial set to 'just nice' for working in the vegie patch scattered cloud polka-dotting the sky regulated the sun from overheating keeping conditions adjusted to quite mild….
Coming from left field I stood gob smacked in questioning disbelief when a light hail shower started falling. To assist with convincing another two follow up hail sprinklings lead into a fourth hail burst lasting ten minutes, stoning a quick 2mm we were then dropped back into sunshine, a real mixed bag ☺ ????
After a few termite bites I could walk away today shutting the gate on turning soil in the vegie patch, it's inwardly pleasing to see it looking so healthy and satisfying on the eye ☺ ….

Sunday 14 & Monday 15 November 2004
Looking for something relaxing to do off my feet Monday afternoon, being a day behind with the journal instigated catch up freeing a second consecutive night to myself ☺ ….
To stay on top of a fast disappearing yard Sunday was consumed mowing, mowing some then mowing some more. Offering initial resistance to start, once going there was no stopping cutting loose emptying six tank loads. Buzzing over the entire burnt out house yard around the cottage and a good length of the driveway I extended beyond expectations. The poor old mower is just holding together, wire holds bits where a bolt should be and other bits vibrate loose with every use, its a case of 'gotta know your tools' to keep them operating ☺ ….
Covered in sweat, dirt, bruises and anything else the mower threw at me, it always feels brilliant on skin afterwards to be clean and supporting fresh clothes….
Relaxed with my tired 'mowers feet' up and Ms Tia curled up snoozing nearby, from my position of comfort the 'tiredies and brain dead' moved in, unable to string a sentence together put sore muscles to bed instead….
Monday and the working world back on deck I phoned making doctors appointments for both me and Ms Tia for Thursday, I'm in need of asthma puffers, Ms Tia's up for injections….
A tricky one in paradise wind arrives with a chill and the sun is hot, constantly toggling from hot to cold makes it hard for a woman to pick her wardrobe right for outdoors ☺ ????
The mower was probably grateful only enough petrol remained to fill the tank twice before completely running out, those two tanks made quite an impression along the driveway strip….

Tuesday 16 November 2004
Revived with a drink, I tossed a bit of water over the covered strawberry plants now full of life and fruit, possums haven't been able to reach them to snack out. The fruit tree trying to set-up home amid overcrowding and fierce competition in the elevated garden, now with room to breathe, it's also showing signs of life dotted with a sprinkling of immature fruit. I'll add a bit of water and see what happens ☺ ….

Tinkering with small jobs I stayed with the water theme, bucket after bucket went to the cottage to activate my hands into washing and spin-drying. Nature responded to my limp wristed clothes wringing effort, on and off the line the same day requires bloody good drying conditions ☺ !!!!

Taking the lightweight off my feet spent a cool afternoon in the bungalow hazing my brain over finalising a letter to the State Revenue Office applying for land tax exemption and for former payments to be recognised for reimbursement. Continuing the paperwork trend took steps to get the ball rolling for 'NEIS' (New Employment Initiative Scheme), a brainchild of Centrelink assisting new business ideas. Might be just the injection of inspirational push needed to get book editing and publishing dreams rolling with assistance ☺ ????

Wednesday 17 November 2004
Four days without going beyond the front gates we were getting pretty low on life's little necessities to feed my obsession. Out and about, most importantly the first stop was for mower supplies where I crossed paths with Rita and Ian for a natter….

Petrol cans full, a stop at the bakery, Post Office, supermarket and drinking water, back home it was a quick change from street wear to yard wear and out with the tortured mower. Not coming as a shock, halfway through the second tank the mower just stopped it wasn't going to let me push it one step further. Getting harder and harder to start, now it just won't, the mower has certainly been instrumental in the unearthing of Rainbow Falls ☺ ….

Forgoing walkabout to journal write freed the evening as mine to relax with after returning home from the 'Save South Sister' meeting in town. Placing the pen down with enough time left up my sleeve to relax over a glass of red and feed our habits prior to leaving….

Thursday 18 November 2004
Skink lizards beat us out of bed, being active on the rock pile early is a good indication of ideal conditions for reptiles both large and small…. Stay alert!!!!

Expanding our morning routine of opening up and Tia reclaiming real estate, our ritual also includes watering the strawberries and fruit tree, now identified as a peach tree, before breakfast. Doctor day for both of us there was no dilly-dally it was go, go, go, go….

With first appointment time, and after a catch up of the 'who's who' of the movie world in the waiting area, I was turned around quickly only needing a prescription for asthma puffers….

A very reluctant Ms Tia was honourably led into the vets aware and not happy about her surroundings. Unwilling to co-operate with being poked and prodded, Ms Tia was sedated so all her sensitive bits could receive a thorough going over and injections updated without resistance.

Oblivious to the world, and given a clean bill of health, I carried a snoozing girl back to a waiting Destiny. With no muscle active to assist with her floppy weight, supporting Tia in my arms I opened Destiny's back door four times, the wind blew it shut on me three ☺ !!!!

Ensuring my little mates comfort, I briefly left a snoozing Tia making short stops with both Phillip and Loui. Loui proudly toured me over her exciting purchase of a ride-on mower. No longer having use for it Loui offered me her push mower for Rainbow Falls, yahoo, timing is everything ☺ ….

Getting a sedated patient home to sleep it off, I feathered her nest in the familiar surrounds of the bungalow and kept a doting nurse monitoring and on the ready. Showing signs of controlled life 8p.m.-ish, attending to an itch, Tia sat up then just as quickly nodded off again, it pulls at my heart-strings to see her so vulnerable. Later, on wobbly legs, Ms Tia wanted out for wee's, returning back inside she sniffed at her food bowl then adjourned to bed for another snooze to face the world later☺ ....

Friday 19 November 2004
Waking hungry in the middle of the dark hours Tia devoured the food in her bowl then gave me an unrelenting paw tap on the shoulder for a comfort trip outside ☺ .... Definitely recovered from her trip to the vet....
Any news is new news, giving yesterdays paper a browse indoors was a smart place to be, a mixed weather bag was better viewed from the inside looking out. First up, a blast of cold air was blown in on gale force winds adding threatening cloud on occasion to the rush of air. Staying for the entire performance, wind blew in a brief shower hitting around lunchtime, afternoon sun was quite warm and early evening it was calm with clear skies????
An afternoon in the yard exercising the shovel edging around obstacles the mower couldn't get near turned into a discovery of treasure. Bringing to light a rusted file and unknown metal pieces, they too were stored like trophies with other unknown pieces of metal in the shed. Fiddling around between the cottage and bungalow chipping at woolly bits, the shovel clunked on and found a series of flat surfaced rocks hidden below. What, where, how and when, is a voyage for another time ☺ ????

Saturday 20 November 2004
Buildings opened, watering complete, breakfast and dishes over, ready to strike a blow and thoughts of Mum steered a course. Having a chat with Dad first before he went to golf, no stone was left unturned by the time Aunty Claire called in to share lunch with Mum ☺ ....
Tinkering around down the shed Tia slipped into her body action saved only for the ringing phone, doing the running toward the bungalow door looking back at me routine. Doing the fifty-yard dash I caught a welcome call from Stacey and easily slipped into another lengthy family chat ☺ ....
Spending the lions' share of time by the heater on the top section of the shed the lower front section comes a poor second, except where Destiny stood, her entire bedroom was swept out, easily filling an afternoon between phone calls. Breaking out beer o'clock I quietly sipped away on the first simply drinking in the tidy shed ambience then took a second thistle kicking and walkabout....

Sunday 21 November 2004
A repetitious start but one I don't mind, opening buildings it was a pleasure entering a clean shed.
A bit of water tossed around outside, I then got busy on another job finding the daily roster before breakfast, bungalow de-furring, Tia's winter coat is starting to make an exit. Light, free floating fur, at times are finding their way into my nose and mouth....

Reading over the paperwork for the 'New Employment Incentive Scheme', the associated form is a mini business plan, it's no five minute fill out. Giving it some thought drafted answers to the many questions....

Procrastinating down the shed over an after lunch cuppa, psyched myself for the task awaiting attention. Unable to relocate it, the loo was due for an empty. Grey ash added eliminates most of the unpleasantness the hardest part is convincing myself just to do it ☺!!!!

Tidied up, it was time to rip the lid off a coolly and wander enjoying accomplishments and planning new ones, an occasion for dreaming and scheming ☺....

Monday 22 November 2004

Morning bits accomplished to just enough, I got absorbed into finalising the lengthy NEIS business proposal form destined for Mission Australia. When I finally get this book published its history will be documented from many and varied directions. Without letting the grass grow under my feet, once the envelope was stuffed with inked paper it was immediately delivered to the slot in the wall at the Post Office. Now serious thought has to be applied to editing 'Inside my Skin'!!!!

Roaming with a coolly, Tia lured me into kicking a ball, booting it near a couple of bones she stopped, sniffed, then sat down for a chew. I guessed from that action our ball game was over ☺????

A small piece of Rainbow Falls history has been reached, journal folder number seventeen has found completion, a total of 680 hand written pages accounting for 681 days ☺.... Unbelievable!!!!

Tuesday 23 November 2004

Running about before bed last night Ms Tia got a little overheated, laying in the cool water that the cattle trough offered she then expected to hop into my bed wet, ha, ha, think again ☺!!!!

Rostered morning bits ticked off the list I then got busy on the phone to the Anti-Discrimination Commissioners Office. My mind won't let go of the radio station bullshit until I feel the scales of justice have been balanced, to put it behind me I must first face it....

Feeling as flat as a shit carter's hat there was no active response to the shovel from my body, accommodating a good dose of the 'can't be bothereds' rested my heavy bum putting fingers to work on the keyboard ☺....

Wednesday 24 November 2004

Flinging open the bungalow door onto a real warm one undesirable to be out in, we it migrated anywhere there was a roof. Beginning in the kitchen cooking, lighter on an active dog's stomach and free of artificial bits, I've been supplementing Tia's diet with rice....

Avoiding severe UV rays, taking respite under the bungalow roof is where hours melted doing the keyboard finger dance. If only for a brief moment in time the moving target journal is yet again up to date. There was plenty of company inside the bungalow, skink lizards are making themselves quite at home roaming through at leisure ready to make a meal out of any fly daring to enter ☺!!!!

What was panning out to be quite an ordinary day finished with a rush!!!! Taking a glass of red into the yard basking in the last warmth on offer Tia and I were joined by a tiger snake, the three of us didn't play well together. Introducing the snake to my best friend the shovel, its now viewing life from inside the dam fence....

Thursday 25 November 2004
In need of a little social airing, during horizontal wake up thoughts decided to take up Loui's mower offer and go for a drive....
Bloody hot, I was reduced to a singlet top, throwing a cardigan in Destiny as an afterthought. Within three kilometres of the front gate climbing up between the Sister's, driving into a mass of low thick cloud, mountain fog replaced the hot sun, equally as impressive was the temperature drop, reaching out for the afterthought cardigan????
Indulging in leisurely time in Loui's company lawnmowers and music filled our idle chatter☺....
Posting off the paperwork involved for land tax exemption last week, and being my principal place of residence, sitting inside the Post Office box was a land tax bill for $91.30, one of us isn't getting it right????

Friday 26 November 2004
Responding to a 2a.m. paw tap we walked out onto the set of a movie scene, stepping out the door into the forbidden moors where heavy fog hid that within. Walking anywhere outside was done purely by memory. We were so densely fogged in water dripped from the bungalow roof, not enough moisture to form rain or measure in the gauge but enough to wet Tia's socks before hopping back into bed ☺....
Spending the day sheltered under a roof was established long before the morning open up and watering was complete. To initially step out sun hat and t-shirt clad, lawns were put on hold a cooler option was to tackle the envelope of paperwork received from the Anti-Discrimination Commissioners Office....
Using it as supporting evidence to my sexual harassment and discrimination issues with Break O'Day FM, I sparked up the computer and compiled a file from relevant journal references, offering only a small insight into a trail of improper management practices....

Saturday 27 November 2004
Such a hot one last night shoes were forced from my feet, an event very rare and a trait learnt from my Father. I certainly spent a lot of time observing Dad's habits growing up proudly I'm his clone ☺....
Prior to turning in last night we made the last comfort-stop outside before bed. Torn between her loyalty and stomach, Tia looked for a compromise by attempting to bring a carcass inside, my expression alone gave her an answer☺!!!! With what I saw Tia put in her mouth before bed I wasn't surprised to find she had spewed at some point during the night, staging the scene for a domestic blitz on the bungalow....
Even under the cover of cloud heat again drove the boots from my feet. In sheer desperation for something to do inside I pulled out the vacuum cleaner. A convincing reason to leave the vacuum cleaner alone is being plagued by hayfever after using it, my runny nose got to the point I felt like shoving a tampon up each nostril!!!!

Stepping out on a limb, liberating myself out of a brain set comfort zone, left my shoes on the shelf enjoying the drop in body temperature without them, going to the extreme of stepping outside into the yard uncovered. Reflecting back, initially arriving I wouldn't have considered taking my shoes off inside, progress has rewards ☺....

Sunday 28 November 2004
Monitoring the progress of one ripening strawberry in the vegie patch, having survived possums and stumpy tail lizards, it looks like I'll taste my first surviving home grown....
Being closer to the end than a start, and minus the luxury of time, got my brain and hand into gear focussed on finalising the package of information received by the Anti-Discrimination Commission for tomorrows post.... A long and hard thought out decision to make and standby, but for closure I must act or forever carry a piece of baggage and be haunted by regret....
The covering letter was finished and stacked on top of the other completed bits 4p.m.-ish, a bloody big task I feel pretty damn good about having the courage to tackle. A little yellow envelope arrives home amongst post and once opened kept me busy for the following three days....
Excessive pen pushing caused my thumb muscles to start complaining making me aware of the overtime they've put in.... It's now time to knock off for beer o'clock, cheers ☺....

Monday 29 November 2004
A most welcome phone call raised me from bed and into action. Kerry rang simply for family catch up, her new job is agreeing, energy and life has returned in her voice ☺....
With the big Anti-Discrimination lead up, and time invested over the past few days, what else was a girl to do but get organised for a trip into town to finalise the posting side....
Without the luxury of a printer, and prior to posting, a trip to the library was essential to finish stuffing my fat envelope with the last vital bits. Greeting a closed door, the library was shut for lunch and reopened 2p.m. taking any rush out of the trip. I was beaming happy to have the final product in an addressed envelope and posted, opening the path to head home and spend a week under a rock!!!!
Taking a stroll after dinner simply to enjoy the evening cool I pulled up at the vegie patch picking and eating the strawberry I'd been so keenly watching. Juicy and sweet, sadly there was only one, the up side there are more on the way ☺....

Tuesday 30 November 2004
Strong gusts had my eyes open at some stage through the night, brain active, Ms Tia gave me the paw tap on the shoulder, not sleeping I got up with Tia and went for a stroll. A full moon having just passed the large bright moon illuminated the yard nicely. Taking the weight off my feet I sat in the shed entrance for three-quarters of an hour watching life pass by before again trying for sleep....
Greeting a hot morning, heat started to lose its sting by noon with the onset of change, several small fronts passed through, none offering enough liquid for a break from garden watering....
Left feeling as weak as last week's tea bag, a period starting strips my body void of stimulation, particularly the brain cells harbouring concentration, I'm unable to stay focussed on anything for long. Tired and weak and attempting to use the handsaw, breaking down

prunings didn't hold me for long, opting instead to hit the kitchen preparing bits 'n' pieces, starting with rice for supplementing Tia's meals....
Creating a nice distraction, Pam and Terry came up to release a couple of possums and install a halfway house release box. Once rehabilitated fauna was catered for I flicked the switch of the kettle and filled our hands with a warm cuppa....
Kicking back with the bungalow door open enjoying a red, light rain and the dimming of the day, adding to the magic a wallaby hopped from the dam area across our view into paddocks.... A priceless moment in paradise ☺....

Wednesday 1 December 2004
A generous 5mm of free moisture struck garden watering from the 'to-do' list limiting the number of buckets to cart. Progress with the strawberry and potato plants is keeping me interested; the strawberries are loaded with fruit at various stages of ripening.... Yumo....
A refreshing cool change put the spring back into Tia's step her stamina had an obvious increase, the elements also lured me back out into them. The driveway side of the cottage was getting a bit weedy and wild screaming out for shovel attention, beginning to make a noticeable impression, and unable to ignore the amount of moisture falling any longer, we retreated under a roof, a clear signal to stop for lunch. What's a girl to do when rain persists, but put her feet up relax with a pie and little mate and watch it from comfort ☺....
Without fear of me getting too comfortable rain hung around only long enough to wet the ground. Diverting from the shovel, Tia and I took our sweet time carting water to the cottage, which incorporated our usual water collecting games. Scooping water into the bucket from the cattle trough I then toss it for Ms Tia who's always ready in anticipation, on warmer days I aim to give her a soaking ☺....
In the cottage brushing my teeth before locking up Ms Tia was strong on the scent of a rodent, rooting it out, a frightened mouse scooted past at a rate of knots giving me a start causing a moment of aerial acrobatics ☺!!!!

Thursday 2 December 2004
Bungalow door swung open to the elements, a cool 'perfect for mowing' temperature beckoned ☺....
With a batch of fuel mixed, the new addition Loui mower was ready for just turning the fuel on and pulling the cord for its maiden Rainbow Falls voyage. Needing a few pulls of encouragement to get started, the mower didn't miss a beat when it got cracking keeping up with me carving its way through run after run. Leaving a beautiful finish, the yard resembles that of a bowling-green. The Loui mower may not have a catcher, which is useless to incorporate pushing through great amounts of grass, the major bonus of this mower it throws out to the right, meaning less flying debris to impact on my shins and in turn less bruises ☺!!!!
A spooky thing happened out mowing, the Loui lawnmower stopped dead in the exact same place the Viking died. Feeling a bit 'how bizarre', noticed that pushing it under the elevation of the cattle loading ramp slid the throttle to the off position, phew, however it will take more than a throttle adjustment for the Viking ☺....

Friday 3 December 2004
A fast approaching weekend with hungry mouths to feed meant a trip between the Sisters to town....
Friendly Christmas mail was tucked inside the Post Office box from Sheila and Peter and a second card was thoughtfully sent from Doris Lohrey. On the business side of friendly mail a cheque waited from State Revenue for overpaid land taxes, they finally got it right. Petrol for the mower, bakery, supermarket, drinking water, and last stop, home....
Excited by the bowling-green look left behind yesterday, home and unpacked, the mower was wheeled out of the shed to tackle the yard and me once again. Standing up to me well, the mower further impressed by starting first go every go ☺....

Saturday 4 December 2004
With interesting looking cloud formations hovering I got up and organised and got straight into mowing aiming to beat anything that may hinder momentum. A shingle back lizard sunning itself in the front yard of the burnt out house didn't take long to disappear with the approaching noise....
Three consecutive days of mowing, and finding a bottom to three tanks of juice each day, it took a total of nine tanks to clear the entire housing area spanning from the shed to the front gate of the burnt out house. Destiny's trip meter measures one hundred metres from the shed to the front gate, that being the case, with my best friends' contribution I have pushed the mower and kicked the ball several kilometres.... Mowing our lawn is just a walk in the park ☺....
A body as clean as a whistle, it must be time for beer o'clock and walkabout....

Sunday 5 December 2004
Having a body ready for time away from the mower, pushing the bugger through some tough stuff over three days my hands copped a punishing, soothing them today in cool water reeling in the pile of washing ☺!!!!
Between laundry loads a snake got comfortable sunning itself by the side of the cottage, with Tia safely tucked behind a closed door I tried introducing it to the shovel. The snake's feet didn't touch the ground and it was out of reach under the cottage; even a dull old washing day can be kept interesting....
A blistery rash developing on my hands and stomach woke me from sleep several times being extremely itchy looking for a scratch and it didn't give in at sunrise. Getting pretty warm mowing yesterday I was stopped in my tracks feeling a wave of heat pass through my body, I'm guessing a heat rash has developed....

Monday 6 December 2004
Out on a mail collecting and food buying expedition, walking from the supermarket to Destiny parked in the shade noticed something amiss. Rattling down the hill on the rough trip into town, and left dangling only by wires, the front right indicator lens had vibrated out of the socket; Destiny looked a bit sad ☺....
Switching on a bloody warm one outside, I buried any thoughts of mowing to the back of my mind and reprogrammed it for the keyboard finger dance, adding another few pages of history to the computers memory bank....

Still a little sore from pushing the mower my hands enjoyed another day of rest from physical labour, constantly demanding a scratch, the heat rash isn't doing them any favours either. The rash is showing up at hot spots over my body, the palms of my hands, soles of my feet and stomach, itchy skin is blistering then peeling like sunburn....
Journal updated, finally beer o'clock came around, making it back outside Tia was keen on a game of kick the bucket. I give the bucket a boot and Tia rolls it all over the place nudging it along with her nose, adding special effects, she nudges it into the air and rolls it back to me so we can do it all over again ☺ ....
Tia's energy spurt catered for I eased into a more passive pastime of watching the setting sun while sipping a beer. Seeing Ms Tia wander into the paddock and roll, at that precise moment I received a memory flash of the odour brushed from her last night, it just revisited, shit ☺ !!!!

Tuesday 7 December 2004
Itchy hands and feet refused to offer any respite for a sleepless chunk of time in the wee baby hours. Vinegar seemed to ease the itch, but something gave in, maybe exhaustion, releasing me to get back to sleep!!!!
Initially cool and cloudy, and with a determination driven by visual progress, covered from head to toe protecting all skin I emptied another three tanks from the lawnmower. The gutsy little Victa has unearthed a bloody lot of ground....
I was the lucky recipient of another couple of plump ripe strawberries lovingly grown in the vegie patch, they were of the usual high, sweet and juicy standard now expected ☺ ....
Showing versatility and flexibility, nuggeted my farm boots to shine for city slicking in Launceston tomorrow. Then there wasn't much left to do but to give in to beer o'clock and walkabout ☺ ....

Wednesday 8 December 2004
Rarely a sound to get excited about, rising with the bloody alarm steered a course for a Work Directions appointment in Launceston....
Leaving home widespread dense cloud produced a little misty rain, listening to a weather forecast on the way Launceston was expecting 25° and fine. Stepping into different worlds within 140kms, stripping off skivvy and windcheater, arrived in Launceston wearing a t-shirt????
Ensuring shade for the team, I parked under cover to guarantee my little mate remained cool and comfortable the entire time I was away....
The Work Directions interview was a surprisingly pleasant experience Jennie was practical and realistic, adding a human touch to a cold system. Assisting with a step forward in achieving my goal of publishing the journal, after hearing my story, Jennie accepted the request of printing a hardcopy of the entire document so I can start an edit....
Not being familiar with the flow of one way streets in the city, before hitting the highway home went to fuel Destiny in Charles Street. Following a parallel road going the desired direction, turned when I thought I'd gone far enough to duck across to Charles Street, veering into four lanes of one way traffic not in favour I bailed the mission quickly ☺ !!!!
Successfully fuelling and free of the city we headed homeward. Only a few kilometres out of Launceston Destiny's alternator began playing up and the dash gauge dropped its reading,

thinking I was about to lose power and breakdown, miraculously she got us home. Destiny may have been suffering but not in silence, a continual whirring noise staying constant with engine revs escaped from under the bonnet, increasing in intensity with motor load. Taking a relaxed breath making it back to our little hamlet, without deviation it was straight to St. Marys Caltex to book her in, noisy but driveable, we took her home until her appointment time comes around....

Thursday 9 December 2004
Low cloud and mist lingered. Kicking the ground, surface soil in the vegie patch was still dry, anything under a canopy got nothing. No need to bother checking the gauge, mist only leaves droplets of water clinging to the edge of the tube nothing to rattle around in the bottom to measure....
Letting themselves in through the front gate and driving around back, Aurora Energy staff were on a mission to chop a tree down growing next to powerlines by the falls, I'd prefer the powerlines removed!!!!
Unperturbed by the light mist drift, the shovel, my little mate and me returned to the driveway side of the cottage. Chipping away at ground reclamation sun broke through bathing us in uncomfortable heat, being a smart woman with choice, retreated to shade following it edging around bits the mower couldn't reach....
Giving Mum and Dad a tingle we settled in for a healthy chat. The latest Mildura happening is Uncle Len touched down visiting from Canada, he's staying over Christmas and into early New Year with quite a social calendar of events packed in. Dad proudly announced he's picking tomatoes and beans from his own garden.... Very rewarding ☺....
For a dash of evening decadence, thoughts went to setting up a canvas chair in the shed to relax with a glass of red and purely enjoy achievements inside the termite hole. Putting the plan into motion with a glass of red in hand, I'd thoughtlessly left the chair in the flight path of nesting swallows and they left me a clear message.... For a little bird, they sure are full of it ☺!!!!

Friday 10 December 2004
Leaving the box out to visually pester me for a week, last night I broke out and wrote in Christmas cards, the next big achievement is to post them ☺....
Just doing the water carting routine made clear it was too bloody hot to get serious outdoors, a site for any whim, mood or environmental condition, escaped to entertain myself down the shed. Tired of sore hands, and helping myself, I taped foam rubber to the mowers handle to absorb vibration and cushion my grip it can only be an improvement....
Still deterred by heat, grabbed the vacuum, dismantled my bed and gave the bungalow a thorough going over. Tia and I have been bringing too much work home with us ☺!!!!
A bank of cloud drifted in robbing the scorpion's tail of its sting, affording choices, I instigated the initial plan of mowing. Gathering heavy low clinging cloud had me with one eye on the sky, closing in on the tail end of tank three Mother Nature decided it was time to give mowing away, but not before I made an impression in and outside the cattle yards....
Closing the shed gate on the working day 7p.m.-ish told myself I only had to bath, eat and write, how long would that take ☺....

Saturday 11 December 2004
Inaudible on the tin roof and gracefully adorning the range, low moisture laden cloud drifted a sprinkling. Opening the bungalow door onto the sight, as if time momentarily froze, that very instant a shed day was declared ☺ !!!!
Sun tried pushing through occasionally to steam things up, only to again be stifled by dense cloud persistent with its mission of delivering a gently misted 7mm, so delicately delivered it surprised me to see that amount sitting in the gauge....
Making my body earn its keep, a pretty impressive dent was inflicted in cutting a pile of prunings down to size creating organised shed chaos ☺ ....
Tia's fur from last seasons' fashions is like decorations, found hanging everywhere, turning the lamp on to start writing fur was dangling from it like a frill. De-furring the bungalow is currently a daily event to remove surplus ☺ ....

Sunday 12 December 2004
Delivering my body one serious overheat, bloody itchy feet, hands and a peeling body are still driving me to distraction, initially settling into bed they scream for scratch attention. At wits end after trying an assortment for relief from specially designed cream, oil, moisturiser, vinegar and cold packs, nothing is offering long-term relief the heat rash is really giving me the shits!!!!
My hands, a little swollen and sore from being scratched, and a red itchy body calling out for some quiet down time I declared 'physical labour free' respite....
Steamy, overcast and adding an occasional misting just to maintain humidity levels, sun broke through for five minutes creating an uncomfortable environment that only a plant could love!!!!
Bungalow de-furred and dishes done I remained under its roof to continue the constant refining of our living quarters, fluffing the day away moving bits 'n' pieces around....
Always great to hear from family, Stacey phoned we shared our views on life and talked until we ran out of conversation, then talked some more ☺ ....
If there are idle times in my day Ms Tia certainly knows how to fill them, applying her weedicide program to paddocks she returned on two occasions with fur covered in buzzies. Wet fur added another element of difficulty to remove the matted seed, while I tended to removing buzzies from her fur Ms Tia snoozed, not a bad trade off ☺ !!!!

Monday 13 December 2004
Sheets well and truly warmed, I'd been asleep for around an hour when the desire to scratch itchy hands woke me to respond, and that they did for almost two hours, I wanted to scratch skin off.
Clutching at straws I rubbed in ointment and held the freezer pak, resorting to slapping the itchy area while I still had skin, nothing helped until the itch was ready to ease of its own accord. Bloody heat rash, my stomach is peeling like sunburn, boiling my blood I internally microwaved myself....
Tortured broken sleep caused a bit of a slow stride out of the starting blocks, getting my sorry arse moving I took Destiny in for Grant to have a look at. Heading off to the car doctors Destiny let the neighbourhood know she was around, her alternator screamed under load with

the second gear climb to pass between the Sisters and the highest point of the drive. Reaching the point of down hill all the way, we quietly crossed town using minimal engine revs. Leaving Tia with Destiny, I boosted the economy of St. Marys. Christmas cards posted supermarket then bakery, I was organised and back at the Caltex waiting for a lift home with Ross after school got out....

Dropped home Destinyless, Tia and I went walkabout, stopping at the vegie patch I contemplated the need to hire harvest labour to pick the healthy crop of five plump ripe strawberries ☺ ....

Tuesday 14 December 2004

Stirring through the night to scratch itchy feet I heard the most convincing rain of late, making a quick 5mm deposit and disappearing by morning. Still looking like anything could happen it did, Mother Nature gave a fair sample of her repertoire....

Filling the bungalow with a nice aroma, the freshly picked strawberries only made it to breakfast that saw an end to them ☺ ....

Finding direction with the soft option of sitting on my bum, I was kept busy until mid afternoon doing the keyboard finger dance. Emerging back outdoors to cold and overcast with passing showers I headed to the shed with thoughts of finalising prunings and sparking up the heater. Cutting short one thought, doing a complete turn around sun poked its head out warming things up, still more pleasant to be indoors, prunings were finalised and Destiny's bedroom was swept awaiting her return ☺ ....

Wednesday 15 December 2004

A stupid promise made to myself that the next day sun shines was the one for laundry, today was it?!?!

Nose down bum up washing, not a sound easily disguised and returning every twenty minutes, a helicopter did repetitive trips to the top of South Sister. Simultaneously, welcome roadworks were going out front, feeling more like city living with industrial activity rather than our semi-remote hamlet. The answer to the outstanding activity on the mountain came with Ross. The helicopter was dropping gear required for building another transmission tower on top of South Sister....

Starting a tag team, Loui popped in on the way through from Hobart and drove out the front gate with me and Tia on board, destined for the 6p.m. Council run public meeting responding to the Save South Sister petition. Encountering a first we had problems finding a park, a figure of around 170 people attended the public meeting, that's big for St. Marys ☺ !!!!

Two well-presented motions were unanimously received, without an ounce of acknowledgement no debate was entered into. The meeting was short and sweet and non-committal, and almost a non-event, a beautiful fence sitter by Council????

Tia and I transferred to Lesley's car for a lift back up the mountain. Lesley and Ross stayed long enough for a cuppa and a walk to the top boundary to take in the view ☺ ....

Thursday 16 December 2004

A sinus blocking brain pain dose of hayfever in the company of a wriggly restless heat rash itchy night, as flat as a shit carter's hat, I lacked the energy to make much of a difference in the world.... I hit the wall....

Continual blowing using tissues took its toll, making my nose sore and sensitive they started to feel like sandpaper. It wasn't until the damage was done before I gave a thought to changing over using a softer chux cloth, offering me the staying power required ☺....

Only the absolutely necessary was considered to expel my precious little energy on, today incorporated quite a few rest breaks, food breaks and a bloody lot of sneezing and nose blowing!!!!

Friday 17 December 2004

Last night was the best sleep had for over a week. Before bed I massaged moisturiser into my hands and feet settling those irritations while still awake....

Mother Nature's moisture assistance has dried up thus returning plant watering to the morning regime. I enjoy the open up, bum scratch, look around, and watering routine before breakfast, it's a relaxing way to ease into a start ☺....

A courtesy call from Grant to say Destiny was ready got me revved up for independence. Phoning Ross, I made arrangements for a lift over the mountain when it next suited. Thankful for the lift, I was even more thankful for Destiny's doctors' bill, coming in way under budget at a tiny $22. It seems a bolt holding the alternator in place had rattled its way out.... A bloody reasonable, honest service Grant operates ☺....

In the process of boosting the economy of St. Marys, a check of my Post Office box found it generous, sheltering a waiting gift from Mum and Dad and Christmas cards respectively from Kylie and Lyndall. Although, hiding amongst the good stuff was an electricity bill ☺?!?!

Bakery delights and groceries safely packed in the car it was onward to the pub to break the drought on beer. Destiny's repair coming in under budget left a few extra pennies in the piggy bank, the flow-on effect permitted beer o'clock to be a happening thing ☺....

Calling with appreciative thanks, and making the event as personal as possible, I opened their sent gift while talking to Mum and Dad via the phone. Legacy of Uncle Len and a few thousand kilometres, the treasure consisted of a box of genuine Canadian maple syrup cream cookies and a Christmas card with $100 slipped inside. Dad referred to the two fifty dollar notes as a beer vouchers so Christmas won't be dry ☺....

Cosy in the bungalow after beer o'clock and walkabout, glancing out the window I saw a snapping kookaburra offering resistance to swooping swallows. A kookaburra perched itself on the powerline running parallel to the face of the shed, territory annually claimed by swallows, looking for peace the kookaburra grudgingly left....

Saturday 18 December 2004

Sleeping well, I'm convinced the worst of the heat rash has passed, continually applying moisturiser to peeling body skin I'm on the mend....

Unwilling to dive head first into it, when the watering, de-furring, breakfast routine was complete I took yesterdays newspaper for a walk down the shed browsing it from cover to cover. The main story featured a tragic read of a guy eaten by two white pointer sharks not far from Glenelg, SA. Several years back I did an advanced SCUBA diver course, most dives were off-shore Glenelg, back then, conversation with the boat operator confirmed a six metre white pointer had been spotted in our dive area a week prior?!?!

Quickly progressing into 'reptile active bloody hot', we remained under cover, not only were shoes driven from my feet, stepping extreme left, I was compelled to wear shorts also ☺!!!!

Content with the tidy computer corner of the bungalow having rationalised stationery, I then let time slip away battling with the newspaper crossword. I've never got any better at doing crosswords I just enjoy the challenge of stretching the muscle and sometimes having a win ☺....

Sunday 19 December 2004

Tia expressed a convincing objection to distant thunder rumbles in the wee baby hours. Before shooting through the front offered short bursts of moisture, only managing to raise humidity on an already rather tropical night!!!!

Night turned into day and a hot dry wind stirred grass pollens creating optimum hayfever conditions!!!! Undeterred, Tia and I spent cooler moments moving rocks from the bottom to the pile to the top, adding to the creation of a wall rather than a pile, it also gave me clear access to the line of grass and weeds the mower couldn't reach ☺....

Feeling pretty happy with life, and ready to trade the shovel in for beer o'clock and washing my hands for the transition, Tia walked into the cottage with her undercarriage covered in buzzies. Beer o'clock was postponed for a half-hour. Within five minutes of opening my first stubby she returned in exactly the same buzzied condition ☺!!!! Tia's weedicide program is very efficient!!!!

In response to a card, I rang Lyndall and Geoff. The good thing about Christmas and major events causing celebration, it's a time to reflect on absent low maintenance friends that sustain long bouts of neglect....

Monday 20 December 2004

The worst of the insane, uncontrollable itching seems to have passed leaving behind the ongoing legacy of peeling skin, from scalp to feet, my entire body shed.... Not a pleasant experience to have gone through!!!!

A dig around in the vegie patch upturned enough self-sown spuds to put mash on the evening menu.... Yumo ☺....

Flowing with Mother Nature and the generous shade offered under the canopy of the walnut tree, I worked from west to east keeping pace with shade movement clearing fenceline within the cottage yard boundary.... A skin saving action in the furnace!!!!

Tia's weedicide program is still operating well, on a regular basis she returns covered in a 'thought for the environment' ration of buzzies!!!!

Empty stubbies take up so much room in the rubbish I decided to challenge myself seeing how much household waste can be compressed into one. Squeezing down the narrow neck a stash of buzzies, tissues, a plastic six-pack wrap and a biscuit wrapper, surprising at just what can fit inside an empty ☺....

Tuesday 21 December 2004
Filling in the mini business plan was simply an exercise in time wasting. A bloke representing the 'NEIS' scheme phoned to let me know they can't help with my book, an outcome I wasn't real impressed with at the time. Reasoning behind the decision is because I'm not showing any dollar turnover so they're not interested. Although, it was mentioned after I successfully publish they will help. Now is when help is needed not after I've achieved????
Lucky I believe in me, at least it takes any book ownership away from Centrelink and its contractors. The most this bloke was prepared to offer was a suggestion to speak with Neil at the Business and Employment Centre in St. Helens, handy, being the chairman of the radio station he might be able to help me with a radio career also????
Harbouring some negative energy that needed expressing, I tucked Ms Tia into Destiny and dusted the brushcutter off, after a long sit and good for my frame of mind it fired up quickly and easily. Well-irrigated, and a tough patch, I cut loose on the long grass surrounding the leaky irrigation pipe by the driveway....
In the absence of rain, and the spring rush over, lush green paddocks are browning off under the magnifying glass of hot stinging rays. Emptying one tank of brain therapy from the brushcutter I retreated indoors, still recovering from heat rash I wasn't ready for another dose....
Only when the evening cool airflow came in was I enticed back outdoors. Over a couple of beers, my little mate helped move many more kilograms of rock reshaping the stack. Hollowing the centre of the pile should create an ideal spot protected from wind, affectionately known as 'the rock room' ☺ ????

Wednesday 22 December 2004
Ongoing brushing and de-furring, Tia's moulting body is slowing but still capable of enough to decorate the bungalow daily. Tia must also be making some sort of impression in the paddocks with her buzzie weedicide program too because enough have been removed from her fur ☺ ....
Quiet moments are easily filled at Rainbow Falls....
Following start up bits 'n' pieces was a trip over the mountain to burn CD copies of 'Inside My Skin' for extra insurance and peace of mind that alone easily occupied idle hours. Petrol, bakery, then pub is where I crossed paths with Ross, realising there was only five minutes before the Post Office closed cut our natter short. Packing a CD into a protective posting box, addressed and mailed an entire copy of 'Inside My Skin' to Jennie at 'Work Directions', having accepted my ask of printing a hardcopy so I can start editing.... Day at a time, it's slowly evolving ☺ ....
Close to curtain call returning inside the home gate of Rainbow Falls, 6p.m. I cracked the lid off a favourite beer 'Tooheys Old' and got on the phone, calling Mum and Dad to share the fate of the vouchers ($100) they sent. The purpose of the money was so I could have a beer at Christmas, phoning while quietly sipping away on one of them. The pending fate of the greater half of the voucher will be wisely invested pampering myself with tips and a haircut. Mum and Dad were both happy to hear their actions gave so much pleasure ☺ ....
The phone was definitely a friend tonight, after much talking with Mum and Dad a call came through from Pam, inviting me to share Christmas lunch, no thought required for an answer without hesitation the offer was accepted ☺ ....

Rolled and tossed across and around the yard, in the last light played kick the bucket with Tia. Doing a few modifications with the broken bits and sealing tape, I re-formed the bucket to best resemble a circular shape to hold the game together. Tia's bucket has been loved to death ☺….

Thursday 23 December 2004
I'm falling apart. With all recent ailments healing, for something new a toothache stole prime sleeping hours!!!!
Rock pile tidily edged, cottage fenceline, and high growth area around the leaky irrigation pipe cleanly knocked down, it was time to fully complement the termite holes by mowing their surrounds….
Having a tug on the mower's ripcord and the anticipated sound that knowingly represents, Tia went racing through paddocks excitedly barking returning absolutely matted in buzzies.
Putting in a good effort removing a bloody lot herself, but like the caring sharing soul she is Tia saved me plenty ☺….
Emptying four tanks in and around housing made a huge visual impact. Edging away bringing the whole area to the one length, today I could lower the mowers suspension down two spaces giving it a very close shave, a number two I reckon ☺!!!!
It's hard to believe we're only days away from 2005 I started writing in 2002 and am now stunned at the size of the journal, unbelievable to have stuck at it this long documenting our lives. Jotting daily events is something I now don't know how to stop; my brain has been programmed ☺….

Friday 24 December 2004
Stepping outside to greet the new day shortly after 7a.m. with a brain psyched for more time in the company of the mower, Mother Nature stopped me in my tracks. Quietly doing its job, low cloud and misting rain had wet everything up. My whole psyche was thrown into chaos taking a couple of extra milo's to reconsider a direction, nothing else come to mind other than filling the throat of the heater with wood in hollow optimism moisture would continue. Failing to justify my shed existence beyond a few hours, I found purpose moving rocks remoulding the stack….
An incoming courtesy call from Jennie at Work Directions was to inform a hardcopy of the journal had been printed and is awaiting pick up. Impressed at the efficient pace the printing process was turned around my luck was certainly in, friends of Ross' were in Launceston and were able to bring the entire printed document home with them…. Merry Christmas to me ☺!!!!
Jennie also mentioned she had taken the liberty of reading ninety percent of the journal and was happy to offer some editing tips from her perspective, my use of the word 'fluffing' was a little excessive and writing a little disjointed at times. Nothing earth shattering or unexpected, it's good to receive and take onboard constructive criticism….
Storing hay in the shed, Ross and Lesley turned up with a stacked trailer. Unloaded, we shared some bullshit over a cuppa and a few laughs, before leaving Ross and Lesley extended a dinner invitation, a smart woman couldn't say no to someone else cooking ☺….
Walking in the door at Ross' to take up my dinner invitation I was handed a wad of envelopes containing the hardcopy of 'Inside my Skin', actually holding it sent an amazing uplifting

sensation through filling my heart and leaving pasted a permanent smile ☺!!!! Yahoo....
Coupled with a delicious meal and great company, quality living ☺....

Saturday 25 December 2004
Ho, ho, ho, ho, Santa's day started 8:30a.m.-ish with Christmas wishes from Sheila and Peter. The elements gave a parched earth some festive season cheer, beginning with a drop of moisture that had slipped a quick 8mm in overnight. Rain Christmas day always takes my thoughts to the kids who get bikes and are met with lousy riding weather....
With breakfast settling in our tummies, I then settled into a healthy chat with Mum and Dad slowing their preparations for lunch with Aunty Claire. Two text messages waited with Christmas wishes, one from Ian and Kirsten and another from Loui dude, plus a couple more Christmas cards were tucked into the Post Office box. It's heart-warming when friends go the extra yard when thinking about you to act out thoughts with contact. Compounding, the day just kept getting better. Over a turkey lunch with all the trimmings that flowed into afternoon seated at the table, I had a lovely time with Pam and Terry, their hospitality put a bit of special into Christmas ☺....
In keeping with the eat, drink, and be merry theme, I maintained a wound down mood at home, taking a beer for walkabout I willingly participated in giving the battered bucket a boot upon request by Tia. Unable to deviate from a straight line, Ross drove over the bucket yesterday putting us into damage control, out with joiners tape and stanley knife, and to Tia's pleasure, its roughly circular and rolls again ☺....
Randomly trying Kerry's landline only got an engaged signal, my final attempt to reach the other side of Bass Strait 9:30p.m.-ish connected, confirming her phone had been out, persistence was rewarded speaking with Kerry and all three nieces ☺....
Having just spoken only hours earlier and coming as a surprise to everyone, especially Tegan, 5a.m. she started labour four weeks premature....

Sunday 26 December 2004
How quickly the hype and build-up passes, Christmas over again for another year we've got 364 days before having to think about doing it all again ☺????
Overcast, and beginning with a blanket of low cloud, progressed into bloody hot hitting us from pure north, any conditions that has hand washing tended to by my wrists on and off the line in the same day is impressive ☺!!!!
Leaving an empty trailer after unloading hay Ross offered to take a load to the tip, drying laundry saturated hands considered what to load it with. Sorting out what was useful and what can remain down the shed, and easily sidetracked, began decorating the shed in treasure found by the shovel. Making trophies of rusty old metal tools I displayed shovel heads, a rabbit trap, pick heads and a toilet flush chain, all finding a spot. Staying with interior improvements I rolled the last 44-gallon drum out to reside at the side of the shed.... Another transformation slowly evolving....
Ready to put a yawning body between the sheets didn't quite go to plan, calling the girl in, Tia brought three-quarters of an hour worth of buzzies packed in her fur for picking out!!!!

Monday 27 December 2004
Nothing to cause a newspaper scoop and rather uneventful, spent most of it burning fossil fuel stirring up grasses and hayfever, hayfever is useful trying to mow. Excluding the burnt out house yard, the entire housing area plus a solid strip travelling halfway down the driveway has been given a number two, the visual rewards make every minute worth it ☺ ....
Mower had been put away and I was halfway through bathing when the first of a series of brief showers began.... Timing ☺ !!!!
Content for another evening, Ms Tia snoozed beside me as I wrote at 10p.m., and with still no word on Tegan and the baby, I'll have to wait until tomorrow to be a Great Aunt ☺ ....

Tuesday 28 December 2004
Airflow from direct south brought with it a splash of rain and kindly cooled our world down making for a nice night to snuggle under the doona, pleasantly having a brief return to winter....
Lately there is enough rain to sound soothing on an uninsulated tin roof but rarely enough to make much of an impact on ground. The rain gauge wouldn't have measured much last night blown from its moorings it was left laid out horizontal. In search of a more appropriate location for the gauge I moved it from the rock pile to Tia's oven, a pile of sand long ago dumped in front of the shed; a suitably exposed site....
Part and parcel of life, and regularly taken in stride, Tia and I took our positions in Destiny doing the mountain run to town, losing the morning getting ready and the afternoon going ☺ ....
If I have one small achievement to report outside shopping it was to dig out a piece of timber from the lawn only recently surfacing. The yard surface was upgraded to lawn after the last mowing the cutting blade adjusted down low gave the yard its closest cut yet, agreeably leaving it looking very tidy ☺ ....

Wednesday 29 December 2004
Wind blowing in the wrong direction brought the neighbours' screaming match to my door, stretching their lungs and vocal chords their anger reached everyone in a five-kilometre radius.... Ouch!!!!
What I incorrectly misunderstood to be the neighbours' arguing was actually a shout to the heavens for rain, bringing on some lasting measurable moisture. More pleasant on the ears, I enjoy lying in bed waking to the sound pattering on a tin roof. With the equipment in place and an enthusiasm for checking the gauge, I'm inspired to fill out the rainfall chart at the back of the 2005 calendar, it can only be useful????
Treading gently, I tinkered with the shovel at the excavation site tidying around large slabs of paving stone brought to light near the bungalow. Never letting progress sit idle, or afraid to tackle change, removed weather buckled cardboard from the angle iron surround on the bungalow door updating it with foam rubber.... The cardboard cubby is being modernised ☺ ....

Thursday 30 December 2004
A message delivered late last evening confirmed Tegan had gone into labour, inspiring me to get straight on the phone to the hospital offering a message of caring thoughts. Without another word, Kerry phoned this morning still without birth news. Staying with Tegan through the night, Kerry said contractions got as close as one minute apart but the baby refused to budge from its safe warm environment. Making the world wait until 1:30p.m.-ish this afternoon, Dekira Jayde burst her way into being at a meagre 5 pounds 6 ounces. Family communication on a high wave, a very excited Kristy-Lee couldn't wait to share the news also. Mum said she arrived at the hospital not long after bubby was born and almost broke down and cried to see Dekira receive an injection and stretch her strong little lungs in protest. There's not much of her tiny little frame to poke an injection into ☺!!!!
All water needs catered for, dishes done and de-furred, the morning was spent. Losing the p.m. bit sitting in front of the computer updating Rainbow Falls history, severing power 6p.m. for beer o'clock....

Saturday 1 January 2005
Midnight having passed on Friday, and officially into the New Year, enabled the starting date of the fresh year to head the entry. Initially planning the night off writing I still had the energy and inclination when visitors left after midnight....
Friday morning was nothing out of the ordinary, although, watering in the vegie patch Tia brought my attention to a freshly shed snakeskin, a clear message to keep my eyes open....
Besides a couple of businesses, town will be pretty much closed for the next few days, so an obvious survival trip in to stock up was scheduled, keeping it matter of fact and to the point did only the necessary....
Sitting down in disbelief to read a newspaper running a full feature on the devastating tsunami, no words can capture the devastating enormity. New Years thoughts went to everyone affected by the horrific event. Without buying regular newspapers, never watching television and only occasionally listening to the radio, I wasn't aware the disaster occurred until long after the event. When Ross, Lesley and kids arrived, finding our positions around the fire we raised our glasses dedicating the moment and thoughts to the victims of the tsunami....
Bringing with them a fire ring and hot plate, we got a barbecue going and Lesley brought the weather for the occasion perfectly calm and mild. Complementing the good food was the company....
Guests departing just shy of the New Year, Tia made sure I saw it in spending the following hour plucking mattered clumps of buzzies from her fur, her weedicide program did overtime!!!!
Reckon its time to call it a night, 2a.m. has come around I'm feeling myself begin to wind down and bed is looking good ☺....

Saturday 1 January 2005
An event available only if a combination of conditions align, achieving a first, managed two journal entries on the same day. Yesterday's entry written after midnight in a tiny hour of this morning, today's being at a more reasonable p.m. hour, my brain won't function on a regular basis writing at 1a.m. ☺!!!!

Finally surfacing, a hot day greeted the New Year waiting outside our door. Not feeling overly hyperactive I eased into it gently scraping the barbecue hot plate down, the aroma flared Tia's nostrils and without hesitation she vacuumed the area of tasty treasures ☺....

Seeking UV refuge in the bungalow I activated the memory bank for the year ahead transferring 'must remember' dates into the 2005 calendar before hanging it, then eliminating the festive appearance, put Christmas cards into the journal for historical reference....

After lunch a full blanket of cloud cooled things down, but not for too long, drifting in and out intermittently, the elements followed a pattern of intensely hot and sanely cool. In the moments of sanely cool only then could we be lured outdoors. Still intrigued by the dig site in the hunt for more large slabs of stone used as pavers, and buried below a light layer of soil, I had a poke around with the shovel. For my toil a few small pavers came to light but unearthed nothing groundbreaking....

Sunday 2 January 2005
Just like the sensation of initially adjusting to daylight saving, the beginning of a New Year demands a dash of concentration writing the date, requiring a little brain adjustment....

All the fanfare of the festive season over, it's back to reality no more public holidays on the farm to hide behind. Still not operating at full production I eased back into making a difference in our world ☺....

Usually in the cool of the evening Tia runs through the paddocks and buzzies up and I spend the following three-quarters of an hour before bed plucking them out, spoiling me to extreme, she returned in the same condition throughout the day also!!!!

With a trailer at my disposal for a tip run a load of corrugated iron from the burnt out house made priority to fill it. Clearing a path to access the trailer on site I first dismantled a small roof structure from the kennel in the cottage side yard, only consisting of four sheets of iron and a couple of pieces of wood I had it apart in no time. The bungalow curtain rod came into use, the metre long jemmy bar pulled nails from the iron with ease. In reasonable condition and an ideal length, one sheet of iron was taken to the shed with the intention of later fixing the toilet roof. Something to look forward to, a loo friendly in most climatic conditions ☺ !!!!

Hooking the trailer up to Destiny had it on site and unhooked in minutes, happy with my trailer manoeuvring skills it's now waiting patiently to be filled....

Monday 3 January 2005
Phoning to hear how they filled their New Year, Mum and Dad went up the bush with friends for a peaceful time to avoid loud party revellers in town. A hot topic taking the most interest in our conversation, they mentioned Tegan has been released from hospital, because of her premature arrival into the world Dekira will remain in hospital until her body weight comes up. Most importantly they are both happy and healthy. Talking gardens, Dad gave me a good recipe for liquid fertiliser using cow dung ☺.... Yummy for the plants....

Environmental conditions not ideal for handling corrugated iron, the heat and breeze instead sent me back inside out of it. Tia chose to snooze while I momentarily caught a moving target completely updating the journal to computer, it won't sit still ☺ !!!!

I think Tia is planning to do a solo effort clearing the paddocks of buzzies I've certainly removed enough from her beautiful outfit. Along with Tia's fur decorating furniture inside, buzzies too are also finding their way around I smiled to see two hanging off the lamp writing this evening ☺.... I love my girl....

Tuesday 4 January 2005
Overcast cool and calm were perfect elements for moving corrugated iron it was time for action. Purposefully stacking each piece I managed a reasonable load, making a significant difference on the strewn mess inside the burnt out house. Hitching the trailer onto Destiny, two takes, I had it manoeuvred into the shed out of winds reach and unhitched all before lunch heated. Good trailer reversing skills ☺!!!!
I hadn't swallowed the last bite of lunch when the first shower began and the weather closed in, what timing, I'm definitely in sync with the universe....
Topping the neatly stacked trailer load parked in the shed, I filled nooks of remaining space with unwanted bits clearing out rubbish. Satisfied no more could be done I shut the shed gate and walked out 7p.m.-ish into moisture....

Wednesday 5 January 2005
Flowing on from yesterday, rain pulled up through the night enabling a start at filling in the rainfall-recording chart. It will be interesting to see how the microclimate of Rainbow Falls compares with local averages. Falling moisture sent thoughts to the sheet of corrugated iron sitting in the shed put aside for the toilet roof, causing me to reflect on how useful it could have been recently ☺....
Yahoooo, the working world back on deck its 'find my head under the mass of hair and disguise the grey' day! The closer we drove to St. Helens the more threatening cloud looked and didn't take long to produce a drop. But it didn't matter, anything could have been happening outside; I was being pampered at the hairdressers in the capable hands of Kellie ☺....
Feeling pretty good I popped in on Nana Raye and Charlie for a long overdue cuppa and yack, lovely people who come from the heart, when the time came, they sent me on my way with a bag of plums ☺....
Boosting the economy of St. Marys I purchased the 2004 Collection of Australian Stamps to add to the annual growing collection. Another small but meaningful purchase was that of a pencil and eraser, they have an important future roll of editing the journal for publishing, there is nothing stopping me now ☺!!!!
In our absence another 12mm fell into the gauge, far from letting up, and if the forecast is true to form wet conditions should hang around, and they're very welcome. The only place to watch Mother Natures live theatre performance was in a box seat from behind glass nursing a 'cool ale'. A mass of heavy moisture laden cloud pushed up from the valley below, hitting the huge resistance of the rock face at the falls forced a definite line of cloud skyward. Under its own sheer weight, cloud then fell onto and blended into South Sister Range thickening to produce another shower. It's magic living with a little altitude ☺....

Thursday 6 January 2005
There's not too many mornings at breakfast my little mate doesn't help with a bit of my toast, just a gentle reminder she was waiting, Tia placed her head on my knee in expectation leaving behind a wet patch of drool.... That's real love ☺ ....
Doing usual morning things, I caught a phone call from Ross teeing up a time for a trip to the tip for me that's a new experience I've never been there before. Load secured, I followed Ross into unknown territory to help unload and that's where we said our farewells, leaving the tip I pointed Destiny's nose back at the mountain....
Clunking and rattling a few kilograms of rock into new positions created a hollow in the centre of the rock pile. Finding ground that hasn't felt sun for the minimum of five years created a termite hole large enough to set-up a canvas chair, a big step in a large challenge ☺ ....
Rain threatened to regularly stop play but didn't succeed until after 5:30pm with the arrival of a brief hail front followed by a series of small passing showers. For all the atmospheric theatrics, between them were lucky to produce 1mm, lacking lasting power it was over and done with in no time....
I'm starting to feel pretty damn good about progress occurring at Rainbow Falls our little hamlet has moved beyond catch up and is offering an inner feeling of progressive forward movement ☺ !!!!
Life may be going on but it's difficult not to think of the victims of the tsunami and the staggering death toll, it's unimaginable to get my head around the extent of personal loss. Emerging stories of woe and survival, it's a bloody horrific time. There are those working around the clock just to get food and basic supplies to the worst affected areas is admirable!!!!

Friday 7 January 2005
Determined by fate, a course for the day was set. Without having such a smooth start, I made and spilled a fresh milo over the bungalow window box, initially I cursed the spill, but it turned into a blessing in disguise inspiring a spring-clean. Re-juggling and refining the interior to suit needs I left the bungalow looking and feeling good ☺ ....
With the festive season over and no excuses left, coupled with a number of small fronts passing through, some trying to produce rain others only threatening, determined I finally make a start hardcopy editing 'Inside my Skin'. Holding the sharpened pencil, with eraser on the stand-by, I stared blankly at the wad of paper in front unsure of exactly how to tackle it. Merely feeling the water, I made a start wearing out a bit of lead fumbling to get my head around the task at hand ☺ ????
When my brain failed at concentrating on the sheets of paper before me I didn't resist, instead, moved a few more rocks from the interior of the pile for think therapy before breaking out beer o'clock.... Life however, is feeling positively good ☺ ....

Saturday 8 January 2005
From the array of jobs on the go I selected the shovel as my tool, for the purpose of knocking down a bit of lawn at the excavation site near the bungalow for ease of mowing. A site that never ceases to thrill, a clunk of resistance on the shovel head divulged solid rock, uncovering two more large slab stone pavers along with a series of smaller ones ☺ ....

With all good intentions, I planned on editing, but the paver find kept me intrigued and shovelling. Its exhilarating transforming the excavation site, possibly unearthing a piece of history linked to the cottage and bungalow. Close to both buildings, I'm daring to think the large slabs of rock could have been laid by Rainbow Falls, and Dublin Town's first registered settler, the Irishman, Edward Young????
Enough adventure and discovery, the shovel was put away making way for my usual evening of eating and writing, oh, and answering the phone. Kerry phoned with an excited grandmother courtesy update, thrilled that Tegan has embraced motherhood. Dekira is still in hospital, her body weight is up but she'll remain in hospital until she's capable of suckling by herself that apparently could be a couple more weeks ☺....

Sunday 9 January 2005
The sheet of paper torn from the writing pad, signifying an end to last night's journal entry, finalised another folder used to store Rainbow Falls' history, making number eighteen in the series. The detailed history recorded makes up a staggering 720 hand written pages, quite a number of supporting photographs, letters, cards and collectable bits add to the extensive documentation. Far beyond any expectations, to be perfectly honest it's nothing I ever thought about doing, by chance it just happened and kept on happening ☺ ????
A rare morning Tia woke me wanting outside, not ready myself I let her out and returned to bed. When an adequate amount of stretching and yawning was done, I got up and focussed on being at the base of South Sister Mountain 11a.m.-ish to participate in a fundraiser / awareness day....
Loaded with camera, water and ventolin had me organised to go, leaving Tia to babysit Destiny in shade, I made my way along the track leading up to the Sister....
Managing to catch a lift with passing traffic to a base area where the masses gathered saved my legs for bigger challenges. Well-organised, a crew of people had cuppa's, cakes, savoury and salad meals along with the familiar aromas of a barbecue sizzling away to raise funds. Unable to walk past a double chocolate muffin, burnt the calories tackling the remainder of the distance to the top of the mountain, a goats track ascending steeply tested my fitness level. Taken to exhilarating heights, 831 metres to be exact, I climbed to the fire lookout base to be greeted by a spectacular 360° sweeping view, taking in a rambling mountainous inland that traced out to the ocean, a magic part of the world....
Well supported in all areas, I contentedly left a successful awareness day. Slipping back into comfortable home-wear, and with my little mate keenly on the ready helping, extended the reshaping of the rock pile. After a couple of hours and many, many kilos moved, having exerted enough physical energy was ready to call it quits to rip the lid off a coolly ☺....

Monday 10 January 2005
A date of importance for us Rainbow Falls' folk, signifying five years to the day my name went on the land title. Living in Wollongong I tried, and nearly succeeded, in selling this piece of paradise. September 10, 2001, a firm offer was faxed through to the real estate agent, the following day, tragically, the September 11 disaster struck America causing global economic instability and the offer of sale was withdrawn. Well, here I am, content now to live here forever, funny how life works ☺ ????

Leaving whites to soak I took time out for breakfast to psych myself for the task ahead. Loui phoned between loads, sharing her plans of leaving the district for a while in need of fresh inspiration. Wearing the job down, I pegged the last load on the line in time for a final rinse courtesy of the heavens above….

Warming stiff muscles after yesterday's workout mountain exploring, I played around with the shovel at the excavation site. Finding some pace to the project another three pavers were exposed to add to the growing tally, extending the path to six large slabs of paving rock in length. Both the dig site and rock pile are taking on shape and keeping me interested….

Tuesday 11 January 2005
Void of clear direction to fill idle hours, doing morning things the excavation site kept attracting my eye and curiosity got the better, so I grabbed the wheelbarrow, shovel and broom, on the hunt for more stone pavers. Shovel load after shovel load of soil filled the attentively waiting wheelbarrow the soil was ferried off to fill pitted gaps from rushing water where the brushcutter struck the irrigation pipe those many, many moons back. Satisfying my lust for discovery more flat stone was revealed, extending the path in length to nine sequenced neatly laid large stone slabs; I'm impressed ☺ …. A job that's going to keep me amused for many hours to come….

The single millimetre dribbled overnight was enough to keep clothes wet on the line, looking like they'd be there for days the afternoons blistering heat forced upon us changed that, having everything dry, folded, put away and ready for the next round ☺ ….

A bloody niggly toothache is hanging around striking randomly with no thought to time I'm hoping extra oral attention may help overcome the ache without a dentist visit, maybe that's just plain wishful thinking ☺ …. And the good fairy may grant me another wish too xxxx….

Brushing my teeth after dinner gazing out the window toward the vegie patch, sitting in the gateway looking back at me was the black cat originating from Wendy's. The day prior a rabbit was watching me at the clothesline from the safety of the burnt out house, rare to see either of them here….

With grand intentions, I wrote in the journal early having it in the complete stack by 7:45pm freeing the evening for editing. Lights still not clearly on as to exactly what it is beside grammar and logic that editing entails, pencilled through a few more pages, but the desire to get myself to bed 11p.m.-ish won over ☺ ….

Wednesday 12 January 2005
Supporting my body weight on aching legs rising off the floor getting out of bed, until they're warmed, leg muscles let me know they're not accustomed to steep climbing having stretched out that bit further than normal….

Combined into the usual water collecting at the cattle trough, leaving the bucket to dangle and fill under the tap, I scoop mosquito wrigglers out of the trough tossing the water onto the lawn much to Ms Tia's delight. Snatched from Tia's snapping jaws and opening my eyes to wide whites, a strong gust redirected tossed water right back at me!!!! Refreshing ☺ ….

I'm getting better at staying home for longer duration's and probably wouldn't wander far if food found its way to me. Life on the farm done to its basics, a trip over the mountain slipped onto the roster. One of the beauties of living in a small country town is a park in shade is easily found, bloody hot and unfair to be out in I didn't muck around getting wilting shoppers home....

Catching a weather forecast on the radio driving the mountain, with no change in pattern for the next few we're in for a real taste of summer scorchers. Anywhere indoors being the preferred location, without complaint from my little mate, I took respite in the bungalow sorting through the latest processed photos putting them in appropriate places through the journal. With no intentions of leaving the shade cover the roof provided I read through the entire newspaper on the same day I bought it, sadly though reading through more tragedy. This time lives were claimed by bushfire, bloody awful way to die, the following stories were of the tsunami tragedy.... Unbelievable despair that would melt the hardest of hearts....

Losing its skin damaging searing sting 7:30p.m.-ish, Ms Tia and I emerged from our cocoon to splash some water around, using Dad's liquid manure recipe the results have been outstanding with strawberry fruit set ☺....

Scraping leftover schnitzel crumbs onto the lawn, never one to let a chance go by and on a treasure hunt, Tia was like a kid in a candy store vacuuming leaving no crumb unturned ☺....

Thursday 13 January 2005

As the forecast predicted 'uninviting to be outside unnecessarily', looks like a bit of editing may occur....

Actively filling the morning preparing for the day, included in preparations was a call to Mum and Dad. Slowing the reunion socialising, a reluctant Uncle Len was taken to the airport Sunday to start the first leg of his journey home. Leaving an Australian summer he touched down in Vancouver to be greeted by snow and a temperature of -9°. Giving me room for thought and reflection, Mum also mentioned Janine, a friend from secondary school, had died. My memories of Janine are only fond....

Happy to be perched out of the nasty elements of wind and heat, finally got my bum stuck for a good run at editing putting pencil marks in a language only I can understand over a few more pages. Each edited page is one small step forward each small step gets me closer to an accomplishment. Editing is providing a few laughs, looking back at good intentions and promises made, June 8, 2002, I first wrote about fixing the loo roof, it was only a week ago in 2005 a piece of tin was even put aside for the purpose. I don't rush into things but they will get fixed eventually ☺....

Tia sniffed out a decomposing carcass and gave her jaws some exercise on it. Snoozing quietly by my side the carcass' spirit revisited through her arse, snapping my concentration from editing through singed nostril hair and watering eyes that robbed the bungalow cocoon of breathable oxygen; the aroma being parable to the fly blown, sun scorched carcass laying in the yard, she knows how to literally spoil me rotten ☺!!!!

Friday 14 January 2005

Leaving a bucket to fill painfully slow at the tap, I took the few strides to the top of the dam levee, showing an obvious slight drop in pool level explains the loss in pressure. It's far from the end of the world....

Seated out of heat and wind with pencil and eraser in hand before noon, more sheets of paper with etchings of logic and flowing order of sequence were put in the edited stack. Reading over earlier journal entries is giving me a sensation of looking over my own shoulder☺....
Easier to protect for safe keeping and close by for convenience sake Tia parked the putrid carcass next to the bungalow, a situation that had to be remedied.... She's a little treasure☺....
The good fairy dropped her wand, after a spell of relief the bloody toothache rejoined me and persisted. When the sting left the suns rays I distracted myself from the ache having a go at the rock pile making another termite impression on its shape. Sitting on my bum for most of the day it was nice to give other muscles a workout....

Saturday 15 January 2005
Playing around with water and fertiliser is paying dividends. Dad's fertiliser recipe is making a notable difference the strawberries and sprinkling of potato plants are looking dangerously healthy. At a quick count, impressively, there is somewhere between thirty to forty set fruit on just two strawberry plants alone. I'll be even more impressed when they ripen and I get to taste them☺....
Wishing to get to the supermarket before noon closing I got straight to the point then back over the mountain. A couple of letters waited for my hand to reach into the black hole of the posting box, one of particular interest from the Anti-Discrimination Commission. I was elated to read the words in bold type 'possible breaches accepted for investigation'. What was endured at the radio station now feels real. I'm simply in search of closure so the experience can be put in the past. I wanted to jump up and punch the air, just the three bold typed words 'accepted for investigation', made me feel better about myself....
The bulk of the day behind and knowingly wasn't going to make any significant changes in the literary world, headed to the kitchen to satisfy another ongoing passion starting the long slow cook of a stew. Leaving the pot to simmer away doing its own thing Tia and I had a play at the excavation site unearthing more paving stones. The more I dig the more there is to find the area is a minefield for discovery. I'm particularly impressed by whoever originally laid the stone slabs their sheer weight is to be respected!!!!

Sunday 16 January 2005
There's no more collecting water from the cattle trough it stopped flowing, to access the precious liquid I've reverted to the hose connection coming off the 2-inch irrigation pipe by the driveway....
The entire week has been stereotypical bloody hot and windy, with another repeat performance today I want to move further south. Consecutive months of being randomly hammered by wind all temporary repairs are showing protest signs getting close to the end of their use-by-date....
Without fear of straying or getting sidetracked, harmful UV rays shoved along in gusts was all it took to keep my mind focussed on the editing job. Investing several hours into clarifying and making Rainbow Falls written past flow logically....
Changing down a gear in the brain, I migrated to the magnetic force of the excavation site relocating a few more wheelbarrow loads of soil. The site has the potential to expand in size and consume time it'll be a gradual ongoing project....

Monday 17 January 2005
Funny how us humans become habitual with thinking. I enjoy the morning therapy routine of watering plants, which meant a few return trips to the cattle trough. Forced into a change in thinking because water stopped flowing, now source water at the 2-inch irrigation pipe by the driveway which is only metres away and more convenient to the vegie patch????
The 19mm length of hose connected to the 2-inch pipe has a good strong flow rate, it would be even stronger if the hose wasn't split, thinking differently, Tia on the other hand enjoyed a bit of water fun with the fine stream shooting from it☺....
Activated by heat skink lizards make themselves quite at home feeding inside the bungalow, territorial little critters, the window ledge is a prized position to feed and a high insect traffic spot.
I've been witness to many a scrap had over rights to the window ledge and flies, and there's a healthy population of the buggers to be had☺!!!!
Lost inside the bungalow in self-preservation from extreme elements, sharpened my pencil and had another go at placing etchings on paper, a very slow, time consuming process but entertaining. Unable to hold my concentration beyond 4:30pm I rested an 'edited out' brain to make a start on dinner☺....
Glancing out the kitchen window sighted an oblivious Tia only a few metres from a snake, calling her in, she responded without fuss. Leaving Tia secure inside I went and shooed the tiger snake away with the shovel, wriggling lickety split deeper into the paddock and tall grass it eluded a lifetime inside the dam fence....

Tuesday 18 January 2005
Always getting a double set of prints processed I use the second set as a letter with pictures for sending home to Mum and Dad. Getting my pen busy, etched comments on the back of each print before tackling the mountain. A bit shy on food variety and out of bread meant no toast for breakfast, from petrol to the Post Office I got it all, enough to keep our lives moving forward in a healthy direction for a good stretch of home hermiting....
Unable to bring myself to sit and edit, for a thoughtless change of pace typed journal entries recently written giving the keyboard finger dance a go, its amazing how quickly time passes and I fall behind....
Pulling the plug on the computer for beer o'clock, on such a perfect peaceful and calm evening, I simply appreciated the moment sitting on the step of an open bungalow door cherishing the softening temperature. A nice way to wind the day down, I ask, did it wind up☺????

Wednesday 19 January 2005
A chronic nail biter ever since I grew teeth, the plaguing toothache has caused me to relent from the habit giving them opportunity to grow, creating yet more work to keep the buggers clean and trim. Riding the wave of the toothache it subsided and fulfilled my wish of avoiding the dentist. The good fairy, after letting me endure considerable discomfort again came good☺!!!!
Leaving Tia by the shed with a juicy bone having a chew, obviously intent on saving a bit for later, she returned to the bungalow with a grubby nose covered in dirt☺....

It's been a funny old day weather wise, waking to low cloud and some mist, finished hoping it would return. Shortly after severing power from the computer a bloody hot northerly blew in, warm enough to drive the shoes and socks from my feet, a very rare occasion. My habits are imitations of my father's ☺….
Chasing and catching the moving target gave my fingers a good workout being unwilling to give in until the journals digitised version was updated. Winding up the keyboard finger dance gave myself what remained of the day off just because I bloody well can, then gave myself permission to crack open a coolly and declare beer o'clock ☺ !!!!

Thursday 20 January 2005
The warmest night from memory this summer was a prelude to a bloody hot start, the predicted afternoon showers didn't arrive to hiss and cool. Low cloud containing a good load of moisture pushed only as far as South Sister Range, running out of puff to go the extra distance to share with us its offerings. However, moisture found ground 9p.m. but only enough to wet the footpath, hardly worth the anticipated wait….
Because it was Loui's final radio shift prior to leaving the district I made a point of listening juggling morning bits 'n' pieces around her program. Loui thoughtfully dedicated dog songs for Tia, for me, I got 'Pink's - Trouble'…. May she find happiness in greener pastures ☺ !!!!
Willingly putting the pencil down when Ross drove around back, over a cuppa he asked to store misplaced life possessions in the shed for a while until he settles in a place of his own. With plenty of available space I gave Ross the green light for two years storage ☺ ….

Friday 21 January 2005
Today is possibly one of the most placid put in for a while. Knowing I wouldn't be doing any dirty work outside I organised the day to the extent of only having to eat, leaving minimal to distract away from editing….
A few special moments have arisen while editing that stop me in my tracks to reflect, working the pencil through a section that proudly made mention of reaching a milestone, to quote the moment exactly, 'a second journal folder jam packed with our life's adventures is now complete'. Excited then about finalising folder two I've now commenced folder nineteen, wildest dreams have been imagined!!!!
A long afternoon spent in a small space I was getting a little restless, breaking out a cool ale I went walkabout with my little mate. Still in earshot of a ringing phone I got my legs moving to catch a call from Stacey, family support is important. A little splintered for a while, it's warming to see family unification; the birth of a child is good for softening hearts ☺ ….
Remaining light until 9p.m.-ish tricked me into staying outdoors longer, evenings in turn then evaporate and I struggle getting to bed before 11p.m.….

Saturday 22 January 2005
Putting the anchors on I had a day off literary dreams to catch up on everyday general stuff. In staying with a placid mood, started morning therapy splashing a bit of water around and monitoring plant growth progress. A small handful of peaches are beginning to size up and I've managed to put a dozen walnuts aside already, to this point that's eleven more than last year ☺ ….

Acting on thoughts, I sent Loui a text message to wish her well, flying out of Tasmania today destined for the biggest smoke taking time out to contemplate her future. She deserves some happiness....
Getting shy on wardrobe variety and tuning into a favourable weather report laundry got a guernsey....
While Mother Nature took over doing her bit to the dangling laundry, it freed me for a bit of a roam and fiddle. Garbage went to the shed then I washed dishes, de-furred the bungalow, gave myself a pampering, and spruced up Tia's bedding with a fresh doona. To wind down I moved a few rocks and emptied the clothesline, it's nice to know that everything besides what's on my back is clean and put away....
Calling Ms Tia in with the idea in mind of catching an early night, those plans changed dramatically the moment she stepped paw inside the bungalow. Matted in buzzies like I've never seen, Tia's entire tail looked like one lumpy dreadlock. I didn't know where to begin, from her ears to her arse they were everywhere, her body peeled from the carpet like tearing velcro apart. Taking an hour and a half to find Tia's body under the plastering, I pulled buzzies compressing down to the size of three cricket balls from her fur, one job I'm happy to have in the past!!!!

Sunday 23 January 2005
With all the fur and buzzie action recently the bungalow was feeling a little ordinary, remedying that sensation with a long slow vacuum. Close to finished, the vacuum started mucking up struggling to pick up, I had a go at tracking the blockage but the solution didn't fall into my lap and it began giving me the shits. Before taking it down the back and shooting it I put the vacuum away for another time....
A skink lizard turned on the lunchtime charm by snatching a fly from the window ledge, within ten seconds that one was devoured and it was on the lookout for a second. The fly was half the size of this lizards body I was suitably impressed with its first effort☺!!!!
A few hours were invested putting several more pages into the first edit stack, a very consuming slow process. Ready to rest my brain I made a start on dinner. It never fails to put a smile on my face seeing vegie peelings disappear near on as fast as they're put on the garden, the only bits left are onion skins, obviously not a favourite with the locals....

Monday 24 January 2005
Curious about last evening's vegie peelings, an ever growing collection of onion skins was all to be found everything else disappears without a chance to begin composting....
Void of moisture for a few weeks the yard and paddocks have browned off, most commonly walked areas are beginning to crunch underfoot....
Only enough milk for the morning breakfast milo foretold of a trip over the mountain. Taking accumulated loose change into town converted it at the bank for paper then converted it to a more useful commodity, food....
Heat has driven me indoors for that long I couldn't face anything literary. Occupying an idle mind I pulled the hair dryer apart removing its rattle, a piece of hard plastic floating loose had been mucking around with performance. An old fashioned model with screws for dismantling, and bonus, rattle free, it still worked when reassembled ☺....

Tuesday 25 January 2005
Little out of the ordinary happened. I met the world with a short temper, stifling humidity and heat didn't help matters at all!!!!
Putting myself in a place I could release a hissy-fit if one occurred I occupied a short fuse at the excavation site. Removing a few wheelbarrow loads of soil under the cover of cloud it was still bloody humid and sticky, when the sun poked its head out to stay, hungry, sweaty, sticky and uncomfortable I downed tools bathed and ate…. Fortunately leaving my cranky mood at the excavation site….
A stifling furnace in paradise forced the drastic measures of stripping shoes and socks from my feet. Sitting idle, I found relief in the bungalow with the pencil, eraser and little mate, putting a few more pages in the first edit pile ☺ ….
The only window being westerly facing, late afternoon the bungalow was an oven. Lacking the slightest breeze to move the thick stagnant air drove me to assemble the boxed fan given by Mum and Dad. The instant the fan was assembled I shared the big moment with the people that made it all possible, testing it in a power source speaking to Dad ☺ ….
Tia's actions said it all for both of us, with no desire to be outside preferring instead to enjoy the cool air circulated by the fan. Taking into account the amount of loose paper in the bungalow careful planning went into the fans final positioning!!!!

Wednesday 26 January 2005
Springing to mind on January 26 is A.B's birthday, the only Australia Day baby I know, well not such a baby anymore in his seventies ☺ ….
Getting a bit excited bursting out of the bungalow to see draped low cloud and wet ground, offering hope for the potential of rain, being generous because it's the smallest increment, I recorded the overnight moisture drop as producing 1mm. The few drops in the base of the gauge may have evaporated if I wasn't quick enough to witness their existence ☺ ….
Even with cloud cover to take the edge off heat, butter took no spreading at breakfast, definitely a fridge day! Poking its rays out to wilt the most-hearty of flowers the wild radiation generated convinced me not to go outdoors to play at all!!!! Extreme enough to drive shoes and socks off and to take the next step by giving my legs an airing…. Woohoo….
The only sensible pursuit was to give the pencil and eraser a workout. A small but significant editing milestone, fifty hardcopy pages have now found their way into the first edit stack….
To keep a stinker tolerable the fan came into its own circulating still air, and as an added bonus flies don't like wind, deterring them from settling only added to our comfort ☺ ….
Ross popped in late afternoon in ideal timing on a hot day to share in a beer. Making a start at clearing his former workshop in town for renting Ross brought a few pieces to store in the shed, mentioning I'd be seeing more of him in the coming weeks….

Thursday 27 January 2005
To keep stifling air moving and me and my little mate comfortably sane the fan wasn't turned off at all last night. Without respite we greeted more mongrel uncomfortable hot, steamy, humidity in paradise!!!!
About to settle into the usual morning watering regime a snake only metres from the hose caused a minor delay. Tia patiently waited in the cottage while I nervously moved it on,

making contact once before the snake, more fearful of me, took off at a pace into long grass and out of sight. Thinking that was enough large reptile activity for one day, enjoying a cuppa gazing lazily out the door, had my cage rattled seeing the tail end of another snake heading into the rock pile…. Two in one day, the buggers are active!!!!

In a nutshell it was a hot, thundery, steamy, humid, overcast bastard of a day. Thunder joined in early afternoon making a lot of noise without moisture and lingered until evening. Looking for respite from all the elements retreated to the bungalow with my little mate, spoiling myself rotten with a few more hours of pencil pushing by the fan….

A slow editing pace was made even slower by young Tia's concern over thunder, stressing and barking in the confined area of the bungalow wasn't to be ignored. Going a little stir crazy, I downed tools and on cue Ross pulled in with another trailer load of gear, bearing the gift of a cool beer, a rare offering, I took the top off one and gave him a hand to unload into the shed ☺ ….

Friday 28 January 2005
More of the same steamy uncomfortable fucking humidity!!!!
Placing self-preservation as priority one, I readied the family for a trip over the mountain predominantly to post my payslip and top up consumables. Collecting drinking water being high on the list I found Lesley in, stopping then for a cuppa and a chat. Taking in the cool breeze the shaded veranda offered to sit with a brew, a march fly did a belly-whacker into my cup psychologically robbing the contents and enjoyment of a nicely brewed coffee!!!!
The fan has proved itself invaluable in moving thick, humid, stifling air around, helping my sanity and the comfort level filling more hours with a poised pencil and eraser on the ready….
Eagles have had a visual presence this side of the mountain of recent. Today I sighted a pair circling above the burnt out house, last week a single eagle flew directly above and stayed pace with Destiny for a hundred metres on the drive to town…. Very strong elegant creatures….

Saturday 29 January 2005
The fan has been a sanity saver it wasn't turned off at all again last night. Oppressive, stifling humidity won't budge, hearing a brief shower before getting up was just enough to keep bloody humidity operating at peak performance. Air hangs so heavy and thick it even offers slight resistance to walk through!!!!
Getting my arse into gear, I was sitting in the oscillating path catching air movement editing by 10:30am. Breaking flowing thoughts, Tia barked her way through a thunderstorm, producing one short outburst of 3mm pushed humidity levels off the scale. Remaining threatening, the elements only offered a couple of follow up light showers lucky to add another millimetre to the total, although more pleasantly cooling life down….
Getting confident that rumbly conditions had passed I left the bungalow door open, caught by surprise, a fresh clap of thunder sent Tia racing through paddocks barking to return wet and buzzied. Humidity brings out my worst, and feeling a bit testy, Tia remained model still until she was brushed and plucked free of the offending pests, I'm tired of the sight of fucking buzzies!!!!
A bit stir crazy trying to juggle thunder and editing escaped for a dose of therapy in the vegie patch, breaking out beer o'clock I found strawberries under competing weeds….

Sunday 30 January 2005
Rapt with results from Dad's cow dung liquid fertiliser recipe on strawberry production, I made time to take a couple of photos of results, next set of prints sent off as a living letter they too can see the outcome of that little bit of green thumb knowledge shared ☺ ….
Getting water carting on the move with company never far off, Tia began sniffing the air with neck extended by the vegie patch giving me the 'I'm looking at a snake' body language. Instinct called her away, and taking a peek confirmed Tia to be spot-on. With Tia safely tucked away in the cottage I leant over the vegie patch fence and did my best with the shovel. Injured and not in a real receptive mood the tiger snake came at me with revenge in its eyes giving chase. Moving faster than the snake and pumped full of adrenalin, I was kept on my toes and we finished our altercation outside the vegie patch. It now has permanent residence behind the dam fence!!!!
Extremely happy to tuck away in the bungalow away from all elements I wore down the pencil and eraser. Preparing my psyche to continue the large task ahead, I've got over the first hurdle putting fifty pages under my belt, now to get myself passed the 'there's a lot of pages to go' next hurdle ☺ !!!! Phew….

Monday 31 January 2005
Thank the lord the bloody humidity has passed, its disheartening to bath up and have skin feel just as clammy within five minutes. Changing water collection points, following a long dry spell and a delivery line that could use flushing, water quality is starting to get a bit ordinary its not real flash to be washing whites with ☺ ….
Carting a bucket of water through the cottage, I smiled to see a skink on the kitchen window ledge with a couple of entwined pieces of Tia's fur sitting on its head: she's even decorating the lizards ☺ ….
Managing at this point to patiently etch pencil marks over a few months of the journal, either I'm sharpening to the task or my writing style and logical flow are improving, but the pace has lifted a little….
Having had enough excitement to last, today in contrast was simple and uncomplicated. I'm pleased to say there's nothing outstanding to report. The biggest event was Ross rolling up with another trailer load from his former electrical engineering business in town. Ross happily accepted my invitation to stay for dinner….

Tuesday 1 February 2005
Taking extra time during watering I deviated to dig up a self-sown potato plant, producing enough for a couple of feeds was bloody useful….
A hot northerly, quite gusty at times, coupled with direct sun kept me confined to barracks again with pencil and eraser forging forward with dreams….
Rarely checking their phone message bank I left a message Sunday for Mum and Dad, in part, along with the day and date, saying "see how long it takes you to check your messages". Answering a call this afternoon the familiar voice on the other end just said "two days", a moment of recognition and we burst into laughter ☺ ….

Finally cooling enough to be comfortable outside a bee-line was made to pick the prized strawberries. Tossing an over-ripe strawberry over the fence, Tia sought it out and played with it before sinking her teeth into it unsure of the flavour she dropped it like a hot potato ☺ ....

Wednesday 2 February 2005
The mercury plummeted in the past twenty-four hours, last night sitting by the fan tonight beanie and rugged up by the heater, I love versatility ☺ ???? A cooler air temperature has been refreshing to charge wilting batteries....
One brief shower passed while I was still laid out flat in bed, and the presence of rain never strayed too far off. A threatening sky prompted action straight into the daily outside bits, just getting sorted in time to beat a brief passing front, then that was it; there was no need to rush....
Preparing for a mountain dash, Ross and Lesley arrived with another trailer load, leaving them to it kept on my merry way. Looking for a change of pace I scheduled an impromptu rostered day off self-imposed literary pursuits. With the exception of the obvious daily journal entry I chose instead to idle over someone else's printed words, reading the newspaper and fumbling through the crossword....
The bloody cold southerly blast produced no moisture instead invested all its energy into generating wind, strong gusts gave us a real hammering at random, good to be out of and warm and comfortable indoors ☺ ....

Thursday 3 February 2005
Other than wanting to blow the roof off, wind proved useful late evening driving in a drop of moisture to hiss on hot parched soil. Powerful bellows pushing torrential rain wasn't a good recipe for relaxing a brain to sleep. Belting down all night and unable to stay in bed, brolly'd up, my little mate and I did a dash for the shed stoking the heater by 7a.m.-ish to contemplate what was happening around and what best to do with myself????
Hand in hand with destructive ferocity temporary repairs were left in need of work, the blue tarp nailed to the cottage wall protecting the power board was left flapping by a couple of nails. Up until 10a.m. 110mm had poured into the gauge, tuned in to an ABC news report 100 km/hr winds escorted rain in. The same news broadcast also reported the Spirit of Tasmania ferry that left Melbourne last night sustained hull damage from large waves, in addition windows were also broken by the rough sea, for safety reasons the ferry turned back to Melbourne....
Beauty created from a destructive night the falls could be heard from the loo, the sound alone was a lure to take a look at the strong flow bursting over the rock face and plunging below ☺ ....
Due to sleep deprivation my concentration power was zilch, turning the editor off, and requiring minimal thought, elected instead to tango my fingers over the keyboard. Putting in solid time and almost done, Ross and Lesley rolled up with another trailer load, leaving them to it, and finishing simultaneously, they took up the offer of a beer before heading back over the mountain....

Friday 4 February 2005
Absolutely worn out, I had my little mate and me tucked in by 10p.m. then slipped into a coma sleep. Responding to a paw tap, Tia woke me at some stage for wee's, putting the light on to co-ordinate my drowsy body also illuminated quite a rather large spider above the head of my bed. Everything has its place!!!!
Still as flat as a shit carter's hat, I did only the necessary then settled into the bungalow picking up the wad of paper revisiting the pencil and eraser....
Sun poked its head out on a couple of instances but not for long, emptying 12mm from the gauge late afternoon rain was still far from finished. I'm hoping we get enough to raise groundwater up to pumping level in the bore. Not only would flowing water change our lives I'm also looking for a big event to draw the book to a close, water on tap would be an ideal ending ☺!!!!

Saturday 5 February 2005
Reduced to a cranky mood last night it was heightened by a series of fucking trials. Wishing only to relax, the first trial came as no surprise, Tia returned covered in buzzies. Making a start at removing buzzies the lamp fell blowing the globe and leaving us in darkness. With the aid of a lighter I replaced the globe, without casting light when plugged in only highlighted the entire bungalow had been fused into darkness. To regain power meant a trip into the cottage to flick the switch on the power board. The comedy of errors continually shifting the goal posts further out of reach left me frustrated and ready to scream!!!!
Fortunately, sleeping the shit off my liver, I woke in a better frame of mind and was able to enjoy the finer side to life, appreciating a rare occasion the falls could be heard flowing from the bungalow ☺....
Feeling a bit ordinary of late, struggling with appetite and energy, I put it down to the heat, however, a welcome turn around this morning, an appetite found me for breakfast....
Unwilling to part company a threatening sky released another 6mm. Keeping a keen eye on groundwater movement again measured the bore, void of any sign of encouragement water is getting further out of reach rather than rising. A parched earth is swallowing water just as fast as Mother Nature can provide....
Doing only the required to get life operational, I retreated to the bungalow out of the elements for a continuation in editing pursuits. The entire journal print-out was parcelled up into four envelopes, close to the end of envelope one, its pretty exciting with the knowledge I'm almost a quarter of the way through the wad of paper ☺!!!!
Brain dead, I put pencil and paper down, and like a light bulb going off the rather appealing thought of sparking up the heater, far removed from anything literary, gained my full attention. Turning on the atmosphere Mother Nature resumed supplying moisture justifying ideal shed elements ☺.... Beer and bullshit coming up!!!!

Sunday 6 February 2005
Happily stuffing the face of the heater last night the beers were going down easy, on the cusp of one too many left me a little ordinary first up....
Due for heart and gut worm tablets, and aware of what was about to happen, Tia gave me a wide berth. Placing myself one step ahead using the knowledge of Tia's weaknesses, I poked

the tablets into pieces of leftover turkey and macadamia sausage and they disappeared without a struggle ☺ …..
The 135mm total, legacy of the past few days, has brought water quality back up. A strong flow from the tap at the cattle trough has also returned!!!!
Extremely short on clothes, Ross gave me the green light to use his automatic machine. Dials turned and pressed on the first load, I ducked the remainder of the way down the mountain for one of Evelyn's chicken camembert pies to settle my tummy, and it worked miracles ☺ ….
Socialising and washing complete, I toddled back over our side of the mountain determined to finalise the contents of envelope one and that I did. A bloody huge accomplishment I'm proud to have behind…. A quarter of the way there ☺ !!!!

Monday 7 February 2005
Being the eternal optimist I checked the bore again, taking a peek down the narrow tube I didn't think my piece of rope was long enough, five inches of rain did little more than green the yard up. Running water at Rainbow Falls isn't going to happen from this deluge, also failing in delivering an end to the book ☺ ????
I put an honest day in on the computer transferring pencil edits to digital form. My writing in its infancy was at times disjointed and earliest pencil edits not so well practised, creating a slow but meaningful start….
Nothing too dramatic usually happens seated in front of a computer screen, never one to let a dull moment pass by my little mate snoozing nearby certainly added colour. Tia's burping and farting resembled the aroma of the dead wallaby she's been having a chew on that has a cloud of blowflies hovering above. Pretty bloody ordinary rising from near your feet!!!! Phew….
Tia's foul arse drove me from the bungalow on several occasions. To avoid dry retching I brought the priceless fan into play compromising a heavy situation. There's never a dull day at Rainbow Falls ☺ ….

Tuesday 8 February 2005
Living in a democratic society is a bit questionable at times, told you're equal, that is until someone stands behind self-regulating business laws deciding you have to do what they want. The Electricity Company has powerlines running the full length of the top boundary, cutting in front of the waterfall and dangling across the gorge. People employed by the company drive inside the front gate without a moments notice, or any courtesies whenever it suits and chop trees down without question, I find it extremely rude to take those liberties on private land. With the forceful amount of wind we're exposed to up here, to create windbreaks and heal erosion along the powerline strip, it's at my expense to reverse the situation to remove poles and wires to revegetate. Outside of money collecting the Power Company take the responsibility of a slippery eel….
Earliest attempts at editing, cutting my teeth, haven't made a great deal of difference, my writing style then wasn't that sharp either, determining the pace of entering the edited version onto computer to be relatively slow. In the journals infancy I never considered transforming our lives into a book, now dedicated to the cause I put another solid day into the computer to pull up brain dead….

Switched off, I sat and enjoyed the one and only beer before burning off energy moving a few kilos of rock on a much cooler day....

Wednesday 9 February 2005
Crying wolf on a few occasions, Tia's got me out of bed just to have a chew on a bone or chase something she heard in the yard. Ignoring her pleas until I was ready to get up, with the door open she bolted for relief appealing directly to my conscience!!!!
Finding a little computer diversion I gave myself brain cell charging therapy with a relaxing play in the vegie patch. Digging self-sown garden fresh potatoes for dinner I kept on scratching around with the garden fork digging out a few weeds.... Ahhhh....
Lost to the computer and leading into brain shut down digitising the edits of 'Inside my Skin', a phone call from Stacey gave me reason enough to draw a line in the sand and turn off. The bearer of good news, as from Monday she starts a new job closer to Melbourne Central, transferring within the same company to their Richmond branch. Stacey's settling well living in the big smoke....
With dinner on the simmer I grabbed the shovel for a dig around a paving stone between the cottage and bungalow, the outcome being of no surprise and a familiar scenario, 'but wait there's more'. Patches of paving stones unearthed are beginning to paint a larger picture, there appears to be quite a bit of history to find buried under years of shifting and shifted soil....

Thursday 10 February 2005
Absent of communication for over a week I phoned Mum and Dad before turning the computer on. Dad mentioned he's been having success at golf, hitting well recently for a first and third field placing, as part of his cache of prizes he's put aside another white peaked cap for me. During the course of our chat I heard Tia growling, before continuing I had to satisfy my mind, ready to have a go at it she was growling at a copperhead snake crossing the driveway!!!!
Locking Tia in the bungalow with me out of harms way monitored her behaviour and thankfully she showed no signs of having been bitten. Tia eliminates the possibility of quiet uneventful times, keeping life interesting playing co-author she managed to wrap the mouse lead around her head having page after page of text scrolling on the screen ☺ ????
Without my little mates input I would have had very little to write about, I just press on keys losing time to the computer. Progress slow and steady and never planning to write a book, I don't know what I expected, but anything worthwhile is worth waiting for ☺ ....

Friday 11 February 2005
Plagued by restless sleep the past couple, it was around 1a.m. when I last looked at the clock last night. Given cause to be pissed off, I was woken early by bloody squawking currawongs raiding and damaging the soft limbed trees and anything else they latched their beaks onto around housing. Shifting the horrible mob of birds on, while up and on the move stayed up, hoping a 7a.m. rise would encourage sleep tonight!!!!
In need of food and a little human interaction I prepared for town to blow the budget. Dropping in on Pam and Terry for a hot brew and a chat brought to my attention just how much I needed time away from the computer. It was a refreshing change to be temporarily surrounded by a different set of four walls and good company ☺ ....

Hungry, I cooked dinner and snacked out early. Relaxing afterwards with a cuppa I received a phone call from Ross inviting me for dinner…. Win some lose some ☺ ….
Collecting brain cells rather than investing them into book dreams, prescribed a dose of mind therapy in the vegie patch. An ideal temperature and soft UV I took my top off and savoured the sun's warmth on skin turning in weeds….

Saturday 12 February 2005
Once again the horrible squawking of currawongs on a damaging rampage stirred the camp early to piss them off. Currawongs have the ability to be quite arrogant, standing their ground noise alone isn't enough at times to move them on, it's necessary to throw my beloved shovel into a tree in a stand off situation. Along with arrogance they are also well versed in persistence, determined to take what they want continually return on raiding missions, they've met their match with me as equally determined to save the termite hole from destruction!!!!
With a rest day behind one didn't need to crystal ball gaze, the writing was on the wall, predictably returning to the editor's seat. Following me through life from early high school I'm regularly reaching for the dictionary; although improving, my spelling isn't sharp….
During a cuppa break a pair of eagles entertained effortlessly gliding above South Sister Range, I've observed the pair on several occasions either leaving or returning to the same location passing over the range….
Easing into knock off after slaving over a hot computer I retreated to the vegie patch to eat ripe strawberries, scare off currawongs, turn soil, and kick the ball for Tia…. And so winds down another one in paradise….

Sunday 13 February 2005
Up again with the mongrel, destructive, thieving currawongs 7a.m. sharp when they commence noisy vandalising and pillaging. To discourage currawongs from getting comfortable I utilise the time of their feeding frenzy being present outside watering the garden. By the time the garden's finished even the most persistent of the worthless pests has given up….
After enduring a cool one-dog night we lavished in morning sun playing with the shovel edging along paths. Life organised and psychology right only then was I lured indoors to turn the computer on to chip away at a little more of our documented story….
From the moment the digitising beast is turned on time disappears, unlike the pages of the journal, they tick over consistently and slowly. It's a psychological challenge retraining my mind to ignore measuring output to stay focussed on preferred quality, more and most for least is an industry skill we're trained into participating in the economic world….
Once again, heading to the vegie garden after slaving over a hot computer for a little wind down, not only keeps frustrated currawongs at bay but I also dug up another handful of potatoes. Spending regular snippets of time in the vegie patch is beginning to pay dividends, getting weed growth under control before seeding or flowering is keeping the area manageable and tidy….

Monday 14 February 2005
The good fairy that took my toothache away also let it return, making its presence known preparing for bed last night it returned with vengeance today causing grief!!!!

A frustrating habit, Tia and I got up again with the mongrel squawking currawongs, forcing myself out of bed to save the destruction of trees around housing. Being more persistent than them will pay dividends, maybe I'll get to harvest the walnuts????
Finishing off an average, quiet, yet painful computer session then went in and made a start on dinner. While dinner simmered I took a walk to the shed to lock-up. Checking the mobile phone propped on Destiny's dash for messages, one of the few spots I get reception, movement directly beside attracted attention. Within arms reach a tiger snake was raised and ready to give me a nip, taking off like a startled gazelle my feet didn't touch the ground. With Tia secure in the cottage, the aggressive tiger snake had me running from the shed for the last time in its life!!!!

Tuesday 15 February 2005
I'm bloody-well snaked out!!!! After a long day slaving over a hot computer I headed to the garden for brain relief, watering 'Peaches' the fruit tree I met yet another healthy tiger snake. Thankfully the snake was in a good mood going separate ways, however, it left me unsettled after too many encounters. I've had enough!!!!
Phillip recently posed the question, "what do you write about when you're writing, ha, ha". I wish life was just as simplistic as his question, even getting up through the night for a wee is becoming an event. Putting the light on before wandering outside last night revealed another huge spider had come out of the woodwork and positioned itself above the head of my bed. I'd be happy to just write about writing, which actually did occupy most of the day….
Adrenalin is a good cure for toothache for a while I forgot about its throb, by choice I'd prefer to deal with the toothache bypassing the activity causing adrenalin!!!!

Wednesday 16 February 2005
Psychological mind games with currawongs is beginning to reap rewards, I may have endured more early mornings than desired but the persisting number is lessening. Following the initial morning 'piss off' only one pair refused to leave, returning randomly, it's at least a manageable amount….
Getting up with currawongs assisted with reaching town at an early hour, pushing against the pub door it wouldn't budge, learning via the newsagent it doesn't open until 11a.m.. Still with plenty to do I returned when the doors would freely swing open ☺….
Having had more than my fair share of snake encounters I spent a quiet afternoon with my little mate safely tucked away basking behind glass in the bungalow. Giving my brain a rest I kept it amused reading the newspaper and having a go at the crossword, following other peoples literary pursuits left my own tucked away….
A piece of advice imparted first arriving at our new home is 'your shovel is your best friend', next to Tia that statement proved to be spot on, during the summer months I rarely wander without it, its pretty much strapped to my hip….

Thursday 17 February 2005
Through contact time I've observed currawongs to be intelligent birds, sadly for them they're destructive, having bad habits along with a shit awful squawk. With the help of my little mate we're doing our utmost to keep them feeling unwelcome. Observing my habits, currawongs too

are getting smarter, leaving their squawk behind they arrived to raid in silence, it was the sound of wing flapping from a large bird that woke me to get out and be part of the action 6:30am!!!!

A major plus about being up that early is we're active before reptiles, getting through the outside bits without my eyes constantly scanning on the look-out I'm able to keep my mind on the job at hand. A handful of currawongs were annoyingly persistent returning, me being the most annoying and persistent of all made it bloody difficult for them to satisfy hunger!!!!

Amazingly, clothes were washed and drip-drying before 11a.m.. Although impressed with what's achieved being up so early, I can't wait for all the fruit to ripen to revert back to staying in bed until I'm naturally ready to rise!!!!

The good fairy waving her magic wand got the painful recurring abscess under control within three days, pushing through the pain barrier I've put a lot of effort into cleaning between the tooth and gum; may it clear up and clear off!!!!

Before getting absorbed by white goods, for a chance at avenues unexplored, I phoned the ombudswoman representing the electricity supplier to get a finger on the pulse regarding poles and powerlines on private land. Simply confirming my understanding, the electricity company have self-legislated to abscond any responsibility, having no recourse unless I pay for their removal. Unclear on legislation and policies, the woman I spoke to is going to send appropriate related documents in the post. That should be a nail biting read ☺....

Friday 18 February 2005
Determined to psychologically beat currawongs before they trash the yard, Tia and I were up awaiting their arrival and like clockwork they flew in to feed shortly after sunrise. Not allowing one bird to settle made it hard work to satisfy a hunger, but being cunning persistent thieves we had an ongoing battle of wits, I took out this round!!!!

Before taking up my position next to the whirring hard drive I let my fingers do the walking on the keypad of phone technology, dialling through for a catch up yarn with Mum and Dad. I've had plenty of promises, but Mum and Dad have come-good actually putting photos of Dekira in the post, they also said Dekira features in a Mildura Sandman bedding commercial. Barely able to open her eyes and she's a media celebrity ☺....

Applying all available brain cells to first edit, I escaped afterward to retrieve a fresh supply at the vegie patch turning in weeds and continuing to frustrate pesky currawongs. I hope their power of endurance is beginning to feel the same as mine, worn down!!!!

Saturday 19 February 2005
Continuing the psychological warfare, again, I forced myself out of bed ready to meet any intruder wishing to pillage after sunrise. Persistence is beginning to reap rewards, only one scout bird tested the water three times before giving in, the unwelcome message is sinking in!!!! Mother Nature assisted with the 'piss off' message by turning on a stinker, any bird in its right mind would be resting in its nest, heat certainly drove me into mine....

Up early enough to enjoy time outdoors, keeping a currawong vigil I turned soil in the vegie patch daring them to return ☺ !!!! Airing my skin to the cool morning elements weeding around strawberry plants I disturbed a frog making itself at home in foliage, it was the steadily rising mercury that drove me out of it to seek refuge...

Washing my body free of the morning's exerted effort I then retreated to the bungalow to further advance a dream. Thoughts of unwelcome currawongs momentarily dismissed, instead, demanding my full concentration is the mongrel toothache returning with vengeance. As fast as the abscess is drained it refills with a throb, unable to stay focussed on the computer I called beer o'clock to medicate the problem.... Hic....

Sunday 20 February 2005
My body gave in to a bit of a sleep in remaining horizontal dreaming away until 7a.m.-ish, by then a few pillaging thieves were active but the number has certainly dwindled. I think they're as frustrated with me as I am with them. I'm winning in the annoyance stakes! To the benefit of the vegie patch, I again turned soil while biding time through their feeding habits. Tossing the shovel at arrogant birds challenging and staying put in trees I've been damaging the timber handle causing grief with splinters.... Ouch....
When finally the last persistent thief gave up pillaging, only then did I head indoors to put in a solid afternoon advancing a few more slow moving pages into the completed stack....
Checking the status of currawongs in fruit trees late afternoon, the sheer size of a pair of eagles perched on a branch by the water tank stood out in the landscape. On cue, focussing on them with the zoom lens one eagle leant forward releasing a poo, unsure if that's what it thought about having a photo taken ☺ ????

Monday 21 February 2005
Encountering one bird on three occasions, the trees at least are benefiting from the endurance of many consecutive early rises. All parties calling a truce, I had the family packed in Destiny for a simple trip into town, before rounding South Sister for the descent I pulled off to the side of the road well before reaching the crowd of people, flashing lights, cars and machinery....
Rallying at minimal notice, concerned local residents gathered to voice protest on logging operations commencing at South Sister before having a chance at meeting on an even playing field to object. Legally, only one party has a right, plenty of police made sure protesters left a clear path for logging preparations to continue????
Already having been burnt and scarred by the intrusiveness of logging operations, my spirit to block another truck was broken by being punished wishing only to make people hold true to their word. I drove by sympathetic to some familiar faces clinging to hope at saving the town's water supply, and rare and endangered species found in the mountain, from the greed of the logging giant....
Following a week of absence the Post Office box was full. Anticipated and waiting, eagerly I opened the envelope containing photos of Dekira at differing stages of development, and as confirmed by everyone spoken to, she's a beautiful baby. Dad shocked me by writing on the envelope and the included brief note, knowingly the only written note I've ever received from Dad. I challenged Dad earlier on to write one word in a letter to me for every journal page I've written, time and life passed quickly, reverting to one word per completed journal folder, today we broke even ☺ ....
Also waiting was an envelope from the Anti-Discrimination Commission containing Break O'Day FM's response to my sexual harassment and discrimination allegations, choosing a line of attack rather than recognition and apology. A little overwhelmed by information overload,

chance had me meet Rita, a former station manager, offering her support she invited me home for a chat over a cuppa, it was just what I needed....
A brain too preoccupied to concentrate on editing I took time out to get my head around Break O'Day FM's response to my allegations.... Hmmmm....

Tuesday 22 February 2005
Still persistently pushing myself out of bed, playing psychological warfare has drawn me to the conclusion I've managed to discourage the majority, currawong activity also varies with the weather. There was plenty of squawking going on at a distance, with only two attempts at landing on home soil that were promptly moved on....
Up begrudgingly, after restless sleep at the 'beat the currawong' time of 6:30am dominoed into an early start on the computer, spending a long day inside escaping intense UV rays. Editing into the year 2003, seven months of the hardcopy now contain pencil etchings, twenty-five printed months remaining.... One small step at a time ☺ ?!?!
Ross sent a text message containing an invitation for a barbecue dinner, a girl couldn't say no to that. The elements complemented the evening calm, mild, and heat from the barbecue supplied enough warmth. With an almost full moon lighting the surrounding mountains leading out over the ocean illuminating as far as the eye could see, it was pretty relaxing over food and chat....

Wednesday 23 February 2005
Persistent with my 'save the trees from vandals' early rise, was out there again meeting sunrise, one group of five pillaging thieves flew in and was promptly moved on without taking a berry. Nurturing dear Peaches the fruit tree back to fruit bearing and health she's still holding onto five pieces of sizing fruit, reducing one at a time from the original dozen....
Bathing, the garden and laundry demanding the need to cart water, I didn't stop. Putting washing on the line to drip-dry it didn't take too long, the mercury rose from hot to stinking hot and the fan got a serious workout....
Having a spell from editing for another less desired literary pursuit, swallowing the information load and clearing my head for words, formulated a letter of response to the Anti-Discrimination Commission, losing the afternoon to careful contemplative thought....
Ready for a breath of fresh air I stepped out the door meeting a tiger snake that disappeared fast into the rock pile, shattering my enjoyment of not having sighted one in a while!!!!

Thursday 24 February 2005
Generously offering use of a computer with a printer attached, loaded with floppy disks containing the finalised draft letter to the Anti-Discrimination Commission, I took a fruitless trip over the mountain to Pam and Terry's. The computer refused to read the disks then promptly corrupted both. Adjourning to the On-line Centre I still failed at getting a response from the disks. Calling in on Rita for a cuppa she offered the use of her computer confirming the disks had been corrupted, each attempt ended with the same outcome. Grabbing a few groceries I headed home to hand write the letter, making sure of a copy next time I go near the Post Office....

Its both heart warming and impressive driving the mountain to see a dedicated group of residents have set-up a permanent public awareness campsite opposite the access road to South Sister. Lacking the ability for compromise or giving, the aggressive approach to the 'get out of my way' logging operations, only manages to take from and divide communities!!!!
Pushing the pen for results, the fan got another workout stirring stifling air in the bungalow. Collecting stored camping gear Ross couldn't believe the heat and direct sun having just left a clouded-in afternoon in town????

Friday 25 February 2005
Able to unload by taking the discrimination claim as far as it can for now, a rested mind let me put in the best night sleep in a while….
The ongoing battle with currawongs is all but over psychological warfare wore them down before me. Consistent repetition disturbing their routine has altered raiding patterns, either that or there's nothing left to take, but currawong traffic in our happy hamlet has slowed. I'm near ready to slip back into the routine of getting out of bed when my body is ready????
Editing has taken a back seat to playing politics, only able to stay focussed on one thing at a time to do it justice today it was back to pencil etchings. Retreating for a workout on the shovel to wind down afterwards, currawong activity has certainly been beneficial for the vegie patch, finalising turning the last sod before walking out, it's time to find something else to do ☺ ….

Saturday 26 February 2005
The gentle pitter-patter on the tin roof shortly after going to bed produced 2mm, not enough to cancel the plant watering regime. Sadly, doing the morning rounds found only three remaining peaches clinging to life, my hope is to taste at least one and beyond that is a bonus ☺ ….
Embracing me with open arms again was the bloody toothache, taking the throb for a drive posted the hand written letter as a matter of finalising a loose end. On the return I stopped at the South Sister permanent campsite, at minimum two people are there at any one time to share knowledge. Checking on progress, word is, they're hopeful of a court intervention order Monday to slow things down for a while. A pristine environment harbouring rare and endangered species and source of the towns water supply, having the mountain remain intact and logging operations aborted we all live in hope sanity prevails!!!! If the logging of South Sister goes ahead it's simply a dumb act of greed!!!!
A psychology not ready to dive straight onto the computer I took a moment to wash Destiny, much to Tia's delight, water being splashed around there's always the chance some will head her way ☺ ….
Pain killers and toothache combined the brain wasn't feeling that sharp, able to touch-type without too much required thought, proceeded in digitising the latest hand written journal offerings….

Sunday 27 February 2005
Up and about at 8a.m. the only obvious birds active were kookaburras. The succession of early mornings has returned tenfold, trees are relatively unscathed and look healthy….
Having no set plans, and thinking life was going to be nothing out of the ordinary, the unexpected always keeps life interesting. A peek in the mirror revealed the abscess had

advanced beyond the mouth and taken effect on the right side of my face with some obvious swelling. Wishing to reverse the swelling face syndrome with a course of antibiotics phoned the St. Marys hospital. Offering an efficient service, I was able to get in straight away, particulars and temperature taken, area examined, I was turned around and walked out the door under a half-hour with enough medication to see me through until scripts can be filled Monday....

It's hard to drive past, so I pulled up at the South Sister campsite on the return trip just for a chat....

Swallowing the right pills to start reversing my fat face, and looking to procrastinate, settled in for a solid chat with Mum and Dad and achieved the goal ☺ ....

Replacing a hot receiver, the obvious could be avoided no longer, adding life to the motionless piece of electronic machinery sitting quietly in the corner I burst the computer into life....

Doing an evening watering I was shattered to find I'm down to two chances of tasting fruit from Peaches this season!!!!

Monday 28 February 2005
Sleeping until I was ready to rise, the only currawong sighted was flying overhead their squawking presence in surrounding trees is also becoming invisible, using my head instead of a trigger has worked....

Chipping away editing a sprinkling more pages, I was happy for a change of tack when Ross arrived with the little grey Fergie on a mission to repair the slasher. Playing apprentice got my hands dirty following his lead, a small investment in labour the slasher was together awaiting a test run. Putting labour into action, Ross did a run up and back in a paddock flattening large amounts of long grass in short time. The slasher didn't miss a beat, but with the day a bit long in the tooth, after the initial test run toys were put away for a fresh start. Hidden below long dry tops it was exciting to see fresh green growth exposed, I'm looking forward to the possibilities tomorrow brings ☺ ....

Tuesday 1 March 2005
Tia nagged me out of bed around 8a.m., to sanity's delight not one currawong was sighted at all when so much effort is put in its nice to know it's not in vain ☺ !!!!

Swallowing the last antibiotic at breakfast, and the cupboards almost bare, town made the roster hitting the big metropolis shortly after 11a.m.. Inside the supermarket poking my bit of plastic inside the ATM I stayed there and filled a trolley. Pushing on the door of the make-believe chemist it wouldn't budge, a blunt reminder it has a shut down over lunch....

Filling in three-quarters of an hour constructively, I headed back to the pub where a yarn was had with familiar faces buying a box of Bruce's best, rare to drink at that time, I enjoyed a beer dusting off socialising cobwebs over relaxed chat and laugh ☺ .....

Not long home, and Ross pulled in to demonstrate the tractors idiosyncrasies and I was turned loose in paddocks knocking down run after run of long grass, also giving my arse a pounding on the hard metal seat. Time spent in a tractor seat took me back to my apprenticeship on the farm at the Department of Agriculture ☺ !!!!

Leaving me to it, Ross headed off. After a couple of hours ploughing the little grey Fergie through tall grass and weeds the radiator became blocked with dry grass limiting air flow, protesting by running a bit warm, I packed up toys for a clean up....

Adding to a good day, I caught the news on ABC Radio National waiting to bath, hearing Australia has now beaten New Zealand four games straight in the one day cricket series, bonus☺....

Wednesday 2 March 2005

The elements haven't offered a spell from the watering routine for near on a month. Constant cold wet conditions us mainlanders are led to perceive about Tasmania are a fallacy, the summer here may be shorter but it's just as dry and unpredictable as anywhere....

Sleeping in for as long as Tia would let me, giving in and getting up, again there was no sign whatsoever of currawongs. I'm satisfied to fly the flag of victory☺!!!!

Fed, watered and tidied, I prepared Fergus the tractor for another outing, after checking the vitals of water, oil and petrol I was psyched ready to knock down more long grass. With a crook battery Fergus had to be jump-started, Destiny gave it her best shot but the lightweight jumper-leads began heating up without achieving the desired result. Knowing when to stop, over a quick rethink redirected my psyche to laundry and preparing a big pot of stew to stockpile 'heat and eat' meals....

Thursday 3 March 2005

It was disappointing to find the fat juicy peach I was eyeing off yesterday had disappeared down the guts of some bloody possum! Only the runt of the litter remains, if fruit is to be sampled I've got one chance!!!!

Pumped full of drive and motivation by the mere sight of level ground in the paddocks, it's probably a good thing the tractor couldn't be jump-started I wouldn't have been able to help myself and worked out in the heat. Searing direct sun is hard on human and machinery....

Playing in a sun smart environment refocused on literary dreams. My writing style is beginning to flow beyond merely thoughts emptied out of my head and jotted onto paper capturing fast passing memories, it's now taking on logical sequence, lightening some of the work from shaping our story editing.... Phew!!!!

Slaving over a hot computer keyboard I clunked my way into April 2003, that action brought to attention that the end of March on any year represents a finish to daylight saving; heat, and long daylight hours are about to fade out....

Friday 4 March 2005

Continually exceeding any perceived expectation, the amount of recorded history of life at Rainbow Falls has extended to commencing its twentieth folder, a number I wouldn't have comprehended in the infancy of documenting memories.... Lucky I didn't know what lay ahead or else I would have run for the hills☺!!!!

Taking a stock up trip over the mountain I was surprised by the level of roadwork going on, beyond anything previously experienced. Commencing at the South Sister look-out turn in, and heading in the direction of town, the road resembles a highway, beyond the usual lick over, wetting, grading and compacting is in action. Handy for slowing Destiny from vibrating apart,

but one can't help but feel suspicious its not solely for the benefit of residents, the cynic inside says be prepared to share the road with a lot of heavy vehicles, hope I'm proved wrong!!!!
Pulling up at the campsite on the return trip for latest developments in saving South Sister, court action was in progress in Hobart as we spoke still awaiting an outcome, may common sense be the winner!!!!
Its time to pull the pencil and eraser out again and break out the contents of envelope two, the computer swallowed the contents of envelope ones hardcopy pencil etchings. Officially making it one-quarter of the way through the stack of bulging envelopes, beer o'clock tasted better with a permanent smile ☺ ....
Relaxing with a stubby outside exercising Ms Tia, regularly she would take-off like a rocket into the surrounding paddocks using high spurts of energy, returning hot and thirsty and in need of an instant cool down she squatted in the cattle trough submerging all but her head. Dunking herself at least five times tempted the thought of writing 'Tia's pool' across the front of the cattle trough ☺ ....

Saturday 5 March 2005
Hearing a gentle tap-dance on the roof contemplating getting up, sliding the bolt on the door greeted magic elements in paradise. Low engulfing cloud heavy enough to deliver moisture obscured everything outside a fifty metre radius, nothing to be seen or heard I simply enjoyed the enchanting mood created by nature's elements on those rare occasions that they're offered. A therapeutic stage set also delivered a fit of the 'lazies' my get up and go got up and went ☺ ....
A cool change arriving with rain has slowed reptile activity, offering a sense of freedom walking around without the shovel strapped to one hip and Tia to the other....
Finding no inspiration at all to make a difference in this world, didn't, the biggest achievement was to remove the flesh covering the collection of walnuts to allow the shell to dry. What wasn't allowed for was my ignorance to the stubborn stain left behind by wet walnut flesh on hands, no amount of scrubbing would shift my true walnut coloured palms!!!!
Occupying my brain in an idle body I picked up a radio station broadcasting the cricket, into the final overs the outcome was a for drawn conclusion, Australia beat New Zealand five games straight in the one day cricket series, you bloody beauty ☺ !!!!
Out of the blue Ali phoned, a woman I first met a couple of years ago crossing Bass Strait on the ferry. Our contact following has been sparse but pleasant. Ali and a friend will be in the neighbourhood sometime close to Easter and are going to pop up for a visit. Not only was it lovely to hear from Ali, her company is light and easy to be around ☺ ....

Sunday 6 March 2005
There's a point where bungalow de-furring alone isn't enough, in a better frame of mind to locate the blockage in the vacuum cleaner I screwed off the hose internally removing a solid collection of hair, carpet fibres, a small piece of cardboard and a tissue. Turning loose in the bungalow vacuumed from ceiling to floor, adding final touches went as far as polishing the window inside and out. Returning noisy electrical goods back to its nook in the cottage decided to first clear the window ledges free of carcasses then continued on vacuuming from the roof to

the floor in the cottage also. Not something one deliberately sets out to do, that is lose a day to the vacuum ☺ !?!?

First attempting early afternoon, and managing to connect a couple of hours later, I was shocked to hear the reason Mum and Dad weren't answering the phone was they'd been out looking at cars, it been about twenty-five years since they last did that. For a lot of reasons Mum's lost confidence driving the Kingswood, and is in the market to buy something smaller and lighter she's comfortable driving. They looked at a 2001 model Lancer with all the mod cons that they were about to do some follow up on. The immaculately kept HG Kingswood isn't going to disappear out of their lives it will remain as Lukey's golf car and the car to take bush ☺ ....

Monday 7 March 2005

Tia and I jumped in Destiny making the first achievement a trip to the other side of North Sister to pick up Ross' heavy-duty jumper-leads. A double bonus, he was home to make me a cuppa....

Ready to strike a blow, the jumper-leads did the trick, Destiny added life to Fergus to make more of an impact on woolly paddocks. Only able to do one thing well at a time, I set Tia up comfortably in Destiny then clipped the P.T.O shaft on. Putting Fergus into gear I stalled the engine. Without an ounce of life in the battery, and for a bit of practice, I went through the whole jumper-lead procedure again, this time however managed to gain forward momentum ☺ !!!!

The oil pressure gauge dropping is the only signal Fergus is running a bit warm, with this thought in mind knew when to pull up. Parked under cover of the shed cooling off I went over the radiator, for maximum performance, concentrated on clearing grass packed into the fins doubling air flow capacity....

Out of curiosity I phoned Mum and Dad wondering if they'd made a decision on the car they looked at, an elated Mother was proud to tell me they'd bought it ☺ !!!! The verdict from a test drive was the final selling point, both Mum and Dad had nothing but praise for the cars comfort and handling, only 37,000 on the clock was the icing on the cake, they both sounded pretty excited about the new venture ☺ ....

Tuesday 8 March 2005

Failing in attempts at the NEIS program, and pre-arranged, Paul, the Centrelink psychologist paid me a visit at home. Over a brew we assessed the healthiest path forward, referring me to the 'Personal Support Program' permits breathing space away from job search programs to gain more weight and fully grow into my skin. Paul is a breath of fresh air working for a company with pretty regimented impersonal guidelines ☺ ....

Paul waved off, my little mate and I returned to radiator cleaning. Deciding to join in on shed action Tia gave me the 'I'm looking at a snake' body language and it was in a bugger of a spot next to the shovel! Loved one secure, I threw a lump of wood near the snake trying to gain access to the shovel, that action only managed to fully divert a rush of attention on me. Running on pure adrenalin I sought refuge alongside Tia in Destiny. Losing interest in the chase the snake diverted along the shed wall enabling me access to the shovel. It's now on its way to heaven, but only if it's been good....

Water on the ground under Fergus I thought came from the radiator overflow hose proved different, tracking the slow leak back to the bottom rusted out radiator pipe in need of a solder. Poorly maintained, Fergus gets a rest for a while, I'm not comfortable working a radiator that won't hold pressure….

Wednesday 9 March 2005
Seasonally added to the daily 'before breakfast' routine is collecting fallen walnuts. This time with the use of gloves I took the flesh covering off another built-up stash, my hands still carry the stain from their introductory flesh peeling….
A public information rally scheduled for 11a.m. at the base of South Sister had me rattling my dags to be part of a very peaceful, yet determined air that filled the gathering crowd. Respectively, Fran and David passionately addressed the attentive audience of around 150 local supporters, giving a factual history as to why the mountain shouldn't be logged and the steps taken getting us to where we stood at the rally today. It seems all political avenues accessed to seek sanity to stop the logging, from local Council, forestry, to all levels of government, has been met with shut doors and minds. The final insult to the huge voluntary effort to save South Sister was to be granted a day in court mid June on one hand, then on the other hand permit logging to commence March 21????
The intense sting of the spent summer is softening making it pleasant to wander in the great outdoors, delighted with choice, I utilised it pulling out new growth buzzie runners. Slipping into our working partnership, I threw pulled runners and my little mate sorted, composted and filed. The team still working strong we made a game of emptying the cattle trough of a large population of mosquito wrigglers. A gut full of water from our game coupled with a belly full of wallaby carcass Tia emptied her stomach of its contents, not a pretty sight ☺….

Thursday 10 March 2005
Finding the runt of the litter still intact on the ground watering this morning, I will get to sample the one and only remaining peach ☺!!!!
Making full use of a return to summer, the elements got my weak wristed hand washing dry in the scorching conditions on offer….
Since completing the contents of envelope one I've allowed myself to get a little sidetracked from advancing dreams, other than maintaining the regular daily entry, envelope two still remains unopened….

Friday 11 March 2005
Tia gave me the paw tap on the shoulder until I could ignore her no longer and raised my sleeping body from bed. Wandering in dim moonlight in night time darkness a possum sprang from a tree, and with the sound of approaching feet a couple of grazing wallabies also scattered with the intrusion…. I wouldn't live anywhere else ☺….
Checking on the progress of Mum and Dad's new car buying venture, everything fell into place nicely Tuesday. The Lancer now takes pride of place in their driveway. They can't speak highly enough and with great pride about their new toy with the lot. Mum and Dad have already lined up a tradesperson to extend the carport to accommodate both cars ☺….

Completing all diversions and cornered I couldn't postpone the moment any longer, I ripped open envelope two emptying it of contents. Tightly stacking the wad of paper onto the makeshift cardboard clipboard, pencil sharpened and eraser on standby, I was ready to make a start….

In her generous caring sharing nature, Tia dragged a putrid wallaby carcass past the bungalow attracting every fly and European wasp within a kilometre radius. Unable to concentrate with the stench I emptied a few buckets of water around to settle aromas most importantly slowing winged traffic inside, the place was really humming ☺ !!!!

Having a break away from the return to editing, I sampled the runt of the litter eating the one and only piece of fruit from Peaches, it was of the high standard I'm getting accustomed to producing at Rainbow Falls ☺ ….

Noticing the valleys slowly fill with smoke obscuring mountain ranges, a sad complacency, thought went directly to logging operations not the worrying possibility of bushfire????

Saturday 12 March 2005

Making a flying visit back to the district for the unpleasant occasion of attending the funeral of a friend's 15-year-old daughter, and now ready to leave, I met Loui in town passing through to the airport. A trait of Loui's, always running to a tight schedule, she was able to stop long enough for a ciggy and a quick blurt before leaving, however, it was nice to have physically crossed paths before she resumed her new life ☺ ….

Meeting up with Maggie and Brian at the 'Save South Sister Rally' I was extended an invitation to pop in next time I'm in town, doing just that when Loui parted company driving off into the distance. Favourite times are had over a good brew of leaf tea, basking in sunshine and sharing the company of friends. Staying with the friends theme, stopping for drinking water I caught both Lesley and Ross in, changing tack for a brew of coffee instead ☺ ….

The mercury rose with the days passing, having a return to summer shoes, socks and jeans came off as soon as I walked in the door, giving legs one of their rare outings. A couple more pages made it into the edited pile, my boots felt a lick with nugget, and visibly ripe walnuts were picked before light faded….

Sunday 13 March 2005

In a relaxed frame of mind I idled over applying water in all the right spots, then gloved-up, settled on the step of the bungalow taking the outer skins off the waiting half bucket of walnuts. Still content outdoors and with my little mate always on the ready, Tia followed me into the vegie patch where a good kilo of spuds was added to the food booty ☺ …. yumo…..

A hovering blanket of cloud lifted around lunchtime uncovering a stinging scorpion's tail. Retreating indoors with fan on, window covered, and shoes and socks off, made use of the indoor environment adding to the growing pile of paper having had an eye and pencil waved over it….

The beauty of the changeable climate here is it cools down as quickly as it heats up, the hot sun clung to the very end, setting and sinking, so did the mercury, enabling a comfortable sleep…. zzzz….

Emptying my head jotting thoughts down during the day I ran another pen dry of ink, a phenomenon I'm unaccustomed to. Pens used to come with a lifetime guarantee, guaranteed to be lost or taken long before running out of ink ☺ !!!!

Monday 14 March 2005
Tia woke me for some light relief in the wee tiny hours, while up and roaming I checked the walnut tree, a possum was happily munching and stood its ground when verbally asked to move on. Disliking arrogance, I got the shovel persuader humbling its attitude with a smack on the bum!!!!
Reluctant to dive straight into editing, I spent brain charging time in the haven sweeping up the remaining hay mess Ross left, the bottom level of the shed has seen many sunsets without attention. When I did pick up the pencil and eraser many hours slipped by putting in a big effort....
I've grown tired of neighbour irresponsible behaviour training and encouraging their kids to use the road out front as a raceway and churning it up doing alley rings. Without ever having much luck at communicating with them over courtesy and legal issues, I phoned the police trying to have their behaviour curbed sooner than later. Their continual pushing of the envelope without respect for anyone besides their own immediate need wears thin, without fear, I refuse to accept disrespect or be intimidated by fools!!!!

Tuesday 15 March 2005
The close squawk of a currawong 7a.m.-ish sparked a need to investigate getting up there wasn't one to be sighted. Staying up, I had a play around in the garden, which now includes walnut collecting....
A bit shy on food, I lost what remained of the morning getting ready for a trip over the mountain. Town has become quite a social event; rarely there isn't a familiar face to chat to. Excited about the prospect of buying beer and breaking the drought, following a long weekend the pub didn't have my first or second preference until tomorrow's delivery, choosing to leave the tap turned off I walked out empty handed....
Ready to stay outside in fresh air, I did follow up maintenance to shadecloth that was attached across the southern face of the cottage to stop rain from entering a couple of windows. Beginning to dismantle, I got a fist full of clouts and ladder re-linking the bridge below roofline from the cottage across to the bungalow. The theory behind the shadecloth is to channel water away from the side of both buildings ☺ ....
While cooking dinner I watched, for a third occasion, Tia knock a walnut off out of the bucket of nuts, using them as a ball she tossed it at me to kick. All three occasions the first kick split the outer casing revealing the nut, with the same predictability, Tia took the nut onto the carpet cracked it open and ate the flesh, having developed a taste for walnuts ☺ ....

Wednesday 16 March 2005
With a batch of petrol mixed on the ready, and mower prepared for turning the fuel tap on and tugging on the pull-start, decided first to duck into town and grab a box of beer with the intent of mowing on return. Leaving home 11:30a.m.-ish just for a pub dash I returned home some four hours later still beerless ☺ !!!!

One of those rare occasions the pub delivery didn't arrive on time, as fate has it, I then went to Pam and Terry's for a cuppa. During the course of chat over brewed coffee we got onto the topic of heaters, having two just being weathered at the side of the house they offered one for the cottage, a double bonus, Pam and Terry are willing to bring it up to Rainbow Falls. A wood heater will make a huge difference to our quality of life, a big step forward ☺ ....
Ready to point Destiny's nose back onto dirt roads the pub still hadn't taken delivery of stock, beer o'clock remains on hold....
Stopping at the South Sister campsite Lesley invited me to join her over a hot brew, before parting company I teed up with Ross to try the pub for me tomorrow on his way home from work, my luck can only get better ☺ ????
Immersed in so much socialising I wasn't enthused with the idea of mowing, instead filled the last daylight hours watering, taking the outer skin off a good collection of walnuts to dry the nut, and rounded off a pleasant dose of spontaneity playing ball with Tia ☺ ....

Thursday 17 March 2005
Yesterdays mail contained a friendly letter from Ali confirming the date she and Hazel are planning to visit, included with the letter was a self-addressed envelope requesting directions to Rainbow Falls. Ali wrote she wasn't able to find our little hamlet in the bush on any of her maps.... Odd ☺ .... Following the usual therapy time in the garden I sat and drew a mud map, with no panic to get it posted, Ali and Hazel aren't visiting until April 19....
The little bits 'n' pieces done, accompanied by the usual level of procrastination, I set yesterdays plan into motion wheeling the mower from the shed and putting it to use, making it easier to find fallen walnuts....
I dared to fantasise that Ross would drive through the gate with beer just as the mower was turned off I couldn't have been further away from reality. The delivery truck did eventually arrive yesterday but without one box of Tooheys Old onboard, lose some, lose some!!!! A dry St Patrick's Day heaven forbid....

Friday 18 March 2005
Some little hour of the morning I heard Tia being sick, heaving in her own bed she then hopped into mine, she loves me ☺ ....
Stopping midway over the mountain I retrieved the folding currency from Ross, giving up on beer blew the money on food instead? Stepping in next door from the supermarket, and planning ahead, I made the purchase of a birthday card for Dad and posted the mud map off to Ali. After taking possession of the latest processed photos enhancing Rainbow Falls written history, then meandered the dirt road to home....
Editing took a back seat to a mind preoccupied with a heater arriving, migrating to the cottage I rearranged in readiness. Boxes of possessions waiting to be unpacked that were stacked near the flue now neatly fill idle space behind the door, opening the room. Adding to the décor, I split a couple of wheelbarrow loads of wood half filling the huge woodbox, the lingering aroma of freshly cut timber filled the cottage with a very earthy, homely scent.... Swinging the splitter, an action my body isn't used to, sorted out some long rested muscles.... Ohhhh....
A very elated Ross phoned early evening with the news the judicial system has given S.O.S (Save our Sisters) a confirmed court date recognising there is a case to be heard, community

losses far outweigh monetary gain. This ruling in turn means logging should be put on hold until there's been a fair hearing, injecting an overdue dose of hope back into a long energy zapping trail of closed doors, minds, and rejection....

Saturday 19 March 2005
The amount of intact walnuts to collect has lessened considerably only picking up a handful this morning, possums will soon have to find something else to supplement their diet!!!!
Greeting a beautiful morning in paradise and driven by domestic duties spurred on by yesterdays effort in the cottage, gave the sink and bath a clean, replenished the water supply, resealed a couple of missing window panes and swept the floor....
Pam and Terry drove through the gate shortly after lunch with the heater in tow, a little instruction and grunting and groaning, in short time it was in position to begin a new life at Rainbow Falls. Our guests stayed long enough to share a chat over a brew before leaving us to enjoy the thoughtful, caring gesture of our new addition. The difference today's generous gift made to mine and Tia's lives is enormous, a huge turning-point forward in quality long ago stolen ☺ ....
With every trip into the cottage the dawning realisation of having a free-standing wood heater put a beaming smile on my face. Adding to the ambience, I polished the glass and set a fire ready for when the temperature gets cool enough to spark the heater up for its maiden voyage ☺ ....

Sunday 20 March 2005
All the excitement of installing the heater must have worn me out, surprised at sleeping through to 10a.m., it's something I haven't done or Tia hasn't let me do in a long time. When finally poking my head outside it was a better day for washing than sparking up the latest addition to Rainbow Falls, that's just what happened....
Still taken by the moment, added to the lived in homely feel in the cottage with a wheelbarrow load of light limb wood from behind the cattle yards, increasing an already healthy looking woodbox....
No sooner were remaining clothes taken from the line to finish drying inside and a shower, actually wetting the ground surface, drifted through simply raising humidity, it was soon gone to again expose the suns intense UV....

Monday 21 March 2005
Rousing to the magical sound of rain on a tin roof, showers persisting on and off produced a welcome 7mm by 6p.m. and showed no sign of giving in ☺ ....
Up with the sparrows, rain put me and Tia one step ahead with the morning routine, finding myself in front of the computer updating the latest journal entries by a tidy 8:30am, not wasting a precious gained minute....
A quick phone around took me away from home to the South Sister campsite, ABC television was looking for crowd reaction footage at 12:15pm when forestry were to announce their logging plans at the Sister. ABC got their crowd shot but the decision wasn't handed down until after 2p.m.. A pleasing result, planned logging operations are to cease pending the outcome of a full hearing, buying time until June....

Back inside home soil with a head too busy for editing, instead, utilised the beaut conditions of cool with intermittent showers to give the heater a test run. It was a bit exciting to see the heater throwing off flames for the first time and filling the cottage with warmth, needing to share the moment I phoned the Jones', after all they allowed it to happen. Continually value adding to life at Rainbow Falls I made full use of the heater top by successfully cooking pasta, heating dinner and boiling water for a brew ☺ ….

Tuesday 22 March 2005
Keeping the rainfall chart current I was able to add another 6mm to the tally before it disappeared. Its funny how priorities change, rain has freed up the watering regime instead time saved is put into collecting wood, getting another wheelbarrow load from behind the cattle yards ☺ ….
Making no secret of it Tia has taken a liking to walnuts, helping herself from the bucket she leaves little Tia nests of broken shell strategically placed over the floor. Sweeping discarded shells got me motivated in and around the cottage, again topping up the woodbox, setting the fire, collecting water then I sat on the step cleaning the latest accumulation of walnuts….
With plans of working with 'Inside my Skin' in the warmer, larger space of the cottage, I followed up on thoughts. Leaving the bungalow with a spacious look I moved the computer and desk into the cottage. Preparing a nest to settle in for some serious future literary work, by the time I'd finished lugging furniture the day was beaten and so was I….

Wednesday 23 March 2005
It's been a long summer seemingly locked away and limited indoors. Unprepared to impose self-discipline staring at the screen, I gave in to the whim and perfect autumn temperatures to be lured to the expansive great outdoors….
Walnuts are all but finished, not one nut was on the ground this morning and only a sprinkling are left hanging in the tree, obviously areas possums can't reach!!!!
Disappearing behind the cattle yards collected another wheelbarrow load of limb wood. Taking into account what is dropped by trees, plus the strewn mess at the timber dump site, there'll be plenty to keep us warm this winter, it's just a matter of getting it down to size….
In an outdoorsy mood I stayed out in it giving the lawnmower a run, pushing it around the housing and dam areas tidying before bulbs start shooting. Having walnuts drying in a pan on a fencepost the first thing I did was to bowl them over pushing the mower past!!!! Oops….
Feeling pretty pleased with the revealing outcome I went crazy mowing, sore feet and feeling buggered confirmed knock off ☺ ….

Thursday 24 March 2005
Pulling up a bit ordinary last night nausea robbed me of an appetite, feeling second-hand put myself to bed by 8p.m.. Taking in plenty of fluids I put the sick feeling down to pushing myself too hard, or possibly what was breathed in from the mower in fumes, or maybe what was spat out from the blades from a variety of dry poo to grasses????
Whatever bothered me I managed to sleep off the only lingering affect being low energy. With arrangements to meet Rita at leisure at her studio, I kept pace with my body taking my sweet time getting ready. The purpose of the trip was to pick up a character reference for sending off

to the Anti-Discrimination Commission. As fate had it, Rita at that point, hadn't prepared the reference, after giving recent correspondence thought, if what's been supplied to date isn't enough adding to it will achieve little more except slowing closure. Happy instead to enjoy Rita's company over a cuppa and friendship☺....

Rolling up unannounced, I arrived home to find Terry hard at work with his chainsaw, already having made a solid start cutting into two large logs lying at the top of the hill. Grabbing my splitter I joined in on the action furthering the breakdown process. For Terry's effort, as previously agreed upon, he was happy to trade labour for a load of wood, a great system where everyone wins☺....

Friday 25 March 2005
Simply physical and at the same time relaxing, with hands firmly gripped around the handles I took the wheelbarrow on an endurance run lugging many loads of firewood from the top boundary to the shed. Fortunately pushing the barrow uphill empty, we'll be right for a wet week or two now☺....

Letting my heart rate and energy cross back to moderate, settled my bum next to the phone and partook in low impact light duties giving my jaws exercise getting current with the hub of the family, Mum and Dad. Promptly ahead of time, Dad had received his envelope of birthday goodies, as I phoned he was playing the CD in the new car proudly cleaning his way through both the Lancer and Kingswood☺....

Incorporating domestic duties, a not so warm day in paradise dropped the mercury even further with the setting of the sun, with fading light we headed into the cottage and sparked up the heater for a warm evening in☺....

Pondering the thought of bed, Tia returned reeking from some variety of poo and fur supporting a wet gel look. Impossible to share any space other than the great outdoors while that aroma existed, sitting by the fire thinking for a solution I resorted to grabbing a bucket, gloving-up, and together we adjourned to the cattle trough.... Phew.... Throwing an extra log on the fire so Tia could dry warm, reciprocated the utmost caring consideration shown☺!!!!

Saturday 26 March 2005
Striking a blow on the new day presented it didn't take long for Tia to return wearing that same rotten odour washed off the night before! Ready to track the source rather than fix the problem I followed Tia who proudly displayed her latest trick. Squeezing her way through the dam access gate Tia's been rolling in decomposing snake, it'd come back to haunt me!!!!

Happier to have Tia's odour outside, we made the first job emptying the cattle trough ridding it of its collection of treasure aiming every drop directly at, and saturating Tia. Still inadequate to eliminate the foul scent, 'Plan B' came into play, after securely Tia proofing access to the dam I then gave her a gloved-up scrub!!!!

Going crazy in the cottage I vacuumed it from top to bottom, reset the fire and refreshed the water supply. Without neglecting the bungalow, bedding was aired and sponged over, pretty much retracing Tia's steps and odour of the past twenty-four hours☺....

Sunday 27 March 2005
Enduring a bloody hot one to signify an end to daylight saving, the elements posed a great opportunity to get limp wristed washing drip-drying. Confused as to which way to turn the clock was put straight phoning to wish Mum and Dad a happy Easter ☺....
Heat changed mowing plans, instead, like a magnet, headed for respite under the cottage roof doing a spot more rearranging and cleaning, continually upgrading the comfort and homely feel inside....
Leading on from waning interest in rearranging and cleaning, I sparked up the computer advancing with the keyboard finger dance in the expansive space the cottage provided....
Gradually picking up, late afternoon wind blew the bloody hot UV beams from reach, taking a change in direction swinging south, low cloud clung to the range unable to forge the meagre distance forward to reach home soil, but gratefully plummeted the temperature. Without producing a drop of moisture, wind dropped, cloud dissipated and the front passed without another whimper????

Monday 28 March 2005
Waking a bit pre-menstrual and grumpy and needing to distract me from myself, I worked the mower hard in and around the cattle yards seriously getting into it. After a refuel the mower refused to fire up, running out of energy with the pull-start I conceded defeat. Enduring a trying time of whatever I touched if there was a harder way to do it I certainly didn't find it, is very testing on fragile patience!!!!
Water at the cattle trough has again stopped flowing, managing enough from it for a bath to wash the days sweat from my body and shit off my liver. Until measurable rain its back to the tap at the irrigation line by the driveway for water....
Tubbed up, I had a solid session with the milo tin and a spoon. Following my sugar hit I was left with a smile and feeling soooo much better ☺....
The hot autumn climate deteriorated with the passing of the day so we enjoyed another comfortable night indoors by the heater. The heater is very effective at warming the entire cottage. Still comprehending this warming luxury being available, and spending less time in the bungalow, has increased the amount of carting of bits between buildings....

Tuesday 29 March 2005
After reading the notice in a local Mildura newspaper, Mum and Dad phoned to let me know an obituary had been placed for a dear friend A.B. Always on the ready to share a yarn over a smoke or beer, my friendship with Arthur bloomed as a larrikin apprentice back to 1986 when I started work with the Department of Agriculture. A true gentleman at rest....
Taking rice from the fridge to complement Tia's breakfast I gave the container a shake to loosen grains, the loose lid spread rice like hundreds & thousands through the bungalow, my 'oh no' didn't last long, the Tia vacuum cleaner was promptly on the job scooping them up ☺.... Entrée....
Tidying up loose ends on the wood cutting agreement, I offered Ross a stack to tow a load through the mountain destined for Pam and Terry. Timber loaded and ready for its distribution I followed Ross into town to unload, there we settled in for an appreciative chat over a cuppa once the trailer was emptied....

Striking gold at the pub managed to score a box of my preferred, two days shy of four weeks and beer o'clock is back on the menu. Promising myself if our local didn't have Tooheys Old I was going to keep driving north until finding a pub that did, lucky for me ☺ ....
Returning home, and with Ross' load stacked in the trailer and driving out the gate, I went about winding life down before declaring beer o'clock, taking the first in a while for a walk to the top boundary simply to enjoy the view and reflect ☺ ....

Wednesday 30 March 2005
Wednesday being a religious golf day, I struck early ringing Dad to wish him many happy returns celebrating his 67th ☺ .... Only managing to keep a roof over our head, food on the table and wolves from the door, wishing to be with Dad on his birthday is out of the question at present, living on a poverty budget is limiting on wandering far from home....
After taking the wheelbarrow for a walk behind the cattle yards for light limb wood, I then spoilt myself rotten firing up the vacuum cleaner moving from the bungalow to the cottage. Too much outside stuff had made its way in....
Time disappeared without having anything achieved to brag about, beer o'clock slipped around, dedicating my first to Dad's birthday. Taking it slowly, just relaxing by the top boundary simply savouring the spectacular view, long shadows created from the sinking sun traced contours of the mountain ranges enhancing the exceptionally beautiful scenery ☺ ....

Thursday 31 March 2005
Following up with mutual friends, I phoned Mary and Joan to hear how A.B's funeral went yesterday. Around fifty people attended a simple graveside service and the Carlton Football Club theme song was played as his casket was lowered, A.B. would have been content with that.... Wishing only I could have been there to farewell a true friend....
A bloody warm one in the Garden of Eden encouraged a return of my bum to the seat to resume editing. Making myself comfortable in the cottage with the company of my little mate she let her presence be known every now and again, clearing my sinus with a 'silent but deadly' release of gas ☺ .... Phew!!!!
Delivering Pam and Terry's load of wood yesterday I was sent home with a rain cover for the flue, putting an end to a small but meaningful piece of cottage history. The original rain gauge no longer exists in any form, in its infancy the baking tray below the dangling connected pieces of flue inside the cottage was a 'close to the mark' measure of rainfall. In preference, I'm happy to see waterproofing of the cottage take positive steps forward ☺ ....

Friday 1 April 2005
A period arrived to remind me my body does have a sense of humour and April Fools Day does exist!!!!
Watering done, wood restocked, breakfast had, dishes washed, boots nuggeted and bath complete, I took a brief trip between the Sisters to get those few things we're out of to remain a comfortable hermit at home for the weekend ☺ ....
Turning on a warm one, Mother Nature forced the shoes and socks from my feet to invest more time into 'Inside my Skin', advancing forward and shaping it into existence....

Ahhhh beer o'clock, a time for walkabout to observe, plan and listen, otherwise known as 'smell the roses', entertained tonight by a handful of parrots excitedly vocal drinking at the cattle trough ☺....

Saturday 2 April 2005
Some little creature making a commotion tried to gain entry into the bungalow through the cardboard replacement window during some early hour, bringing all inhabitants to life to investigate and put a stop to the noise making way for more sleep zzzz....
Escaping nature's intense hot elements, choosing to bypass on the physically altering, instead got absorbed in literary change and a few more hardcopy pages made it into the done stack. Coming to an end of another writing pad, I converted the flimsy backing piece of cardboard into a clipboard, catering for edited loose pages....
Again without the need for any form of heating, we spent the evening in the bungalow saving on hard earnt and hard to come by fossil fuels....

Sunday 3 April 2005
Strong gusts pushing in a sprinkling of rain stirred me from sleep 6a.m.-ish, surfacing after lying and listening, opened the door onto a rainbow. Proving the theory of rainbows representing rain clearing wrong, on cue, wandering in for breakfast a steady shower set in, arriving from the west isn't a common direction to receive long lasting fronts....
Following regular news broadcasts, I tuned into ABC Radio National to hear the inevitable death of the Pope occurred 6a.m. Australian time this morning, a huge world event, nine days of mourning has begun in the devout Catholic world....
Procrastinating through any possible distraction before finally cornering myself in the cottage to face the pencil and eraser, a couple of pages in, a good downpour highlighted leaking weak spots in the cottage roof. Drying the work environment I lit the heater....
A margin short on length, the flue isn't drawing well, any wind forces air to flow back down the flue trying as hard to blow the fire out as I am trying to start it. Filling the room with smoke until heat has been generated, the fan has found another purpose it's useful for blowing air directly into the heater's vent to reverse the airflow and clear smoke. Until outgoing heat energy is greater than incoming wind we cop smoke that can turn the enjoyment of making a fire and creating a warm environment into hard work....

Monday 4 April 2005
Waking a little frustrated with my world, I had a day out of life to wallow in the overwhelming frustration at being surrounded by broken or breaking down things in need of repair. Things either waiting on time, or to absorb any spare money in the budget to make it happen....
Grateful as I am for a heater the flue being too short renders it unusable in wind, the amount of smoke I was battling with yesterday was very trying, adding to the feeling of helpless at the inability at maintaining my own life. If the tractors radiator was repaired I could use it, then I'd have to find the money for petrol, Tia's out of heart and gut worm tablets, she wouldn't mind, both mowers are in need of repair, Destiny's due for a service, and a haircut can also wait another fortnight!!!!

I'm so in need of a positive sign of encouragement, money has no value of importance in my life but poverty can be very trying. If I have to survive within the realms of poverty paradise isn't a bad place to do it…. Can't have it all????
When a girl's looking for a change of scenery to soothe the brain, the vegie patch is a relaxing place to retreat. The milo tin and spoon got another workout I'll be content when hormones settle to reclaim clear thinking and energy….

Tuesday 5 April 2005
Wanting the use of shed space to fix his car, swapping abodes with Ross, I bartered shed space for the use of his washing machine. Striking a deal, Ross pulled in 9:30a.m.-ish to make a start, with Destiny packed, we took off to his place to get a load of washing started. Leaving the machine to go through its cycles we ducked into town for bread and milk, checked the post, and took up the offer of grabbing a piece of flue from Ross' former workshop….
Welcome friendly mail waited from Mum and Dad, any word they put to paper is a pleasure to read. A second unwelcome letter was handed on to police, a pyramid money making scheme 'chain-letter' bullshit, that crap irks me!!!!
Unpacking the booty from Destiny I became aware of my wallets absence, the pub was the last point I remember using it, retracing steps it hadn't shown up anywhere. Making an executive decision cancelled the plastic card attached to my savings account, the only bit of value inside, ironically I'd spent the last note the wallet contained at the pub☺….
A little reluctant to start, Destiny's amp gauge gave me the warning sign something electrical wasn't working to its full potential, another thing to postpone until later because it currently is still working. Today had set me enough challenges already!!!!
Giving up on trying to find my wallet I had a go at extending the flue to the heater, with a mind not on the job I failed in the attempt, walking away to a no fail pastime declared beer o'clock!!!! Lately I feel like I'm trying to swim to the surface through honey to stay afloat????

Wednesday 6 April 2005
My brain didn't give in overnight, searching to understand how to mantle and dismantle the flue to add the extension, woke prepared to have another go at it. After feeling beaten there's only one direction to head that's forward….
Preferably a job for two people, I climbed the ladder onto the roof more times than I cared to wrestling with pieces of flue. Dismantling the entire set-up, the flue extension was added inside the cottage without too much effort and I had it entirely reassembled in time for morning tea. Staying with heater requirements, a wheelbarrow load of limb wood was snapped and the woodbox filled with renewed enthusiasm, the heater was also emptied of spent fires and reloaded ready for a fresh one….
While the wheelbarrow was running hot I pushed it up hill to push shit down hill, collecting a couple of loads of dry moo poo by the water tank. The cow pads were emptied in the vegie patch for attention at a later date….
Impeccable timing, a southerly change blew in mid afternoon supplying ideal conditions to test the heater extension effectiveness. Brazenly tossing a match into the heaters face amid the windy southerly, it started to smoke, feeling let-down I shut the vent in an attempt to starve it of oxygen, defying my instruction the small flame persisted, igniting, it began to draw and

burn clean.... Gotta have a win sometime ☺.... An extra metre of flue makes a bucket load of difference....

Thursday 7 April 2005
Preparing breakfast I was amused to see five native hens with their busy little legs run past the bungalow window, a quiet day is never mundane ☺ ....
Supplementing the overnight 4mm with another 2mm, Mother Nature gave me enough time to warm-up on the splitter to replenish the cottage woodbox for a warm dry one inside. Direct sun never made an appearance at all, holding the mercury back: editing was the winner today, happy to be warm and cosy indoors with my best friend ☺ ....
Drawing like Leonardo Da Vinci, the heater took off like a champion, requiring a pot on top to catch a drip travelling inside along the flue with each shower it's at least a starting point for locating the leak....

Friday 8 April 2005
A moisture drop of 14mm found the gauge while we slept a slow soaking delivery is more useful than a fast rush. Remaining consistently steady all day raindrops just kept making their way into the plastic tube. Doing a dash outdoors before sunset the gauge had measured, to that point, 32 welcome millimetres....
Now cooler weather is moving in the heater has come into its own, being naked bathing has risen to a new dimension of comfort, even boiling bath water on top is maximising energy use ☺ ....
Posting the payslip by its use-by-date determined a mountain run, driving between the Sisters friendly mail waited on the other side in town. Mum and Dad had thoughtfully taken the time to send relevant newspaper pieces containing A.B's death notice and tributes, included in the package was a brief note in Mum's handwriting. Incorporated amongst the handful of mail pulled from the box was another from the Anti-Discrimination Commission, containing brother-in-law Bruce's response to my sexual discrimination and harassment issues. With still no mention of his blow-up-doll, he confirmed most allegations, painting a picture of me as being an active participant????
Coming back up the mountain and stopping for drinking water, I found Ross home and we solved the problems of the world over a cuppa....
Sun didn't emerge out from under cloud at all and showers continued increasing only in intensity, content by the heater listening to and catching most of the chorus of musical drips leaking through the ceiling. Warm, mostly dry, and cosy, co-editor and I spent the afternoon in the cottage....

Saturday 9 April 2005
An exhilarating condition I relish the energy of, but keeping us from peaceful slumber beyond an hour, a thunderstorm grabbed Ms Tia's cage and gave it a rattle!!!! Directly above at one point, loud breaking cracks of thunder gave the bungalow foundations a shake along with Tia's nerves. Plenty of pacifying was required....

Waiting in the gauge come morning was another 8mm to finalise the fronts passing. Like chalk and cheese, today layers were being stripping off the past couple we were hugging the heater????

Pressure put on the cottage woodbox recently inevitably carved a path to replenish diminishing stocks, having a play with the splitter first before taking the wheelbarrow for a walk behind the cattle yards....

Balancing an encompassing variety, a token couple of pages also made the complete stack, little by little ☺ ....

Sunday 10 April 2005

Contemplating getting up: the phone burst into life helping with that decision. The call was from a fellow by the name of Mark, inquiring about agisting cows. Unable to help, I'm not interested in livestock they create extra work and are harsh on their surroundings....

Putting my back into it for a couple of hours being a good little squirrel, broke down poor quality timber carted up to dry from the paddock milling site eons ago. Sweating it out building on the 'ready to grab' supply, we're well stocked for a wet week....

No wriggling snake action has been sighted in a few weeks, unwise to get complacent when a late mercury blast was enough to force the shoes and socks from my feet. Retreating out of the weather, I filled my right fist with a pencil and stared down at another of those endless pieces of paper denoting a time passed here at Rainbow Falls ☺ ....

Putting back what was earlier driven from my body, late afternoon the elements did a complete 360°, straight away encouraged shoes back on. Over beer o'clock and kicking the ball for Tia a short-lived front approached from the west, briefly sending us running for shelter in the cottage. Inside leaning on the westerly window ledge I watched cows, once dotting neighbouring paddocks, migrate quickly to lower ground, did they know something more???? Three eagles sighted gliding overhead followed the passing front, drawing an appreciative audience back outside to enjoy their aerial confidence and elegance....

Monday 11 April 2005

Doing a little neglected friendship maintenance I dialled Miriam's number catching the girl for her birthday. Bursting with progressive news to share, I guessed pregnant and being way off track, she resigned from the Department of Agriculture and is leaving Friday to follow dreams. Returning to college, Miriam is moving to Adelaide to do a three-year film makers course specialising in environmental films.... A huge time ahead ☺ !!!!

Taking advantage of the beautiful drying day and good water quality I spoilt myself rotten updating laundry. Comfy in sun behind glass editing, Ross rolled up. Taking a look at Destiny a quick analysis confirmed her battery is on the way out, while under the microscope I spotted a nail firmly planted in the tyre with the slow leak. All part of getting old and wear and tear, but most importantly she still goes in a forward direction ☺ .... Fergus also received some attention having the radiator removed for a dose of overdue T.L.C....

Tuesday 12 April 2005

A better than expected breakfast bonus, running out of peanut butter Tia got to clean the jar, giving it her full attention until even the scent was gone ☺ ....

Cutting loose, I was like a woman possessed doing domestic duties like they were a pleasure, targeting both the cottage and bungalow. Coming to my senses stabilising the desire for mundane housework, and with no obvious distractions left, I retreated to the bungalow enjoying another perfect autumn day with pencil poised and eraser on the ready. Finding pleasure in revisiting fond earlier memories that would now need a prompt to ignite or be long forgotten, the antics of Tia and local wildlife have been a regular source of amusement☺!!!! About to head out bushwalking South Sister Range alone Ross phoned with his details, he was on a mission to attempt to locate an eagles nest in an area a pair have been regularly sighted. Responding to Ross' cooee from home, motionless air carried our voices clearly. A phone call confirmed a very exhausted fellow made no eagles nest discovery but reported on plenty of landscape features, from tracks, streams, rocky outcrops, to plenty of thick undergrowth making for hard walking....

Wednesday 13 April 2005
In the hope a new plastic card was waiting in my Post Office box disappointment again waited after a turn of the key. Unable to access cash and penniless with a tyre needing attention I drew on my good faith. Explaining circumstances, Grant generously allowed me an IOU and repaired Destiny's tyre, Ross loaned money for food and with limited funds the beer ration was postponed stocking up with only the absolutely necessary. Buying a stamp for Sheila's birthday card, and unbeknown to me, registered mail containing one plastic card was waiting inside the Post Office. Excited by the prospect, with the new pin number memorised I went to the hole in the wall inside the supermarket without success! Making a phone call from home, the card is now linked to my account and should deliver a happier outcome accessing cash next ATM visit....
Oddly, on two separate occasions in town was asked if I was returning to radio, it's been a long time between drinks I thought my time on-air was long forgotten????
Roaming the yard late afternoon, twice sun broke through tight cloud targeting the loose rays directly at and bathing only Rainbow Falls in sunshine. It struck me as pretty special being under the spotlight of nature ☺....

Thursday 14 April 2005
Already having supplied a couple of millimetres before leaving the comfort of a warm bed, the distracting chorus of leaks constantly dripping from the roof to the waiting bucket or pot below were robbing the cottage and heater of enjoyment. Between showers, and on a mission, I set out to find and repair where possible, the causes. Water getting in through a poorly sealed window was soon rectified, by tacking on a sturdy plastic sheet covering it from the outside. Up on the roof my attention turned to the obvious flue, the problem area is isolated to the seal surrounding the flue, sadly I could offer the perished rubber no quick fix....
Changing tack, a south-westerly change came in and took the warm edge going indoors without hesitation I put a match to the set fire. Procrastinating by the heater until it was established I then turned attention to the waiting stack of paper on the makeshift cardboard clipboard ☺....

Friday 15 April 2005
Feeling a bit second-hand and not ready to explode into action I basked in the warmth on offer inside the shed entrance over a contemplative cuppa….
Restocking the woodbox after a pretty taxing time, I then focussed on a trip between North and South Sisters, pleasantly incorporating into preparations a call to Sheila wishing her many happy returns ☺ ….
Ready to break free of debt the plastic card again failed. Chance had me meet Pam out front of the supermarket, upon invitation I followed her offer home to use the phone and sort out why? Assured by the bank they had finally done their job right linking the plastic card to my account, was treated to a cuppa before re-entering the commercial world….
Evelyn asked me earlier in the week about Melbourne public transport, buying bread I left behind a street directory containing answers to all her questions. Debts and bill catered for beer o'clock too was returned to the menu ☺ …. Yahoo!!!!
Happy to be home and have Tia released to a larger space than Destiny, the aroma she left behind in the car was raw, bloody close to a poo or needing one, she cleared my sinus anyway!!!!
By the time the day was sorted it was beaten????

Saturday 16 April 2005
Morning walkabout, bum scratch and look around prior to breakfast, I noticed winter bulbs emerging out front of the burnt out house, being northerly facing and with oceanic influences they're always ahead of the rest….
A perfectly ideal temperature to be exposed in outdoors was a magnet. Warming bones I brought down to size a healthy buzzie groundcover established on the face of the dam….
With afternoon sun saturating the bungalow and the body solar panels absorbing maximum warmth, treated myself to vacuuming and dishes????
Beer o'clock came around ever so quickly, over a relaxing coolly out of the fading temperature I watched an outstanding sunset from the comfort of the cottage. Two long slivers of horizontal cloud dividing the setting sun sent a blazing bright orange to filter through trees lining the gorge, peaking in intensity before dimming to soft pastels with its sinking behind the mountain range….
Wood supply replete, the cottage was the place to be after dark, maximising fossil fuel I cooked dinner on the heater top leaving the stove and electricity idle. Concentrating on putting wood into the fire left my right forearm with a memento of the experience, one burn heals there's another to replace it….

Sunday 17 April 2005
Quietly waking and tuning in, the past couple of morning's blackbirds with their sweet call have been making a racket in and around cottage guttering. With Tia's assistance, we flattened a 2-litre plastic milk container, standing tall on the ladder I slid it into the gutter denying access to corner flashing. Kicking blackbirds out before getting too settled, once they've had young I won't have the heart to remove them….

Buried in heavy moisture producing cloud first up, and not seeing the sun at all, appearing as though we were going to be limited indoors, for the lengthy work involved the meagre offering was lucky to produce 2mm....

Falling behind in family maintenance walked my finger over the keypad and settled into a chat that took as long as it needed to with Mum and Dad. With many years wood collecting experience Mum and I had a great conversation about the properties of timber, predominantly the major differences between dry and green wood, from weight to burning ability ☺....

Beer o'clock with us once again, and rain being no threat, my best mate and I went walkabout reaping havoc with buzzies....

Monday 18 April 2005

Through experience it seems the majority of thunderstorms pass at the most inconvenient of times, particularly when sleep is the desired option. Sounding the stress meter 12:30a.m.-ish Tia didn't turn it off until shortly after 3a.m., her reaction kept pace with the storms intensity, foundations were rocked with cracking rumbles on a couple of occasions. With as much purpose as the unsettled noise, showers burst down at the same intensity lashing a fast 10mm through the storms duration....

Following a bastard broken sleep I wasn't in a hurry to dive into the day. Getting life's routine bits complete, I then made an effort to find the cottage floor vacuuming out what Tia and I have spent many an hour trudging in....

Sipping on coolies, with my little mates company, I hemmed housing collecting buzzie seed balls and stunting the groundcover host plant. By the time a couple of beers had been consumed I could close my eyes and still see buzzies ☺!!!!

Tuesday 19 April 2005

Awaiting the arrival of Al and Hazel I busied myself on the shovel tidying a thistle healthy garden bed on the western side of the cottage, beginning to warm up, and not wanting to lose that just bathed feeling, gave it away....

Al and Hazel tread very lightly on the earth taking no energy to be around or have around. Relaxing over a brew I was bestowed with gifts being the lucky receiver of Al's home-made jam, chutney, relish and hand towels, the stash also included apples and biscuits, it was like Christmas ☺....

After seeing photos of the large strawberries grown at Rainbow Falls, and happy to share knowledge, I passed on Lukey's very successful liquid fertiliser recipe to an attentive audience. Taking a tour of the grounds I emptied my head of known details about the upper half of the property from the ocean view to the falls. Holidaying the north-east coast, it was pleasing to hear both Al and Hazel concede their visit to Rainbow Falls as being the highlight of their trip, a very enjoyable afternoon for all inclusive ☺....

Wednesday 20 April 2005

During morning walkabout passing the vegie patch I noticed the fur of some dead animal poking through a gap in a weather-board of the burnt out house, and so did Tia, tugging on the corpse until it pulled free to claim the treasure as her own ☺....

In glorious elements in paradise I got washing drip-drying on the line, then with the thought of keeping warm in the evening ahead the next mission was to fill the woodbox and set the fire ready to put a match to....

Spying a few currawongs back feeding in home paddocks recently, when noticed bobbing around Tia and I make an effort moving them on, its a mission of mine to give them the shits and never make them feel welcome!!!!

A shifting earth's axis, with the changing of season the setting sun has recently been notably outstanding, enjoying this evenings at the best viewing spot on Rainbow Falls by the water tank at the top boundary. It's always a constant source of amusement to see the ocean and surrounding mountain ranges heavily in shadow, while simultaneously watching in the expansive view, a golden glow and lazy shadows slowly fade in the other direction ☺ ....

Thursday 21 April 2005

Getting morning exercise stirring up a handful of pesky currawongs that persistently feed in paddocks, biding time and extending annoyance, I ripped up buzzie fern groundcover to hinder them from resettling. Content to have hampered the horrible birds long enough, the wheelbarrow was then pushed behind the cattle yards collecting another load of limb wood to lose up the flue of the heater....

Migrating to the cottage, after bathing up, a couple more pages were covered with pencil etchings. I'm really struggling to get, and stay focussed editing the contents of envelope two, it's really proving an uphill battle to get through. When I'm started it's fine, it's just a matter of getting my mind past the thought of starting????

Pulling up for afternoon smoko I finished a layer of biscuits in the tin and removed the handful of paper patty pans to reveal the next level. Stacking the pans neatly inside one another for burning, Tia had other ideas for the crumbs they contained pulling them apart she reversed the whole process in her hunt for sweet treasure ☺ ....

The evenings setting sun took on a fiery red appearance with the light spectrum forced through dirty smoke filled cloud. Forestry operations had been busy looking after the economy and environment filling the surrounding mountain ranges with smoke....

Friday 22 April 2005

Air was putrid thick with smoke all night, having a toilet break in the wee baby hours even the illuminated near full moon had a smoke haze. There was no escaping it, even indoors the odour penetrated creating a high use ventolin time, bastard forestry practices!!!! There is a better way....

Not totally giving up on my effort to piss currawongs off, persistently at them this morning hindered their attempts at feeding on ground. The only outcome may be Tia and I get plenty of exercise while reducing the weed population ☺ ????

Monday coming being a public holiday I made an effort, between pestering birds, to take the drive through the centre of the Sisters for those grocery items to see us through. Slipping the key in the post box a parcel pick-up slip was waiting. Expecting nothing, as soon as I saw the handwriting and parcel shape I guessed the contents with a smile. Unbelievable, Mum and Dad sent me a new red leather wallet to replace the one lost, with a tear in my eye and a heart full of love I immediately started filling it with loose paper and plastic bits ☺ ....

Driving to the other end of town Destiny was booked in with Grant for new shoes and a heart starter replacement. Destiny's tyres are beginning to look like a worn patchwork quilt. It will only take another cold snap for the battery to give in: it's just a matter of time....
Destiny unpacked and all the bits having found a place, I called those endeared to me, sharing in my delight at receiving the wallet with Mum and Dad ☺ ....
Losing what remained of the afternoon in the kitchen cooking carbonara sauce, I was then pen down bum up writing and repetitive barking from Tia drew me away to swap comfy slippers for my boots to check out what the issue was about. With torch handy I walked in the direction of the loo and barking, there finding a possum safely taking refuge on the loo roof biding its time watching a frustrated Tia below.... Life here is predictably unpredictable ☺ ....

Saturday 23 April 2005
The scientific engineering feat between Tia and myself, flattening the plastic milk container to the right density designed to fit in roof guttering, seems to have done the trick: blackbird clambering hasn't been heard on the cottage roof since blocking their access point....
Plans of pampering Destiny were shelved. Doing her best work from 6a.m. Mother Nature had other ideas, depositing a burst of 11mm before I thought about getting up. Sun never stood a chance of breaking through, a thick unbudging cloud blanket made sure of that, although looking impressive, the occasional light shower only offered another 4mm....
Rain is not only waking bulbs from dormancy to push spurs out of the ground: mushrooms are also popping their heads out. Anything edible is very useful. The weather change added another bonus. Currawongs made themselves scarce, only seeing one for the day that's one too many....
Heating a pie for lunch movement in the paddock caught my eye, grabbing the binoculars watched the black cat cautiously roaming in the distance, sadly it's still surviving to destroy!!!!
Idling the afternoon away in the warmth of the cottage I cooked a pot of stew over the fire and added more pages to the edited stack. Chipping away at it little by little progress is being made, however envelope two is proving to be an uphill psychological battle....

Sunday 24 April 2005
Fluffy cloud hugged the range and blanketed the sky blocking any solar activity, being generous the small amount of accompanying mist early on would have been lucky to produce 1mm. Giving the illusion there was plenty of juice on offer, elements only upheld an image doing nothing more than look impressive????
Chopping enough wood to keep home fires burning and again having the woodbox looking healthy, next move was to empty the stew pot of its contents making up heat and eat meals to strike cooking from the roster when it suits. With a heart full of optimism and a head full of hope I measured the bore depth, groundwater requires a greater water spillage from above to rise to a level considered worthy of pulling the pump out....
A conscience free alternative to the pencil, attention was diverted to the keyboard finger dance updating the freshly written word that ever so quickly escapes out of hand. One month behind created a long day for my fingers clunking on keys, with eyes beginning to cross I was happy to see the end arrive ☺ !!!!

Monday 25 April 2005
On this 90th anniversary Anzac Day, Ms Tia and I pottered around at home. Greeting a beautiful bone warmer in paradise, ideal conditions saw the return of the same small group of currawongs to ground feed in paddocks. Almost obsessed by their very existence, I got a dose of exercise and weed removal pissing them off....
Satisfied at unsettling feeding pest birds annoying them just by my very presence, then turned the spotlight on Destiny, with contributions from me and Tia there's also been many a trip over the mountain to collect dirt in every crevice. Destiny easily absorbed the afternoon, from vacuuming to wiping over the plastic and metal bits on the inside to a quick lick over the outside....
Putting my back into the last daylight split a large log of wood, breaking it down to cart away a wheelbarrow load from it, effectively warming myself twice with the same wood ☺ ....

Tuesday 26 April 2005
A few currawongs remained persistent until lunchtime to keep me and Tia fit. One thing becoming blatantly obvious in pursuit of pesky birds, is my throwing arm, once very strong in my softball days being able to peg home plate from outfield, is now lacking, demonstrating more strength throwing underarm nowadays ☺ ????
Relaxing over a milo after clearing the paddocks of my obsession, savouring the last mouthful felt a small lump in my mouth. Always the eternal optimist hoping for the lump to be milo, I was shattered to find it was a fly robbing my stomach of the enjoyment factor.... Yuck!!!!
The log broken yesterday and used last night was taken from the assortment of timber behind the cattle yards, exceptionally dry, burning beautifully and producing outstanding heat, I wished to replicate the experience. A fossick out back permitted a repeat, following a small stint on the splitter physical activity was given away for a bath and the more pleasured pastime of putting my feet up ☺ ....

Wednesday 27 April 2005
Stirring through the night the smell of smoke was strong in the bungalow. Getting out of bed in daylight hours the source became evident. Air being so permeated, surrounding mountain ranges were again smoke drenched, if massive burns weren't endorsed by government then low level poisoning of its people wouldn't be legal. It's a bit tongue in cheek when local government has by-laws in place to impose fines for excessively smoky house chimneys, and on the other hand endorse forestry operations and the associated practices within the municipality????
Playing farmers donned my straw hat and went walkabout stirring currawongs wandering. From the bungalow window I've been watching spiny rush, found predominantly around the dam, begin to multiply by the leak at the irrigation pipe, first job was to slide the shovel under that. Doing my bit to reduce the mozzie population emptied both paddock water troughs. The bathtub in the bottom paddock at the end of the road had a thick layer of algae, not pleasant to handle, but its now history along with the active mozzie wrigglers. From my position deep in the paddock looking back toward housing, I was proudly impressed at how lush, green and tidy it looked ☺ ....

Finished playing water games with Tia, we walked into the cottage to catch the boating weather forecast that predicted some strong wind leading up to the weekend, thoughts went directly to a couple of sheets of tin on the carport showing signs of lifting under pressure. Pulling out the drill and ladder a couple of screws were put in to secure the tin, eliminating one less noise amid strong gusts....

Just putting the pencil and eraser away the phone burst into life, when asked if Ms Lucas was in it sounded like a marketing line, I pre-empted asking what are you selling or are you after a donation, the voice replied "no, I'm from the Anti-Discrimination Commission". Feeling red faced and apologetic then put my energy into listening. The purpose of the call was to organise a mediation appointment time best suiting the geography of all concerned, a letter will be forthcoming with a set date and time. A step forward for closure, I'll be happy when the radio station mismanagement experience is being looked back on in the past....

Thursday 28 April 2005

There were more eagles than currawongs active first thing: wind picked up to make flying conditions a little difficult, but as the morning settled a couple of unwelcome birds arrived to test our alertness....

Booked in for new shoes, Tia and I jumped into Destiny taking her over the mountain to Grant. Still starting easily, Grant confirmed thoughts that Destiny's battery was still holding charge and it's possibly the dash gauge that's mucking up, that's not surprising with the rattly rough road....

A letter waited from the Anti-Discrimination Commission confirming a conciliation path, a good start at recognising 'yes' there is a real issue to deal with. Balancing the scales, a friendly card was also amongst mail, Rita and Ian offered their kind thoughts through a trying time standing up in a line of fallen radio station dominoes attempting to bring honesty to the surface. While still in town I made an impromptu visit on Rita in her studio offering thanks for demonstrating friendship and support☺....

Friday 29 April 2005

Strong wind gusts may have stirred me from peaceful sleep regularly but not a whimper came from the carport roof☺....

Only two pesky birds bothered to fly in and were quickly moved on, returning sometime later they were detected by a vigilant Ms Tia, she repeated the action done so many times together. Making a cuppa peering out the bungalow window I proudly watched Ms Tia on the job in the paddock making the pest birds unwelcome. Tia's also still being very helpful at eliminating buzzies, collecting from her environmental rehabilitation termite hole and lacing her beautiful outfit☺....

Running out of distractions I headed in to be seated, ironically pencilling my way through the time I first addressed sexual harassment and discrimination issues at the radio station. Oddly, coinciding with the recent correspondence from the Anti-Discrimination Commission in an attempt at putting an end to the issue once and for all....

Pencil and eraser dulled and put aside, we revisited an old habit come beer o'clock by going walkabout in the paddocks kicking out young scotch thistles. Last seasons effort is paying dividends I'm covering more ground at a faster pace☺....

Saturday 30 April 2005
The beauty of cooler nights is I get to sleep right through without a paw tap from Ms Tia, her bladder makes the distance when its cold, odd it doesn't on warmer evenings ☺ ????
A true taste of winter inspired me out to stock up on wood, heading to the plentiful timber sprawl behind the cattle yards two wheelbarrow loads were pushed up from there and another of limb wood. I've slipped into a habit of taking twice as long to get anywhere around the property by getting sidetracked kicking out scotch thistles as I go….
Without a mouse sighted or a trace left behind for a while, hot on the scent, Tia removed one out of the bath, in moments it artfully escaped her jaws to safety in one of the many nooks the cottage offers, just a little shaken by the whole ordeal….
Catching the tail end of a news story that reported Sarah Henderson had died at the age of 68 from cancer I was saddened to hear of her passing. A woman of personal strength managing 'Bullo Station' in the Northern Territory outback with the support of daughters, Sarah was also the face behind advertising and awareness campaigns for breast cancer. Definitely a person who made a positive difference to this world….

Sunday 1 May 2005
Again, sleep was broken through strong gusts, each one that hit kept me on edge wondering, 'is this the rush of air that will lift the roof off'? Last nights battering dismantled the successful cottage window weather-proofing plastic cover, repairing it and getting washing up to date gave the day ahead purpose….
In Melbourne visiting Stacey before she and Leigh head overseas for a brief tour of Europe, I phoned Kerry celebrating her 44th birthday packing in a big weekend in the big smoke ☺ ….
Clothes dangling from the line, I then focussed more seriously on upgrading window waterproofing by replacing clouts with timber and screws to hold the plastic in place. While still in the mood, I had another go at sealing around the flue on the roof with a spare piece of heavy-duty plastic. Tossing tools clear of the roof before climbing down, Tia shot through with the roll of duck tape playing 'keepies off' the little shit ☺ …. Or as Mum would say, 'big shit'….
Putting in a big day, I finalised it adding a couple more pages to the slow growing edited stack before giving in to beer o'clock and walkabout. While I sunk my boot into thistles Tia was on the scent of a very healthy looking rabbit by the gorge, taking off out of harms way the rabbit shot up towards housing. Tracking it to the burnt out house, and a woman on a mission, Tia fruitlessly rattled around amongst the stack of corrugated iron!!!!

Monday 2 May 2005
A simple day that unfolded neatly…. ahhhh….
Asking a favour of Ross to print one of the digital images he took of me driving Fergus the tractor slashing to make a personalised Mothers Day card for Mum, he was prepared to accommodate. Tubbed up and currawongs regularly stirred, Destiny took us to the other side of North Sister to strike a digital blow with ink….
Happy with the printed outcome, Destiny then took us the remainder of the way down the mountain to get the final product posted, having a social time chatting my way through. Out of

the blue friendly mail arrived from a low maintenance friend, and the woman I'd like to proof my book, Laureen…. Timely correspondence ☺….
Adding Sunday's entry into the journal folder, I have officially hand written 800 pages recording the history of Rainbow Falls. The enormity of this personal achievement is far beyond anything I ever imagined myself capable of. Writing has now become part of daily routine I don't know how to stop. Twenty plastic folders with twenty plastic sleeve inserts, in pairs of varying colours, are now lined up like soul mates on a shelf in the bungalow….

Tuesday 3 May 2005
No currawongs were waiting for our arrival outdoors much to Tia's discontent, instead we got exercise collecting and splitting enough wood to feed the heater for a wet week. Leaving the cottage well stocked and plenty down the shed on the ready….
Completing an honest morning's work and relaxing in the bungalow over lunch putting some petrol back in my motor, two pesky birds flew into my view, without offering resistance they left on the first attempt to get rid of them, too easy….
The afternoon melded reading the pieces of paper that contained earlier action at Rainbow Falls within, remoulding and clarifying past words to formulate the most accurate record of events my brain contains to fill the pages of 'Inside my Skin' ☺….
Getting fresh air after pencil pursuits we went walkabout. Strolling between the vegie patch and burnt out house, I was forced to lean over the vegie patch fence to literally avoid a head-on collision with a determined parrot unwilling to alter its flight path ☺!!!!

Wednesday 4 May 2005
Feeling disillusioned with life, predominantly caused by exposure to people harbouring the traits of greed, harassment, corruption and ego. The more news and politics I'm exposed to the more the human race doesn't fail to disappoint, fortunately not all are driven, or measure themselves by the mighty dollar which keeps my hope alive. Whenever people and money are combined corruption seems to raise its head, blending ego to the equation, is the worst recipe. Any situation can only be as good as its leadership, the radio station is a small time example of 'make it up as you go poor management' combining money and ego. The up and coming conciliation meeting has been occupying thoughts quite a bit lately, I'll be glad when the existence of the sexual harassment and discrimination ordeal becomes a distant memory. Honesty and justice is a hard road to travel!!!!
Not happy with the world I spent it in brain therapy saturation with my little mate and shovel, an antidote to wind down. Focussing on moving a pile of sand becoming overgrown at the driveway side of the cottage, into wheel ruts, expelled some disillusioned energy….
Observing two separate columns of smoke rise in a westerly direction I was shattered when a light wind picked up sending it our way. Today's episode is up there with the worst I've known the aftermath of logging smoke to be, it resembled a fog outdoors, our government proudly looking after the economy, environment and its people!?!?
Putting the shovel away to wash sweat from my body took time out to hear the friendly, trusting and loving voices of Mum and Dad, reminding myself kindness does exist in the outside world ☺….

Thursday 5 May 2005
Starting perfectly, after cuddles and a scruff up with my best friend I opened the bungalow door onto two eagles gliding gracefully overhead, using the wind to advantage they eased out of sight toward the horizon ☺ ....
Its influence working in our favour, wind cleared the air of putrid intense levels of smoke permitting my sinus to clear and regain a full sense of taste and smell....
When I got cracking it was straight into domestic duties, it was out with the vaccy to find the bungalow floor under what Tia and I have uncaringly dragged inside....
All over the place temperature wise, cloud built then dispersed, having a feeble attempt at rain that made very little impact. Better conditions to be inside looking out at through a pane of glass, there several more pages were covered in pencil marks and sent directly to the edited pile. A notable turning point occurred pencilling my way into the year 2004. It injected a badly needed dose of inspiration to feel like I'm now getting somewhere ☺ !!!!
Taking a cuppa break, I sighted an eagle at the bottom of Rainbow Falls being hassled by a couple of ravens, giving me cause to grab the binoculars to bring myself closer to the unfolding event. However, it was the mountain range behind bird action that stole the show. Quite a long strip of smouldering smoke, kilometres in length, appearing like the long trail of raised bulldust left behind after a car has driven over a powdery dirt road, became the focus. Unbelievable what can be justified as jobs and good for the economy????
During beerless walkabout I picked and ate two sweet juicy ripe strawberries, with still more fruit on the way, Lukey's liquid fertiliser recipe worked miracles with the plants. Popping up in the lawn I've also protected mushrooms from passing fauna, at present almost $13 a kilogram in the supermarket, I like the idea of picking home grown ☺ ....

Friday 6 May 2005
The contents of my head gave me a mongrel of a night refusing to wind down for sleep, as soon as it was placed on the pillow my brain kicked into gear going over radio discrimination stuff. Again, stirring this morning my brain started literally tired of trying to sleep I got up early enough to see the tail end of a light frost, a sign of what's ahead.... Brrrr....
After breakfast Tia happily helped out with the dishes by articulately cleaning the empty peanut butter jar ☺ ....
Striving to make town before the pretend chemist closed at noon for lunch made it with time to spare. Lungs catered for with ventolin a while longer, and Rita's quilting studio open, I took the time to visit before loading Destiny with enough bits 'n' pieces to see us through another few....
Basking in afternoon sun behind glass I added a token few more pages to the done stack, the makeshift clipboard is not far off being emptied, it was a slow uphill grind to find this time around!!!!
With a brain hazed over by literary pursuits I escaped outside with my little mate picking the protected mushys to include in dinner. The mercury fell dramatically following sunset, without hesitation I struck a match and got flames blazing, after cooking dinner on the heater top I happily consumed a bowl of mash topped with fried onions and mushrooms surrounded in a moat of gravy.... yumo ☺ ....

Saturday 7 May 2005
At first it seemed as though currawongs were having the weekend off resting on a perfect autumn day, a couple showing up near lunchtime were moved on without their capable dogged persistence. The paddocks are really benefiting from ongoing determination with pesky birds, rarely returning without a handful of buzzie seeds, I've put the collection into an empty beer box and its now three-quarters full, that's a lot of buzzie seeds that won't germinate!!!!
Shy on socks inspired action to get hand washing drip-drying, still playing around in the cottage set the heater ready to put a match to while cooking rice to supplement Tia's diet. Personal grooming and a spot of editing finalised an evolving day leading into beer o'clock, going walkabout in the cattle yards eliminated yet more scotch thistles....
Daylight hours are obviously shortening nearing the equinox and winter solstice: sun is setting 5p.m.-ish and natural light has faded into darkness by 6p.m.-ish, with still a half-hour of evening light to lose before reaching the shortest day....

Sunday 8 May 2005
Finalising a solid Mothers Day chat, the squeak of the bungalow door opening disturbed the only pesky bird feeding in paddocks, Tia and I went for a walk to piss it off totally, giving up easily it shouted currawong expletives at us flying overhead toward the neighbours ☺!!!!
Cause for double celebrations, the outstanding being Mothers Day, secondly I finalised putting pencil marks over the contents of envelope two, a slow grind to achieve. Now ready to repeat the entire process transferring hardcopy pencil edits onto computer, when this book is published it will be a happy day indeed ☺....

Monday 9 May 2005
Cool windy conditions waited to greet the bungalow door opening. Without clear direction wind swirled all over the place, to warm up I got busy with the splitter and stripped a layer off in no time. Driving in cool air, wind dropped and picked up whenever the mood suited having me stripping one moment then rugging up the next????
Not one currawong made an appearance, I'd like to think 'piss off' persistence is taking effect, more than likely being gusty and unpredictable it's a good day to remain in the nest by choice....
Earning beer o'clock while simultaneously staying warm, several hours were sunk into making a little sense of the burnt out house ruins rationalising and sorting roofing iron, lumps of charred timber, and pieces of concrete. When they surface in burnt debris, I remove nails to fill empty 2-litre plastic milk containers....
After a huge physical day I was happy to call it quits with my feet elevated and a cool beer in hand while dinner simmered ☺....

Tuesday 10 May 2005
Around 5a.m., wind gusts strong enough to blow my beanie off blasted across the countryside, they also made sure sleep was randomly disrupted. Surfacing to face the windy reception, and running shy on food, started preparing for a trip between the Sisters....

Grabbing tools from the collection stored in the shed and not in any hurry, both Ross and Lesley had time for a brew, later meeting them in town at Ross' former auto electrical workshop to reciprocate a cuppa....

Preparing the shop for tenants, I got a buzz out of dismantling an unused concrete hearth with the force of a hammer being the demolition crew, Lesley turned loose in the workshop yard with the brushcutter, and Ross measured angle iron for welding. Not having run a weld since apprenticeship days with the Department of Agriculture, I put my hand up to do a run, the rod took off smoothly without fuss achieving a clean weld run I was happy to put my name to ☺ !!!!

Leaving my mess and Ross and Lesley to it, I headed to the supermarket where a chat to Doug confirmed currawongs to be nomadic, I shouldn't be bothered with them at all soon, yahoo, may they forget their way back ☺ ....

Wednesday 11 May 2005

Noticing a healthy crop of young nettles becoming established in the vegie patch, and not wanting them to get too comfortable, put them to work as compost turning them in. Spending time outdoors with my offsider and shovel, with such a perfect temperature and soft UV I took my top off to give skin an airing. Leaving a half job for later through running out of steam, needing to put petrol in the motor headed in to feed my habit....

Remaining indoors, firstly the sweat was washed from my body then turned attention to the computer clunking away on keys playing catch up with the daily written word that so quickly falls behind....

Shadows getting long and natural light fading feeling cool and hunger pangs moving in, without finding an end to the written word turned the computer off to make a start on dinner and get the heater cracking.... And so another day in paradise is spent ☺ ....

Thursday 12 May 2005

Another large evident burn off was ignited yesterday, fortunately elements were in favour only seeing not being immersed in the smoke. Once night fell a clear glow could be seen in the darkness kilometres away. Recurring at the same site today, a column of smouldering smoke billowing up intermingled with cloud....

A big dent in the cottage woodbox predicted one job on the agenda, taxing the wood stockpile in the shed, while on the go with heater things it was emptied of accumulated ash and reset it for the evening....

Moving from priority to optional on the agenda I repaired the vegie garden gate, screws on the top hinge had pulled out of the fencepost staying upright in a vertical position by the bottom hinge only. Replacing 1-inch screws with 2-inch, I got enough length to bite into timber leaving the gate once again free swinging. Continuing on my busy way completed turning soil and nettles, pleasantly closing the gate behind when finished ☺ ....

Letting hard working muscles cool off, I parked my bum in front of the computer tidying the working day and yesterday's half finished effort, briefly catching the moving target of the written word....

Friday 13 May 2005
Still immersed in darkness, we were woken from sleep by a little critter trying to enter the bungalow through the patched up broken window, forcing me up to put a stop to the commotion. My tapping about also disturbed wallabies feeding outside near the window, hearing several sets of legs get hopping in quick time ☺....
The morning was consumed on domestics, cooking rice for Tia I decided on fried rice for lunch myself. Requiring 35 seconds to eat it all, gone for 30 seconds dashing to the bungalow for the wooden spoon, Tia's weakness for bacon was demonstrated, jokingly leaving the cottage I said "don't eat all the bacon", doing what she was told left one eye ☺!!!!
Capitalising on ideal elements, and unable to bear wasting it indoors, I lost the afternoon with my bacon napping little mate making sense of debris at the rear of the burnt out house....

Saturday 14 May 2005
Waiting for toast to pop I stood gazing out the door, Tia's rattling around at the burnt out house caused a rabbit to run across the yard while simultaneously three grass parrots drank at the cattle trough.... Far more stimulating than watching car traffic pass by ☺....
As much as I enjoy being the only human on home soil there are times when it's not enough and the company of others is appreciated. Social doors opened wherever I tried, a sign the time was right. Stopping at the bakery Evelyn offered chrysanthemums from plants she's about to divide, she is a sweetie with a big heart. Ross' daughter working at the supermarket let me know he was at his former workshop. There I had coffee, ate lunch and exchanged a natter. Moving next to Pam and Terry's, I found them basking in the immaculate elements and was invited to join in over a cuppa and cake ☺....
Ross was wishing to store more items from his workshop in my shed, and Pam and Terry decided it was time to have a possum release, chance had us met up at Rainbow Falls later in the day. Having had enough of cuppa's I offered beer to a receptive crew, enjoying the liquid amber we shared conversation and the last warmth the day provided, a fitting end ☺....

Sunday 15 May 2005
After making contact with the birthday girls both Loui and Nana Raye respectively, Tia and I migrated behind the cattle yards to collect a wheelbarrow load of limb wood. Disliking the sound of snapping twigs, omitting a painful frequency hurting her ears, my little mate deserts me usually heading for the security of her safe trusted friend Destiny....
Cooling down considerably after sitting for a long period chatting with Mum and Dad, altering that state afterward I headed to the splitter warming up to stock up....
During evening walkabout I took a stroll to the possum release box left yesterday, a former mail box, its now affectionately named 'number 45 native wattle tree in the bush'. Reluctant to leave the safety it provided, a pair of eyes peeked back at me....
Scouting for mushrooms I picked a couple and put the protective cover around another to size up. Having the great outdoors in order we headed in to stoke up the heater and warm the nest for another night in paradise ☺....

Monday 16 May 2005
The sun is beginning to be robbed of its heating ability creeping toward winter, besides lighting a fire, the most effective way to raise my internal thermostat is to partake in physical activity....
During yesterdays walkabout I noticed a couple of nails almost pulled loose from the roof of the car garage, holding that thought in mind overnight it made priority number one repair job today.
Out with the ladder, drill and screws to rectify the situation before it becomes a problem....
One sure way to really get blood pumping is to push a wheelbarrow loaded with wood or get swinging on the splitter. Expanding on the readily available dry stash I slipped behind the cattle yards sorting and retrieving timber, bringing in a few loads to warm up on with the splitter....
When my body was unwilling to break another piece of wood I changed tack, returning to the ladder, climbed on the shed roof and with a minor modification popped a rain cover over the flue....
Before being tested, waterproofing on the cottage roof was showing signs of wind damage, while the ladder was out I climbed up anchoring the plastic down with a couple of weighty rocks, it'll take a bloody strong wind to budge it now!!!!
As the day began winding down, a stroll to 'number 45 native wattle tree in the bush' found only one remaining resident still claiming the much sought after real estate in a quiet undeveloped neighbourhood ☺....

Tuesday 17 May 2005
Well timing is everything. Heavy cloud clinging to the range greeted the morning and us in paradise. Having already dusted a little mist, it looked like clearing with a halo of blue sky hovering above, only holding open long enough for me to do what was needed outside then healing over for a slow gentle misting rain on a calm, mild autumn day.... Bliss....
Sadly the leak around the flue on the cottage roof isn't solved. It's back to the drawing-board, shit!!!!
Pulling the ladder out I got on the roof while everything was still wet adding another piece of plastic, its obvious I'm going to have to replace the perished seal surrounding the flue, that's the problem....
A meagre 4mm fell up to beer o'clock, steadily dribbling out just enough to wet the ground. Picking a dry time between misting showers to check on 'number 45 native wattle tree in the bush', now vacant, it's a good sign all possum residents have matured enough to face the world alone ☺....

Wednesday 18 May 2005
Washing hanging on the line, dishes done, fire reset, water collected, rubbish taken to the shed, currawongs made to feel unwelcome, dinner cooked and any other domestic thing that got in my way, kept me on the go and broke the back of the daylight hours. If bloody currawongs are supposed to be nomadic a persistent few won't budge: they're continuing to hang around!!!!

The only item managing to dry by 4p.m. was a tea towel: getting the heater cracking I set-up an inside laundry to finish the process off. Once we'd migrated to the cottage I got the computer fired up and made a start at transferring hardcopy edits....

The computer screen wasn't playing ball properly leaving my confidence in its technology waning, the digital display didn't fully fill the screen, wiggling the power connection cord at the rear had the display shrinking and expanding. Nervous something was about to shit itself I fossicked through floppy disks for spares and did back-up's, losing any part of the edited version would literally reduce me to tears. Oh, for the day to have a large brained computer with a CD burner and printer.... Dream on ☺....

Thursday 19 May 2005

Breakfast just settling in my stomach, a call came through from the Anti-Discrimination Commission, the purpose of the call was to set a date in July suitable for both parties in an attempt at conciliation. I'll certainly be glad to have the whole ordeal behind. I can understand why so many harassment cases would go unreported. It's not an easy path to take, happy now there's at least an end in sight....

In home travels I came across a piece of ply board almost perfect size to fit the broken bungalow window. Motivated for change I replaced the perishing duct tape and joined bladders from water boxes, now gaping open, only stop large things from entering. Temporary window mark IV firmly sealed in place, its at least putting a stop to cold air and little critters freely joining us whenever it suited....

While in the mood for change, I headed to the cottage moving the desk and computer to a more suitable location within metres of the heater. Sliding the desk partially under an existing fixed bench increased workspace, and it's in a more solid position, minus spongy floor board movement, eliminated the problems I've been encountering with the screen....

In broken grabs attempting to relax and record the days events, shooting in neighbouring paddocks upset Ms Tia, the explosion of a gun discharging releases a frequency hard on dogs ears, getting through tonight's journal entry was a slow process!!!!

Friday 20 May 2005

Without having shown my face in town since last Saturday, culinary life was a little lean, so the morning was spent preparing to follow the carved road between North and South Sisters. With the family piled into Destiny, reverse parking her up the ramp onto the top level of the shed proved to be a wise action, the battery refused to spark her into life. Pushing Destiny forward until her front wheels started nudging over the ramp, I jumped in as she took off down hill for a rolling start. Ignition on, in second gear, and rolling at a reasonable pace, I released the clutch and she burst into life tackling the mountain destined for Grant's and a new heart starter.... Phew....

Leaving Destiny with Grant I walked the meagre distance to the other end of town to cash up and on the way stopped on the street for a chat with Ian and Rita. Still preparing the workshop for occupancy, Ross and Lesley were in and happy to pull up and put the kettle on. Leaving them for the bakery, Evelyn invited me to visit tomorrow for chrysanthemums. Tomorrow being precisely year three to the day Tia and I officially gave ourselves permission to be Taswegians, I wasn't returning home without a celebratory beer and didn't. Rounding a pleasant venture from home friendly mail sat idle from Ali, included was photos taken from their visit back in April ☺ ....

Steering Destiny back between the Sisters loaded with essentials the afternoon was beaten: using the last sunlight to check 'number 45 native wattle tree in the bush', still empty, then scouted around without luck for mushrooms....

Saturday 21 May 2005

It's hard to believe three memorable years of our lives have vanished into history since we first drove through the gates of Rainbow Falls, poked our flag in the ground, and called it home. Only the journal has witnessed the whole event day to day, fortunately storing our memories never to be forgotten ☺ ....

After coffee, Evelyn and I strolled through her garden then set about loading plastic bags with various coloured chrysanthemums. While digging plants, walking by, Evelyn's adopted Aunt Gwenda stopped for a friendly chat. I was flattered to be introduced by Evelyn as her adopted cousin, a very warm gesture ☺ ....

Arriving back at Rainbow Falls in time to watch the sunset, then a match was put to the heater and a beer or two was savoured cooking dinner. With emotions flowing reflected on how far we have progressed in three years. The day of arrival I was as rundown as the property, life has only moved forward in a healthier direction ☺ ....

A text message came through warning me that by the end of May without paying out on more credit Telstra are going to sever my mobile phone from existence. Unprepared to throw more money at the greedy pricks I'm going to let it lapse, unwilling to feed the gluttonous machine any more than I have to!!!!

Sunday 22 May 2005

A perfect lazy Sunday; I idled time away on the shovel preparing a bed to heal in chrysanthemums until they find a permanent home, placing the flower market garden in the vegie patch....

Spending the better part of the day outdoors basking, retreated in early afternoon, rising wind robbed the moderate temperature offered in stillness. Escaping in, I pleasantly caught up on family life with Mum and Dad ☺ ....

On the hunt for mushrooms come beer o'clock, with my little buddy, we got sidetracked removing another well-established buzzie groundcover from the face of the dam, I pull and toss Tia catches, sorts and files. Still working around the dam I took branches, cut sometime back and left lying on the ground, to the shed for cutting to size and poking in the face of the heater at a later date....

Poor light put an end to outside play, moving with the seasons then reached for the matchbox adding flame to the heater. Happy to rob the Electricity Company of a few cents I cooked the entire dinner on the heater top using free energy wisely ☺ ....

Monday 23 May 2005

Wind picked up to be pretty strong, the latest temporary window replacement has silenced another noise with its existence; less for my mind to interpret trying to shut down for sleep can only be good ☺ ....

Unable to turn a blind eye to it any longer, looking a little ordinary, the vacuum had to come out to find the bungalow floor, Tia and I did a good job trying to bury it. While the vaccy and I were united and running hot, the cottage floor got a lick over also ☺ ….

For a well overdue change of pace the afternoon vanished behind the keyboard digitising hardcopy edits, requiring the investment of many, many, many, more hours…. It's only one small step at a time inside this termite hole ☺ !!!!

Leading into tomorrows full moon tonight's was exceptional, a huge white halo glow immediately surrounded the moon, the halo was encircled with many rings in colours of the rainbow spectacularly rising through the density of trees on the top boundary. Concluding that if the intensity of the ring around the moon signifies rain then we're in for a deluge: may it raise the bore to pumping level ☺ !!!!

Tuesday 24 May 2005

The enormous ring around last night's moon merely offered a token brief shower that wasn't enough even to wet the base of the rain gauge. The action was all over before stepping foot out of bed….

Upsetting a few feeding currawongs, an eagle flew in and circled above for a few minutes, close enough to make eye contact, my eyes watered watching the curious bird directly overhead. Staying with the wind current, with ease the eagle glided out of range ☺ …. A nice experience….

Cloud pushed by wind built-up for rain and dispersed, keeping that pattern produced nothing for effort. Not tempted to be out in it helped with the decision to give my fingers a keyboard workout protected under a roof. Every little bit makes a difference so I keep convincing myself ☺ !!!!

Out roaming after brain and computer shut down I was rapt to find another large emerging mushroom, straight away placing a protective frame around shielding it from competition, preferring to see it on my dinner plate ☺ ….

Wednesday 25 May 2005

The sun may have been shining but a lazy southerly took the edge off any attempts at heat, bloody cool, there was no dilly-dallying bathing, it took a bit of psyching just to get naked and only staying that way for as long as necessary….

Preparing for an overdue restock of the cupboards and a trip between the two Sisters, with Destiny warmed up and heading to the front gate a letter slipped out from under the dashboard. Although not important, the letter's whereabouts puzzled me sometime back. Stopping to open the gate slid my hand inside the dash behind the glove-box where the letter magically appeared, and surprise of all surprises, my missing wallet was also stashed there. The only piece of plastic I hadn't reacted on replacing was my license, waiting long enough eliminated the need…. Un-bloody believable ☺ !!!!

An envelope full of goodies waited at the Post Office; Mum and Dad had taken the time to send recent professionally taken photos of Dekira. She is a gorgeous happy baby, her beauty shines from within. Also included in the envelope was a peaked cap Dad had won at golf, a note attached to the cap and hand written by Dad read, 'if the cap fits wear it', it did and I did ☺ ….

Entering the pub to stock up it was nice to walk into the main bar getting Bruce's personalised service, being predictable, he merely asks "the usual", doubling the personalised pub stop Connie happened to be in for a chat ☺ ....

Helping myself with low mercury I got blood flowing down the back collecting timber, loading the wheelbarrow another eagle passed over at low altitude, accustomed to seeing their large frames at a distance they've been surprisingly low of late????

Another bushfire size burn off was visible in the distance: the only fortunate thing being wind was in favour. If a real bushfire occurs, after being conditioned to seeing regular large volumes of smoke caused from logging operations, I'll probably ignore it....

Thursday 26 May 2005

The remnants of a very light frost still decorated the ground when we stepped foot outside, without letting sayings down, a beautiful day in paradise followed. Taking time to decadently bask and warm the body I made an extra milo, concentrating without spilling a drop headed for the shed. Inside the entrance gates morning sun is at its protected concentrated best, making it difficult to walk away ☺ ....

Getting on the splitter and down to a t-shirt, reduced to heater size timber brought up from behind the cattle yards yesterday, making the quite empty woodbox healthy once again. To wind down some heated muscles I brought up another couple of wheelbarrow loads to repeat the whole experience another time....

Expelling my physical energy supply, and with blood cooling, headed in out of it putting my brain and the computer to use, quitting only to get the fire raging and dinner simmering ☺ ....

Friday 27 May 2005

On occasion throughout the night some pretty wild gusts had me slightly stirred but not shaken, getting the bungalow creaking and groaning it lashed out with vicious energy. Hanging around at a lesser intensity after sunrise wind remained, purposefully just to keep the mercury low. Doing laundry crossed my mind but the thought of wrestling with clothes trying to hang them on the line would only get me cranky, I deserve better!!!!

In a need to warm up, put my back into a job more suited for the elements splitting wood to keep the home fires burning. After finding the heater interior under its load of ash reset it for another night of hot inside action ☺ ....

Voluntarily moving herself to a low care nursing home early this year, the new contact number written in the Christmas card Doris Lohrey sent has always failed. Being proactive I did a telephone book nursing home hunt tracking Doris down, being as welcoming in conversation as usual, we exchanged enough details to re-establish permanent contact ☺ ....

Having communication lines re-opened with Doris, attention turned next to the computer for the following couple of hours. Night after night I forego, by choice, what the outside world offers to document the daily events of life at Rainbow Falls, I can only hope someone other than myself will enjoy the self-disciplined fruits of labour ☺ ????

Fire lit and relaxing with a beer I received an incoming call from Scoot's, regularly in one another's thoughts, she's a genuine low maintenance friend. Still announcing at the radio station, Scoots mentioned my actions have had an impact on management practice, Bruce's offensive behaviour has all but disappeared and the station has cleaned up its act. Unfortunate it had to go to extremes before a forced positive direction is being taken, and sadly at the expense of quite a number of voluntary staff....

Saturday 28 May 2005
Air temperature set on frozen and snow hovering nearby, searching for an extra layer I reached out for the overalls that followed me home last Mildura trip that no longer fit Dad. Obeying the desire to keep warm was lured into the haven, tossing a match onto the heater kept me out of trouble clearing the sheds top level of accumulated prunings and burnable rubbish, a perfect way to warm up and strip layers ☺....
It felt like revisiting a comfortable old friend spending time in the shed. With the handsaw I cut timber to heater size that failed to break with the back of the splitter, generating a nice stack before my protesting arm refused to push it one more stroke!!!!
Starting to get my teeth into, and making progress taking the long road toward book dreams, the bloody computer is mucking up, gremlins are intervening. Before, rather than after it shits itself, being pro-active increasing insurance policies, I rang Ross arranging time to use his computer to burn everything to CD?!?!
The mercury was lucky to rise to double figures, long before sunset the face of the cottage heater was flush with burning timber and hot coals and remained that way until I'd had enough ☺....

Sunday 29 May 2005
Proceeding to plan, I arrived at Ross' mid morning in perfect timing to flick the switch on the kettle, although anytime would have been cuppa perfect. Jumping into Word, patched together 'Inside my Skin' as one large document from floppy disks and burnt copies to CD. It's reassuring for my brain to know the hundreds of hours dedicated to the pen, pencil and keyboard have been backed to a reliable source, gremlins can now strike the pitiful computer at will and I won't shed a tear. Also giving me the green light to use the washing machine, a load silently completed while I played on the computer, it's a far more user friendly model than the archaic wrist wrenching, drip-dry model at home ☺!!!!
Driving the spun load home I then did battle with wind pegging clothes on the line, bypassing the drip-dry stage, left them to flap away and tangle....

Monday 30 May 2005
Just finishing up splitting timber, was pushing a loaded wheelbarrow back into the shed when Ross drove up the driveway. Unpacking a mended radiator and a new battery from the boot we played tractors for as long as it took....
A couple of pots of tea demolished and all the right bits back in place, Ross took Fergus and the slasher for a couple of laps in the paddock. Daring to venture too close to the wet patch by the leaking irrigation pipe Ross bogged Fergus. Nothing too serious, I shoved a plank of wood under the tyre for traction, Ross played the clutch and in no time the tractor was freed to dance again, thinking that to be a good omen to pack up toys for the day ☺....

Tuesday 31 May 2005
I've spent the last couple of evenings reading an old hardcover book purchased in a second-hand shop in Wollongong. The book's contents are a series of short stories on early Australian exploration. Early explorers perished endeavouring to gain knowledge struggling their way across harsh unforgiving country only a few short generations back. Today we can fly across the country in a few hours. What stood out throughout the book with every individual exploration was the reliance on fragile water supplies: the lack of it had fatal consequences and failed many early attempts at exploration; that same fragile theme with water still exists????
A bit cool first up so I warmed in the shed cutting enough timber to last the week out. Carting water, the cattle trough contents stuck out as being a bit ordinary. The menagerie of animals drinking from it, insects breeding in it, plus Tia using it for a swimming pool, I propped the float and to Tia's delight emptied the trough to start afresh. Staying with an outdoor theme continued on to play around pruning and weeding the elevated garden at the rear of the burnt out house....
The neighbours, Troy and Kristy, were busy again teaching their kids how to be irresponsible, inconsiderate selfish idiots. Riding a quad bike sideways out of their driveway thrashed the little thing hard down the road and at the same pace did a U-turn inside my driveway entrance, returning in the same manner time and time again, the more dust raised the greater the praise. Tired of their inconsiderate stupidity, I phoned the police today for the fifth occasion, I don't know if its police inaction or the neighbours are just plain stupid, but very little changes. They finished off a big day of activity across the road after sundown with a spot of shooting????

Wednesday 1 June 2005
If this is winter then keep it coming. A glorious warm, calm sunny day met freshly opened eyes and lured me out into it. Putting in a serious effort I sorted through the stack of timber under the carport left to dry from the milling site. Salvaging a few pieces of timber that still looked okay, then stored a healthy stock in the shed to cut in more suitable climatic conditions, presuming it still knows how to rain....
Leaving the carport looking pretty tidy thought I'd settle in front of the computer, the hard drive had other ideas, refusing to boot up and run windows its only offering was the message, 'primary master hard disk fail', I know when I'm beaten. It was unbelievable timing writing all my work to CD, I'm in tune with the universe ☺ !!!!
Forced to put dreams on hold attention was turned instead to plumbing. Rather than let the sink discharge water directly under the cottage, I climbed under extending the pipe work putting on a 90° joiner and connecting enough 50mm pipe to redirect water away from the cottage. I was left feeling pleased adding another progressive step forward ☺....
The neighbours' kids pushed the envelope one too many times again today being slow learners forced me to call the police yet again. I won't give in until legally satisfied of equality and receiving the respect deserved. Shortly after 6p.m. I received a home visit from the local police constable, very pleasant and helpful he left me feeling confident of moving forward to a resolution....

Thursday 2 June 2005
Without a clear direction fixed in my head I floundered around doing the usual bits 'n' pieces savouring another superb, pleasure to be alive, day. Also gaining leisurely pleasure is bathing, requiring no psyching to get naked, I'm able to take the time to give myself a slow motion pampering....
With the mercury steadily rising to 'bloody hot' found myself looking out for snakes, it feels more like we're leading into summer rather than immersed in winter, I could have been comfy in shorts????
Having all the 'gotta do's' sorted, occupied optional time in the shed cutting the entire stack of timber carted in yesterday, leaving a healthy looking 'just grab and burn' pile on the ready. A hard working best friend made herself comfortable in Destiny until all the activity was over, not a bad life if you don't weaken ☺ ....
Using every last minute daylight offered Tia and I went walkabout: doing a fruitless mushroom hunt I had better luck finding scotch thistles, averting attention gave a few the boot. Standing on top of the dam wall kicking thistles the phone started ringing. My leg muscles unable to stretch out to sprint like they once did I took off at a pace permitted without pulling muscles, arriving in perfect timing to just miss the call. I run more like Cliffy Young these days, body changes have been so slow and gradual I didn't see coming until after change had arrived ☺ ....

Friday 3 June 2005
From around 8:30pm to 9p.m.-ish last night I watched an oversized brightly shining star looking object to the left of The Huntsman's Cap Mountain. At a slow morphing it continually changed colour from green, to blue, and red, seemingly enlarging moving closer then receding. Grabbing the binoculars resting them on a post by the bungalow only enabled me to pick up colours not the object. Around 9p.m.-ish it disappeared behind a mountain range to the south-west, certainly something I've never witnessed before. Wishing to share the experience, whoever I phoned wasn't answering????
We weren't beamed up overnight so life went on. Following nine days without a trip into the big metropolis today was it. Wednesday week ago was the last time Destiny took the panel-shaking journey. It must be near on a record number consecutively spent nestled into our hamlet wedged into the side of the mountain....
Clothes left dangling to drip-dry, we climbed into Destiny and she wound her way through eight kilometres of dirt road to find bitumen on the outskirts of town. Once the Post Office box was emptied I headed to Pam and Terry's solving the problems of the world over a hot brew....
Walking into the main bar I struck up a conversation with Stephen and a friend at the bar, while we chatted Bruce put a box of my favourite on the counter in front of me without a word exchanged, that impressed me. Stopping for bread, Evelyn always works around a brief socialise, continuing on a chatty way met Rita and Pam out front of the supermarket for more conversation. Stocking up on drinking water on the trip home found Ross in and willing to put the kettle on before making it back inside the gates of Rainbow Falls ☺ ....

Saturday 4 June 2005
It was an absolute pleasure ferrying several wheelbarrow loads of ready to burn timber to refill the cottage woodbox, particularly with the knowledge there is still more of the same stored in

the shed. Staying with the heater theme emptied it of grey contents, disposing of the ash where the tractor got bogged to begin filling the deep water filled rut….

Lacking the warmth of the past few today was easily spent indoors. Having the computer out of action I decided to keep progressing forward where possible by emptying the contents of envelope three. Until a change occurs with my predicament I can at least forge forward with the hardcopy wearing down the pencil and eraser. Losing a cool afternoon in the bungalow out of the weather placed edited pages of envelope three into the 'waiting for a computer' pile….

Beside walkabout and ending the life of many scotch thistles today was simply spent, just the way I like to see them pass, quietly yet productively ☺….

Having afternoon smoko I felt a tap, tap, tap sensation on my leg, waiting for her share my little mate had her 'drippy lips' happening, salivating. Love is expressed in oh so many ways ☺….

Heightening that immeasurable love, after gorging on some bloody carcass later in the evening Tia came inside and emptied her stomach contents on the floor, pushing our love to the limits!!!!

Sunday 5 June 2005

Thinking ahead for when the tractors brake is reassembled and tyre again hanging in the right spot, my wish is to take the manual effort out of clearing inside the cattle yards behind the shed. Moving a step closer to achieving that goal, and turning a thought into reality, picked up bits lying in grass that will make noises I don't want to hear in a spinning slasher blade, relocating pieces of steel, plastic pipe and tin, kept me warm on a cool one….

Left in the neglect, non-priority and easily ignored stack, boxes were emptied that contain pieces of life's possessions that have followed me this far. Cluttering and creating an eyesore in the cottage I forced myself to find homes for the contents of the boxes. The sprinkling of boxes represent a lifetime of collected treasure now displayed like trophies in the living area. Pieces of me and the people who have influenced my life in some way, extend a lived in loved homely feel ☺….

Busy creating change, Terry popped in to release rehabilitated possums, over coffee I told him of my computer dilemma, he simply said "have you defragged your hard drive", I said "what, never heard of it, what's that", "it's a hard drive self-clean"???? A simple run of the defrag program and I'm back in business, I was almost ready to take the computer down the back and shoot it, getting a reprieve with its new attitude to life ☺….

Monday 6 June 2005

Filling the woodbox I noticed a kookaburra tugging through the fence of the vegie patch on a long rope like object, stretching like a piece of elastic it was too skinny for a snake and too big for a worm. Disturbed from the object of interest by busy humans the kookaburra flew off. Curiosity took me for a closer look, creating so much attention and mystery was the intestine of some unfortunate animal. Returning from the loo saw the treasure had been removed and claimed, something as precious as an intestine couldn't be ignored ☺….

Keeping the wheelbarrow rolling, bound for snapping a load of limb wood behind the cattle yards, collecting and clearing around the trees the spirit for adventure came over. Following a well worn wallaby track leading down to the gorge below, reckon I got three-quarters of the way down before the relatively easy going track got too difficult to continue. The discovery gave me the sensation of seeing something for the first time, real life exhilarating mystery and suspense ☺….

Early afternoon rain cloud teasingly hanging around produced a light drop, only supplying a little mist but its heading in the right direction. Not overly exciting to be outdoors, I made up my mind to indulge in a deep bath, sparking the heater loaded its top with the largest available pots and kept the face glowing….

Shuffling pots, Ross showed up to reassemble the tractor brakes, joining in for beer and bullshit by the heater, as the last pot came to the boil he left me to the decadent moment to soak in the indulgent amount of water until I was content ☺….

Making a start on dinner, Stacey called to share the adventure from a month travelling around Europe, touring Germany, England, France and Holland, with time also spent in Singapore. Packing a lot in a few short weeks created memories to keep for a lifetime ☺….

Tuesday 7 June 2005

A legacy from the adventurous climb down the gorge following wallaby tracks was sore muscles I'm not as fit as thought….

In need of a rocket up my arse to get moving, my get up and go got up and went. Unable to remain focussed on anything in particular, let the day quietly pass doing a job suiting a numb mind, domestics. Pulling out the vacuum was the most adventurous thought provoking feat???? Assisting with energy conservation Ross took dinner off the agenda. For me cooking is a necessity not a favourite pastime, thankfully a brief drive to the other side of North Sister and it will be waiting ☺….

Tia well catered for and looking after Destiny I shared a delicious meal with Ross, afterwards he challenged me to draughts a game last played with my parents many moons ago. The old rusty strategies surfaced, clawing my way back from an early mistake to draw the game, everyone's a winner. I kept on winning, walking out the door with salmon steaks, yellow, yellow or yellow tulip bulbs, and a Richard Bach offering to read….

Feeling quietly content slowly heading up the driveway, under headlights I drove past an alert owl sitting on a fencepost, unmoved by our close pass it remained comfortable. Rich with a diversity of native flora and fauna, we've definitely landed in paradise ☺….

Wednesday 8 June 2005

Fire still set, woodbox full, and minimal dishes after a night out, freed me early for a trip over the mountain to refill empty shelves….

Getting a couple of Evelyn's best, took a lunch of pies to share with Ross at the workshop, then after achieving goals in the big smoke tackled the mountain to home. Destiny unpacked, I picked up the shovel and planted tulip bulbs, finding a home by the cottage-facing border of the elevated garden to add a splash of yellow, yellow or yellow colour ☺….

With snakes having gone wherever they go through cooler months, hidden out of sight out of mind, offers confidence to enter places like the dam where delicious frogs hang out. Daring to think about raising the intake and empty the line to repair where I hit the pipe with the brushcutter oh so long ago. Getting as far as a brief start attempting to find the rope or remnants of, that on one occasion saw the previous owner tug on and raise the 2-inch pipe intake out of the dam. Never far from the action, Tia followed me inside the gate and drawn like a magnet to water she hopped straight into the dam walking along the edge stirring the water turbid, dropping visibility, I gave the idea away to try again some other time, preferably without help ☺....

Thursday 9 June 2005
Ross' book loan really kept my attention last night, unable to put it down until after midnight, and that was only due to eyes losing focus through tiredness....
Able to count on my hands the number of days since winter began that I haven't been in a t-shirt mild conditions are more like a lead into summer. Yesterday I picked and ate another ripe strawberry - even the plants are still producing fruit????
All luxuries have a use-by-date, and readily available firewood cut to size predictably will run out. To generate warmth for a few more evenings today was nominated for a stint of physical labour swinging the saw....
Keeping an eye on a constipated slow moving westerly change struggling toward us, it managed to reach home soil after lunch. Running low on steam it produced several minor thunder rumbles, placing Ms Tia on edge, and dribbled a minor amount of moisture, not enough to even mist the interior of the rain gauge....
Wandering indoors I sparked up the revitalised computer putting solid time into updating the journals written word, that alone is going to take a couple of goes to get current....
Trying to concentrate on the keyboard finger dance, complacent irresponsible neighbours let their kids push the envelope, venturing back out onto the road flogging the little quad bike. Tired of turning a blind eye, I want their behaviour nipped in the bud to find equality and common ground.
The kids are only going to grow with bigger and faster toys and sadly lacking the responsibility of smart guidance. Making contact again with Constable Cameron, he has been very helpful in an attempt to curb their selfish, irresponsible behaviour....
Ahh for sundown and peace, computer shut down and heater lit I made a start on food. Cradling the book in one hand, dinner was prepared without thought, making the mistake of opening it then struggled tearing myself away....

Friday 10 June 2005
The book kept me up late again last night. Although conquering it before retiring, I'm planning on getting to bed at a far more reasonable hour tonight....
A dismal attempt at rain disappeared before offering a drop to the gauge. Supplied with yet another warm sunny one in paradise it was the right temperature for a play at the dam. Leaving Tia to watch from outside the fence, I successfully found the rope attached to the 2-inch pipe immersed under water. But there was a snag actually several, tall water reeds had grown over the rope laid across the floor of the dam entangling it in their root system. Braving the cool water took my boots off, and with rolled up pants, followed the rope line removing what reeds could be reached. The dam floor being slippery and dropping away sharply made conditions difficult with limited tools. Filing that job for more thought, was pleased however, progress has been made in the right direction ☺!!!!

Before picking up where yesterday left off, I got a pot of stew simmering then called Mum and Dad, that's never a five minute chat. Hot receiver replaced, life was added to the whirring hard drive, then fulfilled determination by not giving in until the journal was updated....

Saturday 11 June 2005
Leaving the cottage for bed last night there wasn't a star to be sighted and the air temperature was warm, all indicators of rain. Taking many hours to eventuate, but proving correct, it's a sound I never tire of and an absolute pleasure waking to steady rain on a tin roof. Set in for a stay, immediately the yard responded livening colour a couple of shades of green. Another scene pleasant on the eye, doing the morning open up, was to find no rain had entered through the cottage roof, the last waterproofing patch up is having some effect, although as the millimetres dropped from the sky chinks in the armour surfaced. Throwing a match to the fire dried the flue and fast tracked evaporation, stopping all moisture except a dozen drops from entering, putting full enjoyment into using the heater by eliminating the pinging and twanging of drips into pots ☺....
Using the heater's energy, water was boiled to clear the sink of the stack of dishes legacy of emptying the boxes storing life's little collection of treasure that once cluttered the cottage. Transferring the washed misplaced items into the bungalow created clean clutter looking for a place they can call home???? One step at a time ☺....
Feeling pretty happy with the state of our home world and content indoors listening to ongoing rain hitting the roof, fired the computer into action putting more valuable time in. Shutting down and confidently defragging with a few simple procedural clicks of the mouse button, these days it only takes a few minutes to complete with less hard drive housework to contend with....

Sunday 12 June 2005
Mother Nature turned the taps off just before diving under the doona last night, unsure of what was on today's climatic agenda, while the sun shone I got laundry up to date....
Demanding to be refilled after a huge taxing the woodbox was responded to accordingly. The readily available supply getting a bit lean, and without knowing what direction the weather was going to turn, a couple of wheelbarrow loads were brought up to the shed for dry storage???? So easily forgotten about when they're gone, a few currawongs made a comeback, they must be confused about being nomadic, Tia and I gave them a reminder that no matter what the season they're not welcome!!!!

Monday 13 June 2005
Taking a peek outside at the morning to determine available choices to fill the daylight hours ahead, the weather looked like it could take any direction. South Sister Range was blanketed from view, its load of heavy low cloud thinned leading toward the north-west, only wind direction would determine the conditions we were going to receive. Jostling about, a northerly influence proved strongest pushing reluctant cloud, resisting all the way, from the range, releasing suns ray's through broken cloud....
Cottage fire set, dishes done, woodbox refilled, water collected, blah, blah, the best place for us girls to play in conditions harbouring such indecision is down the shed. Tia cleared the yard of

anything that moved, excitedly barking and running all over the place leaving me to burn my excitement off with the handsaw restocking the near depleted 'grab and burn' wood supply ☺ ....
Taking a few progressive steps forward I was happy to turn the computer off and socialise when Ross gave me the excuse. Dropping in to finish piecing together Fergus to operational, the radiator once again holding pressure and full of water, I'm free to start using the tractor at my desire. The near future should witness some fast moving change ☺ ....

Tuesday 14 June 2005
Having just warmed the sheets last night, two consecutive short sharp showers burst from the heavens. Stirring from sleep through the night I heard even more moisture falling, 3mm decorated the base of the gauge after the event had passed this morning....
Looking to warm up out of the briskness, and the ground too wet to consider tractor work, instead I picked up the handsaw keeping warm and active cutting timber. With very little enthusiasm for physical exploits I lost interest quickly with the saw, taking less energy to keep warm indoors, took another chip at progressing slow moving dreams forward. The resistance my brain offered to the contents of envelope two is being overcome and barriers are disappearing, assisting with a better-paced forward direction ☺ ....
Wallabies are proving to be very efficient lawnmowers keeping the yard very trim and neat, oh, and fertilised, I'm forever cleaning it out of the soles of my boots ☺ !!!!

Wednesday 15 June 2005
Waiting for grass to finish drying and the weather to make up its mind before bringing the tractor out, put wait energy into cutting enough wood for immediate needs....
Diverting away from half finished paddocks still holding moisture, took the tractor to higher and drier ground using the fuel ration between the dam and toilet. What was achieved in an hour with Fergus would have taken a month and near on murdered homes lightweight equipment, and me in the process. Stoked with the rapid transformation, afterwards, proudly walked the slashed area enjoying it from all angles. Completing a horticultural apprenticeship in Mildura tractor driving was done on flat ground. Working undulating ground took me and tightly squeezed bum cheeks out of a comfort zone on occasion, something I'll have to train my brain into ☺ !!!!
Decision made to reward myself with a luxurious deep bath, while the many pots brewed away on the heater top I fired up the computer utilising wait time constructively ☺ ....
Showing excessive interest in her girlie bits, far more than usual, rolling Tia over confirmed my suspicion that she was in season. Wishing to avoid puppies I'll need to stay alert, although rarely out of sight it's the rare moments that pose the most problem....

Thursday 16 June 2005
Enjoying dying embers before heading into the bungalow for sleep last evening, a convincing spot of moisture fell leaving behind 3mm as a token of its existence this morning. The recent spate of intermittent rain has encouraged bulbs to break ground, with clumps of spurs popping up all over the place it shouldn't be long before the yard transforms into a sea of colour ☺ ....

The morning vanished divided between domestics and lost behind the cattle yards with the wheelbarrow. Once again I'm back into the regular practice of spending time editing. It was still daylight entering the cottage plugging the cord into the power point, turning the computer off I walked out into darkness ☺ ....

Friday 17 June 2005
It was a simple day in Eden. Needing to post the payslip took us over the mountain, feeling a little localised, I rarely fail to meet and greet a familiar face in town willing for a yarn. The few simple needs catered for, and with an open studio door, I popped in further extending social skills to say hello to Rita....
Home, unpacked and sorted, I raised the telephone company's profit margin catching up on family life with Mum and Dad prior to feathering the nest for a cosy one in by the heater. I'm getting pretty content in the snug nest of the cottage the heater has added a level of comfort not known, the flue extension has it drawing like a champion, and waterproofing efforts have made a difference adding to the enjoyment. Utilised to its fullest using the heater for warmth, cooking and boiling bath water, electricity is a convenience I could survive without if need be, there would be no state of emergency here if it failed to exist. Possessions out of boxes and displayed, I too am confidently using the sink after installing and rectifying the plumbing, rodent activity has all but ceased, the cottage feels clean and homely the only missing element is water on tap ☺ ????
Challenged in nearly every thinkable way since arriving three years ago, one by one and day at a time challenges have been embraced, at times begrudgingly, and overcome. Put to the test I've personally grown and feel capable of taking on nearly anything life dishes out ☺ ....

Saturday 18 June 2005
A quiet one began leisurely basking in morning sunshine over a brew or two. Continuing to enjoy sun, nuggeted my boots in anticipation for a big night out in St. Marys, and remaining loitering in the shed, utilised the splitter and handsaw making more heater wood....
Squeaky clean and ready for a taste of St. Marys' nightlife attending winter solstice celebrations in town, I jumped in with Ross and Lesley leaving Tia behind in the company of Destiny out of earshot of fireworks. I haven't witnessed a crowd of that size ever in St. Marys, if I had to guess I reckon there were around 1000 to 1500 people, it brings every mountain dweller down from the hills, including me. Food and drink stalls had their own small sideshow alley. Live entertainment was colourfully alternative, Chinese drumming, belly dancing, shadow puppets, fire stick twirling plus other bits 'n' pieces. Finishing with an impressive fireworks display, we returned back up the mountain after the biggest loudest and most colourful bang....
During times of deep sleep my little mate has been having quite animated dreams, first her paws start paddling accompanying the many and varied facial expressions, eyes open and rolling and on occasion she releases muffled barking. A busy girl, protecting even when she's sleeping ☺ ....

Sunday 19 June 2005
Setting the alarm so as not to be late, however, Tia's persistence had me up before it went off. The sky closed in producing light rain all day, ideal to spend indoors at the e.ScApe Café. Stemming from the passionate public outcry over South Sister, I attended the Greens Northern Regional Conference to hear first hand what is going on both locally and globally. Some of the politics got a bit dry and heavy causing a brain haze over and wander, but refreshingly the majority of speakers held attention. It was enlightening, but sadly not surprising, the magnitude of small communities like ours directly affected by forestry practices, and the importance of voluntary time by locals to keep local icons of interest intact. I support sensible and sustainable logging practices, but we cannot supply the world in a greedy snatch and grab that knows no limits in the name of money where more keeps perpetuating more. The energy, passion and blunt honesty expressed by speakers in politics from federal to local, including concerned public groups, offered reassurance the future ahead wasn't bleak and clear felled ☺ ....
At work in our absence Mother Nature slipped 2mm in by 4p.m. and kept her foot on mercury rising, making priority one to get the heater cracking and warm the cottage. When my fingers freely moved they were put to work dancing over keys, that effort broke the back of the day....

Monday 20 June 2005
Bathed in sunshine all morning, the rays were screened by a blanket of cloud not long after lunch causing a swap from peaked cap to beanie. I can't bear to be without a hat of some sort at home, without having had a haircut since November a hat's worn just to keep bloody hair out of my eyes!!!!
For a change of pace Ms Muffet and I wandered to the front yard of the burnt out house, with serious dismantling tools I broke down what was left of a wall that had fallen. Forced to first prune a climbing plant entwined through the wall to begin the demolition into manageable sized and weighted pieces....
Tia's running and bouncing body language saved for a ringing phone was activated, getting my little legs moving caught the call from the Anti-Discrimination Commission. The courtesy call was to deliver a 'Plan C', to avoid having to travel anywhere for a mediation conference it was asked if I'd be happy with a telephone link-up instead. A link-up is a far preferable option to sitting in a room with Miss Management Maria and her perverted brother-in-law, the station treasurer, Bruce. A tentative date was set for Wednesday, July 13, at 10a.m. to be confirmed, finally an end in sight!!!!
Finishing off a progressive day took another step forward with book dreams....

Tuesday 21 June 2005
Roused at times from sleep, I heard the occasional drop of moisture falling from the sky offering 2mm by morning, with determination to add to that figure, it did. The shortest day of the year vanished quietly under a heavy blanket of cloud unnoticed. Low draped cloud accompanied by showers arriving in waves dumped a load then regained strength for the next wave, slipping into a set pattern created wonderful conditions to stay indoors without complaint....
Home life up and running and the woodbox full, pulling me up for a brew Ross popped in to pick up tools from the shed. Remaining settled in a cosy warm cottage after socialising I

plugged the power cord in and advanced editing. A long session in the cottage feeding the face of the heater chews through a healthy stacked woodbox in no time, today's stretch put a big dent in it....

Wednesday 22 June 2005
A rare natural occurrence that is recognised and appreciated, the capability of hearing the falls from the bungalow is a reminder of the finer things in life. The luring sound of flowing water enticed the curious to its source wandering over to appreciate nature's beauty at work....
Drenched in sunshine perched into the mountainside, the valleys below were an ocean of cloud a good indicator there was, at minimum, fog downstairs in St. Marys. Testing the theory we took a drive into town, and sure enough, losing altitude the weather closed in supplying moisture. Dashing to the dry shelter of the Post Office veranda to slide my key in the little black box pleasantly found friendly mail without the company of bills. Mum and Dad sent pictorial snippets from their local newspaper of an impressive storm Mildura copped....
After ducking between shops in rain and filling Destiny with survival needs, with her sandwich-board sign displaying open, before heading home I called in for a cuppa and chat with Rita and friend Barbara....
Getting comfortable in our absence home wasn't exempt from rain a few millimetres were added to the gauge, and continuing, Destiny was unpacked in the wet stuff. After establishing a fire I then phoned Mum and Dad thanking them for their welcome letter, making myself comfortable, because our calls are never brief ☺....

Thursday 23 June 2005
Dumped overnight, 15mm found ground and pipped 2-inches before retiring. Slipping out in a quieter moment of the deluge, my bit of rope and float were pulled out of cobwebs to measure the bore depth. Disappointed, but not surprised to find the water level still out of reach at the five metre mark, after such a long dry spell soil is going to take some wetting up to raise groundwater levels....
Functioning true to form winter isn't providing too much warmth, keeping my body temperature up naturally I cut wood to size, afterwards headed indoors to use a bit....
When physical activity ceases it doesn't take long for the body to cool, sparking up the heater to create a comfy environment used that comfort affixing my eyes to staring at the computer screen. Advancing the book process forged forward into October 2003, my best friend and co-editor was content to snooze by the warmth of the heater without complaint ☺....
Retrieving everything required for dinner from the bungalow alleviated the need to leave the warm cottage until bedtime, where the phone ran hot for mainland communication.
Responding to a text message I phoned my mate Loui dude in Sydney, the receiver still warm, the phone burst into life with a call further up the coast from Sheila and Peter in Brisbane ☺....

Friday 24 June 2005
Tia nagged me to get out of bed with persistent paw tapping on my shoulder. From the moment my feet touched the floor not one minute was wasted I hit the ground running....
A light frost had all but gone when we ventured out it stepped aside for gorgeous elements in paradise, spoiling myself rotten I got immersed in home maintenance. Doing everything from

dishes, emptied the heater, took ash to the loo, washed clothes, reset the fire, cut wood, refilled the woodbox, spent time on the computer, and brought laundry in to dry by the heater. Taking a breather before cooking dinner I phoned Phillip, not having spoken for a while, he informed me Mary-Anne had resigned from the radio station due to dissatisfaction with management, another statistic????
Cooking a huge feed of spaghetti, making plenty for heating and eating later, juggling leftovers back to the bungalow and fridge, reaching to switch the light on I upended Tia's bowl sending spaghetti flying. Salvaging what could be, then brought the four-legged vacuum cleaner in, already with a belly to capacity she willingly obliged my plight cleaning up what I couldn't.... Shit!!!!

Saturday 25 June 2005
Slowly savouring an after breakfast cuppa in frozen silence, the atmosphere sat motionless as if for that moment time stood still, I was able to hear air passing into my lungs and as easily audible exhaled. Individual sounds could be clearly pin-pointed travelling light and extensively along airwaves, the seemingly purity of the motionless deep silence precisely identified, lifted and carried single sounds as if three-dimensional. The only activity came from birds either calling into the silence or the occasional movement from kookaburras looking to fill their stomach. Kookaburras, of late, are like decorations dotted through trees, there's quite a healthy population here at present obviously plenty to eat....
Waiting for ground to dry to bring the tractor out following yet another frost, I mucked around with firewood, put petrol in Fergus, checked tractor vitals, spent a couple of hours on the computer and moisture still sat heavy, conceding to postponing tractor work until tomorrow. Wandering inside the cattle yards observing ground moisture I found treasure in an old glass cream bottle, partially buried, the historical ornament was retrieved for a shed trophy ☺....
The law apparently doesn't apply to my neighbours, now with zero tolerance I again phoned the police, although now spending the majority of time in their own yard with the quad bike, they're unable to help themselves coming down the road doing a U-turn in my driveway. I've had enough, how many times do they have to be told, I can't decide whether they are irresponsibly arrogant or outright stupid to the law and courtesy to others????

Sunday 26 June 2005
Aside from quiet times spent on the computer, to get things done around the home is very physical and laborious, with very few fossil fuel guzzling tools to assist I can take all day just getting organised for it ☺ ????
Burning fuel in the heater for six hours and upwards daily requires a lot of face feeding with timber, my method of carting in then splitting manually takes a shit load of physical work and regular input. Terry offered to bring his chainsaw up, reckon I'll accept that offer, just one hour's work would eliminate one month's physical labour for me pushing the handsaw or swinging the splitter....
With plenty of moisture lingering and the luxury of time the tractor was again left idle in the shed, affording to wait until conditions are ideal....
Good intentions of achieving a measurable physical accomplishment went by the wayside socialising the afternoon away over the phone. Catching the ear of the European traveller,

Stacey and I got into some serious jaw activity now she's had plenty of time to recover from jet lag. Concluding an afternoon of healthy chat I spoke with Laureen, being the woman I earmarked to proof-read and contribute constructive criticism to the edited version of 'Inside my Skin'. Today's lengthy conversation confirmed her commitment to the task, a very welcome mind and trusted opinion onboard assisting with fulfilment of dreams ☺....
Constable Cameron visited once again in the dark of early evening in response to my call, as usual being verbally responsive and helpful, mentioned he's spoken to the neighbours and they'd assured him they'd keep their kids and motorbikes off the road. Obviously only when it suits them, slow to adopt change they're not the sharpest tools in the shed....

Monday 27 June 2005
Waking with a sense of risqué and recklessness bit the bullet phoning the St. Helens salon for a haircut, being pencilled into Kellie's client roster Thursday week. Calling Phillip to plan a visit when in St. Helens, he offered to organise a morning tea that included Mary-Anne and Scoots. Without having left St. Marys since November last year the big pampering social day out will be a huge event ☺ !!!!
Rainbow Falls is progressing at a phenomenal pace the true hidden beauty is being exposed to the surface rapidly. Working like I owned the place, but simply the privileged caretaker, sorted timber creating a pallet stack made up of large weather-beaten fence posts now awaiting the chainsaw. Behind the cattle yards was a dumping ground for timber of all shapes and sizes, thanks to Dave's early sweat sorting and stacking amongst the disjointed mess, I'm now making inroads, the heaters need for fuel has helped push the process along....
Determined dry enough, spark was added to Fergus making a visually impressive impact finding ground inside the cattle yards, merging into the bordering paddock doing a few circuits. Ready to put the tractor away I jumped out of the seat to disconnect the P.T.O. shaft and nearly hit the deck. Working the tight area of the cattle yards and doing a large amount of clutch depressions for gear changes, including brake presses, my knee was like jelly taking its wobbly time to recover....
On a paddock lap the slasher hit some animal corpse hidden by long grass spreading aromatic bits around, Destiny sitting duties over Tia's nose was straight onto the fresh scent, bite sized pieces saved a lot of jaw work thank you very much. The down side to Tia snacking out on the corpse pieces is now her arse is also bloody rotten. Silently Tia robs the air in her general vicinity from being breathable, rendering air I'm trying to fill my lungs with thick enough to carve through!!!! Phew....
Toys away and tidied up I heard the sound of a rattling trailer being towed up the driveway, a sure sign Ross had more treasures from his workshop to store. Helping him unload, we then caught up on life's happenings over a pot of tea by the heater....

Tuesday 28 June 2005
Both unable to resist for differing reasons, as soon as we were released to the morning me and my little mate were lured into the freshly slashed ground ☺....
Giving morning dew time to dry I took a dash between the Sisters, there a letter from the Anti-Discrimination Commission awaited outlining my requirements and what to expect with the conciliation phone conference process. The onus is now back on me to get busy with a

responding letter outlining an expected outcome, I'll certainly never return to radio with the present Miss Management Maria and some Board Members still in place!!!!
Excited by fast moving progress was unable to help myself, using the last remaining petrol put the little grey Fergy to work polishing the paddock extending from the cattle yards. At first Fergus ran rough being reluctant to play ball, almost ready to quit gave the ignition one more try, being the try that I succeeded in meandering out the shed to make a difference to our world. A couple of hours of carving patterns into grass I was elated with pride at the sharp and open view brought into existence. Having come a long way, when a mere three years ago I got excited carving the termite hole large enough to play ball with Tia☺....

Wednesday 29 June 2005
A quiet unassuming timid time in Eden, unable to help myself was easily enticed into taking the camera walkabout through the slashed areas to record the mementosus progressive steps forward. Every time the view was open my chest would fill with pride at the sight☺!!!!
Using the luxury of surplus cut timber it was time to make more, idling away lazy hours getting extremely warm on a magic one delivered in paradise, doing just that. A gentle northerly airflow in the company of a clear sky delivered ideal conditions making the great outdoors the place to be. Choosing to sit outside and bask, a settlement proposal letter of response was formulated for conciliation, heading inside only when necessary to use the computer for the final draft. While the computer was idling along I remained attentively key-tapping updating the Rainbow Falls bible....
Unless it's a wolf in sheep's clothing, and being only one month into it, winter is going to pass on the warmer side and quietly, aside from cool nights, days have for the most been mild, more like spring and definitely no complaints☺....

Thursday 30 June 2005
Consumed in domestics finding the cottage floor buried under grass dragged in on paws and boots, also incorporated the usual stuff from dishes, water carting, and the heater and wood thing. Stopping the cleaning frenzy to catch up on family life the other side of Bass Strait, phoned the heads of family, giving the call to Mum and Dad all the time required☺....
Replacing the hot receiver and needing to print and post the letter to the Anti-Discrimination Commission, also being Ross' birthday, a woman got herself organised for a mountain run. A quick print, post, and pick-up of processed photos, I returned part way back up the hill to wish Ross many happy returns at a more sedate pace....
Met at the gate by one of Ross' daughters, she secretly informed me of a surprise party organised for him Saturday afternoon, stepping foot inside Ross invited me to stay for dinner, beefing my social life considerably in minutes. I have great difficulty saying no to someone else cooking and didn't☺....

Friday 1 July 2005
Last comfort stop before beddy-byes and unable to see my hand in front of my face in the wall of darkness, Tia disappeared out of view easily. Being a very mild night I left the bungalow door open with light glowing as a guiding beacon to return to. Returning back with a dead animal body part Tia was happy to jump into bed with it for a munch. A quick change of plans

I had other ideas!!!! The little bugger: gotta admire a woman with confidence that's sure of what she wants ☺....

Cloud covering what little light the new moon would have cast, it opened up and began emptying moisture as we put our heads down to sleep, unloading 2mm before again waking. Further adding another 20mm to that total as a welcome wet day continued....

Making arrangements with Barbara to collect a rocking chair she generously offered, I followed through with plans in wet conditions of meeting at Gone Rustic Studio before lunch. Over coffee with Rita and Barbara I was contemplating a reschedule due to climatic conditions, opening a moment of opportunity, rain took a break in transmission before finding the bottom of my cup permitting a follow through with 'Plan A'. The rocker was left on the veranda of Barbara's home for me to pick up sighting it I was overwhelmed by the generosity of the gift. Returning directly back to Gone Rustic, I fumbled to express the depth of my sincere gratitude at the gift of such a beautiful chair ☺....

Again with impeccable timing, rain stopped on cue to locate the rocker into its new cottage home. The moment wouldn't have been complete without a test run, fitting perfectly I was instantly relaxed in the rockers comfortable form, not only does it look good it feels bloody great ☺!!!!

Polishing off a wonderful day spent it in front of the computer progressing dreams of publishing a book further along....

Saturday 2 July 2005

Chatting with Rita the subject of spinning wool came up, mentioning it was something she capably did. Having collected Tia's moulting fur for the purpose of having the fur spun and a beanie knitted Rita said she'd be happy to spin it into a yarn. To assist the cause, in a couple of months Tia will be dripping fur once again ☺....

Another 4mm was dropped into the gauge overnight, having a rest from moisture production Mother Nature turned on a bloody beautiful day, ideal conditions for Ross' surprise party....

Yet another social engagement distracting me from a hermit existence, I spent spare time prior to the 1p.m. engagement doing what was necessary to keep life tidy, warm and comfortable....

Without raising suspicion, Lesley did a brilliant job organising everything from the weather to pulling off the surprise. Further increasing my social life, I received an introduction to new faces within Ross' circle of friends and got further aquatinted with those previously met. No shortage of good food and quality conversation caused time to evaporate ☺....

Winding down reflecting on yet another brilliant day in paradise, I slid my mellow body into the rocker perched cosy and warm by the heater. Assisting with ambience, the oil lamp provided dim atmospheric light helping to create the perfect mood ☺.... Ahhhh....

Sunday 3 July 2005

Clothes worn yesterday smelling of campfire smoke, and drenched in yet another perfect one in paradise, fine conditions were utilised treating my wrists getting washing current. With clothes dangling to dry I moved onward, once again doing the wood thing having a cutting and splitting therapy session....

Staying blissfully ignorant ignoring the inevitable, finding or designing reasons to delay the not so glamorous task, it was time to make some space in the toilet. Grey ash sprinkled in takes

the odour and unpleasantness from the job the most difficult part is the psyching into doing it. Happy now the task won't have to be repeated for quite some months, attention was turned to the computer to round off a full working day....
By the time dinner was cooked, journal written in, and I could sit down calling time my own I was clagged, well and truly ready to relax in the rocker ☺....

Monday 4 July 2005
Decadently basking in direct sun inside shed gates savouring an after breakfast milo I was unable to think of a better way to start. Enduring her way through a bout of constipation, my little mate was content stretching out in full sun snoozing quietly next to me. Sitting in still silence observing the yard alive with activity, scarlet and flame robins dotted the ground bouncing around busily chasing any insect smaller than themselves to make a snack of, their lively presence enhanced the appreciation of the moment ☺....
Daily routine bits 'n' pieces behind, I retreated indoors to burn fossil fuel and stare at the computer screen for a while. In a coincidental timely manner editing through the infancy of trouble with radio station Miss Management, presently I'm working towards finalising the unfortunate event. Preferring to be this much further advanced, now with an end in sight....

Tuesday 5 July 2005
Leading into two consecutive days away from the farm my boots got a lick over with nugget to survive the outings, masking the true work boot look....
Cutting a little bit of wood most days keeps the supply ticking over nicely. Restocking the sheds dry supply bringing timber up to keep a stash under a roof, I let myself get sidetracked behind the cattle yards. Constantly modifying the unruly sprawling timber mess, chipping away at it the area is beginning to make sense, already having achieved a lot there's still a long way to go ☺....
Lending myself to the ultimate pampering I put a match to the heater and loaded the top with water filled pots to create a luxurious deep bath. Intermittently tending to the collection of pots, waiting time was filled constructively staring at the screen and clunking keys....
The phone burst into life drawing attention away from editing, the pleasing voices of Mum and Dad waited down the line to share two messages. Happy recipients of the envelope of goodies I sent, they particularly enjoy progress photos and comments written on the back of each print in the place of a letter. The other piece of news was in regards to my youngest niece Tegan she's now a single parent having left Dekira's father, a healthy move when life could be happier....
With the last pot of water tipped into the bath I eased my body into the hot water and settled in for a recline, once again not judging water depth well enough to submerge my nipples, the only part of my anatomy protruding above waterline. Although there were definitely no complaints, there is nothing more relaxing on the body than a good pampering soak ☺....

Wednesday 6 July 2005
Each morning stepping outside admiring the manicured yard we're fortunate to be surrounded by, I thank wallabies and other herbivore night traffic for doing a brilliant job at keeping it trim and tidy. I'd be snookered relying on an active lawnmower to do the work, neither one of my 'worked into the ground' models are willing to respond ☺ !!!!

Leading up to payday, a time when food becomes scarce, a trip over the mountain is imminent. Mail checked, I called in on Pam and Terry for a brew, asking if the chainsaw offer was still current, and ready to release a couple of possums, we made a date for Friday….

A day lost to sharpening my social skills, after boosting the economy I called in on Ross at his former workshop for a yarp. Then with beer back on the menu, coupled with a reasonable evening, my best friend came walkabout through paddocks as I kicked out scotchies roaming. It was only fading light that sent us in, I was content then to sink into the comfort of the rocker by the heater to contemplate the world ☺ ….

Thursday 7 July 2005

A bloody huge one waiting ahead started in my most unfavouritist of ways, with the alarm, but it only got better from there in leaps and bounds….

Making St. Helens and Phillips by the arranged 10:30a.m.-ish, prior to Mary-Anne and Scooter arriving he gave me a guided tour of his new abode the refurbished former stables on his parents property. Without having laid eyes on one another at minimum for ten months, when Mary-Anne and Scooter pulled up there were plenty of hugs and stories to catch up on. Scoots being the only practising announcer remaining, for all four the morning tea resembled a Break O'Day FM therapy session. Scoots told us of her intentions to shortly resign, Mary-Anne said after consulting with her husband she'll possibly provide me with a letter of supporting evidence of harassment and discrimination claims that occurred at the station. I've tried hard to follow this path of action alone but voluntary assistance with my cause would lighten the load. All reluctantly parting company for various reasons, mine being a haircut with the bubbly Kellie, very skilled with the scissors, the last cut she gave me held shape for ten months ☺ ….

Re-registering Destiny for another year I then walked around the corner to finally purchase another pair of folders for the ever-growing journal. Failing to catch Nana Raye home I did succeed however in dropping walnuts off as promised. Returning to size up trees in the small orchard Phillip asked if I'd consider pruning, not of overwhelming size and comfortably completed in a day, said I'm willing to take it on….

Completing a huge self-indulgent day retreated indoors to the comfortable security of the heater and rocker. Stockpiled loose journal pages waiting on a place to call home in history completely filled one folder and started on the second, also slotting in recently processed photos I put in a big day and evening of catch up ☺ ….

Friday 8 July 2005

What a bloody unbelievable day full of high energy and positive outcomes from beginning to end ☺ !!!!

Leaning peacefully against Destiny basking in morning sun sipping away at an after breakfast milo watching the odd robin flitter about chasing insects, the rowdy pass over of a group of twenty-four yellow-tailed black cockatoos broke the peace. They're somewhat clumsy at flying in a group formation seeing several of them make physical aerial contact, unperturbed they just continued squawking toward their destination….

Depleting the woodbox to the point of being able to sweep the bottom clean forced my hand for the inevitable need to refill. Breaking light timber with the splitter and as pre-arranged Pam and Terry turned up. Terry literally cut loose with the chainsaw reducing enough fence posts to keep me in wood for a month. When the job was complete Pam produced a home baked apple strudel and cream, flicking the switch on the kettle we shared in the culinary delights over a brew ☺ ….

'Number 45 native wattle tree in the bush' release box was replaced with the saloon model, complete with veranda and piss pot area it was placed further up the tree in the red light district. Possums should be very happy with their latest release site and sleazy drunken accommodation ☺ ….

Grateful for the assistance, after waving Pam and Terry off I pushed part of the mountain of wood into the shed with the wheelbarrow, placing enough under cover to last a couple of weeks. Sampling the wares I struck a match and put some to the test ☺ ….

Topping a remarkable day, Mary-Anne returned my call following on from our conversation she confirmed a letter of support, voluntarily adding weight to my discrimination and harassment claims against Break O'Day FM. It's now beyond me against the pack and my word against theirs!!!!

Saturday 9 July 2005

Cooling to a one-dog night last night it's heading the same direction again this evening, it's my fault getting a haircut beckoning wintry conditions to arrive. Drifting light mist showers not registering in the gauge, lingering rainbows and sunshine were the theme of the morning. Driven by a desire to keep warm I ferried all the cut timber into the shed, by no means a small job. It can rain now for a solid month and I'll be right ☺ !!!!

Catching the few glowing coals that persisted from the night before, I got the fire cracking to again keep the cottage cosy for an afternoon of giving the computer a workout….

Pam and Terry popped in to release a couple of possums at the saloon for a life of indulgence, again supplying the carbohydrates for afternoon tea. Over a brewed cuppa they shared in the warmth of the wood they cut by the heater they supplied, that's bloody close to land rights ☺ !!!!

Stepping out on a limb supporting honesty, Mary-Anne phoned reciting her letter of strength adding weight to my claim of inappropriate management at Break O'Day FM. It's a relief to have someone on side strong enough to stand by honesty and their conscience, the path forward feels positive ☺ ….

Sitting quietly in the evening by the heater with my best mate, little critters taking shelter under the cottage floor boards near the heater were having a chat, on such a cool night reckon I'd get as close as I could to a heat source also ☺ ….

Sunday 10 July 2005

What an absolute privilege and pleasure it is going to the shed and having a mountain of stacked wood just waiting its turn to be ferried up to the cottage ☺ ….

Planning on stretching the legs of the tractor ballast, it wouldn't play ball, repeating the pattern of being unwilling to pick up revs smoothly then stalling. On the blower to Ross he suggested its probably a fouled plug, amongst the available tools there wasn't a plug spanner to fit, knowing when to quit headed indoors….

Whatever is available in the meat department at our little supermarket shopping day determines the culinary direction for the fortnight ahead. Shin of beef steered a course for stew. Pitting myself against the manual machine for several hours, I cooked a huge pot of stew on the heater top. Regulating the temperature is the biggest challenge. My aim is to use less electricity the ultimate goal is to wean it out of home life entirely....

Meat, garlic and secret herbs and spices boiling away at the desired temperature, set by the right amount of coals and wood burning, I positioned the boiler for bath water the opposite side maximising the heaters use. Going back for seconds was a measure that both cooking efforts and heat regulation were outstanding, content with full bellies, my little mate snoozed by the heater. After completing the journal entry I reclined in the rocker to finish off another wonderful day ☺ ....

Monday 11 July 2005

A thought sparked, and in search of an answer, I phoned the office of the Anti-Discrimination Commission wishing to know what difference if any Mary-Anne's letter of support will make to the conciliation process. Being enlightened, at this point Mary-Anne's letter makes little difference, I can raise the letters contents during the conciliation conference and it can be submitted as evidence if the case goes to the tribunal, one day at a time....

Another magic, warm, sunny, pretend winter's day in paradise, it would have been a shame to spend it indoors which wasn't something I was guilty of. Doing a variety of things started with the pleasure of bringing wood into the cottage from the stack. Looking at it sideways walking past, the dam got some attention having another go at releasing the rope from under water reed roots, the link to lifting the 2-inch irrigation pipe inlet to the surface. Still causing grief the rope again refused to be freed holding progress back....

Slowly inching forward dreams, I headed indoors mid afternoon and polished another off on the computer ☺ ....

Tuesday 12 July 2005

Constantly looking for ways to be conservative with electricity use, I've been leaving a full boiler on the heater top through the night while the fire takes its time slowly going out, the following morning its contents are a tolerable temperature for hair washing....

Expecting a hardcopy of Mary-Anne's supporting letter, and wishing to have it on-hand for tomorrow's conciliation tele-conference, arrived in town at the Post Office before lunch where it waited....

Channelling a preoccupied mind I let myself get consumed in thoughtless domestics. In impeccable timing I hung washing on the line in time for it to cloud over, not even a tea towel dried before bringing it back inside to finish off by the heater....

I looked like sitting down for a moment while dinner was on the go but Tia turned up after rolling in something rotten, an aroma we couldn't comfortably share in a confined space....

Returning back to the remembered state of relaxation it was the bloody neighbours turn to rob peace, driving down the road and through paddocks spotlighting and shooting anything moving that wasn't a cow. The frequency that each bullet is discharged at hurts Tia's ears and receives a barking reaction, around forty shots is a lot of stressed barking and a bloody lot of dead animals!!!!

Wednesday 13 July 2005
At 10a.m. I was prepared and waiting for the phone to burst into life, punctually it did, and I was linked up with the Anti-Discrimination Commission facilitators, and Chris and Bruce representing Break O'Day FM, for the following hour and twenty minutes. Explaining the process and presenting our viewpoints as a group, the conciliators had private council firstly with me then the radio stations representatives respectively. Unwilling to alter my stance of ever returning to the workplace while current management exists, in turn Bruce and Chris would not acknowledge my harassment, discrimination and victimisation issues, and an impasse was declared….
The outcome from the impasse is the facilitators will recommend to the Commissioner our case is dealt with by the tribunal, finally after twenty months there's an end in sight to a fair hearing. It's been a long, and at times draining, time consuming process, I can understand why many cases go unheard and victims just swallow a bitter pill????

Thursday 14 July 2005
Certainly too pristine to waste under a roof, after chasing a few stray currawongs from the paddock Tia found something delicious to roll in, an aroma I didn't want to share or be confined with…. Phew☺!!!!
Righting my little mate's odour the theme was then wood. When the woodbox was healthy and ash from the heater taken to the loo, I vanished amongst the lessening strewn timber mess behind the cattle yards. Establishing a fresh pallet stack of old rotting fence posts so air can start circulating, so began the process of drying them for a future as firewood. The evolving tidying progress is altering the timber dump site from being a scattered mess and transforming it into something a little more orderly and logical taking shape…. Every little bit is progress, thanks for the inspiration Dave ☺….
Looking at the yard thinking how dry its become now supporting browning patches of grass, rain everyone around us has been receiving found home soil 5p.m.-ish. Cloud containing moisture snuck in while I was head down bum up buried in the computer. The strength of falling showers isn't going to break any records, the misting is unable to be heard on a tin roof without insulation, but most welcome all the same….

Friday 15 July 2005
A pair of native hens let loose with a competing squawking match outside the bungalow in the tiny hours of the night ensuring no one slept, politely they were asked to move on. While still doing my best at the sleep thing, 3mm dribbled its way into the gauge before running out of steam….
Making priority, the fire was beefed up as first job, not only to reheat the idle boiler simmering on top but simply to keep warm. Wind was coming off snow somewhere arriving with a built-in chill factor. Delivered from pure south, the breeze encouraged the beanie snugly down over my ears….
Relinquishing beanie for a hair wash and a trip over the mountain, I posted the payslip by its use-by-date and stocked up on bread and milk. Luckily that's all I needed that simple task alone took over two hours, there's always someone to talk to or a cuppa to be had ☺….

Making myself comfortable before putting time into the computer I thought I'd been sprung with my pants down having a bush wee, a kookaburra tapping its beak on a branch in a rhythmic pattern sounded like someone clapping, spinning my head around for a look it gave me a start ☺ …. Ooooops….

Saturday 16 July 2005
Driving out back to grab tools from the shed, I quizzed Ross about a spark plug tool, handing over the right sized socket from the boot of his car, now Fergus' plugs can be cleaned when the mood strikes. Today, however, had another set course its purpose was to hang a pair of blinds on the two northern facing cottage windows. As with anything done around the home one has to go backward before going forward, a spot of maintenance had to come first before the big event. Missing window panes were resealed, but a piece of reo held by screws and galvanised staples barring a window proved a little challenging to remove. A blockout curtain patched together from water bladders removed, it was novel to see light streaming through the remaining few panes of glass of the rickety window ☺ ….
Hardly rising from the base, the mercury wouldn't have moved in a thermometer, rain threatened constantly but managed to blow somewhere else, a genuine perceived winter's day. Chores complete the cottage and heater was the place to be. Tools packed away, without hesitation I stoked the fire, sliding into the rocker working at establishing the fire my arse got stuck. In the willing company of my little mate we lazed the afternoon away feeding the face of the fire simply doing nothing ☺ ….
Lingering rain cloud finally gathered enough to open up and produce light showers late afternoon, as the evening wore on, and showers more convincing, not one drop hissed on the heater, finally waterproofing is having an effect!!!!
Making a conscious effort of maximising burning wood and minimising electricity use is having an obvious effect, the electric stove hasn't been turned on for over a week now and I'm confidently cooking on the heater top. One beneficial observation is the heater offers use of the entire surface area, giving a uniform cook rather than channelling cooking into the heated strip of the stove element….

Sunday 17 July 2005
A token 2mm sat patiently in the gauge from the night just past. Greeting a fresh one the sun may have been shining but it was far from bone warming the dominant weather stream stemmed from deeeep south….
Its only at Rainbow Falls I can ever imagine being seated on the throne watching a pair of eagles effortlessly glide above the range, even going to the toilet is a pleasure here…. The loo with a spectacular view ☺ ….
With the right tools a job is made easy, assisted by a wire brush and a fine piece of copper wire I had the spark plugs out of Fergus and cleaned in no time, two of the four plugs were pretty ordinary. It's all back together waiting for a test run on a more comfortable day to be driving around in paddocks….
Ross pulled up around back late afternoon on cue to pull me up from editing, shifting only a couple of steps from the computer to the heater for a cuppa and friendly chat, a pleasant way to begin winding down ☺ ….

Monday 18 July 2005
Full of energy and inspiration activated by warm, calm, 'great to be alive' conditions, I psyched myself into hanging blinds in the cottage. All the bits together and spacers made up I managed to play around with two screws before the battery died in the drill, minus the convenience of a charger is a bloody pest, we got separated last shift!!!!
Resigned to hanging the blinds at a later date, attention was redirected to the tractor and slasher. On start up Fergus still ran rough, unwilling to be beaten twice in succession, the plugs were removed once again and sure enough they had again oiled up. Plugs cleaned and replaced Fergus fired up and didn't look back, without complaint the little grey fergie kept up with me putting in a big afternoon. A few more acres were left looking very tidy. Every centimetre of ground now cleared is new territory, focussing on the area out front of the burnt out house leading to the front gate, I'm aiming to make entering Rainbow Falls more visually pleasing and welcoming....
Tools tidily packed away, by the time the fire was started, bath water boiled, dinner cooked and journal updated I was jiggered ☺....

Tuesday 19 July 2005
Thinking winter had set in warm day's again rejoined making the great outdoors a pleasure.... Breakfast had, dishes done, heater reset, woodbox replete and the tractors radiator and fuel topped up, I had the view of complementing work already done. Creating work to use, Fergus is demanding a plug clean before each start, that can't be healthy, making me glad it's only a four cylinder. Cleaning the plugs twice and both times instantly fouling, at that point I was beaten and in need of more knowledge, constantly removing the plugs has become tiresome and ineffective. Quitting that line of pursuit I retreated for the more reliable pastime of advancing dreams....
Phoning Ross to nut out tractor problems his brain didn't take too much picking for an answer, once plugs foul they are prone to repeat and its time for new ones, too easy. While on the blower I also made arrangements to use his drill battery charger....

Wednesday 20 July 2005
Payday I kiss goodbye heading into St. Marys. Drinking water replete, I slipped the key into the Post Office box, pushed a trolley around the supermarket, stepped into the newsagent, whenever possible there's a social visit with Bruce at the pub, all pleasantly followed by a solid chat with Ian. I stood chatting to Ian long enough for Ross and the battery charger to find me ☺....
Outstandingly warm, I left Rainbow Falls in a t-shirt and remained that way until near on sunset. With beer back on the menu Tia and I melded into the great outdoors on walkabout hassling bloody currawongs and giving scotch thistles the boot, staying that way until light faded....
The earth's axis is on the move again, short days have bottomed out and longer ones are on the return, the sun once setting to the right of a distant unknown mountain is now setting on top, pivoting from winter and looking toward spring....
A magnificent day finished on a dumb note. Relaxing to write the neighbours spotlighting along the road broke the peace with stray shots, they're walking violations!!!!

Thursday 21 July 2005
Running low on fire starting and fire enhancing light timber, a load of limb wood was barrowed up and with the back of the splitter head the load was broken down. With the pointy end of the splitter I broke down some of the cut fence posts. Creating a healthy looking woodbox containing timber of varying sizes swallowed up the morning....
Running a smudge bar over neighbouring paddocks spreading cow shit drove bloody currawongs my way and the buggers were persistent. I reckon currawongs roaming nomadically is a myth however their continued presence has been to the benefit of home paddocks by kicking out a bloody lot of young scotch thistles roaming, the experience is made all the more pleasant strolling through clean slashed ground. Rainbow Falls is adopting a rejuvenated healthy look ☺ ....
Able to drag myself away from the wood and currawong theme, and with the help of a fully charged drill battery, I hung blinds. It was sad to see the joined water bladders and shower curtain replaced by neat, evenly hanging blinds, enhancing the cottages lived-in, loved and homely feel ☺ ....

Friday 22 July 2005
Dropping the cardboard curtain from the bungalow window, meeting our early rise, bloody currawongs had already made themselves at home in paddocks, but that was short-lived ☺!!!!
Returning from a thistle kick, currawong piss off stroll with my best friend, a message waited on the answering machine, being a courtesy call from Phillip warning of strong winds. Coming from north-west isn't nippy so I proceeded with 'Plan A' pruning his parent's small orchard....
Fuelling up over breakfast I had to change my psyche to use a different coloured mug, Dad gave me a set of three china mugs won at golf, even in company I use the red patterned mug. The red mug happened to be tied up with dirty dishes in the cottage and I'm standing in the bungalow with a boiled kettle, 'Plan B' came into play. Oddly, milo in the mug with a brown pattern tastes the same ☺ ????
Helping time pass quickly, Phillip's father, Ray turned up at the orchard with his ride-on mower towing a tiltable trailer removing prunings as I cut, he was good company. Extending hospitality, Phillip's mother prepared sandwiches and a hot drink back at the house. The orchard offered a nice moment with nature, a little bird predominantly black of an unknown variety landed at the base of the tree near my feet, we both stopped in our tracks until it realised 'oh shit, a human' ☺ !!!!
No different than anywhere else, returning home wind was at its peak anything that could bang, clunk or rattle was banging, clunking and rattling!!!!

Saturday 23 July 2005
My little mate was a bit on the ordinary side it's an obvious sign when she turns her nose up at food. Not showing a bit of interest in our breakfast ritual, spitting the first piece of toast on offer she also failed to demonstrate much enthusiasm for paddock cruising????
Birds have been snacking out on a dead wallaby that had come to grief on home soil: being timely, I witnessed the visual effects of a kookaburra having the intestine stretched out of the corpse like a piece of elastic, choice!!!!

Knocking off there wasn't too much to write home about beside the persistence of bloody pesky currawongs and the outstanding effort at reducing the scotch thistle population. Threatening on and off, a brief passing shower arrived with Ross mid afternoon, the Ford giving clutch grief he was here again to retrieve tools, fortunately with enough spare time to join me in a pot of brewed tea ☺….

Sunday 24 July 2005
Getting organised and into gear, straight away the wheelbarrow was loaded with wood destined for the cottage because it wasn't going to be overly inviting outside. On a wood trip pushing passed the sand pile by the shed a neat shape caught my eye, a two cent coin being the new-found treasure, a coin I grew up with once having material worth is now a defunct piece of history….
Sun made very few cameo appearances from behind the curtain, leaving a blanket of cloud and the occasional light passing mist dusting to entertain. Mother Nature blew in some wild gusts after lunch sending all creatures great and small to their favourite sheltered spot. Retreating to the cottage I plugged in the power cord and flicked the switch supplying the right ingredients to the computer, simultaneously giving dinner a long slow cook on the heater top. Wishing only to maintain a long slow simmer I couldn't stoke the heater, focussing on warmth it's an interesting experience cooking and self-regulating the temperature to suit varying foods, a skill I'm getting in tune with ☺….

Monday 25 July 2005
Ms Tia's winter coat is starting to loosen, last night she offered one brush full, a small contribution toward the Tia fur beanie ☺….
It was bloody pleasant to drop the cardboard curtain first thing and not see one pesky currawong dotting paddocks anywhere. Its a toss-up as to whose spirit is going to be broken first, I've nearly had enough, managing to deliver the usual level of distraction, the mongrel birds commenced a series of visits starting mid morning!!!!
Dissecting life chatting to Mum and Dad predictably kept the seat warm for quite a while. Leaving my bum firmly wedged in the chair I fired up both the heater and computer to be comfortable digitising documented home life….
Mary, a dear Mildura friend, phoned to inform me Judy passed away early this morning resulting from a long ongoing battle with bowel cancer, today also being Judy's 69th birthday….

Tuesday 26 July 2005
Without a squawk, three currawongs sitting on fenceposts were whistling sweetly outside the bedroom window only to have me piss them off as soon as I got up….
Using the electricity saving practice of leaving a full boiler on the heater top overnight a pot of warm water waited this morning….
The plan in my brain for the day ahead was to simply duck into St. Marys, then as pre-arranged, grab Ross' house key and mechanically update my lagging washing, then return home and give the computer a work -out. Just checking my Post Office box took an hour, meeting Brian out front, Pam and David joined our conversation focussed on our

dissatisfaction and lack of confidence in local Council, particularly with the stand-over bullying by Russell 'the arsehole' building inspector. There were no objectors, but also no action toward the suggestion of forming a breakaway localised Council in St. Marys???? Leaving politics in town, I was content reading the paper while the machine did a far better job than my wrists at washing and wringing clothes, bypassing the drip-dry stage and drying by the heater in quick time....

Wednesday 27 July 2005
Currawongs are up there in annoyance with blowflies, I have to start blocking them out of mind they're taking up too much time. The upside to my obsession with the awful birds, beside the amount of fresh air and exercise, is the scotch thistle population has suffered. Another plus in the pursuit of the bastard bird is I'm getting very familiar with outside changes, frogs in particular have found a voice. Standing above the dam an abundant number of frogs were letting their presence in this world be known. On wanders I've been keeping an eye on the progress of the yellow tulips, nine spurs have now broken through the surface, that's close to the lot planted....
Blocking the mongrel birds from thoughts I headed indoors sparking up white goods to further advance dreams, today reaching a much needed energy boosting turning-point by editing my way into the year 2004 ☺ ....

Thursday 28 July 2005
The more time spent pestering currawongs and observing their behaviour I'm beginning to scratch the surface at understanding their psychology, and almost, predicted movements. They have great teamwork skills using a variety of calls from soft to intense they signal messages to other birds both in and out of view, a strong pack mentality....
More warm dry conditions in Eden, winter so far has made little impression even the nights aren't impossibly cold. A shame to spend such beautiful elements outdoors solely on currawongs so I took my best mate and friend the shovel for a walk to the front gate. Putting myself to work chipping bracken fern and prickly blackberry canes, I tidied the entrance area of bits the slasher didn't reach. Tendonitis in my forearm muscles and recurring tennis elbow were protesting with shovel work, my body is starting to show signs of wear....
Shovel put away and currawongs blocked from mind, by then I was ready to rest aching feet and arms sitting myself down to stare at the white goods screen....
Tia is making regular donations to the Tia fur beanie, the past three consecutive evenings she's donated a loaded brush from her gorgeous outfit ☺ ....

Friday 29 July 2005
One millimetre and five currawongs greeted the morning, happy to see moisture sadly only the currawongs persisted....
With all good intentions at home today pleasantly melted making a social trip over the mountain. In St. Marys, Brian stopped for a chat outside the supermarket, getting my bits done I then popped into Rita's studio. Barbara too called into the studio, giving me opportunity to report back on the rocking chair. Feeling disillusioned by Council also, Rita mentioned that she

and Ian received the maximum fine of $1200 under the guise of illegal building for studio renovations. They have only lined existing walls which doesn't require building permits???? With life matters current I left the studio headed for the next social stop, Pam had made bloody yummy fruit buns to share over a cuppa. Over food, drinks and good company, we made the world a better place creating a utopia in which to live before I headed back up the mountain to that already existing paradise ☺ ....

Turning into the driveway not one currawong was sighted but that excitement was short-lived. I would like an odometer on my boots to tally the kilometres Tia and I have done traipsing through paddocks. Out roaming we made a stop at the car garage where Ms Tia showed interest in Ross' stored haystack. Sniffing around the bottom level of the staircase stacked hay, Tia jumped up, making her way up to the top of the stack where she took her curiosity as a hay bail climber into the roof beams ☺ ....

Saturday 30 July 2005
Changing any thoughts I had, Lesley and Ross popped in mid morning with the suggestion we walk the gorge to the base of the waterfall, never having ever completed the gorge walk in its entirety I jumped at the idea. A brilliant suggestion on a perfect day, within minutes of sharing their idea we were heading to the valley paddock at the bottom of Rainbow Falls to gain access to the rocky stream bed leading to the base of the falls. It was a privilege to be able to leave empty handed because the gorge contained enough high quality water to drink along the way ☺ ....

A short walk along the rocky stream and a dense overhead canopy blocked out sun, from that point a sample of rainforest environment dominated the landscape and the temperature drop forced my jumper back on. The clean air was cool, sharp and crisp, a pleasure to breathe, with plenty of moisture around a variety of ferns, mosses and fungi flourished. Adding to the splendour was the array of rocks in all shapes, colours and sizes, quite a number contained fossils, so much to absorb and discover I had sensory overload. Concentrating on reflections in a rock pool, perfectly on cue the shadow image of an eagle flying overhead crossed over the pool. Another healthy animal experience, Lesley identified poo belonging to a Tassie Devil ☺ ....

We slowly progressed, not wandering far out of the rocky stream bed, Tia on the other hand left no stone unturned she was in her element. Without fear she scaled anything in her path making it to the pinnacle conquering the cliff face with us ☺ ....

Stepping out of my comfort zone of heights, to overcoming a small sharp terrain rise I scaled a fallen tree bridging access and leading up to the base of the main waterfall, victoriously reaching the pinnacle. Scampering up a goats track to the right of the main waterfall we made it back to the top, taking three hours to walk the few hundred metres, I was left fully charged by the full sensory experience ☺ ....

My little mate, hungry and tired after a huge adventurous day out snoozed by the heater leaving me in peace to prepare dinner, not a bad life ☺ ....

Sunday 31 July 2005
A pretty casual time of it at Rainbow Falls doing the usual daily bits 'n' pieces, I split wood, filled the woodbox, reset the fire and hassled currawongs, then for a change of pace phoned my

Mildura home. Mum and Dad helped celebrate Uncle Ian and Aunty Shirley's Golden Wedding Anniversary yesterday, a gathering of the Lucas clan in Red Cliffs with plenty of food, drink and socialising they couldn't help but have a good time☺….

Extending an invitation for 4p.m., David called with details of a 'concerned residents' meeting being held at e.ScApe Café in town for the purpose of opposing the use of our town for timber plantations. The forest pulp making machine has been offering farming families with large acreage $2500 per acre, buying selected properties throughout the state causing their usual level of discontent and fragmenting within communities for the purpose of plantation timber. The main concerns raised from the meeting seem to be excessive chemical use and its aerial application, the use of 1080 poison, slaughter of native animals, a high demand for water and the swallowing up of farming land. I'm unaware of any other unhealthy business that causes so much contention and division within communities????

Monday 1 August 2005

A pretty routine day where the unexpected never occurred. Almost out of light fire enhancing wood the wheelbarrow, me and my best friend, went for a walk out back bringing up a load then put the back of the splitter head to work breaking it down. With plenty of ice and very little available space left in the freezer the fridge also got attention. Defrosting had to be done before shopping Wednesday, with beer o'clock returning to the menu there wouldn't have been room to cool one down☺…. Heaven forbid!!!!

The computer too received time losing the afternoon clunking away on keys….

I'm letting the currawong distraction consume precious time, the positive outcome is thistles have copped a hiding and I now have to walk further and am only finding small stuff. Out strolling it's a pleasure passing through the front yard of the burnt out house. The scent of jonquils lingers sweetly in the air. Densely decorated with flowering bulbs, along with masses of jonquils, bacon and eggs and snowdrops too are also lifting a colourful display ☺….

Tuesday 2 August 2005

Getting through the daily essentials the morning was kissed goodbye….

Running low on ash at the loo, the heater supplied ample to keep deodoriser supplies going for some time. Putting my back into cutting wood, and close to an end, I brought the splitter down with force intent on doing damage, achieving the goal, but was slightly off target and the splitter handle copped the brunt of the impact without faring so well. The crack heard was of wood giving but the wood of the splitter handle, it's still holding together but just, its use-by-date has been brought forward!!!!

A habit I try to keep routine is to head indoors by the afternoon for computer time, staying true to form I took another small step in the big picture progressing the edit☺….

Wednesday 3 August 2005

Through repetitive use and consistency I've taught Tia 'smoko' and 'knock off'. True to my word, each time the word 'smoko' is used we migrate in the direction of the bungalow to share a snack, food is an easy teaching tool. The use of 'knock off' is associated with downing tools finishing what we're doing and straight away Tia loses concentration of the task at hand. Using both 'knock off' and 'smoko' together Tia's response is, you beauty, down tools and lets head to the bungalow and don't be lousy bringing on the food ☺!!!!

Payday and in need of stocking up, Destiny's boots were bouncing over the rock exposed dirt road bound for town by a respectable 10:30a.m.-ish, at that point thought I'd do the return trip home at a reasonable hour and invest in some digital time. Mentioning to Brian and Maggie I'd pop in for a brewed tea, fate directed a course guiding me into some much-needed time away from the life I love at Rainbow Falls....

Shopping complete and loaded, I pulled into the driveway leading up to Brian and Maggie's where it didn't take long to settle into plenty of chat over brewed tea. Sharing our philosophies I was invited to stay for lunch and without hesitation gave the offer a firm yes. While Maggie cooked up a storm she insisted I remain comfortable watching, talking and listening, doing exactly as I was told. Enjoying the red carpet treatment I was surprised to learn the shadow on the sundial had passed 3p.m., with warm groceries and beer I returned home totally pampered to fill the fridge ☺....

Rain cloud moved in with sunset and in a constipated effort made an attempt at a few stray spits and spats. It wasn't until I sat to write mid evening did anything convincing fall from the sky bringing with it some Tia 'cage rattling' thunder rumbles!!!!

Thursday 4 August 2005

Falling into to the land of nod to the sound of steady rain, my brain planned the pending day ahead, my head was filled with the notion of spending a wet day in the shed burning the stack of waiting boxes and prunings. However, dropping the cardboard curtain the fresh morning revealed blue sky as far as the eye could see. Shed plans foiled nevertheless a welcome 11mm gave the parched ground an overdue drink. Not to be robbed of quality shed time, retreated to the haven sweeping and exercising the handsaw making firewood....

At a frustrated feeble attempt at leaving a lasting memory in the minds of bloody currawongs I made a poor replica of a slingshot and it functioned accordingly. Stones I attempted to fling landed two meters in front of me, creating more of a joke than an arse-stinging experience ☺....

Elatedly celebrating the end of envelope twos first edit, having its contents now sitting on the hard drive in the machine, heavy black cloud crept over the range, the temperature plummeted and winter arrived in a flash. Moisture first began falling in its more solid form as small flakes of snow, melting quickly it failed to make an impression on the ground before giving way for the less mystical liquid moisture....

Cloud that looked like swallowing the landscape unsure whether to snow, hail or just rain, cleared doing a complete 360°, as quickly as it popped over the range it left, sun broke through sweetly like nothing ever existed. The only constructive thing for smart beings to do while this mixed bag was occurring above and around was to retreat to the cottage, spark up the heater, bask in its warmth and watch it happen in comfort with the added enjoyment of a beer in hand ☺....

Friday 5 August 2005

The temperature seriously dropped overnight, without a visible trace of frost the ground had frozen, rugged against the elements to step foot outside, the cold airflow had sealed a crust of ice over the cattle trough.... brrrr....

Winding down celebrations from the closure of envelope two I treated myself to a domestic catch up on life's little and big bits, particularly getting laundry current. Now other than the clothes on my back they're all clean....

Willingly doing regular family maintenance, Mum and Dad told me of a friend, Fan, having her 50th birthday advertised in their local paper. Shit, I remember going to 21st's and 30th birthdays, now people I once shared a cool beer with are turning 50! Luck was on my side during the phone call Tegan and bubby Dekira turned up, in Dekira chat she did high pitched 'Mariah Carey' squeals through the landline joining in on the conversation between Tegan and me ☺ ....

When beer o'clock and walkabout came around Tia and I migrated to the top boundary where the ocean and expansive view of the mountains and ranges is at its best. Taking the stroll up hill to the breathtaking viewing point, our movement disturbed feeding ravens, a blanket of them rose into available airspace to evaluate the intrusion....

Saturday 6 August 2005

The privilege of a healthy and readily available wood stack has all but gone forcing me back into 'hunter gatherer' mode, appreciating just how much time the convenience frees up....

Its time to train my brain into giving up on currawongs, my fitness level has risen and the paddocks look cleaner but it's also smart to know when to quit, I'm tired of chasing my tail with no measurable results....

Psyching my brain into keeping the editing flow happening I placed envelope three on display where it will regularly be in my face just daring me to sharpen the pencil ☺ !!!!

Indulging in the luxury of warmth the cottage offered I leant against the westerly window ledge sipping thoughtfully on a beer watching the sun quietly set. Interesting looking blue-black cloud formations passed around putting their energy into the distant mountain ranges, wind drifted a light moisture dusting our direction but nothing measurable made its way this far over until after dark....

Sunday 7 August 2005

The briefest of showers 6a.m.-ish got me all excited for one immersed in the shed, still horizontal in bed it was determined there and then that would be the course ahead anyway. Feeling more like winter lately, with beanie pulled firmly down over my ears the cold westerly trough of air followed me into the institution....

Just tinkering about, I spent the complete day pottering in the haven breaking down prunings and doing a spot of sweeping, it was like revisiting and old friend. Aware Ms Tia had been absent far too long I went to investigate her whereabouts, having shown interest in road kill earlier it was an obvious starting point. Tia had entered next doors paddock under fencing via a well used native animal thoroughfare, the sight sent off alarm bells after having been warned by them next door that, "I'd hate to have to shoot your dog if I found it in my paddocks"!!!! Returning Tia back on safe turf, together we followed fenceline sealing possible exit points ☺ !!!!

Factoring in beer o'clock inside the shed looking out, as I've spent many a memorable moments in the past, was content from my perch watching life pass. A native hen busily darting around caught my interest and amusement, getting its little legs moving fairly picking them up and putting them down ☺ ....

Monday 8 August 2005
Doing a boundary walk checking gaps under fencing, native animal movement through the night keeps re-opening Tia sized holes. I don't mind native animals coming it's Tia's curiosity luring her out that bothers me, grabbing a couple of old bricks I blocked the main Tia problem gaps more securely....
Only managing to whet an appetite yesterday again spent the day in the haven for a double dose of mind therapy. Stopping for lunch a dog, unnoticed by Tia, wandered into the yard. In case territorial rights were displayed I shooed it away averting any potential health risks, failing in contacting the dog's owner Charles I opted more pleasantly to return to the shed....
Shutting the shed gate behind and walking out, the job of breaking down pruned branches for burning is now complete, only requiring a rainy day to send them up the flue....
The Tia stress monitor kicked into action, it's the second consecutive night this week spotlighters have been out shooting native animals in neighbouring paddocks!!!!

Tuesday 9 August 2005
Didn't I get rewarded, exposing its true colours before raising my head off the pillow low cloud had filled the sky and produced light passing showers, in the company of wind, it was a perfectly designed 'spark up the heater' shed day. Not wandering too far from the hot drum I managed to fill its face burning everything desired. Succeeding in a major clean up I found some long hidden floor space that exposed the sheds actual size ☺ ....
Falling to late afternoon, 7mm was delivered in spits and spats, most of those millimetres fell while I was on the phone to Loui dude. In the cottage returning Loui's call I caught one from Phillip, he wanted to know whether we'd received any snow, apparently an extremely cold front with mountain snow has been forecast, winter is finally arriving????
Switching fires near dark I headed up to warm the cottage and cook. Making a start on dinner Mother Nature also made a start on millimetre number 8 and didn't stop, getting comfortably set in....
Without sighting left behind evidence in quite sometime I was getting quietly confident the cottage was close to vermin free, finding a piece of pumpkin a rodent had snacked on is a blunt reminder not to get too confident!!!!
Envelope three has been emptied of its contents and affixed to my makeshift cardboard clipboard, one conscience step closer to getting back into it....

Wednesday 10 August 2005
Reluctant to get out of bed, the planets aligned, Tia too was happy to stay warm and comfy snuggled and daydreaming, remaining horizontal I released my brain to free range to hearts content ☺ ....
A wolf in sheep's clothing, sun may have been shining but the air temperature was a bit ordinary, even currawongs weren't sighted first up. Taking the ritual morning open up and

walkabout 7mm was emptied from the gauge legacy of the night. Visually demanding and attention grabbing was the first cluster of daffodils freshly exploded into flower☺....
Making a quick run between the Sister's and taking no time to complete the desired bits, I pulled up at Pam and Terry's before heading back up the mountain. Able to be sighted from their home, Mt Ben Lomond was snow capped, explaining the cold airflow we're receiving....
Destiny unpacked and wood wheelbarrowed up from the shed, the first of two snow-showers gently touched down at Rainbow Falls melting on landing. The sight of snow falling fills me with the excited eagerness of a child, a sense of something new, fresh and seldom witnessed occurring brings with it a level of strong happy emotion☺!!!!
Radio news reported pretty widespread snowfalls both in Tassie and throughout Victoria, snow fell in places it hasn't been seen for anywhere between twenty and fifty years. A flow of air from the Antarctic is behind the cold snap and unseasonable conditions☺....

Thursday 11 August 2005
It was such a bloody cold one last night I didn't even take my beanie off before bed, and there was still no need to break out the sunscreen today, after combing my hair I simply re-pulled the beanie back over my ears. With a thick crust of ice covering the cattle trough it always amuses me to see mosquito larvae wriggling below surviving the freezing temperature???? brrrr....
Cold elements are certainly no deterrent for new life, after a slow start bulbs are exploding into a variety of colour all over the place, and garlic planted sometime back that I had given up on is also shooting away☺????
Pottering away on domestic duties, which are unable to hold my concentration when there's something more interesting to distract, I easily found a diversion. Surrounded in lush greenery by the cottage, dried up dead hydrangea blooms looked out of place and in need of a haircut, getting heavy handed they received a severe prune. Unloading the stacked wheelbarrow of its booty of hydrangea prunings onto the tidy, freshly swept shed floor, I struggle to keep it clean for long☺!!!!

Friday 12 August 2005
When finally getting to call time my own last night, after dinner, dishes, journal writing and completing my tax return, I parked by the heater to watch wild gusting wind start dismantling temporary waterproofing repair jobs around windows. Needless to say I had the ladder, drill and hammer out again today repairing temporary repairs....
Another thick crust of ice covered the cattle trough, the Antarctic conditions giving us the freezer treatment eased by lunchtime enabling a trade from beanie to peaked cap....
With the luxury of a healthy wood stack gone time was invested into generating enough to keep us warm for another evening. Using myself as a manual chainsaw is bloody hard work, it makes me really appreciate the times wood is just there waiting to be collected....

Saturday 13 August 2005
The blast of icy Antarctic air passed reverting to the mild conditions winter has afforded and we have become accustomed....

Fuelling a habit, I pushed the wheelbarrow behind the cattle yards scouting along the top of the gorge dragging up good sized weighty limb wood then me and the handsaw cut a load to keep the home fires burning another night....

Fulfilling a request, Lesley and Ross stopped by delivering prints of photos Lesley took from our walk through the gorge, assisting in my desire to send memorable photos to Mildura to share with family. Taking a fresh pot of tea outside, we basked in afternoon sun and shared our worldly knowledge. During idle chatter over tea the topic of another gorge walk was raised, this time include others who've expressed interest in the experience with a barbecue to follow.... A day out socialising at home, rather novel ☺....

Sunday 14 August 2005

I had quite an interesting morning getting ready for a trip into town for bread, milk and to post mail. The neighbours' kids again came down the road with their dog off lead, a large black unknown variety, looking for a repeat performance of yesterday. While Tia and I were roaming paddocks yesterday a few kids with dog in tow decided to fill time with a walk along the road, not illegal, but Rainbow Falls' boundary fence is all that stopped this dog from ripping Tia's throat out. Instructing Tia a short distance away, I put space between the dogs and told the kids to move their dog on, with its sheer strength and body mass they had no hope at any control. To finish the stand off I told them to just go so their dog would follow....

Passing on their knowledge, and not real bright, the neighbours' kids attempted the same stunt this morning, once is accidental twice is deliberately looking for trouble. Leaving Tia confined to the bungalow I went to tell the kids not to bring their dog onto the road unrestrained, reaching their desired destination, I met them in my driveway entrance. Not confining its aggression to dogs only, their dog wanted a piece of me through the front gate, plainly a dangerously aggressive beast. Again the kids had no hope of controlling the unrestrained bitch she was prepared to have a go at anyone or anything!!!!

A practice I want nipped in the bud before they turn it into a sport; returning from town I made a stop at the by-laws officer's home to air my concern over the experience too dangerous to ignore....

Accepting their offer to cut the most recent fence post pallet stack, arriving unannounced, I wasn't home when Pam and Terry visited and left behind the calling card of a cut load of wood. Sorry I had missed Pam and Terry to assist their selfless act lightened the load on my very labour intensive life. Playing answering machine ping-pong attempting to phone grateful thanks through we never got to talk personally. What remained of the afternoon dissolved into bringing many, many, many wheelbarrow loads of wood to the shed for dry storage ☺....

Monday 15 August 2005

Wind lifted and darkness hung over the bungalow when I was ready to get up, a good sign the sun wasn't shining. Pushing the toilet around wind gave me a rocking. I was certainly in the right spot for being frightened if some part of the loo decided to blow off ☺....

I swallowed the last bite of lunch. The wind swung from west around to pure south, pushing those rain clouds and cold airflow, that were bypassing, directly at us. Sun that had previously been making cameo appearances was totally obscured. The Huntsman's Cap Mountain, usually up close and largely visible, was no more than a faint silhouette. Wind gusts carrying small

drops of horizontal rain, had a spectacular and dramatic entrance. The performance finished without a whimper and within an hour the theatre was vacant????
The privilege of abundant wood afforded me the luxury to indulge myself in a deep bath, having pots of water boiling on the heater top all afternoon. Sitting close by keeping an eye on things I clunked away on keys updating the journal digitally….
Two paragraphs shy of shutting the computer down I received a welcome call from Anna responding to a message left on her answering machine. Catching up to where we last left off, we agreed to remain in touch ☺ ….

Tuesday 16 August 2005
A native hen caught Tia's attention and she took chase; the hen many steps ahead took refuge inside the dam fence. Gifted with patience Tia waited. Checking Tia's whereabouts after some time found her still sitting upright to attention outside the dam fence, like the hen, just watching and waiting. Luckily for the hen Tia had a date with Destiny….
Loose arrangements with Ross to use his washing machine were so loose he forgot. Pleasantly filling time, I went the remainder of the way down the mountain making final arrangements with Pam over a brew for our trip to St. Helens tomorrow. The driving purpose behind the trip is to support Mary-Anne's first 'Thanks for the Memory' program at Doherty's Resort, a segment taken from her time in radio….
Returning up the mountain I had a chance meeting with Ross out on a horse ride. Taking his house keys I went ahead with a few extra horsepower. The first load was complete when horse and rider trotted down the driveway; over cuppa's snacks, chats, oh, and completing laundry, the afternoon escaped. Returning to Rainbow Falls with enough daylight to get the fire and laundry set-up before night fell….
Checking the answering machine saw my social life increase. Waiting was a dinner invitation from Melanie and family for tomorrow night ☺ …. A definite yes was given in response….

Wednesday 17 August 2005
Picking a variety of flowers from home's selection of bulbs I prepared a bunch for Pam and another destined for Mary-Anne. Life organised on the home front, and as promised, I picked Pam up on the way through to St. Helens and Doherty's Resort. Mary-Anne's 'Thanks for the Memory' program resembled that of a former announcers reunion; including Mary-Anne hosting, Scoots, Phillip, myself and Nana Raye were part of the audience that filled the comfortable lounge. The older music style is not particularly my preferred but the social aspect and atmosphere along with Mary-Anne's personality filled the room ☺ ….
Making home soil 5:30p.m.-ish, and with a dinner invitation at 6:30, I had just enough time to put the groceries away before passing myself on the road….
Living next door, the dinner invitation extended to Ross also, leaving Destiny and Tia at Ross', together we walked to the aroma of a beautiful home cooked meal shared over a bottle of wine in a comfortable family environment created by Melanie. Putting in a huge day of it blew the social cobwebs right off my hermit existence ☺ ….

Thursday 18 August 2005
One of my favourite mood days, very gentle and disappearing at home quietly, it was kicked off with the not so taxing job of changing over Destiny's registration label....
In an attempt at finding the two metre strip of path at the rear of the burnt out house, working from the top of the stack covering concrete, with the help of my little mate took a potential wet days worth of prunings to the shed. They'll have a better chance of disappearing sitting near the heater....
Taking the weight off my feet having a break from outside activities, I kept the receiver warm for quite a while chewing Mum and Dad's ears off sharing life's latest developments. The big news from the family home, after finalising the first weekend of play Dad's sitting in 4th position halfway through Club Championships at golf. If Dad fares well this coming weekend he could give the competition a nudge ☺ ....

Friday 19 August 2005
Pottering around making home life comfortable and clean Tia alerted me to someone arriving. Going out to meet and greet, our guest was aggressive kicking out at Tia's welcome. Coming up the driveway snapping at us just like their dog, I promptly reminded Kristy where she stood, and to respect it. It seems the letter from the by-laws officer arrived, the loving wife, mother and neighbour, Kristy came over ranting and raving looking for an argument regarding their dog waving the letter about in her hand. At least polite enough to park at the gate and walk in, remaining calm I replied with logic and legal fact, flooring ridiculous arguments and leaving little retort. Kristy opted to repeat the line, "next time we see your dog on our property we'll shoot it", replying to her, "you've already used that line on me, I'm aware of that". Looking for another line of argument she went on to say "next time you try running me off the road just remember my cars bigger than yours". Wow, feeling like I was back in primary school that comment really floored me, it deserved a little giggle. She also argued "we're on a public road and the kids are free to use it", that I didn't disagree with, but insisted while in public you must have your dog restrained. She then argued "but we live in the bush we're allowda do what we want", again with a logical reply said "even the bush has rules", I also told her attempts at threats and intimidation don't work. Getting nowhere with her argument she began retreating back down the driveway as negative and unfulfilled as she arrived....
Dull light on an overcast day not generating too much warmth, and being self-indulgent, I sparked the heater up early and hibernated the afternoon away in the cottage. Building a cosy nest I put final touches to a covering letter accompanying Lesley's photos destined for Mildura and Mum and Dad. Keeping literary pursuits on the go I thoroughly went over the contents of the latest correspondence in regards to the radio discrimination case. A pleasant achievement while settled in the warm nest was to phone Doris celebrating her 90th birthday ☺ ....
Unable to let heat energy sit idle the heater top was put to use boiling a couple of pots of water for the purpose of using it as a weedicide alternative to keep fenceline clear....

Saturday 20 August 2005
Our piece of the world was plunged under a thick blanket of low cloud dropping visibility to twenty metres. Blocking everything from view, a miracle day treated me for several hours before lifting and exposing sun patiently waiting a turn on the other side....

Disappearing with the last of morning fog behind the cattle yards I was as good as Tia at disappearing. Collecting limb wood I became aware of Tia's absence, returning after being called for some time puffing hard from the direction of the gorge, conscious of the neighbour's reinforced threats she was kept on a tight rein….

Breaking the mind block I picked up the makeshift clipboard and put the pencil to work on the hardcopy, starting on the contents of envelope three finally cornering myself and realising it isn't that hard….

Impressed at having revisited the pursuits of editing, afterwards, and being multi-skilled, I indulged in the fine art of beer o'clock while simultaneously kicking the ball for Tia ☺ ….

Sunday 21 August 2005

Wind pushed us around like a bully through the night and affected the electricity supply, it decided on a stop work meeting for a few hours. Destiny's clock was the only reliable time source, having only one clock and the answering machine to reset digital life was up and running in no time….

Playing havoc with temporary repairs, strong dismantling gusts had me once again up the ladder temporarily repairing temporary repairs. Wind also pushed a few minor fronts through, it wasn't until the third front blew in I even considered changing my shoes from the pair with a hole in the sole….

With the arrival of the fourth front Ms Tia and I were comfortable in the cottage with a fire cracking, rain pulled up with front four but the air temperature remained hovering in the nippy degrees. Contemplating making a mark in the editing world I parked in the rocker and there my arse got stuck staring through clean glass watching a flickering flame. Prying loose from the grip of the rocker, only for brief spurts, to empty boiling pots collect more water and put wood on the fire…. Not a bad life if you don't weaken ☺ ….

Monday 22 August 2005

An unsettled cement mixer of a stomach woke me 2a.m.-ish, conscious enough to get dressed and make it outside, from the bottom of my boots my stomach emptied its contents. Leaving the ill feeling outside I returned to peaceful slumber until morning. Resurfacing with a more content tummy and not one currawong to be heard or sighted, a perfect start ☺ ….

The woodbox was empty enough to sweep out, ash was taken to the loo with a view, water collected, dishes done, bungalow de-furred and another store of wood brought up from the shed. On a cool day with the fire crackling Ms Tia and I remained snuggy in the cottage all afternoon, shifting my thinking began focussing on hardcopy editing….

Without physical support days can be pretty long, there are no exemptions, from switching the light on to turning it off and everything in between, I have to do it all. Sharing the load would free up time, to walk in on a lit fire or dare I get too bold to say, a meal cooked, is a luxury I have trouble fathoming. Shaving a couple of hours off finishing time, which is anywhere between 9-11p.m., would be pretty special. The future and optimism is a nice place to put wishes, dreams and hope ☺ ….

Tuesday 23 August 2005
Noticing my best mate a little on the lethargic side lately I tracked the reason finding and removing a doozy of a tick comfy inside her right leg. Tia can be tick free with increased energy for turning seven tomorrow ☺ ....
Getting rid of the white toe look on my 'blundstones' literally took them for a walk to the shed lacing them with nugget. Propped inside the entrance out of the breeze basked in sunshine, Ms Muffet and I propped contentedly lazing in the warmth on offer watching wrens busily dance over the yard in their endless search to keep their little tummies full. A few kookaburras cruised about with a keen eye for anything that moved, and frogs in the dam provided a backing chorus of croaks to the activity filling my senses. Aware of enjoying time of perfect bliss, several horrible black and white things flew in putting an end to a utopian moment....
Developing into ideal out of doors elements an executive decision was made to utilise it to the maximum, beginning with a play by the vegie patch taking composted comfrey and other unwanted weeds dumping them in wheel ruts to end their cycle....
Keen on hearing how Dad fared in golf championships I phoned, without hanging around after finishing his round results won't be known until there's a copy of tomorrows paper collected, however, Dad was happy with his performance hitting the ball. Comparing weather conditions, Dad said he's already planted tomatoes I've been waiting for the return of swallows as an indicator to make a start. Following the call to Mum and Dad I returned to the vegie patch with renewed enthusiasm, digging a planting ring for pumpkin seeds then made beds planting tomato and broccoli seeds ☺ ....
The neighbours keep proving themselves as genuine drop-kicks, following a couple of quiet days tonight they fired up the kids quad bike, guaranteed unable to help themselves and head down the road, they're not the sharpest tools in the shed!!!!

Wednesday 24 August 2005
Fitting to celebrate my little mates 7th birthday Mother Nature turned on the elements. After reclaiming real estate doing the morning roam around and start up stuff, supporting a full tummy, Ms Tia was more than delighted to follow sun basking ☺ ....
Ms Tia's birthday was suitably spent outside pottering and incorporating all the bits she joins in on helping. Stripped down to a t-shirt and beanie free by 10a.m. by 11a.m. I even lost the t-shirt for a while. Raising the thermostat that degree too much prompted me to bring the shovel up from the shed and dust it off, having it on standby incase any of our wriggly friends came out of hibernation and paid us a visit....
Watering the pumpkin patch nursery I spied an establishing patch of thistles and gave the heels of my boots a workout, scratching around like an old chook the life was kicked out of them....
Standing out by being nestled amongst her lashes I pulled a tick from the birthday girl, attached to her eyelid she took some convincing to keep still, it won't hurt!!!!
Visible from all corners of the yard, smoke from yet another huge burn is billowing skyward from the direction of distant mountain ranges. Burning now for its second consecutive day, the pattern of the large column of billowing smoke reminded me of an oversized chimney, photos taken from the top of the dam I affectionately called 'Tasmania, Australia's chimney'....

Thursday 25 August 2005
For a third day smouldering smoke filled distant mountain ranges nestled heavy like fog, sadly the only aspect I'm grateful for is climatic conditions were in favour keeping it at a distance giving my lungs a rest. I would like to subject the offices of management who approve these burns to that level of inescapable smoke that's good enough for us to endure. I'd like to share the experience!!!!
The seven year and one day old girl has been running around frisky like a three-year-old with renewed energy since the ticks have been removed. Using part of her rejuvenated energy Ms Tia gave chase to a bush chook, taking refuge under a tight growing holly shrub Tia was smart enough to pull up there and patiently wait, and wait and wait and wait some more. Returning from the chase Tia used the cattle trough for a quick dunk and cool down. Water quality in the trough looked a bit ordinary, stirred up and with quite a bit of fur floating around we had our usual game emptying it out, Tia tries catching the water leaving the bucket load I toss ☺....
With outside life tended to we retreated from the suns warm rays disappearing into the cottage hardcopy editing, and that's where I remained until the next phase kicked in. Cooking, bath, dishes, and journal writing nearly complete, at 10:20p.m. the night is soon to be my own. Some nights I'm more efficient at it than others....

Friday 26 August 2005
Failing to leave Rainbow Falls since Thursday week ago we were due for a few grocery items and to air my hermit existence with a bit of human contact. I really enjoy the friendliness and intimacy of a small town the faces behind shop counters are always ready with a smile and kind word. It never usually takes long to stop on the footpath of the shopping strip to have a yarn. Talking my way through town to the bakery, Evelyn had fresh donuts, grabbing a half dozen, I headed to Pam and Terry's to share them over a cup of brewed coffee....
Having blown the social cobwebs right off hermitism returned back up the hill to the haven and the life I love. Back to using my mouth purely for breathing, with what remained of the afternoon Tia and I pottered around outside maximising another magic performance provided courtesy of Mother Nature. With help, tinkering in the vegie patch always puts me in a very relaxed state, watering the pumpkins Ms Tia just asks for the hose to be pointed her way. Being the water baby she is, whether it be dripping off the end of the shed roof after rain or running out the end of a hose, Tia's there trying to catch it and put it in its place ☺....
Staying outside until the last minute offered the privilege of watching a spectacular golden sunset disappear behind the mountain. Leaving the great outdoors turned attention next to cooking a meal for me and my little buddy, putting petrol in our motors so we can do it all again tomorrow ☺....

Saturday 27 August 2005
Giving Ms Tia the head tilts, sitting upright and full of concern she could hear a puppy from the recently born litter across the road whimpering. Satisfied the puppy's needs had been met and it settled, Tia gave her crutch a lick then snoozed by my side basking in morning sun ☺????
When finally my arse was pried from the chair, bending a tummy supporting the right level of milos, I rose to standing. Walking from the optimum spot in the shed for absorbing maximum

morning heat and sunlight led me to the fate of spoiling myself tinkering in domestic things. Warm conditions again had an impressive go at drying my weak wristed hand washing leaving little to finish off by the heater....

Chasing a moving target is a little energy zapping, looking for an infusion of renewed driving inspiration I've been thinking about a cut off point where I can call my book finished, offering a solid target to work towards. The ending will be signified by the finalisation of something big, odds are in favour for the completion of the tribunal hearing putting an end to the radio bullshit, on an even par for a finish is South Sister saved from being logged. Some long shots which aren't out of the question for a surprise finish would be a joint visit from Mum and Dad, or heaven forbid, maybe some romance in my life, or is that just plain wishful thinking ☺ ????

Sunday 28 August 2005

I'm aware of thistles as I am of those pesky birds, unable to turn a blind eye and walk past I don't even go to the toilet without kicking a few out on the way. Traipsing all over paddocks in travels I'm only finding a sprinkling of juvenile thistle growth. The rejuvenation of Rainbow Falls makes me proud watching it return from a rundown property that once grew thistles taller than me ☺ !!!!

De-furring the bungalow has slipped back into daily routine, Tia's not in full swing hair loss yet but she's leaving a reasonable deposit. My little mate wasn't firing on all cylinders, after a chew on grass she returned for her breakfast. Exerting energy spurts Tia's showing typical symptoms of a tick being attached, searches have found nothing, I only get real concerned when she's off her food....

Obviously winter still hasn't finished, but the oppressive heat associated with summer is already showing glimpses of arriving, driving me to shed clothes. With minimal snow around this season the ground stayed warmer keeping the soil temperature up, winter has made very little impression????

Cloud gathered to take the sting out of the sun but my mind had already been made, retreating indoors opened the electrical circuits to the computer giving it full voltage then let my fingers do the walking ☺ ....

Monday 29 August 2005

With warm conditions continuing the shovel has been a best friend and never far out of reach, it's even been that warm butter is spreadable ☺ !?!?

Putting the shovel to use made my mark on a patch of hemlock becoming established under the blackwood tree in the paddock by the road, particularly concentrating on areas the tractor can't reach. Working under the blackwood tree stopped currawongs from settling to feed, I didn't see or hear one pesky bird until late afternoon, a few tried their luck near sunset and left without resistance....

Before gearing my brain for hardcopy editing I dialled the numbers and got current on family life with Mum and Dad. Feeling pretty pleased, and for good reason, Dad fared well at golf in Inter Club Championships coming second in his age category he also took second position in the overall competition. A rewarded outcome stemming from four days of play over two consecutive weekends of concentrating and consistently playing well ☺ ....

There is a drought on at home for something resembling a semi-decent tennis ball, the situation is that dire Ms Tia knocked off a spud from the vegie patch to play with, a healthy alternative, at minimum the spud had a circular shape and rolled ☺....

Tuesday 30 August 2005
We had just come in from the paddocks after pissing the few pesky currawongs off when threatening cloud released some moisture, sending me indoors to change into shoes without holes, there and then a shed day was declared....
While we literally had our heads in the clouds I stuffed the face of the heater watching prunings disappear up the flue, my little mate kept herself amused pitting her skill catching water offerings dripping off the end of the shed roof. By knock off the top level of the shed was cleared of prunings and after a sweep up it looked pretty damned tidy, it's a desire to keep it in that state until after the gorge walk and barbecue set for October 8.... On a social occasion it's important to look ones best ☺....
A useful 6mm had fallen up until heading in for the evening, whatever else is delivered is more than welcome to add a bit of life to a fading yard, it won't do the newly planted vegie seeds any harm either. Rain adds more life to the soil than any amount of water I put on from the tap....

Wednesday 31 August 2005
Holding my tongue in the right direction, I struggled to pull on a pair of gumboots worn at Lyndall and Geoff's wedding as a joke, to keep my 'blunnies' dry for town. Persisting until lunchtime, 32mm put in a big wet finish to the month and officially the last calendar day of winter. Tia, me and the umbrella went roaming for the pure pleasure of immersing in the beauty of low cloud floating effortlessly across the ground, also absorbing first hand the visual cloud formations draped over both North and South Sisters that at times obscured them totally. Returning from the self-indulgent euphoric stroll in utopia a gust of wind turned the umbrella inside out and it become a victim of the elements, bugger!!!!
Organised early, we loaded into Destiny for a trip over the mountain to save ourselves from starvation. With very little left in stores, and being payday, I had a huge shop that also reinstated beer o'clock to the menu ☺....
Cooking everyday shits me. With plenty, the afternoon disappeared slicing, dicing, chopping and throwing another log on the fire, preparing a pot of stew to see us through a few meals....
Strengthening wind, strong enough to near on blow my beanie off, broke up cloud and temporary repairs and allowed the sun to breakthrough. Gusts raised the carpet, lino and rug in the cottage through gaps in the floor boards, a sign of a nasty night ahead!!!!

Thursday 1 September 2005
First drowned then snap frozen, we're back to being aware of snakes and basking in sunshine all within the timeframe of 48-hours. There's never a dull moment and if there blissfully ever is it never lasts long. An overnight cold snap froze remnants left in puddles from yesterday's rain, and patches of lawn were frozen crunching underfoot stepping out into the first day of spring....

Returning for spring and sighted for the first time, swallows are back to nest in their usual spot in the shed....

All the little bits done to make home life comfortable we adjourned to the haven, joining the swallows. Basking in direct sunshine I wore the pencil down hardcopy editing, kissing the afternoon goodbye. Pencil and paper filed for beer o'clock and walkabout, its not easily missed when a large limb from a tall dead tree falls onto a neighbouring paddock gate leaving it with a deep impression concertina, ouch!!!!

Friday 2 September 2005

Rousing from sleep my brain jumped into gear formulating and planning its way to, and through, the 'directions conference' in Launceston dealing with radio mismanagement, which has been deferred for a month. A letter waiting amongst post Wednesday confirmed a new date and time of Friday, November 11, at 9a.m., getting to Launceston by 9a.m. will mean a bloody early start....

Met by an ominous looking sky the dismantled cottage waterproofing was again repaired just incase, but failing to carry out her threats not one drop of moisture fell, all the same I felt happy being prepared for any of Mother Natures moods on offer....

A deliverer of news, Ross popped in for a visit lunchtimeish, received via his email he printed a hardcopy of a welcome reply e-mail from Anna, the electronic world might be quick but not for me. In no rush, we shared conversation over a cuppa then a garden progress tour. The entire dozen tulip bulbs Ross gave me emerged, several ready to flower, 99% of the garlic planted has also taken off....

Looking for a repeat of yesterday further progressing hardcopy editing, however, to keep warm today we made full use of sun behind glass in the bungalow....

Sun setting on my back winding up walkabout I headed in to spark up the heater. Making practical use of the heaters energy as efficiently as possible I've been continually keeping the boiler raging. Using boiling water as an alternative to weedicide, scorching ground in hard to get at nooks is saving on shovel work. Receiving boiler attention at present is the front of the cottage, scorching around the stairway slabs of rock at the doorway entrance and gradually edging across the front, with little physical input the outcome is perfect ☺....

Saturday 3 September 2005

My little friend was reluctant to rise this morning, the purple ball lying in her bed offered all the answers it only gets dragged out when she's feeling the discomfort of constipation. Silenced by her species Tia communicates effectively when she's feeling off....

The presence of currawongs dominating air space having dwindled and their loud intrusive squawk diminished other birds with sweeter chirps, chortles and whistles could be heard, a preferred option. Never making a currawong feel welcome we moved on a few unwelcome pesky birds, while doing so I noticed a stout little shrub covered in a mass of yellow flowers and thorns, returning straight away with the shovel. Resembling that of the dreaded noxious weed gorse, it's a real environmental threat and a bloody pest if it has the opportunity to take hold. The tap root alone was a test to drive the shovel through causing me to raise a sweat, feeling as strong as a half-sucked peppermint a sweat didn't take much to bring on....

For yet another afternoon, concentration was directed at the wad of paper awaiting attention. Distracted from pencil pushing I did a dash for the ringing phone, puffing, I retrieved Stacey from the answering machine. Picking up where we last left off an easy hour disappeared in chat, returning after a respectable jaw workout to continue on toward dreams of publishing a book ☺....

After wearing out enough lead in my pencil I downed tools to rip the lid off a coolly and go walkabout, wearing out my shoes behind the cattle yards kissing young thistles goodbye until the setting sun doused the lights....

Sunday 4 September 2005

A meek and mild one began gently soaking up direct sun charging my solar panels cradling a milo. Reclaiming the shed, swallows were getting cranky at our intrusion. It didn't take Tia and the swallows long to slip back into their habits, swallows do fleeting swoops beak snapping while Tia in turn tries in vain to round them out of the shed with tail wagging ownership barks!!!!

Allowing time to comfortably have the dishes put away after Mum's traditional Sunday roast, I phoned to wish Dad 'Happy Fathers Day'. Joining the table for lunch, the phone was handed around getting to chat with Aunty Claire also she proudly shared the news of her grandson Jayden winning the Australian junior golf title played in Queensland. Taking the limelight in conversation were the recent photos posted to Mildura, containing the harboured pocket of rainforest and spectacular scenery the prints taken in the gorge by Lesley stole the show ☺....

Playing 'Farmer Sue' I gave the potential author a rest getting busy with the pruning saw along the top boundary fence. I assume planted complements of bird poo, removed some unknown establishing unfriendly looking thorny shrubs entangled through fencing wire, a couple of juvenile holly plants also got in the way of the blade....

Monday 5 September 2005

I wasn't feeling on top of the world first up, the world was on top of me. Having such a physically demanding life is beginning to take its toll on a body trying to recover. Aches and muscular pain are developing through repetition and ignoring it because life has to go on isn't helping....

Walking the boundary pissing off currawongs, two of the neighbours kids roamed onto the road with their dog unrestrained and again it wanted a piece of me and Tia, I firmly said to them 'have you learnt nothing from the last two outings'. I'm now convinced they're outright thoughtless idiots!!!!

In need of a distraction, timely Ross and Lesley turned up to borrow the tractor, a dirty carby contributed to Fergus running rough, with time to spare I put on a brew and we traded our views on life....

Driving her to the hose, Destiny copped a bit of overdue TLC, without having to be asked to play in water Tia helped wash the outside, one splash for Destiny the next for Tia. Continuing with the spoiling, I got windows sparkling and totally going berserk nuggeted the tyres, I'm now reluctant to leave the yard with her ☺....

Without the luxury of an instruction manual, I fiddled around with the knobs of the metal detector left behind to play with using the metal of the shovel blade to calibrate beep volume.

The yard being full of buried bits of metal I didn't have to walk too far for it to start beeping. Reluctant to unnecessarily dig up the lawn willy-nilly I put it away to rethink how to best put the new toy to use????

Tuesday 6 September 2005
Home basics done and the tractor's absence vacating the bottom level of the haven, I seized the moment retreating there for a tidy up. In keeping with a brain therapy theme attention was turned next to the vegie patch. Digging a small pit I made up a compost mix combining straw, ash, cow poo and a dusting of soil, a blend for the future to activate plant growth.... yumo....
Down to straw hat and singlet with hot days back in action, conditions are also bringing back the habits of carrying the shovel and shutting doors not wishing to let any unwelcome visitors in. Winter is phasing out without really getting off the ground????
Eliminating the white toe farm look from my boots with a lick of nugget polished them up in readiness for two consecutive big ones. Renewing my license forced a trip to St. Helens for the nearest Service Tasmania outlet. Maximising tomorrow's trip, I'm sharing lunch with Mary-Anne and picking up photographic darkroom gear offered by Loui and stored with her mum AEnone. An invitation from Ross for Thursday included a barbecue lunch attending the St. Marys School 'community garden open day' where he spends his working life, how could I say no ☺....
When the day lost its sting on went the 'thistle kicking' boots and with my best friend we disappeared into the paddocks. Out walkabout a severe stomach cramping pain moved in and floored me for three-quarters of an hour, for a while I didn't think I was going to see my next birthday, it has however remained on the calendar, codeine obviously doesn't agree with my body!!!!

Wednesday 7 September 2005
Up early for license renewal day, thoughts were directed into making an attempt at getting home from St. Helens without delay to put the afternoon in at Rainbow Falls. With time up my sleeve I leisurely roamed the yard picking a bunch of flowers for both Mary-Anne and Loui's mum. Ready, and with Destiny packed by 9:30a.m. the plan was looking good....
In appreciation of her TLC Destiny sparked into life like a champion, in gear with the desire to move forward Destiny pulled up lame, the passenger rear wheel wouldn't turn. Waiting on mechanical knowledge to arrive with Ross I jacked Destiny up to make a start by pulling the offending wheel off, proving stubborn the answer soon became evident. Caked inside the rim and around the drum was more clay than should have been there, washing Destiny turned the stored clay into a mud pie and when it dried it set like concrete. Managing to have the problem fixed as Ross arrived, contributing to the exercise he put the wheel back on and reminded me of the moral of the story, 'don't wash your car' ☺!!!!
On a second attempt at leaving the front gate I made Mary-Anne's in perfect time for lunch. Contributing to a doubly nice visit Scoots joined us also, there was never any shortage of conversation and as always our time together disappeared in a blink. Helping out with a spot of advertising I took a few 'Thanks for the Memory' promotional posters advertising Mary-Anne's next program at Doherty's Resort, distributing them travelling through coastal towns to the valley home ☺.....

License renewed it was onward to Loui's mum AEnone, AEnone's company being very comfortable I relaxed and again time evaporated. Forgetting the purpose for going there in the first place AEnone reminded me of the darkroom equipment on offer getting up to leave. Taking off to catch the Scamander Post Office before closing to display a 'Thanks for the Memory' poster made it with one minute to spare ☺....

The initial plan of getting home early already beaten by fate I popped in on Brian and Maggie in passing to clarify gorge walk details. Once again settling in with good conversation, we headed back to Rainbow Falls in the dark to relax after a huge 'much needed' day of pleasant social interaction ☺....

Thursday 8 September 2005
Finding and pulling a tick from Tia last night, also observing her do a comfortable poo this morning, she's back to firing on all cylinders with the energy of a puppy ☺....

With more socialising on the agenda we slipped out between the Sisters again, a couple of trips along the dirt road and Destiny's back to square one, time spent cleaning her is now unrecognisable....

Turning on glorious conditions for the schools 'community garden open day', from flowers to vegetables, the garden beds are very tidy and healthy. Losing a couple of hours over a barbecue lunch I simply enjoyed natures beautiful elements on offer....

Before wandering back up the hill to spoil myself lugging buckets of water and doing laundry, I did a spot of public relations work for Mary-Anne delivering posters to a few shops in St. Marys advertising her 'Thanks for the Memory' program....

On a water carting trip, I had a close call with a kookaburra low flying between the cottage and bungalow, startled, evasive action was taken by both of us to avoid a head-on collision and much pain!!!!

Friday 9 September 2005
Bridge maintenance over the stream feeding the waterfall has been in full swing. Taking a look at the finished product on Lohreys Road, I was disappointed to see the cold amounts of concrete that replaced the historical log-bridge. The rocky stream that once flowed under the log-bridge was cleared to accommodate bloody ugly cemented in concrete pipes to let water flow through, a cold sad sight....

A succession of early mornings with long days following saw Tia and me tucked into bed by 10p.m. last night. Heavy eyed, peaceful bliss was disrupted not long after warming the sheets. Distant thunder rumbles shattered Ms Tia's sense of relaxation for around a half-hour before sleep again could be attempted!!!!

For the third day straight a trip over the mountain was on the cards, upon invitation I went to Pam and Terry's arriving at baby feeding time. Rehabilitating several baby marsupials with a high care need, one being a cute little wombat weighing in under a kilo, I was able to cradle him in my palms. At a tender young age, the baby wombat only has a fine covering of fur looking more like five o'clock shadow, what he lacks in fur he makes up for in charisma that melts a heart on sight ☺....

Walking out Pam and Terry's side gate to hit the shops in a feel good mood, doing my bits met up with Brian and Maggie doing theirs. Through the course of our conversation they offered

me a twin tub washing machine, will that make home life easier, there'll be no more wringing my wrists out. What an amazing trip into St. Marys, how lucky am I ☺ ….
Friday afternoon flowing into evening consisted of a hot date with the computer, exchanging it for a pen after dinner, then traded it all in for bed…. Out of control behaviour ☺ !!!!

Saturday 10 September 2005
Rain blew in on wind cooling life down and driving the warm humid conditions away, if only for a short while. Giving humidity a nudge, leading up to 6a.m. passing thunder shattered blissful sleep, in its wake left behind a heavy shower dumping a quick 12mm. After dozing, I surfaced around 8a.m.-ish to one of paradises' best, we literally had our head in the clouds, fogged in with illuminated low visibility removed the existence of an outside world for a short while ☺ ….
For the sake of dry feet I held my tongue in the right direction squeezing into the gumboots then got on with it. Climatic conditions have been ideal urging two tulip flowers to explode into existence, adding even more colour to a bulb filled yard….
Late afternoon sun breaking through was short-lived, low cloud lingered, and gradually gathering momentum a thunderstorm settled in before sunset and was slow to depart. Providing a spectacular light show and a lot of noise for the first hour, the waterworks were eventually turned on to accompany light and noise. Tia's thunder meter went off and needed plenty of pacifying it was working on overload! In a feeble attempt at calming I gave her a brush - that action only managed to contribute to the Tia fur beanie!!!!

Sunday 11 September 2005
The moment the bloody awful squawk of those pest birds can be heard close by my brain kicks into gear and won't return to sleep, this morning happened to be 6a.m. neat. Looking for an up side to getting out of bed that early I saw a beautiful sunrise, and with complements of rain the falls could be heard flowing from deep within paddocks in the motionless quiet on offer….
The sound of running water was a lure to its source to fully appreciate the energy and beauty first hand. Ms Tia's nose took her for a wander nearby leaving me to contemplate the world taking delight in the might of the falls. Calling my little mate to leave she returned with the body part of some animal she claimed, finders keepers. Proudly walking back tail high with the dead bit in her mouth Tia buried her stash in the garden to return to at a later date ☺ ….
Showing all the signs of being host to a tick I gave my best friend a thorough search, finding three little tiddlers happily enjoying the goodness of life inside her thigh. She's certainly been hanging out with the wrong crowd lately!!!!
With little to distract, and organised in record time, I had myself seated and pushing the pencil before noon and put in a solid lead effort….
In a release of testosterone and a feeble attempt at intimidation, one of the smart grown-ups from across the road setting an example, without a helmet, flogged a quad bike down the road doing a U-turn in my driveway and treated the machinery just as poorly returning, nothing ventured nothing gained????

Monday 12 September 2005
A day simply spent at home with nothing earth shattering going on. The squawk of currawongs had the bungalow active shortly after 6a.m. and the small handful took very little effort to move on, the sky on the other hand was more threatening. To take the edge off a pretty ordinary air temperature I declared a shed day just to keep warm. Prunings were dragged up from the rear of the burnt out house to help the cause....
I don't know what stopped measurable moisture from falling out of the sky lingering heavy cloud looked like it would open up at anytime. Occasionally wind pushed in a drift of mist but nothing outstanding, being generous I pencilled 1mm onto the rainfall chart. Returning several times to drag more prunings to the shed to satisfy my need, by the end of a big day put in at the heater a huge dent was put in the mess littering the path out back of the burnt out house ☺ ....
The mercury rose very little, only moving from one heater to the next. There was no dilly-dallying bathing either, I didn't even take the time for a body moisturise. The cottage has no air flow problems. It makes me wonder how I ever managed to get naked the first couple of winters here without a heater and having nothing effective to take the cold edge from the air???? brrrr....

Tuesday 13 September 2005
Hands buried deep in pockets first up, the sun may have been shining but the flow of cold air kept the temperature at the lower end of the scale. The reason behind the bloody cold airflow became obvious. Snow was visible to the naked eye dusting the peak of the most southerly mountain in the distant ranges....
It's a magnet in weather extremes, making a bee-line to the shed pried hands free of pockets and cut a wheelbarrow load of wood. Wind dropping letting the mercury pick up steam permitted me to venture forth with an outdoorsy theme. Taking the broom and shovel to the rear of the burnt out house I had a tidy up of the reduced stack of prunings, allowing the lower buried bits to air and dry pending their fate!!!!
Finding a message on the answering machine from Sheila, I phoned back, without having spoken for some time our ears were glued to the receiver and silence never fell idle for quite a while. I take delight in quality, low maintenance friendships that don't take offence without regular contact, when eventually we do cross paths we straight away pick up where we last left off ☺ ....
Wind dried the ground to enable the lacing on of holey thistle kicking boots to paddock roam with my best friend until sunset, which has now extended to 6p.m. Running out of visibility caused us to head in to throw a match on the heater and get dinner on the go, setting the foundation to do it all again tomorrow ☺ ....

Wednesday 14 September 2005
Trying hard to stay in tune with my journey rather than look for physical measures of achievements, I've resigned myself to the fact that going to St. Marys shopping is a social blow-out day....
Starting at the Post Office, said a quick hello to Ross at his shop in passing, a stop at the police station, supermarket, chemist, and newsagents for another writing pad, pub, bakery, a coffee with Rita at her quilting studio, petrol, then finished the circuit at Brian and Maggie's....

Pushing open the door to the police station in search of a legal resolution to the walking violation of threats and intimidation, playing the neighbours 'struggle for energy' game is easy but negative behaviour never solves anything only perpetuates a bad situation. Both officers being unavailable at a training course, the next suitable time for a chat was after 8:30am tomorrow, looking for a positive direction forward I'll make an effort for it to happen....
Brian and Maggie always turn on the hospitality, with the ability to laugh and share in a good word I never fail to leave charged and ready to face the world again. Taking up their offer of a washing machine, Maggie and I loaded it in the back of Destiny headed for its new home ☺ ....
A living alone drawback is I didn't have the privilege of help to unload the machine at home. Forced to be inventive with thinking, sliding the machine out of Destiny and getting it to the cottage door was easy enough. Protecting the cottage doorway entrance with a towel slid the machine inside then walked it onto a piece of carpet, in position on the carpet I dragged the washing machine to its new home at the foot of the bath, living alone I have to think smarter. With the new addition taking pride and place the day was almost spent, ready for beer o'clock donned my 'thistle kicking boots' and went walkabout with my best mate ☺ ....

Thursday 15 September 2005
Serious about equality and peace, I followed up on the advice given yesterday and made it to the St. Marys police station by 8:30a.m.-ish having an honest chat to Sergeant Mike. Being a good keeper of records I bled my spleen over the history of problems encountered from across the road, wishing only to nip selfish, dumb behaviour in the bud rather than spend years in a negative energy struggle. The most sincere assistance to date, including a wealth of positive knowledge and advice, Mike outlined my options, starting with the logical sequence of events: he's going to have a talk with the neighbours in hope that will solve problems. Leaving the station with a feeling of finally getting somewhere closer to a solution and the peaceful lifestyle I'm entitled to....
Having made enough difference in the outside world for one day I headed back up the mountain to resume life as a modest farmer. Adding change to our home world I loaded the wheelbarrow bringing planks of wood of varying size up from the timber dump site, two loads delivered, Mother Nature released a moisture dusting for a couple of hours. With enough timber to keep me amused I stayed under the shelter the shed roof provided cutting some....
Impressing me with action, Sergeant Mike made a follow up phone call keeping me in tune with progress, mentioning he's paid the neighbours a visit but didn't strike them home. Mike agreed with my thoughts on their dog, admitting he wouldn't get out of the car because it greeted him with the same vicious approach....
Spelling out she's feeling unwell, sadly Tia retrieved the purple ball from its hiding spot, one tick removed and plenty of tummy rubs she's still far from her healthy self. Leaving the cottage door open taking leftovers to the bungalow, Tia went and buried herself under the cottage and took some coaxing to come out. Tia's behaviour is concerning, she's now under the microscope for monitoring her well being which is teetering on a visit to the vet....

Friday 16 September 2005
There isn't an edge of the seat read instore for tonight's journal entry having a simple mental torture story to report....

Currawongs had me out of bed again at the ugly hour of 6a.m.-ish and a sense of real intense urgency made them persistently extreme. In the early pursuit of pesky bird pissing off I saw my little mate have a poo that should relieve some of the discomfort she's been feeling, heading in the right direction for recovery....

Done so regularly, the wheelbarrow could almost do the trip alone, pushing it out back brought up more wood to help stretch the dwindling available stack....

Hanging up the receiver after the usual lengthy chat with Mum and Dad the yard was literally crawling with currawongs in mind torturing numbers. Arriving in a huge mob the awful birds took a bit of moving, to do so raised my fitness level another degree, causing blisters, not to mention wearing my boots out. Driven from housing the pests filled trees lining the top of the gorge and joined in a chorus, their penetrating loud trumpeting squawk filled every available bit of peaceful airspace!!!! Happy to see sunset and an end to pesky birds....

Throwing a salad together with last night's leftover silverside I pieced together a quick early dinner then just as efficiently wrote in the journal, carving a path for a bloody early night catering for my tiredness after a day filled with kilometres of paddock run around!!!!

Saturday 17 September 2005

On hot pursuit of rabbits that set-up home under the cottage Ms Tia is clearing the area of tics, finding yet another happily lodged into her skin, its any wonder her energy is all over the place?!?!

Socks and blundstones sogged up after traipsing through paddocks I traded them for dry socks and the holey 'thistle kickers' when grass dried. Beaten by the elements in footwear, skies opened forcing my hand to reach for the impossibly tight gumboots to paint them on the skin of my feet!!!!

Getting my arm swinging carving up the wood recently wheelbarrowed in, between showers the cottage woodbox benefited receiving a beneficial stack for evening needs....

With each millimetre finding ground the mercury fell a degree to match, driven to seek both a roof and heat, retreated to the cottage making a literary mark sparking up the computer and heater. Delving my fingers over the keyboard getting the written word current, it didn't take too long before beer o'clock knocked on the door ☺....

A sound I've learnt to dread, currawongs squawking nearby drew me out to find a tree in the driveway dripping with the pests. Responding to an approaching human voice the tree looked like a fire cracker exploding with squawking beaks darting off in all directions ☺!!!!

Sunday 18 September 2005

Leading up to a period my appetite takes off and I could eat until my lungs had no room to expand. Yesterday, included in toast and sandwiches, I ate seven slices of bread chased down by a pastie, then cooking enough carbonara to cover two meals I consumed both bowls for dinner. I couldn't afford to keep feeding myself if that level of food intake was constant. Fortunately home life is pretty physical to burn the carb's off????

Bloody glad when the grass dried enough to peel my compressed feet out of the gumboots, regaining toe circulation, donned the friendly old 'blunnies' ☺....

Nothing outstanding impressed upon our day passing quietly with the usual daily maintenance. Disappearing first thing into the shed to cut a wheelbarrow load of wood, intermittently stirring up currawongs, I also managed a couple more pages into the 'hardcopy edited' stack....

Monday 19 September 2005
Up with the dawn, a brilliant moonset preceded the rising sun. The full moon softly sank between slivers of pastel crimson cloud slipping from view behind the Huntsman's Cap Mountain. On cue and at opposite poles, the sun was lifting from behind North Sister. In mountain shadow, the sun's rising drew a definite line of drenching light inching its way across paddocks until touching upon housing and reaching saturation ☺....
Unable to face the thought of squeezing my feet into the crushing gumboots took my chances with soggy socks, walking in well-worn wallaby tracks just prolonged the inevitable!!!!
Pulling out the last pair of dry socks instigated the washing machine having its maiden voyage, and what an amazing difference it made, literally taking the pain out of the experience my wrists were impressed with the spin cycle eliminating all drips. Brian and Maggie fondly entered thoughts on a regular basis ☺....
It was rather fortunate the drip-dry stage was bypassed because the sky closed in producing persistent drizzle. Every available chair was dragged out, draped in clothes, and decorated the parameter of the heater strategically parked next to drying boots!!!!
A regular townie, I phoned Ross early asking if he'd grab me some bread on a trip saving me from going all the way in and giving all the reason needed for someone else to make me a cuppa.
A glance through Ross' bird identification book I correctly identified a pair of birds as masked lapwings that have adopted Rainbow Falls as their home, I've heard them calling out the past couple of nights. Walking in a paddock lining the gorge Ms Tia passed within a metre of the lapwings, full of spunk, they kept their spindly legs firmly planted shouting bird words at her until she left their personal space ☺!!!!
The sun had set Ross' side of the mountain by the time Destiny's nose was pointed homeward, crossing back between the Sisters a halo of light breaking through the tree lined road returned us back into sunshine. Those few kilometres separating us make a huge difference....

Tuesday 20 September 2005
Fast running out of dry shoes forced the painting on of the 'tight arse gumboots', striding out, the rubbery heels even proved fallible the cuffs of my pants wet things up acting like a wick. By capillary action dampness made the short distance up my pants across to socks and travelled down into my shoe. A much slower wetting process but when it makes the distance it's really effective!!!!
Still excited with the convenience of a less manual model washing machine, taking some dread out of the chore, I got back into it. In the olden days of wrist wringing hand washing towels and jeans were a nightmare, now even larger items are painless. Without fear I'm even taking on the jobs filed in the too hard basket, and what a pleasure it is to hear the spinner whirr into life.... Out of control with domestics ☺....
Positively responsive and reliable, Sergeant Mike made a follow up call to say he'd spoken to Kristy next door and she was receptive. Hopefully now the peace message will be taken

onboard and we can find some common ground, and I'll get to enjoy the tranquillity I'm entitled to....

Unable to keep the spoon out of the milo tin of late, having to refrain from just one more scoop to stretch it through to next shopping, burnt the high calorie intake cutting enough wood for the night's needs ☺ ....

Wednesday 21 September 2005

As much as sunrises and moonsets are beautiful it was a pleasure to have missed them, the range and surrounding trees didn't explode like a fire cracker going off with the horrible sound of squawking pests waking to feed. All but given up on them, nomadic, their presence is also lessening....

Developing quickly into a stinger, intense heat from direct sun generated steam on damp ground raising humidity, the shovel sitting idle was retrieved and kept nearby. An amber tinge to the light spectrum, complements of a forestry burn keeping the economy ticking over, suns rays filtered through smoke....

The cottage was the winner choosing to take cover under its roof, channelling time into it spruced everything from the bath to the floors. Pleased with comfortable surroundings, and staying out of the sun, took refuge under the largest roof going crazy cutting enough wood to last a couple of days. So well organised and advanced with personal maintenance I managed to sink a few hours into hardcopy editing also....

Thursday 22 September 2005

Walking in the direction of the loo I experienced the first sign of large reptile activity, scaly skin scraping under corrugated iron raised ears and eyes. Surprised by my reaction the snake didn't cause a rush of adrenalin, the past years of training and exposure I've become less fearful of their presence. The reptile activity indicator pet named 'go-carts', skink lizards, are again active on the rock pile, the air is still and thin due to heat, and lazy old blowies are making their existence known also, all strong signals summer is on the way!!!!

Vegetable seeds planted at the beginning of September have shown no sign of movement, writing them off as failed, I disappeared into the vegie patch raiding compost to have another go at propagation....

Heading under a roof to escape heat Tia was happy to snooze, the reason for her sleepy mood was caused by an outstanding number of ticks, four were attached to her front legs, her social circle needs changing - after all they are rabbits ☺ !!!!

Remaining comfortable out of searing sun, I reclined in the rocker with makeshift clipboard in hand taking another small chip at the editing bottomless pit....

Warmer daily temperatures are finding their way indoors heating buildings, I'm now only sparking the heater up long enough to cook and heat bath water, that's gratefully slowing wood use down to bugger all....

Friday 23 September 2005

The use-by-date reached on the payslip, home life was arranged around a trip over the mountain, with very little to do at shops I leisurely took time over a brewed coffee visiting Pam and Terry. Sitting out back on the veranda we were kept amused by the antics of their latest family addition, an extremely friendly cocky by the name of Charlie, he's quite a character. Charlie took a liking to me, drawn like a magnet, he contentedly climbed over me investigating anything that shone and didn't shine and the attention was duly reciprocated ☺.... Home in paradise, I had just parked Destiny in the shed and Ross almost followed me in the gate on a mission to collect some of his stored treasure, without rushing he had time to share in a pot of tea before leaving....

Getting current with family events in Mildura chatting with Mum and Dad, replacing a well-warmed receiver and giving my lips a rest, with shovel in hand and apprentice nearby we ventured forth on a mission to create space in the elevated garden. With good soil and sun exposure I plan on putting the elevated garden to work growing vegies, Peaches the fruit tree will be happy for the healthy company ☺.... Continually extending daylight hours kept us outside turning soil until after 6:30p.m....

Saturday 24 September 2005
First up, climatic conditions changed gardening plans, instead collecting and cutting wood made the 'to-do' priority, painting the gumboots on my feet off we went. Only managing to bring in one wheelbarrow load before the heavens opened, but enough to keep home fires burning for a while longer....

A quick blast of 7mm stepped aside for a stinging sun to break through generating a steamy high humid environment only a plant could love, using the moment and soil turned yesterday, formed beds and planted beans, corn and zucchini seed. If they survive birds, possums, wallabies, rabbits and all other food chain competition the rewards should be plenty ☺!!!!

Cleaned up after playing in mud the sky again opened, escaping the elements I sparked up the heater, cooked, bathed and wrote a letter. Keeping the heater working and boiler constantly on the go, the scorching water was used as weed killer around the rock pile....

My worst nightmare occurred mid afternoon, a cloud of squawking pests flying overhead landed in the trees lining the gorge, one by one they dropped like darts and dotted paddocks. Walking toward them they lifted and moved on in the same fashion they arrived, loud, intrusive and in a mob, timely making it back to the cottage before the next wave of moisture fell.... Phew!!!!

Sunday 25 September 2005
Sitting quietly daydreaming over breakfast a swallow decided to see for itself what goes on inside. Flying in doing a circuit in the small space of the bungalow the swallow gave me a start, by the time my feet touched ground it had rejoined its mate back outside on the high wire. The swallow must have got a buzz out of the stunt, before breakfast was over it gave a repeat performance.... No fear ☺!!!!

Sniffing below the kitchen sink Tia brought attention to a mouse having had a chew on the end of the wooden spoon; finding candied onion to its liking, bugger it. Slack, not doing the dishes last night I paid the price by luring vermin inside!!!!

Keeping busy with the usual daily bits, added to that a little shovel work doing some edging around the rock pile and bungalow, and had a dabble at editing. Life at Rainbow Falls was a pretty low-key affair....

Monday 26 September 2005
With garden watering edging back into daily routine, I did it first thing while it's cool beating heat and possible large reptile movement. Picking a bunch of flowers on morning walkabout and open up sparked memories of a statement Mum once made, referring to a woman with masses of nasal hair as 'having a healthy bunch of flowers', the blooming fist full offered me a smile ☺ ….
Back from a 'swap meet' in Launceston, the old car Ross towed wanting to sell followed him home, looking for short-term storage Ross and Lesley brought the 'Willys' over parking it in the car garage. The loading ramp inside the front gate was designed for the job, for ease of unloading the old car was able to be driven straight off the back of the truck. Enabling the car to tuck deep into its temporary new home the garage was freed of the majority of stored hay bales. Lesley and I put our backs into it and helped load them onto the truck to sensibly move them closer to the horses….
Not one to enjoy being out exposed in heat I escaped it for respite, feathering the cottage nest found the floor and swept the ceiling of cobwebs. Staying put inside, the machine was sparked into life doing a spot of keyboard finger dancing catching up on digitising the written word and kissing the afternoon goodbye….
Game to venture back out in the evening cool the last of the daylight was put to use, with the willing help of my best friend we finished edging around the bungalow leaving it look very sharp and tidy ☺ ….

Tuesday 27 September 2005
Through the day Tia's bed is put out of the way under the bench in the bungalow, she's usually comfy in it before getting a chance to put it in the night position by the side of my bed. Over time Tia's got used to the idea of whizzies, dragging her bed into its night position with her propped in it enjoying the ride; I'm sure she smiles ☺ ….
Enjoying the convenience of a washing machine I left it doing its own thing soaking whites. Fashioning a crude watering can from a 2-litre plastic milk container I drilled a few holes in the lid and surprisingly it worked well, having its maiden voyage on the newly established vegie beds a nice consistency flowed….
My little mate has been suffering the irritation of nettle rash on the exposed skin of her tummy due to a healthy population establishing amongst winter weeds in the vegie patch. Still pumped after cutting a wheelbarrow load of wood, and looking to change cause and effect, literally turned loose with the shovel making photosynthesising rather difficult for nettles. Giving in to failing light and feeling pretty happy with myself, made a bee-line for the cottage to make a start on the evening bits still waiting ☺ ….

Wednesday 28 September 2005
The sky released a dusting of moisture taking watering out of the scheduled 'to-do' morning jobs, opening opportunity for me and my best mate to get seated for breakfast sooner….
Running our food supply to the bone I was happy payday and shopping day came around. Enduring a run of bills and in need of a little budget catch up, I resisted the pub pull-in stop keeping beer o'clock erased off the menu and all for a good cause, food….

While visiting was still a thought, putting petrol in Destiny Brian and Maggie come roaring into town in the 'troupie'. Chatting in the main street they invited me back, spending the afternoon of my social blow-out day indulging in the healthy recipe of food, drink and laughter ☺....

Thursday 29 September 2005
A hangover from yesterdays overcast drizzly conditions, pleasantly, cool air stayed behind for a while, when the while was up a mixed bag moved in. Experiencing everything from cold to hot and steamy, somewhere in the middle of the temperature changeover included a short, sharp thunderstorm. In a feeble attempt at chasing thunder from the paddocks Ms Tia did a loud lap through, gratefully emptying them of late arriving bird pests doing her circuit.... Gotta be lucky sometimes ☺....
I couldn't have ordered more ideal conditions for seed germination, since sowing we've undergone waves of heat, completing the cycle with a sprinkling of rain for a dose of nitrogen and humidity. Spared from watering, yesterdays 8mm left soil looking rich and alive....
Wallabies are failing to keep up with the spurt on grass growth a few areas are looking a bit woolly. I'm hoping the old 'viking' might miraculously burst into life allowing a couple more tanks of juice to pump through its system???? The eternal optimist ☺!!!!
Finishing on the saw, enough timber was once again cut to spark up the heater, disappearing in I cooked enough food to keep me and Ms Muffet fed for a few heat and eat meals ☺....

Friday 30 September 2005
With the gorge walk fast approaching, and the need for wood to fire the barbecue and extra on standby for both the cottage and shed heaters, overcast cool conditions made for a suitable 'bring a lot of wood to the shed to cut up', day. I love roaming amongst the fast disappearing timber dump site a few treasures have surfaced in an older style door and window trims. Nearing the bottom of a pallet stack Dave formed sometime back, I've burnt my way to a treasure trove of weather-boards and interior wall lining boards once belonging to either the cottage or bungalow. Still in reasonable condition, the boards have been set aside for storage, starting that 'who knows it might come in handy one day' hoard of treasure. Going to the wood dump site is more than just collecting wood ☺!!!!
A laid back day enjoyed at home simply evolved around collecting wood, chewing Mum and Dad's ear off then cutting wood. Good news from Mildura is my sister was successfully hypnotised to quit smoking and is into day eight smoke free ☺....
Feeling like a new woman after a therapy afternoon down the shed, time invested impressed a reasonable start at creating a wood stockpile for gorge walk day....
I love heat and eat meals they return at least one hour to an evening, indulging tonight's gained time in front of the fire oblivious to the outside world relaxed in the rocker with my little mate snoozing beside ☺.... ahhhh....

Saturday 1 October 2005
Sliding down the priority list, I'm able to rest a mind programmed to waking at the sound of squawking bird pests, spending more time sleeping in these days than being disturbed by

raiding pillaging birds. Having seen enough moonsets and sunrises my little mate and I are again getting practised at rising at a sensible hour☺....
The years are beginning to catch up to me, reality hits when my youngest niece, Tegan Termite, has turned 18!!!! Each one of those years led to where I am now, definitely no regrets and definitely no turning back☺!!!!
Working around the ongoing daily needs today was therapeutically lost. Repeating yesterdays mind relaxing time down the shed, plodded away until every post and plank of wood brought up to the shed was cut and left ready and waiting in a pile, creating a few hours of burning.... Come nightfall, and in keeping with the mood set, simply just had to heat and eat a waiting meal, yahoooo☺....

Sunday 2 October 2005
An unrelenting squawking alarm clock had feet on deck by 7a.m., at least while their beak is open trumpeting they're not doing damage. Hitting the ground running we didn't waste time, getting straight into it with my little mate bringing more timber to the shed storing it for another burst of inspiration....
Those mongrel birds probably did a favour waking the household early, enabling outside things to be done while it was still cool and little chance of reptile activity. Little go-carts, skinks, an indicator of reptile activity, were sunning themselves early on the rock pile....
A job just waiting for a cool moment, we slipped into the paddocks eradicating mozzie breeding grounds from the couple of water troughs. I long stopped water flowing to them but the build-up of rainwater in the trough without a drain made an ideal breeding environment. Armed with a scoop and best mate on the ready, emptied the trough of its wriggly, rusty contents....
Driven indoors until the UV sting left, made use of the time giving my fingers a workout over the keyboard then gave my fingers a workout with the pen. Writing comments on the back of a set of photos recently processed as a substitute letter to Mum and Dad, it's timely for their anniversary Friday☺....
Advertising program times on ABC Radio National prior to the news mentioned Tasmania at a different time slot than other states. At a wild guess I'd say daylight savings has started here, that bit of knowledge could have so easily remained unknown, now placing us back in sync with the rest of the world.... Phew☺....

Monday 3 October 2005
Unrelentingly giving me the paw tap some wee baby hour last night, I struggled to wake. Using the clock as a beacon in the darkness I was slightly off course, reaching for the fridge to co-ordinate myself found nothing but thin air, unbalanced, I ended up on my arse on the floor. Jolted awake I successfully finished Ms Tia's need for outside without breaking bones???? Strong dismantling wind, shoving cloud along created a very changeable day and caused the need for damage control to temporary repairs. Wind, for the most, pushed in mild to warm conditions with a couple of feeble attempts at rain. Ideal conditions to wander over the mountain to post the photos destined for Mum and Dad, stopping at the bakery Evelyn said snow has been reported falling in Hobart....

With the gorge walk at the forefront of thoughts I didn't linger in town, returning home just as soon as I was done to have another go at cutting and stockpiling wood for the occasion, lost the afternoon in the shed. Able to remain outside a little later, utilised the extra daylight in the vegie patch....

Tuesday 4 October 2005
Getting up later and running life by the recently adjusted clock the morning was cut short, I splashed a bit of water around in the garden, had breakfast, refuelled the cottage water capacity and it was midday. On the flip side of starting daylight saving evenings seem longer, not sitting down for dinner until 10p.m. last night, needless to say after the journal entry and dishes were done it was midnight before escaping to the bungalow for bed. Without complaint, the sensation of seemingly longer evening hours is preferable, although very little does alter, the time I go to bed and get up doesn't require any shift in thought, the outstanding mindset change is my stomach is out of alignment with average meal times programmed in the brain ☺....
Filling the afternoon, finalised cutting the latest lot of timber carted to the shed, then adjourned for brain therapy where time stands still, the vegie patch, fading light was the only indicator time didn't stand still ☺ ????

Wednesday 5 October 2005
Undecided as to which way the weather was heading, alleviated doubt, ensuring there was enough dry timber to keep the cottage heater burning until Saturday brought up one more wheelbarrow load for cutting. I'll certainly appreciate the handsaw time and love gone into preparations for Saturday's big day out at home ☺....
Bathed in cooler overcast conditions it was ideal to get immersed in the vegie patch to finalise weeding. Discovering an emerging bean seed in the revived elevated garden thought it appropriate to get the wallaby, rabbit and possum proofing done to protect the investment. Remaining outside pottering with my little mate until early afternoon, when heat kicked in we bailed out ☺....
Staying one step ahead of tomorrows 'to-do' jobs, filled the washing machine leaving whites to soak overnight. I'm going to have to get water on tap, between the garden, bathing, dishes and washing machine, I lost count of the buckets carted today, certainly keeping me fit and toned, or is that 'wearing me out' ☺ ????

Thursday 6 October 2005
Murphys law was beaten! Doing dishes a rubber glove had a blow-out letting bitey hot water in, having kept the good glove from the last broken pair it happened to match the one needed, gotta be lucky some times ☺....
Stirring through the night the sound of rain on the tin roof caressed me back to sleep while slipping a quiet 2mm in the gauge. With the thought of waiting domestic duties ahead it didn't inspire movement, resisting the inevitable I was sluggish rising, being happier snuggled in bed listening to dismantling wind, warm and comfy next to my little mate....
Wind picked up to mongrel speeds, going outside with a hat on was out of the question. I was forced to retrieve it a couple of times before giving up, just a fucking awful day! I can tolerate

most conditions but gale force wind sees a cut-off limit, wrestling with clothes attempting to hang them on the clothesline tests even the most tolerant of patience, bringing my temper to the surface. With six pegs holding a towel on the line trying conditions managed to rip it from its moorings and dump it on the ground. My patience were wearing thin constantly untangling clothes and reassembling pegs, although, it was the first time in a while nothing had to be dried in front of the heater!?!?

A token drop of moisture may have fallen overnight but drying harsh wind robbed the soil of that token offering and more, before retreating indoors for the evening a bucket dash was done giving food producing plants a good soaking drink….

Friday 7 October 2005
Using scrap timber from the dump site there must have been a kilogram of nails sorted and removed from the collection of ash extracted from the cottage heater….
A planned trip over the mountain to post the payslip and pick up food ordered for tomorrow's barbecue, I stopped first to fill up on drinking water, finding Ross home to make me a hot brew. By word of mouth Ross could turn Rainbow Falls into a tourist attraction, adding to the invited list, I told him the people attending tomorrow's gorge walk is for those who opened their hearts and homes to me and Tia since arriving on the shores of this island. For a win:win solution I suggested he make a time in the coming week, with the five extras he'd invited, to experience the gorge walk ☺….
Pleasantly reliable, waiting for me at the Post Office were birthday cards from Mum and Dad also Sheila and Peter, returning to Destiny to read the words of thought, I love friendly mail. Stocked with groceries and beer o'clock returned to the menu I called in on Pam and Terry before home. Charlie the cockatoo was roaming the back veranda, like a magnet, while saying hello he made himself at home on my arm. Convincing Charlie to return to the veranda post, I made it inside where Pam asked me to hold the baby wombat while she attended to another baby marsupial ☺….
Before getting my teeth into finalising preparations for tomorrow I phoned Mum and Dad to wish them a 'Happy Anniversary', 45 years together is getting less common now marriage is so easily walked away from. Mum and Dad are reaping the rewards of the work they have put into one another and family ♥♥♥♥….
Phoning through birthday wishes Phillip caught me in the thick of collecting water, and in the midst of cutting onions Loui's mum AEnone phoned. Into genealogy, AEnone did a spot of research on my behalf filling in unsolved pieces of the jigsaw puzzle about the elusive Mr Young, the original documented settler of Rainbow Falls and founder of Dublin Town. Dealing me a feast of information, an important missing link being his Christian name, Edward was born 1855 and died 16 June 1939 aged 84. Adding to the snippets, its documented Edward built the hut (bungalow) 1889, some years later in 1894 the cottage came into being. AEnone is a saint ☺!!!!

Saturday 8 October 2005
Misty rain drifting in before bed only increased with intensity as the night progressed, developing into one heavy shower exposing every leak in buildings!!!!

The message extended with the invitation was 'no matter what the weather gorge walk day will go ahead even for just a get together'. Steady rain didn't relent. Sparking up the cottage heater I created a dry congregating area in anticipation of guests. One by one, cars struggled their way up the driveway slipping and sliding. Greeted with hugs on arrival, Pam and Terry, Dave and Liz, Brian and Maggie, Ross and Lesley, and me and Tia then took a position around the heater and moved nowhere. A gorge walk was out of the question, but the hum of conversation and decoration of assorted pots and pans on the heater top cooking food duly compensated ☺….
Being the last remaining guests, I challenged Ross and Lesley's sense of adventure, extending a proposition to join in a walk to the falls to experience first hand the strong sound from the massive amounts of water rushing over the top. Gearing up for the conditions, with umbrellas in hand we took on the elements without disappointment….
Waving the last guests off a high energy filled my body in appreciation of the hours just spent. Solving curiosity a dash to the gauge found 69mm in it. I didn't think I'd negotiate the task of journal writing after spending a full day with friends, eating, and included with chatting was those couple of extra beers to keep the voice box lubed ☺…. hic…

Sunday 9 October 2005
I don't know how or where the inspiration rose to write yesterday's journal entry, I was lucky to make one - my handwriting was a bit loose and scruffy, all the same yesterday was a wonderful lead into happy birthday to me ☺….
Needless to say the real 'happy birthday to me' felt a bit ordinary and slowwww, on automatic pilot cleaning up after yesterday, the pace didn't alter as the day passed. Concerned there wasn't enough wood cut for yesterday's big day out at home surprisingly ended up with a good surplus, the saw blade can sit idle and cool down for a few moons….
Mum and Dad were first to call extending birthday wishes, Dad and I both agreed that the intensity of rain warranted a bore level check….
Easing off gently after an explosive effort, only a few scattered showers drifted across the landscape dusting minor amounts of moisture, but the 73mm in the past twenty-four hour period made a huuuuge difference to the bore water level. Lowering the float and string for a quick depth measurement roused excitement, focussed on the potential directed my energy and afternoon into setting the pump up over the bore….
Yet again feeling beaten failing to prime the pump was ready to give it away. When the pump was turned off a slow flow seeped from the suction hose connection, coming under investigation, a broken perished rubber washer caused air to enter the intake line. With renewed hope I replaced the rubber washer and fired the pumps motor into life, and in disbelief received a soaking by the pressure of primed rising water, however, my exhilaration was sadly short-lived. Checking the weight along the 2-inch pipe, water managed to fill it three-quarters of the way to the waiting empty tank, a bloody tease being so close to success! The failing problem lies with the bore being sucked dry, running out of water to slurp up. Water sat at three metres in the bore with six metres of suction hose submerged I finally thought recharge odds were in favour ☺ ????
Being a bit free with her fur lately, tonight four brush loads were contributed by my little mate toward the Tia fur beanie. Getting a bit tired of waiting for dinner, Ms Tia went and helped

herself to the cooling snags one way to ensure you get what you want, the naughty little bugger☺!!!!

Monday 10 October 2005
Tidying away toys after the optimistic hope of pumping water, I sealed exposed pipe ends saving them from becoming homes and storing ecosystems until I solve the issue of drawing water from the bore….
The heater top accepted a welcome clean with steel wool, removing oil, cooking stains, and rust from where it copped a constant drip from around the flue during the rain. The heater now has enhanced memories with the combined cooking event that happened on its surface Saturday afternoon, Maggie, Lesley and I got food started with extra cooks stepping in to assist. Allocating myself the pan to cook onions, Dave told me I was stirring them too much taking the wooden spoon from me, without a whimper, I left the spoon with him and retreated to the rocker and beer to watch on ☺….
Heavy machinery doing bridge work disturbed a cloud of currawongs sending them our way, making a bloody ruckus in the trees lining the gorge they were encouraged onward with little effort. Except for an unusual event, their numbers are now few, I'd like to think the time put in disturbing them feeding is having some effect????
The uncomfortable combination of heat and humidity sent us packing indoors after lunch for the more passive pastime of computer adventures, re-emerging to a cooler climate a few pages on….

Tuesday 11 October 2005
From bungalow de-furring to wood and water I had it all done, then armed with screwdrivers and the meagre collection of tools made an attempt at getting a mower running. Both mowers refused to fire into life and I can't say I blame them, working with me unveiling Rainbow Falls they certainly earnt their keep….
Beginning to think the lugging of buckets watering routine may have to recommence, the skies opened with a token more liquid. From the comfort of the cottage I watched a pretty threatening front approach from a westerly direction. Being pushed out to sea as it slipped over the distant series of mountain ranges the front struggled to advance over as far as us, catching the edge of the change, a few spots of hail and a dusting of rain drifted in. The second front, a little later, came direct ahead without deviating influences, taking no time to wet the ground it delivered ongoing relief from garden watering ☺….
Like an expectant mother constantly checking seed germination, I've counted half a dozen beans on the move, things are starting to happen ☺!!!!
The next big event etched on the calendar is the fast approaching 'directions conference' at Launceston Magistrates Court. With very little idea of what to expect on the day I'm just leading from the gut. Doing a little preparation for the time in court got my head around organising a calendar of events and known fact for quick reference. Reading over the paper trail history a blurred brain lost focus, taking time out to let the brain breathe and find direction, walkabout in the paddocks pissing off stray currawongs with my little mate was the antidote. A bit overwhelmed, fresh air generated clear thought and brought the task at hand

back to its true course of honest simplicity by cutting through the irrelevant, 'he said' and 'she said' stuff and staying rigid with the stone I originally cast....

Wednesday 12 October 2005
With grass creeping up, and no tools to remove the spark plug I've been doing mower maintenance around it, thoughts today went into checking for a possible blocked fuel line. Managing to squeeze a murmur of life out of the old 'victa' gave me hope to press on, delving into areas of a motor I know little about but have no fear to tread ☺ !!!!
Four pumpkin seeds burst into life along with a few more beans, I love finding a germinated seed for the first time breaking through soil, its bloody rewarding ☺ ....
Enthused with seeds on the move, during the cooler end of the afternoon more beds were prepared in the vegie patch, planting and watering in brown onions, carrots, tomatoes, silverbeet and spring onions. Certainly creating some bucket lugging work, if I can keep native animals out this years harvest should be plentiful, nothing more satisfying than eating home grown produce ☺ ....

Thursday 13 October 2005
With so much left over food from Saturday's big day out at home grocery shopping could be delayed but drinking water was at dire, unable to be ignored levels. When the manual life I thrive within was prepared to base level a quick trip was taken to the other side of North Sister....
Decorating everything within a five metre radius she walks past, I don't go anywhere without a sample of Tia fur woven into clothing. Each night Tia makes a donation to the fur collection, the little bag of stored fur is getting quite packed in it must be nudging close to enough fur to spin into a yarn and knitted into a beanie ☺ ....
One final go at getting a mower running expired my willing knowledge. It's now filed in the too hard basket, there are some things I don't excel at and mechanics is one. To take in information it also helps to have an interest in the subject, mechanics to me is like cooking. It's done out of no choice, but unfortunately I am the good fairy ☺ !!!!
The six 44-gallon drums leaning against the shed had enough tall grass surrounding them to attract attention. Moving the drums exposed bare ground long covered. The drums were rolled and repositioned to flatten more patches of new spring growth against the shed, with the thought of again repeating the procedure at a later date. Long grass the drums didn't hide underneath was quickly knocked down to size with the shovel. With a cup full, and always displaying optimism, I can tidy areas the mower can't reach until something gives with one....

Friday 14 October 2005
Driven from a warm bed for the first time in many moons by the awful sound of currawongs intruding in the housing area, three of the bloody pests were hovering around the vegie patch. Fortunately everything edible or shooting is covered, there's not much the destructive buggers won't steal to eat! With the bloody mongrels out of sight, and life in an orderly structure, we headed between the mountains to boost the economy of St. Marys....
Sheila and Peter played one of their fun prankster games with birthday cards. As punctual as ever they sent me one for the actual day, the first card received had written on the cover 'Not

only could I not afford a birthday present for you', written inside, 'I'd kinda like this card back after you finish reading it'! Following banter today a heartfelt card with serious words of friendship sat in the Post Office box, they created a monster with the first card sent ☺!!!!
A social stop to return a bowl left behind from last Saturday only found Terry home and we yarped over a coffee. Over idle chat Terry offered to have a go at fixing the better of the two lawnmowers. Terry's fix it words remain etched, "its only a motor that goes round and round, can't be too much to go wrong with it"???? I hope the mower's problems are as simplistic as Terry's words ☺....
A sign of warm conditions well and truly on their way, a go-cart made its way into the bungalow trying its luck at a feed from the window ledge, the first sighted inside in the lead up to summer. As the long day cools, evenings are literally immersed in the therapeutic occupation of preoccupied garden watering. Venturing inside 8p.m.-ish to start the fire, followed by dinner, bath, dishes and journal writing, daylight saving is making me nocturnal....

Saturday 15 October 2005
Squawking pests in the location of housing set off the brain alarm shortly after 6a.m., not getting to bed until 1:30a.m.-ish, we returned to the warm comfort for a few more zeds after pissing them off....
My little mate had claimed the prize of a dead native hen, through the night the carcass disappeared some other critter liked the prize more, this morning Tia could only piss on the spot claiming the ground where it once lay ☺!!!!
Doing the usual bits that keep life ticking over, washing blended into the daily manual tasks, rather more pleasant conditions required only the basic number of pegs to keep clothes attached to the line to dry. Washing, wood and water, water, water was the theme, water for the cottage, water for washing and water for the garden, I was passing myself heading to the cattle trough with bucket in hand....
Thank goodness for a Tia vacuum cleaner, cooking dinner an egg fell on the floor and my little mate had the mess cleaned up in no time, Mum's little helper ☺....

Sunday 16 October 2005
With plans to spend the afternoon socialising helping Pam celebrate her birthday the morning focussed on preparing the home front for time away, particularly ensuring garden needs were attended to....
As pre-arranged, Ross came up early along with the potential new owner of the 'Willys'. Ross stayed long enough after handshakes to share in a brewed pot of cha....
Mower loaded on board and family organised, Destiny's nose was pointed at the mountain to join a relaxed afternoon with friends. With me as apprentice, Terry had a look at the mower and a split fuel hose was detected and repaired, with the spark plug cleaned she fired up, rapt it was so quick and easy, I reloaded a working mower to take home. Ideal conditions were turned on to enjoy the great outdoors, over a barbecue, drinks, delicious food and good company, the afternoon and time dissolved ☺....
Escaping lawn growth was getting me down, being a product of house-proud parents I take pride in the yard, so removing an operational mower from Destiny I couldn't help myself. With

a reasonable amount of daylight remaining to make a start bringing lawn back down to size, I literally cut loose. Feeling uplifted, inspired me to ring Terry to express appreciative feelings of thanks, he suggested being a full moon I could keep going ☺....
As the sun disappeared behind the mountain, with an earned beer in hand and my little mate nearby, enjoyed the start made while strategically planning the next moves with the mower ☺....

Monday 17 October 2005
Heavy dew postponed lawn mowing first thing then a fast rising temperature shelved the thought entirely for a saner time. Avoiding long stays in heat I gave seed beds a good soaking, cut wood for the evening, then got the scraper and steel wool onto the heater top removing evidence from a rice spill....
Ringing Mum and Dad for an update on life Dad told me he has befriended a few top notch pigeons, wishing to buy a small amount of wheat for feed, and living in the middle of a wheat belt, he had trouble finding any locally. Mildura also has citrus varieties growing all year round and local growers are dumping truck loads because of no available markets, yet Dad couldn't get fresh orange juice squeezed on site at his local supermarket because no fruit was available, go figure????
Losing the worst of the bitey celsius close to 5p.m.-ish, I raised the mower as high as it would go and set about reducing a bit more grass to size. My little mate, as helpful as ever, put in a big effort dropping anything available in the mowers path, so dedicated to the cause Tia ended the working day with green socks ☺.... Such a bloody big labour push exerted I didn't pull up for beer o'clock until after 7p.m.!!!!

Tuesday 18 October 2005
It was brilliant, and good for natural feel good energy, to step outside the bungalow to face a fresh beginning seeing the cottage surrounds trim and neat ☺....
Out of petrol to continue the clearing process determined a trek over the mountain. Before doing the mercy dash for mower fuel the usual number of elite athlete trips to the cattle trough carting water, freeing me to continue mowing, came first....
Doing a pretty quiet trip into St. Marys sticking only to the necessary, turned the Tassie Trio team of me, Tia and Destiny around and had us pointed homeward putting the petrol to use in short time....
Ms Tia dropped anything considered fetchable in front of the moving mower, on occasion being very good at her game!!!! Tossing things willy-nilly the game doesn't always go to plan, trees around housing are decorated with lodged bits. A plastic bottle, tennis ball and a plastic bat are waiting for possums or wind to knock them to the ground ☺....
Refuelling after a solid session I wasn't particularly sorry when the mower played hard to start. Feeling jiggered I was happy to push it back to the shed and declare beer o'clock, the universe was telling me to have a mowing break, who am I to argue ☺????

Wednesday 19 October 2005
With Tia's moulting fur in full swing she leaves a beanie load on my bed each morning, clothes are decorated with the appearance of mohair, the first move any given day is to find the bungalow and bed under loose fur ☺ ....
Counting the trips to the cattle trough to water the garden I carted fourteen buckets, all for a healthy cause. A chemical free vegie garden is on the move, the peach tree and strawberries are bearing fruit and seventeen bean seedlings are standing up to face the world, this years harvest is shaping up....
Getting me offside, a rodent left an obvious trail inside, unable to share space the cottage received a clean and suspected entry points were blocked. The local fauna keep life interesting. Currawongs are pleasantly making themselves scarce, but taking care of a quiet moment over lunch, a swallow made another brief appearance inside the bungalow.... I wouldn't want to live anywhere else ☺ ....
Filling idle time I disappeared down the shed cutting enough wood for the evening, while there I gave the mower a few tugs, still refusing to fire gave all the reason to leave it parked. Always looking to maximise any situation, I've started using prunings littering the path at the rear of the burnt out house as fire starters for the heater. Chipping away at an eyesore converting it to a resource and something beneficial....

Thursday 20 October 2005
With the luxury of hindsight currawongs did us a favour getting the bungalow active earlier than otherwise would have. Up and animated in time to collect light fire starting sticks before anything exposed to the elements was wet by a welcome drop of moisture. The gift from the heavens not only gave me the day off excessive bucket lugging, it should also get the vegie garden standing to attention with a dose of nitrogen....
Exposed to favourite climatic conditions, home was left submerged in low cloud for a good part of the day, altering only in density and producing the occasional misting, nothing measurable fell until early afternoon. Perfect weather for frogs, gumboots and the garden. Inspired by ideal conditions, my little helper, up to her elbows in mud, helped me plant out containerised pumpkin and sugar snap pea seedlings....
After cutting enough wood, me and my best friend escaped to the dry comfort indoors and it was at that point the sky caved in. Adding power to the computer several hours were lost leaving Mother Nature to do her thing outside....
Last gauge check before nightfall the fifth millimetre was being worked on, I'm feeling confident that total has long been surpassed rain has remained pretty persistent all evening. My clothes did the usual capillary action thing wetting up, so decorating the heater surrounds with drying clothes and shoes is not an uncommon sight....

Friday 21 October 2005
Unwilling to budge all night, the 76th millimetre had fallen by the time I rose this morning to again check the gauge. Three currawongs looking like they were having a miserable time trying to feed had a worse time when sighted, reminding them they're not welcome and I'm unsympathetic under any circumstances!!!!

Watering the garden has been struck off the agenda until further notice. Freed time and energy was instead invested into cutting enough wood to take us through the afternoon and into the night. It's not particularly cold, the fire is lit more so to dry the cottage ceiling where water gets in around the flue. With dry wood in short supply I raided the barrel of the shed heater, still set and unused from the day of gorge walk....

Hearing the roar of the falls from the shed was a lure in a quieter moisture moment, just shy of inch four Tia and I went for a walk to see what all the noise was about. Juggling the umbrella and camera I snapped a couple of photos capturing the enormous flow roaring over the top. The sheer might is a constant reminder nature is a force not to be reckoned with and very capable of looking after itself....

Changing into dry clothes the afternoon was spent high and dry by a 'reluctant to start' heater preparing for the fast approaching harassment and discrimination hearing....

Fronts coming in off the ocean the north-east is the direction of our big rains, well rain, rain and more rain dropped from the sky. Braving the elements last checked the gauge 6:30p.m.-ish, then it totalled 123mm, giving in is the last thing the sky looked like doing....

Saturday 22 October 2005

Management flicked the switch on power due to the usual area of wall surrounding the power board wetting up, I'd prefer to reset the clock and answering machine and still have the cottage standing. It was an interesting experience for a mind accustomed to living with a clock not to have any idea of time, simply waking when I've had enough sleep, eat when hungry, and just get on with life oblivious ☺ ????

Submerged in low cloud blocking the world from view, moisture gave us a break from the 213mm delivered to date. Staying with a water theme, I was excited to be able to reach down and touch water in the bore, determining one direction ahead. Without hesitation and with a heart full of optimism set the pump up over the bore, this time the pipe filled right up to the water tank, sucking the bore down to the foot valve before one drop entered. Taking well over one hundred litres to fill the line, and minus a one way valve to hold the pipe full of water without the pump attached, 'Plan B' came into play. Leaving the pump in place and line full, let the bore recover then whatever the bore offered after recovery would pump straight into the water tank, and continually repeat the procedure. Thinking 8½ inches was probably enough rain, down it came again with the same intensity, wrapping the pump in one of my raincoats to protect it from the elements headed out of them myself to cut wood ☺ ????

Dumping close on an inch while my little mate and I just stood in the shed looking out hoping for a break that didn't come, wishing only to be rid of tight arsed gumboots and warm and dry by the fire. Another desire was to get dry wood to the cottage, to fulfil the need I bit the bullet and faced the elements. Using the catcher from the mower carted wood to the cottage to keep it dry, happy to once again have the fire going, bathed, and be stripped of wet clothes ☺ !!!!

In a less intense rain moment before nightfall I dashed out and emptied another 52mm out of the gauge, the moving total has now reached an extraordinary 266mm....

Sunday 23 October 2005

Lying in bed last night I drifted off to the sound of waterfalls thundering and croaking frogs in their element. Last sighted Thursday, the sun made an appearance, and with the majority of

deeper puddles dispersed a trip over the mountain was on the cards. Destiny on the other hand had different ideas by refusing to start. Feeling the effects of the saturating amounts of moisture filling the air, willingly turning over she refused to finish the circuit and fire into life. Struggling, I pushed Destiny out of the shed to grab the sunshine on offer, pulling the distributor cap off dried its interior and a short time later she found the spark required....
Driving the hill, remnants of the past few days was evident with plenty of water still flowing along the roadside. Popping in on Pam and Terry they had been tested by the deluge, the St. Marys Rivulet, running through their property, rose considerably flooding their paddocks causing an animal rescue operation. Brought to higher ground they're all a little wet but safe....
Letter posted and bread on the passenger seat it was homeward bound to put 'Plan B' into operation and it worked like a charm. Without a need to prime the pump I just pull the cord and watch the bore empty then amuse myself waiting for it to recover to repeat the experience. New ground was broken finally getting water into the tank, not earth shattering amounts, but 3½ years of carrying buckets I hope is nearing an end, dare I contemplate water on tap ☺ ????
A lesson learned by experience is that possessions are only yours until someone else wants them, for 'out of sight out of mind' insurance I chained and padlocked the pump to the fence for peace of mind....
Just in case the ground looked like drying out late afternoon the sky closed in again, and garden watering remains off the agenda until further notice ☺ ....
Dashing between the bore and water tank I spied a couple of large mushrooms, beating wallabies, relocated them to the fridge to wait for the ultimate destination, my dinner plate ☺ ....

Monday 24 October 2005
Those favourite magical fogged in times screening the outside world from view seem to be spoiling me a lot lately, starting yet another with that same theme. Thundering falls and frogs still fill airwaves with elated energy, oh, and did I forget to mention the sound of rain, rain, rain and more rain ☺ ????
Before wandering out the bungalow door to face moisture I first found it under Tia fur, her beautiful outfit is thinning and I've brushed out countless loads. Fur dripping from her body should start slowing????
Again concentrating on the theme of wood and water, waiting for the bore to recover a good amount was cut. Where the poly pipe enters the access hole into the water tank had kinked offering flow resistance, resolving the problem used a larger piece of plastic pipe as a supporting sleeve. I sure could have used a clone of myself an extra pair of hands would have been useful ☺ ....
With the pump system back to running smoothly, I poked my nose in the top of the tank and was excited to see about 1000 litres lining the bottom. Quite enough water to open the valve and test plumbing, the gremlins didn't take long to surface, taking the next step backward to go forward I repaired leaks in lines with poly joiners. I remember putting the shovel into pipe early on in the piece initially clearing in the elevated garden, another distant memory of taking a swipe at a snake sometime back snapped a poly join in two....
Opening the line again for a take two I near on cried to watch water flow from the tap above the bath, indulging in the moment washed my hands. Sitting idle for years tap washers are in

need of replacing not turning off effectively, and when the hot water service tank was filled water kept spewing from the overflow hose, locating system gremlins, I closed the valve off for ongoing maintenance☺!!!!

The only difficulty with replacing washers is the lack of tools to do the job, the hot water service on the other hand I know little about. I've decided to put an inline tap into the hot water supply so it can be isolated and turned off, when washers are replaced I can open the valve and indulge in water on tap for a while having a well deserved break from lugging bloody buckets☺!!!!

The ongoing deluge has pipped the 300mm stage, now heading into the thirteenth inch it pulled up by the close of business at 304mm, happy to be free of tight arse gumboots and wet clothes I called it a day. For a change of pace the evening rewarded us with a thunderstorm and of course more rain, trying to write with my best friend stressed by thunder isn't much fun, even less for her!!!!

Tuesday 25 October 2005

Having enough carryover wood in the cottage freed the day of that routine. Other than waiting for the bore to recover, it's all that can be done for the moment for water on tap in the cottage....

Still pumped in the 'I can fix it' mode, located and lifted the 2-inch irrigation pipe from the dam, emptied the line past the split where I hit it several years back initially clearing with the brushcutter, finally cutting and repairing the pipe. Fashioning a handlebar shaped hook from copper pipe, connected it to some old electrical cable and cast it into the dam in hope it would snag the sunken pipe. That exercise only managed to dredge water reeds and send the water turbid. Having another tug at the rope connected to the pipe, with a little persuasion it freed, letting me pull the inlet pipe to high dry ground. The hard part done the rest was easy. The inlet pipe having been submerged for such a long period was in need of maintenance. The rope is in a state of decomposition and the styrene float connected to the pipe had sunk; it was left in dry dock to give those repairs more thought☺....

Feeling pretty good finally repairing the irrigation pipe so the surrounding sodden ground can at long last dry, then treated myself to the pile of waiting washing....

A brief shower first thing was just that, brief, cloud lifted and broke letting sun breakthrough generating bloody hot, steamy, uncomfortable conditions, a good climate to grow tropical fruits. An afternoon thunderstorm looking like it was going to dump a load passed by, only sounding the associated bells and whistles to stress Ms Tia!!!!

Another beauty of this ongoing deluge is only a single currawong has been sighted on any given day, one too many but a bloody refreshing change, wherever they've gone I hope they stay!!!!

On a trip up to the water tank I crossed paths with and sent the first reptile this season to heaven, sadly for the snake it was hanging out in the wrong spot near the dam, too close to Tia and housing. Surprised at how calm I remained my large reptile fear has diminished, it's not an action I got out of my way to do or enjoy, except for currawongs, every creature has a purpose and place. The frog population in the dam is the only beneficiary....

Wednesday 26 October 2005

Out of socks, I was happy to have a dry, clean pair waiting in the cottage, adding comfort between sockless feet and boots....

Getting ready for the payday mountain run, a woman by the name of Sandra phoned representing the Centrelink 'personal support program', making final plans we decided on meeting at Rainbow Falls Friday to assess my eligibility for the program, my life is in her hands....

Destiny's wheels still cooling by the curb out front of the supermarket, a very excited David greeted me to share in his uplifting news. David polled second to lame arse Mayor Salter in the local Council election at his first attempt. I gave David my first preference because he freely assisted AEnone in tracking down information, putting together huge pieces of Rainbow Falls' jigsaw puzzle history, in particular relating to Edward Young's background. Again crossing paths with David in the supermarket, on a mission to reward himself for the victory, he purchased a packet of marshmallows. That's over the top clean living ☺.... Just the kind of Councillor I'd like to see represent St. Marys....

Shopping day is taken off guilt free, Destiny loaded with post, groceries, pub supplies, bakery and service station needs, I dropped in on the birthday girl Maggie and happily lost a couple of hours. Firing plumbing questions in need of answers at Brian he willingly filled my brain with solutions. Answers made problem solving obviously easy. Brian said the small copper header tank stolen from outside the cottage would have had acted as a float shut off valve, regulating water flow to the hot water service. The reason for water pouring out of the overflow is the brains telling the hot water service it's full have been removed, sounds logical to me ☺.... Fortunately the cottage wood supply was enough to get through another night following a constructively happy big day out ☺....

Thursday 27 October 2005

Tinkering at a bit of everything doing ongoing survival requirements, I got priorities in order beginning by satisfying a wood need. Gently easing into labour and implementing our mozzie eradication program, Ms Tia escorted me into the paddock putting her heart into helping by catching water tossed from the trough without a drain....

With a fast dropping bore level, I've been wasting a lot of pumping opportunities simply by not knowing how to un-stick a stuck foot valve and retain the water in the line at the same time. Without a one way valve inserted into the delivery line the answer is, I couldn't. Resigned to losing the line full of water I re-primed the pump, connected all the accessories and once again got water moving through the line toward the tank?!?!

A drying wind replaced the deluge fronts approaching from over the distant series of mountain ranges out west never made it this far over, being escorted across the face of the ranges ocean bound. The elements permitted a solid start at mowing the spurt of new growth and keeping it down to size. The existing spark plug demanded a clean after every tank full swallowed, so practised, it took little effort to remove, clean and replace, then fire the mower back into life. Grass is literally jumping out of the ground experiencing ultimate conditions for maximum growth. The down side to the rapidly changing climatic conditions is the bore level is fast disappearing from view....

Friday 28 October 2005
Arriving punctually at the planned 10:30a.m.-ish, watching a little white car go to the neighbours and not take long to return, suspected it might have been Sandra. The outcome from her visit is I'm officially on the 'personal support program'. Eliminating the need to actively source work, my only obligation is six weekly form lodgements and contact with Sandra every third week, I'm now able to fully focus on weight gain, health, home and writing. Two years should buy time to finish my book and move closer to self-sufficiency????
Shutting the gate behind Sandra, strolling back along the driveway I only made it halfway stopping en route to dismantle the pump. The height the bore was recovering to it was a waste of time leaving the system in place, drawing on about a metre at each pumping only pushed a fiddle fart amount up the line....
Without literally letting the grass grow under my feet a solid few hours was put in pushing the four wheeled beast around, the football field of mowing has far from reached the goal posts but an impression is being made. Tired of walking in squares and rectangles the mower was put away while enough light remained to cut wood, gather water and cover the pipe ends of the now finalised pumping effort. Calling it a night to cook dinner, bath, write and hope to make bed before midnight, makes me wonder how I ever found time to watch television????
Stripping for a bath I was surprised to see the toes of my right foot covered in blood, with no obvious reason for the blood I turned my sock inside out and found what remained of a leech. It must have had a bastard of a time keeping up with the kilometres I walked mowing, it was a feat just making it into my sock and down to my toes, the bloody mongrel!!!!
Heading into town Wednesday filled me with optimistic hope our road may get graded, pushing back on what was washed off by rain. The road the mayor lives on was being top dressed and repaired, but it seems the grader doesn't know how to deviate off that road or past his house, rather in your face use of position. I will however eat humble pie if the grader shows up out front but won't hold my breath, call me cynical. Wednesday's trip over the mountain also supplied me with an interesting snippet of corruption. Neil, the former chairman of the radio station has been formally charged and fined $20,000 for misappropriation of funds while working for the Business and Employment Centre in St. Helens. It's self-explanatory why he ran off to Perth on the mainland some months back.... Hmmmm....
Putting in a long, big day, and now after midnight, I can think about bed....

Saturday 29 October 2005
Nature's elements dropping 13mm overnight decided I have the day off mowing, and a worn body wasn't sorry. Garden watering beginning to look like it required assistance was also cancelled. Fortunately having foresight yesterday, as buggered as I was after mowing, to bring a dry load of wood to the shed, cutting it got first priority today....
Gradually easing, rain pulled up early, in the transient changeover foggy cloud slowly lifted and increased the sun's ability to penetrate, heat elevated humidity to uncomfortably steamy, conditions only plants don't wilt in. Environmental factors have certainly agreed with mushrooms; they've been busy spawning. I am finding and protecting several for my stomach rather than that of a possum or wallaby....

Returning a missed call, Mum and Dad were keen to find out how I was going delivering water to the cottage; as far away as they are it's a change they had plenty to do with, supplying the main link the pump immediately springs to mind ☺ ....

Sunday 30 October 2005
Facing an interesting sky first thing, a clear halo above was surrounded by thick fluffy rain cloud. To cover all bases my best mate helped barrow up enough wood to get us through a wet week before breakfast, looking like anything could happen - it usually does here. Still out and about we did the usual garden walkabout. A covered mushroom protected from fauna is doubling in size daily - growth can almost be observed by the naked eye. Needing only enough to cook carbonara one mushroom alone will supply more than required; it's near on the size of a dinner plate ☺ !!!!
The mower's spark plug cleaned ready for another round and the sugar snap peas trellised, the hard working team adjourned to the cottage to avoid wilting in the rising mercury. Out of the elements I got serious preparing for the trip to Launceston Magistrates Court, investing a couple of hours and near on brain melt down, was ready to give the paper chase away when a social time arrived with Pam and Terry. Popping in to release a couple of rehabilitated orphan possums, after another happy outcome we relaxed over a brew, chat and stroll around the garden. The gate hadn't long been shut behind Pam and Terry and Ross made his way along the driveway, willingly parking my arse relaxed yet again over another brew and more conversation ☺ ....
All guests departed I had a go at continuing the mowing process, tired and reluctant, the mower stalled fouling the plug and refused to start. Without having to be told twice I parked it back in the shed, declared beer o'clock and retreated inside to begin dinner. Ingredients cut and establishing the fire, Phillip phoned and I again exercised my vocal cords, Ms Tia was happy to see food in her bowl when it finally arrived ☺ !!!!
Having a spare course of antibiotics on hand I made a start swallowing them a couple of days back, following a ten month reprieve the abscess in my tooth made a repeat appearance, no more delays or relying on the good fairy it's time to have it extracted.... Ouch....

Monday 31 October 2005
Testing my inner strength I tried pulling the tooth containing the abscess myself, unable to tug at the required strength decided the $25 and trip to St. Helens was a less traumatic experience. With a firm decision made I phoned the dentist to hop in the queue and wait for an appointment, then found solitude down the shed cutting enough wood to keep home fires burning....
Still driven by the inner 'girl can fix it' I dismantled taps over the bath removing perished washers, back to a stalemate, left the half job sit idle until I borrow the washer-seating tool from Terry to finalise repairs thoroughly and once only....
Standing tall and its growth peaked I picked the mushroom so careingly protected, its impressive size almost covered a dinner plate, while fresh and moist, carbonara was put on the menu ☺ ....
Throwing a match onto the heater to get the evening indoor stuff underway, I received a pleasant phone call out of the blue from Cousin Mark. Having little to do with one another

throughout life, Mark and I spent time exchanging a brief overview of the past decade to the most recent....
Experiencing a rare occasion over dinner I pulled up full before the bowl was empty it must have been the influence of the bloody big mushroom in the carbonara☺????
My toe still looks pretty nasty where the leech clamped on remaining a little swollen and red, as long as it doesn't end up in the same state as the leech I'll be happy, dying unceremoniously in my sock isn't real dignified ☺....

Tuesday 1 November 2005
It was a 'save little critters morning'. A small moth with its wings plastered to the bath by water was successfully removed and dried, ending in a success story. Hearing a dull thud on a cottage window I reacted immediately to find an injured swallow, quickly racing into the bungalow threw together some sugary water to administer, the swallow sadly died in the brief moment of absence. Cupped in my hand, I carried the swallow's beautiful limp body to a more dignified final resting place....
Shy on drinking water and wishing to borrow Terry's washer seating tool we took a mountain drive. The drive was filled with climatic change, leaving home in stinging sunshine reached the highest point passing between the Sisters and was totally swallowed in low cloud, returning to sunshine in St. Marys. Completing my economy boosting bits I made Pam and Terry's the last stop; after consuming a brew of coffee we migrated to their well-organised shed....
A few kilometres from home on the return trip I was thrilled to see an eagle feeding on road kill. Raising its massive body into flight directly in front, the eagle bided time resting in a nearby tree waiting for the inconvenience to pass to resume its meal ☺....
Popping in a new spark plug made very little difference to the mowers performance, struggling with revs beyond idle, it limped through one tank of juice before refusing to start until more maintenance is done. Waiting its turn for repairs, the mower was parked back in the shed then wore my boots out lugging water....
Tempting fate, I collected a few extra buckets of water filling the washing machine and left whites to soak. Remaining with the water theme splashed a sprinkling over the younger shallow rooted vegetable seedlings. Fading light turned attention indoors to the evening routine of fire lighting, cooking, eating, bathing, dishes, and writing....
I'd like to think the moth with damaged wings dancing over the writing pad and lamp making tonight's journal entry is the one saved from the bath this morning, the thought alone gives me the warm and fuzzies ☺....

Wednesday 2 November 2005
Filling the washing machine did tempt fate, up for a wee through the night misty rain was falling; clearing before re-surfacing it left behind 1mm and created conditions only plants, reptiles and blowflies love. The rock pile was literally crawling with go-carts, a couple scampered into the bungalow looking for a feed on the window sill....
Shit, days are manual and long, getting to bed before midnight is novel, last night was 1:30a.m.-ish, daylight saving keeps me happily distracted outside until 8p.m.-ish when it cools comfortably enough to spark up the heater....

With no airflow clothes on skin felt clingy and bloody uncomfortable in outstandingly hot humid conditions, free of shoes, I wore only a rolled up pair of light cotton pants, I miss winter already. Enduring a series of late and long days, today I hit the wall, feeling as strong as a half-sucked peppermint procrastinated through the washing. When all the material bits were happily dangling on the clothesline, me and my little mate contentedly remained shaded under the cottage roof taking refuge from searing, steamy heat….

Looking to occupy an idle mind in a wilted body on something not too taxing, washers were seated and replaced on the taps over the bath. Before replacing each component it got a scrub with steel wool eliminating many, many years of grime build-up, I was able to see my reflection when finished. Already having the usual water supply organised, saved the big moment of opening the valve at the water tank to test the seated washers for later ☺….

Thursday 3 November 2005
Heading to the bungalow for bed last night at the semi-reasonable time of 12:30a.m.-ish there wasn't a star to be sighted. Ms Muffet and I were settled in our beds getting the nods, and a passing thunderstorm changed that blissful state. Reckoning it was time to get up Ms Tia's thunder meter went off sending fur flying again this morning, staying comfortable in bed I calmed a stressed young lady until it passed….

The same steamy, uncomfortable, warm conditions lingered, my little mate and I took refuge down the shed the coolest building with a most generous airflow. Cutting a wheelbarrow load of wood I raised a clammy sweat, and the occasional sprinkling of rain ensured the humidity level remained peaking!!!!

Ready to test the reticulation system I opened the valve at the water tank and let the precious liquid flow and all seated taps worked like a dream, being extremely pleased with my first attempt at replacing washers. Assuming it still worked, the next big test was the hot water service, flicking the right switches let it begin heating ☺????

Blanketed by cloud mid afternoon offered cool relief, and doing a complete 360° it just kept on cooling. The temperature helped with the enjoyment of a huge outstanding turning-point, it's the first time I've soaked in a bath with water that flowed from a tap and generated by the hot water service. When the in-line tap installed to regulate flow to the hot water service is open, it also robs its brains from registering when it's full the overflow still pours water out. Knowing the work involved getting water into the holding tank it pains me to see it flow onto the ground. We've got a long way to go, but we've come a long way, I'll just keep enjoying the journey one day at a time ☺….

Friday 4 November 2005
Thinking on an early night, I packed up my bat and ball and headed to the bungalow by a respectable 11:30p.m. Leaving the cottage for the building changeover Ms Tia refused to respond to being called, traipsing all over the place calling into the wind, I got serious firing Destiny into life for a broader search with lights. Following Destiny up the driveway a naughty Ms Tia met us at the front gate, happy to finally see her but cranky she ignored my calling, made it to bed an hour later….

Nestling my head on the pillow finally ready for sleep wind had picked up to destructive speeds, up there with the worst experienced, causing a brain to remain alert hoping everything

stays intact. Managing a little broken sleep, gave up on the idea shortly after 4a.m. when menacing gusts refused to be ignored, causing uncomfortable sounds, I preferred to be up, dressed and prepared for anything. When the worst of the gusting front passed, exhausted and fully clothed, I lay on the bed and drifted off to find a couple of hours sleep....
Once again everything held together except me, but everything including me was tested to breaking point! Waking from broken sleep I roamed the yard to see things were still where they should be. Tuning into the radio, news headlines reported Hobart had copped its wildest recorded gusting wind since 1958, leaving a trail of damage!!!!
My get up and go had got up and went, with my arse dragging on the ground had the perfect day to cater for energy, excepting my ask for help, loaded me, Tia and the mower into Destiny and headed over the mountain to Pam and Terry's. A social afternoon away from Rainbow Falls was just what the doctor ordered. Chatting over brewed coffee and freshly baked scones straight from the oven was ideal ☺....
Putting together a video to send Mum for her birthday, I took Pam and Terry's camera for a walk filming the little hamlet of St. Marys. Popping into the bakery, Evelyn was a good sport saying hello to Margaret and Barry on camera. Filming career over I played apprentice to Terry fixing the mower, taking the mystery out of the unknown, simply explaining how components fit into the scheme of things, I absorbed the knowledge on offer like a sponge. The afternoon melted and was heading toward evening, packing a healthier mower and a home baked loaf of bread in Destiny, bestowed in generosity, said farewells returning home to a calmer evening in paradise ☺....

Saturday 5 November 2005
Following seven hours of pushing the mower around I was stuffed and ready for bed. On automatic pilot I focussed on dinner, bathing and writing, my head neatly placed on a soft fluffed pillow being the ultimate goal. Now almost there, with no wind or thunder a reasonably early night is looking good ☺....
Wishing to tidy the yard a little before including footage of Rainbow Falls onto Mum's birthday video, I added revs to the mower as soon as I was organised. The mower was a pleasure to use, besides performance, an outstanding change following repairs is a tank of juice goes a lot further....
If my little helper wasn't dropping something in the mowers path she was excitedly racing through paddocks, when her motor got a bit warm Tia would take a dip in her cattle trough pool then do it all over again, putting in a huge one herself ☺....
Advancing the neat picture perfect look, I went crazy putting in a bloody enormous burst pulling up spent 6p.m.-ish, without variation it was mow, mow, mow and more mowing ☺....

Sunday 6 November 2005
Unleashing a huuuuge explosive physical release on my body yesterday, today I opted for a softer journey plodding around doing whatever looked interesting crossing my path....
Garden watering has crept back into the routine, always finding pleasure and losing time there. Having trouble germinating seed, the strike rate is low, maybe the 400mm of rain for October caused them to rot in the ground. Pumpkins however are popping up all over the place,

Peaches relished in the deluge, overloaded in fruit for such a small tree to get reasonable sized fruit I've been thinning numbers....
Paradise is certainly peaceful with the absence of mongrel birds, on occasion a horrible squawk can be heard in the distance, but we haven't had to piss one off for sometime at home. For a tease, two large black birds landed in a paddock to browse pickings, causing me to take a second look, smiled to see they were ravens. Alternately, my heart sank to find a second swallow dead, discovering this one on the shed floor below its nesting site; united for eternity buried the two together....
Popping in early afternoon to add to the video, Pam and Terry arrived armed with cakes from the bakery to indulge in over a brew, sustaining our energy before walking up hill and down dale. Behind the cattle yards Terry found the obvious poo evidence confirming Rainbow Falls has its own resident wombat, expanding on the known marsupial inhabitants. Other than low lying valley land and the gorge not much was overlooked for filming, talking my way through recording anything that stood before me from housing to the falls. Winding up the recording on a tidy note, Pam and Terry joined me in singing 'Happy Birthday' to Mum. It was a lot of fun contributing to the videos making, I reckon it will rise a bit of emotion within Mum and Dad viewing the final product ☺ ....

Monday 7 November 2005
Placing my head on the pillow at the early dream time of 10:30pm, too much video excitement, sugar and caffeine combined, I last looked at the clock 3a.m.-ish, early nights are just not meant to happen???? Tia had a chew on a rotting carcass before bed and its aroma lingered on her breath, arse and paws; she's a little treasure ☺ ....
Loitering rain cloud and a shortage of wood prompted the decision to cart enough to last a few consecutive wet ones into the shed, remaining in the haven cutting a few nights worth down to size. Mother Nature mucked around putting in lame efforts at dropping moisture then sun would breakthrough, sometimes simultaneously occurring, just fiddle farting around it only managed to raise humidity....
Not feeling overly active I indulged in a pleasant afternoon perched on my bum indoors leaving no stone unturned preparing paperwork for Friday's trip to Launceston. Moving to a more pleasurable pastime of talking to friends, I began with Doris Lohrey in hope she had spare time for a cuppa while visiting in the neighbourhood Friday, and as luck had it 1:30pm was good ☺ ....
Keeping the receiver warm I dialled Loui's number and we seriously got our jaws moving updating absent time, Ross called in on cue to share a chat with Loui also. Replacing a hot receiver Ross and I adjourned to the shed doing damage to a milo jabbering for a while. Lastly, and before seriously getting into cooking dinner, Stacey became the focus of my phone attention to wish her many happy returns. Mentioning in conversation with Stacey that I don't know how to quit writing, she suggested I begin with paper patches to ease myself off stationery ☺ ....

Tuesday 8 November 2005
Diligently working throughout the night and gently delivering 20mm by morning, once again garden watering is struck off the roster. Swinging open the bungalow door greeted the

enchanted 'world of our own' sensation, plunged under a blanket of low cloud blocking anything outside fifty metres from view, initially I couldn't see beyond the shed, perfect in paradise ☺ ....
With the passing of time ultra-violet rays filtered their way through dismantling cloud, heating life up, sun was overshadowed mid afternoon stepping aside for a few more millimetres, totalling 27mm and running out of steam by knock off....
Sitting idle for a while there was some fancy catching up to do adding electricity to the computer gliding my fingers over the keys digitising the journal absorbed the bulk of daylight hours....
Happy to report the shed is still alive with the sound of busy nesting swallows. Following two fatalities my heart sank with the thought of not being swooped while cutting wood, or hearing the cheerful chirping coming from the electricity cable draped across the yard, swallow activity is alive and populating ☺ !!!!

Wednesday 9 November 2005
Payday, and shaving it to the bone to post Mum's envelope of birthday goodies, a trip over the mountain made priority....
Terry expressed interest in the excess cut from the 2-inch roll of poly pipe, looking like the 'Beverly Hillbillies' with twenty metres of 2-inch poly pipe rolled and strapped to Destiny's roof, needless to say dropping it off to its new owners was the first port of call. Relaxing over brewed coffee I watched the final video product, very happy with my amateur attempt, a copy was priority posted to Mum for her birthday ☺ ....
After hitting town and doing the necessary bits, then called into Rita's quilting studio arriving in perfect time, not only for great company, but also to sample a gorgeous apple cake laced with cream ☺ ....
A thank you block of chocolate dropped into to Pam and Terry, and stocked with supplies, developing rain escorted us home the entire distance. Destiny unloaded and returned to her bedroom a passing thunderstorm kept life in paradise interesting, leaving behind in its wake another 5mm break from garden watering. Going walkabout after rain I found and took care of a sneaky slug on a bean seedling, already having done damage, I saved myself from more disappointment in the morning....
A message waiting on the answering machine from the dentist scheduled an appointment time clashing with Friday's court appearance, rectified, I'm now back on the waiting list????

Thursday 10 November 2005
With a brain preoccupied concentrating on tomorrow's trip to Launceston, today converged around preparing the finer details. How I feel about myself is most important, beginning by giving my boots a lick of nugget, and heaven-forbid, after going through the instruction manual pulled the iron out. Only the second time its had an airing since calling Rainbow Falls home, it took some psyching, ironing doesn't enter my vocabulary or 'to-do' list! Adding a shine to my boots, happily being swooped by swallows protecting their shed nesting site, put a pleasing smile on my face ☺ ....
Three swallows maintained nesting site protection taking it in turns swooping while I cut wood. A safe ownership system operates, with a wagging tail Tia barks and attempts to chase

the swallows from what she thinks is her shed, and swallows swoop us both unrelentingly protecting their space. I'm content paradise has resumed a level of normality ☺....
I was unable to move a focussed mind until all thinkable needs for tomorrow were met, with paperwork done, clothes ready, attention turned next to Destiny. Wishing to arrive in Launceston with the least amount of loose Tia fur as possible, I also wiped away unavoidable mountain topsoil decorating panels. Being as prepared as I'm going to be, I could then relax over beer o'clock and the normal evening stuff that waited ☺....

Friday 11 November 2005
A huge one for this happy hermit and the only way to start recording it is at the beginning, and that was at the bloody awful hour of 5:30am. Conscious of everything needing to run smooth without a hitch to make Launceston in comfortable timing, stirred several times through the night checking the clock because getting up bloody early was step one in the success of the plan ☺....
No fog or fallen trees along the road to hinder the plan I picked Ross up by 7a.m. and we were on the way to the big smoke....
It's the first time I faced a set of traffic lights or left our local municipality in fourteen months, I'm definitely a happy hermit. Destiny's odometer turned over to 400,000 kilometres during the journey, celebrating her youth by running smoothly the entire trip, adding step two to the success of the plan....
With Tia and Destiny comfortably together in under cover parking I managed enough time for a nervous toilet stop before presenting myself at the court. Emotions well collected, I dealt with the directions conference comfortable remaining clear headed. Bundled together in the same room before entering Court 2, Bruce and Chris, representing the radio station, also waited. Bruce made a point of extending his hand and saying hello then introduced me to Chris, unfazed we exchanged small talk pleasantries. Ross was able to remain with me for the entire brief proceeding; capable of facing the experience alone, it was however nice to have supporting company....
Seated at a large table opposite Bruce and Chris in the courtroom, and looking side on to the magistrate situated higher behind an elevated bench, the directions conference experience was made pleasant. All questions were directed to and answered through the Magistrate. Spoken to in user friendly terms, without the need for legal jargon, the recommendation and agreed outcome from the conference is report writing and evidence compilation postponed for 56 days allowing time to try another avenue for mediation. This mediator has direct court authority and can advise of my chances if the action proceeds, their job is also to suggest and source outcomes to bring our issue to a close without the need for masses of paperwork. The magistrate confirmed 90% of cases referred to mediation don't return to the courtroom, being resolved in a friendly and easier manner. Agreeing with the suggested direction, we vacated the courtroom in under an hour....
Browsing around town while in the big smoke Ross led me to a few second-hand book stores, favourite shops for time absorption, from stationery to hardware we looked in them all ☺....
The most pleasant stop was to visit Doris, making a hot brew we sat and talked, she loves hearing about changes to our shared home as I love hearing the history of Rainbow Falls. Through idle chat over tea, Doris provides unknown snippets of the past adding to the

comprehensive jigsaw puzzle being pieced together. Being in Doris' company is always a pleasure ☺ ....

Happy to take the passenger seat, Ross steered us homeward, shouting pizza in St. Marys we enjoyed it over a brew at his house before making it back to our side of the mountain 8p.m.-ish. That big trip should see me through another fourteen months, leaving me to resume a hermit existence ☺ ....

Saturday 12 November 2005

Following yesterday's cultural city blow-out a very placid tinkering time was spent in paradise keeping in tune with available energy....

Preparing breakfast ready for the usual toast sharing, Ms Tia returned after reclaiming real estate from night traffic proudly strutting inside plastered in a new scent, her back looked like it had been gelled and spiked. Precious as rotting carcass is, Ms Tia earned herself a shampoo so we could be confined in the small space of Destiny taking a quick trip over the mountain to grab mower fuel ☺ !!!!

Before heading into the big metropolis of St. Marys I phoned through birthday wishes to Mum, catching Dad also before leaving for his regular Saturday golf. Confirming they'd received the video but as yet hadn't been able to sit down together to watch it. Making herself beautiful to be taken out for lunch by Kerry, I didn't keep Mum long, calling back later for serious chat ☺ ....

Petrol tins full and greeting with a warm hug, Brian and Maggie were happy for a casual yarp before we returned back up the mountain. Overcast with the occasional light sprinkling of mist kept ground moist and mower free, a good thing because I didn't harbour the required energy for that level of physical activity....

Tinkering around, I brought in a wheelbarrow load of wood and cut just enough for the evening, staying with heater needs, emptied it of its collection of ash then reset it fresh for the night ahead. Winding down heading toward beer o'clock, I carted in extra water to leave whites soaking overnight, in particular the white shirt worn yesterday because it caught the pizza that missed my mouth, bugger it!!!!

Sunday 13 November 2005

With Ms Tia content outside chewing on a meaty bone, I was savouring an after breakfast milo sitting quietly in the bungalow, being snapped from daydreaming by a swallow taking the liberty of flying into the bungalow for a visit. Surprisingly, the experience was repeated five times within as many minutes???? I wouldn't live anywhere else it doesn't get better than paradise ☺ ....

It was 'strap a shovel to the leg' kind of weather, perfect for reptiles and drying clothes, sun was delivered with a real sting. Getting the last clothes dangling from the line, cloud conveniently moved in on cue making conditions outside tolerable for mowing. Setting seed en masse, I concentrated on buzzie busting, mowing to and around the loo nipped a potential few million seeds in the bud, even now closing my eyes I can still see the buggers!!!!

Pushing the mower around I lucked finding a couple of mature mushrooms for the picking, and doubled my luck by protecting others to harvest later, bonus ☺ ....

Still jet lagged from Friday, it was fortunate having leftovers to heat and eat because I finished up bloody exhausted, exerting a huge effort I pulled up lame with sore feet from pushing the mower up hill. I won't take any rocking tonight, just waiting to put the pen down to retire to bed…. Yawn….

Monday 14 November 2005
If I wasn't on the phone I was mowing. Missing two calls by having the only working phone in the cottage next door, after breakfast I followed up with Centrelink. Saving the best until last, I got comfortable returning Sheila's call before heading down the shed cutting wood waiting for grass to dry….
Once again cloud cover moved in on cue keeping the temperature reasonable to push the mower around. At the end of the first tank of juice I found a message on the answering machine, Mum and Dad had watched the birthday video and the recorded message left simply stated "invite me to your party next time thank you". Calling back, Mum and Dad expressed how much they enjoyed the video. Achieving the desired results I headed back out to destroy more fossil fuel mowing ☺ ….
Returning indoors to catch a phone interview with Centrelink, I found another message from Mum and Dad asking me to give them a quick call. After viewing the video, between them had decided to buy Loui's ride-on mower as a Christmas present, generating a succession of calls, the last one to Mum and Dad confirming the ride-on now has a new owner ☺ !!!! The blisters will now be on my bum, not my feet…. A dream come true ☺ ….
To celebrate the amazing life changing gift I ended the working day emptying a tank of juice pushing the mower around the dam. A string of barbed wire surrounding the dam made short work in the gentle breeze of a flowing light shirt worn for UV protection. Impressed by the outcome of a lot of work for seed eradication, being able to see buzzies when I closed my eyes after mowing yesterday, today their image was etched inside my eyelids ☺ ….

Tuesday 15 November 2005
A well-earned take it easy day, giving poor blisters a rest from the punishing kilometres of following the mower around the yard ☺ !!!!
Returning to the roster, I took my sweet time first up to enjoy the garden watering experience while taking in change. Applying a spot of engineering I used a plank of wood to prop Peaches, the weight of new growth and fruit had her stooped over, the plank carried the weight load for the thin trunk and elevated branches off the ground. Along with garlic and strawberries, quite a number of self-sown potato plants have taken off looking healthy and standing to attention. Octobers deluge has been visually beneficial to many plants in the vegie patch, however took its toll on seed, rotting quite a lot in the ground….
A call from the dentist secured an appointment time in St. Helens for Thursday. With that knowledge I was able to phone AEnone confirming my visit to pick up Loui's ride-on, borrowing a trailer from Pam and Terry to transport Rainbow Falls' new addition…. Ho, ho, ho, ho and merry Christmas, love Mum and Dad ☺ xxxx
With the wood supply behind the cattle yards beginning to wind down I've now turned attention to the charred remains strewn through the burnt out house, it's time to make a start tidying the area and putting the unfortunate mess to a practical use. Having wood organised

and heater set I parked my bum in front of the computer, giving my feet an earned rest let my fingers do the walking over a keyboard instead ☺ ….

Wednesday 16 November 2005
The croaking population of the night chorus of frogs is about to explode. Stepping sideways out of the extensive water collection routine, I took the time to get an overview look at clearing from above the dam, from where I stood glimpsed an outstanding number of large wriggling tadpoles basking in warm surface water. I read in a landcare magazine that 85% of all frog species are found on private land in farm dams, a sad figure for public land. The presence of frogs is also a good indicator of water health. While I'm here frogs are safe from human intervention, its only kookaburras and snakes they have to contend with, life is a bit of a lottery ☺ ….
Summer has wedged its foot firmly in the door, the stir-crazy season, a time I dislike being outside any more than necessary. Tinkering in the vegie garden until the UV comfort level peaked, I then escaped the heat retreating to the shed, Destiny's vitals were checked then she got a tidy in readiness for the big day out trailer towing….
Remaining in the cool the haven offered gave it a sweep then converted my boots from farm use to street wear with a lick of nugget. Still thinking ahead for tomorrow, I rattled amongst the timber collection, cutting to equal length two sturdy planks so the mower can be ridden up onto the trailer ☺ …. Ride-on mower ☺ !!!!
Having to shoot through pretty early in the morning the garden got a soak when the day cooled, if it has to endure a stinker it will survive. Winding down a well-earnt pretty lazy old time, I went walkabout with my little mate taking photos of what is hopefully my last enormous effort with the push mower. Ensuring I have hard evidence to visually remember the good ol' days before life became cushy ☺ …. Hallelujah, and merry Christmas ☺ ….

Thursday 17 November 2005
Another bloody huge day for the hermit dwellers in paradise, up again with the annoying alarm, allowed enough time to complete all requirements to make the 11:30am dentist appointment in St. Helens….
Needing to finance the expedition my plan momentarily hit the wall, the supermarket ATM was temporarily unavailable waiting to be cashed, adjusting to 'Plan B', went to Pam and Terry's hitching the trailer first. With cash, petrol and a trailer following behind we headed in the direction of St. Marys Pass….
Living diagonally across from the dentist, Phillip offered the carport at his unit for Ms Tia's comfort, shade is pretty difficult to find on a warm day and with a trailer attached even harder….
Burying my nose in magazines the dentist was an hour behind, the delay I could live with because getting teeth pulled isn't something to get excited about. Seemingly with his hands and feet pressed against my mouth, the molar root pulled free of the gum creating another gap in my jaw. Feeling fine, the dentist insisted I sit in a nearby room for post extraction observation, prior to leaving was told to take it easy. Taking the advice onboard, reversed Destiny and trailer onto the road then drove the few short kilometres to AEnone's. Sharing a soup lunch discussing the world AEnone said she was having wrist problems, offering a hand, I raked and

removed grass clippings tidying the front yard before loading the ride-on, strapping it down, and heading proudly for home ☺ ....
Catching up with us slowly climbing the last couple of kilometres at the tail end of the Pass, and following me into St. Marys, Connie pulled up in front of me at the bakery greeting with a hug and friendly words. Heading into the pub for a box of Bruce's best Connie had a coolly waiting on the bar, sharing in a drink and a dash of spontaneity her company was perfect for the moment ☺ ....
Manoeuvring Destiny and the towed booty around in the dead-end street I called in on Pam and Terry, by then getting a bit late in the day asked if the trailer could be returned tomorrow. After displaying the prized new purchase I broke open the box of beer, over a stubby Pam and Terry invited me to join them for Christmas lunch and I gratefully accepted ☺ ....
Reaching my driving drinking quota made it back over the mountain to paradise, straight away phoning Mum and Dad to let them know Christmas made it home early and safely, a pleasing result all round ☺ ....

Friday 18 November 2005
Forcing my tired, lazy body out of bed to feed it before talking to the two most important people in my life, Mum and Dad were preparing for dinner when I excitedly called about the ride-on last night so we made plans for more length and detail this morning ☺ ....
Still with my arse dragging on the ground I got it and an empty trailer back over the mountain, visiting in perfect timing for baby bottle-feed time at the zoo. Both baby wombats were looking for tucker and I willingly extended a helping hand to feed one. Remaining curled up with a belly full cradled in my arm the baby wombat snoozed while I indulged in cake and coffee, a perfect moment in utopia ☺ ....
Saying thank you and farewells to Pam and Terry the next stop was at the shops for a few bits. Checking the Post Office box gave me a laugh waiting in the black box was a creative lollie, a 'tangy tongue'. Sealed inside the wrapper was a set of large strawberry lips, forced between the lips a three inch long tongue dangled, Harry at the Post Office had the answers but was sworn to secrecy, his lips were sealed. The only people coming to mind who would think of me with such a gift are Brian and Maggie, and the buggers weren't home to be held responsible, if I'm wrong I'll be surprised ☺ ....
Petrol purchase safely on board Destiny's nose was pointed homeward to put it to use sitting on my bum. The first tank of juice was spent getting co-ordinated with the beast between my legs, by the second tank I'd settled, getting used to the speed and controls we began working together as one. A mere two hours spent seated on my bum steering the beast knocking down grass floored me at the rate of progress. Without raising a sweat or taking my jumper off I condensed two days push mowing into as many hours, yard maintenance has become manageable freeing up days spent sweating it out walking in the park ☺ ....

Saturday 19 November 2005
Waking to face whatever lay ahead, I looked at a blank faced clock and the obvious no power supply. Breakfast not immediately on the menu, I used the last remaining mower fuel and put time into the vegie patch. Stretching and yawning opening the cottage I just walked inside and the phone burst into life, Ross sent the day into a pleasant but unexpected direction. After

viewing a property he's potentially looking at purchasing he extended an invitation to also visit Dave and Liz, I jumped at the opportunity to see their efficient home set up. Living without electricity, they grow most of what they eat including varieties of meat. My high expectation of knowledge gain wasn't disappointed their ability to efficiently manage resources living within their environment impressed and richly inspired my sense of future. Finalising a tour of their well kept impressive market garden sized vegie patch, we adjourned to the bird-net covered orchard arboretum, feeling more like being relaxed in a sun room we lost the afternoon over tea, cake and plenty of questions and answers ☺ ....

Returning to Ross', I stayed long enough to help move Lorraine's two cows to a lush paddock and share in a brew, then a patient Ms Tia was taken home to reclaim real estate and burn off pent up energy.... So ends another perfect day living in Eden ☺ ....

Sunday 20 November 2005

Distracted away from the nest of late and neglecting the hermit life at Rainbow Falls, today the anchors were put on refocusing on home duties and the six W's, washing, wood, water, water, water, and more water. On a stinger in paradise clothes didn't take long to dry. Washing, dishes, cooking, cleaning and bathing, the water supply forever disappears keeping me honest and off the streets, water in the cattle trough couldn't keep up with demand. To avoid wearing tracks to and from the cattle trough I consciously never walk the same repetitive course, flattening a wider area of lawn to avoid trampling a threadbare track....

Carting bucket after bloody bucket, the vegie patch gave a bit back, picking eight ripe strawberries I'm snacking out on their juicy sweetness as I write....

Plodding along with basic daily life maintenance having a quietey doing nothing more than necessary; that alone filled my time. With the fire prepared ready just to light the evening chores requiring heat awaited ☺ ....

Monday 21 November 2005

Summer's definitely on the doorstep, limiting what and when things outside are done, while the morning is still coolish the routine of bringing water to the cottage kicks things off. Water storage begins by filling two 10 litre boilers and repositioning them back on the heater, a 15 litre bucket sitting over the bath is filled and returned to the planks of supporting wood across the bath. Having a permanent position on the floor, the 25 litre bucket remains on stand-by to top up the pots and bucket, also doubling as a watering hole for Tia. The standard old 10 litre bucket, with me attached tends to them all, ferrying water to both the vegie patch and cottage, and in idle times the bucket stores water for use in the bungalow. After carting an average 50 litres into the cottage, I'm then ready to get into the bits making the priority list screaming out their turn for maintenance ☺ ....

Making the 'to-do' list, the heater was relieved of its ash collection and taken to the loo toping up the almost deplete stock of deoderiser. Leaving the heater set ready to face another night of cooking and bath water boiling, I headed outdoors with a firm grip of the shovel handle in my palms, and following the shade of the walnut tree, cleared around obstacles in the cottage side yard. My little mate, always on the ready to help, waited alert for every clump of grass tossed her direction, after wrestling it to the ground she graded each clump then placed them in the compost file ☺ ....

The shovel left my hand to be replaced by the handle of the bucket to again cart water, this time quenching the thirst of surviving vegies. Letting muscles cool over a beer or two I waited for the sun and sting to leave before continuing on with my manual life and the evening ahead....

Relaxing with feet up, I took a call from Cousin Mark, he plans visiting soon from Mildura. I'm going to make him earn his evening beer - there are stored 'two people' jobs he can help with. I'll have a go at sending him home a farmer ☺ ????

Tuesday 22 November 2005

My little mate's dripping fur has reduced to a dribble offering relief from the daily bungalow de-furring, spare time created is easily absorbed by moving to the next item on the priority list ☺ ....

Overcast, cool conditions ideal for mowing cemented the decision to drag the push mower out tidying bits the ride-on can't get to. Midway through the second tank of juice gathering cloud thickened and had a go at delivering moisture, finishing the tank is all I was permitted, steady rain set in....

Needing petrol in my motor I had a quick snack then did a scout of the burnt out house, grabbing an armful of dry scorched timber before again being driven under cover. Retreating to the shed time was filled mixing fuel and putting the handsaw to work cutting more wood. By the fourth millimetre garden watering was happily crossed off the 'to-do' list, a very welcome drop saving my legs....

Preparing dinner, genealogy sleuth, AEnone, called confirming our hot date at Gray cemetery; the purpose for the visit is to attempt to track down Edward Young. Records show he was buried there 1939, the only hope is he still has a legible headstone intact. Tomorrow will reveal the answers ☺ ????

Wednesday 23 November 2005

My little mate, who's been regularly waking me with her persistent 'wake-up!' paw tap, let me stay snoozing. The mercury dropped through the night and she was content to snuggle for a warm cuddle instead ☺ ....

Meeting punctually in St. Marys, unlike her daughter Loui doing her best always ran behind, AEnone and I had a lovely and successful outing. Jumping in Destiny we went out to Gray cemetery on the outskirts of town. AEnone had Edward Young's grave located before I even put water in Tia's bowl. Edward's headstone gave us no more information than was already known, but I was happy to have found him with a legible intact headstone ☺ ....

Dating back to the turn of last century, steeped in history, we took our time looking around the cemetery. Finding marked graves, not positively identified, but more than likely other residents associated with Edward Young's settled Irish hamlet nestled into the mountain. People with the surname of Speers lived in the shingled roof house over the road and adjacent to Rainbow Falls' top boundary. Quite a small community, Doris spoke of the Brittons living down the lane, a dirt road following a fenceline, the lane is located between the Speers and Lohrey homes, on what is now all Lohrey owned property....

A shut padlock on the church gate kept us from looking at the Cullenswood cemetery where a good number of Lohreys are buried. A little cemetery near the Cornwall turn-off dating from

1855 through to 1900 was overgrown in long grass, looking like a foreboding snake haven, we decided lunch was the preferred option....
After stopping at Evelyn's to purchase lunch I took AEnone home to eat so I could show her what all the fuss was about, share local knowledge, and add visuals to all the names and dates putting puzzle pieces into perspective. After having had a lovely time shared together, with information overload, I returned AEnone to her car in town where we said our farewells. Going about the payday shopping routine, I chatted to familiar friendly faces along the way with the realisation the living are only history in the making ☺ ....
Back home in paradise the requirements for the night ahead had full attention, scouting through the burnt out house heater sized bits were collected from collapsed foundations for the evening. A bit of the veranda entrance and kitchen wall went up the flue tonight, turning an act of criminal damage into a resource by cooking dinner, keeping warm and heating bath water ☺ ....

Thursday 24 November 2005
Unable to help myself, my eyes sprang open at 6a.m. to the bloody awful sound of a pest bird squawking on a fence post near the bungalow, up moving the bugger on, Ms Muffet and I made our bladders more comfortable before returning to bed continuing sweet dreams....
I may have enjoyed a comfortable sleep in but made up for a slack start with a bloody huge input, not pulling up for a beer until shortly after 7p.m.....
Unwilling to take the ride-on into unpredictable areas, undulating ground and tight spaces, I completed those classified bits with the push mower. Burning up the first tank of juice tidying around a tree stump the blades rattled over something they didn't like, reducing the number of blades down to one and a bit. Progressing with a nice vibration through the handle, screws made their way loose and disappeared from the top plastic cover. With a determined mindset I refuelled and headed to the front gate entrance, again putting human and machinery alike to the test. With only one and a bit blades and a wild vibration the mower soldiered on doing a gallant clearing effort. I'm very proud of the appearance of Rainbow Falls the entire 150 metre strip from the loo to the front gate is presently looking extremely tidy ☺ !!!!
My little mate was as helpful as ever the tennis ball was kicked out of the mowers path more times than I care to remember. If Tia wasn't keeping me distracted she was racing around paddocks or taking a dip in her pool to cool her motor and recharge the batteries ☺ ....
The front yard of the burnt out house provided a bonus, two mature large mushrooms, unnoticed by night traffic, made it into tonight's wallaby in honey barbecue sauce stir-fry ☺ .... yumo....

Friday 25 November 2005
The past couple of occasions the mower's been brought out it's attracted moisture from the sky. Walking the path to bed last night just prior to midnight there wasn't a star to be seen. Light misting showers fell through the baby hours, opening the bungalow door this morning onto another of those magical, immersed in low cloud days blocking the rest of the world out ☺ ....
Before settling into an after breakfast milo I first set my little mate up with a fresh meaty bone, both content then to have a quality moment to ourselves. As usual Tia strips the bone pretty well, but obviously not well enough, from the dry comfort of the cottage I watched a raven

land in the yard, and as casual as you like, stroll over then shot through with the bone in its beak. Someone's trash is someone else's treasure ☺....

Dominant weather conditions arriving from north-east is a 'I'm going to settle in for as long as I like' front, and it did. Earning a laid back rest, I had a no stone left unturned chat to Mum and Dad. Unable to mow, and with no need to water the garden, the logical place for a girl to head is to her shed. There are no big surprises in store down there waiting: to keep the cottage heater burning I cut a weighty wheelbarrow load delivering it in a lighter moisture moment....

The front was unremitting, not sighting the sun at all by knock off, and the last look at the gauge 22mm had fallen and was confidently heading toward an inch. Heat generated from cooking dinner reduced the patch of wet roof back to the area immediately surrounding the flue, that is until the fire goes out ☺.... A north-easterly front can settle in for days????

Saturday 26 November 2005
What a bloody trying night, next to gale force wind thunderstorms are one of my least favourite sleep time events. I personally find thunder exhilarating, but my best friend has an opinion contrary to that! Ms Tia's stress meter was activated 2:30a.m.-ish sending fur flying and signalling the start, claps of thunder and explosions of lightning hovered overhead for what seemed an eternity and released a booty of some intense downpours!!!!

The orchestra ended its performance drifting out of Tia's hearing 5a.m.-ish, a nagging thought wouldn't let me relax until the main power switch was flicked to off, a correct hunch, the cottage wall surrounding the power-board had wet up. Intense rain eased off with the thunderstorms passing, adding to yesterdays drop, lifted the moving total to 45mm. With a mind and body finally finding peace I caught a few more hours sleep....

Doing only the required to keep normality ticking over, and with as much strength as a half-sucked peppermint, opted for the soft option of passive therapy finding the vegie patch under weeds, with the ground at saturation point they're easy to pull. Scraping the dirt from my boots at knock off Ross cruised up the driveway with impeccable timing looking for a brew and chat, and that we did easily ☺....

Timing as sharp as a tack, I had just finished scouting a supply of wood from the burnt out house and the sky caved in. Mother Nature didn't pussyfoot around opening the main full throttle delivering moisture hard, fast and incessant, enforcing bucket lugging for garden watering remain off the agenda for a while ☺....

Sunday 27 November 2005
Starting to get webbed feet, another 44mm fell overnight, the longer rain persists the more pots and pans required to catch drips entering through the roof around the heater flue. With extraordinary high levels of moisture around the welcome sound of the falls is clearly audible from housing....

Out of bread and energy I gave myself one off. Starting with a chat with Evelyn over the counter at the bakery, I then met up with Ross in town before stopping at Pam and Terry's to deliver a block of chocolate in appreciation for the loan of the trailer. As customary, great coffee enhanced a pleasant visit....

Looking to confirm the givers of the 'tangy tongue' lollie that made it into my Post Office box found Brian and Maggie home. I would have been amiss and worried guessing wrong, a correct guess gave us a few laughs over a brew☺....

Social cobwebs given a dusting, I returned to clean up the water filled pots and pans I turned my back on driving out the front gate, the minimal electrical appliances relying on power for their existence were also reset. The most energy exerted was put into cutting wood for the evening, but before retiring in to burn a bit, I picked the mushroom growing by the cattle trough to add to dinner and the ripe strawberries for after☺....

My period gives me one restless sleep that happened to be last night, exhausted by thunderstorm activity the previous evening, tonight I'm buggered. Getting between the sheets by a reasonable 11p.m. is looking good and all elements are currently in favour☺!!!!

Monday 28 November 2005
Taking it gentle absorbing the realisation of finally getting quality sleep, made all the difference with energy and a desire to want to participate in the world. Setting up the ladder to have a go at the bloody water leak issue in the cottage roof, spotted a car coming up the driveway, its occupant being my case manager for the 'personal support program'. Arriving earlier than expected, but in perfect timing for a brew and chat, Sandra and I found no shortage of conversation....

Back to dealing with possible water entry points around the flue, I smeared a tube of silicon over the perished rubber mat surrounding the flue on the roof, using available tools and sticking to budget, a five dollar investment could solve and seal the problem???? Suck it and see....

Collecting water I just kept going filling the washing machine and soaking whites committing myself to the task tomorrow. The heater got in the way next, emptied of grey ash and reset, I roamed into the burnt out house cutting enough to burn for the approaching evening. Getting me running from woodcutting, Ross phoned suggesting we take a walk up the mountain in an attempt to sort out why water doesn't freely flow to the holding tank from the spring....

A tiger snake cleared our path scaling up South Sister Range. Water was flowing in the pipe at the spring but not finding its way to the holding tank at Rainbow Falls. Buried and unable to track the few hundred metres of poly pipe to find the problem shelved the hunt, putting it in the too hard basket for the time being....

It was ideal conditions for snake activity. Down from the mountain and making our way up hill to the water tank, I caught a glimpse of a copperhead looking quite comfortable near the dam and Ross' feet. Stopping Ross in his tracks, I handed him the shovel but all he did was freeze and hold it in the air saying, "it's eyeballing me". Taking away any decision the copperhead took off out of harms way making an unscheduled rushed dip in the dam....

Following an appointment with her surgeon to set a date for the annual colonoscopy, trying to phone Mum nothing happened. Testing probabilities, I bypassed the answering machine and the phone sprang into life, the answering machine is out of action????

Tuesday 29 & Wednesday 30 November 2005
My visitors were comfortably seated at the bar when I arrived at St. Marys' pub for our scheduled 7p.m. meeting time Tuesday. Following a warm greeting from Cousin Mark and his

friend Gavin, we settled in for a lovely meal over a couple of beers at the pub before returning to Rainbow Falls to kill more brain cells. Its lucky for me the alcohol ran out and Mark and I talked ourselves out, fortunately for Gavin too, he's an early to bed bloke and we managed to wake him from peaceful slumber on a couple of occasions with our ongoing chatter. A lot of red wine evaporated into conversation, shy on intelligent flowing words and a pen only dangerous in my hand I had the night off writing. Still feeling intoxicated waking Wednesday, my little mate took on my hangover. I stirred to the sound of her being sick on the floor....
Turning back the hands of time, I didn't get bathed until after midnight Monday so dishes waited, already behind the eight ball, I kicked off Tuesday enslaved to domestic duties....
It took very little time to test and fail the effectiveness of silicon as the latest attempt at waterproofing the cottage roof. Gaining strength, wind blew a change in overnight Monday, just what we needed more rain, incase we hadn't had enough, down it came again the moment the last clothes were dangling from the line. Cool and wet, I sparked the heater into life early, needing to dry clothes and heat bath water preparing for a 7p.m. rendezvous with Mark and Gavin at the pub....
Having a sluggish start Wednesday, my energy didn't rise, nursing a healthy red wine poisoning I earned the nickname of 'burley' from Gavin for needing a quick stop to eject poison from my stomach. We had a pretty casual time touring a favourite tourist destination route between home and St Columba waterfall, elated to be a passenger it was however the only capacity I was capable of doing the trip....
Punishment for my seedy state: I got to cook dinner after cutting the wood, the boys declared beer o'clock burying themselves in the esky down the shed. Fire lit and throwing out warmth, clutching a bottle of water I made a start slicing and dicing, by the time dinner was complete an appetite finally found me, food added life to a weary body ☺....

Thursday 1 December 2005
All but one day of the past seven has produced rain, in that short space a healthy 167mm has been totalled. Today began with an intense downpour, a quick 14mm dropped out of the sky but staying true to the start of summer the day ended in warm sunshine????
The alcohol effect on my brain killed the cells containing the information regarding gifts arriving from Mildura with the boys complements of Mum and Dad, flying in with them was a very practical and useful cutlery and dinner set ☺....
While Mark had the cottage to himself tubbing up, Tia come walkabout with me putting an end to a patch of thistles in the cattle yards, and Gavin went to work throwing down a couple of beers. A perfect outing for a wet start, I arranged a visit with Pam and Terry for wombat cuddling, pulling up at the bakery first to provide a little something to have with coffee ☺....
The stop at Pam and Terry's was a pleasant experience, but like a magnet, next port of call for the boys was to the pub for 'a quiety' and a game of pool before again tackling the mountain. My pub moment was cut short by a thunderstorm, joining Ms Tia in Destiny in an attempt at calming her stress levels, it's not something I've ever managed to master but at minimum being with her clears my conscience. Apparently I won the game of pool just started in my absence ☺....
A theme set in a groove we had beer and bullshit in the shed entrance, from the open gates we watched and felt the effects of the edge of a thunderstorm clinging to the coastline. When the

thunderstorm finally subsided sun broke through and the weather did a complete 360°, retiring to the bungalow for the night the sky was full of stars, not a sight witnessed in a while ☺....

Friday 2 December 2005
Gavin woke dosed with bronchitis and in need of antibiotics, phoning the St. Marys Medical Centre was advised a doctor was only available until 11:30am through accident and emergency, so the boys got going over the mountain....
Pleasantly returning with a lunch of pies from Evelyn afterward, leaving Mark engrossed in newspapers and Gavin resting his illness washing it down with beer and tobacco, I replaced blades on the Victa push mower. It amused me comparing the old with the new, the blades removed from the mower were only stumps being around a quarter of the size and thickness of the blades replaced, it should make future mowing easier ☺....
Filling in a sun drenched stinging afternoon in paradise we loaded in the hire car doing a tourist drive, meandering the triangular route of Elephant Pass back to Falmouth and returning through St. Marys Pass, taking in another piece of the municipality. Still in the mood to explore we found the Cullenswood cemetery gate open for a wander into the past, and new for me, we detoured into the Cornwall turn-off, consisting of a small community and handful of houses it didn't take long to solve curiosity and complete the exercise....
With an hour to fill before being able to pick up Gavin's medication, time was utilised constructively at the pub, opening a vending machine ticket on Gavin's behalf I revealed $100 making the beer taste even better. A fellow by the name of Malky sitting at the bar said we're due for four inches of rain overnight, mentioning warnings have been issued to boat operators, another deluge is unwelcome I've had enough I'm wanting my socks to dry out!!!!
Without producing moisture the sky closed in once again blocking stars from view, who knows what will happen but for now the earth is still drying????

Saturday 3 December 2005
Pretty casual in paradise, four inches may have been predicted but thankfully not falling here we pulled up at 18mm....
Feeling crook, Gavin stayed in bed resting his bronchitis. Mark and I went into St. Marys sorting out food for the weekend also food for the moment visiting Evelyn for lunch, then I joined Mark down the shed where the afternoon dissolved buried in newspapers....
As day transpired into night the weather did a complete 360°, the bloody persistent north-easterly deluge was replaced with strong wind directly from the South. Going from one extreme to the other warm and wet was substituted by cold and windy????

Sunday 4 & Monday 5 December 2005
Sunday was pretty easy-going. Mark did a trip over the mountain returning with another fist full of newspapers. In keeping with a relaxed pace, and rain finally giving in to sunshine, we sat in the cool comfort of the shed perusing papers. Browsing the newspapers reiterated why I don't waste time buying any. Predominantly, newspapers are the printed view of the elected political party. The Examiner is an outstanding one-eyed bias paper locals inform me its better known as the exaggerator????

After covering our hands with newsprint heavy metals, and being such a beautiful day, Mark, Tia and I piled into his hire car and took a drive around the mountain capturing a few happy snaps to document his holiday. Taking Mark to the top of the falls, unprepared for the sight and view waiting, he was suitably impressed ☺....

It seems when the boys think they should have a go at cooking we end up at the pub. Gavin miraculously rose from his sick bed other than for cigarettes and cans, to take on the arduous journey. The counter meal and red wine routine slipped in again last night offering the same reason to miss another journal entry, but this time more moderately done ☺....

I've been feeling rather ordinary, if Gavin has done anything for me while he's been here that's pass on his cold. Greeting Monday with a sore throat, heady, blocked sinus and hearing cousin Mark calling out "are ya' up"?....

Getting pretty testy with Gavin's non-existent hygiene, failing to bath at all, he also didn't make the toilet and dropped his soiled undies into the drop pit loo. Mark took off with him to Hobart to give me simmer time....

Boys waved off, and with most of the yard dry and the sun shining Ms Muffet helped me for a while mowing. Running all over the place, I couldn't relax with the thought of active snakes so I put Tia in the Destiny babysitter allowing my mind to rest. New blades made an outstanding difference, slashing their way easily through grass left a manicured bowling-green finish....

Happy for a reflective moment, I wandered the garden where pleasingly the sugar snap peas are producing flowers. The ongoing deluge has spurred on some growth, including weeds ☺....

Tuesday 6 December 2005

Plugging the electric shaver in to do my legs it refused to burst into life. Following me around a lot of reliable years, death was acceptable. Disappointment turned to hope noticing the answering machine was also lifeless power had merely gone off, phew, all appliances were alive and well ☺!!!!

Cloud cover slipping in robbed the stinging edge from the sun making exposing elements comfortable enough to head outdoors to fire up the mower, where the only power required comes from petrol and me. To sweat it out thoughtlessly, again Tia and Destiny kept one another company to avoid any chance meeting with larger reptiles. Mostly doing bits that can't be with the ride-on, the housing is looking pretty tidy, the finish new blades create doesn't fail to impress ☺....

Wednesday 7 December 2005

Finally making it through the evening routine, with blocked sinus and feeling very heavy headed I was searching for bed last night. Before even stepping foot outside the cottage Mother Nature tested my patience and powers of staying awake sending in a thunderstorm. In a quiet down time between booms I got Ms Tia and myself into the bungalow and settled in bed, so when the opportunity for sleep arrived we were in the right spot for it. The quick 5mm travelling with the thunderstorm masked a few of the quieter distant rumbles, helping with settling peace....

Testing me at the other end of the sleep scale, noise from a pair of bloody currawongs had tuned ears and eyes alert 5:30a.m.-ish with ongoing squawking near the bungalow. Unable to ignore their presence they were moved on, then returning to the state of comfort I was enjoying slipped back to the contentment offered in bed☺....

The sky looked like it could do anything: while it was making up its indecisive mind Ms Muffet and I did all the required outside bits. Planning a stint inside with the computer I managed to accomplish that goal. Journal digitising had slipped about a month behind leaving a solid amount of catching up to do. Page after page spilled into the hard drive, putting in a huge session, the happy travellers returned giving me all the reason to stop my fingers from dancing over keys....

Ross popped in to meet the guys over a couple of beers, already settled into their routine of beer and bullshit down the shed. Mark and I spent the last evening together again sitting by the heater chatting, tonight however, I did it over ice water finding it soothing on a raspy, dry, sore throat, and less taxing on brain cells☺....

Thursday 8 December 2005

From the moment Tia and I were tucked into bed last evening a repeat performance of the night before arrived with a late shower, this time without the sleep disturbing bells and whistles attached, handing out yet another 2mm. The past two months alone have delivered a staggering 595mm taking the total for the year to date to a whopping 1094mm. Surpassing one metre is an awesome amount of water for soil to absorb!!!!

Setting the alarm so there was no oversleeping, I roused the boys to get ready and pack the car, holiday over it was fly home day. I enjoyed Mark's company - he is welcome to return but Gavin's personal hygiene and habits were to say the least, bloody ordinary, for him the gate is shut! Before parting farewells, I handed Gavin a piece of wire and plastic bag with the words, "if you don't do it I'll have to, I'd prefer it if you did, please retrieve your undies from the toilet and take them with you"....

My hope of getting assistance with two people jobs failed dismally, initially rain hindered any good intentions outdoors, however Gavin struggled walking his large frame to the loo so putting him to work was out of the question. Waving the boys goodbye I got into cleaning the cottage, domestic duties being a least favourite pastime....

Colonoscopy day for Mum, I called home sending loving thoughts. Due at the hospital midday, it would be several hours before anything was known. Cutting wood occupying an idle mind and waiting hours for an outcome, I lucked it phoning one minute after Mum and Dad had walked in the back door. Other than feeling weak from not eating in twenty-four hours, Mum pleasantly had no health issues to report. Leaving the hospital the only advice received was to visit the doctor March 3, another step further out of the woods☺....

Friday 9 December 2005

My brain, body and natural elements united co-ordinating for the best solid night sleep experienced in a while. The combination of Mum's favourable colonoscopy results, no wind, no thunder, no currawongs and no visitors to consider, just me and my best mate and a relaxed mind in a state of utopia did what it does best, snooze☺....

A day for catching the breath and restocking shelves the morning idled away preparing for a trip between the two Sisters....

Not in any rush, after checking mail I stopped in for a brew with Terry before hitting the shops.

With Christmas fast approaching a packet of cards was added to the shopping list, not big on the commercial side Christmas represents cards are about as excited as I get. However, removed from the shopping list to push the budget further was the fortnightly beer ration, covering bills, keeping the roof over our head and survival has priority….

Winding down a day that didn't wind up, my little mate always at the ready gave me a hand pottering in the vegie patch. Drawing a line at grit on the strawberries I packed dry grass clippings under runners lifting fruit off the ground. Shutting the gate to the vegie patch meant making a start on the evening routine….

Saturday 10 December 2005

Unbelievable, rolling over semi-conscious through the night heard the sound of rain once again, first spring and now summer is being drowned????

Making a personal promise last year I wouldn't endure removing that amount of buzzies from Tia's fur again, scaring deeply was that one occasion last season she returned with her body plastered, sticking to carpet, she peeled from the floor like separating velcro. The 4mm dropping through the dark hours didn't interfere with my brain-set daylight mission. The vacant area between the loo and falls was a carpet of buzzies. It was action day for me and the ride-on to get re-acquainted. Millions upon millions of proudly standing green seed heads reaching for sun were severed from the mother plant and unceremoniously tossed to compost in neat rows left behind in the mower's wake….

Blowing the entire petrol ration in a days outing, what was achieved in the few hours on my arse without the manual effort required would have taken me a week with the push mower. From the falls to the dam is an impressive tidy sight, later walking the freshly tidied area with my best friend I was instilled with a deep sense of pride☺….

Undressing to hop into the bath a leech making its way over the kitchen floor stood out to get noticed, I couldn't find a bleeding latch site anywhere over my naked body, either way it won't come inside again!!!!

Sunday 11 December 2005

Tia must have got a bit cool last night, wandering around to give me the cold nose nudge to hop into my bed she had pulled coat-hangers from their moorings, dressing up for the occasion, Tia was draped in jackets attempting to get under the doona☺????

Enslaved to white goods the washing machine had to be filled twice to catch up, beginning with the neglected clothes stack, freshened and refilled for bedding. Fortunately the furnace was activated in paradise and clothes were drying fast enough to keep me in pegs, it's only the cattle trough that struggled to keep up extracting and carting bucket after bucket!!!!

Having a break from laundry, leaning against the bungalow doorway savouring an after lunch coffee, watched a raven that had made itself quite at home feeding in the yard. Strolling casually within five metres of where I stood the raven showed no fear and I offered no threat. Slightly larger and sadly looking similar to a currawong, it's lucky it had no patches of white then it wouldn't have been given any peace. Hanging around where the pickings are good, the raven had a go at a kookaburra intruding on its claimed patch of worms causing a brief moment of territorial squabbling and squawking….

Phoning earlier to make arrangements, Ross called in 6p.m.-ish with a potential buyer for a petrol mulcher stored in the shed. After the sales pitch and demonstration, Ross indulged my showing off the latest mowing feat, by saying all the right things oohing and arring in appropriate spots I gave him the remaining scotch left behind by Mark. In no hurry, I brewed up a couple of milos before Ross made tracks leaving me to the evening ahead....

Monday 12 December 2005
Our adopted friend the raven was back fearlessly roaming the yard again. Peace was momentarily broken when Tia went flying through the bungalow door with jaws clacking in pursuit of an unwelcome fly. Getting the jitters, the raven took the incident in from a safer distance clumsily flying to the cattle yards, where another territorial altercation occurred between the raven and a kookaburra. Unsure if it's the same kookaburra; the raven however is easily identified it has a couple of ruffled wing feathers that don't sit tidily....
Without a single word exchanged since the 'directions conference' in Launceston a month ago, and knowing a couple of deadlines for submitting documents are approaching, I got proactive phoning the Anti-Discrimination Commission. It seems the answers to all questions were posted yesterday. Colleen read the letters contents and deadline dates over the phone - the knowledge reassured my mind it can hover on idle resting until Christmas has passed....
Feeling a bit daunted by the amount of time required to inject into the discrimination case I escaped to the vegie patch with my best friend and shovel, with a cool breeze and scattered cloud it was idyllic to get lost in free ranging thought. Clearing thoughts from the overwhelm of the entire picture got it back into perspective reduced to one step at a time, not only was my mind cleared but so too was half the vegie patch, eliminating weeds and exposing the desired plants and rich soil....
A little easier to remove, green buzzie seeds are managing to attach themselves to Ms Tia's beautiful outfit, plucking a small collection out got a surprise rolling her over to discover her fully in season. Life always remains interesting at Rainbow Falls. Dull moments are rare but appreciated ☺ !!!!

Tuesday 13 December 2005
Hearing in disbelief another spot of rain arrive through the night, to spoil me rotten, at 3:20a.m. precisely a few distant thunder rumbles broke bungalow peace. Fortunately for pillow quality time it didn't last long at all, only a few outbursts of barking were required to chase it away ☺ !!!!
Running out of time fast and unable to put it off any longer, cornered myself into sitting and writing in Christmas cards. Just winding up the Christmas card list, Pete, in the company of Charles arrived to pick up the mulcher for test drive. Mentioning to Charles his dog has been a regular visitor, being even more regular now that Tia is in season. Last night while journal writing Charles' dog, Oke, was whining outside the cottage door, a very receptive tail wagging Tia stood on the opposite side. Obliging, Charles said he'd stop his dog from roaming keeping him home in the evenings for the next couple of weeks until the danger of puppies was over....
Striking while the iron was hot, I placed the Christmas cards on Destiny's passenger seat and took the drive. Popping my booty in the public box, in my private box a card waited from Sheila and Peter. Personally delivering two cards locally, I grabbed custard tarts and popped in

on Terry and also shared in the feeding of the baby wombats and a coffee. Brian and Maggie were card stop two, again not rushed, another couple of hours disappeared in their company. It came as a shock to see Destiny's clock display close enough to 6p.m. heading home ☺ ????
The mountain trip has lost its quiet amble. Due to a land-slip in St. Marys Pass it's temporarily closed to traffic over five tonne, heavy traffic is being diverting through the mountain using Upper Scamander Road. In the brief amount of time it takes to drive the four kilometre strip to our turn-off, I encountered five trucks, that included two B-doubles and one oversize, its like a dirt Bourke Street!!!!

Wednesday 14 December 2005
Waking in bewilderment to hear more rain, a brief passing shower producing bugger all soon drifted aside to make way for sunshine. Whatever happened outside it would be factored into a very placid one home….
It was a tricky weather day, under shade or with cloud cover it was cool but direct sun was like being under a magnifying glass, a real concentrated heat where sunburn sneaks up undetected, referred to affectionately as a 'hot and cold day'. Choosing to stay in the controlled comfort of the cottage, finally got the moving target of the digitised journal version current for the time being????
Content with the computer achievement, and in staying with the indoor theme, I got down and dirty cleaning out the heater. Using recycled timber, I do my best at removing nails from the ash before taking it to the loo as deoderiser, a small price to pay for a seemingly endless timber supply at the doorstep….
Regular moisture dribbles may be finding ground but the soil's surface dries quickly, shallow rooted vegie plants insist I carry a few extra buckets to satisfy their need. By the time trekking to the cattle trough had finished and wood supply sorted, I took the weight off my feet with a nonchalant moment supported by the rocker over a glass of red, before tackling the evening ahead….

Wednesday 15 December 2005
Last evening's written entry saw journal folder twenty-four neatly filled, an outstanding achievement of recording life at Rainbow Falls, surpassing the humble thoughts behind its beginnings. Initially I didn't want to lose all the daily little bits, the memories and moments that are so easily forgotten that make up living and life as we know it that so quietly tick over into oblivion and were happening so quickly. Also needing an outlet to unload my brain, little did I know 3½ years down the track and 960 hand written pages later I'd still write regularly. Lucky the crystal ball wasn't active - if I knew up front what lay ahead it would have been a task I'd see as overwhelming, too big, too long, too hard and better left alone ☺ ….
Our friend the raven is still comfortably cruising the yard, watching through the kitchen window, a chubby kookaburra was sitting on the vegie garden fence while the raven strolled on the lawn only metres away. Aware of one another's presence, they respectively avoided confrontation ☺ ….
Now into the second consecutive hot moisture-free day maybe summer is going to arrive????

During morning roam about and open up I noticed what remains of the bean plants, after slugs had a feed, are producing flowers. A productive sign, there are also two peas starting to size up, a bountiful harvest is shaping up ☺....

Having the Vegies water needs met I retreated to the shed to repair the push mower. Last outing a nail attached to a post in the cattle yards hooked onto the spark plug lead ripping it from its moorings, not a taxing mechanical repair but ideal to keep me out of the sun....

Taking it easy in paradise I headed indoors earlier than usual putting the effort into making wallaby stew, literally slaving over a hot stove so we could eat at a reasonable hour....

The cold may have all but left me but for a change of pace I copped a menacing dose of hayfever, the beauty of regular rain is it kept airborne pollens settled. Life's an ongoing test....

Friday 16 December 2005

It's going to take quite a number of consecutive dry days to evaporate a huge sodden patch in the yard caused by a full dam regularly releasing water from the overflow. The extent of the damp area soggy underfoot has receded from the driveway and is now at the excavation site by the bungalow, slowly retreating back to its source....

Overcast comfortable conditions remained long enough to keep garden watering company, however good intentions of turning soil were postponed the moment stinging sun broke through. Opting for a cooler, sane option I shaved my legs, oddly now the electricity company is reliably supplying power the electric shaver works ☺ !!!!

It didn't take long for bloody hayfever to return causing irritating discomfort once again, with paddocks full of seeding grasses it's hard to avoid airborne pollens. Helping matters, taking the stagnant stillness from the air, a breeze blew in reducing hayfever from insane to tolerable....

Stripping down to undies and t-shirt gave my hairless legs an airing, enjoying the breeze I donned work boots then me and my little mate finished tidying the vegie patch, now only plants that should be are standing tall and proud. Very little direct sown vegie seed survived the deluge, seven spring onions and about the same number of carrots germinated. On the other hand broccoli, potatoes, pumpkin and strawberries are seriously healthy they obviously enjoy extreme elements. Counting five sugar snap peas now sizing up, unless they get plenty of company they'll be eaten before they make the pot....

The raven is in the dog house and barred from the vegie patch after I sprung the bugger ripping a strawberry plant apart, not a smart thing to do if it wanted to stay in the good books!!!!

Saturday 17 December 2005

My little mate relocated a pair of ravens that were creeping up on the vegie patch, then with watering done Christmas came early for Destiny removing the fur and mountain dust covering her interior. Tia and the swallows terrorised one another while Destiny and I got acquainted with the vacuum. Rain clouds hovered around threatening at times, interior finished, Destiny was left out in hope the elements would wash her outside, but not to be, that job was saved for me for later ☺ !!!!

Overcast conditions seem to moderate bloody hayfever, not so torturing, I was only having the occasional sneezing outburst to remind me it's not finished yet!!!!

With the excitement of the vaccy in hand I showed no control, unsatisfied until the bungalow had a turn also. With energy to burn, used the very last available fuel managing one tank in the

push mower dispensing the ration behind the cattle yards cutting buzzies, thistles, sycamore seedlings and bracken fern down to ground level....
Parking the mower back in the shed, by then having had enough myself, parked my bum in a chair outside nursing a cup of tea, looking comfortable and relaxed, my little mate persisted it must be time to play ball. Content just to laze watching late afternoon shadows and spotlight beams randomly target mountains when sun broke through cloud, I got my wish; that is, in between throwing the ball ☺....

Sunday 18 December 2005
Our reprieve from rain was short-lived; threatening cloud that hung around yesterday today carried out its meaning, delivering enough first up to merely wet the ground. Unsure of what moisture may follow, I made cutting wood from fallen charred walls at the burnt out house first priority....
With an uncertain course elements were going to take I played it safe fleeing out of them indoors tinkering with computer keys for a while, attention was then turned on sorting through paperwork relating to the discrimination case. I can't see the point of waiting until due dates arrive to act, so I made inroads at compiling a rough draft of the list of evidence that has to be submitted by January 20. All new ground, and unable to afford to hire expertise to do the work for me, it takes twice as long to get half as far but I plod my way through step at a time being guided purely from the heart and honesty....
Body unwilling to postpone a trip up the hill, as the wave of a second brief front arrived - I copped a misting enjoying the view. A complete roof wouldn't have helped keep me dry; the weather's influence coming from a southerly direction would require a loo door as well ☺....
Winding down an afternoon of literary pursuits and contemplating splashing a bit of water around the garden I was beaten to it. The sky caved in shortly after 6p.m. dumping a quick 10mm....

Monday 19 December 2005
A boiler full of water left on the heater overnight surprisingly still had a sting to it this morning, requiring cold water to be comfortable on the skin, bonus. Bathed and with boots nuggeted we were off over the mountain to meet my 10:20am doctors appointment. Almost out of ventolin and wanting something for hayfever, Dr Luffler left me with a fist full of scripts to deposit at our pretend chemist. Collecting the latest processed photos, I sat in Destiny simply enjoying a bone warming writing comments on the back of a set to send off to Mum and Dad just in time for Christmas ☺.... Pictures of the ride-on will be the highlight!!!!
Sliding the key into the Post Office box found a feast of good news, predominantly Christmas cards, but not one bill waited. I like this time of year when low maintenance friends go out of their way to make contact ☺....
Pulling up at the bakery I saw Rita was in, popping my nose in the door was invited to stay for a cuppa. Sharing where I'm at with closure at the radio station, and bruised also by management and looking for endings, Rita said after talking with her husband she may offer her story as supporting evidence, adding weight to my case. With an ever growing trust and friendship, I was extended an invitation to join Rita, Ian, family and close friends for New Years Day celebrations, accepting the offer without consideration ☺....

Brian and Maggie's bus was in town, heading for a chat saw the dirty old man Allan holding their attention, a bloke who did his pitiful best with many and varied performances to get into my pants: deviating past, placed myself more comfortably in the supermarket. It was down one of the aisles that Allan quietly approached me inquiring whether he'd done something to offend me, responding by saying "I think you are nothing but a dirty old man and what do I have to do to get you out of my life"!!!!

Tuesday 20 December 2005
A lazy blowie buzzing around in the bungalow while me and my little mate were still trying to sleep is up there in annoyance with a mozzie buzzing around your ear, to say at the least irritating, but I was too lazy to do anything about it. The ongoing droning disturbed Ms Tia enough to corner the fly on the window taking the buzz out of its annoyance, giving us both peace bless her ☺ ....
Leaving me to slave over a hot washing machine, Tia either barked at swallows in a futile attempt at chasing them out of the shed or lazed in the shade of the walnut tree, and that was pretty much the norm, other than cutting a bit of wood....
Water, water, water, from the garden to washing machine and bath water I carted bucket after bucket, taking a break from lugging the liquid gold I gave Mum and Dad a call to thank them for the Christmas card arriving in yesterdays mail ☺ ....

Wednesday 21 December 2005
Having a desire to ease blocked sinus and a runny nose took a drive over the mountain to pick up the filled script from the pretend chemist and walked out without it. Leaving overpriced hayfever medication behind, the $40 they wanted to charge for steroids to shoot up my nose I could slash the paddocks for that price, a healthier body choice instead bought extra tissues....
Doing the mountain dash I was pleased to see long overdue roadwork in progress, appearing only to do the worst patches it's at least a token at making bits of the rough as guts road tolerable....
Summer really turned on a corker, walking a short distance to shops to have Destiny totally immersed in shade for my little mates comfort, once groceries were loaded we didn't hang around in it any longer than necessary. Heat took the wind from Tia's sails she wasn't very active at all, the most animated she became was cleaning the dregs from the peanut butter jar. She always finds energy for food. Stripping down to a more comfortable shorts and singlet at home, I couldn't even bare shoes on my feet enduring the hottest summer temperature to date....
The raven was sprung attempting another sweet feed from the vegie patch and was promptly told it to move on, the persistent bugger was later pissed off for a second time but did no obvious damage!!!!
Looking for respite I relocated to the coolest spot mixing fuel and doing a little mower maintenance. Still waiting for the sting to leave before garden watering, wait time was constructively filled over a couple of lead into Christmas beers.... ahhhh....
Just commencing bucket lugging Ross rolled in along with a sea fog, following a good yarp Ross left but the sea fog kept gathering momentum, gaining enough density to drop a little moisture from the sky....

Sitting with the cottage door open capturing the cool evening air on offer, a tail wagging and very receptive Tia greeted her visitor Oke looking to sow his seed. Once again phoning Charles and once again Charles was all apologies for Oke escaping his chain. Although making nice puppies, I mentioned the vet bills will be his if Oke manages to make contact with Tia, hopefully enhancing responsibility????

Thursday 22 December 2005
Sea fog that rolled in late yesterday looking like it was going to engulf the landscape distributed only the one immeasurable sprinkle, remaining quiet, it was well and truly gone by the time we got up, again turning on another bloody hot one!!!!
Responding to the recent searing heat, an impression has been made drying up the sodden patch in the yard reducing the large tear drop shape weeping from the tear duct of the dam overflow. A little more of the same treatment and I'll soon be able to mow around the entire dam to stir snakes up☺….
Not getting to bed before midnight most nights is a set-up for not rising that early either, so needless to say by the time I'm up, organised and garden watered, the morning is usually spent and heat has moved in….
It wasn't until mid afternoon did a slight breeze lift making conditions tolerable for mowing, taking the stand up version into places I'd prefer not take the ride-on. After making a bit of an impression in the yard attention was turned to cutting burnt timber offerings from the house, then revisiting garden watering, I didn't stop for a beer until 7:30p.m. Thoughtfully sipping the golden nectar taking the weight off my feet briefly before starting on the dinner, bath, dishes, and writing routine, I may have a late start but still put in an honest day☺….
Each opening of the heater's door to feed it more wood delivers a hit in the face with a wall of stifling heat, the blast clears my sinus and dries my nose, I wish I could bottle the relieving effect shooting it up my nose as required!!!!

Friday 23 December 2005
Leaving the protective cover off broccoli yesterday didn't go unnoticed, between then and this morning birds have eaten the main larger leaves. I'm pretty confident it's the work of birds because the incriminating evidence of poo was left behind on lower leaves not eaten!!!!
Intentions to put the push mower through its paces completing the entire housing surrounds started off true. After refuelling I left the mower sit for a short while with the fuel tap on and it self emptied three-quarters of the freshly filled tank, from that point it refused to start. Not beaten, switched to 'Plan B' bringing out the sit down to mow option advancing the clearing progress in leaps and bounds. Mother Nature took care of comfort by increasing cloud cover to stabilise the temperature at sane, although still warm enough to be seated mowing in a light shirt and underpants, and of course foot protection. My legs have seen more daylight in the past few weeks than they have in the past couple of years. Gaining more confidence airing my legs since a lift in weight and health, arriving here weighing a meagre 42 kilograms, after bottoming out at 38, growing into my skin I've gained about 13 kilograms since taking up residence at Rainbow Falls….
Stirring grasses with the mower also stirred up my nose which isn't a difficult task, it would be nice to be reminded that a nose is also used for breathing through it hasn't done much of that

the past week. At times I could also scratch my eyes out in the itchiest kind of way, oh, and to regain a sense of taste and smell, the flavours attached to eating food is done purely through memory, the simple things that give so much pleasure....
A couple of days of physical labour and my right shoulder is protesting, I'm falling apart, tomorrow being Christmas Eve light duties are on the roster ☺ ....

Saturday 24 December 2005
Ensuring a follow through with promised light duties 3mm dropped from the sky overnight, without fail, this is the third consecutive time rain has followed after mowing. What little moisture the night provided didn't take long to disappear, a drying wind robbing the gift from the gods lifted with the sun....
Setting a standard for relaxation, I took an after breakfast milo to the shed and contentedly watched my little mate passionately strip a meaty bone of its goodness ☺ ....
The elements determined a continuation to a restful day by producing regular passing showers, just keeping the ground wet dismissed any thought of mowing, keeping it firmly on the Christmas Eve taboo list. Adding to the reduction in work-load the afternoon felt the effects of a serious shower producing a quick 2mm accompanied by a thunderstorm, stressing the bark, bark meter on my girl, alternatively removed garden watering from today's agenda....
Spreading a bit of Christmas cheer I got lost on the phone after the thunderstorm passed, first up Loui copped an ear load from me then it was Sheila and Peter's turn, in the same reciprocal mood everyone was happy for long conversations ☺ ....
Easing from habits I was unable to completely help myself, getting drawn to the shed I cleaned the ride-on ready for next outing. Leaving the comforting shelter the haven offered only then became aware of a huge, dark front approaching from the west its pure image encouraged a race against the clock to bring a dry store of wood in. As the front passed over the series of distant mountain ranges, reaching the drop to waiting valleys below, a dominant south-westerly filling the void above the valleys blew the front seaward, feeling only a spit from its threatening edge....
Tonight Ms Muffet and I shared our Christmas dinner together. If we don't get blown away, wind picking up to gale force at times is either going to blow Christmas right at us or right away????

Sunday 25 December 2005
The big wait is finally over - it arrived ☺ ????
Tia and I literally had Christmas dinner together last night finally having it cooked ready to serve minutes into Christmas arriving. Unbroken sleep wasn't looking good for a while, wild gusting wind menaced, dying down to sensible speeds by midnight it still lingered for Christmas day....
A bit reluctant to get out of bed I lazily started the big event, a great mood to call Ma and Pa Christmas to share feelings of sentiment for the festive occasion, chatting until there was nothing left to say ☺ ....
Ready to get on with it, started by putting petrol in the motor sharing a Christmas breakfast with my little mate, taking the next step for the main event, prepared for the trip over the mountain to join in on lunch with Pam and Terry....

The afternoon vanished seated at the dinner table. Pam generously filled the table with masses of food. Constantly eating, sipping wine, talking, including a coffee chaser, we sat at 1p.m. and seemingly moments later stood up and it was 5:30p.m. A very comfortable homely time put the special into Christmas. I mentioned the bottle of red produced over lunch was courtesy of Mum and Dad, bringing thoughts of family to the dinner table ☺ ....
Returning home the wild wind hadn't left to keep unruly hair out of my eyes donned my Nana Raye beanie, the only hat likely to remain on in the gusty conditions. I stayed out amongst the elements long enough to water the garden before regaining indulgence ☺ ....

Monday 26 December 2005
Temporary repairs have been staying together for longer periods however the latest hammering has taken its toll claiming a couple of victims. Shade cloth linking the cottage and bungalow diverting water away from windows had a few nails removed, staying up but just. A plastic sheet covering a window for the same waterproofing purpose was also in the process of being dismantled. Wind finally abated making it pleasant to be outdoors offering some earned respite. Unrelenting wind robs my energy....
Thoughts of finalising the housing area enticed me to pull the mower out, but listening to the peace and tranquillity the elements offered it was too serene to break, so I pushed it back in the shed for a more appropriate time. Relishing the quietness I unpacked the white dinner set delivered by Mark from Mum and Dad, with a bit of a shelving reshuffle made it a home. The mugs are a good size satisfying my need for a cuppa, the bowls too are nice and deep, giving one a test drive demolishing the take home sample of Pam's Christmas pudding drowned in cream ☺ ....
It was a culinary delight leisurely watering the vegies a plump juicy strawberry just waited for me to eat it, and the sweet climbing mass of tangled tentacles from sugar snap peas also offered a sample. Garlic was showing signs of yellowing and dieback, due for harvesting, and with the help of my best friend dug up the shabby crop. The deluge of October and November took its toll on garlic a-half-dozen corms had to be thrown out but the remainder were fine, just small in size, not going to waste they simply won't last as long ☺ ....
Pottering around outside, Oke again showed up looking to sow his seed and mark ground with a receptive Tia, slack neighbour practices makes work trying to get her through a season without pups!!!!

Tuesday 27 December 2005
Out of bread determined a trip over the mountain. So I could take my sweet time getting ready, and expecting a rush following a public holiday, I phoned ahead asking Cousin Evelyn if she wouldn't mind putting a loaf aside. Rest assured of my purchase when making it into the big smoke....
Battering winds passing through seem to have done a favour stripping the air of pollens, granting my Christmas wish of wanting to be reminded how to breathe through my nose once again. A strong gust must have also blown the raven away, it hasn't been sighted of late, or maybe it shot through sulking for getting told off for being in the vegie patch more than once ☺ ....

Mowing the housing area was again postponed just because it was too bloody hot, on the flip side intense heat has slowed growth. Under the UV protection of the cottage roof attention turned to the computer updating the journal, fingers fluently dancing over the keys glide through pages more efficiently....

Wood and water are just part and parcel of daily life at Rainbow Falls it's rare when they don't need attention. Having bucket after bucket distributed in appropriate spots, I took a break for a coffee down the shed, before tackling the wood. Still parked on my bum Ross pulled up, happily postponing woodcutting remained seated for another brew and chin-wag☺....

Wednesday 28 December 2005
Neglecting to repair the dismantling cottage window waterproofing nature's elements gave me a blunt reminder to lift my game, in the wee baby hour's moisture fell from the sky. To really spoil me rotten at 6:10a.m. exactly Tia's thunder meter was activated, not quitting until 8a.m.. Entering into hearing reach, a couple of distant rumbles had Tia giving the appropriate number of belly growls in return warning the noise off, leaving me hope that's all that would occur.... Optimism☺....

By the time my unwilling body was dragged out of bed sun had already turned up the volume, following a 2mm drop, it made ideal conditions for plant growth only. Wind lifted stirring up some pretty wild conditions, also stirring up my bloody hayfever! The temporary repair of the temporary repairs on window weatherproofing was shelved again because getting blown off the ladder was more than likely....

Wind not being a favourite condition to be exposed in, me and my little mate spent a good part of the day shielded in the calm coolness of the cottage, Tia simply moved from one comfortable spot to another conserving precious energy. Preparing to meet deadlines set by the Anti-Discrimination Tribunal I devoted time to the computer, 90% completing the list of documents and relevant attachments to be used as supporting evidence for the hearing, it's pretty much to the stage of print, copy and post....

Emerging later to a calmer reception, I finalised a serious day with garden watering therapy. Very little produce is going to make it inside because while irrigating I graze, strawberries and peas are being eaten as fast as they ripen, supply can't keep up with demand☺!!!!

Thursday 29 December 2005
Still not completely out of the woods, but Ms Tia's hormones are beginning to settle, her need to reproduce is finally waning returning from over sexed. Creating a domino effect, I'm also able to relax a little, not so diligently on the lookout for Oke jumping the fence and wandering into our paddock....

Filling a bucket at the cattle trough I noticed a couple of scotch thistles on the dam wall almost ready to flower, returning with the shovel literally nipped them in the bud. Remaining sidetracked, I moved onto buzzies also looking too comfortable. Tossing pulled buzzie groundcover for my little mate to file and compost, to her frustration wind blew most of it directly back at me☺!!!!

The persistent wind hammering is wearing thin, refusing to wrestle with shadecloth whilst trying to remain upright on a ladder I held that job over until whenever. Instead, I'm watching the ongoing dismantling progress, the shadecloth only has a couple of nails left securing it to

the bungalow, what remains intact is merely stopping it from blowing away. In keeping with an unsuccessful tone, thought I'd have a go at finalising clearing non ride-on bits around housing but the mower refused to fire into life. After cleaning the grotty spark plug, first pull the mower started but my glory only lasted 30 seconds before it conked out, returning it to the shed for more serious maintenance. The spark plug lead still looked a bit shabby so I tidied that, cleaning the plug again then checked the fuel line was flowing and returned to the work site. Starting first pull, by the time gloves and ear muffs were in position the mower stalled and refused to restart, having had enough it was pushed back to the shed and parked!!!!
In need of time out to lift dispirited energy I turned to a reliable no fail job, trimming and cleaning harvested garlic. Staying with a therapy session, after splashing a bit of water around kept the decoy in place weeding around the bean plants ☺....

Friday 30 December 2005
Opening the bungalow door greeting the morning four swallows were sitting on the electricity cable, I'd say bubbies have left the nest. Learning to fly and survival skills are vital now, they only have a couple of months remaining of their spring / summer procreating vacation in the shed until they move on to wherever they disappear to for the remainder of the year ☺....
Lately it's the usual hot, windy, hayfevery start, with the customary level of discomfort I got on with it. The up side to the bloody awful blowy heat is grass growth that seemingly popped out of the ground after the mower had passed over, has slowed to a virtual standstill, its also starting to lose its lush green appearance also....
Out of bread meant starting Destiny up for a trip over the hill, adding to the drive I wrote brief descriptions on the back of a few photos and sent them off instead of a card for Dekira's first birthday. Getting purely what was needed, stopped long enough for a hot brew and chat with Pam and Terry before heading home to strip down and cool off, getting as comfortable as possible out of the heat. Tassie is supposed to be known for a cooler climate now the South Pole is looking good ☺ ????
The bloody good news is finally wind abated, the down side to its absence it sent the mercury soaring. Barefoot and wilted, Ms Muffet and I headed to the cool comfort the shed offered, Tia cooled her belly on the concrete floor and put in the odd half-hearted attempt at chasing swallows. I had another more open minded go at getting the mower running smoothly, taking the cover off the mower the vacuum hose fell, dangling free, the problem was caused by a small stick wedged in the motor. Still tinkering, Ross made his way up the driveway. Downing tools, we let time hang with our bare feet up sharing our views on the world demolishing a milo ☺....

Saturday 31 December 2005
Putting myself to bed last night with a blocked irritated sinus wanting to break its way out of my skull, needless to say, causing grief!!!!
Deserved calm elements started opening doors, not only could repairs to temporary repairs be considered but calmed my bloody hayfever down for a while also. Cottage window waterproofing finally received attention, while in the fix it mood, I reconnected the drain pipe to the bath. Life's almost back together again. The mower however gave me a repeat performance, running for 30 seconds, stalling, and refusing to re-start????

Pam and Terry came for a drive up early afternoon, predominantly so Terry could offer solutions to my mower questions. A diagnosis between cuppa's and Pam's Christmas cake, the push mower has issues with its accelerator cable and a vacuum hose that won't stay on....
Finished with water carting and woodcutting, I let myself relax with a couple of glasses of red cooking dinner. Sharing the night with my best friend, a more perfect day I could not have designed to celebrate the last one of 2005 ☺ ....

Sunday 1 January 2006
The fresh year began with a cleansing, feeling the effects of passing light showers and a mild dose of bloody hayfever. At least I didn't have to squeeze garden watering in before making the 11a.m. invitation to join Rita, Ian and friends for a barbecue, cake and coffee ☺ ....
Making it perfectly on time, following a chat with Evelyn in passing, around twenty people met at Rita and Ian's, there was a sprinkling of familiar faces to get reacquainted with and a lot of new faces to get acquainted with. The barbecue was supposed to be at the grassy expanse of the St. Marys Rivulet, but climatic conditions diverted all celebrations back to Rita and Ian's home. Conversation, like the delicious savoury and sweet food, was plentiful and three hours got consumed ☺ ....
Ringing Mum and Dad welcoming them into 2006 they mentioned New Years Eve in Mildura was 45° by noon, continuing to heat up, the day would have peaked at 47° easily. Simulating a furnace outdoors, I'm bloody glad I wasn't there to share in that extreme heat!!!!

Monday 2 January 2006
Important dates to remember were transferred from last year's calendar, onto 'my brains and memory' this year's calendar, then the annual symbol was hung on the bungalow wall above my bed. Tearing the rainfall record from the rear of 2005's calendar to slip into the journal I tallied the statistics, totalling 86 days of measurable rain, those 86 days produced a whopping 1158mm or the equivalent of 46 inches, there's certainly no worries of drought ☺ ....
With nothing pressing to distract, and garden watering complete, I was cornered into 'D-day', bugger it, shy on clothes domestic duties found me!!!!
Dropping into the bakery yesterday Evelyn sent me home with a couple of coconut macaroons, polishing them off for smoko I left the cellophane bag on the window box in the bungalow. Returning for lunch, I was surprised to find life in the bag a skink had buried itself at the bottom in search of the remaining sweet crumbs. Nothing goes to waste here ☺ ....
Paddocks bordering Rainbow Falls have been cut and recently baled, since the dust has settled on baling my hayfever has almost been non existent. I'll stand a better chance of eliminating sneezes altogether when home paddocks are tidy also.... Archoooo ☺ !!!!

Tuesday 3 January 2006
It doesn't take much to recharge the dam to overflow to again expand the sodden patch in the yard, each time it starts receding the mere hint of moisture sogs things up again. On the contrary, today zapped the moisture out of everything, having a serious go at reversing the effects....
Leaving me to the repetition of lugging buckets, Tia made her own liquid contribution reclaiming real estate from passing night traffic. It never ceases to amaze at how far she

stretches the contents of her bladder, placing a little squirt here and a little squirt there staking claim to a large expanse of property ☺....

Having enough water in the right spots, a hot drying wind sent me anywhere it wasn't; hanging around, I stayed out of its way and accomplished very little. Pottering about tidying, the most outstanding achievement was to empty the heater of ash, extracting nails from every scoop. Marking an end to the festive season, after creating colourful decorations, Chrissy cards were removed from their random placement on shelves and deposited into their final resting place buried in the pages of the journal....

Reading a reminder message perusing last years calendar highlighted it's been six months since last haircut. To keep the overgrown, out of control, long strands contained and annoyingly off my neck, it's now long enough to gather into a little ponytail ☺!!!!

Wednesday 4 January 2006

My nose is being reminded it can be used for breathing. Sinus sensitivity offered a break, in turn having relief from the drooling and the dry mouth syndrome. Only able to take in air through the mouth I've been waking with it as dry as a chip, totally void of moisture, my tongue is like sandpaper against the roof of my mouth needing a squirt of water to lube things up again. Bloody hayfever!!!!

Almost nocturnal, with midnight being the average time for feeling the pillow under my head, last night or more correctly this morning, being 1a.m.-ish. Each season offers differing opportunities with change. The longer daylight hours of summer keep me outdoors later, then waiting until it's cool enough to spark up the heater to cook, eat on average at 10p.m.-ish. Late nights also domino into late mornings, organised for a trip over the mountain to do the payday stock up shopping thing, early afternoon had already crept in ☺????

It's rare to hit the shops and not strike up a conversation or two, chatting my way through town I got what was needed and headed back over the mountain. A simple outing broke the back of the day ☺....

Shopping purchases having found a temporary home, over a brew I lazed down the shed staring out into the mountainous expanse daydreaming letting my mind go walkabout. A quiet moment void of the sound of any human activity I silently watched natural life busily go on around, kookaburras and swallows were outstandingly active. Breaking the euphoric moment, those ongoing daily bits that couldn't be ignored beckoned attention, to cook and eat needed wood, to bath and grow food needed water; so the merry-go-round of life continues ☺....

Thursday 5 January 2006

Driven out of bed for a 5a.m.-ish wee, a kookaburra was already perched on the electrical cable on the lookout for anything that moved resembling something to eat. There aren't too many hours of the day they're not feeding - kookaburras can be heard fluttering from the ground to their vantage-point above, long after Tia and I have adjourned inside for the evening....

Now the dam overflow sodden patch is fast drying and receding I don't have to walk as far for water, opening a more direct route to the cattle trough. Over a dozen trips carting water from the cattle trough those few diverted metres matter!!!!

Managing to be in close proximity I caught a call out of the blue from Denise in Kiama, still with some of my possessions kindly stored since my shift from Wollongong, we had lost contact through the changing of telephone numbers. Denise and partner were about to move with my possessions in tow, repositioning only a couple of doors down, the courtesy call was to re-establish contact and exchange personal details to keep communication channels open ☺ ....

Heat not being a favourite climatic element, without resistance, Ms Muffet spent the afternoon in the comfort of the cottage taking the weight off her paws leaving me to the keyboard finger dance. Again getting the moving target of the journals digitised version current, then diverted attention to the fast approaching Anti-Discrimination Tribunal 'conciliation hearing'. Putting thoughts into the progression, or regression, of events down on paper, pretty much made a start at preparing a logical sequenced brief for February's hearing....

Resurfacing from literary pursuits 6p.m.-ish I relaxed over a beer and a game of ball with my best friend, a perfect way to call another one over ☺ ....

Friday 6 January 2006
Miracle of miracles, I made it into bed by 11p.m. last night, I struggled to find sleep but still made it ☺ !!!!

I was dealt a quiet simple one home. With all the outside bits reliant on me for their survival catered for, in the willing company of my little mate again escaped stinging heat indoors. Devoting many hours once again, further advanced the chronological report from incidences to correspondence for the conciliation hearing as a reference. Slugging it out on the keys sneezing and sniffing hour on end until brain dead, I then escaped outdoors for beer o'clock and walkabout to breathe in a prescribed dose of sanity and reality....

Out and about, one of the limited number of fruiting walnuts was found rotting on the ground, sadly this seasons harvest can be counted on one hand, Tia got some use of the rotten one using it for a bit of sport.... Kick it again ☺ !!!!

The walnut tree staged its own protest against October and November's 600mm deluge. Very few crops performed at all: it's a learning experience getting to know the limitations to work within for future self-sufficiency. Even the hydrangeas under the walnut tree demonstrated signs of protest against the massive rainfall by setting very few flowers. Like the walnut tree, only the south-westerly fringe of the hydrangeas has shown any interest at completing their cycle????

Saturday 7 January 2006
Happy for a spell from mowing grass, growth has come to an absolute standstill, doing a turn about it's now drying out and browning off at a rapid rate. When the insane rate of grass growth is in full swing it's worse than painting the Sydney harbour bridge. Before the end is reached the start is back out of control!!!!

Returning from an after breakfast milo in the cool comfort the shed provides, a shingle back lizard crossing the yard made me take a second look; reptiles with legs are safe. Mentioning to the lizard in passing that I hoped it hadn't just left the vegie patch snacking out on strawberries, they're quite partial to the sweet juicy fruit....

Raising the thermometer to bloody scorching Ma Nature gave us double barrels, an atmosphere clear and still permitted the sun to give us everything it could muster, driving me into shorts, singlet and ponytail ☺ …. Kept alert, I had the shovel strapped to one leg and Tia strapped to the other….

A must to be sheltered under shade from the furnace, the garden received enough moisture to survive so my best friend and I could get out of it. A carbon copy of yesterday, after irrigating I headed indoors to play poor person's solicitor. Sadly, the simplicity of it is, if my initial complaint was listened to in the interim and responded to by management we wouldn't have had to come this far. Whatever the outcome I'll be glad when the story is merely written history….

Sunday 8 January 2006

It's not common to still be minimally dressed at bedtime, yesterday was a bloody doozy. Reaching out for shorts to get this day underway, I also put a light shirt on to take the sting off my shoulders doing the water thing!!!!

Morning bits complete and setting out the pile of discrimination paperwork in front of me, I couldn't bear to delve into it; instead picked up the phone for a more pleasant pastime talking myself out with Mum and Dad ☺ ….

Leaving no stone unturned in conversation, the paper stack was again left to sit idle, choosing sanity over stupidity I cut a lasting stack of wood. Dry wood rocketed up the priority list as the sky rapidly began to close in, bringing respite with a huge drop in temperature. Pushing in from the ocean, a north-easterly direction is where we receive lasting, big downpours????

Pulling up for afternoon tea I heard an unfamiliar bird whistle projecting from the airspace above, stepping out of the bungalow to put a face to the voice, less commonly sighted than eagles, a goshawk was circling around. Easily identified by being the only pure white native bird, its presence temporarily silenced bird activity in the zone of its flight path….

By 4:30p.m.-ish cloud had built enough density to drape over the range, spilling some of the booty to coat Rainbow Falls in foggy conditions. With enough dry wood stacked inside, I welcomed the passing mist showers, although, moisture delivered to date isn't out to break any rainfall records.

Spared from watering, and donned in long pants and jumper, headed to the haven with beer in hand to make myself comfortable for a spot of self-indulgence ☺ …. ahhhh….

Back to reality, cooking dinner I got a call out of left field from Bonney and Gary visiting from Mildura, staying the night in St. Helens hoped to cross paths tomorrow making their way to Bicheno, and welcome guests they will be too ☺ ….

Monday 9 January 2006

Expecting guests I didn't get my teeth into anything lasting, filling wait time fiddling around with water, setting the fire and domestics. Intuition from previous experience, the need for a couple of day's dry timber proved correct. Producing very little, the front that pushed in yesterday hung around for most of today, not dropping anything that deterred from being outdoors until timely after visitors left….

A warm hug greeting with sincere friends, Bonney and Gary's company was a breeze. Their interest, honesty, enthusiasm, attitude and high energy was infectious, the seemingly brief time spent together showing them around was a pure pleasure ☺ ….

Left in a brilliant feel-good mood, relaxed and as pliable as putty, I disappeared with my little mate into a favourite spot 'the shed'. Staring out into the wide overcast yonder, my mind went walkabout while my physical being kicked its feet up and parked its bum living for the moment. Like moments do they pass - tearing myself away from that demanding diversion indulged in picking and eating ripe strawberries and peas, not one of them has made it indoors. However, the first freshly picked small harvest of beans made it inside and into tonight's fried rice ☺ …. yumo….

Tuesday 10 January 2006
Today's date is of special significance to us humble mountain inhabitants, representing the signing of appropriate paperwork for the deeds to Rainbow Falls six years ago to the day. Not knowing then the extent that act would forever change the direction and destiny of life's little journey ☺ ?!?!
Stinging heat forcing me to venture out in undies and t-shirt, timely softened with cloud cover when a trip over the mountain was organised. Destiny's bonnet protruded into the swallow's flight path having a few stray missiles of poo fired in her direction. The shed floor is also copping an evenly distributed trail of poo, the nest location is no secret, there's a white trail leading from it to the shed exit ☺ ….
Wishing to chat with Rita, made a visit my first move in the little hamlet of St. Marys, setting a comfortable mood, I sat in a rocker with a cup of brewed tea. Agreeing to read over documents destined for the Anti-Discrimination Tribunal for logical sequence, Rita also confirmed her preparedness to write a supporting report. Able now to tell her story outlining the personal, wrongful experience, at the hands of the radio stations current management, is affording Rita an opportunity for closure also….
Bread and milk on board, headed home and got on the phone to Ross teeing up a suitable time to make use of his computer and printer. With timelines closing in, it's become a priority to prepare document hardcopies for posting to appropriate parties; seems tomorrow or tomorrow is suitable ☺ ….

Wednesday 11 January 2006
A sky full of fluffy thick rain cloud, in the company of a cooling wind; again it was better spent indoors, for a change of four walls headed to the other side of North Sister to Ross'. A couple of cuppa's, plenty of chat, and a bit of a play on the computer pretty much describes the venture over the mountain, a fun way to achieve. Printing most of the documents required for posting Friday, I'm looking comfortable to meet deadline one leading up to the conciliation hearing….
A flow-on effect from the cool change is butter, having been pliable and soft, had set firm. A very welcome pleasantly cool, hands in pockets kind of day, and with more time to do it because being exempt from watering the garden reduced the number of buckets needing carting. Other than 2mm delivered overnight, the tap was turned off, not another drop of moisture was added to the total, cloud broke up and cleared before sunset….

Thursday 12 January 2006
A pumpkin runner I've regularly walked past to commence watering I now have to step over, plants can almost be watched growing. Quite a few flowers dotting runners have burst open, during open up walkabout before breakfast I stopped to watch a bee busily investigating inside the brightly coloured flowers, a useful practice for fruit set....
Heat put paid to any thoughts of doing a bit of edging with the shovel, the most action the shovel saw was to dig up a few spuds for dinner....
Gearing up for stage two, and the final step prior to the conciliation hearing, I made time with Mary-Anne for a visit Wednesday to go over her witness statement. While the phone was running hot I also called the office of the Anti-Discrimination Commission inquiring whether the conciliation hearing was open or closed to the public. Most definitely closed and confidential, I am however permitted a support person, a clearly stipulated path forward....
When it was more climatically favourable to be outdoors only then did I dare to be openly exposed at the burnt out house generating more wood, having a go at finishing the burning process of charred remains. For the short period timber has been sourced from the ruins a difference is already becoming evident, within a year the place should be looking tidy ☺....

Friday 13 January 2006
Wishing to make Rita's studio opening, we headed between the sisters 10:30a.m.-ish allowing time to make a stop at the hospital en route. The hospital stop was merely to source copies of medical certificates to use as supporting documentation to add to the wad of paperwork being stuffed into envelopes and sent to all discrimination players. Quite an overworked person at hospital reception got approval, and outstandingly made extra copes for me in her free moments, which were few....
A brave step, Rita had her personal disturbing experience at the hands of current radio station management prepared and printed to add to evidence being presented she also spoilt me with lunch before leaving. Stuffing envelopes at the Post Office I sent many hours of generated paperwork off, step one leading to the conciliation hearing is now complete!!!! Phew....
Ventolin ordered and bread, milk and meaty bones for my little mate sitting on the passenger seat, I aimed Destiny's nose back at the mountain. Back home I did nothing but cart water, then cart some more, beyond the usual things I wanted to soak a couple of towels, filling the washing machine committing myself to the deed tomorrow....
Both satisfying and rewarding home grown potatoes, garlic and beans went into the evening meal. I love having a vegie garden ☺....

Saturday 14 January 2006
Talking to Phillip last night asked if he'd be my support person at the conciliation hearing, he spent most of our conversation giving me reasons why he couldn't. Getting the same response sometime back asking him for a statement to support my case, I'd be standing alone and very lonely if everyone responded that way....
Doing regular morning therapy I was elated to find set fruit on a pumpkin runner, rain may have diminished overall crop success but I've been supplied with a sample of most things planted. The growing season offered a steep learning curve observing shortcomings and challenges the elements create ☺....

Elevating the mercury to uncomfortable heights, turning on a scorcher and committed to laundry, clothes took little time to dry, handy because all bedding got a dunk also. Going berserk gave me cause to fill the machine twice, generating countless trips to the cattle trough....
Home existence pretty well sorted and the last of the clothes drying, Ross and Lesley pulled up pleasantly just for a social visit. Unwilling to let Lesley and Ross relax until they'd indulged me in a garden walk, rewarded them with a couple of plump ripe strawberries. It felt decadently nice to lose a couple of hours with friends simply sitting, laughing, and chatting over a brew or two ☺ ....

Sunday 15 January 2006
A light sea fog pushed its way up from the valleys giving the evening air a cool heaviness, perfect for getting buried under the doona. Quality sleep has returned now hayfever is almost non-existent, the occasional sneezing outburst reminds me a blocked sinus is only an extra sneeze away. The peak pollen explosion has passed; nasal torture too should continually wind down!!!!
Today just happened, melding from one job to another. Brushing my teeth led to the dishes which in turn led to the need for water, watering got me distracted in the garden and that's where I stayed for a while; a place to find great contentment ☺ ....
Wandering indoors the phone receiver leapt into my hand, remaining comfortably seated until family life was current with Mum and Dad, then thoughts swung to the evening ahead. Changing priorities to cutting wood, setting the heater and playing ball.... Round and round we go ☺ ????

Monday 16 January 2006
Helping in the garden sometime ago Tia took a potato from the compost and buried it, her horticultural sense today produced a half kilo of spuds keeping fresh clean food on our plates ☺ ....
Driving it up the priority list, a front pushing in from the North, looking like it could do anything, got my arm swinging on the saw to ensure a reliable supply of dry wood. Topping up the woodbox with fallen charred timber from the dining room ceiling....
Suiting a restful mood I added life to the computer, pleasantly, the spell of key clunking was solely for the benefit of book dreams, refreshingly not for playing politics. Its due time for closure and finalisations returning more of my life back to me, oh to the day politics is a thought merely of the past....
Spending time in the cottage I usually leave the westerly window open, reason being so flies entering through the door on the east side have a thoroughfare on the opposite side to exit from. Breaking with habit assisted a skink and spider feeding on the window ledge, leaving the window closed their combined appetites kept the afternoon almost buzz free ☺ ....
Head down letting my fingers glide over keys, I was surprised taking a breath to see moisture falling from the sky, my initial thought was of happiness, glad to have been smart enough to stock dry wood. Persistent drizzle gave all the reason needed to light the fire early, achieving a first for a while by bathing before dinner ☺ ....

Tuesday 17 January 2006
Taking a brief trip outside in the dark hours I saw three nocturnal lawnmowers feeding in the moonlight. During the spring growth spurt when feed is plentiful wallabies generally remain on the outskirts, now grass growth has virtually stopped good feed is found around housing, bringing grass eating furry critters closer to home. All going to plan, I should only have to tidy the yard by mechanical means once more this summer then night traffic should keep it trim until spring rush arrives again ☺ ….

Our rain front was short-lived, waking to sunshine, scattered cloud and wind, however the 2mm left behind spared me from carrying excessive buckets….

A fair indulgence of procrastination successfully complete, and regular daily bits ticked off the 'to-do' list, then went crazy in the cottage vacuuming everything in sight from the ceiling to the floor; raw timber walls are great web collectors. Small ecosystems inside can be useful, the spider occupying the top corner of the westerly window survived the suction nozzle; anything that eats flies is welcome in my book ☺ ….

Getting the binoculars to gain a closer view of an unknown beautiful bird feeding from the red hot fire poker shrub I copped an eye-opening dose of reality. Having trouble balancing and sharpening clarity through both lenses, getting a clear view through the left the right lens remained fuzzy, a blunt reminder I could use another eye test. From the sharp view through the left lens, I watched what was possibly a honey eater, a smaller bird brushed with precise lines of varying shades of brown highlighted with splashes of white, a brown spot on its throat encircled by a moat of white was particularly outstanding ☺ ….

Wednesday 18 January 2006
With nature's elements sending me indoors earlier the past couple of evenings, last night I experienced a first in a while, sitting to write before lighting the heater freed the evening purely for free range thinking. Not this evening however. Arriving back inside home soil 6p.m.-ish from the direction of St. Helens, there was only time to get daily bits done before the curtain was ready to close….

Readying myself to follow through plans made with Mary-Anne, Sheila caught me on the phone before leaving bursting to share her exciting news. Since hearing the word Vladivostok as a child she's dreamt of travelling on the Trans Siberian Railway. For Christmas a son gave her and Peter the funds to turn dreams into reality, planning the big adventure for mid September, they're literally being sent to Siberia ☺ ….

Knocking at the door of Mary-Anne and Theo's, without fail it was welcoming warm hugs and plenty of homely chatter. Answering a learner's questions, and giving me tips from her 92 years of knowledge, Mary-Anne's Mum first took me for a tour through her very healthy vegie garden, offering a lovingly grown booty of her produce to take home. Following a lovely lunch Mary-Anne and I made inroads with her witness statement, with little more to add we just sat discussing life in general. Through chat she generously offered pieces of furniture that no longer have a place in her home and are getting in the way of renovations. The exceptional furniture gift consisted of an older style armchair, towel rack, and with an offer to pick-up later, a beautiful old dresser with a gorgeous bevelled mirror attached ☺ …. Lucky me!!!!

The heartfelt generous and practical gifts all complement the cottage. With my towel dangling from the rack, I did the new chair the courtesy of sitting in it for the evening welcoming it to its new home. It's a beautifully designed old chair. The front is fixed and the rear is based on a spring giving when weight parks itself within, with little effort it will gently spring up and down giving a rocking sensation. The chair itself is of a solid base and back. The padded material covering makes for a warm winter chair to curl up in and read a book by the fire. Two curved strips of timber tracing from the front of the base rejoin the back midway to make up the arm rests, supporting my elbows comfortably. It was made to order, a very friendly, welcoming old chair befitting its new home ☺....

Thursday 19 January 2006
Summer's failing to get off the ground. It hasn't been an overly warm week, the temperature on offer for a couple of evenings has been ideal to sit by the fire then bury myself under the doona. Today, being content wearing a jumper, without taking it off passed myself walking the water bucket back and forth....
Tidying daily commitments on the inside world then took a drive to the outside world so I could hermit myself up the hill until the need for food drives me back out of utopia again. The rough old dirt road linking us with a postcode and a town, in places is powdery leaving a duststorm trail. Drinking water, groceries and ventolin packed on and around the front passenger seat, I called in at Pam and Terry's perfectly on time to be invited to share a light lunch and be introduced to their visiting grandchildren....
Sun was obscured and lingering mist settled long before sunset, content to adjourn indoors it's feeling more like we're heading into winter????
A healthy diet can be found at the westerly cottage windows. Over a glass of red leaning on the ledge daydreaming out, I found an obvious clue. The resident spider has gone up a size, leaving a shed skin on the ledge....

Friday 20 January 2006
Cloud that moved in, lingering and dribbling away yesterday, did very little overnight. Moisture threatening conditions still hung around this morning - to add a dash of total uncertainty thunder rumbles were included to the equation. Unsure what direction the elements had in mind, beginning with a dribble of rain, the sun was breaking through at times and wind lifted, it was a bit of a liquorice allsort???? Although unsettled, conditions were quite mild a north-westerly influence kept the mercury up, being pushed right up when sun broke through....
Atmospheric uncertainty prompted action straight away by bringing in a dry wood supply and topping up water, with the beauty of hindsight there was no rush, aside from the initial dribble not another drop fell....
A ruckus on a window ledge in the shed drew me over to see three skinks having an aggressive altercation. Unable to watch unnecessary harm letting nature take its course, separated them, being suitably impressed with the strength in their little jaw. One skink had another's front leg in its mouth and its jaw was locked on like a clamp, all three carried scars from the altercation but lived to eat another fly or two....
Bucket just put away and kettle on, my 'personal support program' case manager Sandra drove in, pulling out an extra cup we both relaxed in rockers drank a brew and chatted....

It was certainly a day for fauna. Lunch finished, and replacing the cardboard curtain over the bungalow window, I caught movement of something large in a paddock. An eagle, lucky to be one metre above the ground, pitting its strength against wind gaining altitude, flew over the paddock toward the blackwood tree by the road before disappearing from view. It can only happen at home, magic ☺ ….

Saturday 21 January 2006
Located outside the cottage side yard amongst long grass and too close to the dam and snakey territory, a cool start opened the door to chip out budding scotch thistles. Losing a healthy crop of weeds I gained a bloody uncomfortable splinter in my palm from the shovel, rarely without gloves it only re-enforces why!!!!
While splashing a bit of water around I discovered a third set pumpkin, keeping the fruit off the ground to avoiding rot and slugs, pieces of timber were placed underneath each increasing their odds on reaching maturity….
Noticed by their absence, there's been very few European wasps sighted; like walnuts, they can be counted on one hand. Last summer wasps were as common as blowflies, nomadic, swarming and predominantly exposed to the elements, the deluge obviously didn't favour breeding conditions….
Another busy day for fauna, sitting in a tree by the dam long enough for a boisterous chat, a pair of squawking yellow-tailed black cockatoos dominated surrounding airwaves, drawing me outside with binoculars to observe the visitors through the left lens ☺ ….
The patchy, 'on again, off again' summer turned it on again for a while, with nothing pressing to keep me outdoors, to stay cool, propped on my bum in front of the computer….

Sunday 22 January 2006
Stripping down to undies, light shirt, donning a ponytail and hat, sweat it out watering enduring one of the hottest encountered. Diligently helping me with the water routine my little mate pulled up lame, concentrating her tongue on her front left paw she let me have a look to remove a bee sting…. Ouch…. Continuing to lick her wounds, Tia watched me do a few trips with the bucket….
Blinds pulled, westerly window covered with a towel to keep the cottage as cool and comfortable as possible, we sought refuge. She was a conserve energy self-preservation temperature. Turning up the volume on the bloody hottest this season gave cause to pull the fan out. It was crazy being outdoors any longer than the time required for a wee. My little mate was knocked for a six, like myself, wilts to inactive accordingly with the rising of mercury….
The topical word from Mildura is they're having a stream of days in there forties, so severe the heat, Mum has stopped power walking and Dad is foregoing golf…. Phew!!!!
Unable to contemplate torturing me and Ms Muffet with heat from a blazing fire, first gave myself a bath in cool water, and switched to 'Plan B' putting last nights leftovers on the menu. Despite the extremes, straight cold water was, to say the least, invigorating. It was liberating to remain naked after bathing and walk over to shut the shed, furthering the liberation by sitting on the cottage step sipping a glass of red. That much exposed flesh proved irresistible to a persistent march fly. It made good sport for a game of tennis feeling a few backhanders!!!!

Monday 23 January 2006
Having no fire to light, dinner to cook or water to boil, last night surprisingly was my own by 9:30p.m.-ish, a bloody rare occurrence. The regular evening relief of cool air didn't eventuate so turning the fan off wasn't a consideration, staying on to circulate stifling air all night.
Comfy in shorts and t-shirt first up this morning, cloud cover initially kept conditions pleasant, sadly, cloud lifted letting the furnace kick back in. Reducing my outfit to shorts and sun hat I busied myself with domestics....
Up to my elbows in laundry, Tia was obsessed with the pursuit of catching rabbits both under the cottage and what remains of the burnt out house floor. Intent on a rabbit snack, trying hard but getting nowhere, looks like I'll be cooking again ☺....
Leaving whites to soak, I dug up enough spuds for another week, an appetite whetting taste of self-sufficiency ☺....
In quick time the tea towels had dried opening opportunity to tidy up dishes in the bungalow. At the precise moment I tossed excess water from a plate outside, Tia emerged from a blind corner copping the load fair and square both momentarily surprised being caught unaware ☺!!!!
Unable to bear the thought of lighting the heater to cook, I defrosted wallaby mince for my girl, having the preferred option myself of a garden salad. Sugar snap peas and cos lettuce from the home garden and tomato from Mary-Anne's Mum's, dribbled balsamic vinegar over a fresh bowl full of colour.... yumo ☺....

Tuesday 24 January 2006
Supporting a right shoulder muscular strain, gained by doing a wrong twist picking up 20 litres of water destined for the washing machine, a burst of sneezing adding to discomfort is how I put myself to bed last night. It took a while to find a comfortable position for sleep. Not dragging my tired arse out of bed to face today until 10a.m.-ish, by then two messages waited on the answering machine, and washing the sleep from my eyes Ross came up the driveway....
Overheating on her hunt of rabbits, Tia's been stirring up the lumpy bits taking a dip in the cattle trough. Plants obviously like the lumpy bits too, being rewarded now with five set pumpkins and a head of broccoli ☺....
Dagging in the cottage out of heat with my little mate, I had a bit of a tidy up then parked my bum preparing cover notes and envelopes in readiness to copy and post Mary-Anne's witness statement. Taking the serious edge off, a bit of fun was had doctoring up a birthday card destined for Peter. The card was originally sent to me October last year for my birthday, it read 'not only could I not afford a birthday present for you, I'd kinda like this card back after you finish reading it'. They created a monster, also recycling the old envelope I taped over where it was originally addressed to me, dotting the envelope and card with comments it should create some enjoyment.... I even plan putting a new stamp on top of the old one ☺....
Reluctant to close, the cottage door lock screamed out for attention pulling up limp, turning the door handle no longer sends a message to the bolt to open or close. A bit late in the day for a job requiring time and patience that could be postponed for later, instead gave the garden a top up watering when life cooled down. Planning a trip over the mountain tomorrow, and taking watering from the roster, I'll get there at a reasonable time and with more energy....

Returning to sane evening temperatures the heater got a run, its back to hot water and hot food ☺ ....

Wednesday 25 January 2006
Through conversation during his brief visit yesterday Ross mentioned swallows have already left his side of the mountain. All four, the breeding pair and their addition to the next generation were perched watching us from the electrical cable. Their presence overall is much quieter, I'm seeing less of the swallows, with no nest feeding required they're spending more time away, a walk to the shed doesn't guarantee being swooped anymore ☺ ....
Up until after 1a.m. last night, today was a pretty low-key pleasant affair casually evolving around getting ready for a dash between the Sisters Mountains. On the town side of the mountain an original signed copy of Mary-Anne's witness statement waited in the Post Office box. The statement's presence sent me into action at the library copying, folding, and stuffing more envelopes to then post the bundle on its way. I can now sit back and relax for a while having met the last obligation prior to the conciliation hearing. What a cumbersome, time consuming process honesty is to uphold, although now a load feels like its beginning to shift ☺ !!!!
Chatting my way through town with known faces, I finished at Rita's studio to share in latest developments over a brew ☺ ....
On and off hayfever revisited again bluntly reminding me not to overdo the enjoyment of taste and smell. Snivelling my way around the yard finished a calm day doing the therapeutic jobs of watering and cutting a little wood ☺ ....

Thursday 26 January 2006
Rolling over with the desire for more sleep, a car heard coming up the driveway putting an end to that thought. I'm just going to have to get to bed before 1a.m. In need of tools from the shed to help stranded friends with car troubles, before leaving to go hay-baling Ross quickly blurted out main points and left me with a few apricots. Importantly, as part of his blurt responding to a phone message I left, Ross and daughters are available to join the choir for a surprise visit at the bakery to sing happy birthday to Evelyn ☺ ....
With an amber tinge to the air distant mountain ranges were merely a silhouette obscured by a smoke haze. A blunt reminder of what is happening around the country, Victoria, NSW and Tassie, knowingly are experiencing bushfires, sadly for this area it could just be a forestry operations burn off in progress, its hard to tell the difference????
Tipping what remained of a bucket of water on the chocolate granny's bonnets growing against the wall of the cottage, also enjoying the sun was a tiger snake. With my small dose of adrenalin it received bruised ribs before escaping back under the cottage out of shovels reach. They have a place in this world but not so bloody close to my back door!!!!
Summer has arrived with a full on week of heat. Occupying myself inside I dismantled the cottage door lock to get a better handle on why it won't work. Tightening loose rattly bits, easily sorted out why the one broken rattly bit won't instigate the open and shut mechanism, leaving it dismantled for a solder repair....
Snacking on apricots I filled the afternoon cataloguing the collection of journals, sticking relevant date identification strips on spines. The idea was inspired, predominantly for quick

reference at the conciliation hearing after listing parts of journal entries as evidence. I liked the idea so much continued on to completely label the whole series, taking the search out of finding any particular date....

Friday 27 January 2006
The priority occupying waking thoughts was to get organised and head over the mountain joining the choir in singing happy birthday to Evelyn ☺....
Forming the choir and warming vocals at Pam and Terry's, including their grandchildren, Ross, one of his daughters and myself completed the ensemble. Walking through town it was difficult to refrain choir members from chatting to keep the ensemble on the move. In position when Evelyn walked into the shop front, on cue we burst into song causing tears to well in Evelyn's eyes. Moved, and moving from behind her counter, Evelyn gave each and every choir member a happy 40th birthday hug ☺.... Taking the feel good mood back to Pam and Terry's sampled Evelyn's cakes over a brew....
Reading about the release of Chrissy Amphlett's autobiography 'pleasure and pain', inspired the decision to join the library and today was the day, before leaving town a membership card was safely tucked into my wallet ☺....
Following a very uplifting outing smiled my way back over the mountain ☺....

Saturday 28 January 2006
Nothing out of the ordinary happened - existence quietly ticked over doing the predictable things. With this wave of hot weather still turned on not even the antics of native fauna are giving much to report; they too are only doing the necessary. The intense heat on the westerly cottage window got too much for our arachnid friend, even the spider has been driven from its feeding turf and web. The most outstanding event occurred in the vegie patch. Birth was given to a couple more bubby pumpkins ☺....
Getting through an energy efficient time using minimal electricity when I can't bring myself to throw a match to the heater, sparked by a conversation with Mary-Anne, I located the solar shower bag that's followed me around idle for countless years. Dusted off, washed and filled, laid it flat to catch some rays. The solar shower box instructions had written, 'lay flat with black side up', the solar bag read, 'clear side up'????
For the short time the bag saw direct sun before cloud blocked high level solar activity, the edge was taken from the water, being perfect on skin. For elevation and pressure for showering the bag tucks in nicely at the head of the bath against the wall, supported on a block of wood, it's nestled between the wall and fixed piping of the permanent showerhead.... A potentially very useful item ☺....

Sunday 29 January 2006
A couple of spits hit the roof both last night and early morning. They did nothing more than make a sound on the roof, not even delivering enough to make the heater flue start to leak....
Without clear direction one was selected for me, about to make an outside call an incoming call beat the dial, and Phillip began a social time with the phone. With the numbers punched in I sang 'happy birthday' to Peter on his and Sheila's answering machine, not being surprised they weren't home they always take the time to do something special for one another ☺....

Seed planted in my brain I started the psyching process for shovelling out the toilet, doing a standard check to see if any little critter had set-up camp within, found a team of dung beetles hard at a biological breakdown. A self-composting toilet doing the work for me was a very welcome sight ☺....

A courtesy call from Pam mentioned they would be visiting with the grand kids. Terry and grandson Cody took a walk in the gorge, Pam and granddaughter Rochelle, Tia and me opted for a softer option of eating Pam's home baked cakes, Anzac biscuits, and washing it down with tea comfortably seated ☺.... Looking for suggestions from Terry at how best repair the broken door lock, he offered to tack a weld to put me back in business....

The solar shower got a rest, a cooler evening and with a desire for vegies I sparked up the heater and boiled bath water also. Home life is definitely progressing, particularly now with choice in styles of bathing ☺....

Monday 30 January 2006
Only a couple of hours dry wood remaining in the woodbox, and welcome morning rain wetting the burnt out house standing supply, I headed to the shed to salvage enough to keep the evening fire burning. A collection of pots and pans were strategically placed on the cottage floor by the heater, heading in a southerly direction catching the spreading roof leak....

The visual presence of swallows is becoming less obvious, cutting wood down the shed it pleased me to be swooped a couple of times. One of the swallows swooped close enough to stir air around my face. Their presence adds life to the shed and is pleasantly brain distracting while doing the repetitive sawing action ☺....

It's nice to be given a break from garden watering, downing bucket and stepping aside for a nitrogen boosting drop of moisture, 28mm in fact. Ideal for plants showers all morning sunshine all afternoon, the best of both worlds ☺....

The dung beetles didn't seem to be enjoying the rain, they too were wishing there was a full roof on the loo. Rain however has refreshed everything else though removing the lifeless appearance from the ground, drying grass was starting to crunch underfoot....

Tuesday 31 January 2006
Getting serious about dismantling what remains of the fallen in walls at burnt out house, I pulled out the metre long jemmy bar prying a fallen section of a bedroom wall apart. Off the ground, it's now sitting in the woodbox waiting its turn to go up the flue....

Instigated by cooking the last of the spuds, always ready to help, Ms Muffet and I wandered to the vegie patch and got busy digging then washed this week's supply. The personal rewards from growing your own vegetables only drives me to get better at it; to eat there's a huge difference in the potatoes from the garden to those bought. Home grown is guaranteed chemical free and their flesh is a sharp white and they're crisp and crunchy with outstanding flavour.... It's hard to turn back after being so spoilt ☺....

No amount of money could buy the great feeling I get from lifting potatoes out of the ground, and for that matter, picking and eating anything else that survives the elements to get to me at the end of the food chain. Without ever knowing this much inner contentment, living a dream existence in paradise, the fortunate element is I'm lucky enough to know it and appreciate what I'm unbelievably part of. Tia and I have found our utopia. Life is about how you feel inside

those feelings can only glow through acts of kindness; they can't be bought. Playing around in utopia I turned compost, ate peas and picked beans ☺ ....
The local traffic of lizards, spiders and flies shitting on cottage windows obscured the view a little; careful not to disturb the resident spider now returned to its web, interior windows received a little shit removal and shine ☺ ....

Wednesday 1 February 2006
Managing to keep pace with the simply lazy slow moving mood, time was idled away getting ready for the grocery shopping expedition. Mother Nature enhanced the ambience of an unhurried mood, with no sign of the sun, passing drizzle showers built-up then eased into gently releasing their load, lengthening the spell from garden watering by another 5mm. A good store of dry timber in the woodbox always lifts my mood when there's rain ☺ ....
It was a quiet trip over the mountain for groceries, a couple of brief conversations in the supermarket, a quick chat to Maggie then Evelyn and I got comfortable over the counter before a customer broke our concentration. Expressing her appreciation for last Friday's birthday choir, a kind gesture to someone deserving is always a pleasure ☺ ....
The black hole of the Post Office box contained a Telstra bill at the front and a welcome friendly letter from Mum and Dad at the back. Stashed inside Mum and Dad's envelope was a newspaper clipping with a brief note attached. Thickly blanketing Mildura, the picture in the clipping captured a dense level of smoke blown in from a South Australian bushfire. Through words of experience and exchanged newspaper articles, Mum and I both agreed later over the phone that the smoke black-out was all too similar to my last Christmas in Wollongong. There's always the possibility forestry have bought property in that area - that's the only other time that dense level of smoke is experienced....
Here, however was a different story. At the same time the sun would normally have been setting we were fogged in with low cloud, unable to see far beyond the shed when 50 km's is a potential maximum distance....
Pipping three weeks, beer o'clock again made it back on the menu; a 'bills first' policy sees me go without at times but not this time. All the daily bits done and the fire ready just to put a match to, the rocker beckoned, placing the world on hold sipped thoughtfully over a beer, rocking soothingly enhanced the moments serenity ☺ .... ahhhh....

Thursday 2 February 2006
Again the rhythmic patter of rain could be heard falling during lights out, producing little. It's still brain therapy listening to rain on a tin roof lying peacefully in a warm cosy bed. Ending a fresh one the same way it started, with a drop of moisture, the middle bit was a combination of sun generated humidity that considerately included spells of respite when cloud shaded the ground cooling things down a tad????
Watching their antics whilst carting water, swallows were soaring all over the place chirping. There must be some obvious difference from Ross' side of the mountain; swallows left there some weeks back. What the extended attraction is this side is unknown ☺ ????
A stocky strong tomato plant in co-habitation with beans popped its first bubby out. I'll just keep adding water and see what happens? Tearing myself away from brain therapy I lost the afternoon to the computer....

A spell of cool weather is great for recharging batteries, after a run of bloody hot days it's nourishing to be able to withstand any length of time leaning over the heater cooking. A committed start was made preparing a two-day stew. The meat and secret herbs and spices were cooked yesterday and left to cool overnight, removing a few millimetres of set crusty fat from the cooled brew, returned it to the boil adding a variety of vegies, spuds and beans being the home grown component ☺ ....

Friday 3 February 2006
Lying by my side the moment breakfast was ready, rarely disinterested, my little mate spat out the sample of toast on offer. After watching me fill her bowl with stew and following the scent to the bungalow the offering of boring old toast came a poor second ☺ ....
Putting the week's supply of potatoes into the stew caused the action of bringing more to the surface. I'm treasuring home grown potatoes, not only for taste but also for price, the 5kg bag usually bought at the supermarket has jumped from near on $6 a bag to $10, the reason for the hike is wet conditions failed crops in Tassie's South....
Leaving a feed of potatoes sitting neatly on the ground, let myself get sidetracked turning soil. Having a bit of a tidy up, I was blissfully oblivious to the world until Tia gave me her snake body language, sniffing the air with her neck distended. Securing my little mate inside the cottage I returned to deal with the tiger snake that had moved into the neighbourhood only metres from us. Aware of my presence, the snake straight away flared its neck in aggression like a cobra ready to strike, unable to tolerate such behaviour it went to heaven and is now residing permanently behind the dam fence. The very healthy specimen probably found its condition at the dam, giving a bit back, its now enriching the soil fertilising plants for the frogs to feed from and hide safely within....
Totally emptying the woodbox to the point of sweeping coal from the bottom, with rope and jemmy bar as selected tools, I pulled down frail remains of a wall at the burnt out house. Flexing muscle, I dismantled enough of the structure ready for the cutting stage....

Saturday 4 February 2006
Occupying my mind and idle hands started with dishes, then the stew was divided into meal lots, a fire was set, and getting wood to start the heater is where I got waylaid. With the exceptionally wet season being experienced scattered rain cloud lurking about didn't get ignored, putting an order in for at least three days dry wood, I grabbed the jemmy bar and handsaw and got busy dismantling....
Giving muscles a rest from the recurring wood chase a magic moment happened watching a wanderer butterfly flutter about. Admiring its beautiful markings, as part of the demonstration displaying its beauty, the butterfly landed on my calf resting its wings for a spell ☺ ....
Charcoal on my white top from playing amongst burnt remains instigated carting extra buckets to soak whites overnight. A couple of consecutive warm days has quickly slurped up the recent free moisture gift, today's rain cloud threats went begging, void of any liquid sun had more impact, climatic elements were all over the shop....
Having had enough I pulled up stumps for beer and bikkies. Sliding slippers on, I placed the Mary-Anne and Theo chair by a low set cottage window, propping my feet, gazed into the mountain ranges daydreaming sipping beer and crunching biscuits ☺ ....

Sunday 5 February 2006
Opening up the shed gate Tia went straight in investigating scents left behind from the night just been, desiring to reclaim territory she crouched in a poo position, asking her kindly to take her load outside, she obliged without a whimper. Staying with a poo theme, dung beetles survived the recent soaking to continue their transformation ☺ ….
Existence ticks over just keeping maintenance up to it: proving my theory, I had a pleasant chat with Mum and Dad, did washing, dishes, water collecting etc, and time passed. Humans as a species go racing after some imaginary goal outside of themselves in a search for the elusive happiness, when in the end its only the 'considered' simple things we get the most enjoyment from, its attitude toward daily needs bestowed upon us that determines our contentment. Tia's involvement may increase the time to do things but pleasantly she makes a game out of everything ☺ ….
The earth's axis is well and truly back on the move since summer solstice, the sun is now setting snugly to the left side of the Huntsman's Cap Mountain, and moving toward slipping behind. An all too obvious message the season's they are a changing, days are shortening and cooling saner temperatures are just a few moons away ☺ ….

Monday 6 February 2006
Well bloody hell, when the pen's ink reaches the bottom of this page incredibly it will be the 1000th hand written and journal twenty-five complete, I must be due for holidays ☺ ????
Personal discipline and ongoing commitment at recording life at Rainbow Falls is something I couldn't have fathomed, performing through happy oblivion is a passive way to achieve ☺ ….
Low on bread, drinking water and energy I treated myself to time at the other side of the mountain. While consumed with my routine of doing piss farting around bits first up, I put the solar shower out to catch some rays. The continuous water flow through a shower nozzle sure makes hair washing easier, without a haircut now heading towards eight months it's become quite a long handful….
The only mail waiting was the radio station's full list of documents being used as evidence, a few new additions were listed without forwarding copies, but nothing earth shattering from left field. I'm quite looking forward to this time next week because the conciliation hearing will be over. The best case scenario is the whole business will be complete, worst case scenario there'll be one more step, a day in court…. I'd prefer an end sooner than later….
After talking to Rita I wandered diagonally across the road paying Evelyn a visit, it's rare we don't find time for a chat. Meant to follow the social theme, I found Brian and Maggie home and ready for a brew, a visit with them cannot be skimped. Hugging and bidding farewells Brian called the chooks up, from out of the woodwork it amused me to see around thirty chooks with chicks in tow appear, it was clear they had practised that call for food many times ☺ ….
Returning from town I noticed neighbouring paddocks loaded with feeding ravens and not one sighted feeding at home. The only obvious difference is home paddocks are still full of long grass. I might leave them that way because if it's keeping the ravens out maybe it'll deter the bloody currawongs too ☺ ????

Tuesday 7 February 2006
Experiencing cooler evenings not only is the fire more enjoyable, cuddling into the doona sleeping has become more pleasurable also. With no paw tap on the shoulder or bladder wake up call I was bestowed the rare treat of sleeping uninterrupted right through the night…. zzzz….

Contentedly and peacefully doing regular life maintenance bits, the garden thoughtfully watered, and more of the wall neatly sitting in the woodbox, found and returned a missed call to the Anti-Discrimination Tribunal that took the relaxed edge from my leisure. The call enticed me then to spend a solid eight-hour stint on the computer preparing a report until my brain frazzled. The uninterrupted urgency was to finalise an overdue personal witness statement, I was under the wrong impression that the statements due date was after the conciliation hearing, and its requirement scrapped if we settled at conciliation. Concerned about missing a deadline, I was instructed simply to have copies distributed prior to Monday's hearing….

Pleased I'd had the foresight and already made a huge start with the statement, commencing 3p.m.-ish it was 11p.m. when the computer was finally shut down. Content with the quality of the quickly produced literary offering, trading keyboard for pen wrote in the journal, closely followed by collapsing into bed ☺ ….

Wednesday 8 February 2006
I'll be bloody glad to totally reclaim my life back from the initially mismanaged, long running unnecessary suffering, epic!!!!

Ross pulled up out back to borrow the shed shortly after I'd returned to the computer to run my eye over the rushed witness statement tidying its layout. Over a brew we got events current, getting myself organised I left Ross working on his car and headed to his place to use the computer and printer. Two and a half copies complete, the black ink cartridge ran empty and 'Plan B' was put in motion. Rolling up to Pam and Terry's they were unable to oblige, both their computers refused to read the floppy disk. After sharing a coffee I was sent on the way with a soldered door lock and 'Plan C' went into action, onward to the library and photocopier….

With three full witness statement sets compiled and ready to post, I did gratefully just that, I'm running out of energy for the paper chase and am searching for an end. Reading over the content of the statement I really couldn't think of much else to add given the luxury of more time….

Satisfied, playing poor persons solicitor, I'd done the best I could with what I had, contentedly returned home. By the time Rainbow Falls was again sighted the back of the day was broken….

A copperhead snake wriggling past the bungalow door did a quick turn around when Tia and I crossed its path on a water carting trip. When the shovel and I were united it was well and truly hiding, a safe place to go. Excitement over it was back to watering the garden, then setting the fire, and so it goes ☺ ….

Thursday 9 February 2006
Plans of a leisurely sleep in, followed later by mowing, were both disrupted by the sound of light rain; the knowledge of limited dry wood niggled me out of bed. Up and into it I hit the ground running. Not only cutting enough wood for the cottage I also lugged a couple of planks to the shed storing them as a dry insurance policy. With a brain at ease, my little mate and I put petrol in our motors with breakfast....
What fell from the sky through the morning didn't even get the drip started around the heater flue, saving all its energy for later in the afternoon then showers arrived in waves. Keeping moisture company wind from direct south cooled the ground temperature down a few degrees. The morning's rain did little more than get me out of bed earlier than anticipated....
Finalising the morning walk up the hill I put a roof over the dung beetles, saving them from some elements, I thoughtfully covered the toilet seat with the ash drum ☺....
Being indoorsy elements, reinstating the cottage door lock got a guernsey, replacing screws I also included a rubber spacer to take the slack out of the handle; tightening all the loose bits it's now back and working....
Having observed the road the mayor lives on being graded for the third time without a sighting near home, I was elated to see the grader finally was given directions, working out the front today. The road received its annual 'shove a bit of dirt in the potholes and stir the rocks up' maintenance for another year....
Not good conditions for heating the solar shower, sun never made an appearance, remaining inside cranked up the computer for the more leisurely pastime digitising the life and times of Rainbow Falls' current caretakers.... A quiet, peaceful, energy conserving day ☺....

Friday 10 February 2006
Up with energy after a solid sleep, I got cracking clearing away the array of scattered pots and pans strategically placed catching leaks from the cottage roof....
Meeting the 'personal support program' criteria of contact with a case manager every three weeks, and mutually agreeable, Sandra called in paying a home visit. Over a brew comfortably seated in rockers, we again had a meeting of the minds sharing our philosophies and values....
Waving Sandra on her way, the insurance stash of charred dry wood was retrieved from the shed and cut to size on the burnt and rusted dishwasher makeshift saw bench; a quick 5mm before bed last night dampened anything exposed to the heavens....
In the bungalow preparing afternoon tea Tia did her 'urgency run and bouncing about' activated by a ringing phone. Rushing to the cottage I retrieved a call from the answering machine from the Anti-Discrimination Tribunal. Gratefully it was simply a courtesy call to let me know the witness statement arrived and all reports are completely satisfied....
Quite warm after an exerted effort with the handsaw I took the solar shower bag of warmed water inside out of the sun and put it to use....
Indulging in a therapy session amongst the vegies I ate the last offering of sugar snap peas, collecting the bloated handful of pods scattered through runners for next season's seed, then recycled the plants that regularly offered me a reliable snack in the compost. Beans however are still offering a sprinkling they remain to see a few more moons and litres of water. Well camouflaged, in a search of the south-west side of the tree for walnuts, the number of fruiting

nuts has doubled raising the total from four to eight, double checking I wasn't looking at the same four from a different angle ☺ ….

Saturday 11 February 2006
Restless sleep didn't have me too excited to get out this morning, out of energy and with one foot in front of the other bumbled through the regular stuff inked on the daily roster….
Finding a dash of inspiration I added only a token gesture of time in the vegie patch onto the roster digging up a couple more potato plants, also pulling a few carrots. Six pumpkins are now sizing up; one runner grabbing on with tentacles is climbing up a tree and another has climbed its way over a lavender plant giving birth smack bang in the middle. It will be interesting to taste whether the fruit absorbs the lavender scent????
Tia has developed an obsession with rabbits residing under the cottage. It's sad from my point of view to see her pounce the floor, watching her so vigilant with floor boards separating them. Rarely does Tia relax inside she even snoozes on the floor above the rabbits, she probably thinks similarly of my distraction with pesky currawongs ☺ ????
A din in the usually well-balanced bird world drew me to a window to see what all the fuss was about. Gliding from South Sister toward North Sister, the presence of an eagle rattled the cage of a handful of currawongs urgently squawking warnings. Fear drove the loud-mouthed pests further out of the mountain, quieting airwaves. It would be a blessing to have an eagle present full-time and have no currawongs at all, what a fantasy ☺ ….
Still observing birds, seeing less of them, but swallows are still present, sighting a pair gliding around the yard they then took a spell on the overhead power cable by their shed home ☺ ….

Sunday 12 February 2006
Facing unpredictable conditions, to ensure there was a secure supply of dry wood it made priority one after breakfast. Wind picked up and just kept on pushing cloud through not permitting it time to thicken to do anything other than block the sun….
What has slipped into the groove of a pleasant Sunday ritual, as clockwork as Mum's Sunday roast and equally as nice, is to give Mum and Dad a call for a round-up of the weeks events, both wishing me well for tomorrow's conciliation hearing….
Sadly our conversation ended all too soon. No longer could the most dreaded domestic task be deferred - even worse than vacuuming or shovelling out the loo, is dusting off the iron. Having its third use in as many years I'm in fear of wearing it out ☺ !!!!
Channelling all processed thoughts into leaving no stone unturned, preparing every small detail possible for being well prepared for tomorrow, from compiling paperwork, organising clothes, to giving Destiny a tidy. Being the organised being I am, I was left feeling about as relaxed as one can be about a conciliation hearing. Compiling the witness statement was a blessing in disguise - it gave me the opportunity to totally unload everything from within, emptying the load from my brain onto paper to be used simply as reference when required. Recording the entire chain of events from go to whoa was stage one of closure, now an end actually feels close….

Monday 13 February 2006
Not fazed recognising what the buzzing alarm represented, had no reason to be, there was nothing to get fazed about. The day's experience was pretty much a non-event????
Kindly offering support, I picked Barbara up in St. Marys heading through to the conciliation hearing. The whole clinical, cold process was void of any emotion ending in a few more pieces of paper being generated, too simple. Leaving me at a loss as to what all the personal effort was for, merely to have what occurred to me agreed to on an A4 sheet of diplomatically worded paper, a hollow recognition leaving an empty feeling. I got a piece of paper to take home Bruce and Maria go back to work. Nothing really changed????
Issued with plenty of useless advice, first being my harassment and discrimination allegation, now exceeding a twelve-month timeframe was no longer recognised as evidence. I can't understand why that knowledge wasn't made clear from the start. Why would I bother to pursue a lame duck???? Another useless piece of advice issued was if I was waged rather than voluntary I could have pursued an unfair dismissal claim. It seems my worth as a volunteer can only be measured by the money earned????
Putting in the hard yards to pursue the last available avenue of victimisation, I was advised I'd only gain an outcome similar to today's, more A4 paper. What I expected I don't know, but it's certainly not a fulfilling system. Having the carpet pulled out from under my feet with evidence, and without being waged, received all I could possibly hope for in a 'fair and equal system' by simply making my point and getting it recognised….
Feeling void of emotion, left the hearing promising myself if I ever encounter another idiot like Bruce I'll just knee him in the groin and avoid the paperwork, certainly never complain to his sister-in-law Miss Management Maria☺!!!!
Returning home to wood and water left the sun to set on another day….

Tuesday 14 February 2006
The more I participate in the outside world, without disappointment, it usually lets me down. When some people and money are combined, honesty, pride and dignity go astray, reinforcing the healthy alternative of my hermit existence….
Pottering about getting reacquainted with life outside the cottage, while I've been politically distracted and wasn't looking, maintenance has escaped and everything is in need of attention. The only way to tackle the recovery is one bite of the termite hole at a time….
Low on enthusiasm and feeling as strong as a half-sucked peppermint I took time to just fiddle about. Showing the effects of neglect, I gave plants a good wetting up on what turned out to be a scorcher, but only until sundown ☺….
The rest from bloody currawongs looks like closing in, accustomed to seeing the stray raven today noticed a white tip on tail feathers, unable to help myself, and with the assistance of Ms Tia, disturbed around ten feeding between the dam and loo. Without much exercise outside of housing since sighting the first snake for the season it felt good to stretch the legs, I look forward to again reclaiming paddocks from long grass and reptiles….

Wednesday 15 February 2006
Sadly, to my detriment, the small flock of currawongs sighted yesterday were the entrée of bigger and better things to come, arriving en masse to shatter blissful sleep, their black

squawking bodies dripped through the housing area. Entertaining myself with the mongrel birds, Tia amused herself with another pest hot on the scent of rabbits, both successful at relocating our objectives to more desired sites. There goes the peaceful serenity of the neighbourhood and decadent relaxing sleep-ins. The airwaves were drowned in their boisterous return, bugger it! From observation, long grass in paddocks is deterring currawongs from landing to feed; only littering the ground in mowed areas is a bloody convincing reason to leave it long….

Payday shopping presented an outstanding social trip into St. Marys. Making planned visits to Rita and Pam and Terry respectively, fate put me in the path of more conversations with Peter, Evelyn, and Dave and Liz. Talked out and content and with a loaded car that included beer we meandered back up the hill ☺….

Magic does happen. Standing outside the cottage door early evening appreciating the motionless quiet a light thud on the ground broke the still silence, tracking down a freshly fallen walnut I was meant to find. The odds are pretty short to be standing outside and hear one of the eight walnuts fall. Happy to be part of the moment, I popped the little treasure on a shelf inside the cottage protecting it from the rest of the food chain ☺….

Ready to make a start on dinner Rod returned my call, with calm sincerity told him of my experience at the radio station. Wanting no bitter reprisals, asked if he'd consider running a passive story in the local paper questioning, 'where have all the familiar voices gone'???? Mondays emotions of emptiness are now subsiding I'm finding inner piece with the knowledge of breaking even, its not about winning, managing the castle or restoring life to where it once was, having well and truly voiced my opinion we can't go backward; the direction is straight ahead….

Thursday 16 February 2006
Setting the scene for domestics got whites soaking yesterday, weather being in favour insisted I follow through plans without excuses today. Not only a good one for drying clothes it was great for heating the solar shower, the 'on again off again' summer returned. Liz mentioned yesterday that their cherry tree is so confused with the season it's thrown a second lot of blossom, not even the trees can work this spring and summer out????

Maximising, I completed laundry by stripping my body of clothing to cool down tossing it in to be washed left me standing barefoot and naked. Not taking long to cop a lesson in being without shoes, taking a trip out to the clothesline following the path my left foot took the sting out of something, immediately distracting my mind away from everything…. Ouch….

Keeping out of the reach of harmful UV remained tinkering indoors doing everything from changing a blown globe, leg shaving, to the convenience of bathing early. It was too hot to contemplate lighting the heater the solar shower saved the discomfort….

Friday 17 February 2006
A heavy sea fog rolled in late yesterday evening taking the sting out of UV, still lingering this morning. I took advantage of cool conditions raiding the burnt out house exerting energy swinging my arm with the saw. Continually glancing over my shoulder at the morning sky, heavy cloud pushing in from the north-east inspired a full woodbox and an uncut supply stored

down the shed. On the flip side the afternoon heated the solar shower bag, keeping me guessing, weather is always unpredictable ☺ ????
Focussed on the wood theme, after separating, cutting and storing, I stepped sideways to empty the heater of ash before resetting it, each step taking a chunk of time....
With a few plants looking pale, I asked Ross if he'd grab some nitrogen fertiliser on one of his regular trips into St. Marys, saving me a trip all the way in. Come beer o'clock Ross called to say he was home, armed with a couple of stubbies I tackled the mountain and with ease took in the beautiful view from another angle over a couple of beers ☺ ....

Saturday 18 February 2006
Nothing out of the ordinary to report, I did little more than just getting on with what needed to be done. Doing Tia bits she set about further demolishing the burnt out house kitchen continuing her unrelenting rabbit obsession. Warming up after fruitless rabbit hunting expeditions Tia's been using the cattle trough as her cool down pool, leaving it rather ordinary and requiring regular emptying. Using the stirred algae, fur and mosquito larva water combination, I added to it a dose of liquid nitrogen to give the vegie patch an exceptional feed....
The assumed bee sting received on my foot Wednesday is outstandingly itchy, with optimism I hope it's a sign of healing, but a dash of reality, it's coinciding with puffy eyes I've experienced for the past two mornings. I'm having a reaction to something????
As I do in quiet moments, observe what's going on in immediate surroundings, unable to sight all the familiarly known set walnuts I had a scout about finding another of the limited treasures ripe and intact on the ground ☺ .... Two to me....
The plentiful food source fruiting trees usually provide is having a positive impact with limited annoyance from currawongs in a poor season; with little worth staying for they leave quite readily.... A plentiful year brings plenty a poor year brings notable change in everything ☺ ????

Sunday 19 February 2006
Bung eyes and an intermittent itchy foot again joined me throughout the night. Reckon I'm having a not so pleasant reaction to the sting received in my foot. If I wake in a similar condition tomorrow then it can be ignored no longer a trip to the doctor for antihistamine will make the priority list. Other than energy being down a little and ventolin use at the upper end of the scale I'm still feeling alright, puffy eyes only flare up after being horizontal; maybe I should avoid going to bed ☺ ????
On the search for a wombat release site Pam and Terry asked earlier on in the week if I'd like to join them on a visit to Dave and Liz's: happily accepting, loosely made plans were made for between 12 & 1p.m. today. Comfortably making it on time to be greeted by our expectant hosts, following a home tour we got down to the business of cuppa's, cakes and chat. Content sugar levels were right we went for a walk following a track leading into the mountains, confirming the terrain ideal for releasing wombats. A few happy kilometres later we returned for a repeat performance of cake, cuppa and conversation, topping a nice time away from home ☺ ....

Our 'on again off again' summer was just that, leaving home in a t-shirt and sunshine returned as drizzle started and went looking for warmer clothes to blockout the evening cool air. The planets aligning reiterated it was definitely a day for rest and relaxation, having enough wood cut, there was no need to cook dinner, and the elements watered the garden, the only thing left for me to do was set the fire and put my feet up.... I can get used to living in paradise ☺ ....

Monday 20 February 2006
Concerned, and desiring to wake for the final day with puffy eyes, made priority one a doctor's appointment, not required until 1:50pm in town gave the solar shower plenty of opportunity to warm up....
Following a pleasant morning tinkering around in the garden Destiny was pointed over the mountain. Proceding a consultation with a doctor, I was instructed to the nurses station for further tests. Met by an unfriendly nurse, rudely stating I was to return to reception there are two waiting ahead of me, responded politely and directly as to why I come to be standing there in the first place. Looking for a thoughtful caring nurse passionate about their job wasn't about to happen, unprepared to outstretch my arm for either of them to shove a needle in, I sure as hell wasn't pissing in a jar either, that was out of the question. My feet not being painted on I walked back to the familiar comfort of Tia and Destiny patiently waiting in the shade....
Particularly wanting the antihistamine script filled, hospital reception staff faxed it through to St. Helens pharmacy to be filled and delivered back to St. Marys' pretend chemist for the 5p.m.-ish delivery. With only two hours before delivery, I chose to remain in town spending time over a brew with Pam and Terry. To say the least, I was bloody disappointed arriving after a two hour wait to hear the simple words, "sorry, the pharmacist didn't have time to fill all the scripts, yours was one of them, I hope it's not important, it'll be here tomorrow".
Beaten, I took my bat 'n' ball and went home, trying to regain positive optimism for a life of equality searched for the sanctuary of Rainbow Falls????
Unless there's a dire need, I'm burying myself up the hill into the comfortable hermit life far removed from other humans for the next week until forced back out!!!!

Tuesday 21 February 2006
Needing time away from the energy-zapping element of the human race, with puffy eyes I faced the day at a pretty laid back pace. Happiest at home with my four-legged furry best friend, Tia keeps contentment, sanity and reality into perspective, looking for a good dose of brain therapy Ms Tia followed me into the vegie patch where I never fail to find it ☺ ....
Digging up spuds it's customary to put the shovel through one or two, fortunately they still taste the same. Ripe strawberries dangling like Christmas lights had my name on them, sampling the first peach on offer also, yumo.... Like a good little squirrel I have now collected three walnuts from the ground for my stash, with limited nuts, and being at the end of the food chain at home, I'm doing well ☺ ....
On a bloody stinker serious enough for a westerly window blockout, escaping the afternoon scorcher I picked up the phone catching up on family life. Mum and Dad enlightened me to a shocking tragedy that occurred in Mildura Saturday night, an out of control car ploughed into a group of youths killing five at the site. Known to our family, Nina is in Melbourne with her

son who is fighting for life being amongst the group struck by the car, a bloody horrific ordeal….

Wednesday 22 February 2006
Extending outstanding success, against the odds walnut number four has made my booty, what's even more exceptional four can still be counted attached to the tree. A huuuuge harvest is looking good ☺ ….
Ideal conditions perfectly suited to the job, rain cloud hung around keeping the surrounding atmosphere cool, adding an element of comfort for cutting a supply of wood to keep the home fire burning. Delivering a light dusting, a couple of misting showers was all the heavy cloud could muster, also appreciating the cool change, pumpkin plants didn't fold their huge broad leaves down ☺ ….
Feeling a bit flat, it only takes a small act of kindness to rapidly restore volumes. Ross phoned with news I'd received a response from Anna via his email, topping the call by printing the message and personally delivering it. Over soup bowls of milo and relaxing conversation befitting the size of the mugs, we put our feet up in the shed for a while. Escaping the 'hands dirty' car repairs, I left Ross to tinker with his and escaped to the cottage to do the keyboard finger dance with my little mate tranquilly snoozing near ☺ ….
Sharing moving news, Cousin Mark called early evening, short of selling his Mildura unit the Tasmanian property sale is complete, making way for a second of us Lucas' as a resident, with one at either end of the state….

Thursday 23 February 2006
Giving up participating in the outside world playing politics, with the realisation of just how much of life it consumes, redirecting distracted time back home makes way for other exciting things like ajaxing the bath. Nose down bum up scrubbing away felt a slight twitch in my back, thinking of all the exciting things I do how humiliating it would be injuring myself scrubbing the bloody bath, or even worse still, ironing. Preferring to re-read about myself doing an injury on some outdoor adventure, like completing a repair job or climbing through the gorge ☺ !!!!
Creating a rod for my back, the more accomplished both inside and out it seems the more there is to maintain. With each passing season more ground is reclaimed and tidied generating a larger area to mow. Converting the cottage from storage to homely and habitable has also increased upkeep requirements, spreading myself even further….
The elements offering a spell from watering noticeably frees up a large chunk of time, the vegie garden is an absolute pleasure but a demanding job without water on tap at the site, a situation that will be rectified before next growing season. Every passing season has its upkeep requirements absorbing time and labour; responding to nature and change is a situation I'm happy to be part of. Unable to think of anywhere else I'd rather be ☺ ….
Adding justification to manual watering, spring onions, potatoes, carrots, garlic and one bean included in tonight's dinner were all home grown, a satisfying feeling and taste, although it would be even better if someone else cooked ☺ !!!!

Friday 24 February 2006
Cloud hugging the range obscuring the top from view overflowed some of its load letting varying fog densities and misty rain dominate proceedings. Not good for the solar shower but visually magic ☺ ….
My 'tight arse' gum boots were recruited for collecting water to keep the tired old blundies dry, leaving the python shoes on only as long as necessary, reverted to comfy old boots and withdrew into the shed with my best mate. Taxing into the rainy day stash of dry planks of wood stored down the shed I cut them down to size, my little mate pitted her skill at catching drips of water falling from the roof edge, both happy doing our own thing ☺ ….
Revisiting a trusted friend, I lost most of the day in the vortex black hole of the haven, a first in a while the heater got sparked up to swallow rubbishy clutter lying around. Rounding off a tidy up, I neatly swept the floor before giving in to the magnetic force of the cottage for a wild Friday night home with my pen ☺ ….

Saturday 25 February 2006
Great thunderstorm potential - like yesterday sun wasn't shining but it was far from cold, only reptiles, plants and butterflies seem to be enjoying the clammy conditions. Comfortably seated on the throne enjoying the view from the loo, the paddock in front leading to the falls was alive with butterflies delicately busying themselves flittering about ☺ ….
My mate Loui, long gone from Tassie and submerged in the biggest smoke, resurfaced giving the morning a lift with a dash of friendship maintenance. Thankfully personalities never change after altering our abodes ☺ ….
Confined to anywhere sun can't reach for what seems forever I was starting to go a little stir crazy; it was refreshing to have one delivered perfect for outdoors. Mild and overcast with a gentle cooling breeze, my little mate sorted, composted, and reburied unearthed bones as me and the shovel cleared around the rock pile. Tying hair back to keep my neck cool, the ponytail that once just squeezed into the rubber band now has no trouble at all. My fringe is only centimetres away from joining the confined bundle????
Leaning the shovel to cool down following its workout Ross timely popped in for a visit, parking our bums down the shed we demolished brews leaving the curtain to close on another ☺ ….
On a mild evening, lighting the fire to cook up silverside with all the trimmings, the cottage heated to uncomfortable in no time, leaving the door open only attracted moths not cool air. The fan came to the rescue adding a level of comfort it also stopped the intruding moths from landing on me…..

Sunday 26 February 2006
Searching for bed following a late night, more precisely an early morning after completing evening bits, lead free making the transition from the cottage to the bungalow, Tia refused to respond to calling. Hot on the trail of something more important than sleep, tired of wasting time calling I pulled out the trump card. With the moon in mid cycle and blindly walking around in a black wall of darkness I made my way to Destiny. Returning from a quick drive to the front gate a naughty girl was sighted in headlights waiting by the shed, lead on and heading toward bed, I finally placed my head on the pillow 2a.m.!!!!

Outside watering taken out of my hands with the occasional misty shower, the northerly influence weakened dropping the mercury considerably also. Putting paid to thoughts of washing, feeling a bit aimless and wandering, tinkered until it was time to head over the mountain, having accepted a dinner invitation Ross left behind yesterday ☺....
Ross' talent extends to the kitchen, roasted chicken breast stuffed with garlic, semi-dried tomato, olives, hot salami and cheese, covered in mushroom gravy speaks for itself, bloody delicious. Mains followed by a serve of Evelyn's sticky rice and ice-cream, I was in food heaven. Between courses, chatting and cuppa's, sitting opposite sides of the kitchen bench, in a combined effort we separated, peeled and minced garlic, I told Ross there's no such thing as a free meal ☺ !!!!

Monday 27 February 2006
Come rain, hail or shine the laundry was going to be done and shine it did, even though days are still warm they've lost the summer sting, a changing of season can now be sensed. Not only is there the obvious shortening in daylight hours, clothes are taking longer to dry having to bring some inside to finish off by the heater. I love the many and varied moods the earth's movement, combined with gravity and a multitude of conditions, deliver as a constantly changing climate, our mere existence always remains pleasantly unpredictably challenging ☺ !!!!
Not a single currawong has been sighted in days, only hearing a rare squawk way off in the distance and far enough away so as not to be offensive, the harmony is perfect in paradise ☺ ....
With little interest the laundry was painstakingly done, without moving far from the washing machine I literally just turned around and got into dishes preparing to do it all again tonight. Luckily I enjoy eating because we sure do spend a lot of time preparing to do it, cleaning up after doing it, and thinking about how to do it differently next time ☺ ????

Tuesday 28 February 2006
A real fruit and veg day; I was devastated to find it had rained peaches through the night emptying the tree of all but seven. The couple of dozen peaches strewn over the ground were at varying stages of being eaten - possums and rabbits had had a feast. Failing to reward the buggers for almost stripping the peach tree. I removed the half eaten fruit from the ground and buried them in the compost!!!!
Now managing six walnuts in my booty, I can still see two hanging on the tree, taking into consideration the few walnuts available I've done pretty well in the food chain with the crumbs on offer....
Noticing natural die-off in the few remaining self-sown potato plants, to remember where to find the hidden spuds. Ms Muffet and I dug them up while the dead top still gave a clue to their whereabouts. Checking out a healthy pumpkin runner that had climbed its way up and around a tree I discovered a hatched aerial offspring, that baby is going to need plenty of support growing up ☺ ....
Remaining outdoors I cut enough from the burnt out house front bedroom window to get us comfortably through another evening. Utilising the last daylight, and noticing tracks in grass leading away from gaps in the rock based cottage foundation, made a start at rabbit proofing by raiding the rock pile for gap fillers....

Prior to lighting the fire for the evening Rod called, reading his very diplomatically worded piece for inclusion in the local Valley Voice paper, the small article simply poses the question as to whether the radio station is commercially run rather than community minded????

Wednesday 1 March 2006
Swallows have made themselves scarce, not having been sighted in a few days it appears they too have felt the changing of season and are moving on to wherever they go during the colder months. They'll be missed until September when they once again return; the swallow's occupancy adds life to the shed ☺ ....
After a stint of nine days without a trip as far as town we made a mercy dash to keep our bellies fed. Heading down the mountain it was difficult not to notice roadside slashing done along the road the mayor lives on, one can only live in hope the slasher knows how to find its way up here ☺ ????
The Post Office delivered a parcel of Mildura newspapers from Mum and Dad covering the bloody horrific event of the car that ploughed into a group of youths killing six. Mum warned, "you won't have a dry eye reading the papers, they tear at the heart-strings", just a brief glance with Kerry over the Post Office counter sent chills and goose bumps over my body....
Stopping at the bakery Evelyn asked what I was doing Saturday, pre-empting her question replied "picking you up, what time?". Evelyn's free moments are precious and few, I was stoked she chose to spend some of her very limited free time visiting Rainbow Falls ☺ ....
Car packed with groceries, and without having missed a chat with too many people, we wandered back to our side of the mountain to slip back into hermiting ☺ ....

Thursday 2 March 2006
Beginning to feel more secure wandering about with a bit of distance between me and the shovel. Today it was kept within arms reach. It was bloody beaut for heating the solar shower, summer's having a last hurrah. Retreating out of the sun after watering, Tia did her bit demolishing the burnt out house kitchen after those dreaded bunnies. I on the other hand spoilt myself with last night's dishes....
Betrayed by my body's lack of hyper-activity and enthusiasm I parked my bum with the Mildura papers. Mum was certainly right in saying it's impossible to read the stories and tributes without shedding a tear for those unknown youthful faces killed....
Bathed early and with dinner organised I sat down with a frosted glass from the freezer, filled it with Guinness, and melted into a rocker until reaching the bottom of that can, for that duration the outside world momentarily stood still ☺ ....

Friday 3 March 2006
The last hurrah to summer gave us another hurrah today, getting out of it just as soon as the garden was prepared for the elements it was about to endure. Leaving the solar shower out for a slow cook was surprised at the temperature reached inside the bag it was a shade warmer than I would have had a shower that could be regulated.... Impressive!!!!
Blocking the westerly window to keep indoor life a little saner I found respite from limiting heat by adding electricity to the typing machine. With one day entered onto the hard drive my

case manager Sandra arrived, comfortably seated over a brew we exchanged views on human existence....
After waving Sandra off and closing the gate behind, I phoned home seeking an outcome from Mum's visit to the surgeon. Nothing but good news is all I wanted to hear and that's all I got, Mum's heading in the right direction ☺ !!!!

Saturday 4 March 2006
While my back was turned a handful of currawongs crept in around housing, getting themselves noticed they were given the move on message, with little to argue over they left quietly. The feed shortage must be affecting them, steering clear of long grass and with the trees stripped of fruit they're scratching around in cleared ground for tucker....
A sky full of rain cloud prompted action for a stash of dry wood to be stored in the shed, and with a splash of optimism I put the solar shower out, later requiring some encouragement from the electric kettle to take the edge off....
Pulling up in front of the shop Evelyn was ready and waiting to cram a lot into her spare hour. Following a quick tour, sweet buns and a brew, we walked to the edge of the falls viewing the dry rock face across from the tree line then it was time to return after a short but pleasant visit ☺ ....
Thinking swallows had flown the nest, recent hot thermal currents briefly has them returning. Trekking back and forth with my bucket to the cattle trough four swallows did fast moving, excited, aerial manoeuvres in the open area between the shed and bungalow it felt as though they were bidding me farewell ☺ ????
Reclining in a rocker contemplating the day just passed watched South Sister Range slowly dimmed from view, a southerly change pushed in engulfing the range like fairy floss covering a stick. Appearing as though it was going to share its load at anytime, it almost did, misty rain pushed in only as far as the shed, failing to reach housing the front passed without adding one drop to the garden ☺ ????

Sunday 5 March 2006
Appreciating the view from the loo, I watched a goshawk silently glide its way along the range sending the noisy and most obvious squawking ravens and currawongs scattering. The goshawks beautiful large white frame was outstanding against an ocean of green; paradise has it all ☺ ....
It was a hugely successful scout for walnuts today, the largest cache for any one time yet, scooping another four from the ground boosted my personal collection to ten. Leaves starting to do their autumn thin made it easier to locate four nuts still hanging, far exceeding eight initially tracked down, confirming my poor eyesight ☺ ....
Tinkering on after watering I pulled the bean plants, what fruit remained was let go to use for next seasons seed. Moving from the garden and remaining outdoors I made a start dismantling a bathroom wall of the burnt out house unceremoniously laid strewn on the ground. Staying in tune with energy, I generated enough wood merely to make it through the evening ahead....
Its a dog eat dog world, opening the westerly window to let a few blowies out at that precise moment the black spider made victim of one. Using up a bundle of energy on the kill the black spider took a power rest. Sensing a moment of opportunity, a gangly legged, daddy-long-legs

looking spider did its best to take-off with the catch, bringing black spider back into action to start an 'its mine' tug of war!!!! Black spider easily retained the prized catch dangling in its web☺....

Reflecting on daily routine tasks, it's funny how we strive for a world of glamour and convenience where everything is at our fingertips and readily awaits us, when in reality that's bullshit for most. That kind of consumable lifestyle can be bought, and a carrot dangled that few can afford, for the majority of us mere mortals, whether be it home or at the workplace, our daily contribution evolves around a series of repetitive tasks. Only attitude and environment separate our enjoyment to the journey along life's simple offerings ☺....

Monday 6 March 2006
Finalising the regular 'to-do' things, Ross stopped by, pleasantly for a social cuppa and chat to excitedly share his adventure climbing over North Sister's rocky formation....
Dust settling on his visit I then had the arduous task of deciding a course the afternoon would take. Therapy in the garden got the nod ☺....
Out and about I encountered my worst aerial nightmare, around twenty currawongs flew over South Sister Range landing in the clump of trees adjacent Rainbow Falls' top boundary. Long grass still presenting an element of risk for grass seeds getting into wings, about a dozen of the buggers tried their luck landing in mowed areas of the yard and being promptly short-shifted!!!! A cold reception and not much to hang around for they didn't, phew....
Grabbing bits 'n' pieces from the bungalow in preparation for dinner, stepping outside the door was surprised to see a wallaby grazing two metres from me not looking the least bit perturbed, I could have almost reached out and touched it. Unfazed by my passing presence the wallaby went on grazing, usually flighty, I wondered if it may have been deaf, maybe poor eyesight or possibly accustomed to humans???? Watching from inside the cottage, with seemingly no disabilities the wallaby casually grazed meandering its way toward the dam, adding just another magic moment in paradise ☺....

Tuesday 7 March 2006
With the growing season winding down, not only are plants peaking and dying off, the amount of water lugged is also lessening. I love the pleasure of growing vegetables, but made a solemn promise to myself there will be water on tap before September's fresh growing season symbolised by the return of the swallows ☺!!!!
Skipping a fortnightly beer ration should buy the length of hose needed to reach the vegie patch from the irrigation pipe outlet. My fitness level will drop along with food intake, but it will be bloody wonderful to see water flowing on site without the required physical effort to get it there ☺....
The morning carried a cool edge drifted in on a light breeze, losing that mild summer start and pulling on a jumper, it was fantastic having energy and comfort to want to do something outside. Ideal for dismantling the burnt out house bathroom wall ☺....
Engrossed in dismantling and stacking individual planks for cutting, I became aware of my best mate's absence, failing to respond to anything even the Destiny trump card. Last sighted obsessed with rabbits under the burnt out house, gaining access to holes in the floor of each room failed to find her. Time and my anxiety levels were getting away and from the direction

of the shed Tia returned, whereabouts still remain a mystery, without question and being the upper most of importance I was over the moon to see her back happy and healthy ☺.... The little bugger!!!!

Wednesday 8 March 2006
Mostly calm and with an idyllic blue sky drove the mercury up, not unbearably hot but enough to rob the desire off being outside, just a reminder we're only gently easing away from the reach of the limitations of summer's confining heat. Reassuring and offering hope of more comfortable conditions on the horizon, the black spider on the westerly window is confidently settling in and spinning extensions ☺....
Most of the time Tia's outdoors she can be found at the burnt out house terrorising rabbits, lucky for rabbits they've got speed on side because if it was up to persistence they would come a miserable second ☺!!!!
Pam gave me a courtesy call asking to release a possum, phoning a half-hour too late, I'd finished the vacuuming, a half-hour sooner would have given all the reason needed to leave the back breaking machine idle ☺!!!!
Taking Bonney the possum for release Tia and I remained behind, Tia out of Bonney's way and me preparing brews. In no hurry following another success story released, the three of us reclined in comfy chairs savouring a hot brew and afternoon sun filtering into the cottage....
Long removed from summer solstice, and an obvious shift in the earth's axis, we're looking winter down the barrel, an outstanding time for appreciating brilliantly coloured sunsets. Staging a colour range of rich crimson to soft pastels. Each changing season has beautiful features of nature unique to that time of year, there's always something waiting around the corner ☺....

Thursday 9 March 2006
A morning disappearing on me doesn't take long; without having placed my head on a pillow before midnight for some weeks I've become nocturnal....
The solar shower had the edge off by the time it was required, and with boots shining the Rainbow Falls team headed over the mountain. In town only five minutes and I received a dinner invitation from Evelyn along with an offer of a dressing table both generous gestures were gratefully accepted. Inside pub doors buying wine to accompany the dinner invitation, plans were made with Connie for pre dinner drinks while in the big smoke tomorrow ☺....
Calling in for a brew, Pam turned on the finery with Devonshire tea on the front veranda. Freshly baked scones with home made raspberry jam and a decadent dollop of King Island cream on top washed down with a cup of brewed leaf tea, I would have to say, topped a very pleasant trip into town ☺....
Returning from the outside world to our side of the mountain, and reinstated within the sanctuary of Rainbow Falls, we quietly slipped back into our simple existence. Tia had a chew on a long dead possum carcass between chasing rabbits, and I got on with the usual bits keeping our humble life happily ticking over.... Perfect ☺....

Friday 10 March 2006
On a nice cool 'great to be alive with energy' day, following breakfast Tia resumed her obsession with rabbits leaving me to home maintenance. Standing by the cattle trough filling a bucket I heard movement on top of the dam levee, still weary of snakes, watched where the sound originated and a flighty rabbit sprang from its grass hiding spot and raced back toward the burnt out house for further Tia torture ☺ !!!!
Before joining Tia at the burnt out house to continue cutting the remains of the bathroom wall I received a courtesy call from Connie, all apologies having to cancel on pre dinner drinks, we rescheduled for this coming Wednesday....
The solar shower, electric kettle combination came to the rescue for hot water, leisurely sprucing up following a 'no stone left unturned' catch up chat with Mum and Dad ☺ ....
Driving into town for Evelyn's dinner invitation it was plainly obvious the roadside slasher still hasn't made it this far up the mountain, being the eternal optimist I haven't given up hope yet ☺ ????
Feeling pretty relaxed I rolled up at Evelyn's with the bottle of red, she insisted we first put the lovely dresser on offer into Destiny, juggling it around in Tia's space all the pieces fit snugly. With nothing left other than to sit, eat, drink and chat time away, we achieved our goal. Evelyn made a delicious stir-fry with delicately sliced tender pieces of lamb decorating a bed of soft fluffy rice.... ahhhh, another evening spent in culinary heaven ☺ ....

Saturday 11 March 1006
Being a creature of habit, opening the cottage first thing Tia made a bee-line to where rabbits are making a home under the floor. Usually only sniffing and scratching around at floor boards this morning Tia's habits were out of character, feeling threatened she was barking with tail erect and body puffed warning off the scent of the invisible intruder. Remaining boisterous and guarded for a couple of hours, it'll be a long winter of noisy distraction if a snake has curled up under there for hibernation ☺ !!!!
Literally with the arse out of my pants, it's a blunt reminder on the shortage of clean clothes and a strong message to get the suds stirred up in the washing machine....
Always easily distracted, Ross found me splashing about in suds at the tail end of washing, being happy to stop what I was doing there and then to take-off down the shed to share a chat and brew. Softening me first with a dinner invitation, Ross then asked if I'd help walk the many kilos of steel frame in his tractor mounted carry-all from the shed to load it onto the trailer. I was a little kinder on his back asking for a lift with the beautiful dresser brought home from Evelyn's last night....
Social skills in need of sharpening, when he was off the phone Ross cooked up a storm, cheese and spinach pastie topped with fried garlic, onions, mushroom and tomato. What can I say, I've died and gone to culinary heaven having two consecutive dinner invitations, its been a bloody long time since this little hermit has been out both Friday and Saturday night running ☺ ....
While indoors and oblivious, a sea fog had intermingled through filling the valleys and mountain ranges generating soupy patches and light showers for the return trip from Ross'. The ground could use a drop of moisture; it's parched enough to crackle underfoot. I was also

happy with the decision of decorating the cottage with almost dry clothes before going out ☺....

Sunday 12 March 2006
Brief showers persisted through the night; following a short dry spell the massive drop of 3mm sent the power delivery service reeling for three hours, waking to a flashing clock a stoppage was obvious....
Remaining mild enough to keep butter soft, nature's cooler conditions encouraged me outside until rain cloud did its best at lifting and giving the sun brief glimpses at our bit of the earth. The sea fog, however, refused to budge, keeping the valley and mountain ranges mist hazy. The combination created uncomfortable clammy humidity, taking the cream off being exposed in the great outdoors....
Being only one step away from rain, a very tropical 100% humidity wouldn't finish off clothes put back on the line to dry, returning them again inside, this time to be completed by the heater???? Unbelievable!!!!
Putting in a lazy Sunday, I let myself get sidetracked doing daily maintenance procrastinating time away. In a quiet procrastination moment I increased my stash of walnuts to a staggering fourteen and two can still be seen dangling from the tree ☺....

Monday 13 March 2006
A convincing shower of rain greeting us and the morning looked like and sounded like it was set in, gearing myself up for a shed day, was surprised within an hour to be in full sun ☺???? I struggle to pick it....
Waking not only to rain I also woke to a period, the scheduled one was two weeks back and it finished within three days. Maybe my manual lifestyle is throwing the system out? Hindsight explains why I got the craving for chocolate and ended up eating the whole block yesterday....
A few blasts of wind has given the walnut tree a bit of a shake the past twenty-four hours, picking up another four nuts this morning, and only able to see one nut still attached to the tree, the booty now totalling sixteen is a good snack ☺....
The new Evelyn dressing table found a home fitting nicely with the cottage décor, attaching the mirror it now takes pride of place near the front door ☺....
On average, the things regularly needing doing take up half my time, the other half deals with priorities then further down the line comes optional. Making it to optional I chose to sit my bum down and get the digitised copy of the journal current, it doesn't take long to get away....
Eagles are prevalent in the neighbourhood sighting them on three separate occasions today, further supporting cooler conditions arriving, its rare sighting them this side of the mountain over warmer months. Even Tia has more energy with her one remaining entire ball she instigated a game and was racing around like a frisky two-year-old.... Kick it again, kick it again ☺!!!!

Tuesday 14 March 2006
A cooler start gave me the appetite to revisit a familiar friend and the shelved habit of an after breakfast milo. Retreating to the shed to savour the moment, basking protected pondering the world, an eagle joined the moment effortlessly gliding over ☺....

A moment where I'm kept still, the throne is a good site to notice change, grass has been observed disappearing at a notable rate making an obvious visual difference. Green lush grass is highly prized by night traffic, hopping up for a comfort stop 5a.m.-ish I saw a wallaby grazing in the moonlight....

I'm also feeling safe in saying the swallows have taken off. They haven't been sighted since their farewell aerial performance over a week back. A changing season gives plenty of clues if you're fortunate enough to be able to see them ☺ ....

On ground nothing out of the ordinary happened. The usual bits filled waking hours, the only variation being Ross was joining us for dinner; his presence was a good influence bringing me in to eat at a more reasonable hour. Leading into a full moon, star-gazing, chatting, cooking, cuppa's and eating unfolded the mystery of another evening pleasantly into history ☺ ....

Wednesday 15 March 2006

The edge was just taken off the solar shower making it tolerable for washing hair only. Having plans to meet Connie 4p.m.-ish I left Rainbow Falls with enough time to grab drinking water, groceries, and lastly stop at the pub picking up afternoon tea on the way....

Following groceries, cash was momentarily rattling around in my wallet, priority one I headed to the Post Office paying the regular phone bill and a $60 neat Post Office box delivery service bill. Getting to know me better, Harry questioned whether I was in a service delivery area his questioning thankfully saved me $46. The service fee for non-delivery area is only $14. Lucky I wasn't behind in payments because the previous three years paying full price didn't even rate a mention????

Food neatly packed around bottles of drinking water, made my way to Connie's putting an end to a couple of moderately warm stubbies. Cheaper to buy a box of beer, Connie and I shared in the cost. She paid half earlier in the day and I covered what remained picking them up.

Unbeknown to me Connie had words with the new publican that morning, knowing our arrangement he smiled sending me on my way with a warm box of beer. If Bruce still owned the pub that pretty ordinary service would not have happened, the new bloke doesn't have the personality!!!!

Exploding with bursts of energy in cooler moments Tia has been doing a mad race through paddocks, only returning with a sprinkling of buzzies but nothing torturous like last year. Home following afternoon tea, Tia found a sticky patch of buzzies plastering her legs and decorating her belly, not too bad compared to the worst case scenario ☺ ....

Thursday 16 March 2006

It would seem Tia's taste for vegemite toast returned, her loss of appetite for sharing breakfast had plenty to do with gorging on a dead wallaby fouling the air out front....

A slow moving thunderstorm pushing in from the west got my arse into gear and rendered the solar shower useless. Looking over my shoulder I cut a good load of wood for the night then re-stocked water....

Warm steamy conditions colliding with an approaching cold front vying for the airspace above, between them working up a thunderstorm and a dive in temperature creating the event of a quick shower. All rumbles for a while, it looked like it was going to bypass without a drop....

Rattling my brain for a passive solution, music was trialled as Tia-pacifying thunderstorm therapy. Venturing to the cottage Joan Armatrading supplied the calming sound masking distant and softer rumbles, only barking at obvious loud overhead booms, on the overall Tia was less worked up. Other than a soundproof room, music is a pacifying assistant ☺….
Plans made with Ross to take a photo of me to make a birthday card for Dad was altered by a good bout of hayfever zapping my energy, tentatively rescheduling arrangements for Saturday after voting….

Friday 17 March 2006
Living in Dublin Town warrants a thought on 'St Patrick's Day' ☺….
There's nothing like the sight of rain clouds to get me rattling my dags. Out and about doing the regular bits I made another eagle sighting, they've been busy feeding this side of the mountain the past week ☺….
Usually hot on the trail of rabbits, Tia left me to it, preferring instead to rest her hard working cotton socks in the cottage. Using the burnt and weathered dishwasher as a saw bench I was disrupted from cutting by the sound of leaves crackling behind, the unfamiliar sound pattern attracted attention along with the copperhead snake causing it. Being territorial the housing area for snakes is taboo, it now sleeps inside the dam fence giving back to the frogs….
Step one of many required, it was action day to make life harder for rabbits. Salvaging enough chook wire and anchoring it with rocks I sealed access openings around the base of the cottage. Tia's actions will soon let me know if there's success, her super-sniffer is outstanding at tracking movement below floor boards ☺!!!!

Saturday 18 March 2006
The last time I went to the doctor looking for a cheaper option to manage hayfever it came with a price tag of $40. From the pharmaceutical company displaying advertising across the doctor's computer screen, this time he prescribed a new inhaler, coupled with the advice to inhale the self-administered dose through my nose. Experiencing enough discomfort, and in trust I gave it a go. Since taking a snort Tuesday my sinus has worsened daily delivering the feeling of a massive head cold. The snort created an infection from my ears to my throat, later reading the label the recommendation was to take the inhaler through the mouth and rinse after use. Sure as hell won't be following that advice again, I'd rather endure hayfever, a runny nose and tissue I at least understand the consequences of those actions!!!!
Compulsory voting duty complete, I was sitting in the bungalow on a pleasant day enjoying the view through the open door with a cuppa and piece of Evelyn's cheesecake with my little mate. If that alone wasn't pleasant enough, a pair of eagles flew into view enhancing an already pristine scene ☺….
Leaving the bungalow in an agreeably relaxed state, me and my little mate filled a couple of hours dismantling a fallen bedroom wall relocated on the front lawn….
Contemplating leaving for home made pizza and photo taking at Ross', Tia returned with her socks full of buzzies delaying plans for a half-hour ☺!!!!
Making a quick dash into town on a hunt for places Ross possibly left his camera, which turns out was safely put away at home, the noise from us approaching in the car disturbed a pair of eagles rising from feeding on a road kill in front of us. Delivering another delicious meal,

incorporating it into eating, chatting, kids and dishes, Ross took a photo of Tia and me in Destiny for making into a personalised birthday card for Dad ☺....
Feeling flat with sinus discomfort, I didn't have the lasting power for a big night out and headed back between the Sisters at a respectable hour. The head count of the welcoming committee in the yard picked up in Destiny's headlights consisted of four wallabies and two rabbits ☺....

Sunday 19 March 2006
Waking for a wee during the hours of darkness, an aching sinus and lower back wouldn't let me get comfortable and return to sleep; it was a bloody long night searching for relief. Trying cold packs for a face ache cure I started with the good ol' frozen peas then traded for a cool stubby. It's predominantly the left side of my face effected, the only snort inhaled went off up my right nostril, thankfully the left side failed to administer, traces of blood are now also showing up in my left nostril. Unable to get comfortable and tossing and turning good sleep time away hour after hour, had I'd been outside I could have easily rolled myself to the front gate....
Literally dragging my sorry arse out of bed after noon with a lost appetite, having no trouble eating at Ross' last night, I was unable to face breakfast. Opening a can of two fruit I struggled swallowing, although, a while later a cup of tea went down well. My little mate was a bit ordinary herself showing all the symptoms of constipation; we're synchronised ☺....
Everything aches from my lower back to eyes, the pain in my teeth and gums feel similar to that related to an abscess. This day only received my concentration and energy for as long as it took to do the 'have to's', then I pretty much only moved my sorry arse from seat to seat following sun.
My big spurt of energy came and went with a game of skud ball against the rock pile with Tia, utilising her one and only ball still intact, its fur may be gone but the rubber still has plenty of bounce ☺....
With the luxury of hindsight, snorting the inhaler up my nose sure did cure hayfever, I haven't had any since ☺ ????

Monday 20 March 2006
Once my little mate was brushed last night I dragged my sorry arse into bed. The drowsiness felt sleep should have come easy, being a long time since I was tucked into bed by 9p.m., but sleep still eluded me. Surprised to see 1a.m. arrive; taking with it what little energy I had I slept through sheer depletion, dismantling the bed with fever restless tossing and turning added to the uncomfortable situation....
Waking to the sight of my left eye puffy underneath stemming from the tear duct, looking similar to a black eye, it gave cause for concern. Again just getting myself through the bare bones basics I started to feel like my days were numbered, mustering up the last of what I had in me to make the doctors. Medical staff stretched to the limit and fully booked, I was grateful to be squeezed in and have antibiotics delivered to the pretend chemist within an hour on the same day, all green lights. Time to pop a few pills and sniff tea-tree oil to abruptly reverse whatever is happening inside my body....

My little mate hasn't lost her energy; persistence and patience paid dividends. Tia had a victory rabbit chasing, walking proudly past displaying a bunny snack in her mouth doing her bit for the environment ☺....

Tuesday 21 March 2006
Taking all night just to cook dinner and write, beating the restless time in bed I didn't get there until 1a.m. limiting those hours of roly-poly blues. Following an initial couple of restless hours I slipped into an exhausted five continuous, more beneficial than the five broken hours of the past two nights....
Knowing life won't stop while I get off, dragged my tired arse out of the cot before noon giving my little mate the opportunity to stretch her legs and put some petrol in her motor. Absolutely floored, I had a wash and another go at the two fruits. Draining just to sit upright in a chair, within ninety minutes of getting up, feeling nauseous and with bucket handy, I returned to bed. My best mate was a brilliant nurse remaining faithfully and quietly by my side keeping a caring eye on proceedings. Catching a couple more hours sleep, I resurfaced 5p.m.-ish with another day wiped off the map....
The garden couldn't be ignored any longer; it needed water. A reluctant body unable carry the weight of full buckets I tread softly doing the bare minimum to limp through. The limiting and restricted energy bursts are comparable to when my weight bottomed out at 38 kg, always struggling with low energy and tiredness stripping life of any quality....
What little daylight remained took no time to cave in and a beautiful sunset presented itself, with the full moon out of cycle, a wall of darkness soon fell forcing a retreat indoors for another evening ☺....

Wednesday 22 March 2006
Finally a restful night without the sensation of being in a rodeo, the wild infection broke offering a healing dose of peaceful sleep. While Ms Muffet and I still lazed in bed Mother Nature took care of the watering. Grateful for the meagre offering, it's one thing I could conserve precious strength with and strike off the 'have to' list ☺....
Waking with a shot of energy, and an appetite yearning to fill my belly with vegies, meant cutting wood. Placing one foot in front of the other I took all the steps required to make dinner happen. It was a relief to see the small pile of wood delivered to the cottage, phew....
Tia gave me a hand in the vegie patch digging up the last carrots and a few more spuds. Setting the fire and collecting water were the last links in the chain to attain the food goal, by then my bum was happy to be planted. A healthy serving of mashed potato and spinach decorated with peas, carrots and fried bacon, I ate the bloody lot in a stacked bowl; that'll help the motor pick up steam ☺....

Thursday 23 March 2006
Still not firing on all cylinders, life is however returning to some normality, harbouring a ration of mustered energy, and while it lasted, spent it cutting wood. Slipping enough of the charred remains into the woodbox to see us through a couple, then replaced what was used from the dry shed stash yesterday....

A side-effect of the infectious inhaler blast is my ears have been sensitive to noise; leaving the radio turned off since last week I caught the midday news today, establishing that I've missed nothing. Reported politics is mostly full of self gratifying egos feathering their own nests while empire building and chewing up valuable resources in the guise of short term money gains!!!!
Driven by an ever-increasing appetite I could feel myself improving as the day lengthened. Taking a break away from a return to the physical world I took a spell having a yarn with Mum and Dad, always enjoying our shared phone time I am however longing to see them personally ☺ ….
A south-easter pushed in draping South Sister Range in thick fluffy cloud robbing any warmth that existed, as much as it tried, wind couldn't push the cloud past the range over to us. It's extraordinary to watch a wall of rain only a few hundred meters away and receive none, while simultaneously feeling the effects of sun with patches of blue sky appearing above ☺ ????

Friday 24 March 2006
Grateful a dash of quality is returning to my existence, energy however still isn't running at peak capacity. Catering for my low energy, Mother Nature again thankfully took care of watering delivering a useful 5mm and clearing before Destiny's nose was pointed between the Sisters….
Finalising the bits to pack a birthday envelope for Dad, posting it being the special reason for leaving home, from there on in fate dealt me a good hand ☺ ….
Ross thoughtfully phoned to ask how I was feeling, mentioning I'd be his side of the mountain for drinking water said I'd call in, from our conversation the most I could hope for was a cuppa. Not only was a brew placed in front of me but I also got to share in Ross' speciality of home made pizza, oh, and the company was pretty good too ☺ ….
Completing the envelope stuffing process I tastefully decorated its outer with written comments, 'Bazza the birthday boys' parcel of goodies then started the journey to its destination….
Bread, milk and a bag of bones for Tia tucked neatly next to the water, I called in on Brian and Maggie, home and greeting me with open arms, I reckoned my luck was o.k. for a brew. Maggie left Brian and I chewing one another's ears in chat over tea and returned armed with freshly baked cheese and chives scones ☺ …. yumo!!!! I was certainly in the right spot at the right time to get absorbed into a high spirited day with friends ☺ ….

Saturday 25 March 2006
Depleting the cut wood supply, and with rain clouds lurking about, I headed to the burnt out house and like a woman possessed completed dismantling the bedroom wall. The charred wall remains, lying unceremoniously on the ground, rabbits had turned into a refuge; its removal is step two in my contribution for making it harder for rabbits. Generating a healthy stash of loose timber planks I also increased the dry booty in the shed, storing ample for a wet week….
Returning after a snack to strike a blow sawing dismantling planks down to size, I noticed several grass parrots dotted through the elevated garden. The clicking of beaks feeding was in stereo and evenly spread through the long neglected shrubs: unable to spoil that moment, a well-behaved Tia and myself lightly left giving them a moment of peace to snack ☺ ….

Happily trading peaked cap for beanie the past few evenings the days are noticeably becoming shorter and cooler, sun is slipping behind the mountain not long after 7p.m. and is producing some pretty specky sunsets. The obvious changing of season must be an indicator for snakes to crawl back under their rocks, allowing us to reclaim paddocks confidently, and permitting shovel free liberties….

Sunday 26 March 2006
An ideal tepid temperature, encased under an ocean of blue sky, set the foundation for perfect in paradise; although I reckon they're all perfect. Comfy with my top off, I roamed over the place from collecting water to hanging clothes on the line, soaking up liberating freedoms ☺ ….
Go-carts were darting over the rock pile in their on-going chase for insects, a good sign to keep an eye open for all reptile activity. Fading embers of the season turned on heat, the last ditch effort should help ripen a handful of plump fruit still dangling on the tomato plant….
The neglected and skilfully ignored washing machine tub was overflowing with dirty clothes. Unable to be left abandoned it was relieved of its load today. Dragging me away from whites, Loui phoned for a little friendship maintenance and to share action in the biggest smoke. Doors are now opening in Sydney supporting her music passion - starting Thursday Loui's got a regular weekly gig at a nearby pub ☺ ….
Unable to contain myself I returned to nose down bum up into the washing, still a couple of loads shy of finishing, Pam and Terry called in to collect the last bales of hay stored in the car garage; step three in the 'making it difficult for rabbits' program. Bunnies found it homely under the pallets the hay sat on, just out of Tia's reach. A timely visit, being short on pegs gave clothes time to dry making room for more ☺ ….

Monday 27 March 2006
Leaving the cottage for bed last night the sky was clear and full of stars, somewhere between then and morning rain successfully settled in. The lingering front held us under until lunchtime giving the parched ground a nice soaking 14mm; flowing water could be heard from the falls seated on my throne ☺ ….
The north-easterly front stepped aside for a stronger southerly influence. Cloud was pushed along by a cold wind, all but the wind passed by. Windows of blue sky and glimpses of sun even got a guernsey on this liquorice allsort kind of day????
Bloody magic conditions for us shed dwellers, Mother Nature's way of extending permission to get immersed in the haven, where a solid dent was put in cutting the dry wood stash. Uncertain of what the next few days entail, and with the crystal ball malfunctioning, as an insurance policy I took more planks to the shed to dry off….
Ross popped in kindly delivering a sample of meatloaf, a sweet gesture that complemented last nights leftover veggies, doused in onion gravy it made an afternoon snack. Over conversation he also mentioned daylight saving is due to finish Sunday and mountain snow has been predicted for the end of the week. From past observation, my association of wind accompanying snow is so far true to form….
Unfolding the ladder I picked the last known walnut; seeing its skin split the nut was ready to escape at anytime. Monitoring the nut's progress from inception I couldn't bare to lose it to a

possum, rabbit, or heaven forbid, a currawong!!!! From the original eight nuts spotted growing on the tree I scooped a booty of twenty-two, is it my eyesight or do they camouflage well ☺ ????

Tuesday 28 March 2006
Turning on an ice-box of a night, it was beaut for getting buried under the doona snuggled next to my little mate. With a full belly I contentedly slept like a hibernating bear. On the flip side, today reverted to sunshine and warmth, certainly presenting no lack of variety....
Its rare a day passes that Tia doesn't get me sidetracked with a game of ball of some sort, her favourite being skud ball off the rock pile. I kick the ball into the rock pile and it ricochets off at unpredictable angles, sometimes back at me, but for the most, making the yard with the physics expert in hot pursuit. Tia and her ball terrorise me randomly at any given time, happily taking twice as long to get half as far ☺ ....
Salvaging a fly screen in semi-reasonable condition from the burnt out house bathroom wall I sifted and separated grey ash from coal and removed nails, oh, and threw the ball. Grey ash for the loo, nails for rubbish, coal for re-burning, and ball for Tia ☺ ....
Catching the last evening golden embers on offer I sipped on a beer and watched robins dancing over the yard feeding on twilight insects. Tia's robin watching concentration span didn't hold, movement in the cattle yards became more important, she's now splitting her rabbit obsession between the burnt out house and cattle yards ☺ ....

Wednesday 29 March 2006
Sleeping heavily following late nights sets the stage to snooze until late morning. When finally the family was packed in Destiny and ready for a trip over the mountain afternoon had already arrived ☺ ....
Promising to show Rita and Barbara where the rocking chair made a home, popping into Gone Rustic we etched this coming Monday in the calendar, with finer details to be sorted later, the idea was met with enthusiasm. A sample of Pam's freshly baked coffee-cake and a complementing brew to wash it down with I left for the supermarket. Serious about channelling money used on beer into other more useful areas at the present time, I headed home without the fortnightly ration bypassing the pub ☺ ....
Requiring cut wood for the evening ensured I get home from town with plenty of daylight left up my sleeve, shortening daylight hours creates some obvious seasonal habit changes notable in priorities and thought processes....
At this stage snow by the end of the week isn't looking imminent if today was any indication; a beautiful day to be alive and participating ☺ ....

Thursday 30 March 2006
Following another late night, I pleasantly lost what remained of the morning on the phone to the birthday boy and Mum. Appreciatively, Dad received his birthday parcel of goodies through the post, and like myself, was about to spend the day outdoors, Dad's mission is to plant bulbs ☺ ....
The working day began with a game of skud ball against the rock pile. Putting her usual heart and soul into the game Ms Tia's motor got a bit warm, dropping the skud ball chase like a hot

potato, Tia deviated to the cattle trough for a drink and climbed in giving herself a couple of dunks. I love a self-washing dog ☺ …. Capitalising on Tia's soggy state I wet up her dry bits refreshing the trough's ordinary water quality….

The true sign of autumn stood out as obvious. Rings of fallen leaves are forming on the ground below deciduous trees. Extending the fresh look I brought the ride-on out giving the yard possibly its last tidy until spring. Night traffic should keep it trim until then ☺ ….

From the moment my bum was parked on the seat and earmuffs in position the mower performed like a champion. No matter where Coxy's nose was pointed it went without question. It never ceases to amaze the full extent of area so effortlessly mowed in one outing, from the cottage front yard, encompassing part of the dam surrounds, and across to the loo, all look trim and tidy. Quietly parking the hard working beast with the setting sun….

Stepping inside on dusk I found a pleasant message waiting on the answering machine, Evelyn extended an offer of sticky rice that can be picked up from the bakery Saturday, something to look forward to ☺ ….

Friday 31 March 2006

Stirring to face whatever was presented before me in paradise, the first presented clue a dimly lit bungalow was a sure sign of overcast conditions…. Highly unlikely I'd wake before sunrise ☺ !!!!

Still rubbing my eyes to waking, I had enough time to grab light fire starting timber before drizzle pushed in, the urgency to rush, along with the light misting, left. Following breakfast I returned to the burnt out house, at a far more sedate pace, to add more of the charred bedroom wall to the woodbox….

It was like stepping out into an entire new world leaving the bungalow being greeted by a neatly mowed yard. Definitely in tune with the universe, yesterday mowing and today it's raining ☺ ….

It's a pleasure to be outdoors now cooler weather has arrived. I'm even getting more confident by not carrying the shovel to the loo….

I made a start at composting within a dirt centred, concrete edged, two metre strip running directly parallel with the back of the burnt out house and path. Establishing an organic brew, I raked a few barrow loads of cut grass to combine with the existing plentiful potash, generating a healthy beginning….

Digging potatoes was a grim reminder there are only four plants left; of the vegies grown I shall miss them most. A handful of pumpkins making it through to maturity aren't far off being harvested; another vegie crossed off the shopping list ☺ ….

Saturday 1 April 2006

From the moment my eyes opened thoughts and actions led to Evelyn and sticky rice. Rugged against cold, the warmth of the bakery and conversation was inviting. A traditional Philippine sweet, Evelyn presented me with black sticky rice, unbeknown to me black rice is the pick of the crop in the rice world. A series of customers broke our untroubled chat, wandering diagonally across the road to firm up visiting details, found both Rita and Barbara in and was extended an invitation to join them in a brew. Bringing their visit forward to 1:30p.m.-ish tomorrow, we never discussed whether that was daylight saving time or normal time ☺ ????

The planned trip complete and nothing left to distract the Rainbow Falls trio we wound our way back up the mountain....

Not getting any warmer with time, I kept blood pumping exercising the handsaw aspiring to have surplus wood for a fire to keep our visitors warm if need be tomorrow. Thinking the woodbox was looking healthy, the first of many brief fronts passed through delivering the message to head in and sample a bit of my labour....

During a conversation in town it was mentioned snow was falling to 800 metres. By mid afternoon its effects could be felt - the air temperature dropped down to icy. Each occasion wind picked up and a fresh front pushed through kept me on the lookout for those falling white flakes....

A spoonful sample of black sticky rice gearing up to prepare dinner was a dangerous time, expanding my culinary repertoire. It's a flavour sensation; I was unable to stop the spoon until I could eat no more ☺....

Sunday 2 April 2006

Wishing to tidy the cottage and have a warm fire to greet Rita and Barbara I achieved my goal with time to spare. It felt really decadently nice to use the heater through the day for pure relaxation with company, using its top merely to boil water for a hot brew ☺....

An afternoon of pure pleasure eventuated with the arrival of Rita and Barbara, visiting on time at the newly adjusted normal time.... Daylight saving was so yesterday ☺ !!!!

Treading lightly and taking no effort, time spent in Rita and Barbara's company melted. At a pretty relaxed pace we took a browsing stroll around housing, and taking little encouragement, I emptied my head of the known history surrounding each building. Settling into the warmth of the cottage we shared in the finer arts of comfort, food, cuppa's and knowledge sharing.

Barbara revisited an old friend making herself comfortable in the rocker she generously gave to Rainbow Falls, the spring rocker given by Mary-Anne impressed Rita for comfort. The show stealer however went to Evelyn's black sticky rice it seems my opinion of delicious was unanimously shared ☺....

Having enough energy stored to sustain we loaded into Destiny to put boundaries into perspective, oh, and take the short cut to the top of the falls where the spectacular view never fails to impress ☺....

With a head full of new adventures on a lovely day out at home, the sun set behind settling dust waving our visitors off ☺....

Monday 3 April 2006

Aware of daylight saving finishing is all I was - no thought was put into changing clocks until today. Mattering very little in the big scheme of things anyhow, I slept, woke again and participated in the day. If its end was meant to get me to bed earlier it didn't work last night seeing 2:30a.m.-ish daylight saving time ☺ ????

Leaving me to go about the usual old things, Tia put in a busy time marking territory and alternating between the cattle yards and burnt out house terrorising rabbits. She refuelled with a dunk at the cattle trough and occasionally checked on me ☺....

Tinkering about I was within hearing distance to catch a call from Pam inviting me for a roast dinner Wednesday to celebrate Terry's birthday, without question that was a definite yes. I love socialising over food, even better when it's cooked for you ☺ !!!!

Bird life was noticeably active today. A pair of eagles was sighted gliding high over the range, regular visitors grass parrots darted about, and quite a number of robins were active snapping at insects. Kookaburras are reliably active, and a small honey-eater kept itself busy along with others unfamiliar. Ravens and currawongs verbally made their presence known never being too far away….

Since mowing anything on the ground is easy to see, another two walnuts sitting there large as life made twenty-four for my booty ☺ ….

Tuesday 4 April 2006

Into the dishes before retiring to bed last evening it came as a surprise to hear a steady shower hit the roof, always expect the unexpected ☺ ????

Not real in tune with daylight saving I turned the clock forward instead of back, patterns of habit didn't change what stood out I was getting to bed and rising even later. Back in step with the outside world winding back two hours, I might get to bed at a more respectable hour. Only time shifted, not behavioural routine ☺ ….

Psyching myself for woodcutting over a brew, I was relaxed sipping tea when Ross called in bearing the gift of apples. With room for another brew, we headed to the shed to scan an eye over his printed photo of Rainbow Falls from South Sister lookout. Getting into a paddock mural planning session bouncing ideas we sorted a plan of attack….

Gathering black cloud deleted sunshine and stimulated my sawing arm into action. Cutting weather-boards at the burnt out house a passing shower drove me under the roof of the shed, adding a quick 1mm to last night's 3mm. In the shelter of the haven I cut solid wood, warming up over the 4 x 2 planks that once supported the bedroom wall….

With a shortage of balls Tia's been improvising, taking a liking to the feel of stubby holders in her mouth, she's laid claim to a couple. Without being neglected the one remaining ball received attention saying goodbye to the last daylight by the rock pile over skud ball ☺ ….

Wednesday 5 April 2006

Passing mist showers, wind, and glimpses of sunshine presented the day with plenty of variety ☺ ….

Our trusted best friend the shovel is gratefully being neglected, I'm having to put thought into where it was last left, the obvious changing of season has freed my hands and is safely opening our piece of the world for exploring. Tia's pent up stir crazy inactivity stored over summer is now on release; with new-found energy she's racing around the yard and paddocks like she's discovering them for the first time. We're also back to the butter setting like a brick and bread never moulding ☺ ….

Confidently roaming we went walkabout sourcing wood of the larger, longer burning capacity, needing now to expand on the necessary burning time beyond dinner and hot water with the inception of heating. Staying out and about I went shopping at home for Terry's birthday, expressing interest in seeds from the bloody feral sycamore trees and bulbs from the more

pleasant red hot fire poker, accompanied with a block of chocolate and bottle of red should get me through the door☺....
Going to share in someone else's fire instigated that once in a blue moon occasion the electric stove felt the effects of power to boil water. Spruced up and my little mates belly full, Destiny tackled the mountain delivering me to an ideal night of socialising over my favourite combination of food, wine, good friends and plenty of life knowledge readily shared.
Following coffee and hugs I left culinary heaven returning to a known lifestyle tucked into our hamlet edging the bush ☺....

Thursday 6 April 2006
Everything has a season and returning to the 'to-do' list is de-furring the bungalow. Although less work than her winter crop, Ms Muffets summer coat is dripping from her body guaranteeing a brush full or three of fur each grooming ☺....
The decorations cluttering the heater top, consisting of bucket and pots 'n' pans catching drips entering through the roof, were relieved of their token load from yesterdays couple of millimetres and reinstated to normal duties....
A cooling atmosphere has opened new doors, reptile activity has become invisible keeping me far more relaxed concerning Tia's whereabouts, nothing has to be postponed and there are no limits or boundaries. On the hunt for heavier wood I enjoyed the newly reinstated freedoms. Left to rot behind the cattle yards by the top of the gorge, I brought a few wheelbarrow loads of old fence posts to the shed. Spending as much time cutting as I did carting got the blood flowing, me stripping a layer, and the back of the day broken. Larger pieces of wood made a lasting difference in the heater, slowing the need for face feeding....
Back to reality, there was no roast chicken dinner with plum pudding waiting tonight. Returning to the task of cooking I hit the ground with a thud ☺ !!!!

Friday 7 April 2006
Like Tia, I'm like a kid with a new toy rediscovering the great outdoors; once outside there's no budging ☺ !!!!
Still loaded in fruit the tomatoes just wouldn't finish the ripening process. Sound horticultural advice recently given was to pull and hang the plant and the fruit will finish off.... Words put into action....
Digging the last struggling self-sown potatoes, that lived snugly next to the tomato plant, produced enough for a feed. Picking the one and only offering from the neglected corn plant, I could then turn the patch in. Still shovel roaming, I wandered over to clear grass from around a chocolate columbine that had set up home at the front of the cottage and just kept on going edging right across the front. Unable to be contained, I continued on doing a shovel circuit around the path leading to the clothesline....
Following a perfect outing of garden therapy for the brain, putting toys away Ms Tia managed to distract me at the rock pile. Our day seems to regularly end there kicking the ball until either Tia's had enough or we can't see what we're doing ☺....

Saturday 8 April 2006
Marking territory, a dog passing through in the night has been leaving a calling card for Tia in return she regularly supplies a reply message. Between the two of them the entrance to the loo is looking like a bombing ground ☺ !!!!
Lurking around the past week wind has slowly been picking up momentum delivering doses of punishment with random destructive gusts, not to the point of needing to sleep in the car or have the SES phone number handy, but all the same tiring. Window waterproofing and temporarily repaired temporary repairs are again in need of temporarily repairing ☺ ????
Posting off the payslip necessitated a trip over the mountain, getting my act into gear to get in before the supermarkets noon closing. Waiting to be served in the newsagents the counter conversation centred on wind; it seems I'm not the only one who's had enough. At the bakery I shared with Evelyn my delight and preference for black sticky rice. She wanted to dong me over the head with the pan I just returned because it's the hardest one to make ☺ !!!! With the now, regular ordered copy of the local 'Valley Voice' newspaper neatly sitting on the passenger seat, it was homeward....
The need to feed the heater drove me to the shed absorbed in the haven shielded from wind I cut a small load. Pleasantly, the old fence posts are far cleaner to cut than the charred timber from the burnt out house, however both are welcome in the woodbox....
A recently developed habit is to head indoors come sunset and spark up the heater then recline in a rocker purely enjoying the fires warmth. Until the mug of milo is empty the world doesn't exist; only then am I ready to face the evening ahead ☺ ....

Sunday 9 April 2006
A more, calm peaceful day you would not want, an earned reward for the past few gusty buggers endured!!!!
For some unknown reason the squeaking of the bungalow door closing activates Tia to take-off like a rocket, racing to the top boundary she then runs parallel to the road returning via the driveway completing the circuit. Shutting the bungalow door and destined for the loo, Tia rocketed off doing her circuit arriving at the loo with me, covering some distance in quick time ☺ ....
Down to clothes with holes is the signal to fire up the washing machine. With a predetermined course of action, I gave the whites a chance to soak while I did some fancy chatting over the phone with Mum and Dad. The receiver copped a good workout that near on drowned the whites. Hungry after a healthy chat working my jaws I made a bee-line to the bungalow to feed my habit ☺ ....
Attempting to return to washing, without even managing to glove-up, Ross pulled in saving me from the suds. Loaded with plastic temporary fencing pegs we paced, sited and pegged a love heart pattern guide in the paddock and discussed plans for Tuesday to bring the tractor and slasher into mural play....
My report card on life would read 'easily distracted'. The whites were resuscitated 7p.m.-ish. Finalising the laundry job and low on water and furniture, I pulled the plug on the operation in favour of last nights leftovers, sharing the heater with my little mate and drying the wardrobe ☺ ....

Monday 10 & Tuesday 11 April 2006
My little mate needed me more than ink and paper, the first for a long while I haven't written....
Late Monday afternoon Tia's energy fell in a heap. Checking her from head to toe everything seemed fine apart from her energy. Needing reassurance before taking the fifty-kilometre vet trip I drove to Pam and Terry's for an opinion, they too agreed just to keep her warm and comfy....
Without being active Tia had trouble keeping her body temperature regulated, using my body as a thermostat placed her on my lap in a rocker near the heater. Dozing with Tia on my knee peace was only disturbed to feed the fire, but by 2a.m. the wood supply was looking grim.
Leaving my little mate snug and warm in the cottage I prepared the bungalow, wrapping Tia in a weatherproof jacket, I brought her straight through into bed with minimal body heat loss and tucked her neatly by my side. That comfy arrangement didn't last long. Tia stood and had a spew that came from deep within. It certainly must have made a difference....
Before Tia's health took priority yesterday the makeshift laundry was disassembled then we got on with more important things in this mortal existence. Mum mentioned during Sunday's chat Mildura received a possible frost warning, sparking the brain light bulb that thought prompted action in the vegie patch. Picking the ripe pumpkins they were removed from the elements, then to protect us from them, I got enough water and wood stored in the cottage for the evening ahead....
Desiring nothing but rest again Tuesday I left my little mate in bed where she was content. Doing only what was necessary I returned to the bungalow so Tia could relax reassured the nurse and plenty of love was on standby. The vet is still not ruled out; if recovery means rest and sleep then I'd prefer to leave Tia doing just that rather than endure the many kilometres and vet stress, not being one of her favourite places. It's bloody awful feeling helplessness, unable to alter the way Tia feels other than to keep her comfortable and showered in love?!?!
Remaining attentive, I occupied myself writing to empty a busy brain while simultaneously maintaining comfort and warmth to sick-bay; offering a little help, afternoon sun streaming in from behind glass kept the bungalow quite cosy....
Early evening Ms Muffet got a bit warm buried under the doona, showing signs of animation she hopped out moving to snooze in a cooler spot, maintaining her own body heat was the desired progressive indicator. Tia's momentary absence gave a window of opportunity to de-fur the bed almost in time to turn around and hop back in. Activity entering Tia's body only perpetuated, requesting a visit outdoors for some territory marking she returned to consume the food in her bowl, have a drink then return to the comfort of my bed ☺.... The only way is up☺!!!!

Wednesday 12 April 2006
With my little mate showing all the right recovery signs last night my brain was content and ready for a good night's sleep. Just getting us tucked in and pulling the doona in place under my chin, a brief furiously destructive front blew in lashing out at anything in its way and tossing out a little moisture. Within the hour the wild front blew onto its next destination and I was down for the count blissfully ignorant....

An appreciated sight to see, Tia woke ready to tackle the world, delving straight back into her usual antics lightened my heart ☺ ....

Playing nurse I'd eaten us out of house and home. With my little mate firing on all four paws again a trip to the supermarket was possible, and required to keep starvation at bay!!!!

Having exceptional skills in the kitchen, stopping in for a brew before shopping Pam produced fruit buns fresh from the oven, coated with a light layer of butter. I was somewhere else.

Topping food utopia a loaf of fruit bread followed me out the door ☺ ....

Flicking the switch on a high electricity use day from hot water to heating, putting the need for food ahead of wood, I had nothing lasting ready to burn. Retreating to the bungalow to cosy on up by the electric heater for the evening, I sampled the pleasures of Evelyn's noodles and Pam's fruit loaf with a sliver of real butter ☺ ....

Thursday 13 April 2006

The only hat that would stay on until a wild gusting front passed was my beanie, wind for a time made a strong comeback bringing with it an air full of smoke it could however be a bushfire because a responsible person wouldn't light fires in strong wind????

Devoted to wood, whether I be wheelbarrowing it up, cutting it up, or carting it to the cottage filling it up. Sorting through the timber dumpsite behind the cattle yards, and hidden from view waiting for the right moment to arrive, I was elated to find a small treasure-trove of wood ready to fit the heater, every precious piece represented one less to cut....

Packing it in during a brief visit Ross released a brain blurt, emptying out every word pent up in his head he left me to nod, peacefully sip tea, and savour shortbread. On a mission to collect camping gear from the shed, part of his intense conversation he mentioned predicted snow. Snow being wet prompted repairing temporarily repaired temporary repairs. While actively mobile doing repairs I taped together a weather-tattered plastic sheet to again waterproof a prone window....

Wild blasts of the past week only offered one more walnut, I'm now feeling pretty confident in saying my booty has pulled up at twenty-five, a nice snack ☺ ....

Friday 14 April 2006

Starting out predominantly with a northerly influence and looking like anything could happen, the western side of the sky, including South Sister Range, was full of mountain clinging rain cloud. The eastern side in contrast was clear blue, a real mixed assortment. Cloud and a light sprinkling producing little dominated proceedings for a while, but a determined sun returned hitting ground only to be blocked once again, this toggling repetition continued on all day????

Watching confused outside events unfold from the comfortable position inside by the cottage western window so was our friend the spider. Life has been kind, the spider has gone up another size, the skeleton shell of a former life sits lightly suspended in the web. Without ruling out the theory it's possibly the remains of a trespasser ☺ ????

If snow is on the way then plenty of wood had better be on the standby prompting a repeat performance of yesterday. Confidently putting the saw down with a number of nights burning catered for, freed up a few days to get my teeth into other things…..

Still pumped warm after cutting wood I gave the shovel and secateurs a workout turning soil and tidying the red hot fire pokers, I worked like a woman possessed cleaning up the driveway side of the cottage....
It wasn't until after sunset that moisture again found ground this time seriously with an intense downpour, by then we were snuggy and warm by the heater with pots 'n' pans scattered catching drips from the leaky flue. Stopping briefly once, and on occasion pushed by wind, intense rain, unrelenting, is still giving ground a soaking as I write several hours later nearing midnight....

Saturday 15 April 2006
Quiet moisture moments were rare last evening, waiting for one to make the dash to the bungalow for bed didn't appear promising. Biting the bullet Tia and I did a dash amid the downpour. Arriving in a rush and staying at that intensity rain dropped a soaking 16mm, doing its best work before we closed our eyes. It pretty much pulled up as we hopped into bed.... If only we waited five more minutes ☺????
Content to wake lazily at my own convenience, Tia determined we get up 8a.m.-ish and she made sure of that by spewing on the bed. A cold southerly wind was waiting outside the door, burying my head in the Nana Raye hand knitted Collingwood beanie I just got on with it....
Stopping for coffee and the last of Pam's fruit loaf, television was on. Entertaining the beautiful expansive view from the intact bungalow window was the scene of a pair of eagles using the wind to their favour....
On one of the many trips passing myself for water I noticed something flapping from the toilet. The roll left out to dry had began unravelling, before it created a streamer it was placed back into its tattered bag for safe keeping....
Weighted full of water my doona stayed on the line to drip-dry without pegs, unable to fit in the washing machine it gets a dunk in the bath and feels my weak wristed wringing....
When knock off came around the wind direction had shifted and the air temperature plummeted to icy. Snow was somewhere about....

Sunday 16 April 2006
On this Easter Sunday a quiet one was put in keeping myself busy doing very little ☺....
Conceding defeat, the patched up and patched again cottage window waterproofing gave in and was blown into the side yard; like the rest of us, got tired of being pushed around by wind. That too finally blew itself out, turning the dial to cool, calm, sunny and serene, and a pleasure to participate in....
Pleasantly a good chunk of the afternoon escaped entering into a marathon call to Mum and Dad ☺....
A night by the heater and two days on the line the doona was ready to be returned to the bed. The substitute blanket was toasty and warm but collects and keeps Tia fur too readily. It was choice spending time in the bungalow remaking the bed; sun streaming in from behind glass makes it a naturally warming cubby....
Keeping the flue above the heater as dry as possible, drying clothes, heating water, cooking and keeping warm, I chewed up the optimistic lasting wood stack. To get through another night in paradise the burnt out house made a donation....

This time of year is outstanding for brilliant sunsets. Words fail me to capture and transfer such splendour onto paper. Colours range from a burning golden glow, fiery alive-reds, to soft mellow pastels. The incredible effects when cloud is included are individual works of art. Then there are those moments of shut down magic; housing is completely immersed in shadow from trees lining the top of the gorge, simultaneously, internally the gorge is brilliant with vibrant light and shimmering leaves on trees sparkle like diamonds ☺ ....

Monday 17 April 2006

Rattling about looking for a potential winter nesting site blackbirds woke the household 7:30a.m.-ish making a ruckus at the edge of the cottage roof, sounding more like a heavy footed possum jumping about.... The jackhammer of the bird world!!!!

Filling my existence with the usual wood and water chase replenished supplies yet again, then, returning some of the burnt out house back in a much smaller capacity, I got sidetracked sifting heater ash with the salvaged fly screen. Sifting through separating out nails and other bits from grey ash, I set-up shop next to the recently developed compost pile - a little potash won't go astray....

Autumn hasn't bypassed it's like a wolf in sheep's clothing. As if the harsh tiring wind and cold conditions of the past week never existed today was gorgeous. Stripping down to a t-shirt I put the solar panels out for a shot of vitamin D ☺ ????

Literally rounding-up a simply relaxing laid back time spent in paradise, I played ball with my best friend until her interest and enthusiasm started to wane, then we headed in with the light closing in behind....

Tuesday 18 April 2006

Before heads were raised off pillows 1mm had dropped out of the sky. Although the sun was shining initially getting up, wind pushing cloud maintained an element of uncertainty????

Cool and comfy, ideal for manual labour, with saw bouncing around in the wheelbarrow and always with the help of my little mate, devoted every spare minute to collecting wood. Our venture took us walkabout picking up limb wood out back by the top of the gorge....

Sending out a cooee from the hill by the loo, Ross drew me out of the trees to meet and greet, happily downing tools for a hot brew and chat. Planning on making a lean-to shelter for his horses, Ross accepted the offer of a couple of posts and corrugated iron laying around, giving them a future with purpose....

Walking to shut the front gate after Ross headed east I felt the effects of a temperature drop. Staying with wood devotion I made a horizontal passage to the shed keeping warm swinging the saw....

Mid evening waves of strong wind literally passed through. Drifting in with most gusts was a dusting of rain; combined, they offered nothing too serious....

Wednesday 19 April 2006

Presented with a heavy sky always looking ready to unburden itself of its load, I took precautionary action decorating the heater top with pots 'n' pans to catch any potential drips in our absence....

Down to the last couple of litres of drinking water I made refilling bottles the first move on the mountain pilgrimage, beginning the start to a flowing social time. Unaware of the extended Easter break schools received, I was surprised to find Ross and the tribe home and pleasantly I was extended an invitation to join in for lunch. Sending me off in a nice state of comfort to finalise the rough as guts, in parts second gear only, bone rattling, bolt loosening, trip down the mountain☺....

The Post Office and supermarket were breezed through. Sitting in Destiny I opened the envelope sent from Mum and Dad containing a tribute supplement from their local paper for the teenagers killed, tears started to well so I put it away for later. With the ordered copy of the Valley Voice neatly tucked beside all the other goodies packed in Destiny, then I stopped at Gone Rustic sharing a cuppa and Evelyn snacks with Rita and Barbara☺....

The last stop was to Brian and Maggie's to deliver rescheduled gorge walk invitation details, met with open arms, a couple more hours melted into comfortable chatter. Maggie produced a beautiful home baked cake to accompany the brewed tea; swallowing was the only quiet moment in conversation. Daylight beginning to dim, exaggerated by overcast conditions, I said farewells, saying them for the fourth time I actually left☺.... During our time of absence a steady mist set in turning Destiny's panels to mud going home....

Thursday 20 April 2006
Passing showers arriving yesterday lingered on throughout the night and remained settled until mid morning. Listening to a shower empty its load while we still lay warm and snuggy in bed, I don't know what Tia's thoughts were but I was planning time in the shed☺.... Bungalow de-furred, the doors were flung open and we went out to greet it....

To buy some Easter cheer Mum and Dad sent me a little money in their envelope of goodies. Bypassing the pub again, I phoned Howard the plumber and for the same price as a slab of beer spent the money on a copper header tank, a missing link to water on tap at Rainbow Falls☺....

Gently travelling fronts pushed in from time to time dousing the ground then stepped aside for a full blue sky: either way, I was content lost in the shed only emerging to feed or unload the wheelbarrow....

The flow of fronts regularly dusting the ground with moisture has spurred on a few mushrooms, prompting action to stake a claim to a few with protective coverings....
Bonus☺....

Friday 21 April 2006
Observing a pair of parrots drink from the cattle trough, considering the attention Tia gives it through the day, and night traffic only knowing what happens in it then, Ms Muffet helped out by clacking her jaws trying to catch water, tossing bucket after bucket for a refreshing clean out. I love being on the fringe of nature, privileged to be part of the activity that so naturally goes on. Hanging around of recent, a raven landed in the yard and in its business like manner idly strolled and snacked without a worry in the world☺....

Two consecutive days devoted to wood affords time without giving it a thought, redirecting freed up labour at the burnt out house. Putting my heart and back into it, concentrated on revealing the two metre concrete path bordering the rear perimeter and further developing the compost bed. Shovel, rake, secateurs and broom, I turned, separated, trimmed, tidied and

removed bloody nails, even now closing my eyes can still see rusty nails. Progress moves at a snail's pace, but already a noticeable impact is pleasing the eye ☺….
Always on the go, Tia put in a big one. Deep in sleep she broke out into a snore waiting for dinner - not a bad life having trained me well ☺….

Saturday 22 April 2006
Dripping from her body, Tia's fur is decorating anything she touches, and doesn't touch for that matter ☺ !!!!
When our living quarters looked less like mohair, expanding on progress we returned to the burnt out house. Unmotivated by the sight of rusty nails and broken glass I changed tack carving inroads at making sense of the tangled, overgrown garden. For the future I'd like to see edible plants and fruiting trees introduced establishing a rather sheltered food bowl ☺….
These days being outdated currency, a 2 cent coin literally turned up in the flip of the shovel head, another piece of history to add to the stash of collected treasure ☺….
Working steadily, Ross pulled me up for a milo to keep our voice boxes lubed while we parked our arses down the shed for a yarp. The milo too gave me the energy to give Ross a hand retrieving a few timber planks stored in shed rafters….
Without returning to the garden transformation I packed up my toys, shut up shop, and turned attention to awaiting night time activities….

Sunday 23 April 2006
While I idled over breakfast dishes, a group of passing currawongs thought they'd make themselves comfy in the yard, ha, ha!!!! Gee'd up by me and their squawking, Tia went racing all over the place enjoying the thrill of the chase. With that enthusiasm it didn't take long and their horrible sound was heading toward South Sister Range. Ms Muffet returned with enough buzzie burrs attached to her gorgeous outfit to keep me busy longer than it took to piss the currawongs off ☺….
Outside collecting water, the sound of a rough running engine could be heard lingering out front, taking a peek I saw Ross on his little grey fergie coming through the gate, that sight meant it was paddock art time. Placing the bucket aside I changed tack for exciting change to unfold. Between us we paced, sighted, measured and pegged, doing a dot to dot with pegs as a guide for the tractor and slasher to follow carving the love heart creation….
Making the first cut in the heart Fergus misfired like a mongrel, looking for a plug spanner rattling around amongst his possessions stored in the shed, I asked whether there was a sink washer amongst the treasure, "not here but there's one at home", came the reply from within. Without a plug spanner to fit Fergus, I drove Ross back to his place where the washer to fit the sink and the right tools just happened to be ☺….
Content to have watched the heart makings taking shape, I ducked inside and inserted the washer in the S-bend putting a halt to the annoying leak; there's now a reliable usable kitchen sink!!!!
The thought driving the creation of a slashed love heart in the paddock is for it to be viewed from the top of South Sister. Following the final tractor run the heart neatly presented itself to the world at a magnificent, 40 metres at its broadest, and a length totalling 60 metres ♥….

Each time I catch sight of the heart or remember to use the sink a beaming smile breaks out, although still unable to help myself I look for the 's' bend leak, a habit I'll have to get out of. It's uplifting for self-confidence when a repair is finalised and working ☺ ....

Monday 24 April 2006
The only courteous polite course to take after investing precious time into the idea, giving the concept thought, to planning, right through to the action stage, was to view the neatly carved paddock love heart from its desired vantage-point. Meaning a fitness workout climbing South Sister to her 850 metre summit lookout ☺ ....
Loose plans with Ross: weather permitting I'll ring to make arrangements before heading into St. Marys, which is what eventuated. Freeing up the day to climb the Sister I first did my bits in town. With a personal promise of the first flowers produced from the chrysanthemums would be picked and delivered to Evelyn, a gift that goes around. Today the promise blossomed ☺ ....
Popping a birthday card in the post for Kerry with simple words inscribed letting her know she's in my thoughts, finalised my list of bits. Ross and I shared a feed of hot chips getting carbohydrate levels right: chased down with an Evelyn cake and brew, we were ready then to tackle the mountain....
The road leading into the Sister eliminates a chunk of the walk. The last couple of hundred metres consist of a steep goats track made up of rock steps leading straight up an incline that requires a reasonable level of fitness....
Trying to pack the most in, we got ambitious in our excitement at making the heart as plump as possible, from the top of South Sister the right side is marginally obscured robbing the shapely heart of full exposure. Past the designated viewing area and requiring a mountain goat to pass the monstrous rocky outcrops to capture the right angle to fully see the heart, detracts from the initial purpose, however the carved paddock art was effective and neat ☺ ....

Tuesday 25 April 2006
The atmosphere was so breathlessly silent, overcast and perfectly still: a falling dried autumn leaf rattling its way through a tree to the ground was clearly audible the entire fall; absolute pristine peace ☺ ....
Perched in the bungalow over breakfast gazing out through the window overlooking the carved love heart, a pair of goshawks created movement within my viewing canvas inspecting the heart on their bypass. For them it was more than likely for food. The goshawk's rapid wing flapping and gliding style, being quite different from more commonly observed birds, and obvious colour gave their identity away ☺ ....
Back to reality: leaving the first load to soak in the washing machine Tia and I took the wheelbarrow for a walk out back, where a couple of hours can happily be lost pushing the barrow between there and the shed. Putting enough in the cottage woodbox to see another night out and a stash in the shed awaiting my muscle, I finally returned to washing....
Only breaking through momentarily as it was setting, the sun did very little toward drying anything on the line. It was predetermined the cottage furniture would be surrounding the heater decorated in clothes ☺ ....

Wednesday 26 April 2006
A made to order, perceived paradise perfect climate warranted an extra after breakfast milo to bask appreciating the bone warming dreamy morning. It was that warm even a lazy old blowfly got humming ☺....
Leaving the beanie parked on the shelf I propped a peaked cap on just to keep bloody long hair out of my eyes to see what I was doing! Tired of trying to manage the ten-month growth spurt I got proactive picking up the phone making an appointment for a haircut. Staying on the phone, I set-up a pick up point for the copper header tank at AEnone's and arranged a cuppa with Mary-Anne, filling a day out at St. Helens tomorrow....
Replacing the receiver I couldn't bear to be inside missing one of Eden's best. Sifting ash there was an almighty crack followed in quick succession by the crashing of a falling tree. Locals were certainly on the ball, within minutes the screaming motors of two chainsaws were staking claim, the swift response impressed me....
Rudely, Ross ribbed me about the amount of insect traffic that had shit on the bungalow window. Bugger he was right - removing the UV insulation the view now looks outstandingly clear. Zipping around inside and out, I did all but the original northerly windows of the cottage. Aged, weathered and delicate, the slightest bit of pressure could see them fall out ☺....

Thursday 27 April 2006
The moment I stopped ignoring the alarm and my feet hit the ground the day took me in its stride....
Planning on getting my wish list complete and making Mary-Anne's the last stop I got ready early enough to achieve the goal. The wish list was successfully completed but life set me another course to get there....
Reaching the base of the mountain St. Marys was lined with people, cameras and cars, not a common sight by any means. Just checking the Post Office box answers arrived, both St. Marys Pass and Elephant Pass were closed for several hours due to 'Targa Tasmania', to anyone other than me it's a well known island car event. With no sealed road open leading to St. Helens, and without a haircut in ten months and a header tank waiting to be picked up, I wasn't about to concede defeat!!!!
Heading back up the hill I took the unsealed Upper Scamander mountain road, pretty rough and second gear on many stretches it was a slow preserving journey to reach Scamander and bitumen. Made my destination with time only for a brief chat picking up the header tank at AEnone's before the long awaited haircut....
Feeling less weighted by hair I did my bits at the chemist and vet before knocking on the door of a lovely social time with Mary-Anne and her sprightly 92-year-old mother. Over food and hot brews time slipped away in chatter, reluctantly leaving to complete the 'to-do' list ☺....
The supermarket offered a brilliant special on milo; a 1.25 kg tin for $10. A trance however comes over me in the hardware store; I'm like a kid in a lollie shop. A quick check of the cock and ball thread of the header tank I bought two fittings to suit, also a new rubber cover to waterproof around the flue on the cottage roof and some goo to stick it down. With less fur on my head and a car loaded with treasure under the watchful eye of Tia, Destiny's nose was pointed back home to paradise and bitumen all the way to St. Marys ☺....

Proudly carrying the copper header tank into the cottage noticed the outlet has a female thread I bought both fittings to suit the male cock and ball thread.... Oops....
Bursting to share the news, I called Mum and Dad including them in the outcome of their Easter cheer gift, a header tank instead of a pub visit impressed them also.... And longer lasting ☺ ....

Friday 28 April 2006
Last evening's still silence delivered a continuous low rumble sound almost identical to that of distant thunder, arriving courtesy of surf breaking along the coastline. It was still audible crashing onto sand in the morning motionless atmosphere....
An occasion to be sensitive with the type of equipment used preferably operating something that respects the pristine quiet. Pre job planning, I'd been up on the cottage roof to oil a rusty nut and bolt and sized up and gathered tools when hunger pangs took over. Sitting on my bum sipping tea Pam and Terry rolled up, not only harbouring a possum to release but Evelyn cakes also ☺ ....
Finalising a pleasant social break, our visitors wandered back down the mountain into the valley. Armed with tools I climbed back up the ladder. Battling through lashings of old rubbery silicon to find screw heads, I began dismantling the perished waterproof seal surrounding the flue. The old perished seal was a little reluctant to move from its long seated position, virtually pulling the entire flue apart at roof level to install the new aqua-seal. Lining the newly installed seal seam with black sticky goo, then tacked the edge in rhythm with the contour of roofing iron corrugations, finishing up with a lap around the sealed edge with more goo ☺ ....
Looking over my shoulder running against the clock with a fast sinking sun, I had every piece of the flue back in place, confidently finishing the challenge, with spare time to scout the burnt out house for offerings of timber before being beaten by light....
Its humble origins as the original rain gauge, with a bucket placed at the base of the few linked pieces of flue left dangling through the roof when the original heater was stolen, was again later upgraded to a working heater. Harbouring a flue leak that was a constant source of distraction, trying several half-hearted waterproofing attempts, finally getting serious: if this repair job doesn't reap results I'll be shattered ☺ !!!!

Saturday 29 April 2006
Stripping the cottage woodbox bare, determined it was time to steer some life back into it. Putting repair work on hold, with all good intentions, I migrated to the burnt out house but got sidetracked at the compost heap. The distraction seed was planted just by wetting the heap; breaking down grasses use nitrogen and there was plenty of it just lying around. Fashioning a plastic two-litre milk carton I scooped it full twice with herbivore poo from the yard and mixed it into the brew. Wetting and burying all the goodies under a thick serving of slashed grass, the delicious layers were topped off with three large panes of glass; that should get it warmed up and working....
Taking in a fiery red sunset from the viewing vantage-point of the dam wall, easily distracted, my eyes were more focussed on the sight of nitrogen dotting on the ground. As the evening colour dimmed behind the mountain, grabbing pooper-scooper tools, I used fading light to fill

the milk container once again. Seeing wallaby poo in a whole different light it's now far more than that stuff I sometimes drag inside on my boots ☺ !!!!
My little mate didn't stop; if she wasn't rounding parrots out of trees surrounding housing she was on the trail of rabbits, taking a dip in her pool or, on occasion, hanging out with me. By the time a match was put to the heater Tia was happy to curl up in front snoozing, receiving the odd belly scratch waiting for dinner ☺ ….

Sunday 30 April 2006
The recognised and appreciated few consecutive days of absolute still perfect silence ended last night with the arrival of light wind. Delicate sounds of nature that could clearly and individually be identified have now, for the most, fused….
On the ever going pursuit of heater fuel I ended up tinkering in the dining room of the burnt out house. Pulling a small clump of grass discovered the buried hearth. Grabbing the shovel to divulge the treasure, I landed on my bum when a rotting floor board in front of the hearth collapsed underfoot. Dusting myself off, I revealed the hearth, salvaged some timber then took the wheelbarrow down the back cutting and filling it with fallen limb wood….
Since the pumpkins have matured and the plant died off, it's offered access to dig the last known stash of potatoes, bringing to the surface a good kilo of home grown ☺ ….
Yesterday comfy in a t-shirt today the beanie's pulled down over my ears. Milder easterly conditions shifting pure south, on occasion, looked like rain and felt more like it could snow as the afternoon shortened. The atmosphere being full of smoke created a hazy view blending with the band of cloud….
Come knock off and shut up shop, a fine mist pushed far enough over South Sister Range to lightly touch down on home soil, however, not heavy enough to be heard on an uninsulated tin roof. As the evening wore on wind pushed in a good steady soaking drop, enough to test flue waterproofing, first came the expectation waiting for the roof to leak, as time passed came the realisation it wasn't going to. Sitting quietly in a rocker light-hearted with pride looking at a dry heater top, I'm pretty bloody happy ☺ !!!! Yahoo, one less thing to think about ☺ ….

Monday 1 May 2006   "Happy Birthday Kerry"
Pulling up while we slept rain delivered a useful 22mm, for the moment the falls can be heard flowing from the loo. Over the moon, peeking in on a dry heater top put me in earshot of the ringing phone. Ross mentioned that south-east of town copped nearer to 2-inches, North and South Sisters held quite a load back. The purpose of Ross' call was to deliver good news; Evelyn sent him home with black sticky rice destined for me. Planning a trip over the mountain I didn't leave it behind ☺ ….
To know the full extent of my supermarket budget I started at the Top Shop with hardware first. Tracking pipe joiners and poly pipe, I couldn't get a ½ inch poly joiner with a male thread for the header tank, now the only missing link. Evelyn rarely fails to receive a visit; a black sticky rice thank you was included in today's. I don't know what's in black sticky rice because when I get the taste I can't stop, without fail eating the entire bloody pan full before nights end. A pleasant surprise waited at the Post Office, receiving an invitation to 'Exotica' a quilting exhibition opening at Gone Rustic this coming Wednesday, barring extreme conditions, the evening out is etched onto the calendar ☺ !!!!

Wishing just to be immersed in the familiar comforts of Rainbow Falls I hung around town no longer than had to and saved my cuppa for home. Utilising remaining daylight I scooped poo, tinkered with compost and snacked out on black sticky rice ☺....

Tuesday 2 May 2006
Rain has sent a few additional critters indoors looking for dryer lodgings. A couple of extra spiders came out of the woodwork and the pitter-patter of little feet could be heard scampering within the cottage ceiling ☺....
With the timing of a tuned radio I made it back from the loo before the first of several fine misting showers passed through; sun, cloud, wind and mist took turns featuring. Climatic conditions of late are suiting the love heart, greening up, highlighting its bold presence....
Feeling a bit clagged it was taking twice as long to do half as much. In need of wood I blew my energy ration in the shed. Pushing the last from my body, the wheelbarrow was filled from behind the cattle yards with faster burning limbs from the ground, that lot should keep the home fires burning....
A body in want of a dose of iron, meatloaf made the menu, with creamy mushroom and cheese potato bake and gravy for company. I'm impressed with the selection creatively leaving the heater top nowadays ☺....

Wednesday 3 May 2006
Identical weather patterns with of a dash of everything from wind, cloud, sunshine and the odd shower continued. Being generous pencilling the rainfall chart awarding 1mm to yesterday's total, it's just the smallest increment to work with ☺....
Sitting in the bungalow hugging a cup of tea looking out, I watched a wall of rain approaching and a parrot clinging to a fence post doing a balancing act with aerodynamics resting out a wind hammering. Strong gusts drove the front right at us and the freezing air temperature produced sludgy rain on the cusp of snow....
Preparing for my big night out spotted a large frame on the ground in a bordering paddock, a check through the binoculars with my good eye, I was pleasantly impressed to identify it as an eagle. Keeping my good eye focussed, the eagle lifted its huge frame and equally impressive wing span to find altitude joining its mate already circling overhead ☺....
Between dustings of mist, and always helped by my little mate, we ducked outside removing the perished 19mm hose connected to the 2-inch irrigation line, with the intention of downsizing it with 30 metres of reduced size garden hose. Factoring in hose size and length it should deliver reasonable pressure on site at the vegie patch saving kilometres of bucket carrying, but first, taking a step backward to go forward, an appropriate size adapter is required....
To get spruced up earlier in the day the electric stove got a run boiling up water. Ross phoned asking if I too got an invitation to the exhibition opening at 'Gone Rustic', establishing known facts we settled on a hot date attending together. The plan began by leaving from Ross' in his car because his shock absorbers are in a better state than Destiny's ☺!!!!
Rita and Ian's tastefully displayed exhibit, set amongst beautifully restored older style furniture, was received well. Comfortable, sharing conversation in a warm environment, it was easy to forget about the coldest day of the year lurking outside ☺.... Brrrr....

Thursday 4 May 2006
It was difficult leaving the heater last night to slide a semi-clad body under a doona waiting to use me for generating warmth....
As part of our idle chatter driving the mountain on our big night out, Ross suggested I fossick through his treasure stored in the shed I just might have luck finding the adapter and poly joiners I'm after. Failing with the header tank, on the flip side found an adapter to fit the irrigation line, the outstanding problem was then finding some tool to fit the job and tighten the bits. Demonstrating overkill, a large pipe wrench was the only tool successfully aiding with installation, step one for water to the vegie patch being a reality. Next step was minor repairs to the irrigation inlet at the dam; add a float, bleed air from the line and she's a goer☺....
Using an attached line to drag the inlet pipe via the float to deeper water within the dam, I tugged on the line one too many times, giving the system a few pumps up and down to get water flowing the float with line attached sailed free from the pipe. My knots surprisingly failed and the anchor dragged the pipe under the water surface obscuring it from view. Leaving a valve open down the line in a paddock to bleed air and encourage water through, I tentatively peeked around the corner from the dam to see water flowing. I'm happy to have broken even, with a line full of flowing water, water on tap, and the knowledge of the floatless pipe's location☺....
Tia instantly found use for the idle float. Claiming the 20 litre plastic drum she did a few excited laps around the yard nudging it along with her shoulder and nose☺....
Thirty metres of garden hose doubling back up hill on a gravity-fed system - the pressure isn't going to blow any joins apart but it reaches every corner of the vegie patch for long, slow, bucket and kilometre free watering. A huuuuge progressive step and without one leak in a high standard plumbing job☺!!!!

Friday 5 May 2006
Winter's going to be a long one. Autumn isn't getting much of a mention being pretty much bypassed. Today morphed into more respectable, finally shaking free of the tiring wind for a little calm consistency. Cooler conditions are certainly preferable to the bloody restricting limiting heat of summer, now not only is there access to all areas snake free, I've got energy and a desire to participate and accomplish....
Wanting to achieve a few bits in town I packed the family into Destiny and rattled our way over the mountain. It amused me immensely having to give way, not to one, but two cars turning out of the mountain; usually I'm lucky to pass a single car the entire eight kilometre trip, nearly as much chance of winning lotto. St. Marys Pass being closed for repairs all week has sent a higher volume of traffic through the Upper Scamander mountain road....
Parked outside the Post Office writing comments on the back of a set of photos to send off as a letter for Mum's special day in May, Brian and Maggie strolled into view. Following hugs they invited me back for a brew and with nothing to stop me I went. Sharing our humble journeys latest developments, I spoke of the header tank excitement and frustration of the missing link stopping progress, and being almost ready to take the one hundred kilometre trip to the hardware store just to get the right fitting. Brian opened a box of plumbing bits and said "here, is this what you're after". Every time I see that fitting on the header tank that act of kindness will spring to mind☺....

Making it home with enough light left to unpack Destiny and spend quality time with my little mate playing the latest craze of throwing the 20 litre plastic drum again, and again, and again, and again. Unbelievable, I'm rugged against the cold night air: sprinting around Tia warmed up enough to pull the game and dunk her body in the cattle trough ☺!!!! Brrrr....
Opening the fridge to make a start on dinner a rank smell filled the bungalow putrefying air. What switched my senses off turned Tia's on - she made short work of the browning tray of wallaby mince.... What can I say ☺ ????

Saturday 6 May 2006
With a new rooster on the block to save the gene pool Brian laid the old one to rest, still fresh, its carcass joined us on the trip home yesterday, if Tia wasn't interested in eating it the compost could make use of it. Spilling its body from the bag Tia straight away took claim to the treasure, within ten minutes she had the rooster's body covered in compost, in the oven and cooking. Nagging me out of bed this morning with 'the paw tap', Tia went straight over checking the chooks oven bake progress, marked the surrounding ground, then joined me for breakfast.... There's no stopping a hard working girl ☺....
The concept of having the header tank installed was put on hold; the need for wood took priority. A healthy woodbox and enough of enough to get us through I put the header tank through its paces, testing for leaks and or weaknesses - it failed. Better now than installed in the ceiling. A seeping leak slowly trickled from above the bottom outlet, however there are never problems, just solutions waiting to be found, and the solution walked through the door offering to solder the leak, also bringing a long absent friend with him. Ross had convinced Loui to escape the biggest smoke for a few days of country living. While we sat warm and relaxed talking of where we've been and are now heading, the sun set on another day in paradise. It's always nice to melt in the comfort of the heater laughing with good friends ☺....

Sunday 7 May 2006
Gentle rain massaged my brain into consciousness petering out not long after bringing me tranquilly around, dropping a useful 4mm. Without the heater blazing, a minor, non distracting drip follows the flue down. Wanting to replace it at some stage I didn't seal the flue water tight with goo keeping components easier to pull apart....
My 'personal support program' case manager made arrangements for a visit, so I got life's bits ticking over and complete before Sandra arrived. Staying for a good hour, after a short walk we made ourselves comfortable in the bungalow chatting over milo....
Leading on from Sandra's visit I planted my bum next to the phone breaking the peace at Mum and Dad's, then its a case of covering everything new and all the fine detail associated since we last spoke, that's not a brief task ☺....
Re-emerging outside, the warm airflow that earlier had me stripping down to a t-shirt cutting a little wood had shifted to pure icy south. Seeing the sunset from behind glass with heater blazing, a front burst forth a short shower leaving me lean against the window on the look out for snow.... Brrrr....

Monday 8 May 2006
Come rain, hail or shine the washing had to be tackled, and shine it did, not only good weather wise it was also a good day for eagle sightings. Sitting on my throne, and clear to view, I watched a pair circling by South Sister, later hanging over the washing machine saw another on descent through the cottage window ☺ ....
With one of the fifty loads of washing on the go, Ross phoned with an invitation to join him and Loui for a roast dinner, only a fool would say no. Let's say I didn't shed a tear when Ross broke the news of our mayor dying, now there's more room for progressive thinking on Council, and a little less mateship profiteering legitimately disguised in bureaucracy....
Making it halfway through the fifty loads of washing, I pulled up to freshen the water and left a load to soak overnight, because it was time to get organised for my hot date with Ross and Loui for a roast dinner. Dressing in what few clean clothes were left, Destiny's nose was pointed at the mountain ☺ ....
I so love good food, the enjoyment is heightened when it's cooked for me. Treated to a dream night in utopia, chocolate pudding and ice cream followed the roast and red wine. Handling the pressure, I did little more than relax and consume. The mood of the evening was uplifting, light-hearted and happy. Laughter is good for the soul ☺ ....
Driving home was done in contentment, smiling, reflecting on an evening I would repeat. Caring to repeat an experience is my gauge of an exceptionally good time ☺ ....

Tuesday 9 May 2006
With a stomach still full from the night before I had to earn an appetite for breakfast. As soon as my feet hit the ground the wheelbarrow got pushed down the back and two loads of dry wood had been carted to the shed by 9:30am ready for downsizing. From there on in a course was already chosen, getting back into the waiting washing....
Two brief misting showers set the stage for the cottage and furniture to get decorated in drying clothes. On occasion the skies cleared, but wind gusts were too bloody strong to even consider putting clothes on the line if I wanted to remain sane ☺ !!!!
Leaving clothes to dangle from everything available me and my little mate disappeared down the shed. Tia pitted her skill catching raindrops falling from the shed roof courtesy of a passing shower; I did the usual thing exercising the handsaw ☺ ....

Wednesday 10 May 2006
Stirred from sleep getting the paw tap, reluctantly I raised my body from a warm bed for wee's.
The simple act of opening the bungalow door cleared the yard. A startled possum took refuge scampering up the bungalow wall; having nothing to grip beyond the wall stopped it from climbing onto the steep sloping roof. Like a jack-in-the-box on lead, Tia sprung up after the potential meal getting close enough to sniff tail fur. Tucked back into bed and listening without choice, the slightly stirred but unharmed rowdy possum clawed its way around bungalow eaves, finishing the commotion off with a scene cartoons are designed from. Unable to get a grip on a piece of sloping guttering the possum wore its talons down trying to. A light thud signified hitting the ground and silence fell for peaceful sleep once again ☺ ....

Living on the fringe of nature has many rewards. Daydreaming hugging a warm milo over breakfast I watched an eagle glide into view; keeping my brain entertained the milo disappeared unnoticed.... Not a bad start ☺....

With very little variety remaining in our diet payday came around none too soon - spruced up driving between the Sisters was the target. Doing the regular drinking water stop triggered a spell of socialising, catching Ross and Loui in struck it lucky for a brew and snack ☺....

Momentarily cashed up and loaded with groceries, I paid Brian and Maggie a visit, giving Maggie money to cover hamburger ingredients she's generously making for beer, barbecue and bullshit, following the big day out at home rescheduled gorge walk. Popping in on Brian and Maggie is never a rushed experience, courteously taking the quality time required to enjoy company sharing over a brew or two ☺....

Thursday 11 May 2006

An absolute gorgeous autumn day in paradise, warm enough, in fact, to pry the beanie free, shed layers and don the sun hat....

Preparing a bed to plant garlic a car towing a squeaky trailer turned into the gateway. Ross had turned up with his chainsaw to cut a load of old weather beaten fence posts. Following toasted sandwiches and a brew we disappeared behind the cattle yards, as Ross cut I loaded. Keeping up with the chainsaw pushing a loaded wheelbarrow up a short incline to the trailer, I endured a good workout.... Phew ☺....

Meeting back at the shed Ross helped unload, knowing the hours of hand sawing involved in creating such a stack I was beside myself with such a huge workload lifted. Preferring to barter than leave favours hanging, Ross was happy with a few posts and a small load of firewood for his effort....

With several weeks catered for it's a bloody relief not living from day to day with wood, it's also been a while since I've seen the cottage woodbox overflowing ☺....

Friday 12 May 2006

With a belly already full on carbonara, my little mate topped up on breakfast gorging on a kindly donated possum carcass. Her only interest then was to move from one sunny spot to another snoozing. Tia was half-hearted in the help stakes today. In doggy utopia, a content look never left Tia's face it was seemingly painted on ☺.... Joining in on the possum feast, a kookaburra must have been disturbed, leaving the prized find of an intestine neatly piled on top of a fence post.... Attractive!!!!

My bed copped attention first. With the doona airing I changed over mattress covers. The red sleeping bag went to be washed while the green one got a run. Attention turned next to emptying the heater to make room for another fire; taking one step backward to take one forward, I first relieved the ash drum of its cooled load; sifting and separating I binned another half kilo of nails. I took the drum containing the heater's fresh contents down the shed to cool any remaining embers in readiness to repeat the procedure when it's screaming out for attention again.... The squeaky wheel gets the oil around here ☺....

Putting in a big finish, autumn turned on a t-shirt temperature just magic for being outside doing odds 'n' sods. Heater taken care of, I played around wetting up a garden bed for garlic and tinkered with compost. Doing a zip around the yard I pooper scooped just over two 2-litre

plastic milk containers full of wallaby nitrogen, contributing it to the interesting developing composting brew????
Still content outside, but beaten by fading light, I used the last of it to cart evening food and writing needs from the bungalow into the cottage. A large, bright full moon set in a clear sky made sure visibility outside remained transparent....

Saturday 13 May 2006
A first in many moons; mouse poo was left behind in the cottage. It's been so long - confidence was growing!!!!
To keep my hand in so as not to forget what it's all about, I cut and filled the wheelbarrow with light fallen branches to use as fire starters. Fire and water once again sorted it was onward to the garden ☺....
Both Peaches and the freshly prepared garden bed felt the nurturing of a watered in compost feed, then the garlic cloves were ready to poke into their lovingly prepared new home. Returning a bit of goodness, I scouted around for wallaby poo adding it to the taxed compost heap ☺....
Bursting with pride at the garlic sitting neatly in the ground, at that point the thought of a beer crossed my mind. The cupboard empty, it wasn't about to happen. Calling in to pick up possum release boxes Pam and Terry left me with two bottles of home brew stout; so excited, I went crazy drinking both ☺!!!! Hic, the universe was listening ☺....

Sunday 14 May 2006
Another magic moment with nature occurred over breakfast. Scraping toast crumbs outside the bungalow door I settled back in to finish off my milo. Grabbing at the opportunity, a robin hen bounced around by the doorway snacking on the crumb offerings. I really delight in fauna being close without the need for fear ☺....
Unsure of exactly what direction the day was going to take, before getting my teeth into anything distracting I first took pleasure in phoning Mum for Mothers Day ☺....
A wonderfully simple yet peaceful time home working around usual bits, spending the lions share of daylight hours making a little more sense of the burnt out house elevated garden. Tidying through the first five metres past the garlic bed, severely pruning, turning soil and digging out a couple of shrub stumps, cleared ground past Peaches with the idea for future vegetable plantings ☺....

Monday 15 May 2006
Mother Nature turned on a beanie-free bone warmer in paradise doing her best at perfection; us humans on the other hand, we're hell bent on exploiting anything from it. The drone of heavy machinery could faintly be heard. Smoke filling the valley and surrounding mountain ranges gave away the location of yet another spent logging site and a simple waste of timber....
For a couple of weeks the neighbour's dog has been giving me the shits. Left alone for long stretches it does nothing but call out with a painful, empty hearted, lonely cry. I can't even bring myself to call the by-laws officer because it will only be the dog that'll be punished. Its very existence sounds punishment enough. The saddest thing of all is when the dog echoes its lonely cry when the neighbours are home....

The little rodent leaving an obvious trail of its presence in the cottage made the fatal mistake of getting stuck in the bath and getting assistance from Tia to get out. It's now keeping the composting chook company....

Pushing the ride-on to level ground checked its vitals, then with a spot of pre mowing preparation took my little mate and shovel into the cattle yards to find rocks and other foreign objects the blades might reject. It was there I got sidetracked. Knocking a clump of grass from a rickety internal dividing fence I ended up tidying the entire section on the mission for rocks. Those too large to budge were clearly exposed. Combing the area thoroughly made for slow progress, only managing to scan a third of the entire area. Daylight hours fast closing in, the sun bathed mower was pushed back in the shed and we knocked off to zip between the Sisters before sunset....

Saving me the entire trip, I made a cuppa stop at Ross' to pick up bread and milk he carted back from town. With the basics I'm sweet to remain hermiting for another couple. Ross also created work for me adding a soldered header tank to the take home treasure, woohoo☺....

Tuesday 16 May 2006

Another piece of ground stripped bare in a short term money grab; air was again fouled with smoke. Present day actions will be remembered in the future as a forest cancer, but for today it's an extra puff of ventolin and get on with it. Sadly I didn't even consider the prospect that it could be a bushfire!!!!

Reiterating a dose of reality, I cannot manage or carry the emotion of anything outside of the nucleus of farm gates. I returned my brain back to appreciating the utopian life led inside Rainbow Falls' boundary....

With daily essentials filled, stacked, tidied or cleaned, and nothing left to distract, me and my best friend returned to the cattle yards on the hunt for obstacles mower unfriendly. A concrete ramp tracing across the back of the shed is covered in pieces of steel of all descriptions. Grass and autumn leaves hide the area from sunlight and a patch of sycamore saplings are growing in cracks in the concrete. The area has never made the priority list: including it in pre-mowing clearing I sorted through making a termite hole in a corner for future inspiration....

Resting my bum and shovel I squeezed in one tank prior to the sun setting; it's starting to look pretty good☺....

Wednesday 17 May 2006

My bum cheeks copped a workout, not only from sliding around on the seat but from gripping, squeezing tight. My arse did its bit in keeping the mower upright. The front right wheel got a bit light and was ready to lift on one occasion.... Eeeek!!!!

Coxy the ride-on is a gutsy little machine that makes short work of anything served up. My initial intentions were only to complete the cattle yards. Getting excited I was unable to help myself with my bum comfy in the seat. Getting the bug to spread and expanded asked Coxy to hill climb going places I've never been mowing. Pushing a clearing, Coxy did a circuit of the dam. Ready to level out, I played around just inside the paddock by the shed stirring up weeds and mice, emptying the tank prior to the curtain closing on another one....

Hovering cloud blocked the setting sun from view shortening an already short evening. With lights out by the 5:30pm limit, and minus moonlight assistance, I raced against the clock slamming together a load of wood from the usual haunts, doing it with time to spare ☺ ....

Thursday 18 May 2006
Words fail to spill from the pen accurately describing the moving inner feeling experienced opening the bungalow door the morning after achieving something outstanding outdoors, a sensation felt rather than verbalised. The only fitting thing to do was to go for a walk amongst it and simply enjoy the tidy splendour freshly mowed surfaces provide ☺ ....
Loading drinking water into Destiny Ross rolled up and offered to put the kettle on, bleeding his spleen over work politics hazed my brain over. Finding the bottom of the cup after a verbal punishing I left him to the bullshit to finish the bone-jarring trip into town....
The Post Office box delivered mixed blessings: on one hand there was a welcome card from Mum and Dad, on the other a chain-letter from some idiot that promptly found a bin. Making pleasant but brief stops at Rita's and Evelyn's respectively, we returned back up the hill. After an eight day absence from the outside world I can't wait to get out of it and return to the comfort offered at home....
Abstaining from walking inside the pub doors for the past 6 weeks, today beer o'clock, walkabout and beer burps followed me home with complements of Mum and Dad. Enjoying the great outdoors at the close of business sampling a taste of the amber fluid, my little mate got me doing what I do best; kicking the ball again and again and again and again ☺ ....

Friday 19 May 2006
A light sprinkling may have helped settle lingering smoke filled air, but it wasn't until near on beddy bye's time did anything audible happen on the tin roof. Even then the brief light shower certainly didn't drive the need to start building an ark ☺ ....
Giving resting muscles a slight warm, light timber was cut commencing an afternoon happily lost in the shed. From the haven I watched Tia with interest zigzag, sniffing her way through a paddock, drawing me out to seek what the attraction harboured. The outcome of paddock exercise saw the black cat, still alive and well, flee the scene!!!!
When beer o'clock finally crept in the shed was ready to greet visitors. Both levels of Destiny's bedroom were swept and tidied, and many hours of stacked wood sat idly waiting for gorge walkers to share it ☺ ....

Saturday 20 May 2006
In need of a little brain therapy to boost enthusiasm, I wandered poo scoopering which in turn lead into a play in the compost, putting myself in the right mood to face the remainder of the day. True to habit I procrastinated doing anything representing a distraction away from awaiting domestic duties, and true to form they waited....
Taking ingredients into the cottage, Ross called in delivering the barbecue for post gorge walk entertainment, a pleasant distraction taking the weight off my feet for a short while. Returning to the waiting ingredients, my little mate proved very attentive help: never failing to splatter cream thickening it, Tia willingly cleaned up every morsel splashed within reach ☺ ....

Unleashing my cake making creativity designed a chocolate ripple cake shaped into the number four: the significance - tomorrow is four years to the day we reached the soil of Rainbow Falls to follow wherever it led. 1460 days of growth, learning, challenges, acceptance, progress and importantly finding inner peace, in that time have lived volumes ☺ ....

Sunday 21 May 2006
Very fitting and appropriate for the 4th anniversary of our existence at Rainbow Falls, paradise was just that, 'paradise'. Even the alarm didn't faze the feel good mood. Barely conscious and rolling over to further sleeping, the annoying electronic beep, beep, beep, was hard to ignore after a continuous ten minutes....
At an underlying personal level, aside from the anticipated gorge walk, today presented an air of expectance. Setting both fires with time to spare, I then got the Rainbow Falls large rainbow flag positioned high and proud above the front gate before the planned 11a.m. meeting time. Feeling like a symbol of healing and future, with my little mate, marched proudly to the front gate with the flag tied to a five-metre thin tree limb flapping in the breeze draped over my shoulder. Securing the flagpole to the gatepost, the front gate was then opened for friends to enter and they did ☺ ....
In a steady flow each invited gorge walker arrived and was greeted with a friendly hug, in quick succession Dave and Liz, Pam and Terry, followed closely behind by Ross, pulled up out back. Armed with cuppa's and the number four shaped chocolate ripple cake we headed to the social hub, 'the shed' ☺ ....
Latest events and sugar levels right, we mingled our way, encouraging, assisting and informing through the predominantly dry, rocky stream. All walkers passionate and appreciative of natural nature the gorge presented a lot to a few. Nearing the end of the walk greeting the steepest section leading up to the falls, scaling rocky surfaces, loose in parts, Liz's sheer guts and determination to return to the top of the falls with a gorgeous 5kg rock impressed ☺ ....
Taking the scenic route, Brian and Maggie arrived in perfect timing for the beer, barbecue and bullshit component when activity around the shed heater sprang into life ☺ ....
Tia was in doggy utopia: with the excitement of the walk over, food began dripping out of humans' hands. When that flow stopped and coals cooled she obligingly gave the barbecue a thorough clean ☺ ....
Our guests left, waving the last farewell 6p.m.-ish. Shutting the gate, I again ceremoniously carried the flagpole, with flag flapping, over my shoulder to the shed signing off on a brilliant occasion shared. If I had to put an order in for a designed day it wouldn't have been any different than the one that naturally happened. Leaning on the warm pole only centimetres from the heater hugging dying embers, I knew then it was time to sign off and venture indoors ☺ ....

Monday 22 May 2006
At the same pace I do most things, being one foot in front of the other, began the clean up process, with tidy, civilised friends it wasn't difficult. Tia already put me one step ahead by doing an exceptional job cleaning the barbecue hot plate ☺ ....

Starting the tidy up marathon I found the bungalow then shuffled between the cottage and shed ferrying bits back to where they came from....

It must be due to a huge dose of social activity, not to mention a few beers, causing me to be a little absent-minded. Zapping a Liz home baked roll to eat warm with butter, I opened the microwave door after the cycle finished and laughed at myself to find it empty. Getting the process right second time round ☺!!!!

Warmer autumn weather lasted long enough to see us through the big day out at home, today sun did little other than illuminate our world, the air temperature was on the icy side definitely one to keep hands buried in pockets....

Tuesday 23 May 2006

An empty beer bottle strewn outside the shed door isn't a naturally occurring phenomenon and gained attention, leaving rubbish lying around isn't a habit of mine. A possum was able to claw the bum out of a rubbish bag hanging from a nail on a shed beam; usually critter safe, a plank of wood leaning on the wall next to it provided a ramp!!!!

An ideal magical start, fogged in with mist, the small token of moisture was welcome to a browning off yard, however, not exactly ideal for laundry. Unfortunately the sun broke through, and with laundry up to my armpits, offered no excuses for postponement ☺!!!!

Doing a quick pooper scoop while the weather made up its mind, then began the ongoing trek to the cattle trough. The hose would reach into the cottage but the lack of pressure would slow down a procrastinator, and I'd also have to change my thinking ☺....

I seemingly no sooner got washing on the line than to turn around and bring it back in to decorate furniture. What warmth the sun had made a start drying clothes for the heater to finish off.... Getting through the day gets me through the day ☺....

Wednesday 24 May 2006

A carbon copy of yesterday, starting with about a millimetre of mist before moisture shot through, although in contrast there wasn't much direct sun sighted today....

It felt like visiting a comfortable old friend, slipping down the shed warming up cutting and splitting wood while my best friend snoozed in Destiny. The mercury didn't get too excited so only jobs to ward off the chill made the great outdoors comfortable. When the heater and woodbox were taken care of, like a bee to the honey pot, migrated to make a bit more sense of the elevated garden....

Shortening days and season change have had an obvious effect on thinking patterns and priorities; make hay while the sun shines, the 'gotta be done's' get done first without dilly-dally. Like clockwork, the 5:30pm lights out curfew so quickly takes over sending us in to get into the evening indoor stuff....

Thursday 25 May 2006

There comes a time when one has to leave the comfort of home to make the pilgrimage into the outside world between the Sisters. The rough as guts road linking us to St. Marys received its annual quick lick over by the grader, knocking the top off corrugations and spreading rocks. Some rocks, at a guess, were up to a couple of kilo's in size. Marginally better, but still nothing special....

Wondering who could be asked to sew the bum back into a pair of tracksuit pants was shocked by the answer, nominating myself for the job. It was meant to be: when popping into Rita's studio a woman selling craft supplies was in store. I now at least possess the tools for the job. I haven't plied a needle for at least twenty years, never has been a favourite pastime ☺!!!!
Included in a welcoming hug gorge walk day, I received a gentle pinch below my shoulder blade, the reason behind the gentle pinch came to light when we met in town today. To consider betraying the vows sworn to someone as honest and true hearted as his wife is nothing short of shameful!!!!
Wrapped like a mummy against cold, from a viewing vantage-point at the top boundary my little mate and me watched the final few minutes of sun before it slid gracefully behind the mountain.
Blanketed in cloud, a slit opening above the distant westerly mountain ranges opened a space of opportunity permitting the sun to breakthrough one last time. Edging out through the gap in cloud and tracing its way overland, watched in appreciation sunlight slowly drench the valleys below inching toward us with a flooding golden light. Once again I cast a shadow, if only briefly. Paradise provided a high energy peaceful end ☺....

Friday 26 May 2006
A really odd thing occurred, stemming back to when Cousin Mark visited with his mate Gavin, and they brought with them a cutlery set with complements of Mum and Dad. From the time of the boys visit there has only ever been five teaspoons, doing breakfast dishes teaspoon number six magically returned to the set, how bizarre ☺????
Just as they disappear they come back. On the way to the loo I counted a cloud of 42 bloody squawking pests pass over and land in the island of trees above the top boundary. There was currawong action in the skies all around but none dropping in, that I can live with!!!!
Just a quick scoop around housing every second day gives me a 2-litre container of fresh poo, highlighting a good active population of native marsupial nightlife....
After Ross left with his trailer and barbecue following behind, my brain homed in on making plant food. Scraping up several wheelbarrow loads of mower cuttings added them to the establishing compost pile at the rear of the burnt out house. Packing the grass in I stomped all over the pile then dribbled through wallaby poo liquid fertiliser. Adding a third hose extension got water on site to wet up the delicious brew. Loving the idea of running water from a hose Tia added another game to her repertoire of the big game of life ☺....

Saturday 27 May 2006
Autumn made it clear it hasn't finished; in fact it was warm enough for my little mate to take a dip in her pool; simply gorgeous to be outdoors we did just that. It felt decadent shifting a hose in the garden; the flow rate isn't going to run a sprinkler but it's not going to wear my feet out either ☺....
The ol' empty the heater and sift the ash routine got a run; another milo tin full of rusty nails, staples and useless bits found its way into household rubbish. Staying put on site advanced the slow but progressive tidy up at the burnt out house with a stint on the shovel. Turning charred remains in a concrete edged dirt strip running parallel to the rear of the house, removed unwanted useless bits for the future purpose of converting it into usable ground for planting....

I don't know what it was that caught my attention, but looking up from the shovel saw bloody currawongs quietly feeding around the loo. Unable to leave them in peace, a walk up the hill revealed about forty had sleazed in. Stirring them up they lifted like a cloud flying in the direction of South Sister Range. Leaving with a racket, at least another hundred pest birds in fragmented noisy packs dripped from the island of trees by the top boundary joining the leading pack…. Stuff my worst nightmares are made of ☺ !!!!

Sunday 28 May 2006
Greeting more poo again this morning from rodent activity in the cottage pushed buttons to fire me into action leaving behind a box of feed they'll takeaway only. A harsh move by someone so peace loving, but their presence is extremely unhealthy and our food supply doesn't need any more competition ☺ !!!!
Each time there's something placed on the wish list to achieve, like sewing clothes or sowing seed, plumbing, reading, etc, it's lined up on the bed as a nagging visual reminder for each occasion I walk into the cottage. With all good intentions at starting on clearing the 'to-do' piles off the bed, I didn't eliminate one ☺ ….
Visit day by my case manager, Sandra, lasted the usual average hour over a brew and chat. Still in the sit down frame of mind I ventured to the cottage for a settle in chat with Mum and Dad, leaving no stone unturned from sport, politics, social to family ☺ ….
Reduced to t-shirt and sun hat I remained inside until the glorious burst of sun lost its sting. As the shadow shifted on the sundial layers of clothes continued to increase. Slipping the sun hat from my head reached for the Nana Raye hand knitted Collingwood beanie, Dad said Collingwood is doing extremely well this football season and a flag is looking promising???? Like a magnet, with every spare moment I migrate to the burnt out house continuing the transformation, playing compost maker, garden creator and hose shifter ☺ ….

Monday 29 May 2006
Stirring up the usual rattles and clunks wind moved in yesterday evening. Lifting in momentum, gusts randomly roused me from sleep throughout the night, then to really offer a treat stayed all day….
Looking like anything could happen I prepared for a couple of wet days just incase. For extra insurance brought in several wheelbarrow loads of light limb wood for dry storage, but not a drop fell from the sky. Aside the give-away cold, outside looks more like we're heading into summer, with only 10mm falling for May to this point. U, usually lush and green by now, grass is browning off????
Eagles seem to thrive in strong wind. Almost never failing to see them cruising this side of the mountain in blustery conditions, using wind to their advantage, a pair gained elevation getting a better view on the hunt for their next meal ☺ ….
Slow to get my brain around change, took a huge step by collecting water for the cottage from the hose. Far less effort involved, daydreaming holding the hose for a couple of minutes filling the bucket then simply walking it the few metres inside almost felt lazy. The more I use the hose the more uses I find for it….

Going walkabout through the slashed love heart taking in another spectacular sunset I found a misplaced treasure. Tia's one and only remaining intact furless tennis ball revealed its hiding spot, re-entering circulation put skud ball back on the menu☺.... Kick it again....

Tuesday 30 May 2006
Yesterday's urgency to store a supply of dry wood could have waited. Autumn isn't done with us yet....
Low on milk for my brew a trip over the mountain was absolutely necessary. The boiler left on the heater overnight was cold so I left it in the hands of electricity to power up some hot water. While the boiler did its thing me and Ms Muffet went walkabout, me pooper scoopering and thistle kicking; Ms Muffet wrestled the 20-litre drum and barked at birds☺....
Enjoying the peace and serenity at home I didn't dilly-dally in St. Marys. The longest stop was for a chat with Evelyn then it was straight home. Having the fire set for another night, like moths to a flame, played around in the garden until the sun set on yet another day in life at paradise☺....

Wednesday 31 May 2006
Plans spinning around in my head stirring to consciousness to further progress cottage waterproofing were soon changed. Opening the bungalow door greeting silently falling morning drizzle ended a dry month leading into winter....
The first sign of rain after a dry spell it's almost tradition to head to the shed where the store of dry wood is taxed into, spending a couple of dry hours under the roof simply appreciating the gentle mist. A favourite climatic element, fogged in with the sensation of being cut off from the outside world fills me with energy, luckily because there was plenty of wood to cut☺!!!!
At lunchtime the token moisture fall pulled up at 2mm, by then I'd had a pretty good warm-up on the handsaw also. Roaming outdoors took on a more sedate pace, adding seeds to garden beds I poked broccoli, spinach, spring onions and brown onions under a fine layer of soil, supplying company for Peaches, garlic, and tulips....
Putting pessimism aside regarding fringe benefits for the recently deceased mayor, eternal optimism returned dividends. It seems maintenance equipment does know how to wander this far up the hill. Finishing the job off this morning, a pair of tractors roadside slashing did a tidy job out front slashing within a foot of home fenceline; I'm pleased to say it looks great☺!!!!

Thursday 1 Winter 2006
Waking on the wrong side of the bed and feeling cranky, nature turned that around. Catching sight of a rainbow draped over South Sister Range distracted negative thoughts and took them to a better place. Rainbows require both moisture and sun and for a short while we had both. Limbo was kind enough to hang until I'd visited the loo with a view. Walking back and watching it over my right shoulder, the rainbow was soon clouded in and given a wash. Pushing in from an easterly direction rain set in....
Leaving behind a sprinkling of silver balls is a telltale sign a bearing has collapsed. At this stage I'm unaware if it's associated to a squealing noise related to the mowers forward movement. Without the luxury of a cash flow I parked the ride-on mower on the flat, top section of the shed, preparing to have a go at fixing it myself. Giving grief to start: that was

tracked to a free ranging accelerator cable. Manually giving throttle I started the beast, offering me another puzzle to solve. With poor light to clearly see what I was doing, plus feeling a little sensitive, thought mower repairs were a job better left for some other more suitable occasion☺!!!!

Nothing seriously took my interest down the shed so I wandered my sorry arse to the cottage, self-indulgently sparked up the heater and spent the afternoon burning yesterday's hard work. Fiddle farting around indoors the cottage was reclaimed from vermin giving it that clean sensation once again....

The combination of mowing and recent rain has sent quite a number of tiny pitter pattering feet inside. Having a peaceful moment in a rocker, a mouse pulled up startled near me, it did a quick about turn and vanished through a gap in floor boards. Unable to wait to get their teeth into the next box of 'take-away only', it already had a mouse hole chewed into it before it was removed from the cupboard and opened!!!!

Friday 2 June 2006

The morning rainbow on display really did mean what it represented. Heavy looking rain cloud lurked about but delivered nothing. Spurred on purely by the power of suggestion, armed with roof and gutter sealing black goo, grabbed the ladder and filled a few holes. The roof area above the power-board received attention, and a particularly bad leak in the shed roof was also filled with goo. Happy with the outcome, I returned to the job started before getting sidetracked☺....

Accepting the challenge of rolling up the 120 metres of 2-inch poly pipe, unravelled for pumping from the bore, it had been left laying on the ground for convenience and remained in the too hard basket. Thoughts led to using the car garage as a sensible storage area; taking one look inside at loose hay left littering the floor after storage was finished, decided on a clean up first. Like many jobs, I take several steps backward to make one forward. Putting in a day's work achieved what I initially set out to, patiently winding; strapped the poly pipe to itself binding the roll together and placed it in the freshly swept garage☺....

A huge pack of currawongs still squawking their way over surrounding countryside nomadically feeding definitely can't sneak anywhere. I reckon, by chance, I've been dealt a favour having long grass in paddocks because they're not keen on landing in them. Dripping out of the sky yesterday, the bloody pests filled an adjacent neighbouring paddock. The few encounters at home have only been in cleared ground.... An incentive to leave grass long☺!!!!

Tracking down the source of a rotten poo aroma found it decorated around Tia's neck; gloved up she copped a twilight bath. Pretty ordinary, her neck was shampooed three times.... Phew!!!!

Saturday 3 June 2006

Looking like rain and having tapped into the dry supply, the privileged large cut pieces fast running out and the cottage woodbox needing filling, it was time to gather more limb wood from the ground. Overloading the wheelbarrow and me, only one trip was done because mist began falling before loading was finished the first of many passing fronts added another couple of millimetres to Thursdays sixteen. Steps two and three in the wood process, cut then fill the woodbox, chewed into a good chunk of the daily time offering....

Both contributions to the flue and shed roof waterproofing failed, my cup being half full, saw the shed drip improved by 95% and the flue is frustratingly nearly there!!!!

Winding down from a high energy spurt with the saw, me and my little mate went walkabout adding a couple of barrow loads of lawn clippings and scooped wallaby poo to compost piles. A large metre thick pile with a couple of dead chooks buried within is brewing out back of the burnt out house, and one of a smaller scale developing in the fenced off vegie patch, both receive regular feeds….

Recent offerings of moisture have got bulbs rattling their dags. Clumps of spurs are breaking through ground and reaching for sunlight; activity is most outstandingly obvious across the base of the dam….

Creeping up early and quickly, the curtain closes on light as the sun slips behind the mountain. After enjoying the pleasures of yet another spectacular sunset the experience was topped by putting my slippers on and hugging a milo propped in a rocker in front of a blazing fire…. ahhhh A fitting way for one happy camper to wind down ☺….

Sunday 4 June 2006

Getting back into wood collecting Rainbow Falls' style, with the meagre selection of tools, me, my little mate, wheelbarrow, handsaw and bottle of water disappeared behind the cattle yards fossicking. Roaming in and along the top of the gorge I dragged out a good stash of 2-4 inch limbs in no time. Pushing three wheelbarrow loads of limb wood up hill, not only got me stripping also stripped my get up and go. There's plenty of wood laying around it's just a matter of getting it out. One thing is for sure; its a pleasure going after it the views are spectacular ☺….

Waiting for my energy to regain composure before cutting a few limbs down to size, first played in the compost adding a layer of the finished product to newly formed garden beds. Continuing with the energy recovery theme, my bum was firmly parked for a good session on the phone to Mum and Dad exhausting new and old news. Recently having been to the surgeon for a check-up Mum again returned with favourable feedback. This November will be four years since the nasty operation and thankfully there's not a sign of secondary cancer. Mum's certainly got to be able to take a step out of the woods by now ☺!!!!

Monday 5 June 2006

The first doozy of a white frost decorated the ground and lingered in shaded areas until 10a.m.-ish, not quite cold enough to ice over the cattle trough….

Although a little flighty, robins are a regular visitor at breakfast, bopping around the bungalow doorway after toast crumbs. On occasion a cute rotund hen will hop onto the step, only to shit itself after catching sight of the big monsters inside. It keeps my simple needs amused ☺….

How quickly time passes. Bulging to overflow, the washing machine tub contained most of my meagre wardrobe. Leaving whites to soak I escaped from the waiting chore to the great outdoors. True to form after a frost pristine conditions equal to any autumn offered followed. A regular habit, letting myself get sidetracked, aiming to cut out an established spiny rush where the irrigation pipe once leaked, ended up clearing a few panels of fenceline leading to the recent hose connection….

The mass of washing soon ran me out of pegs, and without enough furniture to accommodate the finishing off process by the heater, I pulled the pin, not before refilling the tub and soaking towels to torture myself again tomorrow ☺ !!!!

Collecting laundry water, erratic behaviour from kookaburras aroused my senses. Looking up I contentedly watched a goshawk circle overhead a couple of times, stirring the local natives before moving on....

Perfectly still where a pin could be heard dropping, nature was active. An almighty crack followed by a thundering crash shattered the silence briefly as another tree found its way to ground. Tia gave the noisy intruder what for, barking her way to the edge of the gorge daring it to come any closer.... My hero ☺ ....

Tuesday 6 June 2006

A coating of frost equivalent to yesterday's dusting topped the ground. A sea of fog filled the valleys below indicating St. Marys was under a blanket, and here I am basking in smoke filled sunshine. A perfect day fucking robbed of quality air by the mass burning of perfectly good fire wood locals should access. The 'Huntsman's Cap' mountain, usually in my face and clear to view, was little more then a smoky silhouette. The lonely, pleading cry of the neighbours' dog created atmosphere to the unhealthy environment delivered to our doorstep....

Putting a spark back into the mood, and true to form, within one minute of clacking my knife over the plate scraping breakfast crumbs a robin arrived to clean up offerings, a routine I can get used to. One daring young hen hopped onto the bungalow step hanging inside the doorway for about thirty seconds pecking around, reminding me life is special ☺ ....

Getting a bit long in the tooth, I tossed a bowl of rice into the paddock for the taking. First in line to retrieve the gift was Tia; like a treasure hunt extracting grains from the grass it kept her very busy.... Stomach first, second, third and fourth ☺ !!!!

Following a healthy play at the evolving elevated garden the air cleared enough to consider returning to waiting laundry. Water, washing and wood kept me honest and out of trouble ☺ ....

Wednesday 7 June 2006

Robins didn't show up over breakfast but crumbs left for them were neatly cleaned up by the time we returned from town ☺ ....

Just before noon Destiny fired into life taking us along that well-worn track between the Sisters, beginning the outing with a favourite socialising recipe of chatting over food and drink. Being school holidays, Ross was home stopping to grab drinking water, enticing me inside with the offer of a meatloaf sandwich and a brew ☺ ....

After loading Destiny's front passenger seat and floor in groceries I headed to pay the phone bill, greeting me with a hug outside the Post Office door is where Pam and I remained for the following half-hour. The only planned stop was for a brew with Evelyn. Between a sprinkling of customers we chatted our way to the bottom of the mugs. Returning home with a sample of Evelyn's beef stir-fry and a pan of white sticky rice, tonight we eat well ☺ ....

Topping a highly uplifting time away from home, driving past I disturbed a pair of eagles feeding not far from Rainbow Falls' driveway turn-in; gliding to a nearby tree they waited for the broken calm to pass ☺ ....

During a visit without his dogs and with Ross' blessing, Tia jumped into his car, sniffing about she found and knocked off a tennis ball with life in it. More lively than the remaining odds and ends in her collection, watching sunset fade we played skud ball with Tia's newly claimed treasure ☺ ….

Thursday 8 June 2006
A quick game of skud ball before breakfast then it was time to put petrol in our motors; robins thought so also. One robin stood tall and proud on top of Tia's knocked off tennis ball, another hopped onto the bungalow step. The pair anticipated breakfast early. Helping the robins with their wait I broke a fruit bun placing it on top of the rock pile and the flighty birds cleared off momentarily. Never one to let a chance go by Tia climbed the rock pile and claimed the bun ☺ …. Stomach first, second, third and fourth ☺ !!!!
Getting high-heels standing in wallaby poo, I did a quick scoop around high traffic areas filling the 2-litre container quickly. Seemingly always going backward to take one step forward, completing daily essentials to free time to return to the burnt out house chewed up most of the day. Fulfilling water needs was shortly achieved; however, the heater was overdue for an empty, in turn meant sifting nails from ash to make room for more. Wood was needed to again fill the heaters face, requiring a trip to the shed to cut more for that very purpose. Essentials done, it left bugger all daylight hours for free time but not one minute was wasted….
Turning and wetting up compost the garden fork pierced a chook carcass and the aroma raised Tia's interest, cooked to perfection, having a dig she tore pieces off like paper. Stirring the pungent odour caused me a short stretch of uncontrolled retching. For as long as I could hold my breath hastily buried the buggers back down deep again…. Phew!!!!

Friday 9 June 2006
The only active bird life at breakfast was a mob of noisy parrots drinking at the cattle trough. Robins arrived shortly after the action was over, probably a smarter move snacking on crumbs in quieter traffic times….
Wood and water organised at a smart pace freed up a good chunk of the day, and like bees to the honey pot, headed to the burnt out house. Leaving the hose to wet compost me and my little mate took the wheelbarrow for a walk into the cattle yards. Extracting a couple of loads of dry, flaked cow dung from inside the small timber structure tucked in the corner, added it to the large brewing pile, along with another dose of wallaby poo…. Yum!!!!
Digging her way to the delicious chook aroma brewing within, Tia contributed to turning the compost pile doing us both a favour, not so with the stench. Taking a break for smoko Tia's dead chook aroma breath forced me outdoors for a brew and snack, a blessing in disguise, getting out from under a roof to bask in bone warming sunshine…. Experiencing the autumn we didn't have ☺ ….
Throughout the day there were plenty of games that included the hose to leach dead chook aromas worn by Ms Muffet. Oh, and what a pleasure it is to stand and water with a hose. While water flows freely my mind wanders contemplating the number of trips to the cattle trough with a bucket it would have taken. My feet are glad it's only a thought ☺ ….
Raising a compost takes a lot of effort, watering, feeding and turning to get desired results. After doing just that and giving the garden beds a sprinkling of water we disappeared into the

fringe of the gorge on the ongoing hunt for timber. Dragging out three wheelbarrow loads of good sized solid limb wood, carted it to the shed creating more work for myself to cut it????

Saturday 10 June 2006
Too large to manage in one piece, and without the saw handy, I left a good stash of limb wood behind yesterday, but not today. Looking like a tightrope walker balancing limb lengths of up to five metres across the wheelbarrow, pushed the load to the shed storing enough to last a week….
A light wind picking up put the feel of change in the air and my arse into gear: returning to the ongoing saga of shed and cottage waterproofing, spread the last of the black goo and replaced a few nails with roofing screws. Reckoning I've now sorted the leak around the cottage power-board by gooing up a gap between overlapping roofing iron, that allowed me to remove the ugly blue tarp tacked to the wall doing little to protect the area anyway. With all good intentions repairing leaks, I gave my right knee a memorable whack on a rung climbing the ladder, pulling up where I stood until endorphins, taking their sweet time, kicked in!!!! Ouch….
Ladder and drill packed away, my body copped a workout pushing the handsaw cutting a barrow load for the evening….
Watching another spectacular golden sunset playing skud ball with my little mate not a threatening cloud was in view, so it came as quite a surprise preparing dinner to hear rain falling. I didn't see that coming at all, and it came down, wind and rain extended some southerly might ☺ !!!!

Sunday 11 June 2006
Rain came and went in a 4mm rush but the harsh gusting of the lazy old southerly lingered on into today, setting up ideal conditions for snow and for a brief moment tried. The compost pile crunched underfoot and the cattle trough had formed a crust of ice, a true winter welcome ☺ ….
The only course for a woman to take was to head to the shed and bask in sunshine out of the icy wind, tucked inside the gates. Warming bones basking quietly out of the way, a team of robins went to work having a major clean up around the bungalow. Cute little rotund bodies with icy-pole sticks poked in their lower backs as tails, supported by fast moving match stick legs, darted around with much purpose feeding ☺ ….
Content to remain lazing, I had to muster all spare animation from within to keep home fires burning to again fill the cottage woodbox. Converting back to going easy on myself, taking it quietly catching afternoon sun I retreated to the bungalow to phone Mum and Dad. Changing over to gas heating last year, and following a heads of family discussion, Mum and Dad were ready to part with their chainsaw and accessories making a left field surprise offering the equipment to me. Due for another trip to the island, they had already made arrangements with Cousin Mark to deliver the treasure. Shit, I'd better be careful one might get lazy mechanising life ☺ !!!!

Monday 12 June 2006
A contemplative breakfast brew idly got me started. With the possibility of Ross coming up to collect, cut and share a load of limb wood, I got my teeth into jobs that could be left at the drop

of a hat. Obviously something more exciting than cutting wood came up because I remained at the burnt out house uninterrupted most of the day....

Looking for an after breakfast snack Tia dug her way to the chooks happily decomposing in the compost, stirring up the buried stench, at times the pungent odour filled my respiratory system like concrete as I pruned Peaches nearby.... Phew!!!!

Shaded out and struggling just to exist for many neglected years Peaches' hard life shows, with strong growth only on one side, Peaches was thinned and shaped to form an arch over the bordering two metre strip of concrete path. Completing a tidy job, prunings were chopped down to size and added to the composting brew. Tinkering around I set the header tank up to fill testing Ross' soldering, now tried and proven water tight, whenever the moment strikes I'm confident to install it in the ceiling to add the remaining infrastructure link for water on tap.... A long time coming ☺ !!!!

Closer to us at this point in the lunar cycle, not only does the moon appear larger it also throws more light, illuminating to the point of casting night shadows. Migrating to bed last night the images of two wallabies feeding midway into the slashed heart could be made out, visibility is outstanding....

Tuesday 13 June 2006
The blustery southerly giving us a solid taste of winter blew itself past within forty-eight hours, reverting to frosts with idyllic days to follow - stuff fairytale books are fashioned around ☺ ....

Co-ordinated with scraping my plate, from where I sat inside the bungalow watched four robins bouncing around outside the door; one popped in for a brief visit. Tia and I sat quietly literally enjoying nature at our doorstep ☺ ....

It's a bit of a trap wandering down to bask in morning sun; inside shed gates my arse seems to get glued to the chair - oh well that's life ☺ ????

Motivated, me and Tia put the wheelbarrow to work carting sand from a lazy pile at the side of the cottage relocating it to the worst worn sections in the driveway, the gorgeous day quickly stripped me down to a t-shirt and straw hat. Sand weighing in bloody heavy there was no filling the wheelbarrow to the brim, we both creaked and groaned under half a load. Slowing erosion at the worn bottleneck around the front gate, it received the sand attention, being just a mass of exposed small rocks. Sand laid sometime back shows favourable results for stability....

GST included, taking into account the driveway length being around one-hundred metres, I must have covered at least two kilometres pushing the wheelbarrow. Fortunately for half that distance it was empty and no uphill work required ☺ ....

Wednesday 14 June 2006
Burning the last of the luxury surplus cut wood provides it was back to reality. Preparing to migrate to the shed, I found a message on the answering machine from Ross ready to pay us a visit with his chainsaw. At that precise moment the handsaw idea was given the flick ☺ ....

Lining the back of Destiny with a tarp, drove to the edge of the gorge pulling up near a large fallen limb, it alone supplied enough wood to fill Ross' boot and place a good stack in the back of Destiny. It's wonderful to be temporarily removed from the day to day drive for wood. By

1:30pm a good load was stored in the shed. I'm sweet now for a solid week, freeing time to get my teeth into other things☺!!!!
The bearer of good news, Ross mentioned the ideal weather we've been experiencing is about to get blasted away by a rush of winter in the next twenty-four hours. Putting that knowledge to use, like good little squirrels, got prepared for it. Eliminating the need to walk anywhere for water tucked the hose through a gap under the cottage front door then neatly ran it along the wall to the bath. With all the bits mantled, I turned the main on and walaa, with the twist of a nozzle there's a tap full of water at my convenience inside☺....
Staying with the water theme, Ms Muffet and me took a quick trip between the Sisters to replace an almost depleted supply of drinking water. With enough food on hand staying up the mountain until Friday is a happening thing, by then it will be day nine since the last sighting of town. That suits this happy little hermit☺....

Thursday 15 June 2006
When the sun sets my working day is still far from over. First cab off the rank each evening is to get a fire cracking closely followed by dinner, bath, dishes; and writing is the final step. Without being a martyr, there's a moment when the world stops and I momentarily get off. For as long as it takes to reach the bottom of the mug I savour a milo buried in a rocker basking in front of the fire. Migrating to the bungalow for the night it's not surprising I sleep soundly!!!!
Focussed on treating myself, I concentrated the day around having a rare night off. A real time consumer, I got the fire ready just to throw a match to. Further easing my load, leftovers sat on the heater top simply waiting to be heated; even water for a milo was perched ready on the heater, then at a mere 3:30p.m.-ish the pen found my hand to sit down and write. By the close of business bathing was the last thing left. I kicked a goal☺....
It wasn't surprising robins were a bit quiet on the feeding front. Wind hanging around would be enough to blow their light body off the perch☺!!!!
Free ranging wandering and tinkering, after moving past the heater's needs a couple of containers of poo were scooped to feed compost. I also supplied a feed for mice noisily rattling through foil insulation in the bungalow wall. They seem to be active all day and bloody night: anyway it's my hope to slow the traffic flow. Removing a little aerial ugliness out of the line of sight from the open bungalow door, I cut wires from the shed roof that linked it to an unused telegraph pole. Rotten at the base, the pole is earmarked to finish a distinguished career as firewood....

Friday 16 June 2006
Gazing out the west facing cottage windows watching fading light on my night off, five wallabies could by seen feeding in the love heart from my warm comfy spot....
Woken abruptly from a snooze in a rocker, once the quota of bullets was used on animals across the road, and Tia was settled, then my head was softly planted on my pillow by an amazing 10p.m.-ish....
Oddly, Doris told me that when she first arrived in the mountain there weren't such large populations of possums or wallabies, but with more land cleared and grass available their numbers flourished.... One imbalance created another????

Bread nine days old, milk three days past its use-by, the weekend supermarket shut down meant a trip into the big smoke. Even having myself ready earlier than usual to take the drive I still managed to break the back of the day on the other side of the mountain socialising. The top end of town can't be rushed. Chatting between customers, I left Evelyn and walked across the road to Rita and Ian. A pleasant trip was topped with one of Pam's beautifully brewed coffees ☺ ....

Included in the Post Office box scoop was an envelope from Mum and Dad containing recent photos of Dekira, now 18 months old. Showing appreciation I phoned just as soon as Destiny was unloaded. Any call home to Mildura takes as long as it takes. My little mate made herself scarce while I chatted: leaving a window down in Destiny still parked by the bungalow, Tia was quite comfortable in her trusted friend ☺ ....

Walkabout prior to knock off I discovered water on tap had already been sabotaged: draped across the driveway, Destiny managed to split the hose to irrigate wheel ruts. When water is flowing to the cattle trough it's now solely used as a watering hole for the local natives. Parrots are regulars perched on the edge, and of course it's a swimming pool for my best mate ☺ ....

Saturday 17 June 2006

A below average rainfall is beginning to show chinks in the armour: usually to capacity, the dam is about a foot down, and winter's customary lush green grass is dry and browning off???? The accumulation of reminder jobs in individual piles on the cottage bed waiting to be done finally got the better of me. It was 'stop procrastinating and start clearing the bed' action day! Step one in finding the surface of the bed came with eliminating the drill. Its existence was a reminder to take the possum release boxes down. Next priority was to poke a joiner in the hose I ran over and split with Destiny. Opening the line to release a water flow only revealed a second split, oops. Back to the drawing-board, a second joiner did the trick to get the hose up and flowing to the cottage again....

Turning ignoring and invisibility into an art form to avoid sewing I took the plunge reaching for the needle, cotton and daks. Basking behind glass in the bungalow I patiently joined threads. Far more pleasant to the senses, gliding in thermals, a pair of eagles in view briefly distracted me from the thread-joining task at hand. Sewing is certainly not something I'd like to turn into a career. It's a bit like cooking, done purely out of need. When Destiny is cleaned, more vegie seeds planted and the header tank installed the bed will be cleared, but that's for another day ☺ !!!!

Ending a bit of an everything kind of day and dry enough for my thistle kicking boots with the holy tough sole, I laced up and went walkabout in the slashed heart eliminating young thistle growth. A seasonal habit returning ☺ ....

Sunday 18 June 2006

Yesterday my arse was dragging on the ground and it's sitting no higher today either. Whether I wanted to or not life dictated to take it easy. Sadly the air was blue with smoke and calm atmospheric influences weren't in favour. A forestry fire that's been smouldering now for a week without directly affecting us let us know we weren't forgotten.... Pretty ordinary!!!!

A small tube of glue easily hidden on the cottage bed revealed itself as another reminder job waiting for action. Once open a tube of supa-glue is a one-use item. Poking a bit around the toe of my blundies to hold them together a bit longer, a couple of spurts of air and a dribble of liquid a rubber foot grip was stuck back on the ride-on; the tube was empty and job's neatly done....

My little mate and I covered a few kilometres on foot and paw through paddocks on a general observation, forward planning and thistle kicking walkabout. Skud ball finished outdoor activity until dark time took over. I'm not sure which part of the game represents the skud, my kicking the ball into rocks or Tia's haphazard ball returns? It amuses me to watch Tia stop in her tracks sprinting after the ball, as casual as you like stroll to the cattle trough have a drink and take a dip, and with the same casualness idly return to the ball and game ☺ ???? Gotta love her ☺ ....

Monday 19 June 2006

Feeling the cold last night it was definitely a one-dog night, and lucky for me I willingly had one prepared to snuggle seeking some extra warmth herself ☺ ....

A personal promise; if another sunny day was on the cards Destiny would benefit, and it was meant to be. Sun's rays filtered through forestry logging operations smoke....

Working through the quicker, more easily achieved reminder jobs on the cottage bed, I've now reached those with longer timeframes required. A simple towel placed on the bed in my mind represented a replacement for the grubby one covering Destiny's back seat; to achieve that simple task first required a detailed clean inside and out before the exchange could take place. Seemingly the greater the duration between washes the more time required to bring Destiny back to natural: sinking a few hours into the job included ongoing random ball kicking and hose squirting for my helpful offsider ☺ ....

The heavens aligned catching me unawares. Coming from left field the seed was planted and germinated to finally fill the gap in the loo roof. Lugging the ladder and a piece of corrugated iron up the hill, I drilled and screwed the sheet firmly into position to alter a rainy day experience on the throne. Washing the car should tempt fate for rain but a sky full of stars certainly isn't a convincing indicator of moisture ☺ ....

Tuesday 20 June 2006

With the entrance facing south and its back to the sun the entire day, the most obvious noticed change a complete roof makes to the loo with a view is it has a darker interior edge to it....

Disobeying a period by continuing with manual activity I pay the penalty with depleted energy. Harnessing my brain around light duties I fiddled with a series of small jobs. After filling the woodbox, vegie seeds received a sprinkling of water, the compost was fed with scooped poo then my recently glued boots got a lick of nugget preparing them to re-enter the workplace before I brought a shine to Destiny's windows. Glistening, I'm reluctant to move Destiny from the shed only to get dirty again ☺ ....

After darkness had thrown its blanket over us, a wind of change picked up pushing in cloud and breaking the dry spell spilling a drop of moisture. Nothing to have me racing to the shed building an ark but to a browned off yard and dropping dam every drop is very welcome ☺ ....

Wednesday 21 June 2006
Last night's huge deluge spilled a total of 5mm doing precious little other than wetting the ground surface; every valuable drop of moisture was rapidly slurped up....
The yard isn't the only thing to be browned off lately. Yesterday the grumpies found me. Today the lid of the milo tin was flipped and spooning didn't stop until I'd had enough. The dreaded menstrual cycle lets a force take-over my body: taking control of the reins it steers emotions in any direction at will!!!!
Threatening heavy lingering cloud is a condition that uncompromisingly beckons the shed, and like a magnet I was drawn into its force. Drizzle tried to find ground noonish but South Sister Range held the load back as if on a piece of elastic. Happily immersed in the haven, I remained until the last of the limb wood was cut and left in neat pieces stacked in the wheelbarrow. For me it's a logical sequence to clean up after myself. Following a stint on the saw I got out of control sweeping both levels of Destiny's bedroom. Giving the shed a makeover I went as far as removing intruding grass from across the front wall ☺....
The curtain well and truly drawn on daylight and dinner sizzling away on the heater top, rain returned to supplement already damp ground. The moisture offering is spurring on bulb activity - they're beginning to rattle their dags ☺....

Thursday 22 June 2006
Last night's dribble amounted to a sample 2mm. The heavens have been doing quite a bit of work for little reward until today steady drizzle eventuated into convincing showers. A trip to the loo was made pleasant without the need for a third hand to hold the umbrella; the dry environment only took four years to come about ☺ ????
Payday and shopping day, we piled ourselves in Destiny for the big excursion and she remained clean only until we got to the front gate. Leaving the damp grass surface for mud she decorated herself nicely. Tia takes care of clean windows; the rattly dirt road takes care of the outside shine and creates repair work????
Heavy moisture laden cloud clung to the top of both North and South Sisters producing mountain fog, existing only at the highest point of the drive. Slipping between the Sisters, it was pure enchanting magic ☺....
Last trip into St. Marys I quizzed Kerry at the Post Office about reimbursement for overpayment of my Post Office box, saying she'd look into it. Broaching the topic this visit Kerry said there's nothing they can do for me; having the business for just over a year and being a privately owned franchise frees them of liability. Through persistence, Harry said he'd phone Australia Post and inquire.... Ahhhh, hope keeps me going....
Invited by Evelyn to join her in a brew, I made the bakery the social stop this trip and the last port of call before returning home to organise a warm fire ☺....
Oke's been making a pest of himself here again. To avoid being constantly on the phone to Charles about his dog decided I'd only call after every fifth sighting. I've had enough of Oke's pissing, shitting and encouraging Tia to wander, and Charles' lax duty of care as a pet owner!!!!

Friday 23 June 2006
Looks like another occasion to be comfortable and dry under a roof; the sun poked its head through spelling an end to the front that slowly dribbled a total 18mm over three days....
First cab off the rank following sighting five, Charles was called and in a friendly manner made him aware of Oke problems. While the receiver was running hot family life was caught up on with Mum and Dad, a call that rarely goes under an hour and is always a pleasure ☺ ....
Ready to strike a blow inroads were made at bringing the old telegraph pole down. After a dig at the rotting base I tied dangling cable, still connected to the top of the pole, to a drag chain. Ensuring Destiny was a clear distance away with Tia inside, the drag chain was hooked to her towbar to begin a slow tug, under a load the drag chain and cable separated. I took that as a sign to leave pole felling for another occasion ☺ !!!!
Heeding the advice to change jobs, I ventured into the cottage for a more passive pastime lightening the load of webs appearing within; one of those once in a pink fit tasks. Sweeping the ceiling and walls, rough cut raw timber grabs hold of anything floating around and the small gaps in the boards let in anything that will fit. The spider that set-up permanent residence inside the westerly window is exempt from removal; it's part of the furniture to be left to do its bit with the insect population ☺ ....
Days are just disappearing. I seem to get geared up then find myself racing against fading light getting evening needs sorted before lights out by a sharp 5:30p.m.-ish. With winter solstice now past, it shouldn't be long until the earth's axis gets moving again and more daylight hours are on the way ☺ ....

Saturday 24 June 2006
The privileged stack of cut wood will be lucky to see us through another couple of days, and the heavens still looking uncertain, Tia and I, with wheelbarrow, saw and bottle of water, scouted along the edge of the gorge on the hunt for fallen limbs. Well, I hunted for wood filling my load; Tia tracked after scents coming up empty ☺ !!!!
Slurping up moisture from the recent rains added weight to the wood; splitting the load in two delivered it to 'destination shed'. Needing to add to the dwindling stack sooner than later and wood dries faster in smaller pieces, I kept myself warm cutting a bit....
Playing dodgems pushing the wheelbarrow in a polka-dot yard full of soft animal landmines led then to pooper scoopering. Deposits of native animal poo are pretty consistent averaging one 2-litre container full daily; any day missed has the equivalent amount built-up and waiting ☺ ....
Driven in by fading light as another short day caved in, after watching the accustomed high standard sunset then simply with the twist of the hose nozzle filled the washing machine. Unable to ever bring myself to rush into laundry, left a load to soak overnight. Why do today what can be put off until tomorrow ☺ ?!?!

Sunday 25 June 2006
Struggling to reach the end of a rather waffley book on loan from my case manager, 'Adventures of Wim' is a story that could have been condensed by a quarter. With Sandra due today I put in a big reading effort the past twenty-four hours. The biggest sacrifice was to bask

in morning sunshine down the shed to find its end. Tia laid her heat absorbing solar panels out and snoozed with one eye open, a pattern she maintained ☺....

Absorbed in full sun reading, the phone was heard calling out for response; with Tia excitedly bouncing around at my feet my reluctant legs got moving. Catching a brief call from Cousin Mark, his first words were "guess where I am, standing in your Mum and Dad's backyard"; replying simply "I wish I was standing next to you". The purpose of the call was to establish drop off plans for me to inherit Dad's chainsaw. Arriving on the island Tuesday to start life afresh in Cygnet, Mark and I confirmed crossing paths at Epping Forest Roadhouse. The brief call was finalised with a chat with both Mum and Dad before returning to basking and the book ☺....

Through morbid curiosity and persistence I found the book's end and had a fair crack at laundry before Sandra pulled in. Giving her the one-hour Rainbow Falls therapy session, Sandra was returned back out the gate with a higher energy level than she arrived with....

Washing has no longer got limited hours. After replacing a blown globe and with unlimited water on hand, I got back into it after the 5:30pm sharp nightfall. Running out of furniture put an end to play. Refilling the machine left towels to soak ready for a fresh start tomorrow ☺....

Monday 26 June 2006
The remnants of a light frost still remained when Tia and I poked our heads out the door. Pristine weather following didn't fail. By lunch, a westerly influence drifted blankets of cloud in occasionally cooling life a little; maybe a half-hearted frost represents only half a guaranteed sunny day????

With my one foot in front of the other pace returned to enslaving white goods adding power to the washing machine. The convenience of unlimited water on tap inside is brilliant, until I got distracted filling the 25 litre bucket!!!! Bugger!!!!

Knowing how to treat myself to a spoiling, the two-day stint of laundry was finished to further indulge wearing down a worn handsaw carving up a weighty load....

Showing quite a bit of interest in her girlie bits recently, and if I'm not mistaken, Tia's freshly in season. A ripe girl in the neighbourhood proved too difficult for a fella to resist; sitting quietly by the fire last night a very interested Oke was outside the door. A busy night for neighbours; I then heard Charles whistling him up from the road out front ☺.... He's trying????

Disturbing the peace while cooking dinner, a few odd, angry shots cracked through the silence from across the road. Seems animals were getting in the way again. Since the move to Tassie regular exposure to guns being discharged and air thick with smoke, sadly, now hardly perturbs....

Tuesday 27 June 2006
Beating the awful, offensive, droning, ongoing beep of the bloody alarm got up before it preparing for the 11a.m. meeting time with Cousin Mark. Pointing Destiny's nose out of town it was a gorgeous morning for a drive - the valley was alive. Heading towards it, I'd been watching a lingering rainbow in the distance knowingly having been brightly illuminated for a half-hour. Close to the rainbow and Avoca an eagle joined the view; visually there was certainly plenty of uplifting ingredients to generate a great mood ☺....

Out the other side of Avoca a twin cab Ute drove up along side tooting, a pretty woman in the passenger seat was smiling and waving: ahead of time, Mark and Joanne drove into the valley. With me oblivious to their earlier attempts at gaining my attention, they managed to slow me down to stationary within a few kilometres. Having no time to spare, with the removalist truck already an hour ahead of them, we exchanged brief pleasantries by the roadside before parting with goods and company. With moisture all around, nearing St. Marys a vividly strong rainbow shadowed by a lighter softer arch decoratively mirror imaged, presented a double rainbow resting against a mountain backdrop. Proudly home having taken possession of Dad's well-maintained prized chainsaw and hoard of accessories, phoned the family home with news of delivery ☺....

Creating a blank canvas to cut mine and the chainsaws teeth on, my back and the shovel went to work, like a termite chiselled away at soil surrounding the telegraph pole. Fashioning a good surrounding airspace at the pole's base, brought Destiny and the drag chain back into play to have a tug at the towering structure. The weakest link again snapped, preferring it to be cable and chain join rather than Destiny's clutch, but not before the pole shifted to a 45° angle. Returning to digging at the base, dry and hard the ground refused to release its captive. Beaten by light, not determination, I emptied a few litres into the hole to soften things overnight....

Wednesday 28 June 2006
Emptying a bag of bread, the crumbs and crust bits were sprinkled at a comfortable distance from the bungalow and it took little time for flighty wrens and robins to move in, it was magic to watch over a breakfast brew. The crusts however were only safe until Tia sniffed them out, without giving it a second thought down the hatch they went ☺....

Oke's roaming and thinking with his dick has worn thin, following today's visit I drove around to see Charles to rationally discuss solutions. Eye contact makes more of an impact than a courtesy call every fifth sighting. For Oke, losing some of his manhood could be on the cards, for the short-term he's going to be put on a run....

Applying water at the base made no difference to the telegraph pole. It hadn't moved an inch beyond its 45° angle by morning. With Dad's instruction for use, coupled with reassured confidence after reading the manual, and the pole already having made its mind up which way to fall, I decided to drop it with the chainsaw. Preparing for the big moment a wide girth was dug surrounding the base of the pole to keep the chain free of dirt. Nervous, excited and a little scared, without looking back I gloved-up, put ear-muffs in position, and with high revs smoothly spinning the chain made my virginal cut. Any doubt was eliminated once the bar effortlessly started chewing its way into the timber, instead of being the first cut it felt like I'd been doing it forever. As the chain carved its way deeper, the gap at the base began to open, one light crack, I stepped back to watch the pole neatly lay on the ground without fuss. Having my way with the pole until the petrol tank emptied, it also drained with it the last available two-stroke oil ☺....

Storing the cut stash of large cross-sections in the shed the remaining uncut section of pole was left to lay idle. Packing up tools, I didn't give the job away until refilling the gaping hole created by my fancy shovel work was complete. Cutting the pole below ground level allowed the remaining stump to be buried out of sight to compost over time....

Adrenalin pumped by successfully daring to step outside my comfort zone and break new ground, made possible by their generosity, I shared the entire experience cut by cut with Mum and Dad over the phone ☺ !!!!

Doing a quick water heat, the boiler was tossed on the stove to burn electricity. Bathed up I made St. Marys with minutes to spare for a 6p.m. exhibition opening at Rita's quilting gallery 'Gone Rustic', having a lovely time blowing off social cobwebs ☺ ….

Patiently waiting with an empty belly I took my little mate home to feed her habit. The wood cooking tonight's dinner and keeping us warm had a solid depth of meaning to it, watching pieces of the pole burn, knowing the love given to get it there left me quite emotional. This particular fire felt somewhat special ♥….

Thursday 29 June 2006

Waking for another chapter in life, still lying peacefully and warm in bed resting hard working bones, heard the soothing sound of light mist falling. Lately I'm feeling very in tune with my journey of accomplishments, getting dealt enough of enough at just the right time. Rain in any quantity is nature's way of changing the pace every now and again determining a physical slow down; reckon I would have had one in any case today ☺ !!!!

Mist that so peacefully roused me into consciousness shot through early and only left behind a wet smear in the rain gauge….

Dropping from an excited fever pitch, today the pace was wound back to sedate, reflecting, basking in yesterday's personal development and deep lasting sentiment ☺ ….

Making the remaining chunk of telegraph pole chainsaw friendly decorative ornaments were removed, winding up cable and levering off a metal label and insulators, prepared it ready for the next onslaught. Wandering the yard and playing dodgems with poo lead into a poo scoopering tidy up….

Migrating to the shed I placed Dad's chainsaw on the bench, and with pride, cleaned it to Dad's standard as guided over the phone, from the air cleaner to carby throat ☺ ….

Following a thorough search skud ball's off the menu until the ball resurfaces ☺ ????

Friday 30 June 2006

Refusing to burst into activity I happily remained horizontal leaving my mind to free range, not solving the problems of the world but planning home life, in particular the daylight hours waiting ahead. Getting a little restless with an inactive human, Tia helped with the decision to get up and greet yet another mild start. Dad mentioned in conversation Wednesday that he has a daffodil ready to flower. They haven't even began to move here; the only signs of bulb movement is from snow drops ☺ ….

I seem to be suffering from domestic blindness; Tia walked into the cottage had a sniff, light scratch, then proudly displayed the treasured tennis ball in her mouth, she's been watching me get fit looking for it. The little bugger was probably sitting back laughing, saying, "you're cold, getting warmer, nowhere near there, ha, ha, ha, ha" ☺ !!!!

Shy on bread and payslip posting time a trip over the other side was inked in. Pulling the key from the Post Office box, and long overdue, the Rainbow Falls team took off to book Destiny in with Grant and to stock up on 2-stroke oil. Grant is a person that will be in business for as long as he likes because he operates from the heart and is refreshingly honest….

Meeting the birthday boy crossing the street we stopped for a hug and I let Ross know I'd left a small gift at his house. Returning possum release boxes ready for the next generation of orphans I had a brew and a sample of Pam's home baked fruit buns on today's social stop ☺ .... I manage weeks at a time without grog but only days out of milo and I'm feeling its absence. Sampling a nice boxed red at Rita and Ian's exhibition launch I broke the drought replicating a box of the same for home. The bloke serving at the pub continually repeated the line, "I can't believe how cheap it is", $12 for four litres and palatable; I'd have to agree ☺ .... Cheers....
Breaking the back of the day away from home, I slipped back between the Sisters to ease myself into knock off over a glass of red. Appreciating the enormity of the many hours freed labour returned by the convenience of a hard working chainsaw, simply walked to the shed rolled out a couple of logs to split and in a jiffy had the woodbox brimming ☺ .... Too easy!!!!

Saturday 1 July 2006
A couple of days Oke free my little mate's erratic behaviour is returning to almost predictable again. Usually a regular, Ms Muffet has shown little interest in my bed lately preferring her own bed and company. Spoiling me with a morning snuggle, we had just settled and the pleasant experience was heightened. Leaning out of the doona with a huge heave, Tia regurgitated indigestible bone - lucky me ☺ !!!!
Cloud placed a shield against any hope of sun's rays hitting ground. Light passing showers left me a bit undirected, aimlessly wandering. I put my back into splitting another cross-section of the telegraph pole to contemplate what to do with myself. An incoming call bearing good news kept my social skills alive; Stacey's been promoted to an Executive Assistant by choice of management - no job application required, just pure skill recognised ☺ ....
Concentrating thoughts, focus was found snipping prunings into compostable size at the burnt out house. Fiddling near the garden I discovered a sprinkling of baby garlic and onions poking their heads through to greet the world ☺ ....
Trying hard for an hour, rain eventually drove the hard working team for refuge indoors. Mountain fog sealed us in eliminating any possibility of a sunset then a convincing steady drop made an impression; the skies opened. Hoping the rain gauge doesn't get worked too hard, it copped a hit playing splitting the seam from the 3 inch mark upward. That's not good for accuracy ☺ ....

Sunday 2 July 2006
Pulling up by morning, the 15mm delivered sent the power supply into chaos. Waking to a flashing clock asking to be reset, sometime through the night power was out of circulation for a couple of hours. Seated at the loo with a view a sound that's been absent like a good friend, returning to fill a space in the quiet calmness - water could be heard dribbling over the edge of the falls ☺ ....
Following a brief warm-up splitting wood I made room for more ash in the heater; nail free clean wood takes little time to sort and sift before moving onto its next faze as toilet deodoriser. Everything is used to its fullest potential ☺ ....
Caring only for a passive 'gentle on the body and brain' way to occupy idle hours, a bit of everything was sampled from pruning to composting at the burnt out house. A few empty milo tins loaded with broken glass, rusty nails and other useless bits from the fire aftermath have

slipped through with general household rubbish, chipping away at small pieces of a big picture....

A call from Evelyn sparked generosity with the offering of food, phoning through the exceptional offer of sticky rice for Ross and me. Passing the message on, not only did Ross pick the rice up for me he also extended a dinner invitation ☺ .... I'm in heaven, life can be very kind ☺ !!!!

Monday 3 July 2006

Suitably impressed, I cut and stored the remainder of the telegraph pole finishing the entire job off. Splitting rounds in half to make their weight manageable I keenly watched a front drape itself over South Sister Range. Thickening up, it began moving toward. Continually looking over my shoulder got my arse into gear with the wheelbarrow shifting the load into the shed. Three-quarters complete, and filled with determination, braved mist to finish off, being satisfied only when the last piece was stacked under cover. Definitely a clone of my father; determined habits and actions mimic Dad's ☺ ....

A southerly meaning business slipped over the top of the range converting the air temperature to refreshing and invigorating icy. The weather repeated the same pattern from there on in. Wind picked-up and South Sister Range would thicken with cloud without making it over to reach home soil. Only feeling the effects of snow nearby, never actually seeing any.... brrrr.... Remaining in the haven, the chainsaw was cleaned prior to retreating to the cottage to take the edge off nippy putting some fresh cut timber to use ☺ ....

Tuesday 4 July 2006

Ripe and prepared to increase the doggy population, overactive hormones are driving Tia into some uncharacteristic behaviour. Sitting outstretched on the bungalow window box sipping an after breakfast milo keeping an eye on Ms Muffets movements, she created a beautiful moment in time. Joining me inside on the window box, Tia gently leant on my outstretched leg and together in still silence we watched wrens and robins busily skipping over the yard feeding. Vocally joining busy activity, kookaburra and parrot calls were heard dotted through trees; ravens and currawongs also got in on the act from a distance. A hawk has been a regular oral contributor of late. I've been hearing it consistently in the same area; being a recent arrival my hopes are pinned on it being a fledgling setting up home. Tuning in to all the outside activity I went and joined in, just getting on with it also ☺ ....

Working independently, my body has been delivering a period every second week and stripping physical energy to the bone. Doing the best to cater for waning strength I take it easy wherever possible but some things just have to be done????

A healthy stockpile of poo polka-dotting the yard was scooped and transferred to compost, giving the massive load a turn while playing. The mix of goodies making up the pile are beginning to breakdown and resemble compost rather than individual bits waiting to transform, worms are also getting active in the tasty concoction.... Yum ☺ ....

Yesterday's snow threatening icy southerly retreated, leaving calm and overcast in its wake. Come knock off and skud ball, Tia and I were pleasantly smack bang in the dry centre of a halo of mist, only briefly budging, but for the most we were surrounded by moisture reluctant to move away from trees into open ground ☺ ....

Wednesday 5 July 2006
Emotionally and physically flat, plans of grocery shopping were put aside. Following the mood, instead had a therapy session making advancements at the burnt out house. Slowly converting from pure mess, the termite hole's expanding to a usable and functional area. The many hours of toil put in are showing but many, many, many, many more are needed ☺ ….
A huge bank of cloud filled with moisture travelling in from the west stuck to South Sister Range, sharing part of its load mid afternoon. Sent indoors long enough to stack the fire and draw a blank with Telstra in an attempt to put an end to bloody pest marketing calls, another two today prompted the action. Each Telstra solution offered comes with a price tag: pay extra on my account per month to block all overseas services, pay for an unlisted number, change my number all together without guarantees, buy or rent a caller id phone…. Hmmmm all financially geared for a Telstra win:win responsibility free!!!!
The passing shower pulled up letting sun again breakthrough and we were immediately drawn back out of doors. Working nearby and within sight, I took renewed interest in removing the door and poles wedged in the walnut tree as a tree hut: grabbing the ladder followed through with the thought clearing the debris….
A couple of wines over dinner combined with tiredness. I went down for the count. Feeling wasted I lay down on the cottage bed stirring 12:15a.m.-ish cuddled next to the chainsaw. Mustering enough life over a milo, I stoked the fire, wrote in the journal then ventured next door to finish the snoozing process….

Thursday 6 July 2006
Still a bit flat, took my sweet time getting organised for groceries but eventually when the family was packed in, Destiny took us over the mountain….
Paying a couple of bills in the Post Office was pleasantly surprised by Kerry and Harry's positive action, having written to Australia Post they're now awaiting reply regarding my posting box overpayment. Expressing gratitude told them of how much I appreciated their effort, taking responsibility and going the extra yard to assist customers is a rare quality ☺ ….
Refreshing….
With Tia taking care of a grocery laden Destiny the last stop before home was for my own personal indulgence - chatting over a brew with Evelyn at the bakery. Sampling a delicious chicken garlic ball for the first time driving home, I copped a steep learning curve; the liquid centre decorated every piece of clothing worn. Lucky I like garlic ☺ ….
Wishing to participate in the evening and bypass chainsaw cuddling I abstained from red wine and stuck to the safe option of milo, staying awake and active long enough to even get the dishes done ☺ !!!!
Unable to muster up any sort of reasonable whistle, trading the pathetic inaudible noise I've taken to clapping for Ms Tia's attention, a system that seems to be working more effectively for us both. Greeting Tia warmly every time she responds to a clap is also improving the frustrating habit of her ignoring me - she's willing to return for a happy greeting, I'm a slow learner ☺ !!!!

Friday 7 July 2006

Enduring an extra period is making me extra cranky. Burning off the overload of negative energy I grabbed the sledge hammer and wedge and smashed a couple of logs apart. It's always good therapy doing something physical. Splitting another load to fill the woodbox, Tia did her usual excited race all over the shop running to extreme boundary points barking. Sprinting a few quick kilometres heats her motor in no time and she doesn't fail to take a dip in her pool. As a team we are becoming predictable - knowing one another's habits there aren't too many surprises ☺ ….

Wiping out a complete outfit with juice from garlic chicken balls, and almost needing a ladder to add them to the laundry stack, cornered me into filling the washing machine to torture myself with the mundane task!!!!

Against better judgement I hung clothes on the line in gusty wind; only having to reassemble two pegs far exceeded expectations. Niggling all day, strong gusts pissed off the moment the line was emptied and remaining clothes were draped over furniture decorating heater surrounds. Murphy's law ☺ ???? Shit I find washing an inconvenient pain in the arse ☺ !!!!

Saturday 8 July 2006

Left at an empty house, the neighbour's dog began its painful howling 6a.m.-ish. As much as I feel for the dog's sad empty existence, its behaviour due to neglect is finding a cut-off point. An entire long day of howling and whining on and off continued after humans returned 6p.m.-ish!!!!

A pair of hawks making themselves at home in the surrounding vicinity got too comfortable near a nesting raven. Without extending the welcome mat, the raven gave them the move on message loud and clear. I have to admire the spunk of a raven - there's not one bird it isn't prepared to take on….

A huge time for bird activity; a particularly vulnerable little wren battling against a shed window permitted me a good deed. Gently picking the hen up in a towelling tea-towel, exhausted, the little tyke sat calmly in my cusp until reaching shed gates then it didn't look back when the great wide open was sensed…. Those transparent bloody human contraptions are a dangerous mystery!!!!

Brain sensitivity has eased but left me feeling as strong as a half-sucked peppermint. Going quietly on a tired body, the yard was cleared of poo and what was missed packed into the tread of my boots….

Dry enough for thistle kicking boots, I laced up and went walkabout into the sunset with my best friend and a glass of red. Only purchasing one box of beer in a three-month period my tolerance to alcohol has dropped ☺ …. Hic….

Evenings are starting to lose their sense of urgency now days are beginning to feel longer with another season change on its way…. Just when I'm getting used to the idea of no bloody active snakes ☺ !!!!

Sunday 9 July 2006

Still hugging a contemplative after breakfast milo: Ross pulled up out back, grabbing bits from his stuff stored in the shed he then joined me in a brew. I proudly showed Ross Dad's chainsaw, his first words were, "shit, it's well looked after", replying, "Dad's taught me how to keep it that way" ☺ ....

Sadly, a wallaby doing a rare freaky leg tangle in fencing lost its fight for life. Its carcass left hanging unceremoniously didn't escape Tia's attention. Releasing its body, I then cleared growth from the nearby paddock gate for the purpose of shutting it, making the horizon paddock inaccessible for Tia who is too easily distracted by her curiosity. She can get into too much trouble down there!!!!

Wallaby removed and extremely proud of the cleared gateway, feeling good with the job complete and simply adding finishing touches to the gate post, couldn't believe my eyes to see water trickling from a poly pipe hose connection just found with the shovel. Applying boiling water was futile, as was struggling to insert an internal joiner with a low pressure of water still flowing. Sorting through limited plumbing supplies tossed a hose nozzle on the flowing end applying a band-aid fix to the problem????

Extending the life of a simple job, I could finally down tools for a yarn with Mum and Dad. Discussing plans for an up and coming trip to Mildura, Mum mentioned she'd like to return with me but has a surgeon's appointment scheduled for the 15th August. Postponing travel plans a fortnight until Wednesday 3 August, massaged arrangements to suit everyone ☺ ....

Enjoying it so much yesterday the procedure was repeated. My little mate, me and a glass of red went walkabout thistle kicking in cool evening air. Long after sunset we retreated to the heater when thistles could no longer be clearly identified, or hands buried any deeper into pockets ☺ ....

Monday 10 July 2006

Fortunate for native wildlife there are stretches where there are no carcasses on offer, but not currently. A possum came to grief in the yard overnight keeping Tia extremely busy guarding it and marking claims. With a wallaby and possum on the go a girl is kept on her toes guarding her booty from all competing identities....

Cornered into the very last available opportunity to pay Destiny's registration I was forced into taking the 100km round trip to St. Helens to Service Tasmania....

As a rule of thumb the first stop at the bottom of the mountain is to check the Post Office box. One piece of today's booty lifted out was a $138 money order from Australia Post, reimbursing me totally for every last cent of overpayment for the Post Office box since 2002 ☺ .... Un-bloody believable!!!! Nothing at all was deducted for so-called administrative fees, a refreshing, honest experience and a good turn goes a long way ☺ ....

With Destiny's registration sorted for another year I took a stroll around the corner to the travel agent. Setting in concrete August 2 as the travel date for the Spirit of Tasmania to start our Mildura trek, the wheels were put in motion ☺ ....

Making the most of travelling away from home, after completing business I caught up with rarely maintained friends. Scoots, Mary-Anne, Nana Raye, Lesley and I met at the Village Store picking up from where we last left off. Whether we had one hour or five there's always more to share than time to be had....

A personal promise made that if anything came into fruition from Kerry and Harry's effort I would buy them a bottle of wine as a thank you. Coming good with my personal thoughts I stopped into the Post Office returning from the day out. While cashing the money order I presented Kerry and Harry with a bottle of wine before heading home, a win:win situation ☺ ....

Tuesday 11 July 2006
When shooting finished across the road last night and their dog finally shut up sleep only progressed as far as the nods before forceful wind demanded I remain awake and listen. Shoving us around and blowing in horizontal rain spurts, my brain was exhaustedly happy to collapse into solid sleep after the worst of the lashing front passed!!!!
Re-confirming arrangements made with Pam, I phoned regarding the acceptance for help getting Destiny into Grant for a revitalising service; all about to start breakfast, we made loose arrangements for about an hour. Going close to on time, I rolled up with Evelyn snacks for smoko, Pam got the kettle on the boil and we settled into a yarn. Placing our bums on seats in Destiny we meandered back up the hill to deliver me and my little mate home. Hearing the comfortable familiar sound of our best friend getting further away, separated from the team, Tia looked quite miffed watching Pam drive off in Destiny ☺ ????
Turning from cold to bloody icy, I split enough wood and retreated indoors to indulge in an afternoon of pleasure. With all the required bits on hand I broke open the tax pack short cut tax return and poured ink over its contents. Filling in blank spaces and marking X's in the right spots an envelope was stuffed ready to post for another year....

Wednesday 12 July 2006
Wild wind pissed off, taking the absolute bitter wind chill factor from the equation, assisting the temperature to remain steady at tolerable. Definitely a one-dog night; for the second occasion this winter a crust of ice covered the cattle trough....
Blissfully basking in full morning sun inside shed gates protected from air movement, hugging a milo, I was content watching busy bird activity. Robbing the serene moment a pair of currawongs flew into the picture and immediately triggered the 'piss off' mechanism inside ☺ !!!!
As part of up and coming travel plans, to bring Mum home, the need to uncover the bed returned thoughts to the reminder jobs cluttering its top. Starting with the least desirable job, again I picked up the dreaded needle and cotton, this time keeping the stuffing inside a pillow....
Venturing out to catch some sun and wind, oh, also a couple of attempted late showers. Remaining exposed to all on offer once again I put time into 'project burnt out house'. Taking little to keep me busy, I took another small snip at revealing the bordering path. By cutting littering prunings down to compostable sized bits reduced the impeding pile to a manageable height....
Bringing Tia into view to keep track of her movements, I dragged the dead wallaby that tangled in fencing to the centre of the slashed love heart. Its life is certainly not going to be wasted Tia's had a few goes at the wallaby, returning after each snack with her left front paw blood stained. Appreciating a particularly vivid orange and gold sunset over a glass of red shielded inside the cottage, gazing out a westerly window I watched a raven land near the carcass. The raven's actions were funny to watch. Finding ground about ten metres from the potential feed it remained motionless for several minutes, beginning to feel secure it did the

serious, rigid raven stride pacing toward the evenings full belly taking in one healthy gorge ☺....

Thursday 13 July 2006
Feeling a little amiss not running on all cylinders lately, I spent my ration of physical energy splitting enough wood to keep home fires burning. Hard at my burst of work I missed a call from Pam to say she was on her way with Destiny with Evelyn snacks on the passenger seat ☺....
Tia was happy to be reunited with Destiny hopping straight in familiarising herself checking the fingerprints of scents left behind by other humans in her absence. Content then to join Pam and me in the bungalow waiting for snack samples to come her way, Tia's never disappointed ☺....
Returning Pam home in a round about way first stopped into Grant's for Destiny's prognosis, in a nutshell said she's holding up well for her age, know how she feels. With groceries on board and in no rush, I accepted Pam's offer of a brew before the reunited Tassie Trio returned to our cubby hideaway in the mountain....
Long after sunset on a beautiful evening, with a glass of red in hand and thistle-kicking boots laced up, remained walkabout doing just that. Leaving me to it my little mate opted for the company of the dead wallaby, stomach first, second, third and fourth ☺!!!!

Friday 14 July 2006
Any gap in the doona let in a flow of cold air that was bloody icy: also being one of the rare occasions Tia insisted on a visit outdoors through the night, getting up was done with reluctance.
Opening the door, little legs of all native shapes and sizes scattered. I was forced to dodge a couple of scampering pademelons racing toward me in the darkness looking for an escape route. It couldn't have been much fun being herbivore feeding from the ground last night, grass crunched underfoot with a covering of frost....
Finally daring to surface from under the warm doona, with my little mate busy chewing on a beef bone, I sat quietly with a milo gazing through the window. I've been amused watching a raven's antics landing and approaching the wallaby carcass for a chew, then Christmas! The pair of hawks that have been vocally present in the neighbourhood lately both landed for a snack. All was going well until Tia finished her bone, it's a dog eat wallaby world ☺!!!!
Needless to say breakfast took some time to get through....
Standing idle twiddling thumbs wasn't an option; one had to stay on the move to keep warm in the cool, overcast, moisture threatening, surrounds. Opting for a soft option to conserve precious energy, after topping up the woodbox I awarded myself a day off for personal pampering and self-indulgence. It wasn't all decadence, working many hours feeding the fire, refilling pots and the water supply, simply to get some depth in the bath for an hour of soaking luxury. Can't say there were any complaints reaching the goal ☺....
On and off, moisture tried finding ground until finally succeeding. Mountain fog and a steady gentle misting rain settled in justifying my existence being in by the heater....

In an idle moment from bath preparation I phoned Ali for a chat, with the intention of visiting on the way to Devonport as part of the trek to Mildura. Ali generously extended the offer to join her in a meal before boarding the boat; she knows how to treat a friend ☺....
Lying peacefully and innocently snoozing while I made a start on the nights journal entry, Tia's additional dietary intake caused the release of some nasal hair scorching, sinus clearing gas, its going to be fun in the confined space of the bungalow tonight…. Phew!!!!

Saturday 15 July 2006
If anything my ignorant neighbours will give me plenty to write about. Still peacefully snoozing, the sound of a chainsaw ripped through the motionless air at a disrespectful 7:45am. Extending a courtesy call across the road politely requested of Kristy to ask her husband to refrain from using the chainsaw until a more courteous legal hour, the request fell on deaf ears, it only received a couple of hard revs before continuing. Looking to be heard and the legal hour respected I phoned the police asking them to call on my behalf. That action seemed to gain the desired results. I don't know what makes those idiots tick but it's certainly not any thought beyond their immediate need ☺ ?!?!
Taking time-out for a dose of brain therapy had a play in the garden, being stoked to find tulip spurs breaking through soil giving the neighbouring infant garlic shoots company. Slow moving, but earlier work is being rewarded ☺....
Low cloud and misting showers hovered while expanding on a start made at unearthing buried concrete wheel tracks leading into the car garage: adding to yesterdays 5mm, falling moisture determined that job be given away. What began as light mist graduated into some bloody outstandingly heavy downpours ☺ ????
Retreating in I did maintenance on a long neglected personal dream by putting a few hours into the computer, not touched since mid March; there are many more hours still waiting….

Sunday 16 July 2006
Being the direction of our heaviest and longest lasting rains, the visiting easterly front peaked yesterday with 25mm falling from the sky. The drop is second in line to January 30th's 28mm for the highest recorded rainfall in a twenty-four hour period this year to date, and not a single drip entered through the flue. If moisture arrives from south-west a few drips find their way inside. When finalising waterproofing the flue ever makes the repair list again its behaviour has given me plenty of clues….
Heading into the shed to grab wood for splitting, I first put three large slow moving worms stranded on the wet concrete floor back outdoors where their survival rate is higher, unless spotted by a kookaburra. Loading logs into the wheelbarrow for downsizing noticed movement behind one; returning that particular log back into position for the frog seeking shelter behind it ☺ ....
Expecting a contact visit from Sandra 2p.m.-ish, I got chatting to Mum and Dad exhausting our news beforehand. With impeccable timing I managed to get a warming fire up and burning before both Ross and Sandra pulled in within minutes of one another. Loading their fists with a brew of choice, we found positions around the heater hugging hot cups ☺ ....

True to her word, and delivered on Ruth's behalf, Ross brought a copy of her delicious lemon slice recipe, a flavour I was fortunate enough to sample at Rita's gallery exhibition and wanted to replicate ☺ !!!!

From Sandra's seated position, she pointed out rainbow activity outside as the mixed basket of a day produced the right variety of elements. Waving Sandra off, Ross alerted me to the end of an arch resting faintly on the ground by the water tank. Racing up the hill chasing the tail of a rainbow like an excited child tried to immerse myself in the prism, being no sprinter I missed the moment. However, the other end of the arch remained strongly fixed into South Sister Range and had developed a double shadowing…. A magic moment shared in paradise ☺ ….

Monday 17 July 2006

Tia's more interested in the wallaby carcass than her crotch lately, a good sign she's ending her 'in season' womanly attractiveness…. Hallelujah ☺ ….

A very popular spot for carnivores; removing the cardboard curtain the first sight to view was of a pair of ravens in the love heart feasting on carcass ☺ ….

The dense bank of cloud giving the ground a long overdue soaking started its retreat revealing patches of the colour blue, leaving outdoor life refreshed and rejuvenated. The dam is a good indicator of unseasonable drier conditions. Following 34mm over the past three days it still hasn't risen to pool level. However, the friendly soothing sound of a flow of water dropping over the falls has returned ☺ ….

Looking for by-law solutions to the ongoing selfish, ignorant actions from across the road, I contacted the local Constable Cameron making a time for Wednesday to have a sit down chat to resolve all issues of concern. I just want to find middle ground so me and them can reside harmoniously happily ever after????

Completing the ol' heater ash empty and sift routine, seemingly spent a lot of time busily going nowhere fast. Filling the washing machine I wasn't tempted to return to its drudgery until long after walkabout; decorating available furniture then left a load soaking to spoil myself again tomorrow. Out wandering, we roamed through the love heart and couldn't find any trace of the wallaby. Its life wasn't in vain - not one morsel was wasted….

Tuesday 18 July 2006

Migrating from the cottage to bed last evening Tia retreated. Barking her way back from the side of the shed to the bungalow, she unsuspectingly crossed paths with something unfamiliar. Tia probably encountered either a wombat or devil, because signs of the existence of both have been found in the yard. Still barking and fur fluffed, Tia took some settling safely back inside the bungalow…. My hero ☺ ….

Wind picked up before retiring to warm the doona, stirring through the night the sound of a sprinkling on the tin roof could be heard. This occasion being nowhere near as mild as the easterly, pushing in from pure south, the only place the mercury reached double figures today was in front of a heater…. brrrr….

Running out of the simple things that pleasure-add to life, like food and water, drove us to a trip between the Sisters. Tickets for the ferry waited at the Post Office, food was gathered next then over and above my treat at Evelyn's, an apple pie given from the heart made it onto the front seat.

Picking up my copy of the Valley Voice I was pleasantly surprised by a letter to the editor article printed. Following Rod's earlier story that posed the question 'is the radio station run commercially or community minded', a reply story from the radio station placed them on a high moral standing. A letter to the editor in today's Valley Voice bluntly and honestly publicly fired 'dirty laundry' double barrels. The article said everything that has long needed to be said knocking the radio station from a self-made false pedestal, something I would have liked to do but long run out of energy for; a positively uplifting outing ☺….

Returned to paradise we readily slipped back into routines. I split wood for the evening and Tia covered kilometres racing up hill and down dale barking at extreme points until the splitter was returned to the shed. Avoiding it long enough, I couldn't bring myself to even look at the washing; getting a good chunk of the wardrobe dried by the heater yesterday, soaking towels were left to drown ☺!!!!

Today seemed somewhat special, beginning by watching a pair of eagles on the horizon gliding above the valley paddock. Taking a timely peek at the setting sun, a single eagle was sighted gliding low over bottom paddocks; doing a loop it returned via the gorge before disappearing from view ☺….

Wednesday 19 July 2006
Having seen so very little of it of late, a bee-line was made to the shed to bask in a dose of direct sun over a long slow milo. Adding atmosphere, kookaburras dotting surrounding trees broke into chorus on occasion entertaining us morning baskers. Tia took a spell from chewing her bone only long enough for me to remove an unbudging pesky piece of meat wedged between her teeth, putting an end to the full-time salivating and tongue slapping ☺….

Refreshing the laundry water then myself, I shot through over the mountain for a 2p.m. scheduled chat with Constable Cameron. Getting myself to the appointment on time only to hear the words "Cameron is in Launceston". A quick call to his mobile and we rescheduled to meet later at Rainbow Falls, a nice compromise….

True to his word Cameron called by. Talking at length, we discussed the best possible course of action looking for long-term lasting solutions to all issues raised. For the short-term Cameron's going to clarify laws from gun to recreational vehicle use for a clear-cut path forward. I can help myself by keeping an incident specific diary; lucky I've already made a reasonable start ☺….

Thursday 20 July 2006
Intentions of getting straight into the washing got somewhat pleasantly waylaid returning Sheila's missed call. We have a solid sincere friendship that doesn't require high maintenance. When we do talk we pick up where last left off and that takes as long as it takes ☺….

Throwing the drowning towels a buoy brought them back to life, refreshing the water yet again; also washed long-term storage out of sheets, rejuvenating them in anticipation of Mum's visit. The hand sewing on my daks has survived wear and tear and a few dunks in the washing; machine, credit to a long forgotten skill, and may it stay that way ☺!!!!

Exhausting the supply of laundry detergent and clothes waiting to be washed, was bloody elated to pack the white monster back in its corner until the next time I'm forced to recognise its existence….

Lightening a mundane load, I filled a glass of red and disappeared into the paddocks with my best friend investigating nearby. Wandering in the mild evening air until poor light forced us indoors for another night of the usual routine of heating, eating, dishes and writing....

Friday 21 July 2006
When plans were made some weeks back, I mentioned to Charles I'd bring a snack to go with a cuppa visiting to trade electric fence insulators for Destiny bits. Setting a time for today, I absolutely went berserk last night; following Ruth's lemon slice recipe to the letter, had the first attempt neatly tucked into the fridge before bed. A simple recipe - the only bit that gave me the shits was crushing biscuits to a pulp. My hand copped a punishing but all for a good cause.... Eating☺....
Beginning 7:30am, blackbirds looking for a nesting site made one hell of a ruckus dismantling last years blackbird proofing in the cottage roof. A piece of timber filling a gap in the roof was pushed out of the way by the determined little buggers, but they have matched it with the most determined bugger of all.... Me☺!!!!
Delivering heart worm tablets to cover Tia for our time away in Mildura, Pam called in on her way home from St. Helens pulling me up from splitting the last of the telegraph pole. In need of sustenance we sampled the lemon slice over a hot brew. Proving to be a winner, for giving the right response Pam got to take some home☺....
A reliable trait, being as punctual as ever, wandered in the direction of Charles' for our 1p.m. arranged meeting time. Parking by the tidy looking Camira amongst his collection of cars, I needed no more than to see the configuration of an entire working tailgate lock and indicator to realise no spare parts were needed. Reassembling Destiny's bits to functioning with minimal fuss eliminates the need to climb over the back seat to release the tailgate, after poking things in the right spots I opened and shut the tailgate a few times just because I could☺.... Time for a brew and more lemon slice....

Saturday 22 July 2006
Leaving the bungalow door open working around the yard; wrens and robins have been roaming in make themselves at home accepting anything on offer, and depositing evidence of their visit on the door step. Entering the bungalow last week I had to duck as a robin made a quick exit over my head... ahhhh, paradise....
With my little mate safely tucked into Destiny I took a trip outside my comfort zone. Tackling the job of levering a telegraph pole sized tree trunk from its elevated perch, held by gravity, nestled in V-notches across the top of two poles of similar size. Three poles make up a square frame standing tall within a metre of the shed. Not keen on heights, my footing was sure and steady tackling the elevated, horizontal tree trunk, from on top of the shed roof....
Getting the required reach across using a star picket to lever the delicately resting pole, couldn't wedge the picket far enough under to disturb the pole from its V-notch resting position. Never beaten just thought challenged - grabbed a second star picket. Using one as a wedge and the second as a chock, combined with a dose of adrenalin, permitted me to lever the pole to the edge of no return. The realisation of the telegraph pole sized log finding air and beginning to fall, and that I'd successfully achieved my goal with such a large structure, was

an awesome sensation. Throwing the star pickets to the ground I returned jelly legs confidently to the ladder☺!!!!

Plummeting from five metres above only seconds earlier, the monster of a log that so quickly and quietly found ground scarred it with only one small divot. It was just a matter of time before the structure fell independently, mobile at the base and with dry splits my fist could fit in, I prefer the frame came down in a controlled manner….

With the chainsaw cleaned and maintained to Dad's specifications, it was time to strike a blow. By the close of business the pole had left its resting site, was cut into pieces, stored in the shed, and work site tidied. Another month of timber created within a few hours, too bloody easy☺!!!!

Sunday 23 July 2006

I certainly know how to pick the days. Within minutes of getting out of bed a light shower gave paradise a moist covering and went on to do nothing more than that; great conditions instead to clean and maintain the chainsaw after the event☺….

Proudly returning a clean chainsaw to the cottage found and returned a missed call from Lesley, we left no stone unturned. Keeping my bum in the chair let my fingers keep doing the walking, next dialling Mum and Dad's number. We were still immersed in conversation when Ross pulled in to top off a social afternoon☺….

Running water was once again sabotaged splitting the hose by being driven over; sure, it's not designed for running over, but seemingly cheap hardware store bargains are generally just cheap shit. Water delivered stinks of resin used in the hoses' manufacture and the rubber dries and goes brittle quickly. If the price fits into a tight budget then 9 out of 10 it's rubbish, proving the saying 'you get what you pay for'….

Nestling in for the evening, a dear thoughtful and long time Mildura friend, Mary, phoned to let me know we have known one another now for ten years. Today celebrating its 10th anniversary, we met at the first ever Fergie Tractor Rally, with near on three hundred entrants attempting to enter the Guinness book of records and only seven drivers being women. It was destined we meet. Leaving tomorrow to cross the Simpson Desert with members of the Land Rover Club, Mary will return home while I'm still in Mildura so we planned to cross paths over a couple of beers….

The telegraph pole denoting my virginal chainsaw cut reached its use-by-date, cooking its last meal, heating water and the cottage for the final time. A long and distinguished career spanning a few decades now enters its final step as toilet deoderiser, to its existence I give many thanks☺!!!!

Monday 24 & Tuesday 25 July 2006

As the date suggests, ink never made paper last night. I had no words willing to present themselves for the journal….

Concerned about a lump discovered inside Tia's right thigh, adjacent her bottom nipple, I made a date with the puppy doctor for 3p.m. Monday in a search for answers. My little mate wasn't showing any signs of discomfort; life was going on as per usual but rarely things ignored go away. Before leaving for the trek to St. Helens and vet, I'd just finished a blow wave and was shocked to hear a freaky shower of hail pelting the roof; drenched in sun I didn't see it coming. One large cloud passing over lightened part of its moisture load on the way past????

In Tia's resisting 'I hate the vet' manner, she initially put on a struggle receiving a cool response from the woman examining her, having nowhere near the calm personality of the business owner.

Settling enough for a vet probe, standing in the small room surrounding the cold stainless steel examination table, it seems only I could feel the deep hurtful stabbing pain the clinically delivered words provided. The word cancer, and the probabilities of malignant, benign, aggressive, contained, doesn't feel good, and may have it early enough spun without finding a place to rest in my brain. A head still reeling to come to grips with its new-found unwelcome knowledge, moved onto the next step. Cutting straight to the chase, the lump needed to be removed sooner than later, also insisting Tia be desexed at the same time, all this for a mere $415, money I sure as hell didn't have....

Feeling my pain, without hesitation Mum and Dad came to our aid allowing Tia's surgery to be scheduled for Wednesday. Organising details prior to leaving an emergency entered the front door. The broken body of a dog hit by a car was rushed through; I sure could feel their pain....

Stunned with numbness the drive home was done in auto-pilot, tears of realisation fought their way to the surface from time to time, desiring only to be home protected with my little mate to let them flow freely, my heart sure felt bruised....

Body numbness incorporated my brain; totally uninterested in anything other than Tia's immediate need not one word of ink would flow from the pen....

Waking with cried out telltale puffy eyes, tears eased gaining strength in hope rather than despair. As if yesterday's stinging words evaporated, while I split wood my little mate raced excitedly all over the place, our life together resumed its happy normality, from the outside looking in everything appears fine....

Adding to my buckets full, 2mm of tears dropped from the sky. Feeling fitting, it was delivered in waves during the afternoon. Unfocussed, I could do little more than the requirements to keep life ticking over. Coming to grips with what Tia is about to endure my mind rarely wandered from her plight, wishing only to endure her load....

Wednesday 26 July 2006

Tia slept obliviously warm and peaceful by my side all night. It was only my mind that regularly stirred looking at the clock watching slow hours pass to the sound of drips falling from the sky then 6a.m. came around all too soon. My heart felt for the active little body so contentedly sleeping snugly. Telling her all I knew wouldn't prepare her for what was waiting ahead and the purpose of the pain she was yet to endure....

Unable to have anything to eat prior to the pending operation I couldn't bring myself to eat either. One look into those eyes and swallowing would have been out of the question, because it's rare Tia doesn't sample anything I'm having. Still pitch black outside we disturbed a couple of wallabies feeding on the trip to the loo; a day I wasn't looking forward to but faced with strength and forged forward....

My wish was granted. Jeff was in the surgery and the atmosphere friendly when we arrived. Receiving satisfied answers to Tia questions that had spun to the surface of my brain since Monday, I then asked after the dog hit by a car. With no internal damage its body will heal with time. A well-practised craft of separating pets from their humans, with swift professionalism Tia and I were parted without stress. With AEnone's blessing, her phone number was left as a contact point to reach me after surgery was complete....

A beautiful mind and a generous heart - time in AEnone's company evaporates. Following a brew in town we returned to her home. There the call came through prior to noon to say Tia was fine and the lumps name had been changed from cancer to lipoma. Those words releasing Tia of any potential death sentence lifted my heart to the point of feeling light and airy. Sharing the news and a celebratory hug with AEnone elevated the level of strength between two strong women, while the third strong woman recovered from anaesthetic ☺....

Never a lull in conversation time elapsed. Grateful to have spent it with AEnone, we hugged farewell so I could excitedly pick my little mate up and bring her home to familiar surroundings ☺....

Once the patient was comfortable, my first move was to share the day's knowledge with Mum and Dad, fumbling to find words of gratitude to thank them for making today possible. At times I find the English language inadequate for words to describe deep inner feelings received from heartfelt giving that is truly life enhancing; the word love alone is not enough ☺????

With the luxury of hindsight and clear thinking, 'lipoma' is just a fancy name for an accumulation of fat cells; if the female vet initially examining Tia performed her job correctly and did a simple biopsy there would have been no need to operate at all!!!!

Thursday 27 July 2006

My little mate came to life long enough to share a bite of toast, swallow a disguised painkiller, devour a meaty bone and have a wee. Compulsory to remain quiet for a few days and only walks on the lead permitted, she sure isn't going to buck the system, happily returning to bed snoozing off her burst of morning activity ☺....

Mother Nature assisted our plight. The lingering easterly cloud mass that's been playing around gave us double barrels all morning. Eliminating the thought of battling the downpour and splitting a load of wood, opted instead to remain snuggy in the bungalow. With Tia already settled in there snoozing it was pointless altering an established peaceful environment, sensible only to join in ☺....

Staying attentive by my best friend's side, I had a rare complete day off indulging in the luxury of reading. Restful hours together quietly passed ☺....

Friday 28 July 2006

The only problem I'm encountering in Tia's healing process is stopping her from licking the stitches, like a mother tuned into a crying baby, my brain snaps into gear with an inkling of her licking the wound....

Close to two days enclosed in a small space, it was time to freshen the bungalow and catch some sunshine. Compromising with my little mate, a small extension was added to her lead keeping her nearby at all times, but limiting the temptation to stride out and split stitches. It's hard to believe Tia's just endured major surgery, without a whimper she's gaining ground ☺....

With enough flow to get washing started, between loads I once again repaired the hose. This time being a little smarter, I threaded the section of crumbly stinky hose, draped over the driveway, through a piece of snug fitting PVC pipe retrieved from the burnt out house. Let's see how that survives traffic ☺ ????

Taking one of the many trips to the clothesline I stopped for a look at the garlic. Shoots have doubled in size following the deluge of the past few days - all but about two of the planted cloves have taken off ☺ ....

Powering through the laundry it came to an abrupt halt. After a refreshing refill the machine seemed to want to remain on drain. The spinner slowly turned ploughing its way through sudsy water and refused to alter that mode. Taking that as a sign to stop, towels were left to soak, deciding to look at the problem with a fresh mind tomorrow avoiding any negative emotion at that precise moment ☺ !!!!

Reducing the higher than usual electricity use, I reverted to nursing the patient in the wood-powered living of the cottage for an evening with the feeling of space....

Saturday 29 July 2006

The splitter head and sledgehammer wood cutting system merely bounced off the latest pole downsized by the chainsaw, the timber's very springy and tight. Not to be beaten, I replaced the splitter head with a rusty axe head. Driven into the wood by the sledgehammer, the keener edge of the axe penetrated and split the logs willingly. Following the impact of many hits the axe head handle surround split in two limiting the surface area to impact on, but the system still worked. Leaving Tia to rest her socks in Destiny, I went about breaking up several logs to dry and air because they're not burning so well either....

Wearing down and considering packing it away, doing a final cut the sledgehammer skimmed off the axe head finding my thumb where it was perched stabilising the piece of timber, endorphins created an instant numbness. Removing the glove not only found an instant fat bruised thumb, but was surprised the impact split and bruised the underside, also weeping blood. Confident it wasn't broken, didn't consider getting it seen to it would eventually heal. If a x-ray was required it meant either a trip to St. Helens or Launceston, St. Helens send the x-rays off to Launceston for processing where they also have to be picked up.... Making me think twice before considering medical help beyond basic!!!!

Cleaning blood from my thumb spotted the washing machine patiently waiting to be dealt with, and like a gift from the gods it worked accordingly, permitting me to finish up and pack up without fuss ☺ ....

Unprepared to do battle with unwilling wood to light the fire I plugged in the electric stove cooking up a feed for my little mate and me. Food is a great way to administer Tia's medication. Painkiller tablets disappear wrapped in minced meat, and the liquid anti-inflammatory medicine is invisible incorporated into her food bowl. Nothing gets spat out ☺ ....

With the necessary daily bits complete we retreated to the bungalow to settle by the electric heater. Tia snuggled in her bed, I completed the book started; there we kissed the day goodbye....

Sunday 30 July 2006
Pushing us around like a swaying tree, wind unrelentingly nudged at us right through the night delivering a punch with several 'WAKE UP' strong gusts. Arriving with company, wind brought with it bloody cold air at the same punishing pace....
Blustery conditions also bring bird activity to a screaming halt, only seeing two ravens bothering to do battle and they moved at speeds that would sure supply a head rush; very little wing flapping was needed ☺....
Not excited to rush into it, I contentedly observed elements from behind glass hugging a milo or two, with no complaints from my little mate still happily curled up in bed. Having no room for error, from the simplest task to thinking through my every move, Tia's safety, comfort and patchwork quilt belly must come first. Of utmost importance to be kept quiet, one unthinking moment of habit could cause a brief sprint and burst stitches. With each passing day we're moving further out of the woods toward full mobility. My wishes of no gun shots, thunder or other noise causing stress have so far been granted....
For the sake of limited mobility and rest the bungalow is the preferred room to hang out, idling the morning away over a milo or two protected from the lashing front outside; watched Ross' car pass the window. Doing what he needed to down the shed, we shared a brew and he shared a horror story. Ross' gory knowledge related to splitting the stitches of a spay cut. If it occurs digestive juices and the bowel come into contact, digestive juices then go about doing their thing breaking bits of food down, the bowel is seen as just a piece of meat and death results in a slow unthinkable manner. By no means am I slack in the care area hoping his horror story is nothing but useless information!!!!
No need to wind down from this day because I didn't wind up. Keeping my best friend and me rested in the bungalow nest I picked up the phone to Mum and Dad. The words I enjoyed most through our conversation was "the next time we speak I'll be looking you in the eye". Being in the company of Mum and Dad's physical presence is a pleasure I haven't had for almost two years; come on Thursday ☺....

Monday 31 July 2006
A pretty simple day; aside from copious amounts of rest I factored in a trip to St. Marys. Short on food and out of milk a trip over the mountain couldn't be avoided. Sparking up the electric stove I got water on the boil for showering....
To avoid Tia's initial excited race around the cottage barking when the blow waver starts up, a cool windy day in paradise, I had to think outside the circle of routine to dry my hair. Leaving it wet was plain silly. In no hurry and taking the passive option, avoiding the excessive stir up, my hair was dried slowly by the electric heater in the bungalow, leaving my best friend to snooze stress free ☺....
Getting straight to the point in the big metropolis the Post Office box check and supermarket were complete in minutes, incorporating in that a chat to Maggie. Pretty much a walk in walk out at the newsagents for the ordered copy of the Valley Voice; a short chat with Evelyn was the lengthiest stop. Filling my face and sharing samples of bakery delights with my little mate we drove home ☺....

Surprisingly, since giving my thumb a whack with the sledgehammer endorphins kicked in and they remained. Without a throb my thumb has only protested being used for any physical movement, reminding me, 'hey, I copped a blow, how about a few days rest'!!!!

Tuesday 1 August 2006
Stirring into consciousness, I've regularly woken to a blackbird whistling sweetly from the cottage roof. The same whistling procedure was occurring this morning, but a sudden calamity brought the sweet sounds to an abrupt halt and a flat line silence followed. The ruckus left behind not a shred of evidence of blackbird proofing being dismantled????
Being cornered, it was either today or today to prepare for the big holiday trek to Mildura. Wind finally giving us a bloody rest, in impeccable timing the sun broke through, leaving Tia to bask on the extended lead I went about preparing for our time away. From cleaning to dragging out maps and preparing travelling meals, no known stone was left unturned....
Dangerously close to running out of drinking water caused a run over the other side of North Sister. Inviting me in for a dunked tea bag Ross bled his spleen over personality differences and work politics. Happy to leave his side of the mountain, which was fully shaded by 4:30p.m.-ish, headed home. Nearing the pass between the Sisters a halo of light beamed through the avenue of trees lining the road as we approached; crossing back over to our side there was another hour of full sun waiting - unbelievable ☺!!!!
Capitalising on our extra daylight, and limited on lead, Ms Tia happily steered me on a wander re-marking turf. Tia's alertness, brightness and energy are rising in leaps and bounds; her high priority appetite is also returning with vengeance ☺....

Wednesday 2 August 2006
Refusing to take onboard any emotion of anxiety, I put one foot in front of the other preparing for destination Mildura on the first leg of the journey, simply just letting time evolve and unfold in a relaxed casual manner. Aware of something different happening with changed patterns of behaviour and an air of excitement, Tia's extended lead reached into Destiny; securing a place, she wasn't about to budge. Tia kept a watchful eye on proceedings as our belongings were neatly and strategically placed or wedged in the contours Destiny offers ☺....
Flicking the main power switch to off and shutting the front gate behind, I magnified the appreciation of the beauty of the mountain drive to fill my heart in absence. Taking the day in stride I walked into the local salon for a haircut with the lovely Kellie. Saving me a trip to St. Helens she's taken over ownership of the St. Marys salon - lucky us. Making Evelyn's the last stop before clocking up the kilometres, from the generosity of her heart she put together a travel pack sending me on my way with fruit buns and sausage rolls. I sure love my new home and adopted family ☺....
Driving Destiny within her limits she went smoothly, making it to Ali's at Port Sorell just after our loosely targeted 3p.m.-ish. Ali who loves cooking and I who loves eating combined for a feast of delicious food and great company, eating and chatting our way through three hours easily. One way to impress me, Tia was also thoughtfully included in Ali's culinary skill and generosity ☺....
Fed, watered and exercised, we did a dash for the boat. Making the 7:15p.m. cut off and being one of the last to arrive there was no waiting in queues, pretty much locking up shop behind.

Striking it lucky boarded the Spirit of Tasmania III, put to use from the failed Sydney run while one of the regular ferries was in dry dock. After comfortably settling Tia in Destiny, not only was there an escalator ride to level 7, but there was a reading room away from bars, TV's, pokies and most noise. Able to escape every brain polluter, except the public address system that intruded at will, for the most my brain was free to think. Joined by several other people in the reading room, and me being the only one writing, thought maybe in the future I can be the one to provide them with the reading material they were so absorbed in ☺????
Floating around in Bass Strait, with little choice but be separated from those who truly love me, may the morning come around quick, reuniting the Tassie Trio and bridging a long absence from family ☺….

Thursday 3, Friday 4, Saturday 5, Sunday 6, Monday 7 & Tuesday 8 August 2006
Moored on the other side, the Tassie Trio were reunited and turned loose to terrorise traffic in the big smoke. Doing well with directions I got myself over Westgate Bridge and smoothly approaching the exit to Western Ring Road. Following a truck in the rain and committed to turn, saw a sign ahead for the Western Ring Road exit another 300 meters further along. Shit, there was no doing a U-turn. Incorporating my usual level of wrong turns finally got bearings and back on track; entering the Calder Highway I was home and hosed ☺…. Well almost, just 500 kilometres to go….
Destiny performed without missing a beat; towns and changing scenery got further apart and on she went taking us to our destination 2:30p.m.-ish to be met with open arms. My eyes welled with happy tears, after an absence of two years we had plenty of 'let me look at you again to see what's changed' and loving conversation to share, kissing Thursday goodbye in wonderful company ☺….
Making a conscious decision to be on holidays, even from writing, other than brief prompt notes permitted myself to relax from the regimented habit to simply immerse in family and be spoilt. Meals magically appeared, hot and cold water on tap at my convenience and a fully automatic washing machine that beeps when the laundry is complete ☺…. ahhhh….
A relaxing, warm Friday disappeared playing apprentice to Dad, beginning the knowledge trade by being handed down the skill of replacing a splitter handle, fixing the one I broke through a few miscues. Then I was taken through the verbal and practical technique of setting up the jig and sharpening the teeth on a chainsaw chain. Our father, daughter, bonding session also included any other tip not already covered in chainsaw maintenance ☺…. Content sharing in person with Mum and Dad, is a privilege that rarely comes by ☺….
While Dad played his regular Saturday golf round Mum took me on a shopping expedition. Taking in every new shop, expansion and business relocation in the City shopping centre, then furthering the tour we drove out to the massively enlarged Centro Plaza on 15th street.
Following lunch in the food court to boost my energy Mum toured me through the complex. Feet worn threadbare, only then was I allowed to take us home, returning to a patiently waiting Tia and Destiny shaded under sails in the carpark….
Unable to be by her side 100% of the time, and beside myself with the increasing developing gap in Tia's stitches, frustrated at my inability to stop the regressed healing process I looked for assistance. Having the convenience of 7-day trading, I took Mum and Dad's new Lancer for a trip out to a pet supplies shop, and unfortunately for Tia, purchased an Elizabethan collar

to give reassurance in times of absence so Tia isn't able to reach the stitches with her tongue....

With the collar sadly fitted to my little mate's head I then couldn't find my wallet; not in the car or inside the house I returned to the pet shop, driving home empty headed and handed to find it on a chair where I'd fit Tia's collar!?!?

Giving an absent mind a recharge I indulged in one of Mum's traditional Sunday roasts I've so long craved for, and having my brain and batteries charged spent time tidying Destiny. Cleaning windows I noticed the old rego label still affixed was a month out of date. Windows glistening and registration label rectified I then got interested in mantling the loose pieces of the cigarette lighter. The annoying rattle held together by a peg to be silenced is no longer required, leaving it sitting flush and firmly intact against the dash....

Come Monday I was beside myself in helplessness with an inability to stop Tia licking loose stitches and increasing the stomach hole in the moments I can't be there. The medium sized Elizabethan collar purchased Sunday failed the tongue test, devoting every night and most of the day being attentive to Tia's healing needs was failing and feeling beaten. Again with me as apprentice, Dad and I had a go at adding an extension to the collar but Tia sabotaged our attempt as soon as it was returned to her neck. Feeling pretty low and unwilling to leave her side to prevent tongue action and more damage, Mum did a mercy dash to a pet shop purchasing a larger collar. Finally a stop was put to Tia's ability to reach the stitches, turning the healing process around and giving me confidence to leave her side to participate in family life, which swelled for a while. Tegan, boyfriend Kevin and bubby Dekira called in. Now twenty months old it was my first ever sighting of Dekira, Tegan had versed her up to say 'Arr Sue', as she and all nieces had referred to me growing up. 'Arr Sue' sounded so pure and fresh from such an innocent, tender, honest little bub still stumbling over an ever-growing vocabulary. Dekira has an energetic, easy going happy personality, very loveable and very loving☺....

Tuesday Mum hit the pavement power walking, Dad tinkered around doing maintenance chores outside; with life organised and ticking along I took time out to visit a lagging journal on holidays....

Looking for a little extra brain reassurance I rang a vet explaining Tia's predicament; responding to questions without an examination, the answers were within my capability. Simply restraining Tia from licking the site and with time the gap will close over. I was also advised to use a diluted iodine solution to keep the area clean, further easing my mind.... Now it's up to time to do its thing....

Wednesday 9 August 2006

Enduring an extremely restless night restraining Tia from licking stitches, woke worn out from hours of broken sleep. I can only imagine the alien discomfort she's bearing. Facing the days early light Tia was not at all ready to play ball, resisting all the way in fruitless attempts at pressing studs together putting the cumbersome Elizabethan collar on; in a fit of frustration and cussing quit the idea. Needing a more user friendly system, Dad headed to his shed cut the base out of a bucket and it slipped on painlessly without a struggle, doing the trick in a quick friendly manner????

Leaking fluid, the opening hole into Tia's stomach gaped a little further apart. An uneasy brain needing further reassurance I again called a vet in search of answers to questions floating unsettled. The fluid leaking gaping hole, looks like it will never heal, which apparently is not uncommon in a mobile area containing stitches. An experienced reply said it should close over in two to three weeks. I don't like wishing my life away but look forward to the hole being covered in skin. Until that occurs, Tia must not be allowed to access the area and must be kept, quiet adding to her displeasure….

With no immediate health threat and a brain at ease, I rescheduled a caddying date with Dad leaving Mum to baby-sit the patient as per our original arrangements☺….

Heading out to the golf course Dad pulled in to a service centre and within minutes had the chainsaw bar dressed, sending me home with a total chainsaw makeover. Following introductions to all pleasant personalities, by midday Dad and three of his golfing buddies teed off and we walked the 18 holes in peaceful surroundings. At times the winding course edged onto the River Murray and the variety of trees edging the fairways lured diverse wildlife. Nearing the latter part of the game, waiting dutifully by Dad's clubs while the fellas tackled a green, three hawks kept me entertained; overall a very relaxing afternoon out☺….

Returning home I relieved 'nurse Mum' and resumed patient care duties. Sterilising a small pair of scissors I removed stitches threaded through the nicely healed spay cut, doing the right thing after their 14 day cycle, saw one wound completely healed and stitch free. I'll be a happy camper when that can be said for both surgery cuts obviously no one would be anymore happier than Tia☺!!!!

Thursday 10 August 2006

Being a little selfish and badly needing solid consecutive sleep without a mind on constant licking standby, I left the modified bucket on Ms Tia's head while we slept in our cosy nest in the back of Destiny. Able to relax and combined with exhaustion I fell into an instant coma. Healing discomfort and the bucket combination, at times, are causing my little mate moments of frustration restricted from the natural instinct of helping herself heal. I expect Tia will be shy of red buckets for a while once she's free of this one!!!!

Tia's leaking liquid stomach contents reeked over her body and extended to all the bedding. The scent had to be turned around. Starting with my little mate, I sponged the affected parts of her body and dabbed a diluted iodine solution over her stomach. Next in line was all of our combined bedding. The aroma had to go to make room for more hole in the belly fluids. Looking for a positive aspect I consoled myself - Tia is one day closer to finding an end to the healing process☺….

Dad took the reins of babysitting duties, freeing Mum and I to follow through with plans of meeting Tegan and Dekira at J.C. Park so Dekira could burn a little energy on playground equipment. Taking no convincing, Mum was easily led to the corner store for an ice cream on our walk to the park; without wandering too far from the shop Tegan and Dekira picked us up en route. Each time Dekira wanted a sample of ice cream she just called out "Nana", and a willing hand reached over to satisfy the need. Wide eyed and excited; the park offered more than enough for an energetic child to wear any adult out. Dekira however managed to wear out three. After two hours and a dirty nappy, yawning broke down any resistance to leave☺….

Dropped home and after bidding farewells I once again sponged Tia's stomach, applied diluted iodine, and prepared our beds to do it all over again ☺ ....

Friday 11 August 2006
Following Tia's most restful night sleep snuggling by my side, near on every spare moment of the day ahead was devoted to hygiene. Daily, Destiny is emptied, sponged, aired, and all bedding gets the level of attention required. Adding to the three times a day ritual of sponging bitter smelling body fluid from Tia and applying diluted iodine, I made a start removing stitches from the lipoma surgical cut. Beginning at healed extremities, two stitches were snipped and threads pulled free. It's my intention to progress removing stitches moving toward the stomach hole and total healing, which is now another day closer to being ☺ ....
At last the stomach hole regressing has peaked. Now my little mate is making ground in the right direction. Previous experience, following Mum's cancer operation that resulted in splitting stitches and a gaping stomach hole, has helped me through Tia's comparable condition without sending me into a state of shock. If the stomach hole syndrome was alien I reckon the sight would have freaked me out. It's something else having a keyhole peek at internal organs at work....
The only movement outside the front gate today was done by the heads of family. Dad, the hunter gatherer, battled the grocery shopping, and Mum took off like a startled gazelle pounding the pavement for kilometres power walking. For me nurse duties dominated; remaining put, I kept the home fires burning ☺ ....
From the time humans get active in the morning until they're ready to wind down in the evening, the most noticeable difference living in suburbia to my Tasmanian home is the unrelenting sounds saturating airwaves. Every imaginable power and petrol driven machine known to humans can be heard randomly at any given time, dogs of all shapes and sizes dotted in most backyards also have their say....
The density of the dog population presents itself blatantly with the intrusion of the occasional hot-air balloon passing overhead. Sitting quietly with my best mate last night two balloons passed over shattering ground peace: not one dog, including a grumpy Ms Tia, saw the pleasure I did in watching a parachutist jump from one of the balloons!!!!
To an observant eye, ear and mind, nature can be seen and heard intermingling with competing human and dog sounds; most activity in residential living comes from birds....

Saturday 12 August 2006
Wriggling too much, any attempt made at removing a stitch was foiled by Tia at the first two tummy cleaning sessions. Thinking out why I've been successful until now, realised I'd begun wearing a disposable glove, leaving it off for the final cleansing managed to remove another stitch with minimal effort. One suture closer in completing the total process, along with my little mate, agree that day won't come too soon ☺ !!!!
Leaving me, Mum and Ms Tia to spend a lazy afternoon simply basking in sunshine, Dad took off for a ritual Saturday round of golf. Taking on the serious end of the stick Dad's competing in Club Championships. The competition will consume two consecutive full weekends. With our solar panels fully exposed to the sun and immersed in on another's company Mum and I idly chatted - beats the pants off the once a week chat over the phone ☺ ....

In a quiet moment early evening I gave Tia free time off lead, she celebrated the new-found freedom by quietly strolling her way down the backyard having a poo then voluntarily returning to her bed, no point over exerting one's self☺....

Sunday 13 August 2006
Waking to the sound of a chorus of dogs at a distance saw the culprit hot-air balloon pass overhead at a Tia-safe distance through Destiny's tailgate window☺....
Almost carbon copy to yesterday, Dad went to golf leaving Mum, Tia and me to spend another relaxing day home together. Just for a small taste of pampering I massaged Mum's feet☺....
Tending to my little mate's needs, another two stitches found their way out of her body. Thinking I'm looking at the goals and getting ready to kick the rules took a twist. The healing stitches are adding an element of frustrating itchiness so I added lanolin rubbing to the cleaning, stitch removing, antiseptic anointing routine. When Tia's leaking pasty stomach juices were at their worst I thought 'shit, where do I start', now, little if any fluid is leaking and if I'm not mistaken the hole has slightly reduced hallelujah. Dad's modified couple of dollar plastic bucket has been invaluable in the healing process☺!!!!

Monday 14 August 2006
All finding a niche and slipping into a non-intrusive comfortable morning groove, keeping it simply flowing; when Mum and Dad finish in the bathroom I take over. Following a stroll chatting with familiar faces in the neighbourhood collecting the paper from the corner store Dad escapes outside. After doing a bit in the house Mum regularly takes off for a power walk, if I can't contribute I stay out of the way and migrate to my best friend restricted to the great outdoors....
Particularly after Tia food, for a change of scenery I did a brief trip into town grabbing only listed items and returned immediately like a homing pigeon to family....
Patiently and extremely carefully, another two stitches were extracted from the fast healing wriggling body of Ms Tia, the remaining strands of body intruding nylon surround the hole, a delicate area I'll tread carefully with. Tia's limited lifestyle is rapidly healing its way to an end. The gut hole is closing over at a suitably impressive speed it has now reduced to half the original gaping size. I'm that comfortable with Tia's progress that in the evening she's enjoying time off lead☺....

Tuesday 15 August 2006
Wishing to accompany Mum to her 10:30am appointment with the surgeon, I waited patiently in reception for the outcome. Pleased with Mum's progress, Mr Mason has scheduled an annual colonoscopy for November 2. Time to once again face the dreaded 'fleet', a liquid taken to clear the bowel before any procedure; three horrible litres forced down the throat out of sheer have to, just the mention of the word makes Mum shudder!!!!
Home long enough to freshen up, I resumed my position in the passenger seat and we took off to lose a couple of hours over lunch and plenty of chat with Betty, a relation on the 'Ford' side of family. Able to obtain it at rock bottom prices, or free, Betty sent us on our way with port and red wine; very welcome and useful☺....

Rounding the bend to home I saw a brushcutter at work next door. My thoughts headed straight to the word a-oh!!!! With a zero tolerance for brushcutters, Dad was pacifying a cranky Ms Tia. Three bordering neighbours have fired up their machines the past week, chances of a spell from the disturbing noise is looking good.... Phew....
Relieving Dad of pacifying duties I went to work cleaning and soothing Tia's belly, not as relaxed as she could be. Removing any more stitches from the delicate area was out of the question. Getting Ms Muffet's tummy comfortable as possible is all tonight permitted....

Wednesday 16 August 2006
Dad left us to smash a white ball around. Mum, Aunty Claire and I shared an afternoon out while my little mate looked after her best friend Destiny parked not too far off. Beginning with lunch at Coomy Club, after feeding ourselves then fed the face of poker machines, having that once in a pink fit where money is wasted on gambling....
Following a lovely meal I was stunned to walk into a wall of cigarette smoke in the gaming room, apparently new laws in force prohibiting smoking in public buildings is exempt in NSW, my lungs bucked up tarnishing the enjoyment of a nice afternoon out????
There was a big haul with stitches today, managing two with the morning tummy wash and another two with the last antiseptic cleaning. Through wriggling and a paw pushing my hand away, there appears to be just a single stitch left in the sensitive area at the open hole, now two-thirds reduced. Initially my brain wasn't excited with the thought of doing the nylon snipping. One stitch at a time in quiet wriggle moments, along with a good dose of patience, is closing in on a job, a role far preferable for someone else to have relieved me of. It would be nice on occasion to simply say, "I don't wanna do it", and have a good fairy take up the slack, but only in my dreams ☺ ....

Thursday 17 August 2006
After conferring with the heads of family and contributing to household maintenance, spruced up, I took off, not only to do the rounds shopping for specials grabbing non perishable bargains to take home, but also booking and confirming travel arrangements. Travel plans of leaving Sunday 27, to avoid busy work day traffic and spend a couple of hours with Stacey in Melbourne, unfortunately had to be put forward until Monday 28, because the ferry had no room spare for Destiny....
Out and about still roaming I called into Jacko's getting contact details for Helen, a school friend I hadn't had contact with for many years. Taking a chance mid afternoon I dropped in and was greeted with open arms. Flicking the switch on the kettle, Helen pulled out school photos and we reminisced sharing what knowledge we had of those pictured young faces full of life; exchanging contact details, I left to resume nurse responsibilities ☺ ....
Giving my little mate the days final antiseptic tummy wash, sitting perfectly poised Tia exposed her belly long enough for me to take advantage of the instant to snip that last stitch, a moment that brought a feeling of elation. Ending my least desired Tia job ever, the last leg of the healing process is now for the tummy hole to finish closing over. While all this went on around me another cooked meal magically appeared ☺ !!!!

Friday 18 August 2006
Laid out flat and concealed in the groove of a surgical scar, one hidden intact stitch came to light with the morning tummy clean, however, it didn't last any longer than the antiseptic wash, a few kicks and wriggles and it joined the other fifteen in the bin. Three stitches held Tia's spay cut together, thirteen for the lipoma surgery. Thankfully they're all now part of history, making up memories. Instead of an open window to Tia's intestinal organs the hole is now forming an internal cone, healing from the inside out.... Halle-bloody-lujah!!!!
Being cautiously thorough and phoning a vet looking for an answer as to when Tia can have freedom to her body, sadly for my little mate, I was advised to leave the bucket in place until a scab covers the void.... A couple of days????
Come beer o'clock, Dad dropped me over the other side of town to Pauline's, a low maintenance friendship spanning several decades, established from my after school job at 'New World Supermarket' when I was a tender fifteen year old. Pauline has clocked up 25 years service with the supermarket and four kids, my life, on the contrary has been nowhere near as consistent. Spending a few hours chatting over a couple of ales, all the gaps were filled on where we've been and what we're doing.... Hic ☺....
Strolling back to the home side of town I made a brief stop to pick up processed photos that included the pictorial, step by step, demolition work achieved with the chainsaw at Rainbow Falls. The prints generated a bonding time with Dad, discussing timber and its behaviour from cutting to splitting and burning, sharing our knowledge of experience ☺....

Saturday 19 & Sunday 20 August 2006
A night out at a party put paid to any thought of writing Saturday. In logical sequence starting with yesterday's events, Dad did the regular golfing thing and I shot through for a several hours visiting friends. Other than Tia's company, Mum had some pleasant and precious time to herself ☺....
Visiting unannounced, I started at Fred's. Finding no one home and with nothing to scrawl a note on I stacked shoes by the back door as a calling card. I'll solve the stacked shoes mystery with a phone call at a later date. Next in line for a visit were Mary and Joan, being met there with open arms. Keen to hear everything Mary had to share from her recent crossing of the Simpson Desert, her well documented adventure was soaked up and time evaporated; forced out the door to leave for a family social outing, Camo's 60th....
Before taking off to Camo's party Dad received a pleasing call from the golf club. After three days of play in Club Championships, in his grade, Dad's a contender in a three-way tie ☺ !!!!
Serious about his state of health for Sunday's golf, Dad designated himself as driver. Camo's party was one of plenty; plenty of unknown faces willing to chat, accompanied with plenty of flowing deep fried food and alcohol....
Returning from Gol Gol and the party, Dad turned in front of a car onto the roundabout approaching the bridge, not tight enough to cause an accident but earned him a toot, the unmarked police car he took on, for good measure, pulled us over for a routine check. Tucked together in the glove-box, Dad had an identity crisis, offering Mum's license instead of his own. Clearing the confused look on the officer's face, and passing the breath test, Dad took the tribe home for bed, finishing a good day with an element of excitement ☺....

First thing Sunday Dad prepared golf gear for the three-way showdown; during his psyche time Mum and I slipped out to Cardross for a market. Satisfying my purpose of going to the market to buy local dried fruit to take home, reasonable priced thick socks were also scooped. With little to offer other than a couple of conversations, it took Mum and me a short time to turn around and return home to relieve Dad of babysitting duties. Opting for a quiet afternoon while Dad golfed, Mum buried her nose in a book; I put two days thoughts down on paper and also aired and de-furred bedding making room for Tia's next load ☺ ....
Gently idling the afternoon away, Pauline phoned checking if we were home, calling in with daughter Amanda to be punished with the Rainbow Falls' home video and latest photos. Still in the company of our guests, I broke open beer o'clock. During that time Lukey returned home without a golfing outcome. Tired of trying to finish the round, following a late start on a slow moving busy course, he walked off with 6 holes uncompleted recording a DNF (did not finish) foregoing any placement or recognition; a disappointing finish to two full weekends of competitive golf????

Monday 21 August 2006
Healing from the inside out and unable to see intestinal workings, Tia's stomach hole has a concealed covering. Making an executive decision, Tia's head was released from the confines of the bloody limiting bucket returning her freedom. The moment that red pesky head decoration hit the ground in front of her Tia gave it a punishing chase over the yard pounding the bucket into the ground. It's certainly not how you would treat a friend. It was a pleasure to watch ☺ !!!!
Crossing paths with Pauline this trip returned a long forgotten memory for me that was etched in her mind, willingly reminding me of the time I worked for the supermarket and we had to wear a smock blue dress for a uniform that fit where it touched. I would throw a pair of jeans on underneath the baggy blue uniform, for the purpose of riding my motorbike to work then I would drop my daks out back before hitting the shop. That image left a lasting impression with Pauline. Camo's party also rekindled another supermarket memory; a customer I had regular contact with who was always happy, bubbly and smiling. Fate gave me the opportunity to re-live that time sharing many conversations with Bianca Saturday night ☺ .... Outstanding people leave lasting impressions ☺ ....
Overall, today was a pretty lazy ol' time spent home doing the bits that hold us together for another day, a perfect occasion I long to share when home at Rainbow Falls following a long absence from family. Breaking the slow pace of a quiet afternoon Tegan and bubby Dekira turned up; Dekira added a high burst of energy keeping us all on our toes. Dividing her attention between Dad, Mum and myself, Dekira lovingly wore us out one at a time; a beautiful little person supporting a loving nature I'm glad to have finally met ☺ ....

Tuesday 22 August 2006
Tia made the sin bin within twenty-four hours of her newly found freedom off chain. Without a destructive nature, Tia enjoyed the soft cool soil beneath her toes having a dig in a beautiful groundcover carpet of baby tears, not an action to influence and impress!!!! Escaping from the crime scene, Ms Muffet was taken for a reasonable length walk; I know one of us burned off some energy, exercise being something I've done little of lately ☺ .... Phew....

With plans to have lunch with Betty, Mum and I made a couple of stops on the way. Stop one was to place an advertisement in the 'under $100' free of cost classifieds for Thursday's edition of the local paper, in a plan to relieve Dad's shed from the clutter of surplus tiles. Making a couple more turns, we drove on to the mower centre in Orange Avenue to fill my 'visiting Mildura wish list', attempting to obtain a manual from the 'Cox' mower dealer to assist with waiting repairs on the ride-on at home. What a pleasant experience popping into 'Sunraysia Mowers' turned out to be. There was no manual available but the guys offered dismantling tips and also photocopied appropriate pages from product part sheets on file that demonstrate what part goes where. Charging nothing for the helpful service and pleasant experience, those acts of kindness get my loyalty and recommendation as a great shop to do business ☺!!!!

Turning up at Betty's, the afternoon was pleasantly lost in dissecting Saturday's party, food, tea and conversation ☺....

Returning home, I washed the tea down with a cool beer while kicking the ball again, again, again and again for my best friend until my bare foot was grass stained. Active mobility isn't regressing Tia's stomach holes progressive healing, heading closer to history. I look forward to the entire unpleasant and unnecessary operation experience being just a written memory ☺!!!!

Wednesday 23 August 2006

With Lukey gone to golf and the driveway clear, me, Tia and Destiny reversed out behind on a mission of specials shopping to load up with good priced buys destined for home. After doing over a couple of supermarkets for bargains, I popped into the Cheesecake Shop grabbing a teacake for the planned Aunties afternoon....

I'd just finished plucking Mum's eyebrows when Aunty Shirley and Aunty Glenda pulled up out front. Sitting around the kitchen table over a brew, cake, photos and plenty of chatter, they expressed a desire to watch the Rainbow Falls home video. Adjourning to the lounge the footage held their concentration. Expressing interest in seeing my uncles, their other halves, we set Friday afternoon as a date to reciprocate a visit. Generously, Aunty Shirley offered an assortment of her recently made preserves to take home when we come out ☺....

After waving more than welcome guests off, I got set to take Ms Tia for a walk. Meeting Lukey returning from golf at closed gates, we each opened a side gate leading to the house, letting him in and us out. Both walking Tia and driving about have opened my eyes to the extent of the urban sprawl that has replaced fruit blocks. Houses have, and still are, popping up like mushrooms in spawning season ☺....

Thursday 24 August 2006

Kicking off Tia's 8th birthday celebrations, following a wake up scruff, breakfast was served consisting of a bowl of fresh chicken on a bed of rice; she made short work of the offering. Oblivious to what the date even represented, I took the birthday girl for a walk to give Dad a free go with the edger and mower without her included opinion on buzzing machines. Out and about, the clear line of a front almost on top and moving quick, kept a regular glance over my shoulder and a pace in my step!!!!

Home high and dry, giving Dad ample time to zip over the lawn, the noisy wet front followed us up the driveway; minutes separated our return before the heavy cloud released its load.

Bloody thunder rumbles the front brought with it did nothing to impress, pissing the birthday girl off! I got cranky in my feeble attempts at pacifying the booming, stressed voice of Ms Tia. Seemingly lasting forever, the thunderstorm finally drifted off in the distance!!!!

My best mate's heart rate back to normal following thunder action, Mum returned from the hairdressers to pick me up for lunch, before walking my legs off fulfilling her holiday shopping list ☺ ….

No stone left unturned, Mum permitted my spent body to head in the direction of home. Sitting long enough to catch my breath; don't know where the mustered energy rose from, but with one foot in front of the other pounded the pavement taking the big 8-year-old for another walk. Rounding off Ms Tia's evening, balls of premium mince mixed into rice and topped with a chicken thigh cutlet were served for dinner. The most effective way to please a girl is through culinary delights ☺ ….

Friday 25 August 2006
Deep in sleep dreaming, Tia's retching brought my wandering brain into consciousness in perfect timing to hear the follow through of indigestible bone…. The dear love ☺ !!!!

All but showered, Tegan and Kevin brought the excitable ball of energy, Ms Dekira, for a final visit before they took off to Victor Harbour visiting Kevin's mother. Taking into consideration my average visit to Mildura being two years, Dekira will be almost ready for school next time we again physically meet. I am glad to have met the exhilarating ball of energy. Like a sponge, Dekira's brain absorbs everything, hopefully leaving the little chicken with pleasant memories of our first encounter ☺ ….

Days of the convenience of white goods, hot and cold running water, and meals magically appearing are fast caving in….

Showered, and the last load of clothes dangling from the line, while Dad, the home body, babysat my best mate, Mum and I took off to Red Cliffs visiting Aunty Shirley and Uncle Ian. Greeting us out front as we arrived, Uncle Ian stepped up to met me with a warm, firm, honest hug, shortly followed by a hug as solidly sincere from Aunty Shirley. Both Aunty and Unc accommodated my wish to photograph them together standing amid their colourful, manicured garden. Aunty Shirley being brilliant at anything she puts her hand to, from cooking to craft, I greeted with enthusiasm the offered selection of her preserves along with a lovingly hand knitted square patched throw rug. Uncle Ian, an avid garage sale patron, ensured a piece of him followed me home offering a selection of varying sized secateurs. Before leaving, Aunty Shirley rang her daughter, Cousin Linda, in Melbourne to join in on the happy family gathering for a natter ☺ ….

Stopping in on Aunty Glenda and Uncle Brian on the return trip from Red Cliffs found only Uncle Brian home. After taking his photo and chatting for a short while, Mum and I ventured the final few kilometres to home, rounding off an afternoon out I thoroughly enjoyed ☺ ….

Relieving Dad of babysitting duties I took my little mate out to stretch her legs. Absorbing the many changes and extensive development in the neighbourhood holding my most tender of memories, I've taken Ms Tia walking in a different area each outing. After claiming much real estate pissing next to and sniffing those many fence posts and nature strips, I walked us in the direction of home to call it a day for beer o'clock ☺ ….

Saturday 26 August 2006
Time to realign focus and prepare for the fast approaching return trip home. Avoiding it to invisibility until the last minute, removed from my blind spot, I faced the boring old laundromat to wash bedding. That action forced me out of the car and inside to sleep, leaving my little mate, now 95% healed, to look after Destiny alone for a few nights....
Initially arriving at the laundromat in a quiet moment I had my pick of machines; loaded with $2 coins they bloody well wanted to be fed $1 coins. Rounding up enough coin to get two loads going, in the short time it took to duck home, hang the doona and Tia's bedding and accept Mum's offer of coins, an influx of customers arrived. The only machine capable of fitting the king size blanket had a twenty minute wait. Unprepared to twiddle my thumbs for that duration Ms Tia and I disappeared doing a little Fathers Day shopping - splurging on a new bucket filled the wait time neatly. Finding the laundromat about as much fun as watching my toe-nails grow, was elated to see the blanket finally dangling from the clothesline at home. At last, I was freed up to fulfil more pleasurable arrangements with Pauline for a farewell drink, also affording Mum thought space alone to start packing her bags☺....
Stumbling onto some old relics through the week, Pauline produced a sprinkling of photos from our supermarket days, conjuring up more memories of a time long forgotten. Instead of regulation uniforms, fancy dress themes occurred on occasion. The photos depicted a school theme - still at school myself I didn't have had to work too hard to dress up☺????
Before walking out the door for home, Pauline presented me with a beautiful home baked fruit cake made with loads of friendship, accompanied with instructions of 'don't touch until Mum and I reach Tassie'; a difficult ask when it smelt and looked so bloody great☺!!!!

Sunday 27 August 2006
Getting sleepy heads ready for bed last night an ambulance in close range got Ms Tia howling, seemingly fitting for the occasion however it's the sirens screaming frequency hurting her ears that causes the reaction. Reassured and settled, I adjourned inside for bed, separated only until 7a.m. when a handful of happy hot-air balloonists passing overhead upset every fucking dog, dog owner, and contentedly sleeping person in a 500 metre pass over radius!!!! Welcome to Sunday, at that precise moment would have happily watched the balloon shot out of the sky!!!! Searching to add a bit of life to a tired lifeless body I took my little mate for a walk to get the blood flowing; from there on in sparking up, with the inclusion of Mum's traditional Sunday roast my body began firing on all cylinders☺....
Finalising a couple of last minute supermarket requests for Mum, while out and about I wandered across town calling in on a long time friend Fan, visiting a piece of the past that refreshingly never changes. Arriving home not long after Aunty Claire's expected visit, an aunt I have plenty of time for, before farewells she wished both Mum and me a safe and happy trip to Rainbow Falls. After seeing Aunty Claire to her car, I spent the following couple of hours carting stuff too, and packing what could be packed into Destiny under the watchful eye of Ms Tia, supporting a much healthier load than we arrived with☺....

Monday 28, Tuesday 29, Wednesday 30 & Thursday 31 August 2006
Packing in a few consecutive big days created a brain so worn out it couldn't think outside its head to put words on paper....

Following a kiss and hug bidding Dad farewell, we tooted our way out of Jenkins Place Monday taking off from Mildura for destination Melbourne. From there I drove and bloody drove making Melbourne with enough time to get lost and get re-found. Not sure of exact directions, in the City and close to the Port, Mum couldn't see to read the map, there was nowhere for me to pull over to help myself thick in City traffic, creating a rather hapless situation. Stumbling across a signpost ferry symbol, cutting a fine line, Tia was limited to five minutes for wee's and we boarded with three minutes to spare.... Phew!!!!

Bunking in with Mum in a 4 berth cabin, the fourth occupant rolled in late after the three of us were horizontally settled, stating she was a snorer; she did an impressive job!!!! Waking the only snoring occupant to roll over on several occasions so the rest of us could have a go, she left the cabin 3a.m.-ish, and we did!!!!

Waking in the ugly wee hours of Tuesday morning the ferry had returned us to Tasmanian soil. Finally driving free of the boat and quarantine inspection, Mum and I grabbed fruit, veg and meat, stocking enough of life to keep us comfortable up the hill at Rainbow Falls for a few days of rest....

Finding homes for the bits unpacked from Destiny's tight load, and comfortably settled for a night in we phoned Dad to share the news of our safe arrival ☺....

Before spoiling ourselves, Wednesday began with a familiar scenario of having to take a step backward to go forward, repairing two splits in the hose. The repair work created was complements of Ross; removing his stored motorbike from the shed he towed the load over the garden hose breaking the PVC surround in half also....

Taking on a more pleasurable sharing experience, Mum and I picked a bunch of flowers from the mass of bulbs decorating housing ☺....

Working around fire lighting and cooking the phone beckoned attention. Miriam started a succession of calls, very pregnant and one day past birth date we caught up on the past two years of our low maintenance friendship. Packed with local knowledge and the best tour guide in the district, Lesley returned my call and we planned a trip to the 'Big Tree' at the Blue Tier Mountain Range to convert Mum into a tree hugging greenie. Hot receiver replaced, my case manager, Sandra, was next in line making time for a visit Sunday. Then out of the blue, Kylie, a friend from my Wollongong life called after a several year silence. Now five months pregnant she gave me an update on her life. With all the chat complete a meal managed to miraculously appear ☺....

Thursday I was excited to see swallows had returned for another season of nesting in the shed, sighting one on the high wire while carting wood to the cottage ☺....

A few consecutive days ahead with pleasant social distractions luring us away from home, I gave myself a solid workout splitting enough wood to see us through those times. Once the perspiration had dried and lunch filled my empty stomach, Mum, Tia and I tackled a walk from home to North Sister. Uphill all the way the few kilometres were hard going; returning however was another kettle of fish. Motoring down hill legs took off ahead of our bodies ☺....

The only encounter with wildlife, as we raced down hill, was brought to attention by Tia's sensitive sense of smell, briefly crossing the path of an echidna. A month of eating and minimal exercise, my body felt clagged following the big spurt.... Phew ☺!!!!

Putting one foot in front of the other, I first lit the fire then fulfilled my promise of making meals magically appear for Mum; it is she who is now on holiday my turn is over ☺....

Friday 1 September 2006
Picking up late yesterday and gaining momentum through the night, some bloody ordinary gusts shoved and rattled us around and persisted for most of today, slowing only when a front producing a little rain distracted the mood....
After removing aching leg muscles from bed, legacy of yesterdays punishing hill climb, we prepared for a town run. This time tackling the mountain was sensibly done seated in Destiny. Re-introducing Mum to part of my friendship circle in St. Marys started over a coffee with Terry, expressing thanks for him and Pam checking on Rainbow Falls in Tia's and my absence ☺ ....
Instantly adopting Mum as Aunty Margaret, Cousin Evelyn's for lunch was next. I'm never in a rush entering the bakery - there's always time for a chat even if it means serving around customers to do so; Evelyn is a solid friend. Walking across the road from the bakery found Barbara holding the fort at Gone Rustic in Rita's absence, further expanding introductions and conversation with strong and thoughtful friends ☺ ....
Blowing off some social cobwebs, and still battling strong wind, the final stops were to the supermarket and Post Office prior to casually making our way back to Rainbow Falls to settle for another cosy night in by the fire. Leaving Mum in a holiday mode state relaxed in a rocker soaking up the heater, I cooked a meal on top while we chatted over a glass of wine bonding as a mother and daughter should ☺ ....

Saturday 2 September 2006
Up and into it; with an air of excitement we got ready for a big outing to the St. Marys market. A simple but pleasant small town country affair, conversations always on the ready from friendly faces, consisting of only a sprinkling of stalls the market took little time to get through. Winding down after the big event we rested our feet over a coffee at e.ScApe Café ☺ ....
With the latest Valley Voice local paper waiting at the newsagents we followed up on an advertised garage sale in Mathinna, however, it provided nothing of interest to either of us. Never having been to Mathinna, the thousands of hectares of plantation timber and the denuded logged mountains reduced only to dirt was an absolute eyesore; for the most a very ugly drive into and townscape, a bland lifeless area I could never live....
Checking out a couple of old historically significant graveyards on the return drive, then satisfied hunger feeding it with bloody delicious Coach House Restaurant takeaway hamburgers, washing them down over a cup of tea at home ☺ ....
With what daylight remained it was spent at Rainbow Falls once again getting the cottage woodbox brimming over and the water supply replete. Leaving Mum to her book, Ms Tia and I went walkabout thistle kicking until it was time to change tack re-directing thought patterns into evening needs. Holding up my end of the holiday bargain, Mum is receiving a well earned break from cooking and most other ongoing chores that don't include self-indulgence ☺ ....

Sunday 3 & Monday 4 September 2006 (Happy Fathers Day Dad 3/9/06)
Feeling a bit tired last night after relaxing over an extra glass of port, I lost all enthusiasm for anything other than putting my head on the pillow. The thought of picking up the pen raised no interest....

In the tiny hours of Sunday morning Tia's thunder meter exploded into life, her booming voice snapping me from sleep. Fortunately the distant thunder only disturbed blissful snoozing for ten minutes. Arriving shortly after the bells and whistles much needed rain began falling and stayed comfortably settled for several hours. A welcome sound following the driest August ever recorded!!!!

The moisture drop pulled up at the same time as we got out of bed leaving behind in its wake a cool windy start. Without hesitation I stoked up the heater, creating a warm spot for us to hang out. Mum expressed the desire for a deep bath sometime during her visit. With the heater cracking early I took advantage of the moment, stacking the top with pots to fulfil the desire ☺....

Following introductions to my case manager Sandra, Mum left us to chat retreating to soak in her scorching deep bath. Almost passing Sandra at the front gate, Ross pulled in next, unable to offer Ross any more than to warm himself by the fire and a brief chat, having to leave ourselves to make our invited arrangement with Julia for a garden walk at her home. The many thousands of hours are obvious that have lovingly gone into designing her extensive, colourful creation, we followed Julia from one garden bed to the next chatting our way around. Winding up our visit we were treated to tea and home baked biscuits before driving back over the mountain in the last of the day's light to again migrate to the heater ☺....

Mother Nature couldn't make up her mind Monday morning: mist and rainbows decorated South Sister Range, the sky's north-east side displayed blue. In the middle, we copped a mix of everything. Weather may have been indecisive, but Mum and I knew what we wanted to do. Getting a roast lunch on the cook, we pumped loads of washing through then pampered ourselves with hair washes preparing for an afternoon in St. Helens ☺....

Barely a spare moment to have a scratch in the morning the afternoon was in contrast. Taking a gentle drive along the coast we stopped to amble through a few shops of interest. My big splurge was purchasing seed potatoes for this season's harvest. Wishing to introduce Mum and AEnone, while in St. Helens, we met over coffee and as usual we have plenty to share and time evaporated ☺....

Returning to Rainbow Falls after whetting Mum's shopping appetite, used fading light to refill the cottage woodbox then take our positions for another warm evening by the fire ☺....

Tuesday 5 & Wednesday 6 September 2006   (Happy Birthday Kristy-Lee)
Well shit, here I go again, another two days down the track before making time to spill ink onto paper....

Tuesday we were on a mission, up and into it getting ready for a big day out at Pyengana in the pleasant company of Lesley. Lesley was happy to play tour guide showing and sharing the magnificent 'Big Tree' ☺....

Wind had picked up and low cloud was clinging to surrounding mountains creating light drizzle. Arriving near our desired location, stepping off the side of the road leaving the car we were immediately immersed into another world, as if we had stepped into the pages of a fairytale book ☺!!!! Magic ☺....

Submerged under the dense, tall canopy, it protected and shielded us from the elements beyond. Internally calm and dry we were given front row seats to the hidden inner beauty. Slowly strolling through the outstanding scenery I wondered how I would find appropriate words in the English language to convert what my eyes were seeing into description for paper, and still I wonder????

Lush vivid greens illuminated this magical place; mosses of all varieties dripped from an assortment of ferns and trees, whose canopy blocked the sun completely out amid the moist rainforest environment. The dense overhead canopy, competing for sunlight, blocked direct light from touching the forest floor. The flow-on effect limited understory growth; all thriving plants were tall and stretched skyward, free of anything introduced. It was a piece of pristine rainforest ☺....

The purpose of the walk was to be introduced to the 'Big Tree', so inappropriately named, at 19.5 metres in diameter it projects magnificent splendour. Dating back at least 500 years, 'Big Tree' is not appropriate; 'bloody awesome' is more apt. Simply touching the tree sent a shiver through my body. Its exhilarating energy offered a natural high lift, an experience, a walk into another world that will never leave my mind, a memory etched forever ☺....

Taking a moment to catch our breath and absorb the magical surrounds, we sat on the bank at the upper catchment of the Groom River next to the crystal clear rippling stream meandering its way down through moss covered rocks; an ideal location to eat lunch over a cuppa. Sadly, our government sees this piece of paradise as wood chips and pulp - it's targeted for logging????

From the moment of stepping into this enchanting environment I fumbled for words to express feelings: those emotions lingered on re-emerging from the magical wonderland returning to the car for home....

Pulling into St. Marys shy of 6p.m., we grabbed a takeaway from the 'Coach House' and enjoyed it over a glass of wine or two by the fire. After bathing, bed proved far too tempting ☺ zzzz....

Sleeping in a coma, following a big day out in the enchanting rainforest, I slept through most of the 4mm falling from the sky through the night, again shooting through before we rose to face the new day waiting ahead....

Home wood supply being at a dire level, counting the available pieces on one hand determined a day home to make more. Digging at the base of another of the telegraph sized poles from the structure by the shed divulged how seriously rotten the base was. Pushing the pole its foundations were quite easily rocked, with the assistance of the shovel as a lever. Without difficulty I snapped the pole at the base dropping it to the ground without the need to even start the chainsaw!!!!

Once the cottage woodbox was again full, and with Mum's help, the remainder of the pole is waiting its turn for the heater in cross-sections stacked neatly in the shed. Testing out the freshly cut wood on a cool afternoon, Mum stayed warm and cosy feeding the heater's face reading her book. Escaping to the shed I cleaned the chainsaw in readiness for its next outing....

Thursday 7 September 2006

Feeding Mum's shopping fetish we took off for Launceston stopping at every antique shop along the way and every other not far off the beaten track. Ensuring best of friends, Tia and Destiny, were together in under cover parking, Mum set about wearing my boots out beating the pavement all over town. My big out of control splurge of $7 was showered on bulk pens and pencils; economically better than what I've been doing individually, a dozen pens and three pencils should see me through many moons and words ☺....

Stopping at Coles Supermarket on Wellington Street driving out of the City, after grabbing our desired bits, pulling out of the park and obscured by the tailgate I reversed into a large round, solid concrete, traffic stopper. Not as tall as a 44-gallon drum but similar in circumference, I clipped Destiny's driver side rear bumper giving us all a small jolt. Expecting a broken taillight at minimum, Destiny's bumper took the impact keeping us roadworthy to return home. Rolling into St. Marys I just caught Evelyn for bread and Grant to again refuel; this full tank is destined to take us to the Salamanca market in Hobart Saturday....

When in town for the market last Saturday I posted a note, jotted on the back of two photographs, wishing Sheila and Pete happy travels for their up and coming trip on the Trans Siberian Railway.

Over many conversations counting the days down to their big adventure, I guessed at 'only five days to go' at the time of posting. Phoning with a rather impressed tone, Sheila received the photos in the post today, perfectly sequenced with the five days to go count-down ☺!!!! Hey, what can I say ☺....

Friday 8 September 2006

Leaving Destiny to cool the oil in her motor, also extending me one drive free, we merely had a token speed-hump day of rest barely letting me catch my breath before tomorrow's trip to Hobart.

So far travel plans have certainly been in sync with the weather, not being hindered or stopped from any planned outing. With the exception of today's series of passing showers, rain has fallen through the night. The cottage woodbox was re-stocked before the first shower arrived, not effecting the restful game plan at all....

Between showers me and my little mate wandered into the slashed love heart pissing off a pair of persistent pesky currawongs. Walkabout, a trance took over sidetracking me into putting an end to a lot of new thistle growth with the heel of my boot. Excited re-visiting outdoor life during dryer times, while Mum tended to the fire and progressed her book, Ms Tia assisted weeding the garlic bed taking aerial specky dives catching weeds tossed in the direction of the compost heap ☺....

Returning inside I kept the boiler working on the heater, first pot for hair washing. Waiting for the second pot, I plucked Mum's eyebrows; when boiled it created bath water. The last bugger boiled was for pissing the dinner dishes off before retiring the pot for another night ☺!!!!

Saturday 9 & Sunday 10 September 2006

Struggling from day to day to muster enough brain power to write by the day's end quite often don't, last night being a don't ☺!!!!

My first wake up call Saturday was at 5:19am precisely. A wild gust created a quick ripping sound similar to roofing iron lifting; woken bolt upright, couldn't ignore it. Getting up to investigate I found nothing out of the ordinary, returning satisfied to warm the sheets until the designated alarm time of 6a.m.....

The night and morning alive with steady rain, an executive decision was made to take a chance and head to Salamanca market anyway. Exiting St. Marys, with sun breaking through misting cloud the valley was alive with rainbows, offering hope for a dryer path ahead ☺ ????
Without one wrong turn I made it directly to 'Salamanca Place'; a car backing out of a park neatly secured us a 2 hour park. Happy with the situation we wandered the couple of hundred metres to the market....
Only five minutes into browsing market stalls we surprisingly crossed paths with Chris, a woman I'd been in the same Rotaract group with in Mildura over two decades earlier. Happily sharing company, we exchanged the minutes of our lives since then and up until how we managed to cross paths on this particular day ☺ ????
A couple of brief showers followed us to the market; prepared for all occasions we completed stall browsing high and dry. Been, seen and conquered, leaving the market we sighted a sign advertising an open to the public tour of 'HMAS Adelaide', in port for a few days: we took up the offer ☺ ....
Returning within the designated 2 hour parking time limit, failed to notice it was meter parking copping a $20 parking fine, a rather unsocial act!!!!
Already having endured the parking fine, worked out where the meter was to feed it, then with another 2 hours up our sleeve Mum and I went walkabout into the Elizabeth Street Mall and surrounds feeding Mum's shopping fetish. Dragging tired feet returned to Destiny and Tia, again making it out of the City without one wrong turn and safely back to our side of the state ☺ ....
Starting yesterday at 5:19 am precisely after wind roused me a few times, then officially waking 6a.m. with the alarm, crossed state, shopped and returned by days end. By then my brain was content to rest over a couple of wind down beers; kissing anything constructive goodbye....
Short on jeans, socks and any inspiration for driving, started the laundry, split wood; chatting to Dad and refilling water abundantly occupied some of my time. Come beer o'clock, currawongs and thistle kicking filled in more of the available space, then headed indoors for the regular bathing and dinner cooking stuff.... Life goes on ☺ ....

Monday 11, Tuesday 12 & Wednesday 13 September 2006
Mum said to blame her for not writing in the journal. Getting comfy in rockers by the fire chatting I've let it fall by the wayside making night two without an entry.... Oops ☺ ....
Returning to Monday, we remained local just slipping over the mountain into St. Marys and sharing one of my typical shopping days. Adopting Mum as Aunty Margaret, we started the big adventure having a chat with Evelyn satisfying hunger pangs at the bakery ☺ ....
Wishing to see native animals up close other than the masses of broken bodies from road-kill scattered along the highways, after coffee, Pam and Terry introduced Mum to the many orphans being rehabilitated for release. Putting a bit back into the community working in the school op shop, Brian and Maggie completed the day's introductions and social chats. Groceries, Post Office, and a look around St. Marys finalised the big outing ☺ ....
Daring to roam a bit further in Destiny, Tuesday we lost a few lazy hours investigating the shopping offerings in Bicheno, failing to cater for Mum's requirements, it didn't take long to complete the task and revisit Elephant Pass and the deep valleys edging the roadside. It was

only at the absolute longest of drops that guard rails were linked by the side of the road. Mum and I decided the existence of guard rails was a measure of severity ☺ !!!!
Safely returned to the flatter ground in St. Marys I further advanced Mum's introductions calling in on Rita, catching both her and Barbara at the studio before resting Destiny back in her bedroom for a few quiet hours of personal time ☺ ....
Leaving Mum to being boss of feeding the fire, I fulfilled her dinner request for creamy bacon carbonara cooked on the heater top while we shared our views on the world and the block of parmesan cheese ☺ ....
Filling the final day together for a while, Mum, Destiny, Tia, me, and luggage took off to Launceston a few hours prior to the scheduled flight to further feed Mum's insatiable appetite for shopping. Commencing with lunch in a nice café, I put in a last big City effort before my sheltered hermit life returns. Walking the length and breadth of Launceston City in a hunt for baby clothes fulfilling Mum's desire to buy Dekira a present, managed to track down every shop selling baby clothes in the CBD ☺ !!!! A short stop at the airport to book in luggage and sort a boarding pass, packing it in, then visited another two known antique shops in Evandale before take-off ☺ ....
Kissing Mum farewell to enter the boarding lounge out of bounds to visitors, separated by a sheet of glass, I remained attentive until the very last minute. With a tear in my eye waved as the plane whizzed by watching it until it was merely a speck in the sky. Reflecting on our time together driving home made it inside Rainbow Falls gates 6:30p.m.-ish: opening buildings, the cottage feels empty in Mum's absence ♥♥♥♥....
Since that day early August when Tia, Destiny and I wandered out the front gate of Rainbow Falls on our pilgrimage visiting Mum and Dad in Mildura, up until some six weeks later taking Mum to Launceston Airport, Destiny quietly ticked over another 3000 kilometres without complaint ☺ ....

Thursday 14 September 2006
Phoning last night to ensure a safe trip home, not only was my mind put at rest, a very uplifted father was elated to share his dream score winning round of golf, it must have been the excitement of Mum's homecoming ☺ ????
Causing enough chaos amongst traffic for a while it's now back to reality. Exploding into life 7:30a.m.-ish, I was immediately drawn to the great outdoors to do a little hands on with those maintenance jobs hanging in limbo....
Banks of passing cloud pushed by wind displayed some very interesting features; varying in density they were also lined in shades of grey, silver, black and white. An uncertain weather direction pushed the advancement of waterproofing to the top of the priority list. Eliminating the need to slurp incoming water with towels along window sills I carved up a piece of sturdy blue plastic, from an old tarp, externally covering the worst offending cottage window. One less leaky thing to consider adds to the enjoyment of a rainy day ☺ ....
Next cab off the rank, preparing ground for planting potatoes got a guernsey. Doing the hard yards first strawberry plants were removed and soil turned until I could turn no more. Blood pumping shovel work coupled with a warm day got me stripping. Hearing a car stop at the front gate prompted a quick t-shirt slip on to cover exposed skin. An Aurora employee pulled in to read the electricity meter, a sure sign a bill is on the way....

Friday 15 September 2006
With local knowledge of most businesses in town closed from lunchtime tomorrow until Monday, the family was packed in the car to make the trip over the mountain to shop at a leisurely pace.
Starting at the pretend chemist, processed photos were picked up then I grabbed the latest edition of the Valley Voice paper. Standing outside the newsagent I settled into a chat with Peter and Ian. Post Office box checked, the Hobart parking fine paid and groceries done, I rounded off the shopping trip with a visit to the bakery. There I'm never in a hurry ☺....
Desiring to remain clean and sweat free, after a feed and read of the Valley Voice, I remained indoors out of the hot sun tidying paperwork. With mail appropriately dealt with, the latest batch of photos were dated, one set finding its way into the journal and another set put aside for posting to Mildura....
While on the Mildura theme, I phoned the district responding to an invitation received in the post from Fred to help celebrate his 60th. Having to decline, mentioning I was recently in the district and didn't find him home on an unannounced visit and stacked shoes by his door as a calling card. That action he recalled clearly now solving who the culprit was ☺....

Saturday 16 September 2006
Prior to leaving for Mildura and still persisting some seven weeks on, my sinus has shown all the symptoms of infection, identical to the early stages when it was recommended to snort that bloody inhaler. Remaining solely in my sinus and lingering, the flu like symptoms I guess in time will go away????
Both, heading over the mountain yesterday and today playing ball before breakfast with Tia I happily spied a goshawk gliding around; its presence sure silences bird activity ☺....
Hot enough to entice larger reptiles out of winter hideaways to feel sun on skin; an indicator and sure sign reptiles are on the move; a go-cart was spotted climbing over the rock pile. Time to strap the shovel to one hip and Tia to the other ☺....
The sudden lift in temperature caused the tulips, garlic and peach tree to scream out for moisture. Returning to regular watering, I satisfied their need. Direct sun delivered enough sting to warm the solar shower bag but merely taking the edge off....
Parking the shovel by the shed gate escaped heat under cover in the haven directing attention to the ride-on mower. Jacking the rear-end elevating it off the ground left the mower suspended on bricks offering access from both above and below. Unsure of how to release the tension on the drive belt and coupled with inadequate tools I didn't get far - however, it was a good starting point ☺....

Sunday 17 September 2006
For three consecutive days the air has been full of smoke. Unable to do laundry, (that I don't mind), I just take an extra puff on the inhaler and get on with the lifetime of work waiting. Leaving the solar shower to do its thing, I stripped off my t-shirt, finished the beds and planted potatoes....
Following a chat to Mum and Dad I finished the afternoon by stoking up the frying pan and roasting a leg of lamb for me and my little mate ☺....

Wearing thin, and tired of the constant ongoing barking from their dog, I phoned across the road. My call was met by the lines, "what's ya problem?", "we've been here longer than you". Going nowhere, and before hanging up said, "I'd prefer to deal with you than the by-laws officer", but they only seem to listen to someone in authority wearing a uniform.... If only they were law abiding citizens; oh to have considerate neighbours ☺ !!!!

For me now another circle is complete. During my absence in Mildura the boat was rocked at the radio station - my guess is by the last damning article printed in the Valley Voice paper publicly highlighting the many skeletons in the closet. Coinciding in timeliness following the printed story were resignations from the radio stations Miss Manager Maria and her brother-in-law Bruce the sexual discriminator. I've long let go of the issue; their resignations have offered absolute closure. Ends have been neatly tied ☺ !!!!

Monday 18 September 2006
Getting all the creaks and rattles activated, I escaped the hot gusting northerly having another roll around on the shed floor looking over the ride-on. Helping my vision past obscuring panels a small mirror was used to take a peek at the hidden bits. Not beaten, my brain is prepared to undo bolts but not until I have tools to fit, shelving the job till then....

Wishing to send a couple of thank you letters resulting from Mildura travels, and with Tegan's birthday fast approaching, plus a set of photos sitting idle with Mum and Dad's name on, the afternoon was toiled away in the cottage preparing the lot for posting....

A sudden rush of heat has ground both my and my little mate's energy to a halt and stirred skinks into life, driving a couple inside to check out what the window sill's have on offer....

In the evening cool we re-emerged from our cocoon for exercise. I tossed toys on demand, and clearing her yard, Tia chased a couple of bunnies proving only to be a bit of sport certainly too quick to be a meal ☺ ....

Tuesday 19 September 2006
Last night the dam was as dense and alive with frogs as the night sky was with stars. In the hushed evening stillness it was a pleasure to be exposed to the elements. Responding to a paw tap several hours into sleep, I stirred out of bed; the clear sky had been obscured and a half dozen drops of moisture were squeezed from the constipated cloud mass. The sudden elevation in temperature is keeping my little mate confined to her own bed, uninterested in adding to her body warmth at all!!!!

Preparing breakfast Ross phoned extending a dinner invitation. It's a rare day I refuse a meal cooked by someone else ☺ ....

Mother Nature had a bit of sport at my expense. Watching the washing get started she turned up the dial on wind to strong and gusting extending practice at mantling pegs, although on the up side clothes dried in short time ☺ !!!!

Pam and Terry blew in mid afternoon to release a rehabilitated possum. Leaving them to it, Tia remained behind with me waiting for the kettle to boil and preparing a snack to share over conversation on their return. Waving Pam and Terry off, I then casually prepared for my dinner invitation. Over red wine, food preparation, chatter and eating, the evening also escaped, adding a very social end to a quiet laundry day ☺ ....

Wednesday 20 September 2006
The clear sky full of stars I last saw on my way to bed last night, in the company of some pretty ordinary wind, was covered over to produce 2mm by morning. About 5a.m. my brain was kept alert by a rush of wild bullying from the elements. Unwilling to back down and lingering all day, the bloody tiring strong gusty wind helped make the decision, when possible, to remain indoors and out of it....

On the regular pilgrimage up the hill to the loo I spotted the minimal remains of some unfortunate critter, guessing it had been the meal of a devil. Other than gizzards there wasn't a strand of fur or piece of bone left behind. Whatever worthless bits were left Tia claimed - those bloody ravens hanging around weren't going to rob a girl of anything of possible food value!!!!

Retreating inside another small step closer was taken in realising a personal goal; with my psychology realigned, I returned to the computer investing several hours into digitising a couple of weeks of past life at Rainbow Falls. Waiting for some big event to signify completion, searching for an ending to the book, I've come to the realisation it may never happen - life just keeps ticking over from day to day. Reckon I'll just start editing and when that's complete I've found my ending and that will bloody well do ☺!?!?

Thursday 21 September 2006
From midnight wind rattled me apart working on my brain and sleep deprivation. It's the expected that plays with my head. First comes the noise of wind gaining momentum roaring up from the valley, then the sound of forced air rushing through trees. At that point I knowingly wait for the impact on the housing. With each destructive gust I listen intently for any new, or worsening existing, dismantling sound, always in hope it will soon ease off!!!!

Exhausted wanting only to return to a warm bed and relaxed sleep, 2a.m.-ish horizontal rain falling seemed somewhat calming; masking the torturous sounds it presented a harsh burst of 4mm, from that point taming the lashing beast. Slipping into exhausted sleep I woke 4a.m. fully dressed on top of the bed. Brain and buildings still intact, I crawled into bed capturing a few more hours under the doona....

Lurking not too far off, 9a.m.-ish harsh elements found us once again with more punishing gusts, my brain can deal with it better through daylight hours. Gratefully, trying conditions faded as the day progressed. A side-effect from the past twenty-four hours, my finger tips were a bit tender from biting my fingernails back to the elbow ☺!!!!

Mould decorating the remaining two slices of bread determined a trip into St. Marys. Conversation in town centred around wind. Talk has a mean front worse than last night predicted for Friday. It's supposed to absolutely hammer us - I say bring on Saturday ☺!!!!

Armed with Evelyn treats a social stop was made at Pam and Terry's. Offering a loan of an assortment of tools enabling a more convincing go at repairing the ride-on, Terry filled a tool box full catering for most obstacles that may present themselves ☺....

Just filling space in his shed, last Mildura trip Dad sent me home with an electric drill, today it got its maiden voyage at Rainbow Falls, utilising what remained of a calm afternoon up the ladder. Assisting in brain reassurance, I pulled out the extension cord and put a dent in a packet of fifty 2-inch roofing screws distributing them between the cottage and bungalow. If a nail showed any sign of movement it came out and was replaced ☺!!!!

Friday 22 September 2006
Once my head has received a cage rattling, the sound of the slightest breeze lifting animates sleep and activates the brain dominoing on to open eyes. Woken briefly a couple of times through the night, I was left to sleep peacefully until 6a.m. Not so lethal, a front pushed us around for a few hours but nothing severe enough to force me out of a warm bed, merely hindering quality sleep. Yesterday's labour with the drill silenced a few squeaks and creaks, an insurance policy for reassurance and calming the brain. Going to the loo however was like taking a show ride, being rocked around paid my fare getting off☺!!!!
Keen on knowing what the next few days entail I caught a weather report on the radio. The outcome was for no end in sight; wind will continue to hit randomly. Just keep enduring and it's bound to give in one day. An interesting fact mentioned during the weather report is the gale force winds we've been experiencing are officially measured between 63 and 87 kilometres per hour; we have been treated☺!!!!
Making a bee-line to the shed to play with kindly loaned tools, opening the tool box of treasure revealing its contents endeavouring to repair the rear end of the ride-on, not one socket fitted the first targeted bolt. Too confined an area for spanners or a shifter I was snookered again but only momentarily. Desiring to make a start I phoned and arranged a loan of Ross' socket set. Limited with no budget freedom, the hardest part of the job for me is getting tools to do it. Packing up my bat and ball and good intentions I retreated to the cottage escaping wind and passing showers adding fossil fuel to the computer....

Saturday 23 September 2006
Of the extremely short list of positive aspects, to say the least, of ordinary weather conditions lately, one would be the usefulness of the wind's might at extracting dead limb wood from trees. Seeing the neighbours spotlight illuminating the clump of trees bordering the top boundary last night, shooting inside the 500 metre limit, I took a walk along there this morning thankfully finding no corpses. Making the walk worthwhile, I filled my arms with recently deposited limb wood for the stroll back☺....
Taking possession of Ross' socket set it was only appropriate to put them to use so back down the shed we marched. Sited plumb beneath a top horizontal shaft, there was no easy access to the one bolt to loosen and release the bottom vertical shaft where the offending noise, instigating this work, emanates from. First the seat was taken off for light and access. Second move was to extract attached bits decorating the top horizontal shaft so it could be taken out....
Going great guns dismantling reached a stalemate, a small cog wheel that propels the drive chain wasn't attached by a thread, refusing to budge from where it was seated it didn't respond to any tried measure, the small cog stopped me in my tracks until a solution is found!!!! Bending over the ride-on near on broke my back and the day☺!!!!

Sunday 24 September 2006
Woken lightly from sleep 5a.m.-ish by a nudging nose looking to find its way under the warm doona, I also became aware of the sound of rain starting. Vertical rain settled in for several solid hours. Only when I was ready to rise from bed did a light wind blow it somewhere else, simply making way for the next approaching front....

Pulling the beanie over my ears, I moved in the direction of the shed to cut limb wood collected yesterday, adding it to the remnants of the last pole cut in the woodbox....
When Ross was up here Friday collecting bits from his stored collection he left his car open and Tia jumped in making herself at home. Offering a laugh today, Tia produced a tennis ball she knocked off casing his car for anything useful, what good timing because the last one she pilfered recently fell apart ☺.... That's my girl ☺....
Retreating to the cottage escaping an all seasons occasion, parked my bum wrapped in the Aunty Shirley hand knitted throw rug, and had a lengthy chat to Mum and Dad. Ending our conversation, sun and serenity had replaced wind and rain outside. Starting the fire and dinner, hail, rain and light wind popped back over the mountain; not a dull moment ☺ !?!?
Leaving snags to cool while vegies finished cooking I sat them on top of the boiler on the stove thinking they were dog-proof; think again!!!! Tia had eaten her share when sprung stretching her body beyond its reach in her obsession for food, receiving only vegetables for dinner when the time came around.... The little shit, or as Mum would say, 'big shit' ☺ !!!!

Monday 25 September 2006
Around 3a.m. my free ranging brain being analytical woke me with a proposed solution to removing the cog from the shaft. Before following through with the thought and getting my hands dirty the answer arrived with a trip over the mountain to post the payslip....
Ross was home stopping for drinking water, speaking of the hold-up in the works dismantling the ride-on, he said being able to turn the cog on the shaft the key had been snapped and the cog requires a bearing puller to take it off. The key is merely a small sliver of metal slipping into a groove between the cog and shaft stopping it from turning, and keeping it rigid and aligned....
A quick stop at the Post Office and Evelyn's, on a mission, I went straight back up the hill. A name recognised from the tools on loan was a 'three jaws forge steel gear puller', or more simply known as a bearing puller. With my fresh knowledge and the right tool for the job, a dose of hit and miss and the cog was off within a half-hour. It was a pure pleasure with each turn of the bearing puller to watch the cog slowly pry loose from its anchorage. Quietly proud, placed it on the ground with its broken key next to the chain and in the sequenced order each piece has been removed ☺....
Another topic I know very little about the mechanics of is free spinning bearings. One at either end of the top horizontal shaft stopped me from removing the top shaft to gain access to that 'one bloody bolt' on the vertical shaft below that houses that noise. Reaching the next stalemate, the bearing puller wouldn't fit the job. The bearings aren't on a thread and they can't be physically pulled from their seated position - I'm again looking for a clue to the next step ☺ !!!!

Tuesday 26 September 2006
Reluctant to get motivated I remained procrastinating over my milo. Not only was the returned wind foreboding, but the first job assigned was to shovel out the toilet. The hardest part of emptying the toilet is getting my brain around the task, always completing the job in less time than the thought going into planning it ☺ !!!!

Putting the shit spade away I grabbed the grown-up's shovel and stayed with the shovel theme all day. In short supply of wood I began grown-up's shovel work digging around the base of the sole remaining pole left standing by the shed. The ground was like concrete; bringing the pick into play created a moat at the base, then I thought 'bugger it, this could be easier' and filled the moat surrounding the pole with water leaving it to soften....

My little mate and I then shot through to the vegie patch turning soil - three-quarters of the entire area is now very tidy. My back by this time had had enough; my brain however had other ideas. Seeing weeds screaming out for attention in the elevated garden my brain forced my body to continue and like a puppy it followed. Leaving the small area surrounding the garlic and peach tree weed free for the time being, I'd had enough and packed up the toys and the day like me was beaten.... It was time for a red and relax ☺....

Wednesday 27 September 2006

Starting as a snack yesterday, and finishing up as the same today, I ate all of last season's booty of walnuts. Not a difficult task when the duds are extracted from the entire harvest of twenty-six nuts ☺....

Disappearing over the mountain to make a dent in the pay packet grocery shopping, I stopped for a yarn to Rita, then Ross, before doing a quick turn about....

The terms 'strong and gale force' are wearing thin. We've had quiet times but not a day has passed lately without wind of some measured description. I'll be happy for a spell so my fingernails have time for growth. Weather wise today was a wolf in sheep's clothing. Giving a false sense of security it started off comfortable enough to be naked bathing; during the morning the shovel was kept at hand; by afternoon I was rugged up in warm waterproofs ☺ ????

Home from town, wind strong enough to blow your beanie off picked up pushing through a brief shower. Groceries unpacked and Destiny returned to her bedroom, I had a dig at the base of the remaining post earmarked for the chainsaw, getting a bit of mobility pushing the post merely by hand; wet it up again for another soil softening soaking....

Inspired to have another go at extracting the bearing from the shaft stopping mower repair progress; these particular bearings are in a bugger of a position - I'm denied access with the bearing puller, I can't get at it to give it a hit and it won't be worked free???? Nuts, bolts and screws I have no trouble dismantling but when it comes to bearings I'm caused grief!!!!

Contemplating the day just gone quietly giving my best friend a pat savouring a glass of red, my probing fingers found and pulled the third tick from Ms Tia in as many days; she's certainly been playing host lately ☺ !!!!

Thursday 28 September 2006

A very rare occasion Tia wasn't interested in joining me over breakfast she was intent on catching her own at the burnt out house hot on the scent of rabbits. Giving her location away from time to time by jumping on the stack of corrugated iron, failing in her pursuit of a rabbit breakfast; when hunger set in she tracked me down for a feed ☺....

Having another play with the last pole standing, softened soil was dug from its base and again a few litres of water were dropped in to continue softening the deepening surrounding moat. Leaving water to penetrate, I disappeared inside to get reacquainted with the computer....

Having a short break from the square machine giving eyes a rub and stretching my legs, was gob smacked to see the pole had tilted over and was left leaning on a 45° angle in the softened ground. Now I'm sure of how it's going to fall, at leisure, the pole is ready to be tackled safely with the chainsaw and brought down to size....

Friday 29 September 2006
On pursuit pissing off currawongs eliminating weeds on the way, and working up an appetite for breakfast, opened the gate entering the horizon paddock and was shocked looking down the valley. Clear to the naked eye, Mathinna was outstandingly recognisable merely by being just a large barren patch of ground; thousands upon thousands of hectares of threadbare dirt carved into a hilly vegetated surrounding landscape.... A sad sight....
Impatient with my dilly-dallying around, waiting for breakfast Tia knocked off a piece of bread sitting in the toaster to fill a hungry belly.... The little bugger!!!!
Waiting for bath water to get itself stirred up on the stove I had a scratch around at the base of the last remaining pole. Without even raising a sweat, and already halfway there, in minutes I'd eased the poles massive weight calmly the remainder of the way to meet ground ready for the next step with the chainsaw, but not today ☺ ....
As a matter of course Sandra paid her regular contact visit, and as requested she gave me a copy of her report from the time we have shared. Not long out the gate behind Sandra we too made our way over the mountain headed for my doctor's appointment....
Remaining in town, for the purpose of Mum and Dad's approaching anniversary, set myself up by the photocopier in the library copying appropriate pages from the journal of the recent Mildura holiday for sending; starting from the date of leaving Rainbow Falls until the 3000th kilometre later taking Mum to the airport returning home herself ☺ ....
An appropriate envelope selected and the bundle posted, following a visit to Rita then Evelyn respectively, then moved on to the newsagents, Post Office and supermarket before again returning to familiar soil through home gates....
During my absence Ross had called in, over the phone later said he'd taken a look at the ride-on and recommended Allen-keys should fix the stubborn shaft problems. Knowledge from experience saves hours of fumbling frustrating learning. I have however taken in a wealth of knowledge during the learning phase; part of that knowledge is mechanics doesn't excite me ☺ !!!!

Saturday 30 September 2006
On a rare wind-free day blissfully enjoying the calm silence and sounds of nature over a milo or two, living next to morons that peace was soon shattered. Beginning with the sound of heavy machinery, a chainsaw was then included, followed closely behind by two motor bikes with minimal exhaust systems stirring up cows. Getting cows bellowing added to the commotion overload. Robbed of any tranquillity, they went ADD for two hours - they probably could have made more noise but extra people would be required; only guns discharging was absent from their repertoire!!!!
Unable to do anything about noise intrusion, I just got on with my own business distributing a dose of compost to the garlic and peach tree and watering the goodness in....

Patting Ms Tia in passing noticed a slight imperfection on her face. A tick had lodged itself onto her eyelid and only lasted seconds beyond being noticed. Hanging around with rabbits she's a magnet for tics lately!!!!

With plenty of other more interesting things I'd prefer to be doing on such an overdue perfect day in paradise, the drudgery of laundry made the priority list pumping out load after load ☺!!!!

Tuning into a 5p.m. news broadcast, was bluntly reminded of that one big day in September and the dying minutes of the A.F.L. grand final. West Coast Eagles beat Sydney Swans by a measly point, an evenly matched 'edge of the seat' game….

Sunday 1 October 2006

My idiot neighbours did their best to test me again this morning. As with their dog, I can only feel sorry for them; to be so outwardly angry and negative must be a tortured body to live within. Both motorbikes were revved up and a ride-on lawnmower was in action accompanied by loud music. They can't seem to make enough noise simultaneously????

Encountering similar symptoms experienced when recommended by the doctor to snort the prescribed inhaler, eight weeks of a sinus infection has gradually advanced to swelling around eyes. Usually leaving during the morning, swelling around my right eye remained; again looking to reverse the problem I started a course of antibiotics leftover from the inhaler snorting effects!!!!

Friday's long-term weather forecast predicted rain for Monday; after watering peaches, potatoes and the compost, I got me and the chainsaw fired up. Cutting the last and largest log, measuring 400–500mm across, I was happy to have the last piece of cross-section rolled into the shed waiting splitting. Worn out by just cutting the log I didn't bother cleaning up; that was left for later….

Showered and spruced up I took off to Ross' to re-borrow his tools. Over a brew he mentioned daylight saving had started - lucky because I was oblivious. I'm back in tune with the outside world ☺….

Phoning Tegan for her birthday, Dekira joined in contributing "hello Arr Sue" and "luv you" to our conversation; she is a sweet personality. Tegan had to cut our call short happily leaving for work in the dining room at the Gateway Tavern, a job she's had for a week and as an added bonus is enjoying ☺….

Monday 2 October 2006

Like my neighbours, currawongs too were quiet. The blessing of a work and school day, life at home was ideal. One can only hope they move near like minded people!!!!

Taking up the offer of Ross' push mower put it to use today tidying housing buying time to repair my own, not one is operational at present, that situation is on the priority list to rectify ☺….

After a stint on the chainsaw yesterday and a workout with the push mower today, following a shower I hit the wall. Feeling as strong as a half-sucked peppermint nothing else reportable happened in paradise ☺….

Tuesday 3 October 2006
Greeting the morning opening the bungalow door to a tidy, freshly mowed yard, is to say the least uplifting, low on energy it was just the antidote needed ☺....
After playing with all the toys it was clean up and maintenance time. Every minute was accounted for today. With the shovel strapped to one hip, the solar shower was put out to cook, from there moving onto cleaning out the heater. Sifting and sorting the heater's contents the task was completed by taking the grey ash to the loo....
With a high turnover of GP's locally, a new health caring doctor I had an appointment with Friday sent me home with a print-out of the side-effects to using aldactone; a read explains my irregular period, breast soreness and lumps, prompting a call for a breast screen appointment to rest my mind, next time the bus visits St. Marys. Continuing on the phone, a suitable time was confirmed to chat to the local Constable looking for a solution to regular and ongoing recreational motorbike noise problems from across the road....
Phone back on the hook, I then raked a pile of grass, for the purpose of adding it to the establishing compost pile at the rear of the burnt out house. Leaving compost to wet up I cleaned the sawdust trail left behind by Sunday's chainsaw activity. Sweeping out the shed came next, removing the track where logs were rolled in for dry storage. Not standing still, the chainsaw and loaned mower were cleaned prior to splitting a wheelbarrow load of wood. Without having the right sized Allen-key to fit the bearing on the shaft of the ride-on mower, it gave me the 'pull-up and have a shower' message ☺!!!!
Over a glass or two of red I finished watering the compost, Peaches and garlic, while kicking the ball for Ms Muffet. Content to call it quits I headed indoors, lit the fire, cooked dinner, ate and did dishes. The pen is replaced and I've finished writing; elated, the day is then mine to lazily relax, or maybe just go to bed to recharge my batteries to do it all again tomorrow ☺....

Wednesday 4 October 2006
First cab off the rank, I loaded Destiny with the equipment borrowed from Ross, from push mower to tools. The socket set is only sitting idle until the shaft is removed; there's no point hanging on to anything when again I can't progress with the ride-on....
Totally out of physical energy, a thought rose about washing Destiny before putting her back in her bedroom but that's as far as it got, a thought ☺....
On a passing pat noticed Ms Tia's eyelid attracted yet another tick, again it lasted as long as it took to grab tweezers pluck it off and squash it!!!!
Before getting immersed on the computer with data entry I called Kiama speaking to Denise: she kindly stored possessions I was unable to take when leaving the State. Embarking on a six week trek on the mainland in her campervan, and potentially the last stop being Kiama, AEnone and I lightly touched on the topic of loading up the last of my stored gear and bringing it back with her. Both AEnone and I are invited to Ross' for dinner tomorrow there I shall ask if her potential offer still stands ☺????

Thursday 5 October 2006
Unable to tolerate the sound of a beeping bloody alarm I woke by pure instinct and got up a couple of minutes before it was due to go off. The purpose of getting organised early was to

catch Constable Cameron looking to, once and for all, solve neighbour motorbike noise issues....

Driven by the courtesy of punctuality, Tia had made herself scarce when it was time to leave being out to get her fair share of a carcass on offer - food is of foremost priority. Destiny was warmed and so was Tia's arse when she hopped in; the air was thick enough to carve creating a window down drive into St. Marys.... Phew ☺ !!!!

Cameron has listened on several occasions with neighbourhood problems. Searching for peace my request for resolution was to enforce the law of 'no gun or recreational vehicle be used within 500 metres of another dwelling'. Off duty from 6p.m., Cameron said he'd visit across the road at home resuming duty this coming Wednesday evening. There is now light at the end of the tunnel....

Reaching into the black hole of the Post Office box was rewarding. It contained birthday wishes from Mum and Dad; with the inserted cash gift I made a hair appointment, a pampering to look forward to Tuesday. Also included in mail was a postcard from Sheila and Peter dated 14/9 sent from Moscow, the day before they were due to reach Sheila's childhood fascination, Vladivostok, and the end of the Trans Siberian Railway journey ☺ ....

Following a chat and hot brew with Rita and Barbara, a chat, cuppa and scones with Pam and Terry, I then returned back up the mountain investing time into the computer....

Later, flicking the switch on Destiny's windscreen wipers, wandered back over the mountain to join Ross and AEnone for dinner; over a glasses of red or two, conversation never sat idle. Ross cooked up a treat adding to a quality night. AEnone confirmed her willingness to pick-up the last of my possessions from Kiama. I kept my promise of giving her the Melbourne street directory. At evening's end I took a quick trip home picking up the directory. As she was leaving Saturday, AEnone and I said our farewells at the Dublin Town Road junction before calling it a night ☺ ....

Friday 6 October 2006

The puffy swelling has finally left my eyes. With only two days antibiotics remaining they finally kicked in doing the trick - even my sinus has stopped being a bother ☺ ....

Making room for her new outfit Tia's winter coat is on the move. Her scratching is randomly distributing fur and de-furring my bed and bungalow has returned to daily routine ☺ ....

Ready to move onto something more challenging, I took off to the shed trying my luck with recently borrowed Allen-keys from Terry. Cracking the four nuts with the 3mm key, and with some light, gentle persuasion, the top shaft was removed within fifteen minutes offering clear access to that 'one bloody bolt'. Wanting his tools for the weekend I won't be able to borrow Ross' socket set again until Monday, I'm just bloody elated to be at the point of needing them ☺ !!!!

Going as far as I possibly can with the mower for the time being, once again sparked up the computer. Parking my bum in the cottage is where I lost the remainder of the afternoon. Then came the evening; slicing, dicing, chopping, stirring, boiling and stoking the fire, tossing in every available vegetable, I brewed up a huge pot of stew and it was well worth the wait ☺ ....

Saturday 7 October 2006

A rare feat in these times; today Mum and Dad celebrate their 46th wedding anniversary. They're going for gold ☺ !!!! Phoning early to catch Dad before golf, and going all out for the big event, Dad's grabbing fish 'n' chips on the way home from golf for a quiet night in together ☺ ....

Planning ahead for an evening in myself, another log was rolled out of the shed and my back was put into splitting it. Emptying the load into the cottage woodbox the fire was then set ready just to throw a match to....

Looking for a passive change of pace, grabbing shovel and water bottle, Ms Tia and I headed to the vegie patch. Wetting up and loading a bed with compost I took my top off to soak up the warmth on offer planting out bean seeds. Assuming I beat all competition and reap the fruits of labour, this seasons harvest consists of garlic, potatoes and beans. The walnut tree and Peaches have set and are loaded also, a good start ☺ ....

Still with a pot full of stew; Ross accepted a dinner invitation to share in the tasty feast. Arriving bearing gifts, Ross presented me with a birthday present of four claw feet to replace those long removed from my bath. Leaving the stew on the heater top simmering, when our bums pried loose from rockers we'd grab a scoop at will. Other than admiring a rising full moon illuminating the yard we remained propped in front of the fire in rockers yapping ☺ .... Perfect ☺ ....

Sunday 8 October 2006

Sleep disturbing gusts struck at random giving me and housing an occasional rattle. Arriving with one rush of high energy, wind showered a burst of moisture. There was nothing more us girls could do but remain snuggy and warm in bed sleeping through quieter times....

Wishing to celebrate my birthday with a beer I took a trip over the mountain to stock up in advance of the big day, enabling a practice run with a couple of coolies tonight ☺ ....

A quick run for a drop of the liquid amber chewed into a chunk of the day. Starting at the Post Office, a good yarn was had with Evelyn, and my reason for doing it all, the final stop being the pub. Turning myself around meandered back up the mountain, dropping in to re-borrow his socket set I caught Ross home. While Ross flicked the switch on the kettle and clanked a couple of mugs on the sink, I sang happy birthday to myself and blew the candle out on the cake given to me by Evelyn, sharing birthday cake over a brew ☺ ....

Home and unmotivated, conditions steered me in the direction of having a day off to fully please myself. Unable to find the small wire brush that fits into the end of the drill to begin the clean up of the claw feet for the bath, exhausting all potential haunts, ended the extensive search with the scientific finding of, 'I don't know where it is' ☺ ....

Uninspired to get down and dirty with the ride-on, and talking myself out of any other work thought, I was lured into games with Ms Tia and her stash of slightly battered about, self-collected toys. Only when she had enough play did I treat myself to a coffee and more Evelyn cake, sharing a sample with my little mate ☺ ....

While Tia entertained herself at the burnt out house for hours on end terrorising rabbits, basking in sunshine behind glass doing bloody nothing beyond just plain relaxing, I quietly sipped on a beer or two. Tiring herself of rabbits, Tia returned to the bungalow and lovingly spewed then settled into bed snoozing waiting for dinner ☺ ????

Monday 9 October 2006
For every load of fur brushed from Ms Tia she has another on the ready to drip onto anything in her path. Fine floating pieces of fur hovering in the air, whipped up by the slightest atmospheric movement find their way into my nose and mouth. At times it's like having a streamer connected to my nostril; fur latches on and flaps around in air movement purely from breathing, tickling its way over my nostril ☺ ….
From deep in the bottom paddock with my best mate, I watched Terry pull in for the purpose of reclaiming a piece from his loaned tools. Before he left, together we had a go at getting the nut to budge on the ride-on but it was in no hurry to leave its seated position, giving it a good dose of CRC left it to soak….
In my absence two missed calls with birthday wishes flashed for attention on the answering machine. The first thoughtful birthday message was delivered courtesy of Mum and Dad, the other from Tegan coaching Dekira. Picking up the receiver and pressing the numbers on the keypad I started with Mum and Dad; preparing to babysit, Tegan and Dekira turned up. Catching them all at the one spot for a chat, some conversation was more audible than others ☺ …. Gotta love the bubba ☺ ….
The nice thing about a birthday is those that care stop to think about me. That's the start and finish of it; life still continues as per normal. As part of my normal, I nutted out the configuration for removing that final bottom vertical shaft from the parts breakdown sheet given to me in Mildura, deducing how to remove the entire shaft in one piece. Unprepared to even look at the bloody thing out of the mower decided that 'one bloody nut' a maintenance dealer can deal with. Happy with my personal learning curve and skills attained, I've patiently served my apprenticeship ☺!!!!
Hearing from Mum, Dad, Tegan and Dekira, a cake from Evelyn, a set of claw feet to restore for the footless bath, and completed dismantling the mowers rear-end releasing the shaft from its anchorage of attached bits, left a birthday girl contentedly fulfilled ☺ ….

Tuesday 10 October 2006
The neighbours not only revved up motorbikes Saturday and Sunday they also expanded to Monday this week. Working in favour, wind carried some of the irritating noise off. Left to their own devices their unsociable behaviour continually increases. My saviour and ability to block the irritation of the invasive noise out is in the knowledge of Wednesday's visit from Cameron. If they and I give a bit and meet in the middle we should be able to find common ground legally ☺ ????
Tia parted with seven brush loads of fur last night. My cup being half full I see it as seven less loads I don't have to remove from the bungalow, and that's a lot of de-furring ☺ !!!!
The hype and euphoria of another birthday passing has returned my adrenalin to simmer; letting myself down gently I had a pampering at the hairdressers in the capable hands of Kellie. Having my first colour to cover a dusting of grey hair after 44 years, like my Dad, there's a strong gene for natural hair colour. I'm still predominantly black….
Making my way back up the mountain I remained in relaxation mode occupying an idle mind leading up to beer o'clock holding the hose watering. With no heat and eat meals left the heater was sparked up producing a healthy load of spaghetti ☺ ….

Wednesday 11 October 2006
Sure of my actions, euphoria is felt pulling bits from the ride-on. Not one bearing from the bits removed appears to be seized - that outcome, however, is kind on the budget. Nothing extracted bares its soul to take responsibility for the free ranging ball bearings. Feeling confident the sound I was hearing led me in the right direction, concluded the grinding sound heard, similar to that of metal on metal, is where the drive wheels from the top horizontal shaft touch down on the bottom vertical shaft. The drive wheel's point of contact on the bottom shaft, similar in appearance to a tapered grinding wheel, is looking a bit beat up. Its outer surface is scarred and under side has flaking chips; I'll have it looked at before reassembling my handy work ☺ ????
Strong gusting fronts determined a course, eliminating the ridiculous thought of laundry. I escaped out of the elements to stare at a computer screen. Focussed with brain and hands clunking keys I digitised twenty-two journal entries taking the sting out of July and most of today....
At day's end looking for fresh air and sunshine Tia kept me occupied either with her 20 litre drum or tennis ball: the latest tennis ball she knocked off from Ross' car has got plenty of bounce; it's obviously not a cheapy because they hit the ground with a thud ☺ ....

Thursday 12 October 2006
Lately, waiting for a wind free sane day to do laundry, it's just not going to happen. If I had to describe today's weather in one word it would be 'mean'; unrelenting destructive gale force winds accompanying a scorching hot temperature was pretty darn ordinary!!!!
The up side to the energy robbing conditions is the clothes dried in quick time; wrestling them on the line against the wind, some tangled, some stayed, a few made the ground, but they all dried and within an hour to be folded and put away ☺ .... My right index finger became sensitive just putting pegs back together again!!!!
Being outside unnecessarily was absolutely avoided. If this is an entrée to summer then it's going to be a doozy; thoughts of moving to the South Pole are looking attractive. Usually ADD, even my little mate put the anchors on conserving energy amid the wild, windy scorcher ☺ !!!!
Shielding under a roof against the elements, and easy to be without clothes, I gave myself a pampering. Following the white goods torture the electric shaver was pulled out to find legs and armpits. By this time the solar shower was borderline too hot; body and clothes clean, I surrendered to beer o'clock ☺ ....

Friday 13 October 2006
Waking with a pain in the neck refusing to leave, it was only my lefthand turns that were taken at a slower response ☺ !!!!
Destiny packed with payday purchases her nose was pointed back up the mountain. Being out of the ordinary shopping on a Friday, turkey and macadamia sausages were available - they should go well with Aunty Shirley's home-made plum sauce ☺ ....
Relieving Destiny of her load I put everything away in appropriate spots under the watchful optimistic eye of Ms Tia. Parking my arse, I went through mail then read from cover to cover the Valley Voice staying in touch with local happenings. My little mate's patience and

optimism paid dividends. Hitting the switch of the kettle I broke out cake with my coffee and without fail she received a sample ☺....

Belly at peace for a while longer, I kept my arse parked, this time for the purpose of dating and inserting processed photos picked up today into the journal. Staying with the parked arse theme I merely shifted spots into the cottage adding animation to the computer. Working my way through July, I'm reliving the emotion associated with Tia's unnecessary operation to remove fat cells.... I'm glad that is fading in the ol' memory bank....

Being Pam's birthday Monday I splurged shopping to give the gift of nice savoury food; salami, olives, cheese, cocktail onions etc. With all good intentions those foods too are my favourite - breaking out beer o'clock I just had a sample. The olives had a solid dent put in the contents and the salami didn't last the evening. Like Tia, my heart is in the right spot but my stomach betrays ☺ !!!!

Saturday 14 October 2006
In windy, hot, drying, trying conditions the garden screamed out for another watering. Advice given by locals for growing garlic is to plant on the shortest day of the year, forget about it then harvest on the longest day of the year; not a good rule of thumb this season....

The spring rush of growth just isn't happening. By now I'm usually flat out mowing and watching it shoot up behind. Without a good drop of moisture soon grass won't reach maturity to produce seed heads containing the nutritional value. For those relying on cut hay to feed livestock, without a spot of moisture in the immediate future the cut will be near on useless; we're in for interesting times ahead???? Doris told me that there was a time there wasn't a blade of grass up here at all!!!!

Until Rainbow Falls imposes water restrictions I held the hose watering the spuds, beans, salvaged strawberry plants, self-sown lettuce, garlic, then left it to run freely on Peaches. As a tease the wild wind pushed a couple of cloud banks in from the west, giving it a generous measurement for effort, recorded 1mm only because its the least amount the gauge can record. The beetles rattling around in the bottom of the gauge were capable of drinking what went in ☺....

Going indoors out of the elements I put in a big afternoon with the frying pan cooking a shank roast, as Ms Tia will agree it was well worth the wait ☺....

Wandering out of the cottage my presence frightened a bunny back to the burnt out house and straight to the snapping jaws of Tia rattling around on the stack of corrugated iron. How the rabbit escaped is beyond me! Persistently and patiently doing her bit for the natural, native environment, and pumped full of adrenalin, Tia later had a victory catching an afternoon bunny snack....

Sunday 15 October 2006
In a likely snake active area, each walk taken to the throne I look over at the pesky sycamore saplings marking their patch of ground; meeting a cooler start made them number one priority for elimination. With long handled secateurs, pruning saw, my little mate and shovel on the handy, meandered along the fence leading to and behind the cattle yards leaving it looking more attractive naturally native ☺....

The only thing wind has done is change direction. Instead of hot northerly gusts it's channelling some cooler stuff at us delivering a desired temperature to want to be outside. The vegie patch became the focus of attention after smoko, losing a couple of hours turning soil. Closing the vegie garden gate behind complete and satisfied, filled my belly, then got comfortable in a solid session on the phone to Mum and Dad covering last week's notable activities ☺ ….

Cameron obviously has spoken to them across the road because today motorbike noise was kept behind the legal distance of 500 metres, making continual operation of bikes with limited exhaust and hard revving operators nowhere near as intrusive. Thanks to Cameron's intervention maybe we've found a balance for us complete opposites to live harmoniously within the same kilometre as one another ☺ ????

Monday 16 October 2006

When my lazy old body was prised out of bed I then took the time to appreciate the long overdue calm, sunny day. Taking a second milo to the shed to bask in the luxurious sunshine I propped my bum on Tia's 20 litre plastic drum adding a dash of comfort to the moment ☺ ….
Reluctantly tearing away from the shed perch, in the same unrushed manner idly did dishes and de-furred the bungalow. With one foot in front of the other got ready for a trip down into the valley and town specifically to wish Pam many happy returns ☺ ….

Sliding the key into the Post Office box took from it what I believe to be a birthday card from Sheila and Peter. They have obviously put their Russian translation book to work. Every single word printed or hand written on the card is in a language foreign to me; the buggers are always up to some antic ☺ !!!!

Prior to visiting, I called into the supermarket to replace the salami and olives eaten from Pam's savoury gift, staying at the birthday girl's long enough to enjoy good company over a cuppa and home-made biscuits. Social activity expanded to Maggie sitting parked at the library as I pulled into the curb nearby destined for the bakery ☺ ….

Typing my way into August, a gentle day was finished off seated behind the computer….
Sadly, it's funny how complacent I've become living in Tasmania having been exposed to so many large forestry operation burns. Last week, even being a day of total fire ban, I didn't raise an eyelid seeing smoke fill the valley below and it was an actual scrub fire at Beaumaris. Tonight the valley has continued to thicken with smoke sparking the thought, 'maybe it could be a bushfire, but then again maybe not'???? hmmmm….

Tuesday 17 October 2006

A commotion outside the bungalow before sunrise triggered one off inside. A cat-like squeal followed by heavy thudding feet outside got Ms Tia's warning voice activated inside. The burst of activity was over reverting to quiet all within the space of two minutes; in the third minute I was back sleeping ☺ ….

Lately the hose has a higher demand outside to keep up with the garden; rather than dragging it in and out I've left it outside. It's easier just bucketing the cottage water supply in. That's how the morning started, watering the bits outside needing a drink, carting a few buckets inside and putting the solar shower out to cook….

Standing filling a bucket with a slow flow rate there's nothing better to do than look around; spying a couple of weeds drew me under the walnut tree. There I discovered another 2½ pegs had been blown from last wash day ☺....

Putting my body to work swinging the splitter nineteen pieces were carved out of a pole cross-section. Placing the fresh cut load in the woodbox, the simmering solar shower was then put to use washing the sweat from my body. Cleansed, dry and comfortable, returned to key clunking and staring at the screen digitising more of August....

When digitisation is current, my brain is ready to unleash the preface already having spilled a few thoughts onto paper. The remainder is swirling around in my head almost ready to ooze out; dreams of publishing a book keep moving forward ☺....

Wednesday 18 October 2006

A couple of spits of rain were blown in 3a.m.-ish. If wind didn't wake me the whole event would have passed completely unnoticed. The few token drops were also blown away just as quickly without relieving a parched ground or recording anything at all measurable....

Daily, I've watched brown patches in the yard increase. Spring is nowhere to be found; the characteristics and behaviour observed of grass growth resemble that of the lead into summer????

Following a series of calmer days I get a false sense of security thinking 'yeah, the worst of the wild gusty wind has passed', then Mother Nature gives a blunt reminder not to get relaxed. Paradise turned on another one of those times it was hard to keep a hat on. Wind paid out on us randomly all day; now near on 19 hours on, as I write, it hasn't let up!!!!

Environmental elements determine how time is spent; similar procedure to yesterday, dealing with water then retreating under cover. Offering the potatoes and bean seed garden beds a survival soaking, topped up the cottage supply, then escaping the drying elements sheltered inside again seated in front of the computer....

After many hours of the keyboard finger dance, resigned myself to having a cool beer staring out the bungalow window. Letting my brain free range, I don't know why the thought popped into my head, but in a quick grab for paper to jot thoughts, not only did I use the back of it but also burnt the piece of paper I began the preface on!!!! There's no getting that back....

Thursday 19 October 2006

Preparing for bed last night wave after wave of wind roaring up from the valley, barging its way through the tree lined gorge found us to push around. Hopping into bed 11p.m.-ish thought I'd just lay there in readiness to doze off when it subsided, because just like it started it would stop sooner or later. Three hours later and wide eyed I was still waiting for it to relent!!!!

With each violent gust impacting on housing my brain would rush around accounting for every squeak, rattle or creak; stock-take done it would then wait for the next wave to arrive to repeat the procedure. Practising mind and body relaxation kept reassuring my brain there is simply nothing that can be done; we're in the hands of the elements. Bright eyed and waiting for the worst of the front to pass, I brushed three loads of fur from my little mate who ironically was content snoozing ☺ ????

The meanest of the lashing gusts passed 4a.m.-ish, and once again I woke fully clothed on top of the bed. Everything held together one more time; exhausted and ready to crawl into bed, did. Today it's hard to believe last night ever happened ☺ ????

Gordon from Clive Street, St. Marys, got my dozing body out of bed knocking on the cottage door. Pleasantly delivered, but not preached, his message was from god. I'm lucky enough to know how to live my life's journey honestly and fulfilled already….

Pulling the plug on the computer and heading down to shut the shed gate I was amused to see a 'sit down to walk' push-bike rider pedal past, a first time observation since planting my roots here ☺ !!!!

Friday 20 October 2006

Pissing off a handful of currawongs just passing through, I got sidetracked in the horizon paddock chipping temporary, well-established scotch thistles and hemlock weeds….

A much cooler overcast day presenting the possibility of rain got me into action repairing wind-dismantled temporary waterproofing temporary repairs. Stopping for coffee after repairing repairs, gazing out the window I watched a front push in from pure south. By the time my cup was empty the air temperature had dropped ten degrees and rain was finding ground ☺ ????

Leaving the bungalow with extras, beanie, jacket and Aunty Shirley throw rug, I made my way to the cottage to fraternise away more hours with the computer. Playing catch up digitising the journal's past 6 months, it's an extraordinary experience reliving the thoughts, actions, feelings and emotions of any one given day. Being able to place myself back into recent history is like having my own personal time machine ☺ ….

During a late afternoon visit Ross mentioned a lot of local fruit crops have been badly damaged through a severe frost encountered last week. I remember a couple of cold nights but saw no trace of the white stuff; nothing here is showing any sign of frost burn. As a leaving thought Ross asked if he could borrow shed space to change over motors in his daughter's car next week, promising to use tarps to protect the shed floor. If I don't have to clean up after him or he doesn't leave a scar of some sort it will be a first, but I answered yes….

Yesterday the solar shower cooked borderline too hot and my limbs were dangling out of bed to cool; tonight we're huddled by the heater and wouldn't be surprised to see snow ☺ ????

Saturday 21 October 2006

Aimlessly gazing out the bungalow window over breakfast was amazed to see a raven, a bird that will have a go at eagles and hawks, be chased away by a kookaburra????

Playing around with water easing into motivation was rapt to find nine bean seeds have started to take off. A place I'm easily distracted, the garden kept me longer than planned doing follow up on the latest weedicide program. I've been putting surplus boiling water on a patch of ivy getting established within the prunings, coal and ash pile littering the path at the rear of the burnt out house. With its dying back, me, Tia and the shovel helped the scorched ivy along by digging most out. In the ground ivy is a noxious weed; like comfrey, it doesn't take long to expose the bits missed ☺ ….

A woman on a mission, again let my fingers do the keyboard finger dance not giving in until turning into the pages of October; catching up is so near it's coming into view ☺ ….

My brain has been uncomfortable with the thought of placing a block and tackle over the shed beam to assist Ross' motor removal exercise so I phoned to express my feelings. All I did was save him a call because he managed to borrow a more suitable venue elsewhere, a win:win situation....

Sunday 22 October 2006   'A spark of hope can ignite big dreams' ☺ ....
Getting up bloody early for a Sunday, not only did I see remnants of a light frost but at 7:30a.m. there was also a pair of ducks feeding by the base of the dam, the same pair I saw fly from the dam yesterday. They're not a breed recognised, smoky blue, grey and white in colour????
Managing to gain attention the heater copped a clean out; a quick sift sorting coal from ash the ash went straight up to the drum at the loo. Harbouring a glint of determination in my eyes to find an end to journal digitising, electricity was added to the white goods and I began advancing toward the target. Claiming victory will have to wait for another time, because 148 minutes on the phone to Mum and Dad left me too relaxed to even look at the computer again. Dad and I spoke plenty, but Mum and I put in an exceptional jabber covering everything ☺ ....
Leaning on the wire fence bordering the burnt out house supporting a glass of red at dusk, enjoying progress and planning future moves, I glanced below the walnut tree finding another 1½ pegs. The more available pegs the more washing that can be done. I'm going to have to stop looking ☺!!!!

Monday 23 October 2006
Up by 7:30am yesterday and not giving in until midnight, I stayed warm under the doona a bit longer this morning. Doing the usual 'get the day started things' I then took a drive into St. Marys following a week's absence....
With little money and few needs it didn't take long to complete the list and blow the budget. Last stop before home, and inviting me to sit down over a cuppa, I took up Evelyn's offer. We made it through our brews before a customer drew the moment of relaxation to an end ☺ ....
Like metal filaments to a magnet I was drawn back to my mission. Punching the air through victory I walked away from the computer, for a few hours at least, totally up to date with digitisation ☺ .... Yahoooo....
With the concentration span of a snake, already those across the road are breaking the distance agreement with motorbikes by riding in the paddock in front of the house. It was a good week of peaceful consideration while it lasted. They're far from bright and definitely not the sharpest tools in the shed....
Taking a freshly cooked pot of rice to the bungalow spotted Tia literally on the tail end of devouring a rabbit, ridding the burnt out house of another introduced pest!!!! Good girl ☺ ....

Tuesday 24 October 2006
My intentions of doing laundry were shelved by the presence of a smoke haze in the air. I reckon why do today what can be put off until tomorrow or the day after ☺ ....
Having a half peg surplus without a mate stored inside the cottage, reaching for a shirt being sun smart after lunch, I was amused finding a matching half peg attached to the shirt. Now maybe last washing day is finally complete ☺ ?!?!

Giving time for the dust to settle on jet lag I gave Sheila a call for some pretty serious holiday adventure chat. Scratching the surface of the amazing adventure, I was given a brief overview of highlights fulfilling a childhood dream aboard the Trans Siberian Railway travelling through Russia then on into China☺....

Stepping inside to see a skink feeding along the bungalow window signifies high reptile activity; with Tia strapped to one leg and the shovel to the other confidently we made our way to the garden. Affording a dose of brain therapy outside, me and the hose were put to work; one hot day and the entire garden is screaming out for a drink. Everything from the beans to the walnut tree received a generous soaking. Starting to take off, I raised the mounds and weeded the spuds just leaving their heads poking out of the ground to keep reaching skyward☺....

Wednesday 25 October 2006

By 9:30am the drought was trying to break; ideal conditions to trigger thoughts of returning to lawnmower repairs so the drive was taken to St. Helens to make it possible....

Holding back, granting enough time to do the necessary bits, the mildest part of the day was first up when bare skin could be exposed before the first of many showers settled in adding life to a ground that had set like concrete☺....

Entering St. Helens first stop was to pull into the mower centre. Walking in with the bottom shaft Jamie said "the cone is worn", in its state it caused the noise that's concerned me, cone is the technical term for the stone disk at the end of the shaft the drive wheels touch down on. He also mentioned most people would take one look at a Cox mower and say "no way" to fixing it, replying, "I did". With a cone in stock he was happy to replace it if I could kill an hour shopping, striking a deal. I was told later they had to heat and snap-freeze the shaft to strip it free of pulleys and bearings to reach the cone. I would have turned that exercise alone into a career at home, the new cone clearly demonstrated the wear being double the size of that removed☺!!!!

Filling in time while the mower part was repaired I let my imagination get excited rummaging through the hardware store. A wire brush to fit the drill was bought for the purpose of tidying up the feet for the bath. Going all out breaking into the budget also splurged on film for the camera☺....

Leaving our local packed with groceries I started the trip toward the mountain. Before leaving bitumen the thought of chocolate ripple biscuits for Maggie's birthday cake turned me around for one last farewell☺....

A patch of blue sky broke through 5p.m.-ish but by then a useful drop of 14mm had relieved me from watering. Before the cardboard curtain went up in the bungalow for the evening there was more blue than cloud covering the sky; however a strong pure southerly influence prevailed.... brrrr....

Thursday 26 October 2006

Tia thought it was a one human night, not leaving my side from go to whoa. Following yesterday's rain I wouldn't have guessed a frost would follow; traces of the white stuff lingered up until 9:30am. A pan lying around in the vegie patch collected a sample of rainwater and the overnight freeze formed an ice crust across its surface. At this stage no crop damage is evident????

Avoiding one of my least favourite jobs, and no one to relieve me from it, it bites me on the bum at some stage. Daylight hours were filled sending load after load to the clothesline. Planning ahead organising for a spaghetti cook up, the splitter took my last available energy breaking down another pole cross-section ☺ ....

Speaking to Lesley a couple of nights back she mentioned the area surrounding the 'Big Tree' has been tagged for logging. Tape tagging the walking track was removed along with the visitors book sitting inside the hollow of the 'Big Tree', Lesley also said Mum and I were the last to write our appreciation in the visitor's book. It pains me with the environmental guidelines logging practices must follow to preserve sensitive areas and endangered species. Looking down the valley from the bottom of Rainbow Falls over to Mathinna at the thousands upon thousands of hectares of land stripped bare and not one thing was worthy of preservation.... I've got to question that????

Friday 27 October 2006

On just another occasion wind roused sleep; coming from south a direction more protected, the scantily clad tree lined gorge took the sting out of its impact before reaching housing, leaving me stirred but not shaken ☺ ....

Watching front after front blow past, rain was all around but it could be counted on one hand the drips that fell in our direction. Relaxing with a glass of red knocking off 6p.m.-ish, a bloody cold blast from the Antarctic delivered with it a light snow shower that melted on contact hitting the ground. Blowing past in the same rush as it arrived, blue sky was once again exposed timely for the sun to break through before disappearing behind the mountain to set for another day????

Taking up space in the fridge, I got organised to deliver the chocolate ripple cake to Maggie for her birthday, but before taking off anywhere first honoured an appointment with my case manager Sandra. Arriving unannounced I didn't find Maggie in; instead the cake was left on her sink awaiting her return. Being more in touch with spontaneity, I found Ross in on the way home to again take possession of his socket set....

Cleaning the work area in the shed preparing for a fresh start on mower repairs in the morning I began to tinker. One tinker led to another, I finished up by totally reassembling the bottom vertical shaft and assembling the top horizontal shaft to the point no more can be done until a woodruff key is tracked down to replace the one I sheared on the cog.... Getting ready to kick a personal growth goal ☺ !!!!

Saturday 28 October 2006

Winter, like the wind, is reluctant to leave. Rising from under the doona, I pulled the beanie over my ears, put on an extra couple of layers and got on with it. That'll teach me - getting confident buying real butter; of late it can only be used as a weapon ☺ !!!!

In my 'girl can do it' determined state of mind, a large woodruff key offered by Jamie was the right thickness, easier than trying to chase one up. Using a grinding wheel I fashioned it down to size....

This tiny piece of metal I'd been so articulately and lovingly fashioning, nearing its completion and reduced to taking fine slivers, let it slip through my fingers during a fitting. Lurking below unsuspectingly, and accommodating of a tiny piece of metal, was the open mouth of the rear brake drum willingly harbouring the fugitive in a single swallow. Totally surprised and in disbelief my instant thought, following shit, was it was probably trying to lead me to the unsolved mystery of the collapsed bearing???? At that point it was time for a lunch break and re-think....

Unable to let myself wake up tomorrow with the first thought being to find the home fashioned woodruff key within the brake housing, reversed any thought of leaving it for later. Wandering back to the shed to, at minimum, have the key retrieved ready to progress forward in the assembly department....

Dealing with each presented challenge individually, once the key sat in the palm of my hand I tightened every bolt undone for its retrieval to revert to where I left off. Further lifting my spirits, secured all the components along the top horizontal shaft leaving only the key, cog, and calibration of the large disk drive wheels to face later. The collection of loose parts is dwindling, all are accounted for and the end is near ☺....

Sunday 29 October 2006

Bungalow de-furred and teeth brushed, the shed gates were opened and like a woman possessed walked straight up to the top level....

Shaving a few more slivers from the home-made woodruff key, the cog was sat flush on the top shaft with the Woodruff key seated in its groove, and with a little encouragement, it was driven home. Using thin cardboard I set the gap between the large drive disks hovering above the new cone and fastened the final nuts on the top horizontal shaft. In excited eagerness I used the pull cord to supplement a tired battery to fire the mower into life. Everything worked accordingly but the mower itself refused to budge. Taking little time to nut out I hadn't put the chain back on the cogs ☺!!!! Oooops....

Guiding the clip that secures the chain with my finger tips got it to snap over the link, also snapping onto my thumb like a clam, taking in its grip only a small piece of skin but it refused to let go. Opening the clip with my left hand and a screwdriver released my captive thumb and the blood blister it sported, replacing the clip to the desired position this time without any accessories ☺....

Before stopping for lunch, and without any spare parts, I quietly and successfully rode the mower around in the shed. One thing's for certain - I'm glad it's only a flat tyre stopping me now. From getting the cone repaired to the last nut tightened, Mum and Dad relived the whole mower repair job step by proud step in our regular Sunday catch up on life call ☺....

Monday 30 October 2006

Recently being devoted to ride-on repairs, I caught my breath having a bit of a tinkering time with other things....

Nearly kissing the ground, Peaches was propped back up onto the timber plank that's keeping her supported in a firm upright position. Drinking water and cottage water replete and the solar shower on the cook, Ms Muffet and I took a quick drive to Ross' returning the socket set....

The wire brush was retrieved with the intent of putting it into the drill to make a start cleaning up the bath feet, but the job never went beyond good intentions. On a timely trip between the cottage and bungalow I chanced to see an eagle fly past directly overhead, giving an acknowledging call on its pass over ☺....
The novelty still fresh and unable to resist the indulgence I lifted the seat of the ride-on to expose those two reassembled shafts, the moment sent a shiver down my spine, a task I never thought I was capable of ☺!!!!
Walkabout with my little mate until it was time for nocturnal animals to claim the paddocks, I checked on how the dam was travelling. The waterline is sitting at least 30cm below capacity - quite a way to go before running out is a threat....

Tuesday 31 October 2006
A habit developed on the walk back from the loo to prevent mozzies from building up in the cattle trough - I splash water out with the shovel and Tia tries catching it. Sadly for Tia, the dam level has dropped enough for her gravity fed swimming pool to stop flowing. The float is doing sweet little other than just hanging limply inside the trough....
Picking up the electric drill, and without a chuck key, the bit for driving home roofing screws refused to leave its position to step aside for the wire brush. A challenge I couldn't be bothered dealing with when it can be done simply in seconds, the bath feet cleaning was shelved once again....
Playing in the garden with my best friend while re-programming my brain and thought processes into doing something else, a sky full of rain clouds doing nothing but blocking sun and dropping the mercury, helped steer a course to the computer to keep journal digitising at manageable levels....
Indoors and protected from another snap freeze, I made a start sorting out how to be legally buried on site at Rainbow Falls. Damien at the Department of Health straight away hand passed me to our local Council. Rebecca offered a call back once she chased up and deciphered the information. Tony, versed with on site burial knowledge, called me back citing the steps to achieve my goal. A letter compiled by me, to Council, stuffed with appropriate pieces of paper is step two, step one outlining the criteria for envelope stuffing is in the mail and on its way. Not sounding difficult or out of the question, being at Rainbow Falls forever with my little mate side by side is a step closer to happening ☺....

Wednesday 1 November 2006
Making a habit of brushing at least one load from my little mate each night before turning in her body is now getting reluctant to part with fur the winter coat drop is on the slow down. Although, I'm still far from ready to remove bungalow de-furring from the daily 'to-do' jobs ☺....
Coming out of winter into spring last year, for the months of August, September and October, we had an exceptionally wet transition copping 525mm - for the same three months this year 71mm???? Mother Nature pulls the strings ☺!!!!
In the lead up to Mum's colonoscopy tomorrow, I phoned for details on a theatre time and to share loving thoughts. In preparation for theatre Mum's last food intake was 3p.m. today, from 7a.m. tomorrow absolutely nil intake until returning from her theatre booking time of 2:30pm,

a long 24-hours with an empty stomach. With Dad at golf there was no sharing the phone, Mum and I settled right in going over the new and old ☺ ….
Resting my ear and receiver, and following a quick game of skud ball, my little mate and me wandered out the front re-visiting a job started sometime back. Buried under a good layer of soil, the concrete wheel tracks leading into Doris and Norm's car garage were unearthed. I tossed clumps and Ms Tia filed and sorted the surplus soil into driveway wheel ruts; we're a co-ordinated team ☺ ….
Watching the last light fade from the comfort of the bungalow I saw four wallabies stop and graze passing through the slashed love heart; television had a wildlife program on tonight ☺ ….

Thursday 2 November 2006
Cloud that has been passing all around spent the night banking up and shortly after 7a.m. released a slow, gentle, consistent spill. A quiet couple of millimetres over a few warm, wet and steamy hours combined for brilliant plant growth conditions….
Whatever was happening with the elements outside I had planted the seed early in my mind lying in bed at making inroads writing the preface for 'Inside my Skin'. I've talked about writing this book long enough its time for action ☺ !!!!
Thoughts constantly reverting to Mum's colonoscopy, I phoned prior extending my love and thoughts for the pending discomfort….
Setting the right relaxed state of mind to get words flowing, I first disappeared with my best friend into the garden. After transplanting a couple of salvaged strawberry plants, I once again mounded the potatoes and distributed compost ☺ ….
Procrastinating until I could procrastinate no more, me and my little mate got comfy in the bungalow, the warmest spot in the afternoon. Pencil and paper on the ready, I hadn't even finished my coffee before words were ready to spill. Feeling totally relaxed words streamed from the pencil held in my hand and naturally flowed with ease, releasing the pent up words that stored themselves in my head waiting for this moment to surrender ☺ !!!!
Left feeling inwardly content, placing the pencil down I retreated outdoors and waited like an expectant Mother to hear news of Mum's outcome. Occupying a pacing mind, wait time was filled moving two slabs of timber that once represented a bench seat and table in the cottage side yard. Bases rotten and long fallen to the ground, rather weighty, I flipped, twisted, tilted and walked these solid pieces of timber to concrete, resting them against the back wall of the burnt out house. Coincidentally, where they once sat by the fire pit in the side yard of the cottage is a site considered for Tia and I to terminate our material existence and be buried side by side together forever as promised ☺ ….
Of all the words released today, the ones I most wanted to hear were Mum's home and fine ☺ ….

Friday 3 November 2006
After breakfast, lazily and leisurely, I put a pot of water on the boil to spruce up for a trip into the big metropolis of St. Marys to gather enough stocks to see us through until Wednesday's pay….
Bringing to my attention local attractions, Maggie and Brian's 'troopie' parked in town was a chalkboard of information advertising tomorrow's Maypole Festival. Town was a hive of

activity with a tepee and tents being erected on Faulkner Green for the much-anticipated festival. Festivities beginning 10a.m. tomorrow, a small parade will pass through town 2p.m. and Maggie will display her belly dancing skills directly following the parade. An experience to be had at minimum once ☺ ....

Prepared for a splurge on a push-bike pump for the mower's tyre it just wasn't meant to be. There wasn't a single pump hanging from the supermarket shelves. Maybe the drought has other plans for me besides wasting fossil fuels on mowing ☺ ????

Kerry at the Post Office told me that both walnut trees leading into their driveway in the township of St. Marys were so badly burnt by late frosts they blackened and look dead. Listening to the disheartening stories of crop losses I'm grateful at how lightly Rainbow Falls has escaped the severity; we're still growing without any sign of damage....

Evelyn was more than ready to sit down for a brew; still chatting long after my cup was empty, her honest giving aura is easy to be in the company of. The demand on Evelyn's time drew our chatter to an end, from there I wandered back up the hill to continue sweet bugger all and didn't falter from the same laid back mood ☺ ....

Saturday 4 November 2006

Emptying the clothes brush in the process of de-furring the bungalow, the gentlest of breezes lifted the discarded contents into the air. A robin watching attentively from the electricity cable flew at the floating fur playing with it doing a few flying passes until the fur lodged in a nearby tree.... Ahhhh, utopia ☺ ....

Having a few hours up my sleeve before heading out, and following a couple of consecutive hot days, the hose was pulled from the cottage to make a difference outside. The meagre rain offerings of the past week have only offered immediate moisture benefit, nothing lasting. Leaving the hose to spill its life giving revitalising liquid I filled a few milo tins with rusty nails, pieces of glass and other bits of small valueless crap from the burnt out house sliding them into the household rubbish for disposal.... Every little bit makes a difference ☺ ....

Faulkner Green, where a taste of the Maypole Festival waited, drew us away from home for a first time experience. By-passing face painting and the mornings kids' activities I targeted arriving for the 2p.m. street parade. Larger than life sized puppets, brightly coloured clothing, a procession of decorated kids and adults, accompanied with an array of non-mainstream instruments, added life to the parade making its way onto Faulkner Green to the coloured streamers encircling the maypole and entertainment tent. Stopping for a hug in passing, Maggie participated in the parade representing gypsy dancers, aside all the pieces decorating her body that jingled dancing around, she played a happy uplifting rhythmic beat crashing bell like disks together with her fingers. Plenty of food stalls, socialising and entertainment - everyone had at least one of their senses satisfied ☺ ....

Weather wise it literally shifted 180°. I spent a lovely afternoon out comfy in a t-shirt at the Maypole Festival drenched in warm sunshine from a north-westerly airflow. Returning to Rainbow Falls a south-easterly pushed in and South Sister Range fluffed up with misting cloud. From that point the temperature plummeted before wind entered into the equation. South-easterly is our most protected direction - I'm certainly glad we're not living on the other side of the 'Sisters' tonight.... Who would have thought ☺ ????

Sunday 5 & Monday 6 November 2006
Cosy in front of the fire on a freezing night my elbow got a bit excited with the wineglass, getting very happy; so happy, in fact, I went in search of bed rather than the pen. Starting tonight's entry in logical sequence I'll go back to the day of the wine☺....
Sunday went from cold to bloody icy - it could have been any one of our coldest winter days three weeks short of summer, real butter off the breakfast menu stuff☺?!?! A sky heavily laden with cloud did nothing to help with the long dry spell....
To supplement what was already in the woodbox for the evening ahead, I had a reminder of how wood was cut in the olden days before a chainsaw. Following a remedial stint with a blunt handsaw I then treated myself to the pleasures of domestic duties, ranging from removing corpses from window ledges to sprinkling a dusting of ajax in the bath....
When domestics gave me the shits, which doesn't take long, I propped my bum for a yak with family. Mum mentioned she didn't bounce back so readily from this colonoscopy, but is slowly heading in the right direction. Up to date with my Mildura life, I then sparked up the computer updating the journal. Creating a new file captured all the spilled words of the preface just in case I decide to toss that piece of paper into the fire; its loss this time would bring me to my knees and there will be tears!!!!
A bit slow to fire on all cylinders Monday morning, I eased my body into the day fiddle farting around pulling weeds until my brain cleared the red wine fog and kicked into gear....
Fixing another bloody hose leak, and serious about doing the job properly this time, Ross proofed the section draped over the driveway. The broken PVC pipe was retired. A tough job requires tough equipment, I threaded the hose through a length of galvanised pipe for drive over assurance☺!!!!
In a conversation with Mum some weeks back I spoke of how I'd like to rid the last of the shed look from the cottage. Finding myself traipsing from building to building in search of scattered tools, rationalising the distribution a start was made at storing the lot in one spot. Reclaiming shed space amongst Ross' stuff I cleared the fixed bench, cleaned it, and like trophies displayed my united bits☺....

Tuesday 7 November 2006   'Happy Birthday Stacey'
Working on getting the most from the rapidly growing potato plants, their mounds were pushed even higher. Grabbing soil adjacent to the plants to fill their growing need I've created a pit☺....
In sheer optimism the solar shower was put out, battling against the odds. Moments of sunshine surprisingly took the edge off the water. Exiting the nice conditions of morning, south and west had a shoving match for weather dominance; proving strongest south blew in another bitter blast.... Brrrr....
With our nest feathered I returned my unsatisfied mind to the ride-on and that elusive bearing. After much contemplative thought decided I'm unprepared to continue a witch-hunt dismantling until there's a clue via a noise or unfamiliar movement. Not overly fond of mechanics, my brain refuses to go on doing a lot of work to possibly find nothing. Jacking up the mower's front end I spun, twisted and wriggled every moving part but nothing showed any sign of once owning those loose silver balls???? Resigning myself to wait, the tools on loan from Terry were polished and tool kit packed for returning....

The southerly rush failed to weaken. Cooking dinner in the frying pan without the company of a heater it was so bloody cold I had my beanie pulled down to meet two windproof jackets????

Wednesday 8 November 2006
I ought to bring the hose back inside; since taking it out of the cottage one could be mistaken in thinking we've returned to winter. Following yesterday's rush of cold air today was replaced with broken cloud, poor attempts at drizzle, the occasional burst of sunshine and rushes of cold air, but any day is a good day to fatten the fridge and shelves with food ☺ ....
Heading off shopping I shut the front gate behind to keep out large black animals, proving to be a smart moooove; seeing a single cow grazing wandering along the road leaving, I returned to four. Can't blame them escaping their boundaries; there's more feed along the roadside than in their paddocks. Tia took little time from getting out of Destiny to politely move cows on, driving them down the road from within her paddock fence confines ☺ ....
Returning kindly loaned tools, and being the official rainfall record keeper for St. Marys, I asked Terry for a copy of August's figures to fill in the blanks on my chart for the time away from home visiting Mildura. Conversation regarding the obvious dry year we're having led us into the past; the driest year since records were kept was 1908, delivering a total of 488mm. We need 121mm to fall before December's end to even equal that figure. Anything less will set a new benchmarking record for an all-time low dry year????
Hitting the shops, a photo enlargement along with the negative sent away for processing a month back, to be ready in time for Mum's birthday, managed to get lost in the incompetence of our pretend chemist. My intentions were good however; the smaller version made today's post?!?!
The Post Office was kind offering hand written friendly mail, my favourite kind. Sheila and Peter sent several postcards with descriptions from their travels along with a gift. The tubby envelope revealed a beautifully and decoratively painted set of varying sized timber dolls, each fitting neatly inside one another, traditionally Russian ☺ ....
Loaded with food I stopped for a yarn with Evelyn. After getting mower fuel home was put in my sights; with very little of the working day left it was time to shift thinking to the working night ☺ ....

Thursday 9 November 2006
Sitting for breakfast, I thought a grain of bread had dropped onto Tia's head but it wouldn't budge, I pulled a huge tick from above her eyebrow. The tick's removal slowed Tia's desire for participation, spending most of her day snoozing shifting from sun to shade....
No matter what elements were happening outside laundry had to be done. A perfect spring day accompanied by a sprinkling of cloud, and of course what's laundry day without a dash of wind ☺ ....
Tearing me away from a favourite chore, washing, ha, ha, my friend and bank manager, Helen, gave me a courtesy call. An oversight by the bank; the land title wasn't secured to the mortgage giving the bank no security. Promising Helen I'd honour my end of the bargain and assist with rectifying the issue.... Ooooops....
The sun's rays highlighted the yard's amber tinge. The first sign of warmth depletes any available moisture from the dry, hard soil. Taking the hose outside after laundry everything

edible was given a long slow soaking. Taxing my body, I stood in the shade watching water trickle out the end of a hose, shifting from my cool vantage-point only to move the hose and return to my shady spot. Ahhhh, I'm going to enjoy those spuds and beans ☺ ....
Inside the bungalow putting dry clothes away I was initially startled by the speed and wing flapping of a robin doing a quick lap inside. To settle me it did another couple of entries checking out what goes on indoors ☺ .... Utopia ☺ ....

Friday 10 November 2006
Sheila wasn't home to receive a natter of thanks for the letter and gift recently received. After a brief chat to their answering machine I escaped outside watering the bits that missed out yesterday. Easing into activity I quietly played around in one of my most favourite places for relaxation. For the time being the garden will need plenty of hose attention, the ground is so depleted of moisture that walking around beds in the vegie patch powdery soil is raised underfoot. An upside to the establishing drought is it's indiscriminate. Weeds are also suffering, from weeds to mowing. For this usually busy time of season my work-load has been lightened....
Stopping Ms Muffet from racing through paddocks on a high reptile alert day, while I split another pole cross-section she looked after Destiny. Breaking one of those stumps down requires a good level of fitness. Each dismantled cross-section makes the wheelbarrow creak under its weight delivering a split load to the cottage....
Having teeth issues raising their head again I decided to be proactive and make an appointment. The surgery was happy to make a time for me but I now have to travel to Launceston to see a dentist. Shifting the round trip travel distance from 100 km's to 240 km's makes it a bit more prohibitive to get dental care.... Bugger!!!!
Fossicking for the dentist phone number I also picked up another scrap of paper with contact details for Stacey. At that moment the penny dropped why I only ever received a disconnection message trying to ring for her birthday - I'd been trying her previous address. Leaving a message on the answering machine explained my blunder. Maybe Stacey can pick up the birthday thoughts posted to her former address also ☺ ???? Ooooops ☺ ....

Saturday 11 November 2006
Low cloud clinging to the surrounding mountains blocking the sun just dampened the ground having about as much impact as a fog. The bare minimum moisture offered is just keeping a green tinge on the yard and paddocks, also offering weeds and grasses enough hope to continue trying to grow....
The immediate area surrounding the loo looks like a bombing ground. Sitting on the throne enjoying the view I spot buzzies setting flowers. Tia and I then make their struggling lives even more miserable, taking on average an hour to return from the loo.... Life just happens ☺ ....
Escaping to the shed I parked Destiny on the top level side-on to the ride-on. Plugging the mini compressor into the cigarette lighter filled the mower's tyres with air; however, mist once again found us striking a test ride off the menu. Remaining in the haven a solid start was made sweeping and cleaning my scattered sprawl, putting most of Ross' stuff in one of the side rooms to utilise the other, I found a permanent home for my growing collection of bits ☺ ....

Writing some thoughts down over a cuppa a large bird landing on the cottage roof caused me to take a look. Food is getting that scarce a bloody currawong was attempting to raid a blackbird nest tucked into flashing to snack out on the bubbies. When ruffled feathers settled and blackbirds returned to the nest they were met by the squawking of hungry mouths competing for a feed. Out in the open you're either prey or predator. The strengthening drought is showing in the desperation of animal behaviour; there's less to go around with still as many mouths to feed????

Sunday 12 November 2006   "Happy Birthday Mum" ☺ ....
A raiding pillaging gang of currawongs mobbed housing 6:30a.m.-ish. Unable to ignore the ruckus Ms Tia and I got up and didn't return to bed until they'd moved over South Sister Range. Head settled back on the pillow, a steady, soaking, welcome drop of rain found ground reducing that total of 121mm to equal the driest year on record, down to 117mm. Falling that gently not a single drop of moisture drifted in on the toilet seat ☺ ....
The only course of action for us women to take in the current uncertain climatic conditions was to retreat to the shed, further enhancing the impact on yesterday's big tidy up and rationalising effort....
Having a spell from the broom and haven, I left the cottage door open for Tia to roam in and out at leisure while I chatted to the birthday girl and Dad. I told Mum the fate of the photo enlargement destined as a birthday present lost somewhere in the big wide world; maybe it will surface in time for Christmas? Dad and I were buried in conversation when Tia's reaction to a clap of thunder directly above us stole the show. By the second clap Dad and I said our farewells; at that stage Tia was deep in a paddock warning the intruding noise off, and she did a grand job, because two claps and a dribble of rain and it was all over. I reckon not enough warm air was available robbing the thunderstorm of its correct operational recipe????
Staying with a sure thing us girls returned to complete the makeover of Destiny's bedroom finishing the bottom level. Wondering what to do with the broken Woodruff key and few loose silver balls from the mower, I added them to the time capsule, a Blundstone shoe box I've stored pieces of memorable treasure in and placed in the rafters of the shed. The shoe box contents should give me a laugh or teary eye; sometime down the track they'll certainly spark off a yarn or two ☺ ....

Monday 13 November 2006
A front that's been lingering about now for its third day, today fogged us in; rain started 8a.m.-ish delivering a most convincing 11mm drop. Assisting the main front along, wind kept it on the move; doing its best work in the first three hours it spent the rest breaking up and petering out. Spring is all over the place. Ringing me to finish yesterday's interrupted conversation, Dad said Mildura has only received 1mm the past two months but received a drought breaking deluge of 5mm overnight????
Making inquiries to have my teeth looked at got the facts. The Launceston clinic is only classified as an emergency department and there's no booking ahead. The procedure to see a dentist is to call weekday mornings at 8:30am to see if an assessment appointment is available on the day. Travelling a 240 kilometre round trip, I'm permitted one 45 minute consultation at maximum at any one time. Well I guess the guidelines are clear....

Being the least of my worries with ride-on repairs, Ross took me through the principles behind the throttle and choke because a couple of bits had come adrift. Knowing where they go and what they do I lost the afternoon down the shed putting things back where they belong. Pull starting the mower into firing, not only does it propel back and forth without a squeal the throttle is also responsive. I'm ready to cut grass☺!!!!

Tuesday 14 November 2006
Tia sniffed out and claimed a dead wallaby which had taken its final breath near the blackwood tree by the road. Wanting Ms Muffet closer to housing to keep an eye on her, I busted my pooper carrying the wallaby 100 metres on the shovel into the slashed love heart. Paddock travels in blustery wind strong enough to blow a beanie loose from its moorings brought to an end the lives of many budding thistles....
Desiring to remove blood and an aroma that had me retching from the shovel, I followed through with thoughts of further mounding the potatoes, simultaneously cleaning the shovel blade slicing it into soil. Enlarging the pit, many more kilos of soil and compost were tossed onto the healthy growing potato mound. From weeding to feeding everything except the beans got a complete makeover. As if I had the luxury of turning on the heavens tap at my leisure, shutting the garden gate when finished, wind, that had menaced, pushed in a bank of cloud delivering a quick rain burst wetting up freshly turned soil and watering in compost. Fifteen minutes later, bang, the wind eased and we were back in full sunshine, ideal for plants☺....
Nearing sunset relaxing over a cup of tea I was peacefully watching about a dozen blackbirds and a pair of ravens feeding in the love heart. Blissfully oblivious to the world snoozing in sunshine behind glass, Tia opened one eye taking a peek out the bungalow window; spying a raven tearing strips off her wallaby she cleared the paddock in short time☺!!!!

Wednesday 15 November 2006
Hearing the sound of raven activity outside Tia gave me the paw tap to get up, I thought she only wanted to protect her wallaby from intruders so I ignored her ask. Surfacing sometime later from the warm comfort of bed I felt a right mongrel to discover Tia was forced to pee on the floor, copping a hard fast lesson in assumption!!!!
A tooth, left of the top front, long ago crumbled following a root filling; an artificial tooth attached to a metal plate these days fills the gap. Plate wires wrapped around existing teeth have rubbed their way through enamel finding raw nerves, causing me to nearly hit the roof when the plate goes near my mouth. Until I can get to the dentist, and self-conscious of gaps in my mouth, I phoned asking Pam if she wouldn't mind helping me out by grabbing a few bits from the shops; without hesitation she was more than willing....
Tubbed up, I made it over the mountain in time to share a traditional Devonshire tea with a fresh batch of Pam's home-baked scones; double bonus, I received a sample pack of scones to take home☺!!!!
Far more pleasant to be protected from elements in the comfort of Destiny, I drove Pam to the shops because Mother Nature threw traces of snow and hail at us between sunny periods. Nothing measurable fell; a small cloud mass would pass over have a bit of a spit at us and move on, merely stopping the mercury from getting too excited.... Brrrr....

Thursday 16 November 2006
Some wild southerly stuff kicked up a fuss last evening. Lashing wind had a bitterly cold edge; leaving the heaters comfort was a 'have to' situation and lasted only as long as necessary.... Preparing the yard for an onslaught with the revitalised mower, with my little mate on the ready, I got busy with the shovel edging around obstacles. A well-earnt nice day had me stripping down to a t-shirt as it progressed....

Pulling up from shovel work for smoko, and waiting to sample scones, Tia burped filling the bungalow with the aroma of second-hand dead wallaby. The raw odour robbed the moment of any sweetness. Doing what comes naturally, after three days of gorging Tia has eaten her waistline away; rather rotund she's as full as a public school, having some fancy digesting to do. Tia's lungs can't have much room for expansion; I wouldn't be at all surprised to find stretch marks on her belly. Her gas release from both ends has been, to say the least, ordinary.... Phew!!!!

Aiming to co-ordinate travelling to Launceston together, Pam called to say her dentist appointment was rescheduled for this coming Monday. Phoning the dental surgery explaining our situation, I was pencilled in for an appointment 15 minutes after Pam's. Monday is a goer to begin turning the comfort of my mouth around....

I wasn't the only one enjoying the great outdoors; it was a brilliant day too for fauna activity. Kicking off the extraordinary action an eagle effortlessly glided its way over and out toward the horizon. Some time later a squawking currawong gave me cause to look up. Observing two different flight patterns, I was suitably impressed. The commotion was caused not by one but a pair of goshawks. Taking an armful of grass clumps to dump in driveway wheel ruts movement caught my eye. I was stoked to see an echidna idly making its way across the driveway to again disappear into the paddocks☺.... Ahhhh, only in paradise....

Going walkabout with the long handled secateurs prior to dusk, short work was made of bloody feral sycamore saplings edging the fringe of the gorge behind the cattle yards. As a bonus for effort some nice limb wood was scored; now safely stored in the shed, rounded a very complete packed day ☺....

Friday 17 November 2006
Eliminating frostbite and lashing wind it's beginning to finally feel like summer's approaching. Soil is that dry any benefit from recent rain disappeared in an instant; the first sign of a bit of heat everything screamed out for a drink. Appreciating the manual past, for me it's always a pleasure holding a hose giving the vegies a drop of liquid. It's a luxury just to be able to hold a hose. How quickly it's forgotten, the number of trips once made to the cattle trough with a bucket carting water back in the olden days ☺....

Leaving the garden content, Tia and I returned to where we left off yesterday with the shovel edging. Together we finalised clearing the base of the fence bordering the cottage side yard knocking down hidey spots for snakes, not to mention looking bloody tidy. The usual routine occurred with my little mate; I dug and tossed, Tia sorted, filed and composted. Pulling up lame at one stage Tia's paw picked up a spike from the boxthorn. Without sustaining a puncture she was back ready and waiting for the next tossed sod ☺....

Hot and sweaty searching for a wash, the solar shower also felt the effects of the sun's rays, having to add cold water to the bubbling brew to bring it back a few degrees: a big effort all round today ☺ ....

Saturday 18 November 2006
For the past week I've only had two individual puffs of ventolin. Such minimal use is a time my memory doesn't take me back to. In fact many years, happiness and health go hand in hand; I'm learning how to get the balance right ☺ ....
A first in many months - my legs got an airing; dashing about in undies, shirt and boots, I did a bit more shovel work. By the time Tia and I had edged around the long deserted dog kennel, moved a couple of large rocks, cleared and tidied the fire pit, heat drove us to find a cooler location to fill the afternoon. A perfect spot on a hot day, or any occasion for that matter, is the shed. Taking Destiny to Launceston Monday it was her turn for some attention. All the vitals under the bonnet checked and topped up, I ventured inside removing deposited Tia fur, window tongue-lashings and mountain dirt....
Who would have believed that shortly after 6p.m. wind picking up would send my freshly bathed scantily clad body searching for more clothes. Beanied-up, I watched a front cling to South Sister Range looking and feeling like it could do a snow dump at any moment. Seeing the action a couple of hundred metres away, feeling as if I could just reach out and touch it, the front clung to the range like velcro. Doing a stint on the rat-shit blunt handsaw to warm-up, I waited in anticipation for some action from above but was left hanging????

Sunday 19 November 2006
Yesterday's late southerly blast lasted not long after putting the pen down from writing about it. The lasting legacy of its existence was the cloud it left behind, remaining mostly overcast minus the icy blast. A check of the rain gauge in the morning found it still as dry as a bone; nothing fell while I was blissfully oblivious sleeping....
De-furring the bungalow is certainly not off the menu but the severity of Tia's fur dump is starting to put the anchors on. In the process of de-furring the bed I saw what resembled a small red seed, picking it up for closer examination found it to be a blood bloated tick, popping like a pimple it's since gone to heaven....
Taking a few minutes out with my little mate quietly sitting nearby, I watched the world pass from the sanctuary of the shed. Amid the silent peacefulness the scraping of scaly skin on corrugated iron robbed the reflective moment; a copperhead snake stole the show making its way along the shed wall. Priority one, Tia was put into the safe comfort of Destiny, in the short time that took the snake was nowhere to be found, a search failed to track it down. Returning after a chat with Stacey, sadly for the snake it re-surfaced inside the shed, lying by Destiny. It ended up at the same destination as the tick....
Walking back from the dam having just laid the snake to rest my case manager Sandra pulled in. Following our usual pleasant routine of a brew and chat, I kept my vocal chords active after Sandra parted company. Staying put on my bum, letting my fingers do the walking dialling up Mum and Dad's number, we rarely pull up under an hour because there's all those little bits that matter to share ☺ ....

Having a lazy Sunday I did little other than practice social etiquette, drink cuppa's and eat. I deserve a slack one every so often ☺....

Monday 20 November 2006
At 6:45 precisely the alarm annoyed me into animation, bathed up, cashed up and fuelled up I was there to pick Pam up at our designated 9a.m.....
With plenty of time up our sleeve before having to head to the dentist we deviated, Destiny was steered into fantasyland. Blowing the meagre spare budget offerings at the hardware store on a bucket, lawnmower filter, and 20 metre rolls of 13mm poly pipe for a mere $3.57 couldn't be walked past. Leaving via Kings Meadows we did over both supermarkets fulfilling my mission of tracking down milo on special ☺....
With appointments fifteen minutes apart we got immersed in glossy bullshit magazines until our individual turn in the dentist chair came about. I walked out more comfortable with one less mercury filled tooth in my mouth....
Playing navigator, Pam introduced me to shops in Launceston I never knew existed. Carefully negotiating my numb mouth through lunch, we then began a slow journey toward home. On our travels stumbled across Cripps Bakery, makers of the best shortbread biscuits, currently no longer stocked, and a dollar per packet cheaper than our supermarket had them. Loaded with bulk animal feed for Pam and Terry's animal menagerie, I made an impromptu stop and introduced Pam to Doris. Doris was happy to greet visitors over a cuppa and chat - a pleasant way to cap a big day out ☺....
After an extremely long day covering 270 kilometres I was buggered, but a lot more bloody comfortable in the mouth, and happy to return the plate for the purpose it was meant - to fill the holes in my face....
At home I flicked through the much travelled mail, reading a letter from Telstra. Initially a service offered to me for $24, to maintain, I now have to pay $49.90 per month, reducing three hour capped STD calls from $2 to $1 being the bargain. Using Telstra's advertising slogan 'Now your family can get even more from your home phone', being a smart person I'm having trouble seeing the benefit offered in that glossy brochure. What my family gets is a greater burden of an extra $25.90 per month to stay in touch for our regular Sunday chat. A monopoly turned into a pack of thieving greedy bastards - only shareholders seem to be benefiting!!!! Just four months of Telstra's fees alone without making a single call, for the same price, I can fly the two legs to Mildura and visit family personally????

Tuesday 21 November 2006
My dear old doona is showing signs of weariness having seen many full moons and swirls in the washing machine. The material pulled up under my chin is fraying and the small hole took no time to become a big one. Helping our life of poverty limp along a bit further the holey bit was transferred to the foot of the bed, tricking me into the sensation of the doona having a refreshed newness about it ☺....
Feeling as flat as a shit carter's hat, my body totally refused to respond to the thought of anything physical. Propping on my arse I turned fingers loose to glide over the keyboard. Already a couple of weeks behind, catching up on journal digitising filled any spare time....

Smoke filling the valley thickened as the day passed, hardened by my initiation as an observer to the logging and private clearing training ground; it caused little concern. As with most smoke filled days it's usually only our government making money and creating jobs all for the good of the community????

Wednesday 22 November 2006
Before I even got out of bed thoughts of tackling the stack of laundry were shelved for sanity sake. Wind strong enough to torture me through the entire event cemented a change in direction and a 'Plan B' was formulated. Prior to the doona being lifted mowing made it onto the agenda....
Earmuffs hadn't even made it onto position when a hot running phone kept me indoors for a while. Calling to inquire how I got on after the dentist Monday, Mum and Dad started the succession of calls. Helen, my friendly bank manager, gave me a brief follow up courtesy call in relation to documents posted out. Before escaping back outside Pam finished the run of calls, inviting me for a crayfish and salad dinner tomorrow night, an offer only a fool would refuse ☺....
Effortlessly Coxy fired into life, minus the screeching grinding noise. The revitalised outing began at the base of the dam. Charging at the face of the dam doing short runs up the slope, time stood still momentarily as the centre of balance between me and machine teetered almost to the point of no return. Charging the steep incline the front wheels lifted, the lowered blade housing kept us upright, or maybe it was the grip of my tightly squeezed arse cheeks as I leant forward ☺????
An obvious change following maintenance was the incredible fuel economy. Amazed at the acreage covered, I managed two hours in the seat on a single tank of juice. Previously Coxy was giving one and a half hours. Covering a week's work with a push mower in a single afternoon of sitting down polishing the seat with my bum, too easy ☺....

Thursday 23 November 2006
It had just gone 11p.m. last evening when Tia and I went out for last wee's before beddy byes greeting a sky dense with stars. Admiring the scene before me, I stood bewildered by what appeared to be a glowing star, outstanding because it was lower and larger than the average. This star in particular moved at a pace from west to east above South Sister Range. Due to airport locations all domestic flights pass over using a south to west path, it wasn't something I could easily identify with???? Maybe it was just time the star had a change of scenery ☺....
Not removed from this planet and taken to some unknown place overnight, we woke in the familiar surrounds of the bungalow to put another day in at Rainbow Falls. Utilising freshly mowed grass I raked and deposited a few wheelbarrow loads destined to create compost. A serve of nitrogen rich pooper scooped wallaby poo was also included in the developing brew. Again combining skills, I stood idly holding the hose wetting up the new heap. Tia jumped and snapped at the flowing water compacting doused grass clippings ☺.... What a team ☺!!!!
Turning on a bloody stinker, I had to add that much cold water to the solar shower there was enough water to wash my body and hair from the one cook. Sprucing up early for a great cause, I called into the pub for a bottle of red on the way....

Before indulging in the many culinary delights on offer Terry knocked the top off a bottle of home brew stout. Kicking our feet up we partook in a sample. Pam treated us to crayfish, a selection of salads, home-baked focaccia bread and tasty condiments to suit. The indulgent meal was topped off with Pam's own chocolatey, chocolate mousse ☺ .... Totally bloody yum ☺ !!!! What more can be said, a perfect evening shared ☺ ....

Friday 24 November 2006
Idly over breakfast I watched through my window to the world blackbirds busy feeding in the freshly mowed areas. Dashing about full of life they constantly returned food to screaming young waiting in the nest. That one weak moment of procreation indiscretion created an abundance of daily work - their life currently is just spent flying to the nest with a beak full or flying from the nest to fill it, resting only from sunset to sunrise to do it all again the next day....
The animal world gave me a lesson in learning. Out pooper-scoopering waiting for bath water to boil I noticed a large furry animal, identified later as a Bennett's Wallaby. Watching the wallaby almost motionless and exposed in the open through daylight hours is rare to see. Concerned, I phoned well-known wildlife carers. Potentially injured, Terry came up to assess the situation and within two minutes walked out of the paddock smiling. It was a huge old male around four foot. Its sheer size and life experience gave it nothing to fear in the animal world except humans; grazing exposed through daylight hours is a luxury it can afford ☺ ....
New knowledge absorbed and taken onboard, I spruced up and made it over the mountain early afternoon. Following the taxing trip to the dentist I blew what remained of the budget on food, with the exception of a small indulgence on a new writing pad and journal folders. Chatting my way through our friendly little town did my bits and pointed Destiny's nose toward home. The dirt road is not only dry and powdery but in parts corrugated and rocky, rough enough to rattle loose change about!!!!

Saturday 25 November 2006
Currawongs raiding the blackbird nest had me jumping to attention too late. Arriving 6:30a.m.-ish without making a sound, it was wing flapping from a large bird and juvenile squeaky screeching travelling overhead that roused attention. Ridding the yard of unwelcome intruders, this raid the mongrel birds succeeded, nests lost their young lively activity. It was sad to see parent blackbirds return in search of the demanding little mouths that had kept them so busy....
I thought little of currawongs - following today's desperate cowardly attack they have sunk lower in my books, doing nothing to bridge differences!!!!
A raiding group of currawongs returned just as my toast popped. Drawn into the horizon paddock to piss the last of the mongrel bastards off, I got a surprise at how very little useful grass is left alive. Both paddocks closest to housing are faring best. All the same native animals will be right for feed for a while longer....
Up and alert I didn't return to bed. Lagging waaaay behind with laundry there was no more excuses. It had to happen, chaining myself to the white monster all day. The noisy ruckus of hungry mouths in the cottage roof that would give me the shits at times was sadly deathly quiet while me and the washing machine did our thing....

Playing around, or more rightly once the first load was pegged out, cuddly clouds draped over and clung to both Sisters. On occasion mist drifted in the air but made no impact on ground, just hindering attempts at drying washing. Giving up on the clothesline I split a load of wood and sparked up the heater. Draping clothes on every piece of furniture by the fire, there was also a pile waiting its turn. The inside clothes dryer was well established when a sprinkling of hail was prelude to a hard fast dump of 4mm, the heaviest rain experienced in some time but unfortunately not lasting….

Sunday 26 November 2006
From pissing off unwanted birds, to washing, splitting wood, operating the manual clothes dryer, cooking, dishes, and topping it all off writing, yesterday I put in a seventeen hour day. After pissing one pest off rifling through the burnt out house at 6a.m. this morning I returned to bed affording myself a decadent sleep in. Having no big job with my name on screaming out for attention the day was tinkered away on optional bits waiting on spare time….
Relieving the cottage of last night's laundry booty, I returned furniture to appropriate spots then did whatever inspired. Feeling a bit sensitive and testing my patience, if there was a hard or clumsy way to do something I found it. Initially feeling as flat as a shit carter's hat, and a bit grumpy to boot, thought brain therapy was a sensible option and it did the trick. Getting distracted I forgot about the grumps…. That can only be a good thing ☺!!!!
Requiring minimal thought, brain therapy began with pooper-scoopering that led into a play in the compost. The beans welcomed overdue attention, weeding, feeding and filled in blanks replanting seed that failed first time round, then lovingly watered it in ☺….
Any trace of yesterday's rain evaporated by lunch; quite warm, it was however pleasant tinkering outside. Early evening a bloody cold southerly swing had an outstretched arm reaching for the beanie; changeable by the hour, Mother Nature keeps me guessing ☺????

Monday 27 November 2006
Having done a day's work before the sun popped its head over the mountain to greet us, my eyes instantly sprang open at the mere sound of a black mongrel squawking - that occurred 5a.m.. As soon as the bungalow door was open Tia shot through behind the cattle yards after a rabbit. The plan was to merely check the housing area and return to bed….
Noticed by her absence, taking a walk out back found Tia happily pulling the fur from a stiff, chilled small marsupial, having come to grief through the night and waiting patiently for the first carnivore to claim. The thought of Tia hopping on my bed at that point wasn't an attractive option, so I began pulling flowering buzzies from the concrete drain leading from the rear of the shed. Leaving to wash my hands I followed on by filling the cottage water, putting the solar shower out to wait for sunrise then left the hose running at the base of a stressed walnut tree. The walnut tree has dropped a huge amount of nuts, now with as many in the tree as on the ground. Cramming it in all before 7a.m., I had also jotted down thoughts and was lined up for breakfast, and just for the record not one currawong showed ☺!!!!
Tia was showing considerable interest just inside a paddock. Checking the attraction discovered a dead wallaby. It was a night of carnage for native animals; something had a killing spree????

The driveway side of the cottage was getting a little unruly so after breakfast the team of me, my best friend and shovel made an impressive impact before searing sun and heat drove us to do something saner. Intermittently robbing flowing water from the walnut tree I sat my bum down under shade filling bucket after bucket, slowly and casually watering the vegie patch ☺ ....

A furnace of a temp, I could have cooked a meal in the solar shower, doubling its contents to cool it down. Copping damaging late afternoon sun inside the cottage, the three-quarter-size timber bed was dismantled and its pieces leant against the westerly wall out of intrusive elements, then the computer was fired into action. In addition to the usual data entry, previously written thoughts for 'Inside my Skin's' ending were neatly tucked underneath the digitised preface for safe keeping, now being a bit more than just a loose piece of paper ☺ ....

The positive aspect of being up at the ridiculously early hour of 5a.m. - I packed two days work into one, not a habit I plan on maintaining. A person could wear out twice as fast ☺ !!!!

Tuesday 28 November 2006

I'm struggling to get half a brush load from Tia in the evenings, and the bungalow now taking less effort to de-fur; I'm guessing the winter coat has randomly distributed itself out of her body. The collection of a few seasons fur is to the point where I'm ready to seek out a spinner to get a couple of balls of fur spun and have a Tia fur beanie knitted up ☺ ....

The world of nature offered a peaceful morning, letting me remain in bed to get up at my own leisure. The only five unwelcome birds I saw today was at p.m. ☺ !!!!

To eliminate the nagging doubt that keeps re-surfacing in my mind, I went rifling through plumbing bits and put a new tap above the cattle trough. The washer replaced in the existing tap was a different size. Preferring a sure thing than live in hope the countersunk seating etchings to fit the smaller washer would work, now there's no doubt....

Each visit into the cottage, a letter deliberately left out to annoy me into responding to got the desired results. I finally stopped glancing at it in passing and put words into action. Adding electricity to the computer, a letter was formulated to Councils General Manager requesting a home burial, taking a positive step at being together forever, side by side with my little mate at Rainbow Falls ☺ .... although neither one of us is in any hurry to be planted ☺ ....

Cooking dinner watching a blue haze and mandarin sunset, the colours enhanced already amber paddocks. Mid afternoon smoke began filling the valley and only thickened, silhouetting surrounding mountains until the most distant were totally obscured. Making a quick call, Pam confirmed a bushfire in the Tamar Valley. I may have gone two consecutive weeks with only three individual puffs of ventolin in each, but thick smoke filled air will test my new-improved lungs out????

Wednesday 29 November 2006

Starting in the early hours random wind gusts struck at will. Two meagre traces of that elusive liquid were shoved in on the rough stuff but only had brief dances on the roof. What the elements did manage to do, for all the effort involved, was to clear the air and valley free of the dense smoke. My brilliant run with asthma medication fell in a hole administering three individual puffs in a 24-hour period - gotta have it!!!!

Milk and bread being closer to the end than start prompted a re-stock trip into the big smoke. During my chat to Evelyn she mentioned the price of flour is rising by 48% due to drought and crop losses, taking the cost of bread alone from $3 to $4. A coffee with Terry, an attempted visit at Brian and Maggie's, Post Office and supermarket filled the big outing ☺ ....

The front left tyre of the ride-on was deflating and threatening to roll off the rim putting it away last outing; a situation requiring rectifying. Needing only to undo one nut to release the entire wheel from the steering arm, and remove a split pin from the top of the rod neatly holding the wheel in position, with that done the wheel, in theory, should easily slip free independently of the mower. No job done on the mower has been easy so far and the wheel was no exception. Without being removed or greased in quite a while the rod had almost seized inside the cylinder. Treated to spray on lubrication, plenty of twisting and some gentle persuasion, it was released. A nagging thought that couldn't be erased is why would the rod and cylinder on the right hand wheel be any better off???? A job to follow up on another time....

Easing into the day's end my little mate busied herself on the scent of rabbits leaving me to roam the garden enjoying progress. A blackbird going off its head at the burnt out house alerted me to three currawongs that had quietly slithered in for an evening snack on bubbies; barely having time to land they were sent packing!!!!

Thursday 30 November 2006

When my brain returned to a conscious state from sleep, first thoughts went immediately to the right front wheel of the mower. Obviously a priority fixed in my head, to get it out for the sake of peace made up my mind lazing in bed it was to make the first job, well it nearly made it; playing in water robbed the first couple of hours....

A small colony of fluorescent green, chlorophyll packed, triangular shaped, succulent sap sucking winged insects were setting up home amongst the much prized potato patch. Dying shoots aroused my inquisitive mind. Easily finding the culprits, a few escaped the grip between my gloved fingers but the majority didn't. Going over the potato patch that thoroughly I couldn't find a single one several hours later ☺ !!!!

Nothing was overlooked with water. Everything copped a drink, from vegies, to fruit and nut trees, compost, cottage, Tia and solar shower; only then was I ready to take-off to the shed. Well almost; needing petrol in my motor, pulled up for smoko first ☺ ....

In a round about indirect way I made it to the shed escaping the stinging heat to lube, wiggle and firmly encouraged wheel number two loose. Cleaned, greased and slipped back into place the mower now feels like it has power steering. Those grease nipples aren't attached to the wheel cylinders for ornamental reasons ☺ !!!!

Friday 1 December 2006

The call of a currawong, seemingly at a distance, had Tia jumping to attention 7:15am. Wanting to believe it was far enough away not to be a threat beckoned Tia to settle back into bed. Refusing to respond to my request I reluctantly got up, finding a small group of the marauding mongrels draped over the burnt out house trying to further reduce the blackbird population. Peace restored to paradise, existence returned to its tranquil bliss still with the sound of some demanding young waiting to be fed ☺ ....

There was no point in returning to bed. With one foot in front of the other I got on with the bits that occupy the day. Fed and watered I picked up the shovel to strike a blow. Dressed in sun smart attire, sun hat, long sleeved cotton shirt, undies and boots, I got busy clearing around the base of the rock pile. Stirring up seeding grasses hayfever was torturing me internally. Stifling heat began torturing me externally; job incomplete and my feet not painted on, me and my little mate escaped inside. With bugger all seeding grasses around maybe the hayfever season won't be as lasting in a drought year????
Following up on yesterday the spud patch was given the once over. Tracking down and squashing only a small number of the succulent sap sucking insects, a re-check before knock off found nothing and that's the right number....
An afternoon inside was filled between the computer and a stop and start catch up chat with Mum and Dad. Unable to afford the newly restructured monthly fees, for the same $2 price I once got a three-hour capped call anytime of the day, is now capped at $2 for twenty minutes. For an extra $25 per month I can have the service back I once had. The limit is frustratingly annoying taking the relaxation out of calling for our preferred arvo yarn!!!! Thanks a lot greed!!!!
First day of summer and I'm still waiting for spring. The cold of winter seemed to morph into heat bypassing the middle bit and associated soaking rains. I'm hearing stories of people having to buy water in; usually a predictable high rainfall, dams, springs, streams, and water tanks relying on roof run off are bone-dry. Still coasting at home with water for the time being, I saw the dam lower when I split the irrigation pipe with the brushcutter, losing thousands of litres over a couple of days. Even then running empty wasn't a threat....
Emptying my head of a passing thought I wrote an ending to 'Inside my Skin' early November. The ending involved AEnone returning from the mainland loaded with the last of my stored possessions from Kiama. Cooking dinner this evening I answered a call from AEnone. Our brief conversation basically established that she's aboard the ferry in Melbourne, inquiring whether I'll be home early afternoon tomorrow so she can stop in on her way through to St. Helens. From the call I found myself not sure whether to laugh or cry tears of joy, coming to terms with the realisation, potentially, there's closure to the book tomorrow ☺.... I don't think AEnone knows the magnitude of what she's achieved ☺!!!!

Saturday 2 December 2006
A bloody strong westerly took command of Friday evening blowing every piece of pollen from the stifling stillness to kingdom come. It relieved my hayfever but didn't create a relaxing sleeping environment. Anything that would creak, rattle, shake, grate or rasp, did!!!!
Aggressive and determined like a bloody currawong, it was up there with the strongest gusts experienced. The usual routine in such unsettling circumstances unfolded, waking fully clothed on the bed at some wee baby hour; and again only I was rattled apart - the housing remained intact!!!!
Beginning feeling no different than any other, subconsciously knowing I was waiting for something special to occur, a little anxiety built in the wait time that ended in a euphoric high; no better way to end 'Inside my Skin' ☺....
Filling time like an expectant parent in anticipation of AEnone's arrival, I grabbed the shovel on a far cooler day to occupy a restless brain. Finalising edging around the rock pile, then I

split some wood, did dishes, fiddling around with short-term jobs until the loaded expected campervan drove around back ☺ ....

Camera on the ready, I captured AEnone's arrival. Hugs and blurts of emotional greetings we packed many hours of conversation into one, a generous gift from an honourable person uniting our life and delivering an ending to my book. Leaving to walk across her next welcome mat, I waved AEnone off and returned to rummage through every box like an excited child at Christmas. Re-discovering pieces of my life long forgotten ignited a very emotional voyage of discovery. Overcome by a euphoric happy numbness, searching for appropriate words to ink on paper, nothing raised its head to capture the emotion ☺ ????

Way beyond my current financial capabilities, driving to Kiama to retrieve stored possessions was so far out of reach I could only hope for one day. By just passing through the area with spare car space AEnone so easily turned one day hopes into reality ☺ ????

A box containing a few older collected wines arrived amongst my previous life storage - a Cabernet Merlot lost its cork to celebrate the life-turning auspicious occasion. We're now completely united in the one spot at Rainbow Falls for forever ☺ ....

Delivering the remains of a scattered life, now reduced down to two states because there will always be a part of me left in Mildura, it now seems everything that is going to be is here in the one place totally united. And so, that brings us to a happy ending. Forget romance, forget water on tap - I have few heroes or mentors held close and dear to heart, but AEnone, her four legged best friend 'little legs' and touring campervan are the heroes at the end of this book ☺ !!!!

Content with 'Inside my Skin's' ending, but worth a late mention; continuing harsh drought conditions combined with a thoughtless human playing with matches generated a bushfire unlike anything seen in the area. Within hours of ignition on the tenth day of December, and rated as high impact, Rainbow Falls was in its path; it roared through home like the sound of a freight train in passing, but that's another story....